THE ROMAN WORLD:

**Names of Places
Relevant to Ignatius of Antioch**

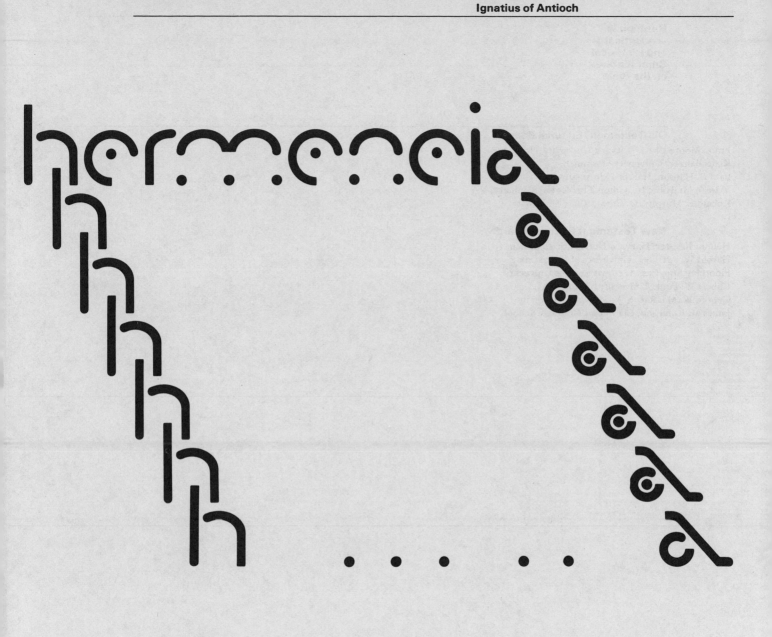

**Hermeneia
—A Critical
and Historical
Commentary
on the Bible**

Ignatius of Antioch

A Commentary on the
Letters of Ignatius of Antioch

by William R. Schoedel

Edited by
Helmut Koester

**Fortress
Press**

Philadelphia

Library of Congress Catalog Card Number
ISBN 0-8006-6016-1

Printed in the United States of America
Design by Kenneth Hiebert
Type set on an Ibycus system at Polebridge Press
K979G84   20-6016

The Author

William R. Schoedel, born 1930 in Stratford, Ontario,
Canada, received his theological training at Concordia
Seminary, St. Louis, Missouri, and at the Divinity School
of the University of Chicago. He taught at Valparaiso
University, Valparaiso, Indiana, from 1955 to 1957, and
at Brown University, Providence, Rhode Island, from
1960 to 1970. Since 1970 he has been a member of the
Program in Religious Studies at the University of Illinois,
Urbana, Illinois. He has contributed to the study of the
literature of the early church—the Apostolic Fathers,
the Gnostics, the Apologists, the anti-Gnostic Fathers,
and others—and has given special attention to the
relation between aspects of early Christianity and the
Graeco-Roman world.

Contents
Ignatius of Antioch

The name *Hermeneia*, Greek ἑρμηνεία, has been chosen as the title of the commentary series to which this volume belongs. The word *Hermeneia* has a rich background in the history of biblical interpretation as a term used in the ancient Greek-speaking world for the detailed, systematic exposition of a scriptural work. It is hoped that the series, like its name, will carry forward this old and venerable tradition. A second entirely practical reason for selecting the name lies in the desire to avoid a long descriptive title and its inevitable acronym, or worse, an unpronounceable abbreviation.

The series is designed to be a critical and historical commentary to the Bible without arbitrary limits in size or scope. It will utilize the full range of philological and historical tools, including textual criticism (often slighted in modern commentaries), the methods of the history of tradition (including genre and prosodic analysis), and the history of religion.

Hermeneia is designed for the serious student of the Bible. It will make full use of ancient Semitic and classical languages; at the same time, English translations of all comparative materials—Greek, Latin, Canaanite, or Akkadian—will be supplied alongside the citation of the source in its original language. Insofar as possible, the aim is to provide the student or scholar with full critical discussion of each problem of interpretation and with the primary data upon which the discussion is based.

Hermeneia is designed to be international and interconfessional in the selection of authors; its editorial boards were formed with this end in view. Occasionally the series will offer translations of distinguished commentaries which originally appeared in languages other than English. Published volumes of the series will be revised continually, and eventually, new commentaries will replace older works in order to preserve the currency of the series. Commentaries are also being assigned for important literary works in the categories of apocryphal and pseudepigraphical works relating to the Old and New Testaments, including some of Essene or Gnostic authorship.

The editors of *Hermeneia* impose no systematic-theological perspective upon the series (directly, or indirectly by selection of authors). It is expected that authors will struggle to lay bare the ancient meaning of a biblical work or pericope. In this way the text's human relevance should become transparent, as is always the case in competent historical discourse. However, the series eschews for itself homiletical translation of the Bible.

The editors are heavily indebted to Fortress Press for its energy and courage in taking up an expensive, long-term project, the rewards of which will accrue chiefly to the field of biblical scholarship.

The editor responsible for this volume is Helmut Koester of Harvard University.

April 1985

Frank Moore Cross
For the Old Testament
Editorial Board

Helmut Koester
For the New Testament
Editorial Board

Hermeneia identifies itself as "a critical and historical commentary on the Bible." The letters of Ignatius of Antioch are not now and never have been among the biblical books. They are, however, close to the canonical writings of the New Testament in time (I argue for the authenticity of the so-called middle recension) and are in many ways still part of the same world. Thus they frequently put us in touch with developments that have roots in the first century, and they often set features of the New Testament writings themselves in clearer perspective. The decision to include a study of Ignatius in this series reflects the conviction that a historically sound understanding of Christian origins requires attention to such sources. The theologian may believe that "by recognizing the existence of a canon, the church declares that especially in its proclamation it realizes that it is not left to its own devices . . ." (Karl Barth); but canonical lines do not correspond in any very precise way to historical demarcations, and there can be no escape from including the widest possible range of relevant material in our investigation of the emergence of the church in the Graeco-Roman world. In this regard a precedent is provided by the *Handbuch zum Neuen Testament* edited by Hans Lietzmann for the inclusion of Ignatius and others of the so-called Apostolic Fathers in a critical and historical commentary on the New Testament.

The letters of Ignatius not only look back, however; they also point forward. More clearly than any New Testament writing they proclaim Christ as God and treat the incarnation as the touchstone of theology. They reflect, then, shifts of emphasis that have remained constitutive of traditional Christianity to this day. But it is not only in terms of theological substance that the letters of Ignatius have proved important. The fact that we can speak of the letters of Ignatius as a body of literature with any confidence at all represents the conclusion of some of the most brilliant and painstaking research on any ancient text; and, as Robert M. Grant has observed, this research played a decisive role in the establishment of the modern study of the church Fathers.

Ignatius is also interesting in his own right. He is, for example, the earliest witness to the threefold ministry of bishop, elders, and deacons, and reflects complex views of the nature of their authority. Other aspects of his thought are less well known but equally striking. Thus Ignatius works creatively with the Graeco-Roman commonplace about matching words with deeds and in this and other ways significantly qualifies the otherworldly (and sometimes Gnosticizing) tendencies of his thought. Also important in this connection is his interpretation of the flesh/spirit polarity which represents a remarkable departure from current usage and has far-reaching implications theologically, ethically, and socially. Perhaps the heart of Ignatius' Christianity, however, is his exposition of the life and thought of the church in terms especially of unity and love which he expounds with exemplary conviction and intensity. These same themes, as we shall see, are closely linked with Ignatius' reflections on his role as (embattled?) overseer of the church of Antioch and as victim of the hatred of the world in his acceptance of (if not enthusiasm for) the martyr's crown. It is a story, as I understand it, of the risks that attend an appeal for solidarity and the exercise of leadership in a religiously intense milieu. To put it bluntly, the charge of fanaticism is not entirely without foundation in the case of Ignatius. Nor does he entirely avoid a kind of spiritual blackmail in his dealings with the churches. A writer who claims that "loves constrains" him to give advice and make demands risks deceiving himself and trading on the good will of others (as Lucian so clearly saw in his account of the life and death of the Cynic philosopher, and quondam Christian, Peregrinus). At the same time, culturally creative figures are precisely the ones who run such risks, instinctively recoiling from what Dante called *il gran rifiuto* (*Inferno* 3.60)—"the great refusal" to shoulder responsibilities whose exercise involves moral and spiritual ambiguities. To state matters in this way is perhaps to attribute more to Ignatius than is appropriate. Yet few have read these letters without finding in them much that rises above other Christian writings of the period and that harks back especially to Paul, whom Ignatius admired so deeply. Indeed, a reading of Ignatius serves as a useful introduction to aspects of Paul's ministry that are often lost sight of in the face of the traditional preoccupation with the apostle's theology. Thus when Helmut Koester speaks of Paul's mission as "a well-planned, large-scale organization that included letter-writing as an instrument of ecclesiastical policy," he is drawing attention to factors in the situation that should be even more obvious in the case of Ignatius.

The introduction to this study is longer than usual for a commentary. Its purpose is threefold: to give some idea of the relations between our investigations and the research of others; to summarize our conclusions, drawing attention to those parts of the commentary that contribute most directly to them; and to develop certain matters that are hard to deal with in the commentary itself.

The translation of Ignatius' letters offered here inclines to "the literal." This should not, I think, be seen as a drawback. "The translator enriches his tongue," writes George Steiner, "by allowing the source language to penetrate and modify it. But he does far more: he extends his native idiom towards the hidden absolute of meaning." And if from this point of view the King James Bible can be hailed as "the most successful domestication," I need fewer apologies. I do not, of course, claim to have produced anything comparable to the King James Bible; and I did not even try to approach "the hidden absolute meaning." My purpose was more didactic: I wanted to provide a sense of Ignatius' range of vocabulary, his characteristic ways of expressing himself, the length of his sentences, and so forth; and I wanted the translation to contribute as directly as possible to the commentary. There are translations of Ignatius available today that are so adventuresome that readers can locate standard items of discussion only with great difficulty. There is the special danger, to be sure, that the traditional translation of some terms may suggest a distorted or anachronistic range of meaning. I can only hope that the commentary will help alleviate the difficulty.

The commentary is largely "philological" in character, for it remains true that "the fundamental science for history is philology" (Wilhelm Dilthey). At the same time, I have attempted to keep the general lines of interpretation constantly in view and to integrate philological detail as much as possible in the flow of the discussion. Comments of a more sociological, phenomenological, or theological character also occur and sometimes strain the limits of what can be accomplished in this form of literature. Finally, the need to be brief will not, I trust, unduly obscure whatever it may be that the commentary achieves.

The works of Theodor Zahn and J. B. Lightfoot still represent inescapable points of departure for work on Ignatius (particularly for those who accept the authenticity of the middle recension). Among other things, they provide a rich collection of parallels that has become the common possession of subsequent scholarship. It is symptomatic that Walter Bauer's commentary on Ignatius in the *Handbuch* often reads like a selection and condensation of the materials gathered by his illustrious predecessors. I have continued the practice of reporting such items without acknowledgment to avoid endless footnoting, especially when they are now reinforced by other parallels and have been taken up into a broader stream of discussion. My introduction will give a reasonably clear idea of the advances that I hope this commentary has made in this regard.

My interest in Ignatius and especially the peculiar density of his language was first stirred by Arthur Carl Piepkorn, formerly of Concordia Seminary, St. Louis, Missouri, to whose memory I dedicate this book. Robert M. Grant is ultimately responsible for many of the strategies adopted in this study but can be held accountable for none of the ways in which I have fallen short in applying them. Friends and acquaintances who are members of the Midwest Patristic Seminar (Chicago) and the North American Patristic Society have encouraged me in this work and forced me to rethink many points. Wayne Meeks asked me to prepare a paper on Ignatius some years ago for the Society of Biblical Literature that helped me see the importance of exploring the interaction between Ignatius' thought and the events in which he found himself caught up. Bruce Malina responded to that paper and made a number of interesting suggestions. And E. P. Sanders provided a forum in which I had an opportunity to develop these ideas more fully.

Members of the editorial board of *Hermeneia* are responsible for broadening the conception of *Hermeneia*'s task to include figures like Ignatius and for approaching me to undertake this task. The one person who has read the entire manuscript for this book as carefully as patience permits is Helmut Koester (whose own work on the Apostolic Fathers has left a decisive mark on these pages). It is difficult to find words adequate to express my appreciation for his generosity in this regard.

Finally, I wish to thank the John Simon Guggenheim Memorial Foundation, which in 1976–77 supported the research that is reflected in this book.

Urbana, Illinois
March 1984

William R. Schoedel

1. Sources and General Abbreviations

Abbreviations used in this volume for sources and literature from antiquity follow the *Theological Dictionary of the New Testament,* ed. Gerhard Kittel, tr. Geoffrey W. Bromiley, vol. 1 (Grand Rapids, Michigan, and London: Eerdmans, 1964) xvi–xl. Some abbreviations are adapted from that list and can easily be identified.

The following abbreviations have also been used:

'Abot R. Nat.	*'Aboth de Rabbi Nathan*
Act. Arch.	*Acta Archelai* (GCS 16)
Act. Ioann.	*Acta Ioannis*
Act. Paul. et Thecl.	*Acta Pauli et Theclae*
Act. Phil.	*Acta Philippi*
Act. Thadd.	*Acta Thaddaei*
Act. Thom.	*Acta Thomae*
ACW	Ancient Christian Writers
Aeschines	
Ctes.	*In Ctesiphonem*
Aesop. prov.	*Aesopi proverbia*
Agobard	
Sermo de fid. verit.	*Sermo de fidei veritate*
AnBib	Analecta Biblica
Ap. John	*Apocryphon of John* (NHC 3,1)
Ap. Jas.	*Apocryphon of James* (NHC 1,2)
Apol.	*Apology*
Apollonius Rhod.	Apollonius of Rhodes
Argonaut.	*Argonautica*
Appian	
Bell. civ.	*Bellum civile*
Aristotle	
E.N.	*Ethica Nicomachea*
Interp.	*De interpretatione*
Arrian	
Anab. Alex.	*Anabasis Alexandri*
Asc. Is.	*Ascension of Isaiah*
A. Seneca	Lucius Annaeus Seneca (the elder)
Suas.	*Suasoriae*
Athanasius	
Contra Arian.	*Contra Arianos*
Gent.	*Contra Gentes*
Synod.	*De synodis*
Virg.	*De virginitate* (TU 29,2a)
AThANT	Abhandlungen zur Theologie des Alten und Neuen Testaments
Athenaeus	
Deipn.	*Deipnosophistae*

Athenagoras	
De res.	*De resurrectione*
Augustine	
Tract. in Ioann. evang.	*Tractatus in Ioannis evangelium*
AUSS	*Andrews University Seminary Studies,* 1963ff.
BAG	Walter Bauer, *A Greek-English Lexicon of the New Testament and Other Early Christian Literature,* ed. William F. Arndt and F. Wilbur Gingrich (Chicago: University of Chicago; Cambridge: University Press, 1957)
Barn.	*Barnabas*
b. Ber.	*Babylonian Talmud,* tractate *Berakot*
b. Yebam.	*Babylonian Talmud,* tractate *Yebamoth*
B.C.E.	Before the Common Era
BDF	F. Blass and A. Debrunner, *A Grammar of the New Testament and Other Early Christian Literature,* ed. Robert W. Funk (Chicago: University of Chicago, 1961)
BEvTh	Beiträge zur evangelischen Theologie
BFCTh	Beiträge zur Förderung christlicher Theologie
BLE	*Bulletin de littérature ecclésiastique*
BZNW	Beihefte zur Zeitschrift für die neutestamentliche Wissenschaft
c.	century
ca.	circa, about
can.	canto
Can. Hipp.	*Canones Hippolyti*
CBQ	*Catholic Biblical Quarterly,* 1939ff.
C.E.	The Common Era
Celsus	
De medic.	*De medicina*
Cent.	*Centuria*
cf.	confer, compare with
CH	*Church History,* 1931ff.
Chalcidius	
In Plat. Tim. comm.	*In Platonis Timaeum commentarium*
Chariton	
Chaer. et Callirh.	*Chaereas et Callirhoe*

Chrysostom
   Hom. in 1 Cor.   *Homiliae in epistolam primam ad Corinthios (PG 61)*

Cicero
   Ad. fam.   *Ad familiares*
   De fin.   *De finibus*
   De off.   *De officiis*
   De orat.   *De oratore*
   In Pis.   *In Pisonem*
   Pro Cael.   *Pro Caelio*
   Pro Roscio comoed.   *Pro Sexto Roscio comoedo*
   Resp.   *Res publica*
CIG   *Corpus Inscriptionum Graecarum,* ed. August Böckh (4 vols.; Berlin: Officina academica, 1828–77)
1 Clem.   *1 Clement*
2 Clem.   *2 Clement*
Clement Alex.   Clement of Alexandria
Ps-Clem   Pseudo-Clement
CMG   *Corpus Medicorum Graecorum*
cod.   codex
Con. Gangr.   *Concilium Gangrense*
Con. Laod.   *Concilium Laodicenum*
Const. Apost.   *Constitutiones Apostolorum*
CSCO   Corpus Scriptorum Christianorum Orientalium

Cyprian
   De habit. virg.   *De habitu virginis*
Ps-Cyprian   Pseudo-Cyprian
   Pasch. comput.   *De pascha computus*
Cyril Jer.   Cyril of Jerusalem
   Cat. bapt.   *Catechesis de baptismo*
DACL   *Dictionnaire d'archéologie chrétienne et de liturgie,* ed. Fernand Cabrol, Henri Leclercq, and Henri Marrou (15 vols.; Paris: Letouzey et Ané, 1907–53)

Demetrius
   De elocut.   *De elocutione*
Demosthenes
   Coron.   *De corona*
   Olynth.   *Olynthiacs*
   Philip.   *Philippics*
Didymus
   In Psalm.   *In Psalmos*
Digest.   *Digesta*
Dio Cassius
   Hist. Rom.   *Historiae Romanae*
Diodorus Sic.   Diodorus Siculus
Diogn.   *Diognetus*
Dioscurides
   De mat. medic.   *De materia medica*

Ps-Dioscurides   Pseudo-Dioscurides
   De venen.   *De venenis*
Disc. 8–9   *Discourse on the Eighth and Ninth* (NHC 6,6)
Dit., Or.   Wilhelm Dittenberger (ed.), *Orientis Graeci Inscriptiones Selectae* (2 vols.; Leipzig: Hirzel, 1903–5)
ed.   editor, edited by, edition
Ep.   *epistula,* letter
Epictetus
   Gnom.   *Gnomologium Epicteteum Stobaei*
Epiphanius
   Pan.   *Panarion*
Epist. apost.   *Epistula apostolorum*
EtBib   Études Bibliques
EThL   *Ephermerides theologicae Lovanienses,* 1924ff.
Eusebius
   Eccl. theolog.   *De ecclesiastica theologia*
   Hist. eccl.   *Historia ecclesiastica*
   P.E.   *Praeparatio evangelica*
exc.   excerpt
Exeg. Soul   *Exegesis on the Soul* (NHC 2,6)
frg., frgs.   fragment, fragments
FRLANT   Forschungen zur Religion und Literatur des Alten und Neuen Testaments
Galen
   Ad Glauc.   *Ad Glauconem de medendi methodo*
   Ad Pison.   *Ad Pisonem de therica*
   Aliment. fac.   *De alimentorum facultatibus*
   Antidot.   *De antidotis*
   Compos. medic.   *De compositione medicamentorum*
   Method. med.   *De methodo medendi*
   Sanit. tuend.   *De sanitate tuenda*
   Sect.   *De sectis*
   Vict. rat.   *De victus ratione in morbis acutis*
GCS   Griechische christliche Schriftsteller
Gos. Nicod.   *Gospel of Nicodemus*
Gos. Pet.   *Gospel of Peter*
Gos. Phil.   *Gospel of Philip* (NHC 2,3)
Gos. Thom.   *Gospel of Thomas* (NHC 2,2)
Gos. Truth   *Gospel of Truth* (NHC 1,3)
GRBS   *Greek, Roman, and Byzantine Studies*
Great Pow.   *Concept of our Great Power* (NHC 6,4)
Gregory Naz.   Gregory of Nazianzus

Gregory Nyss. — Gregory of Nyssa

Heliodorus
- *Aeth.* — *Aethiopica*

Herm. — *Hermas*
- *Man.* — *Mandata*
- *Sim.* — *Similitudines*
- *Vis.* — *Visiones*

Hippocrates
- *Aph.* — *Aphorismi*
- *De art.* — *De arte*

Hippolytus
- *Antichr.* — *Demonstratio de Christo et Antichristo*
- *Comm. in Dan.* — *Commentarium in Danielem*
- *Contra haer. Noet.* — *Contra haeresin Noeti*
- *Theoph.* — *De theophania*
- *Trad. apost.* — *Traditio apostolica*

Ps-Hippolytus — Pseudo-Hippolytus
- *Pasch.* — *Homilia in Pascha* 6 (*PG* 59. 735–46)

HNT — Handbuch zum Neuen Testament, ed. Hans Lietzmann

HNTSup — Handbuch zum Neuen Testament, Supplement-band

Horace
- *Ars poet.* — *Ars poetica*

HSW, *NT Apocrypha* — *New Testament Apocrypha,* ed. Edgar Hennecke, rev. Wilhelm Schneemelcher, tr. ed. Robert McL. Wilson (2 vols.; London: Lutterworth; Philadelphia: Westminster, 1963–65)

HTR — *Harvard Theological Review*

Hyp. Arch. — *Hypostasis of the Archons* (NHC 2,4)

ibid. — ibidem: in the same place

idem — the same author

Ignatius
- *Eph.* — *Ephesians*
- *Mag.* — *Magnesians*
- *Phd.* — *Philadelphians*
- *Pol.* — *Polycarp*
- *Rom.* — *Romans*
- *Sm.* — *Smyrnaeans*
- *Tr.* — *Trallians*

Ps-Ignatius — Pseudo-Ignatius
- *Mar. ad Ign.* — *Maria Cassobolorum ad Ignatium*

inscr — inscription

Interp. Know. — *Interpretation of Knowledge* (NHC 11,1)

Irenaeus
- *Adv. haer.* — *Adversus haereses*
- *Dem.* — *Demonstratio (Epideixis)*

Isaeus
- *De Philoctem. hered.* — *De Philoctemonis hereditate*

Isocrates
- *Helen.* — *Helena*
- *Phil.* — *Philippus*
- *Plataic.* — *Plataicus*

JBL — *Journal of Biblical Literature*

JEH — *Journal of Ecclesiastical History*

Jerome
- *De vir. ill.* — *De viris illustribus*

JES — *Journal of Ecumenical Studies*

Josephus
- *Ant.* — *Antiquities*
- *Bell.* — *Jewish Wars*
- *C. Apion.* — *Against Apion*

JTS — *Journal of Theological Studies,* 1900ff.; N.S., 1950ff.

Ps-Justin — Pseudo-Justin
- *Cohort.* — *Cohortatio ad gentiles*

Kühn, *CGO* — Carolus Gottlob Kühn, *Claudii Galeni Opera Omnia* (MGO 1–20; Leipzig: Cnoblochius, 1821–33)

LCL — Loeb Classical Library

LPGL — *A Patristic Greek Lexicon,* ed. G. W. H. Lampe (Oxford: Clarendon, 1961–68)

LSJ — Henry George Liddell and Robert Scott, *A Greek-English Lexicon,* 9th ed. Henry Stuart Jones (Oxford: Clarendon, 1940)

LTK — *Lexikon für Theologie und Kirche* (11 vols.; Freiburg: Herder, 1957–67)

Lucan
- *Phars.* — *Pharsalia (Bellum civile)*

Lucian
- *Calumn.* — *Calumniae non temere credendum*
- *Dial. meretr.* — *Dialogi meretricii*
- *Nav.* — *Navigium*
- *Pisc.* — *Piscator*

Lucretius
- *De rer. nat.* — *De rerum natura*

LXX — Septuagint

Lycurgus
- *Leocrat.* — *Leocrates*

m. 'Abot — *Mishna,* tractate 'Abot

Mart. Andr. pr. — *Martyrium Andreae prius*

Mart. beat. Petr. apost. a Lino episc. consc.	*Martyrium beati Petri apostoli a Lino episcopo conscriptum*		
Mart. Lugd.	*Martyrium Lugdunensium* (Eusebius *Hist. eccl.* 5.1)	*P.Grenf.*	*New Classical Fragments and Other Greek and Latin Papyri*, ed. Bernard P. Grenfell and Arthur S. Hunt (Oxford: Clarendon, 1897)
Mart. Pet.	*Martyrium Petri*		
M. Aurelius	Marcus Aurelius		
Methodius			
Porph.	*Contra Porphyrium de cruce*		
MGO	Medicorum Graecorum Opera	*P.Hamb.*	*Griechische Papyrus-urkunden der Hamburger Staats- und Universitäts-bibliothek*, ed. Paul M. Meyer (Leipzig and Berlin: Teubner, 1911–24)
Minucius Felix			
Oct.	*Octavius*		
Mon. Ancyr.	*Monumentum Ancyranum*		
n. (nn.)	note(s)		
N.F.	Neue Folge		
NHC	Nag Hammadi Codices	*P.Lond.*	*Greek Papyri in the British Museum*, ed. F. G. Kenyon and H. I. Bell (5 vols.; London: British Museum, 1893–1917)
NHS	Nag Hammadi Studies		
no.	number		
NovT	*Novum Testamentum*		
NovTSup	Novum Testamentum, Supplements	*P.Mich.*	*Michigan Papyri*, ed. C. C. Edgar, A. E. R. Boak, J. G. Winter and others (Ann Arbor: University of Michigan, 1931ff.)
N.S.	New Series		
NT	New Testament		
NTS	*New Testament Studies*, 1954ff.		
Odes Sol.	*Odes of Solomon*	*P.Oslo.*	*Papyri Osloenses*, ed. S. Eitrem and Leiv Amundsen (3 fasc.; Oslo: Dybwad, 1925–36)
Or.	*oratio*, oration		
Orac. Sib.	*Oracula Sibyllina*		
Oribasius			
Coll. med.	*Collectiones medicae*	*P.Oxy.*	*The Oxyrhynchus Papyri*, ed. B. P. Grenfell, A. S. Hunt, H. I. Bell, and others (London: Egypt Exploration Society, 1898ff.)
Origen			
Comm. in Cant.	*Commentarium in Canticum Canticorum*		
Comm. in Joann.	*Commentaria in Joannem*		
Comm. in Matt.	*Commentaria in Matthaeum*	*P.Ryl.*	*Catalogue of the Greek Papyri in the John Rylands Library Manchester*, ed. A. S. Hunt, J. de M. Johnson, V. Martin, C. H. Roberts (4 vols.; Manchester: University Press, 1911–52)
Comm. in Rom.	*Commentaria in epistolam Pauli ad Romanos*		
De orat.	*De oratione*		
Exhort. Mart.	*Exhortatio ad martyrium*		
Hom. in Luc.	*Homiliae in Lucam*		
Hom. in Jer.	*Homiliae in Jeremiam*		
Hom. in Ies. Nave	*Homiliae in librum Iesu Nave*	*P.Teb.*	*The Tebtunis Papyri*, ed. B. P. Grenfell, A. S. Hunt, J. G. Smyly, and C. C. Edgar (3 vols.; London: Frowde, 1902–38)
OT	Old Testament		
Ovid			
Heroid.	*Heroides*		
p. (pp.)	page(s)		
P.Flor.	*Papiri greco-egizi pubblicati dalla R. Accademia dei Lincei, Papiri Fiorentini*, ed. Girolamo Vitelli and D. Comparetti (3 vols.; Milan: Hoepli, 1905–15)	*Paraph. Shem.*	*Paraphrase of Shem* (NHC 7,1)
		Paroem. Gr.	E. L. von Leutsch and F. G. Schneidewin (eds.), *Paroemiographi Graeci* (2 vols.; Corpus Paroemio-graphorum Graecorum; Göttingen: Vandenhoeck
P.Freib.	*Mitteilungen aus der Freiburger Papyrus-sammlung*, ed. Wolf Aly,		

Matthias Gelzer, and Josef Partsch (3 vols.; Heidelberg: Winter 1914–27)

	& Ruprecht, 1839 and 1851)
Pass. Perp.	*Passio Perpetuae et Felicitatis*
Persius	
Sat.	*Satyrae*
Petronius	
Satyr.	*Satyricon*
PG	*Patrologia Graeca* = J.-P. Migne, *Patrologiae cursus completus*, series graeca (162 vols.; Paris: Migne, 1857–66)
PGM	Karl Preisendanz (ed.), *Papyri graecae magicae* (2 vols.; Leipzig: Teubner, 1928–31)
Phlegon	
De mirab.	*De mirabilibus*
Photius	
Bibl.	*Bibliotheca*
PL	*Patrologia Latina* = J.-P. Migne, *Patrologiae cursus completus*, series latina (217 vols.; Paris: Migne, 1844–55)
Pliny	
Paneg.	*Panegyricus*
Pol.	Polycarp
Phil.	*Philippians*
Pollux	
Onom.	*Onomasticon*
Ps-	Pseudo-
PSI	*Papiri greci e latini*, ed. G. Vitelli and M. Norsa (Pubblicazioni della società Italiana; 14 vols.; Florence: Ariani, 1912–57)
Ptolemaeus	
Ad Flor.	*Ad Floram*
Ptolemy	
Apotelesm.	*Apotelesmatica (Tetrabiblos)*
PW	*Paulys Real-Encyclopädie der classischen Altertums-wissenschaft*, ed. Georg Wissowa and others (Stuttgart: Metzler, 1894ff.)
Q	Qumran documents
1QH	Thanksgiving Hymns from Qumran cave 1
1QS	Manual of Discipline from Qumran cave 1
RAC	*Reallexikon für Antike und Christentum*, ed. Theodor Klauser and others (Stuttgart: Hiersemann, 1950ff.)
Ratramnus	
De corp. et sang. dom.	*De corpore et sanguine domini*
RevScRel	*Revue des Sciences Religieuses*
RHPhR	*Revue d'histoire et de philosophie religieuses*, 1921ff.
RVV	Religionsgeschichtliche Versuche und Vorarbeiten
SAQ	Sammlung ausgewählter kirchen- und dogmen-geschichtlicher Quellenschriften
SB	*Sammelbuch griechischer Urkunden aus Aegypten*, ed. F. Preisigke and others (Strassburg: Trübner; Wiesbaden: Harrassowitz, 1915ff.)
SBLDS	Society of Biblical Literature Dissertation Series
SBT	Studies in Biblical Theology
SC	Sources chrétiennes
sc.	scilicet, word supplied from the context
SEG	*Supplementum epigraphicum graecum* (Leiden: Sijthoff, 1923ff.)
Seneca	
De prov.	*De providentia*
Sent. Sext.	*Sentences of Sextus*
Serapion of Thmuis	
Euch.	*Euchologium*
SJLA	Studies in Judaism in Late Antiquity
SJT	*Scottish Journal of Theology*, 1948ff.
Socrates	
Hist. eccl.	*Historia ecclesiastica*
Stobaeus	
Ecl.	*Eclogae*
Suetonius	
Calig.	*Gaius Caligula*
Domit.	*Domitianus*
SUNT	Studien zur Umwelt des Neuen Testaments
s.v. (s.vv.)	*sub verbo* or *sub voce*, under the word (entry)
Tacitus	
Ann.	*Annales*
Tatian	
Ad Graec.	*Oratio Ad Graecos*
TDNT	*Theological Dictionary of the New Testament*, ed. Gerhard Kittel, tr.

	Geoffrey W. Bromiley (10 vols.; Grand Rapids, MI, and London: Eerdmans, 1964–76)
Teach. Silv.	*Teachings of Silvanus* (NHC 7,4)
Tertullian	
Ad mart.	*Ad martyras*
Ad uxor.	*Ad uxorem*
Adv. Jud.	*Adversus Judaeos*
Adv. Marc.	*Adversus Marcionem*
Adv. Prax.	*Adversus Praxean*
Adv. Val.	*Adversus Valentinianos*
Anim.	*De anima*
Apol.	*Apologeticum*
Bapt.	*De baptismo*
Carn. Christ.	*De carne Christi*
Idol.	*De idololatria*
Monog.	*De monogamia*
Orat.	*De oratione*
Praescr.	*De praescriptione haereticorum*
Pud.	*De pudicitia*
Virg. veland.	*De virginibus velandis*
Test. Abr.	*Testament of Abraham*
Testim. Truth	*Testimony of Truth* (NHC 9,3)
Theodoret	
Hist. eccl.	*Historia ecclesiastica*
Theophrastus	
Hist. plant.	*Historia plantarum*
Thom. Cont.	*Book of Thomas the Contender* (NHC 2,7)
ThQ	*Theologische Quartalschrift*
ThStK	*Theologische Studien und Kritiken*, 1828–42
tr.	translator, translated by
Treat. Seth	*Second Treatise of the Great Seth* (NHC 7,2)
Trim. Prot.	*Trimorphic Protennoia* (NHC 13,1)
TS	*Theological Studies*, 1940ff.
TU	Texte und Untersuchungen zur Geschichte der altchristlichen Literatur
UPZ	*Urkunden der Ptolemäerzeit*, ed. Ulrich Wilcken (2 vols.; Berlin and Leipzig: De Gruyter, 1927–57)
VC	*Vigiliae Christianae*, 1947ff.
Vegetius	
De re milit.	*De re militari*
Vitruvius	
De arch.	*De architectura*
v.l.	*Varia lectio:* textual variant
ZKG	*Zeitschrift für Kirchengeschichte*, 1877ff.
ZNW	*Zeitschrift für die neutestamentliche Wissenschaft und die Kunde der älteren Kirche*, 1900ff.
ZThK	*Zeitschrift für Theologie und Kirche*, 1891ff.; N.F. 1920ff.
ZWTh	*Zeitschrift für wissenschaftliche Theologie*, 1826ff.

2. Short Titles of Frequently Cited Literature

Bammel, "Ignatian Problems"
C. P. Hammond Bammel, "Ignatian Problems," *JTS* N.S. 33 (1982) 62–97.

Bartelink, *Lexicologisch-semantische studie*
G. J. M. Bartelink, *Lexicologisch-semantische studie over de taal van de Apostolische Vaders* (Utrecht: Beijers, 1952).

Bartsch, *Gnostisches Gut*
Hans-Werner Bartsch, *Gnostisches Gut und Gemeindetradition bei Ignatius von Antiochien* (Gütersloh: Bertelsmann, 1940).

Bauer, *Ignatius*
Walter Bauer, *Die Briefe des Ignatius von Antiochia und der Polykarpbrief,* in *Die Apostolischen Väter,* vol. 2 (HNTSup; Tübingen: Mohr [Siebeck], 1920). References to Bauer without further specification are to this volume.

Bauer, *Orthodoxy and Heresy*
Walter Bauer, *Orthodoxy and Heresy in Earliest Christianity,* ed. Robert A. Kraft and Gerhard Krodel (Philadelphia: Fortress, 1971).

Betz, *Plutarch's Ethical Writings*
Hans Dieter Betz, ed., *Plutarch's Ethical Writings and Early Christian Literature* (Studia ad Corpus Hellenisticum Novi Testamentum 4; Leiden: Brill, 1978).

Betz, *Plutarch's Theological Writings*
Hans Dieter Betz, ed., *Plutarch's Theological Writings and Early Christian Literature* (Studia ad Corpus Hellenisticum Novi Testamentum 3; Leiden: Brill, 1975).

Beyschlag, *Clemens Romanus*
Karlmann Beyschlag, *Clemens Romanus und der Frühkatholizismus* (Beiträge zur Historischen Theologie 35; Tübingen: Mohr [Siebeck], 1966).

Bjerkelund, *Parakalô*
Carl J. Bjerkelund, *Parakalô: Form, Funktion und Sinn der Parakalô-Sätze in den Paulinischen Briefen* (Bibliotheca Theologica Norvegica 1; Oslo: Universitetsforlaget, 1967).

Brown, *Authentic Writings*
Milton Perry Brown, *The Authentic Writings of Ignatius* (Durham, NC: Duke University, 1963).

Corwin, *Ignatius*
Virginia Corwin, *St. Ignatius and Christianity in Antioch* (Yale Publications in Religion 1; New Haven: Yale University, 1960).

Daniélou, *Jewish Christianity*
Jean Daniélou, *The Theology of Jewish Christianity* (London: Darton, Longman and Todd; Chicago: Regnery, 1964).

Deichgräber, *Gotteshymnus*
Reinhard Deichgräber, *Gotteshymnus und Christushymnus in der frühen Christenheit* (SUNT 5: Göttingen: Vandenhoeck & Ruprecht, 1967).

Dibelius, *An die Kolosser, Epheser*
Martin Dibelius, *An die Kolosser, Epheser, An Philemon* (3d ed.; Heinrich Greeven; HNT 12; Tübingen: Mohr [Siebeck], 1953).

Dibelius/Conzelmann, *Pastoral Epistles*
Martin Dibelius and Hans Conzelmann, *The Pastoral Epistles* (Hermeneia; Philadelphia: Fortress, 1971).

Dictionnaire des antiquités
Ch. Daremberg and Edm. Saglio (eds.), *Dictionnaire des antiquités* (5 vols.; Paris: Hachette, 1877–1919).

Dölger, *Antike und Christentum*
Franz Joseph Dölger, *Antike und Christentum* (5 vols.; Münster: Aschendorff, 1919–36).

Elze, *Untersuchungen*
Martin Elze, *Überlieferungsgeschichtliche Untersuchungen zur Christologie der Ignatiusbriefe* (Tübingen: Univ. Bibl., 1963).

Exler, *Greek Epistolography*
Frances Xavier J. Exler, *The Form of the Ancient Greek Letter: A Study in Greek Epistolography* (Washington, D.C.: Catholic University of America, 1923).

Foraboschi, *Onomasticon*
Daniele Foraboschi, *Onomasticon alterum papyrologicum* (Testi e documenti per lo studio dell' antichità 16; Serie papirologica 2; Milan: Istituto editoriale cisalpino, 1967).

von der Goltz, *Ignatius*
Eduard von der Goltz, *Ignatius von Antiochien als Christ und Theologe* (TU 12,3; Leipzig: Hinrichs, 1894).

Grant, *Ignatius*
Robert M. Grant, *Ignatius of Antioch* (The Apostolic Fathers 4; Camden, NJ: Nelson, 1966).

Harrison, *Polycarp's Two Epistles*
Percy Neale Harrison, *Polycarp's Two Epistles to the Philippians* (Cambridge: University Press, 1936).

Heinimann, *Nomos und Physis*
Felix Heinimann, *Nomos und Physis* (Schweizerische Beiträge zur Altertumswissenschaft 1; Basel: Reinhardt, 1945).

Hercher, *Epistolographi Graeci*
Rudolph Hercher, *Epistolographi Graeci* (Paris: Didot, 1873).

Joly, *Ignace*
Robert Joly, *Le dossier d'Ignace d'Antioche* (Université libre de Bruxelles, Faculté de Philosophie et Lettres, 69; Brussels: Éditions de l'université de Bruxelles, 1979).

Kattenbusch, *Das Apostolische Symbol*
Ferdinand Kattenbusch, *Das Apostolische Symbol* (2 vols.; Leipzig: Hinrichs, 1894–1900).

Koester, *Synoptische Überlieferung*
Helmut Koester, *Synoptische Überlieferung bei den Apostolischen Vätern* (TU 65; Berlin: Akademie-Verlag, 1957).

Koskenniemi, *Studien*
Heikki Koskenniemi, *Studien zur Idee und Phraseologie des griechischen Briefes bis 400 n. Chr.* (Annales

Academia Scientiarum Fennica B, 102,2; Helsinki: Suomalainen Tiedeakatemia, 1956).

Kühn, *CGO*
Carl Gottlob Kühn, *Claudii Galeni Opera Omnia* (Medicorum Graecorum Opera 1–20; Leipzig: Cnoblochius, 1821–33).

Kühner/Blass, *Grammatik*
Raphael Kühner and Friedrich Blass, *Ausführliche Grammatik der griechischen Sprache*, 1. Teil: *Elementar- und Formenlehre* (3d ed.; 2 vols.; Hannover: Hahn, 1890–92; reprinted, Leverkusen: Gottschalk, 1955).

Kühner/Gerth, *Grammatik*
Raphael Kühner and Bernhard Gerth, *Ausführliche Grammatik der griechischen Sprache*, 2. Teil: *Satzlehre* (3d ed.; 2 vols.; Hannover: Hahn, 1898–1904; reprinted, Leverkusen: Gottschalk, 1955).

Lightfoot, *Ignatius*
J. B. Lightfoot, *The Apostolic Fathers*, Part 2: *S. Ignatius, S. Polycarp* (3 vols.; London: Macmillan, 1885, 2d ed. 1889). References are to the edition of 1885 for vol. 1 and to that of 1889 for vols. 2 and 3. References to Lightfoot without further specification are to the text and commentary contained in vol. 2.

Lohse, *Colossians and Philemon*
Eduard Lohse, *Colossians and Philemon* (Hermeneia; Philadelphia: Fortress, 1971).

Martin, "Pneumatologia"
José Pablo Martin, "La Pneumatologia en Ignacio de Antioquia," *Salesianum* 33 (1971) 379–454.

Pape/Benseler, *Eigennamen*
W. Pape and Gustav Benseler, *Wörterbuch der griechischen Eigennamen* (3d ed.; Braunschweig: Vieweg, 1863).

Paulsen, *Studien*
Henning Paulsen, *Studien zur Theologie des Ignatius von Antiochien* (Forschungen zur Kirchen- und Dogmengeschichte 29; Göttingen: Vandenhoeck & Ruprecht, 1978).

Perler, "Das vierte Makkabäerbuch"
Othmar Perler, "Das vierte Makkabäerbuch, Ignatius von Antiochien und die ältesten Märtyrerberichte," *Rivista di archeologia cristiana* 25 (1949) 47–72.

Petermann, *Epistolae*
Jul. Henr. Petermann, *S. Ignatii patris apostolici epistolae* (Leipzig: Vogel, 1849).

Peterson, ΕΙΣ ΘΕΟΣ
Erik Peterson, ΕΙΣ ΘΕΟΣ: *Epigraphische, formgeschichtliche und religionsgeschichtliche Untersuchungen* (FRLANT N.S. 24; Göttingen: Vandenhoeck & Ruprecht, 1926).

Preisigke, *Namenbuch*
Friedrich Preisigke, *Namenbuch* (Heidelberg: Selbstverlag des Herausgebers, 1922).

Rackl, *Christologie*
Michael Rackl, *Die Christologie des heiligen Ignatius von Antiochien* (Freiburger theologische Studien 14; Freiburg: Herder, 1914).

Rahner, *Greek Myths*
Hugo Rahner, *Greek Myths and Christian Mysteries* (New York and Evanston: Harper & Row, 1963).

Rathke, *Ignatius*
Heinrich Rathke, *Ignatius von Antiochien und die Paulusbriefe* (TU 99; Berlin: Akademie-Verlag, 1967).

Resch, *Agrapha*
Alfred Resch, *Agrapha: Aussercanonische Schriftfragmente* (TU 30; Leipzig: Hinrichs, 1906).

Schlier, *Untersuchungen*
Heinrich Schlier, *Religionsgeschichtliche Untersuchungen zu den Ignatiusbriefen* (BZNW 8; Giessen: Töpelmann, 1929).

White, *Form and Function*
John Lee White, *The Form and Function of the Body of the Greek Letter: A Study of the Letter-Body in the Non-Literary Papyri and in Paul the Apostle* (SBLDS 2: Missoula, MT: Society of Biblical Literature, 1972).

Zahn, *Epistolae*
Theodor Zahn, *Ignatii et Polycarpi Epistolae Martyria Fragmenta* (Patrum Apostolicorum Opera, ed. Oscar de Gebhardt, Adolph Harnack, and Theodor Zahn, 2; Leipzig: Hinrichs, 1876). References to Zahn without further specification are to the text and commentary in this volume.

Zahn, *Ignatius*
Theodor Zahn, *Ignatius von Antiochien* (Gotha: Perthes, 1873).

1. The Letters of Ignatius in the Christian Tradition.

Ignatius' letters were written at a time when the diverse achievements of first-century Christianity were beginning to be consolidated and the organizational and theological uncertainties of the second century confronted. Because of their relatively early date these writings have played an important role in the theological reflections of the church and represent a central point of contention in the scholarly discussions of Christian origins.[1]

1.1. The Theological Role of the Letters of Ignatius.

The earliest quotation from Ignatius' letters shows that the Antiochene bishop was widely admired as a martyr who had caught up the meaning of devotion to Christ in his letter to the Romans: "As one of ours said (ὡς εἶπέ τις τῶν ἡμετέρων) who had been condemned to the wild beasts because of his witness to God, 'I am the wheat of God and I am ground by the teeth of wild beasts that I may be found pure bread of God'" (Irenaeus *Adv. haer.* 5.28.4; cf. Ign. *Rom.* 4.1).[2] Such admiration eventually

led to the production of a number of (historically unreliable) accounts of the martyr's death and an encomium of him by John Chrysostom. A more general account of Ignatius is provided by Eusebius who approaches the bishop's letters with the range of questions that he usually brings to his sources (*Hist. eccl.* 3.36). Other quotations and allusions show that Ignatius was valued also as a theological thinker, particularly in the area of christology.[3] His discussion of the hidden descent of Christ in *Eph.* 19 fascinated some theologians (Origen, Eusebius, Basil or Ps-Basil, and others), and Athanasius thought that the christological paradoxes of *Eph.* 7.2 supported his position. In a later period, Antiochene theologians (notably Theodoret) tried to outflank their opponents by appealing to a series of early writers that included Ignatius. But it was not long before the Monophysites found that the Antiochene bishop's unguarded language about "the suffering of my God" (*Rom.* 6.3) and other matters was compatible with their doctrine. Chalcedonians, of course, were equally convinced that Ignatius spoke their language.[4] The authority of Ignatius

---

1   The following abbreviations are used for the letters of Ignatius: *Eph.*=Ephesians; *Mag.*=Magnesians; *Tr.*=Trallians; *Rom.*=Romans; *Phd.*=Philadelphians; *Sm.*=Smyrnaeans; *Pol.*=Polycarp.

2   For the Greek form of Irenaeus' statement see Eusebius *Hist. eccl.* 3.36.12. This material may have been mediated to Irenaeus through a source (cf. Friedrich Loofs, *Theophilus von Antiochien Adversus Marcionem und die anderen theologischen Quellen bei Irenaeus* [TU 46,2; Leipzig: Hinrichs, 1930] 303–5). In any event, his failure to mention Ignatius by name does not indicate that he was doubtful about its authorship (cf. Robert Joly, *Le dossier d'Ignace d'Antioche* [Université Libre de Bruxelles 69; Brussels: Éditions de l'université, 1979] 100–101). Rather, the reference to Ignatius as "one of ours" aligns the bishop of Antioch with the other nameless Eastern figures to whom Irenaeus appeals as his theological authorities. Compare especially *Adv. haer.* 4.17.4 where "one of those who preceded us" (τις τῶν προβεβηκότων, *quidam de senioribus*) is mentioned. Pagan sources also quote lines introduced by the expression ὡς τις εἶπεν "as someone said" (Demetrius *De elocut.* 188) or something similarly indefinite (cf. ibid., 187; Athenaeus *Deipn.* 8, 336b; 10, 433f; Aelius Aristides *Or.* 25.45; 27.15; 28.91–93; 28.117 [ed. Keil]). Especially interesting perhaps is an appeal

to "one of the reputable and ancient sages" (τις τῶν ἐλλογίμων καὶ τῶν παλαιῶν σοφιστῶν) by Aelius Aristides at the beginning of one of his orations on concord (*Or.* 23.2 [ed. Keil]). The unnamed predecessor, Isocrates, was not obscure; and there was nothing problematic about the authenticity of the writing alluded to. (Nothing can be made of the fact that Irenaeus or his source carefully specifies the circumstances under which Ignatius wrote the line. That was more or less necessary for the sake of intelligibility.)

3   For the material see J. B. Lightfoot, *The Apostolic Fathers,* Part 2: *S. Ignatius, S. Polycarp* (3 vols., London: Macmillan, 1885, 2d ed. 1889) 1. 127–221; cf. Adolf Harnack, *Geschichte der altchristlichen Literatur bis Eusebius,* Teil 2: *Die Chronologie* (2 vols.; 2d ed.; reprinted, Leipzig: Hinrichs, 1958) 1. 400–4; Michael Rackl, *Die Christologie des heiligen Ignatius von Antiochien* (Freiburger Theologische Studien 14; Freiburg: Herder, 1914) 348–75. Note in addition that the *Didascalia Apostolorum* works with a hardened version of Ignatius' treatment of the three orders of the ministry (cf. A. A. McArthur, "The Office of Bishop in the Ignatian Epistles and in the Didascalia Apostolorum Compared," *Studia Patristica IV* [TU 79; Berlin: Akademie-Verlag, 1961] 298–304).

4   Cf. Robert M. Grant, "The Appeal to the Early

was such that already in the latter part of the fourth century a long recension of his letters appeared that reflected the religious and social realities of the time.[5] This recension is apparently not cited until about 570 C.E. by the Monophysite Stephen Gobarus. But it was especially the orthodox who thereafter found it to their liking. Both recensions are still reflected in the *Parallela sacra* of John of Damascus, but the long recension gradually ousted its rival, i.e., the original letters of Ignatius.

The modern study of Ignatius may be divided into three periods.[6] The first of these was dominated by the problem of the authenticity of the letters. It was especially Reformed theologians who denied their genuineness or recognized (with various degrees of acuteness) that the materials with which they were dealing (the long recension) had been interpolated.[7] An important motive here was to deprive Romanists of evidence in favor of an early date for episcopacy or Roman supremacy. The brilliant discovery of the existence of an earlier form of the letters by the Anglican bishop James Ussher[8] laid the foundation for Pearson's work[9] and later for the great studies of Zahn and Lightfoot[10] that secured general

recognition for the authenticity of the letters contained in what is now called the middle recension. The second period saw a turn to the exploration of Ignatius' letters from the point of view of the history of Christian thought. This culminated in the still valuable (though one-sided) work of the liberal Protestant scholar von der Goltz.[11] Attention was given in the third period to Ignatius' place in the history of religions. The important work here was that of Schlier who uncovered what he believed to be the Gnostic dimensions of Ignatius' thought.[12] A later, more cautious work by Bartsch has also been influential.[13]

More recent studies of Ignatius carry forward the lines of research just discussed and reflect in addition many of the new interests that have emerged in New Testament studies: reassessment of the religio-historical situation; analysis of the history of traditional materials; investigation of rhetorical strategies and epistolographical conventions; social and psychological perspectives. Recent studies of Ignatius also attest to the continued importance of his letters as a theological resource or a point of departure for critical theological reflection.[14]

Fathers," *JTS* N.S. 11 (1960) 13–24; idem, "The Apostolic Fathers' First Thousand Years," *CH* 31 (1962) 421–29.

5   For studies on the theological orientation of the long recension see Arnold Amelungk, *Untersuchungen über Pseudo-Ignatius* (Marburg: Otto, 1899); Othmar Perler, "Pseudo-Ignatius und Eusebius von Emesa," *Historisches Jahrbuch* 77 (1958) 73–82; K. J. Woollcombe, "The Doctrinal Connections of the Pseudo-Ignatian Letters," *Studia Patristica VI* (TU 81; Berlin: Akademie-Verlag, 1962) 269–73; Reinoud Weijenborg, "Is Evagrius Ponticus the Author of the Longer Recension of the Ignatian Letters?" *Antonianum* 44 (1969) 339–47; especially important is Dieter Hagedorn, *Der Hiobkommentar des Arianers Julian* [Patristische Texte und Studien 14; Berlin: De Gruyter, 1973] xxxvii–lii.

6   Cf. Hans-Werner Bartsch, *Gnostisches Gut und Gemeindetradition bei Ignatius von Antiochien* (Gütersloh: Bertelsmann, 1940) 1–7; Virginia Corwin, *St. Ignatius and Christianity in Antioch* (Yale Publications in Religion 1; New Haven: Yale University, 1960) 3–13.

7   See especially Nicolaus Vedelius, *S. Ignatii episcopi Antiocheni et martyris quae exstant omnia* (Geneva: Rouiere, 1623).

8   James Ussher, *Polycarpi et Ignatii epistolae* (Oxford:

Lichfield, 1644).

9   John Pearson, *Vindiciae epistolarum S. Ignatii* (Cambridge: Hayes, 1672; reprinted, Oxford: Parker, 1852).

10   Theodor Zahn, *Ignatius von Antiochien* (Gotha: Perthes, 1873); Lightfoot, *Ignatius.*

11   Eduard Freiherr von der Goltz, *Ignatius von Antiochien als Christ und Theologe* (TU 12,3; Leipzig: Hinrichs, 1894). An important response (though in its own way also one-sided) came from the Catholic scholar Michael Rackl (*Christologie*). A more even-handed treatment of Ignatius' thought (yet still more or less in a liberal Protestant vein) was provided by Cyril Charles Richardson (*The Christianity of Ignatius of Antioch* [New York: Columbia University, 1935]). In spite of its date, this book did not yet fully address itself to the challenges posed by Schlier's work of 1929 (see below).

12   Heinrich Schlier, *Religionsgeschichtliche Untersuchungen zu den Ignatiusbriefen* (BZNW 8; Giessen: Töpelmann, 1929).

13   Bartsch, *Gnostisches Gut.*

14   Ignatius played a role in the efforts of modern Catholic scholars to contribute to a renewal of spirituality and theology through an investigation of the early fathers (cf. Marcel Viller and Karl Rahner, *Aszese und Mystik in der Väterzeit: Ein Abriss* [Freiburg:

1.2. The Three Recensions.

Three recensions of Ignatius' letters are traditionally listed: (a) short, (b) middle, (c) long. The short recension, preserved only in Syriac,[15] is nothing more than an abridgement of the letters to Polycarp, Ephesians, and Romans (with a paragraph from Trallians) constructed from the middle recension for monastic purposes.[16] The middle recension (the text brought to light by Ussher) is represented in Greek by only one manuscript of the eleventh century (*Cod. Mediceo-Laurentianus* 57, 7) or copies of it.[17] It lacks the letter to the Romans which had at some point been detached and incorporated into an account of the saint's martyrdom (for which the Greek text is preserved in *Cod. Parisiensis-Colbertinus* 1451).[18] There is also a papyrus for the Greek of (roughly) *Sm.* 3.1–12.1.[19] Several important versions of the middle recension are found: Latin,[20] Syriac (three sets of fragments are known),[21] Armenian (close to the

---

Herder, 1939] 22–27; Gustave Bardy, *La vie spirituelle d'après les pères des trois premiers siècles*, ed. A. Hamman [2 vols.; Tournai: Desclée, 1968] 1. 69–90; Jules Gross, *La divinisation du chrétien d'après les pères grecs* [Paris: Gabalda, 1938] 122–25; Adalhard Heitmann, *Imitatio Dei: Die ethische Nachahmung Gottes nach der Väterlehre der zwei ersten Jahrhunderte* [Studia Anselmiana 10; Rome: Herder, 1940] 71–74; Karl Hörmann, *Leben in Christus: Zusammenhänge zwischen Dogma und Sitte bei den apostolischen Vätern* [Wien: Herold, 1952] 21–82; Émile Mersch, *Le corps mystique du Christ* [2 vols.; 3d ed.; Paris: Desclée, 1951] 1. 296–307; Guido Bosio, "La dottrina spirituale di Sant' Ignazio d'Antiochia," *Salesianum* 28 [1966] 519–51). Rudolf Bultmann, on the other hand, discovered a close relation between Paul and Ignatius in terms of the "existentiell attitude" for which this Protestant theologian became the spokesman ("Ignatius and Paul," in Schubert M. Ogden, ed., *Existence and Faith* [Cleveland and New York: World, 1960] 267–77). And the influence of Neo-orthodox thinking is evident in Virginia Corwin's (*Ignatius*) account of Ignatius' Christianity. Other Protestant commentators, however, have argued that there is a fundamental cleavage between Paul and Ignatius in their understanding of Christian existence (cf. Th. Preiss, "La mystique de l'imitation du Christ et de l'unité chez Ignace d'Antioche," *RHPhR* 18 [1938] 197–241; Leonard Stählin, *Christus Praesens* [BEvTh 3; München: Lempp, 1940]). A somewhat different range of issues is taken up by Wolfhart Pannenberg in discussions of the theologically problematic character of Ignatius' doctrine of God ("Die Aufnahme des philosophischen Gottesbegriffs als dogmatisches Problem der frühchristlichen Theologie," *ZKG* 70 [1959] 1–45) and his view of the incarnation (*Jesus—God and Man* [2d ed.; Philadelphia: Westminster, 1977] 118–19). Recently the task of von der Goltz has been taken up again by Henning Paulsen in a form that is theologically sophisticated and in full dialogue with the religio-

historical and literary issues (*Studien zur Theologie des Ignatius von Antiochien* [Forschungen zur Kirchen- und Dogmengeschichte 29: Göttingen: Vandenhoeck & Ruprecht, 1978]).

15 First published by William Cureton, *The Ancient Syriac Version of the Epistles of Saint Ignatius* (London: Rivington, 1845); idem, *Vindiciae Ignatianae* (London: Rivington, 1846); idem, *Corpus Ignatianum* (London: Rivington, 1849). The letters to Polycarp, Ephesians, and Romans (with a paragraph from Trallians) are involved.

16 Fairy von Lilienfeld, "Zur syrischen Kurzrezension der Ignatianen: Von Paulus zur Spiritualität des Mönchtums der Wüste," *Studia Patristica VII* (TU 92; Berlin: Akademie-Verlag, 1966) 233–47.

17 First published by Isaac Voss, *Epistolae genuinae S. Ignatii martyris* (Amsterdam: Blaev, 1646).

18 First published by Thierry Ruinart, *Acta primorum martyrum sincera et selecta* (Paris: Muget, 1689). There are corresponding Latin and Syriac versions.

19 Carl Schmidt and Wilhelm Schubart, *Altchristliche Texte* (Berliner Klassikertexte 6; Berlin: Weidmann, 1910) 3–12.

20 Two manuscripts of this version were located by Ussher and served as the foundation of his work on the text of Ignatius: *Caiensis* 395 and *Montacutianus* (the latter has since disappeared). Editions of the Latin version are available in Lightfoot (*Ignatius*, 3.5–68), Theodor Zahn (*Ignatii et Polycarpi epistolae martyria fragmenta*, in Oscar von Gebhardt, Adolf Harnack, and Theodor Zahn, eds., *Patrum apostolicorum opera* 2 [Leipzig: Hinrichs, 1876]) and elsewhere. These manuscripts also contained an account of Ignatius' martyrdom corresponding to the Greek account in *Cod. Parisiensis-Colbertinus* 1451.

21 For discussion see Zahn (*Ignatius*, 167–240) and Lightfoot (*Ignatius*, 1. 89–101), and for the material Lightfoot (*Ignatius*, 3. 93–124). Included in this collection of material is a Syriac version of the acts of Ignatius corresponding to the Greek acts in *Cod. Parisiensis-Colbertinus* 1451.

Syriac),[22] Arabic (also close to the Syriac),[23] and Coptic (two manuscripts in fragmentary form).[24]

There are several Greek manuscripts of the long recension and several of the corresponding Latin version.[25] The long recension contains an expanded version of the seven letters of the middle recension and six additional letters (one to Ignatius from a certain Mary of Cassobola, the others from Ignatius to the same Mary, to the Tarsians, to the Antiochenes, to Hero, and to the Philippians). All or most of these additional letters also came to be associated with the letters of the middle recension as preserved in Greek, Latin,[26] and Armenian. At least one or two of them were included in the Syriac and Coptic materials. But the Arabic does not have them.

The order of the letters varies widely in all these sources. Modern editions of the middle recension of the letters follow the order suggested by Eusebius (*Hist. eccl.* 3.36), though there is reason to believe that he was wrong about the first three of them (see on *Mag.* 15).

The following standard system of symbols is used in this commentary for the discussion of textual materials:[27]

G   *Cod. Mediceo-Laurentianus* 57. 7 (XI c.).
L   The Latin version, including *Caiensis* 395 (L₁) and *Montacutianus* (L₂).
P   Berlin papyrus *cod.* 10581 (V c.).
g   The collective witness of the Greek manuscripts of the long recension.
l   The collective witness of the Latin manuscripts of the long recension.
S   The short recension (Syriac).
Sf   Syriac fragments of the middle recension.
A   Armenian version.
C   Coptic version.

I have referred to the *Arabic* as such to avoid confusion (Basile suggests the use of the letter B).

The letter to the Romans requires additional symbols because of its separate textual tradition:

G   *Cod. Parisiensis-Colbertinus* 1451 (X/XI c.).
H   *Cod. Hierosolymitanus S. Sabae* 18 (X c.).
K   *Cod. Sinaiticus* 519 (X c.).
T   *Cod. Taurinensis Gr.* A 17 (XIII c.).
Sm, Am   The Syriac or Armenian version of the letter as contained in accounts of Ignatius' martyrdom.

Quotations of Ignatius by later patristic writers are also of value and are identified by name.

The Funk/Bihlmeyer/Schneemelcher text is the point of departure for this commentary but is not adhered to slavishly.

1.3. The Modern Consensus.

The modern consensus concerning the letters of Ignatius may be said to have been established especially by the work of Zahn and Lightfoot.[28] The textual problems

---

22   The Armenian version appears to have been derived from the Syriac sometime in the fifth century (Lightfoot, *Ignatius*, 1. 84–89). For its bearing on the text of Ignatius, see Jul. Henr. Petermann, *S. Ignatii patris apostolici epistolae* (Leipzig: Vogel, 1849). (The letter to the Romans appears not only along with the other letters of Ignatius but also in a distinctive Armenian account of his martyrdom.)

23   The Arabic version also appears to have been derived from the Syriac. It is known to us from a thirteenth-century manuscript (*Sin. ar.* 505). See Basile Basile, "Un ancien temoin Arabe des lettres d'Ignace d'Antioche," *Melto, Recherches Orientales* 4 (1968) 107–91; idem, "Une autre version Arabe de la lettre aux Romains de St. Ignace d'Antioche," ibid., 5 (1969) 269–87. We have made as much use of the Arabic as possible on the basis of a literal translation of the problematic passages.

24   For the Coptic material see now L.-Th. Lefort, *Les pères apostoliques* (2 vols.; CSCO 135–36; Scriptores Coptici 17–18; Louvain: Durbecq, 1952) 1. 44–66 (text), 2. 38–62 (translation). (It should be noted that

the retroversion of the Coptic into Greek by C. Wessely is unreliable.)

25   Cf. Lightfoot, *Ignatius*, 1. 102–26 (discussion); 3. 127–273 (Greek text); Zahn, *Epistolae*, 174–296 (Greek and Latin texts).

26   The Latin version omits the letter to the Philippians and has four other spurious letters not otherwise attested.

27   Cf. Karl Bihlmeyer, *Die Apostolischen Väter: Neubearbeitung der Funkschen Ausgabe*, 2d ed. Wilhelm Schneemelcher (SAQ 2. 1.1; Tübingen: Mohr [Siebeck], 1956) xxxv–xxxviii.

28   Zahn, *Ignatius*; Lightfoot, *Ignatius* (see n. 10 above).

were thoroughly explored and the authenticity of the middle recension was upheld to the satisfaction of most. In particular, it was recognized that the presumed anachronism in *Mag.* 8.2 (where the expression "the eternal Word *not* proceeding from Silence" had been taken as directed against Valentinianism) represented a corruption of the text.[29] And it was shown that all other significant features of the world of Ignatius were compatible with a date somewhere between (say) 100–118 C.E.[30]

These conclusions were attacked a number of times in the late nineteenth and early twentieth centuries. But the critics (notably Völter and Delafosse) damaged their own cause by the unduly speculative character of much of their work.[31] Nevertheless, doubts have once again been revived by three recent challenges to the scholarly consensus.

1.4. Challenges to the Consensus.

Two of these studies are also exceedingly speculative and are unlikely to prove convincing to many. The third represents a more serious challenge.[32]

(a) Reinoud Weijenborg argues that the middle recension (M) represents a shortened version of the long recension (L).[33] His method is to take L and M (of the letter to the Ephesians) and to compare them line by line, asking which of the two appears to have been derived from the other. Unfortunately for the thesis advanced no single example speaks decisively in favor of the derivation of M from L, and the cumulative weight of the evidence is not impressive. Moreover, some of the

possible counter-examples are striking. Thus in *Eph.* 7.2, M naively proclaims that "one is the Physician [Christ], both fleshly and spiritual, begotten and unbegotten. . . ." Our fourth-century writer (L) recognizes that Christ ought not to be referred to as "unbegotten" and provides the following elaborate correction: "Now our Physician is the only true God, he who is unbegotten and inaccessible, the Lord of all things, but Father and Begetter of his Only Son; we have as Physician also our Lord God Jesus Christ, the Only Son and Word before the ages, but later also man from Mary the virgin. . . ." Weijenborg also misleadingly claims that the quotations of Ignatius provided by Eusebius are derived from a primitive form of L rather than from M, and he is compelled therefore to suggest the wholly unlikely view that the *Church History* of Eusebius is a forgery written sometime after ca. 360 C.E. Weijenborg does not recognize that Eusebius and L agree in some details simply because L was derived from a text of M that predates by several centuries the earliest Greek manuscript of M. Indeed, he shows an amazing reverence for *Cod. Mediceo-Laurentianus* 57. 7, going so far as to take obvious orthographical slips as indications of Ignatius' state of mind. Weijenborg also fails to discuss the significant differences between L and Eusebius that remain one of the strongest arguments in favor of the authenticity of M.[34]

(b) Rius-Camps joins everyone in rejecting Weijenborg's work, but he presents a no less difficult reconstruction of his own.[35] He believes that although M is prior to L, it is not what Ignatius wrote. Originally there were four letters (to the Romans, Magnesians, Trallians,

---

29 Lightfoot, *Ignatius*, 2. 126–28; Zahn, *Epistolae*, 36–37.

30 This is the date suggested by Lightfoot (*Ignatius*, 2. 435–72). Harnack came to agree that no decisive argument could be made against a date for Ignatius' arrest in the days of Trajan (as suggested by Eusebius' *Chronicon*), though he was inclined to put it in the last years of Trajan (110–17 C.E.) or somewhat later (117–25 C.E.). Cf. Adolf Harnack, *Geschichte der altchristlichen Literatur bis Eusebius*, Teil 2: *Die Chronologie* (2 vols.; 2d ed.; reprinted Leipzig: Hinrichs, 1958) 1. 388–406.

31 Cf. Corwin, *Ignatius*, 3–10.

32 For a discussion of the three works referred to below see William R. Schoedel, "Are the Letters of Ignatius of Antioch Authentic?" *Religious Studies Review* 6 (1980) 196–201.

33 Reinoud Weijenborg, *Les lettres d'Ignace d'Antioche* (Leiden: Brill, 1969).

34 Cf. Joly, *Ignace*, 12–14. For reviews of Weijenborg's work see P.-Th. Camelot, *Biblica* 51 (1970) 560–64; Antoine Wenger, *Revue des études Byzantines* 29 (1971) 213–16; Ilona Opelt, *Gnomon* 46 (1974) 251–55.

35 J. Rius-Camps, *The Four Authentic Letters of Ignatius, The Martyr* (Christianismos 2; Rome: Pontificium Institutum Orientalium Studiorum, 1979).

and Ephesians) composed at Smyrna. The three letters associated with Troas were later creations: the primitive letter to the Magnesians was broken up and part of it developed into a letter to the Philadelphians; similarly, the primitive letter to the Ephesians was broken up and part of it developed into a letter to the Smyrnaeans; the letter to Polycarp contains one wholly new part (sections 1–5) and another (sections 6–8) derived from the ending of the primitive letter to the Ephesians. Ignatius himself probably lived about 80–100 C.E. and never knew Polycarp. The forger represented the interests of the bishop of Philadelphia. In addition to inventing the scenario that made it possible for him to comment directly on the situation in that church, he also interpolated statements into the other letters in favor of the monarchical authority of the bishop.

According to Rius-Camps, the forger tips his hand in several ways. Thus Ignatius calls himself "bishop of Syria" in the letter to the Romans (2.2); but since the forger did not have this letter in his collection (which explains its distinctive textual tradition), he was free to regard Ignatius as a deacon by misinterpreting his professions of humility (cf. *Sm.* 12.2; *Phd.* 4; *Eph.* 2.1; *Mag.* 2). Nor did the forger realize that at first a bishop was no more than a spiritual guide over a large area (like Syria) rather a virtual dictator in a single locality. That is why Ignatius' church is spoken of as being "in Antioch of Syria" only in the forged letters from Troas (*Phd.* 10.1; *Sm.* 11.1; *Pol.* 7.1). From such points of departure Rius-Camps goes on to show how passages from different letters of Ignatius fit together without difficulty and how in their present arrangement they are often awkwardly interrupted by interpolated material.

But this is all exceedingly tenuous.[36] It is unclear that Ignatius is presented as a deacon in any passage (see on *Eph.* 2.1; *Mag.* 2). And the unusual textual history of the letter to the Romans is likely to owe more to its ultimate inclusion in accounts of Ignatius' martyrdom than to its unavailability earlier.[37] Other explanations are also

possible for the mention of the church of "Antioch" only in the letters from Troas (see on *Eph.* 21.2). In any event, references to "Syria" alone as Ignatius' place of origin also occur in the letters from Troas (*Phd.* 11.1; *Sm.* 11.2; *Pol.* 7.2; 8.2). Moreover, Rius-Camps' unusual understanding of the evolution of the episcopate gains scant support from the external evidence adduced (the Greek text of Irenaeus *Adv. haer.* 3.3.4). Finally, it is not especially remarkable that letters written under such circumstances within so short a time should not always follow as consistently as we may like or that they should contain passages from different contexts that fall easily together.

(c) A more sober assessment of the evidence is presented by Joly, whose views on some matters have already been noted.[38] Joly's conclusion is that the letters of the middle recension are a forgery from about 160–70 C.E. He first attempts to dispose of the evidence for the authenticity of Ignatius' letters provided by Polycarp (*Phil.* 13), who mentions making a collection of them for the Philippians. In this connection, Joly argues not only against the integrity of Polycarp's letter to the Philippians,[39] but also against the division of it into two separate communications.[40] The point of the argument is to show that the reference to Ignatius' letters represents an interpolation. The issue is too complex to be explored here. It will be enough to say that although Joly's arguments are strong, they are not decisive. More important, then, is his examination of Ignatius himself. This examination is taken to show that the scenario presupposed by the letters is impossible (Joly emphasizes especially Ignatius' failure to write back to Antioch and the gravitation of everything around Smyrna) and that an accumulation of more or less impressive anachronisms are to be found: allusions to relatively late writings such as *Hermas*, the use of technical Christian terms that seem too advanced for the early second century (such as "Christianity," "catholic," and "homily," as well as two expressions that Joly refuses to recognize as mistakes in

---

36   Cf. Joly, *Ignace,* 121–27; C. P. Hammond Bammel, "Ignatian Problems," *JTS* N.S. 33 (1982) 66–69.

37   Cf. Lightfoot, *Ignatius,* 1. 263–66; 409–14; Bammel, "Ignatian Problems," 64–65; Joly, *Ignace,* 122 (where however the reference should be to Tarsians rather than to Trallians).

38   See nn. 2, 34, 36, and 37 above.

39   William R. Schoedel, *Polycarp, Martyrdom of Polycarp,*

Fragments of Papias in Robert M. Grant, ed., The Apostolic Fathers, vol. 5 (Camden, N.J.: Nelson, 1967) 3–43.

40   Percy Neale Harrison, *Polycarp's Two Epistles to the Philippians* (Cambridge: Cambridge University, 1936).

the Greek manuscript: "martyrdom" in *Eph.* 1.2, and "the eternal Word *not* proceeding from Silence" in *Mag.* 8.2), the highly developed monarchical episcopate, clear Gnosticizing tendencies, indebtedness to *4 Maccabees*.

Most of these and other points are traditional items of debate, some more significant than others. The uncertainties have to do not only with the meaning of the text of Ignatius but also with the state of affairs in the church at the beginning of the second century. Joly has done a service in summarizing succinctly and more or less accurately the items that present difficulties. Yet the conclusion of our commentary is that there is nothing in the middle recension of Ignatius clearly anachronistic and that the cumulative weight of arguments against its authenticity is insufficient to dislodge it from its place in the history of the early church. This commentary also works with a reconstruction of Ignatius' situation that helps explain the curious relation between the bishop and his church in Antioch and the centrality of Smyrna and Polycarp in his mind.[41]

2. Literary Character of the Letters of Ignatius.

The judgment of Norden concerning the style of the letters of Ignatius is still essentially correct: "of the highest passion and formlessness. There is indeed no piece of literature of the time that violates the language in such a sovereign way. Use of words (vulgarisms, Latin words), idiosyncratic compounds and constructions are of unheard of boldness; long periods are begun and recklessly broken off; and yet one does not gain the impression that this is to be explained by the inability of a Syrian to express himself clearly and correctly in the Greek language any more than Tertullian's Latin can be explained from the Punic; in both instances it is the inner

fire and passion that frees itself from the normal bonds of expression."[42] Further specification, however, is possible.

2.1. Epistolary Form.

Although Ignatius has absorbed at least one of the Pauline letters and imitated features of the apostle's epistolography (cf. *Tr.* inscr), his letters are much closer to Hellenistic (and at times Hellenistic-Jewish) models.[43] At the same time, Ignatius is fond of elaborating the traditional formulae and Christianizing them in the most astonishing ways. This procedure reflects the practice of Paul, but it is characteristic that the substance of such elaborations in Ignatius owes little directly to the apostle.

The most obvious passages for the study of these features of Ignatius' epistolography are the salutations and conclusions of the letters. We have also succeeded, however, in uncovering peculiarly Ignatian (and totally un-Pauline) transformations of standard elements in the transitions at the beginning and end of the body of the letters. Other transitional devices scattered throughout the letters are also commented on. Equally interesting are such features of the letters as the following: the use of the παρακαλῶ ("I exhort") formula (see on *Tr.* 6.1); the identification of the function of the letters as a matter of "conversing" with the addressees (see on *Eph.* 9.2); the habit of driving home requests by ascribing the fulfillment of them to Ignatius' addressees in advance (see on *Eph.* 4.1: "which you indeed do"); and Ignatius' reference to being loved both "when absent and present" (see on *Sm.* 9.2).

2.2. Ignatius' Rhetoric.

A significant advance for our understanding of Ignatius' style was the careful demonstration by Perler that

---

41 For further discussion of Joly's work see Bammel, "Ignatian Problems," 69–97.

42 Eduard Norden, *Die antike Kunstprosa* (2 vols.; 2d ed.; Leipzig: Teubner, 1909) 2. 511: "von höchster Leidenschaft und Formlosigkeit. Es gibt wohl kein Schriftstück jener Zeit, welches in annähernd so souveräner Weise die Sprache vergewaltigte. Wortgebrauch (Vulgarismen, lateinische Wörter), eigene Wortbildungen und Konstruktionen sind von unerhörter Kühnheit, grosse Perioden werden begonnen und rücksichtslos zerbrochen; und doch hat man nicht den Eindruck, als ob sich dies aus dem Unvermögen des Syrers erklärte, in griechischer Sprache sich klar und gesetzmässig auszudrücken, so wenig wie man das Latein Tertullians aus dem Punischen erklären kann; bei beiden ist es vielmehr die innere Glut und Leidenschaft, die sich von den Fesseln des Ausdrucks befreit."

43 Cf. Hermann Josef Sieben, "Die Ignatianen als Briefe: Einige formkritische Bemerkungen," *VC* 32 (1978) 1–18.

Ignatius reflects a stream of popular rhetoric that may be conveniently (though loosely) referred to as "Asianism."[44] The purists of antiquity saw in the tendency "a scholastic and perversely ingenious mannerism."[45] Its aim was the expression of pathos. Consequently it was characterized by unusual diction and poetic color. Sentences were generally built up by the accumulation of short cola, often in parallel construction. In this connection, the use of anaphora and homoeoteleuton and other such devices was common. Antithesis is also frequently found. Indeed, figures of speech of all kinds were popular (metaphors, comparisons, oxymorons, paronomasia, hyperbole, etc.). And Asianic rhetoric was famous for a distinctive use of prose rhythm regarded as decadent by the purists. Most of these features (with the possible exception of any clear pattern in the use of prose rhythm) are abundantly illustrated in the letters of Ignatius. Indeed they seem exaggerated under the impact of the bishop's religious fervor and his impassioned reflections on the significance of his impending martyrdom.

The images used by Ignatius deserve special attention in this connection. As Riesenfeld pointed out, Ignatius reflects especially the Hellenistic world in this regard.[46] Some of the bishop's images, to be sure, are elaborated in such a way that they acquire (or seem to acquire) mythic (or Gnostic) overtones.[47] But one purpose of this commentary is to widen our awareness of the Hellenistic (and traditional Christian) component in Ignatius' images and to show that the Gnostic element in them has often been exaggerated (a good example of this is provided by

the image of "filtering" in *Rom.* inscr). Also relevant in this connection is the extent to which Ignatius falls back on Greek proverbial material (about which we have made a few new suggestions) and his acquaintance with standard rhetorical themes. Thus his treatment of the relation between words and deeds reflects specifically Hellenistic turns of thought and (if I am correct) deeply colors his treatment of the theological idea of divine silence (see on *Eph.* 14.2–15.2). Note also his concern for "concord" in the church which to an extent echoes an old civic (and inter-civic) ideal proclaimed by the orators (see on *Eph.* 13.1; cf. 4.1–2). In this regard Ignatius seems aware that in calling for unity and harmony he was building on standard rhetorical practice (see on *Mag.* 1.2).

2.3. Semi-Credal Patterns and Hymnic Elements.

Ignatius' rhetorical background makes it difficult to identify semi-credal patterns or hymnic elements in his letters with assurance. We must be especially cautious about the possibility that he has quoted early Christian hymns (see on *Eph.* 7.2; 19.1–3).[48]

More fruitful has been the investigation of semi-credal patterns in the letters. The material is concerned with the figure of Christ and may be provisionally divided into two main types: (1) lists of christological antitheses (*Eph.* 7.2; *Pol.* 3.2) and (2) lists of the events of salvation in the ministry of Jesus (*Eph.* 18.2; *Tr.* 9; *Sm.* 1.1–2; cf. *Eph.* 20.2; *Phd.* 8.2); in addition, we find (3) summary christological formulae (*Mag.* 11; *Phd.* 9.2) and (4) the ὑπέρ ("on

---

44 Othmar Perler, "Das vierte Makkabäerbuch, Ignatius von Antiochien und die ältesten Märtyrerberichte," *Rivista di archeologia cristiana* 25 (1949) 47–72. Ignatius shares these stylistic features with *4 Maccabees*, as Perler suggests. Yet it is uncertain that Ignatius is as peculiarly indebted to that work as Perler believes. An important link between them is provided by the application of the term ἀντίψυχον ("expiation") to the martyr in both instances, but Ignatius may well have derived it independently from Hellenistic sacrificial terminology (see on *Eph.* 8.1).

45 D. A. Russell, "Rhetoric, Greek," *The Oxford Classical Dictionary* (2d ed.; Oxford: Clarendon, 1970) 921.

46 Harald Riesenfeld, "Reflections on the Style and the Theology of St. Ignatius of Antioch," *Studia Patristica IV* (TU 79; Berlin: Akademie-Verlag, 1961) 312–22.

47 Cf. Heinrich Rathke, *Ignatius von Antiochien und die*

Paulusbriefe (TU 99; Berlin: Akademie-Verlag, 1967) 48–53.

48 For (questionable) suggestions along these lines see Josef Kroll, *Die christliche Hymnodik bis zu Klemens von Alexandria* (2d ed.; Darmstadt: Wissenschaftliche Buchgesellschaft, 1968) 20–21; Gottfried Schille, *Frühchristliche Hymnen* (Berlin: Evangelische Verlagsanstalt, 1965) 39–40, 117–19.

behalf of") formula and related matter (see on *Rom.* 6.1; *Sm.* 7.1). There is evidently much in all this that is traditional, and some of it may have crystallized about the rite of baptism (see on *Eph.* 18.2). Moreover, it seems possible at some points to uncover traces of an older, more or less adoptionist christology. Yet it is bold to attempt to follow out the growth of the material in detail.[49] Moreover, it is likely that Ignatius himself contributed more to its formation than is often allowed.[50] Rhetorical elaboration of a few basic items seems probable especially in the case of *Eph.* 7.2 (cf. *Pol.* 3.2). Some of the lists of the events of salvation also seem to have been constructed by Ignatius himself or a source close to him for anti-docetic purposes (see on *Tr.* 9). On the other hand, a previous point of crystallization for some of this material also seems possible. For there are a remarkable number of contacts between *Sm.* 1–3 and Christian apologetic themes. Similarly, the philosophical categories invoked in *Pol.* 3.2 (cf. *Eph.* 7.2) evidently presuppose an apologetic environment.

2.4. Quotations and Allusions.

It is generally recognized that Ignatius reflects scant interest in the Hebrew Scriptures. Three quotations are found (see on *Eph.* 5.3; *Mag.* 12; *Tr.* 8.2). Curiously, the first two are from Proverbs; and they alone are marked as Scripture by the formula "it is written." A number of allusions are also found (see on *Eph.* 15.1; *Mag.* 10.3; 13.1). The evidence suggests that Ignatius derived such materials primarily from secondary sources. In an unusual passage he shows that he once confronted

Christians who held a Hellenistic-Jewish conception of Scripture as "archives" (*Phd.* 8.2).

Much more difficult is the problem of the bishop's use of writings produced by the early Christians. Of the Synoptic Gospels a strong case can be made only for Matthew as a source for Ignatius. Even in this instance, however, we are inclined to agree with Helmut Koester that it was oral material to which Ignatius was indebted (see especially on *Sm.* 1.1; *Pol.* 1.3).[51] Nevertheless, it remains significant that the Antiochene bishop was acquainted with tradition primarily of a Matthaean type. Beyond that there is one striking use of material with affinities to Luke (see on *Sm.* 3.2–3), and there are a few passages that have a Johannine ring (see on *Phd.* 7.1; cf. *Rom.* 7.2; 7.3; *Phd.* 9.1). But dependence on the Gospel of Luke seems excluded, and it is also unlikely that Ignatius was acquainted with the Gospel of John.[52]

Certain usage by Ignatius of Paul can be established only for 1 Corinthians (see on *Eph.* 16.1; 18.1; *Rom.* 5.1; 9.2; *Phd.* 3.3).[53] But Ignatius knew that Paul was the author of more than one letter (cf. *Eph.* 12.2), and it is possible that we should be more generous. Barnett, for example, states: "It is clear that Ignatius knew 1 Corinthians, Romans[54] and Ephesians[55] and that he probably

---

49 For such an attempt see especially Martin Elze, *Überlieferungsgeschichtliche Untersuchungen zur Christologie der Ignatiusbriefe* (Tübingen: Univ. Bibl., 1963); cf. Paulsen, *Studien*, 46–54.

50 Cf. Hans von Campenhausen, "Das Bekenntnis im Urchristentum," *ZNW* 63 (1972) 241–53.

51 Helmut Koester, *Synoptische Überlieferung bei den Apostolischen Vätern* (TU 65; Berlin: Akademie-Verlag, 1957) 24–61. For an opposing point of view see especially Edouard Massaux, *Influence de l'évangile de Saint Matthieu sur la littérature chrétienne avant Saint Irénée* (Universitas catholica Lovanensis 2. 42; Louvain: Publications universitaires, 1950) 94–135.

52 On the vexing question of Ignatius' familiarity with the Gospel of John see especially von der Goltz, *Ignatius*, 131–44, 197–206; Paul Dietze, "Die Briefe des Ignatius und das Johannesevangelium," *ThStK* 78

(1905) 563–603; H. J. Bardsley, "The Testimony of Ignatius and Polycarp to the Writings of St. John," *JTS* 14 (1913) 207–20, 489–500; Walter Burghardt, "Did Saint Ignatius of Antioch Know the Fourth Gospel?" *TS* 1 (1940) 1–26, 130–56; Chr. Maurer, *Ignatius von Antiochien und das Johannesevangelium* (AThANT 18; Zürich: Zwingli, 1949); Paulsen, *Studien*, 36–37.

53 Rathke, *Ignatius*, 28–39.

54 Note, however, that the parallels to Rom 1:3–4 in Ignatius (*Eph.* 18.2; 20.2; *Rom.* 7.3; *Sm.* 1.1) probably stem from semi-credal material and that other possible contacts with Paul's Romans are faint (cf. *Eph.* 8.2; 19.3; *Sm.*4.2).

55 Note especially *Eph.* inscr (for other possible echoes see *Eph.* 1.1; 12.2; 20.1; *Mag.* 7.1–2; *Sm.* 1.2; *Pol.* 1.2; 5.1; 6.2).

knew Galatians,[56] Philippians,[57] and Colossians.[58] He may also have known 2 Corinthians, 1 and 2 Thessalonians, and Philemon."[59] But in many of these instances we are more inclined today to reckon with the possibility of the use of traditional materials.

Ignatius also shares a theme with 1 John (see *Eph.* 14.2), but here again a common source is more likely. Parallels involving other late NT writings such as the Pastorals are almost certainly to be explained without recourse to literary dependence one way or the other. Also highly problematic is the possibility of the use by Ignatius of *1 Clement* (see on *Rom.* 3.1; 4.3; *Tr.* 8.2), *2 Clement* (see on *Tr.* 8.2; *Phd.* 7.2; cf. *Pol.* 5.2), *Hermas* (see on *Eph.* 6.1; 9.1; 10.1; *Phd.* 9.1), and the *Preaching of Peter* (see on *Sm.* 3.2).

Of all this material Paul seems to have exercised the profoundest formative influence on Ignatius, not least because Ignatius found in the apostle a model for understanding his own sense of rejection. But Ignatius' Paulinism has been shaped by two somewhat antithetical yet ultimately reconcilable developments: (1) the emergence of more "mystical" strains of Christianity (to which Ephesians and the Gospel of John are also indebted in different ways) and (2) the modification of Christian life and thought occasioned by a growing emphasis on discipline and ministerial authority (to which the Pastorals and the Gospel of Matthew also bear witness in different ways). All of this has flowed together in Ignatius and has been organized according to principles that have yet to be indicated.

3. Historical and Social Context.

Ignatius draws an explicit connection in two passages between his theology and his self-understanding as a martyr (*Tr.* 10; *Sm.* 4.2). This is but one of the more obvious indications that the situation in which Ignatius found himself left its mark on his thought and brought to the surface some of the deeper currents of his Christianity. A major aim of this commentary is to trace the interaction of thought and experience in Ignatius as best we can at this remove.[60]

3.1. Ignatius and the Church in Antioch.

The traditional view of Ignatius is that he was arrested during a general persecution of the church in Antioch and sent off to Rome to suffer special indignities. Thus the good news brought to him in Troas that the church in Antioch was now at "peace" (*Phd.* 10.1; *Sm.* 11.2; *Pol.* 7.1) has been taken to mean that the persecution had come to an end. Under such circumstances it is possible to view Ignatius as embodying the highest ideal of ministry and martyrdom—that is, he is seen as selflessly devoted to Christ, spontaneously admired by all his fellow Christians, and calmly instructing the churches about theology and church order as he is taken to Rome. Of course it has been recognized that his passion for martyrdom (especially in the letter to the Romans) has a fanatical ring, but it seems understandable under the circumstances and may be taken as evidence of the depth of the bishop's convictions.

The historical Ignatius, however, was a more complicated person. Emphasis on his presumed fanaticism, to be sure, is superficial and misleading. But it is superficial and misleading largely because much more was involved. We shall argue that the bishop's reactions to his situation reveal a person whose self-understanding had been threatened and who was seeking to reaffirm the value of his ministry by what he did and said as he was taken to Rome. One probable cause of Ignatius' self-doubts was his loss of control of the church in Antioch and the emergence of a group opposed to his authority. This view was convincingly argued by P. N. Harrison[61] and is adopted in this commentary. Thus the "peace" that was restored in Antioch is taken to refer to a resolution of problems in Antioch that favored Ignatius' cause (see on *Phd.* 10; *Sm.* 10–11). No doubt there were other reasons for the bishop's anxiety, but an unhappy relation with

56 Cf. *Rom.* 2.1; *Phd.* 1.1.
57 Cf. *Mag.* 10.3; *Phd.* 10.1; *Sm.* 4.2; 11.3.
58 Cf. *Eph.* 2.1; 10.2; *Mag.* 2; *Tr.* 5.2; *Rom.* 5.3; *Sm.* 6.1.
59 Albert E. Barnett, *Paul Becomes a Literary Influence* (Chicago: Chicago University, 1941) 170.
60 Cf. Samuel Laeuchli, "The Drama of Replay," in *Searching in the Syntax of Things,* essays by Maurice Friedman, T. Patrick Burke, Samuel Laeuchli

(Philadelphia: Fortress, 1972) 71–126; William R. Schoedel, "Theological Norms and Social Perspectives in Ignatius of Antioch," in E. P. Sanders, ed., *Jewish and Christian Self-Definition,* vol. 1: *The Shaping of Christianity in the Second and Third Centuries* (London: SCM, 1980) 30–56.
61 Harrison, *Polycarp's Two Epistles.*

elements of the Christian community in Antioch seems to be presupposed in many passages and probably explains the indirectness of his mode of communication with his own church.

It is likely, then, that the secular authorities of Antioch chose to try to frighten Christians into conformity or maintenance of a lower profile (cf. *Eph.* 10) by removing their leader. And it is not impossible that Christians disaffected with their (imperious?) bishop (see on *Mag.* 12) were willing to interpret his arrest as deserved.[62] In any event, a threat to Ignatius' authority by some Antiochene Christians evidently played a significant role in determining what Ignatius was to do and to say.

3.2. Ignatius' Journey as History and as Theater.

If we accept the authenticity of the middle recension, the course of Ignatius' journey may be sketched as follows:[63] He was possibly taken first by ship from Antioch to a port on the southern coast of Asia Minor. From that point on if not before the band travelled by land. The plan may have been to go on to Ephesus and to disembark from there to Rome. But the group turned north at the fork in the road near the juncture of the Lycus and Maeander rivers, passed through Philadelphia (where Ignatius had the opportunity to meet with Christians of that community), and reached Smyrna sometime in August (where there was a providential delay). Ignatius gained the support of the local Christians and Polycarp, their bishop. He received visitors from Ephesus, Magnesia, and Tralles (who may have expected to contact him

closer to home), and he wrote letters to each of these communities in return. He also wrote to the church of Rome at this time. The next step was Troas where the stay was apparently shorter and abruptly terminated. There Ignatius learned that "peace" had been restored to the Christians in Antioch. And there he wrote letters to the Philadelphians, the Smyrnaeans, and Polycarp. The abrupt departure was for Neapolis, the seaport of Philippi; and we learn from Polycarp's letter to the latter community that two other Christian prisoners had been added to the band by the time Ignatius was received by the Philippians (Pol. *Phil.* 9.1). There we lose sight of him. Presumably he was taken by the Egnatian way to Dyrrhachium and from there by one of the usual routes to Rome. There is no reason to doubt that he died a martyr's death in Rome as he had expected, but we have no certain knowledge of the event.

Ignatius was transported under the guard of ten soldiers who were apparently picking up other prisoners along the way to be taken to the capital. There are features of the situation for which it is difficult to find exact analogies, for we do not often see life from the prisoner's point of view in antiquity. What we do know about such matters indicates that there is finally nothing impossible or seriously improbable here.[64] Moreover, Ignatius' failure to comment at greater length on the concrete conditions of his captivity or to discuss fellow prisoners is not remarkable in view of his preoccupation with the deeper meaning of his bonds.

Ignatius is in fact far from seeing his journey in sober historical terms. He views it rather as a triumphant

---

62 The split in Antioch may have had theological dimensions. Although there is no reason to doubt that Ignatius learned indirectly of Judaizers active in Magnesia and confronted them personally in Philadelphia and that the threat of docetism was not inconsiderable especially in Tralles and Smyrna, he seems to have been more or less prepared with arguments. Thus he had probably known such groups already in Antioch. Yet if we can read *Pol.* 1–5 not only as a statement about Polycarp's role in Smyrna but also as a reflection of Ignatius' experience in Antioch, personality conflicts were evidently at least as important as ideological disagreements. In any event, Ignatius could have hoped to change the hearts and minds of the Christians in Antioch by his triumphant reception in Asia Minor (and Rome) only if he had in mind those

who (as he would see it) had not yet excluded themselves from the Christian community by their false teaching. For we shall see how he breaks off contact with those whose theological tendencies make it impossible for him to command their respect (cf. *Eph.* 6.2; 7.1; 9.1; *Phd.* 3.1; *Sm.* 4.1).

63 Cf. Lightfoot, *Ignatius*, 1. 31–37.

64 Cf. ibid., 341–59; Bammel, "Ignatian Problems," 78–79. (The historical questions are dealt with at various points in our commentary on the letter to the Romans.)

march (see on *Rom.* 5.1) of mythic proportions (see on *Rom.* 2.2). He thus invites fellow Christians to see beyond appearances and to grasp the hidden meaning of his wretched condition. It seems obvious that Christians who had been nurtured on the story of the crucified Lord and who had experienced rejection by society in their own lives (see on *Eph.* 10) would be prepared to welcome such a figure.

Not so obvious are the indications that the spontaneity of the recognition and support accorded the martyr depended in part on careful planning by Ignatius or his friends. Consider the following evidence of the time and expense involved in bringing Ignatius' situation to the attention of others: Messengers had been sent to Rome already from Syria to inform the Romans of the bishop's arrival (*Rom.* 10.2); another (perhaps Crocus) was to carry to Rome the letter written by Ignatius in Smyrna (*Rom.* 10.1); en route across Asia Minor someone had gone on to Ephesus, Magnesia, and Tralles to alert the Christians of those communities to Ignatius' arrival in Smyrna; they in turn sent representatives to greet the prisoner (five from Ephesus; four from Magnesia; one from Tralles); the Ephesians and Smyrnaeans cooperated in funding a deacon to accompany Ignatius as far as Troas (*Eph.* 2.1); Philo and Rheus Agathopous served as liaison between Ignatius and Antioch; they followed him through Philadelphia (*Phd.* 11.1) and Smyrna (*Sm.* 10.1), finally catching up with him in Troas, where Philo apparently stayed somewhat longer (cf. *Sm.* 13.1); finally, Ignatius asked all the churches with whom he had been in contact to send letters and/or personal messengers to Antioch to congratulate them on their "peace" (*Phd.* 10; *Sm.* 11.2–3; *Pol.* 8.1); and we learn that Ignatius later made the same request at Philippi and met with some success in these endeavors (Pol. *Phil.* 13.1).

It is evident that Ignatius and his friends took their cause seriously. It is equally evident that they understood the importance of embassies, escorts, and letters in gaining recognition and support. To a certain extent events were "staged." At the same time, there was a profound earnestness in all this. Our suggestion is that events unfolded as they did largely because the journey to Rome gave an opportunity to Ignatius and those closest to him to bring to expression their deepest hopes and fears and to channel them effectively.

3.3. Boundaries Within the Church.

Ignatius' letters reflect the conviction that the success of his martyrdom depends on the establishment and maintenance of peace and concord in the churches. Thus he calls for obedience to bishops and avoidance of false teachers, and his views on these matters are uncompromising. Ignatius was not alone in regarding the elimination of dissent as the path to unity. Yet it can also be shown that he went beyond local expectations in drawing the lines between those whom he considered authentic Christians and those he did not.[65] Our discussions of his reaction to the "Judaizers" of Philadelphia and to the docetists of Smyrna are especially relevant in this regard. If we are correct that it is Ignatius who polarized these situations, it is no doubt because he saw a threat (real or imagined) to the central significance of suffering (the Lord's and his own) for the Christian way[66] and because he sensed an independence of mind in his opponents that threatened the unity that he regarded as essential to the success of his own martyrdom. Consequently he insists on the authority of bishops in what appears to be unprecedented ways (cf. *Mag.* 4). The presumed threat to his own leadership in Antioch could only have increased his sensitivity to the disruptive possibilities of theological novelties and loose forms of organization.

It is important to note that Ignatius is more harshly disposed to Christians of whom he disapproves than he is to pagans. Thus he has higher hopes for the "repentance" of the latter (*Eph.* 10.1) than he does of the former, and he recommends that communication with false teachers cease utterly (*Eph.* 9.1; cf. *Sm.* 4.1; 7.1).

---

65 Words like "heresy" (*Eph.* 6.2; *Tr.* 6.1) and "heterodoxy" (*Mag.* 8.1; *Sm.* 6.2) now acquire at least a quasi-technical sense.

66 We argue that Ignatius probably confronted two distinct groups in these opponents and that it was he who provided the few points of contact that seem to exist between them. It is all the more significant, then, for our understanding of what is important to him that he saw the centrality of the Lord's birth, death, and resurrection threatened in each instance.

We have in this a classic illustration of the principle that whereas antagonistic outsiders more often than not serve to drive people together, those who "seem worthy of trust" yet "teach differently" (*Pol.* 3.1) represent the real threat to a group's coherence.[67]

3.4. Ignatius' Self-Effacement.

Peremptory as Ignatius sometimes is, he nevertheless frequently effaces himself before the churches. Especially relevant here is a cluster of ideas that revolves around the bishop's references to himself as the περίψημα ("lowly offering," "offscouring") and ἀντίψυχον ("expiation") of those to whom he writes. This in turn intersects a series of antitheses that contrasts his being "condemned" and their being "shown mercy" (*Eph.* 12.1), his being "in danger" (cf. *Tr.* 13.3) and their being "strengthened" (*Eph.* 12.1), his being "condemned" and not being an "apostle" (*Tr.* 3.3; *Rom.* 4.3), his being a "slave" and the apostles being "free" (*Rom.* 4.3). We also find Ignatius doubting his own "worthiness" (cf. *Eph.* 2.2; *Mag.* 12.1; 14.1; *Tr.* 4.2; 13.1; *Rom.* 9.2; *Sm.* 11.1) and referring to himself (more or less in Pauline terms) as the "last" of the Antiochenes (*Eph.* 21.2; *Tr.* 13.1; *Rom.* 9.2; *Sm.* 11.1; cf. *Mag.* 14) and a "miscarriage" (*Rom.* 9.2).

Some of this language (notably the term περίψημα, "offscouring") verges on polite self-depreciation ("your humble servant"). But that will not account for the complexity of its development (see on *Eph.* 8.1; 12.1). The fact that in this connection Ignatius modelled himself partly on Paul has been taken to suggest that like the apostle he had once persecuted the church (or at least had long been an outsider). But that has no support in the context of the letters, and it seems more likely that we have another instance of Pauline terminology being put to new use. That Ignatius was "in danger" of losing his nerve in the arena is also certainly true (cf. *Rom.* 7.2). But that appears to be a symptom of a deeper sense of unease. The suggestion of Schlier[68] was that Ignatius regarded his "bonds" as symbols of his enslavement in matter. Schlier was right to sense deeper elements in the bishop's self-effacement, but the solution is no doubt forced (see on *Eph.* 3.1). Also forced is the suggestion that Ignatius spoke as he did because he had been deprived of participation in the eucharist, the one channel of salvation (see on *Rom.* 7.3).

The view developed in this commentary is that Ignatius had in fact experienced a blow to his self-esteem and that this is reflected in his dealings with the churches. Conceivably it was his arrest that had shaken him and that had forced him to wonder about his worthiness, especially since he sensed doubts about the firmness of his resolve. But again more seems to be involved. For it appears unlikely that the hostility of the "world" would be so unexpected and shattering an event to a person like Ignatius. Moreover, it is puzzling that whereas he regards his own arrest as but the beginning of discipleship (*Eph.* 1.2; 3.1; *Tr.* 5.2; *Rom.* 4.2; 5.3; *Pol.* 7.1), he can consider churches that sit quietly on the sidelines as spiritually his superior. Can we believe that they are not "in danger" simply because they are not now facing a comparable crisis? Can we believe that this is merely an exaggerated form of politeness? Our suggestion is that Ignatius' self-effacement is connected with the unsettled state of affairs in Antioch, that what the other churches and their bishops have that he lacks is a clear claim to having preserved what he regards as the supreme blessing inherited from the apostolic age—namely, concord and unity (see on *Eph.* 11.2–12.2; cf. *Rom.* 4.3; 7.1).[69] Thus a challenge to Ignatius' authority in Antioch would be the clearest evidence of disunity and would call into question the value of his ministry there. Fiercely convinced of the rightness of his cause, however, he and his friends would seek recognition from others and would use it to deflate opposition in Antioch. His commendation of those who saw beyond his "bonds" (see on *Sm.* 10.2; *Pol.* 2.3) would reflect his conviction that his loss of respect in Antioch was not destined to last. For he uses his captivity to define his relations with the churches in terms of both the prestige that his bonds represent and the potential disgrace and unworthiness that they symbolize. If this is correct, we would expect his self-doubts to lessen on hearing about the reestablishment of "peace" in his church, and reasons are given in the commentary for thinking that this is so.

The patterns of personal interaction and theological thinking that come to expression here could hardly have

---

67 Cf. Lewis Coser, *The Functions of Social Conflict* (Glencoe, IL: Free Press, 1956) 87–110.

68 *Untersuchungen*, 153–57.

69 Cf. Corwin, *Ignatius*, 25–28.

emerged for the first time during Ignatius' journey through Asia Minor. But evidently his arrest brought them into sharper focus. In any event, the centrality of the passion and the vigor of the anti-docetic polemic in the letters may be regarded as corollaries of Ignatius' view of the Christian bishop as one who must endure much at the hands of the people in his charge and his view of himself as one whose bonds are to be seen as paradoxical signs of God's favor (see on *Pol.* 1–3). In short, the shape of Ignatius' Christianity owes much to his quest for personal identity and the social conditions of the church that (with some prompting) made his martyrdom a source of admiration for the Christians of Asia Minor.

3.5. The Church and Hellenistic Society.

As we have seen, the boundary between true and false Christians is drawn more sharply by Ignatius than the boundary between the churches and their immediate environment (cf. *Eph.* 10.1). Ignatius is aware that Christians meet with hostility from their pagan neighbors (*Eph.* 10.2). Yet he advises Christians to prove themselves "brothers" of the unbelievers about them (*Eph.* 10.3).

This attitude is also grounded christologically by Ignatius. Again it is the Lord's suffering that provides the model. For Christ was also mistreated, yet he did not fight back (*Eph.* 10.3). Included here is a faint echo of a view that is expressed more openly by Ignatius elsewhere—namely, that Christians are to cause no offense to pagans and to offer no grounds for criticism of the church (see on *Tr.* 8.2). Ignatius, in short, is prepared to come to terms with the world. The relative openness of his attitude is further suggested by the extent to which elements of popular culture have penetrated his thought. We have already mentioned some of these in our discussion of the literary qualities of the letters, and others will be considered later. Here we note in particular that Ignatius' conception of the Christian community seems to owe something to models provided by the Hellenistic club[70] and the Hellenistic city.[71] Although Ignatius significantly modifies all that he borrows, his indebtedness to his social and cultural environment cannot be ignored. This corresponds to one of the deepest currents of the bishop's thought—that in Christianity things otherwise opposed are united. Of fundamental importance here is his treatment of the "flesh" and the "spirit," which he regards as complementary. In one remarkable passage he even declares that what Christians do "according to the flesh" is "spiritual" (*Eph.* 8.2). Here another aspect of Ignatius' christology is involved. For the union of flesh and spirit is found preeminently in Christ (cf. *Eph.* 7.2; *Sm.* 3.3). Christology, then, illuminates both the negative and the positive sides of Ignatius' view of the relation beween church and society. The reality of Christ's death confirms the value of Christian suffering, and the reality of his incarnation confirms the value of what Christians do in the flesh. In a curious way, then, martyrdom proves to be not a denial of this world but a final affirmation of the significance of what is done in the flesh.

Yet the term "world" in Ignatius is always used in the negative sense familiar to us from the NT as that which stands opposed to God. We now turn to this darker element in Ignatius' thought.

3.6. Ignatius and Rome.

It is significant that with but two exceptions (both in *Mag.* 5.2) all uses of the term "world" are found in Ignatius' letter to the Romans (2.2; 3.2, 3; 4.2; 6.1, 2; 7.1). Thus it is primarily where Ignatius thinks of his martyrdom in the capital that a negative attitude toward those outside the church comes to expression. It is Rome that slays the martyrs. And it is the representatives of Rome—the ten "leopards" (*Rom.* 5.1)—that are deprived of a human face. It appears, then, that Ignatius divides his positive and negative feelings about the world in such a way that the immediate environment of the churches is seen as

---

70 See on *Pol.* 4.3 (the redemption of slaves); cf. 5.1–2 (the sexual ethic of the group).

71 See on *Eph.* 13.1 (the theme of "concord"); *Mag.* 6.1 (the "council of elders"); *Phd.* 10.1 (ambassadorial language); *Pol.* 2 (the images of physician and steersman of the people); *Pol.* 4.1 ("nothing without your consent").

ultimately hospitable and the Roman power alone as diabolic. It is conceivable that in this regard he unconsciously deepens negative attitudes toward Rome shared by many an eastern inhabitant of the empire (see on *Pol.* 2; cf. *Rom.* 2.2; 5.1). In any event, we can recognize in the distinction implicitly drawn between Roman power and Hellenistic culture a stage along the way by which Christians, while never forgetting the ultimate antagonism between the church and the "world," gradually claimed more and more of society as their concern.

The capital, of course, also has positive significance for Ignatius. For one thing, he already possesses a tradition that links Peter and Paul with Rome (*Rom.* 4.3), and he praises the Roman church in extravagant terms (*Rom.* inscr). But the Roman church is not yet Rome for Ignatius. The capital is the goal of his journey only in a paradoxical sense: he will "attain God" there through martyrdom. Yet Ignatius' conception of martyrdom remains distinctive precisely because it is given an interpretation in universal geographical (or even mythical geographical) terms (cf. *Rom.* 2.2) made possible by his selection as a victim for the games in the capital. In this connection, he could build on tradition that told of the journey of Paul and others to Rome as martyrs (see on *Eph.* 12.2). But his universal outlook (cf. *Sm.* 8.2) was no doubt reinforced by his own quest for recognition and support. For his praise of the Roman Christians is extravagant and his expectations of them are high precisely because they form the last link in a chain of churches that is to lend his martyrdom significance (see on *Rom.* inscr). Thus we may say that Ignatius' negative evaluation of the capital begets a positive image of the universal church.

4. Religious and Intellectual Background.

One purpose of the previous discussion of the historical and social context of Ignatius' letters is to suggest that many problems of interpretation are illuminated by attending to the interaction of life and thought that they portray. At the same time, it is clear that Ignatius takes a religious and cultural world for granted and that it includes elements not readily classifiable as biblical. In this connection, scholarship has followed developments in NT studies.

4.1. Ignatius and the Mystery Religions.

The first major study of Ignatius from the point of view of the history of religions was Gillis P:son Wetter's reading of the letters in light of current interest in the Hellenistic mystery religions.[72] Wetter assumed (with many of his day) that ritual is primary in religion and that consequently attention to the eucharist provided the best way into Ignatius' world. In particular, he believed that Ignatius conceived of the eucharist as the reenactment of the Lord's passion. Wetter's view of the matter passed over into Bartsch's study of Ignatius, though in a modified form. For Bartsch proposed an unconvincing distinction between two lines of eucharistic thinking in the letters—one that suits Wetter's analysis and another that reflects a more purely magical (or sacramental) mode of thought.[73] The texts have been subject to renewed scrutiny, however, and it seems highly unlikely that Ignatius anywhere presupposes a view of the eucharist as the reenactment of the Lord's passion.[74] This commentary touches on the matter only in discussion of some of the more problematic passages.

The fact that Ignatius is the first to use the term πάθος ("passion") for the Lord's death and does so frequently[75] has also been taken to point to the influence of the soteriology of the mystery religions.[76] It seems not at all impossible, however, that the use of the noun emerged more or less independently in Christian circles where the corresponding verb had long been in use with reference to the crucifixion. In any event, it happens that when

72   Gillis P:son Wetter, *Altchristliche Liturgien: Das christliche Mysterium* (FRLANT 30; Göttingen: Vandenhoeck & Ruprecht, 1921) 116–42.

73   Bartsch, *Gnostisches Gut*, 99–132.

74   Cf. Ton H. C. van Eijk, *La résurrection des morts chez les pères apostoliques* (Théologie historique 25; Paris: Beauchesne, 1974) 104–12.

75   *Eph.* 18.2; 20.1; *Mag.* 5.2; 11; *Tr.* inscr; 11.2; *Rom.*

6.3; *Phd.* inscr; 3.3; 9.2; *Sm.* 1.2; 5.3; 7.2; 12.2.

76   Cf. Elze, *Untersuchungen*, 62–64. Note that the term also appears in *Barn.* 6.7.

Ignatius speaks of the Lord's "passion," it is not in eucharistic contexts.[77] A more significant link is with martyrdom (cf. *Rom.* 6.3). For Ignatius is preoccupied with affirming the significance of his own death by proclaiming the reality of Christ's suffering (cf. *Tr.* 10; *Sm.* 4.2).[78]

4.2. Ignatius and Gnosticism.

The Gnostic thesis has made a deeper impression on Ignatian studies. Still fundamental is the work by Schlier, who first examined *Eph.* 19 in light of Gnostic mythology and then extended his analysis to other features of Ignatius' thought.[79] Schlier's parallels are often distant, and his exegesis strained. Yet he succeeded in identifying the spiritual milieu that is apparently reflected in a number of Ignatian themes and images. Bartsch proposed a different way of describing the Gnostic dimension in the letters.[80] Finding very little evidence of genuine Gnostic mythology, he suggested that the point of contact was the doctrine of God. In particular, he argued that Ignatius' concern for unity reflected the Gnostic conception of the harmony of spiritual powers within the divine fullness (as opposed to the biblical conception of God's oneness).

These works have made it difficult to deny the relevance of Gnostic sources for an interpretation of the letters of Ignatius.[81] Yet there is scant evidence that the bishop was familiar with Gnosticism in a developed form. It is probably best, then, to consider the Gnostic religion a distinctive articulation of a widely diffused otherworldliness that variously affected forms of mystical and semimystical movements of the period. It is presumably such a spiritual climate that has left its mark on Ignatius. Even so, we are doubtful that some important themes in Ignatius apparently of mystical provenance—that of unity,[82] for example, or that of silence[83]—are as deeply rooted in this soil as may at first seem likely. In any event, the emphasis in this commentary is on the extent to which potentially mystical or marginally Gnostic images and ideas have been made to subserve more concrete religious and social concerns.

4.3. Ignatius and Jewish Christianity.

Daniélou's treatment of Ignatius as a representative of Jewish Christianity illustrates some of the problems of definition just discussed.[84] For Daniélou quotes Schlier approvingly on important aspects of Ignatius' thought yet affixes the label of Jewish Christianity to materials regarded as Gnostic by his authority. One reason for this curious situation is that Schlier had invoked the *Ascension of Isaiah* as a major source in his exploration of the background to *Eph.* 19. Schlier seems to have been correct on this point, but it is surely arguable that the *Ascension of Isaiah* is more apocalyptic than Gnostic.[85] The discussion indicates that sharp distinctions are out of place. But it seems justified to locate the roots of the theology of *Eph.* 19 in a form of apocalyptic Jewish Christianity that has a family resemblance to Gnosticism.

Beyond that, however, little that is specifically Jewish or Jewish-Christian can be found in Ignatius, and Daniélou's method is too loose for us to rely heavily on other observations that he makes. The literature from Qumran represents a special disappointment in this regard. An occasional parallel puts a passage of Ignatius into perspective. But (despite Corwin)[86] the connections are few and marginal.[87]

It is also worth noting here that although the *Odes of Solomon* seem closer to the spiritual world of Ignatius, a literary connection is unlikely (see on *Tr.* 6.2; *Rom.* 7.2; cf. *Eph.* 19.3).

---

77 The exception here is the use of the verb in *Sm.* 7.1 (which scarcely represents a key to interpretation).

78 Cf. Paulsen, *Studien*, 180–85. The link between martyrdom and eucharist is not sufficiently strong (see on *Rom.* 2.2; 4.1; 7.3) to treat the two as interchangeable.

79 Schlier, *Untersuchungen*.

80 Bartsch, *Gnostisches Gut*.

81 Paulsen (*Studien*, passim) has integrated materials from the Nag Hammadi treatises into his study of Ignatius' theology. This commentary also attends to these sources.

82 See on *Eph.* 4.2–5.1; *Mag.* 1.2; 7.1–2; *Phd.* 5.2; 8.1.

83 See on *Eph.* 6.1; 14.2–15.2; 19.1; *Phd.* 1.1; *Mag.* 8.2.

84 Jean Daniélou, *The Theology of Jewish Christianity* (London: Darton, Longman & Todd; Chicago: Regnery, 1964) 39–43.

85 Cf. ibid., 12–13.

86 Corwin, *Ignatius,* passim.

87 Cf. Herbert Musurillo, "Ignatius of Antioch: Gnostic or Essene?" *TS* 22 (1961) 103–10.

4.4. Ignatius and Hellenistic Judaism.

Rather different is the problem of the relation between Ignatius and Hellenistic Judaism. Parallels involving Philo, Josephus, and others are frequently noted in this commentary. Philo, of course, is particularly well represented. It is often the case, however, that references to pagan sources seem as relevant as references to Philo; and in any event, the cumulative weight of the parallels is not overwhelming. Yet it would be wrong to underestimate their importance. Thus one clear source of Ignatius' treatment of the theme of unity is Hellenistic Judaism (see on *Mag.* 7.1–2), and it is likely that the philosophical elements in his doctrine of God were mediated through Hellenistic Judaism (see on *Pol.* 3.2; cf. *Eph.* 11.1). It should also be noted that the bishop confronted opponents in Philadelphia who worked with a Hellenistic-Jewish conception of the Scriptures (OT) as "archives" (see on *Phd.* 8.2), and it is likely that Hellenistic Judaism provided some of the background for docetic ideas (see on the expression "both ate and drank" in *Tr.* 9.1). Moreover, Philo provides parallels for some of the language in Ignatius that has a dualistic or mystical ring. Thus one conclusion to be drawn from such material is that Hellenistic Judaism rather than Gnosticism often provides the background for an understanding of Ignatius' spirituality.

4.5. Ignatius and Popular Hellenistic Culture.

Ignatius was a man of the Greek city and (as we have seen) seems to have been relatively at home there. A major purpose of this commentary is to show the extent to which he had absorbed elements of what may be loosely called popular Hellenistic culture. We have already discussed the literary character of the letters and noted their author's acquaintance with Hellenistic epistolography and rhetoric. We have also commented on the extent to which our bishop seems to have absorbed conceptions of communal life from the Hellenistic club and city. And we have seen that it is often hard to distinguish Ignatius' debt to Hellenistic Judaism from his debt to Hellenistic culture itself. Beyond that are a whole range of items too numerous to list here. The parallels from Plutarch collected by Hans Dieter Betz and his colleagues have proved enormously helpful in this regard.[88] For their research shows that matters such as Ignatius' views on boasting (see on *Tr.* 4.1) or his hints about God's reasons for delaying punishment (see on *Eph.* 11.1; *Sm.* 9.1; *Pol.* 6.2) and many other points reflect the Greek world. Still other parallels culled from Plutarch are noted in this commentary (see on *Mag.* 5.2; *Rom.* inscr; *Pol.* 2.1–3; and elsewhere), and new materials from other Greek sources of the period have also been collected. One result is that some expressions—such as "common hope" (see on *Eph.* 1.2), "I sing the churches" (*Mag.* 1.2), or "nothing without your approval" (*Pol.* 4.1)—gain a new or more definite resonance. At times what seems at first more or less original—such as Ignatius' description of his prophetic outburst in Philadelphia (*Phd.* 7.2)—is shown to follow a Hellenistic model closely. And when a stock theme like "concord" is lifted from the civic to the ecclesiastical level, we discover that the transformation is effected in part by other themes and images of Hellenistic provenance (see on *Eph.* 4.1–5.1). Sometimes a Hellenistic commonplace has become so much part and parcel of Ignatus' theology that an awareness of it can help guide the interpretation and prevent false conclusions from being drawn. We believe that that is so particularly with Ignatius' treatment of the theme of words and deeds and related polarities (see on *Eph.* 14.2–15.2; *Tr.* 10; *Rom.* 2.1–3.3).

Ignatius, to be sure, transforms everything that he has absorbed. And thus exegesis is still more important than parallels. Yet the spirit of popular Hellenistic culture remains more alive in his letters than is generally recognized. We correlate that fact at the social level with the bishop's relative openness to his immediate environment (see on *Eph.* 10) and at the theological level with his conviction that what Christians do according to the flesh is spiritual (see on *Eph.* 8.2).

5. Ignatian Themes.

The special mark of Ignatius' theology is the centrality afforded the incarnation and crucifixion of Jesus Christ. Relatively weak by comparison is the emphasis on

---

88 Hans Dieter Betz, ed., *Plutarch's Theological Writings and Early Christian Literature* (Studia ad Corpus Hellenisticum Novi Testamenti 3; Leiden: Brill, 1975); idem, ed., *Plutarch's Ethical Writings and Early Christian Literature* (Studia ad Corpus Hellenisticum Novi Testamenti 4; Leiden: Brill, 1978).

creation (see on *Eph.* 15.1; *Rom.* inscr), the unfolding of the divine purpose in history (see on *Mag.* 8–10; *Phd.* 5–9), and the coming of the end (see on *Eph.* 11.1). This has given rise to the view that, in Ignatius, biblical conceptions of God's dealings with the world have been replaced by a concern for personal salvation which subordinates all other purposes to it and which finds its best analogies in Gnosticism.[89] But the discontinuity is scarcely that sharp. Ignatius' Christianity presupposes a kind of dialectical development: it is rooted in primitive Christian conceptions; it has fallen under the influence of a variety of mystical or quasi-mystical modes of thought (which have also left their mark in the NT, particularly in such books as Ephesians and the Gospel of John); and it has found a certain resolution of these diverse tendencies in the idea of the incarnation. The result is an attenuation of traditional historical and eschatological elements, but at the same time a significant modification of the otherworldly tendencies of the age.

5.1. God.

(a) The greater part of the language about God in Ignatius is compatible with the assumption that God is a personal agent. God resists the proud (*Eph.* 5.3), he is concerned about us (*Mag.* 3.2), he knows all secrets (*Mag.* 3.2), he offers unity (*Tr.* 11.2), he "wills" (creates?) all that is (*Rom.* inscr), he deems a person worthy (*Rom.* 2.2), he dwells with those at peace with one another (*Phd.* 8.1), he provides assistance (*Sm.* 11.3), he pays attention to people (*Pol.* 6.1), he is patient with them (*Pol.* 6.2). We hear of Christians subordinate to him (*Eph.* 5.3), a plan prepared by him (*Eph.* 19.3), nations gathered to him (*Mag.* 10.3), a church beloved by him (*Tr.* inscr), a person honored by him (*Sm.* 9.1), a bishop overseen by him (*Pol.* inscr). Christians are said to love him (*Eph.* 9.2; 15.3; *Pol.* 5.1), fear his patience (*Eph.* 11.1), inherit his kingdom (*Eph.* 16.1; *Phd.* 3.3), please him (*Rom.* 2.1; *Sm.* 8.2), pray to him (*Eph.* 10.1; *Rom.* 1.1; *Phd.* 5.1), thank him (*Phd.* 6.3; 11.1), die for him (*Rom.* 4.1), repent unto him (*Sm.* 9.1), acknowledge him (*Sm.* 9.1), praise him (*Pol.* 1.1; 7.2), wait on him (*Pol.* 7.3). We hear of God's purpose (*Eph.* 3.2; *Rom.* 8.3; *Sm.* 6.2; *Pol.* 8.1), his will (*Eph.* inscr; 20.1; *Tr.* 1.1; *Rom.* inscr; 1.1; *Phd.* inscr; *Sm.* 1.1; 11.1;

Pol. 8.1), his plan (*Eph.* 18.2), his grace (see on *Sm.* 6.2), his power (*Mag.* 3.1; *Sm.* 1.1; 13.1), his church (*Tr.* 2.3; *Phd.* inscr; 10.1; *Sm.* inscr), his mercy (*Tr.* 12.3), his commandment (*Tr.* 13.2; *Sm.* 8.1), his word (*Rom.* 2.1; *Phd.* 11.1; *Sm.* inscr), his love (*Phd.* 1.1), his kindness (*Phd.* 1.2), his voice (*Phd.* 7.1), his work (*Pol.* 7.3). People and things are said to be "worthy" of God when they conform to high expectations (*Eph.* 2.1; 4.1; 7.1; *Sm.* 11.3; *Pol.* 6.2). And we hear of things done "to the glory of God" (*Mag.* 15; *Rom.* 10.2; *Pol.* 4.3; 7.2; cf. *Eph.* 13.1), or "to the honor of God" (*Eph.* 21.1, 2; *Sm.* 11.2; *Pol.* 5.2; cf. *Mag.* 3.2; *Tr.* 12.2). This representative selection is enough to show that the substratum of the bishop's view of God is conventional enough.

(b) At the same time, Ignatius' God is not vividly personal. References to his activity often seem more or less stereotyped or come alive through association with religious realities of greater immediacy (such as Jesus Christ, worship, or the ministry). The point may be illustrated by Ignatius' references to God as "Father." There are some forty-five instances. A few of these have to do specifically with God as the Father of Jesus Christ (*Eph.* 2.1; *Mag.* 3.1; *Tr.* inscr; 9.2; *Rom.* inscr; *Phd.* 7.2). About the same number seem to have to do specifically with God as Father of his people (*Eph.* inscr; 9.1; *Mag.* 3.1; *Tr.* 11.1; *Rom.* 7.2; *Phd.* 3.1; *Sm.* 13.1). The greatest number apparently also have in view God as the Father of his people, yet consistently make some reference to Jesus Christ in this connection. Thus it is evidently assumed that access to the (universal) Father is only through Christ. The pattern is clearest where Ignatius speaks of being blessed by God the Father "in" Christ (*Mag.* inscr; cf. *Tr.* 13.3; *Rom.* 2.2) or of possessing the stamp of God the Father "through" Christ (*Mag.* 5.2). This is further complicated, however, by the fact that in *Eph.* 4.2 we hear of people singing to the Father through Jesus Christ yet immediately find the latter identified as "his [the Father's] son." Presumably such a correlation between the Father and the Son is not an exclusive one.[90] Even so, Ignatius (like John) avoids speaking of Christians as the "sons" of God. Thus a certain remoteness characterizes God as Father.

Not unexpectedly, then, Ignatius goes further than

---

89 See especially Th. Preiss, "La mystique de l'imitation du Christ et de l'unité chez Ignace d'Antioche," *RHPhR* 18 (1938) 197–241.

90 For two other correlations of the Father and the Son see *Rom.* inscr (cf. *Sm.* 1.1).

NT writers in speaking of God's transcendence in terms that reflect Hellenistic (or Hellenistic-Jewish) thought. He hesitates in speaking about the divine wrath (*Eph.* 11.1), and he finds negative attributes for God the appropriate ones (*Pol.* 3.2; cf. *Eph.* 7.2). Thus God in his being is beyond all temporal and spatial categories.

More problematic is the question whether Ignatius goes still further and adopts the language of Hellenistic mysticism or Gnosticism in speaking of God and his relation with those who know him. For Ignatius speaks of "bearing" God (concerning his name Theophorus, see on *Eph.* inscr), "sharing" God (*Eph.* 4.2), "being entirely of God" (*Eph.* 8.1), being "full" of God (*Mag.* 14), and "having" God (Christ) in oneself (*Rom.* 6.3; cf. *Mag.* 12). We are also told of God's "greatness" and "fullness" (*Eph.* inscr) and find him all but identified with "stillness" (*Eph.* 19.1; cf. 15.1–2) and "silence" (*Mag.* 8.2). But Ignatius does not exploit the mystical possibilities of such language. His conception of the relation between God and human beings revolves not about identification but about communion within the context of the solidarity of the group. (Similar problems are noted below in our discussions of unity, ministry, attaining God, and imitation.)

Dualistic themes are not unknown to Ignatius. Thus he uses the term "world" in a purely negative sense,[91] and he attributes broad powers to "the ruler of this age."[92] In such matters, however, he builds on views reflected in both Paul and John and avoids drawing Gnostic conclusions from them. In *Rom.* 3.3, where he seems to condemn the phenomenal world out of hand, something quite different was intended. A person can become inordinately attached to "matter" (cf. *Rom.* 6.2; 7.2), but matter is hardly evil in itself. Thus elsewhere Ignatius evidently takes a biblical conception of creation for granted (cf. *Eph.* 15.1; *Rom.* inscr), and he finds no

difficulty contemplating the positive use of fleshly things by spiritual people (*Eph.* 8.2). And that includes marriage (*Pol.* 5.1–2).

Problems regarding Ignatius' conception of the relation between God and human beings also emerge in his use of a number of prepositional phrases that must be touched on. Ignatius goes beyond Paul (cf. 1 Thess 2:2) and is perhaps closer to John (17:20–23; cf. 1 John 4:15–16) in his use of the expression ἐν θεῷ ("in God"). The relative frequency of its appearance[93] suggests that he may reflect a tradition in which "God mysticism" had supplemented "Christ mysticism" and thus opened a way to more clearly non-biblical modes of thought. Whether this is so or not, Ignatius' own usage points in a different direction. For the expression has a stereotyped quality and often means little more than "godly" or "belonging to God." In no instance is a profoundly mystical sense evident.[94]

Also fairly frequent in Ignatius is the expression κατὰ θεόν ("in accordance with God").[95] This is less problematic. It has NT warrant[96] and refers to the performance of something in accordance with God's will. Moreover, it too often seems to mean little more than "godly."

References to being "of God" (the genitive)[97] all seem to have in view a relationship of obedience and loyalty. More problematic uses of the genitive are dealt with below in our discussion of unity.

Conceivably all statements about the relation between God and human beings in Ignatius have metaphysical implications, especially in light of his emphasis on the union of flesh and spirit in his account of human salvation. Thus all of the prepositional phrases just discussed may be colored accordingly. At the same time, we must not neglect the evidence that Ignatius still speaks of God

---

91 *Mag.* 5.2; *Rom.* 2.2; 3.2, 3; 4.2; 6.1, 2; 7.1.

92 *Eph.* 17.1; 19.1; *Mag.* 1.2; *Tr.* 4.2; *Rom.* 7.1; *Phd.* 6.2; cf. *Sm.* 6.1.

93 *Eph.* 1.1; 6.2; *Mag.* 3.1; 14; *Tr.* 4.1; 8.2; *Pol.* 1.1; 6.1; cf. *Eph.* 21.2; *Mag.* inscr.

94 More frequent in Ignatius is the Pauline formula "in Christ" (*Eph.* inscr; 1.1; 3.1; 8.2; 10.3; 11.1; 12.2; 20.2; *Mag.* inscr; 6.2; *Tr.* 1.1; 9.2; 13.2; 13.3; *Rom.* inscr; 1.1; 2.2; *Phd.* 10.1, 2; 11.2; *Pol.* 8.3). This too sometimes has a stereotyped quality. Often, however, it plays a more vital role, grounding the possibility of the believer's resurrection, the solidarity of the

community, and the union of flesh and spirit.

95 *Eph.* 2.1; 8.1; *Mag.* 1.1; 13.1; *Tr.* 1.2; *Phd.* 4.1; *Sm.* 11.3; *Pol.* 5.2.

96 Cf. Rom 8:27; 2 Cor 7:9–11; Eph 4:24; 1 Pet 4:6; 5:2.

97 *Eph.* 8.1; *Mag.* 5.2; 10.1; *Rom.* 6.2; *Phd.* 3.2.

as a personal agent and understands important aspects of the Christian's response to him in such terms.

(c) Ignatius knows that "God is one" but affirms the point to mark the importance of God's self-revelation "through Jesus Christ his son" (*Mag.* 8.2). Elsewhere Ignatius refers to Christ as "our God" and evidently attributes divinity to him in the fullest sense (see on *Eph.* inscr). Thus from the point of view of later trinitarian developments Ignatius tends to a "monarchian" position.[98] There are a number of passages that have a "subordinationist" ring, but appearances are probably deceiving in this regard (see on *Eph.* 3.2). In one passage Christ is conceived of as having existed with the Father before the ages *(Mag.* 6.1), but the pre-cosmic distinction between Father and Son is apparently not emphasized. Thus in another passage Ignatius builds (it seems) on adoptionist language and traces the emergence of Christ as God's "son" to the time of the incarnation (see on *Sm.* 1.1; cf. *Mag.* 8.2).[99] But the use of technical language to describe Ignatius' theology runs the risk of falsifying the picture. Images such as that of the word from silence *(Mag.* 8.2) suggest more accurately his concern.[100] What we have here is a mind dominated by a vision of the atemporal and invisible God manifesting himself in space and time *(Pol.* 3.2; cf. *Eph.* 7.2).

Ignatius occasionally uses trinitarian formulae, but he makes little of them theologically (see on *Eph.* 9.1; *Mag.* 13.1–2). In particular he refers to the spirit (or holy spirit) infrequently and tends to deal with it simply as a divine power associated with God or Christ (see on *Phd.* inscr). At the same time, there is no identification of Christ with the spirit in *Mag.* 15 (as has sometimes been thought); and the antithesis of flesh and spirit which plays a role in christological contexts is best regarded as a separate matter. Thus Ignatius has no "Spirit-

christology" in the narrow sense of the term.

5.2. Incarnation.

When Ignatius refers to Christ as "both fleshly and spiritual" (*Eph.* 7.2; cf. *Sm.* 3.3), he has in mind the union of the divine and human in the God-Man and thus anticipates the classical two-nature christology. In this connection a development can be traced from an older two-stage christology (cf. Rom 1:3–4) to a christology dominated by the idea of incarnation (see on *Eph.* 18.2). Here Ignatius is most nearly approached in the NT by John, but he has also moved significantly beyond the evangelist. The development evidently presupposes a description of divine transcendence in metaphysical terms (cf. *Pol.* 3.2; *Eph.* 7.2). For such a description opens up a gulf between God and humanity that requires something as paradoxical as the incarnation for God and humanity to meet.[101] And in such a context it is natural for salvation to be conceived of primarily in terms of the transformation of human nature by the resurrection (cf. *Tr.* 9.2; *Sm.* 7.1).[102]

The anti-docetic thrust of incarnational thinking favors a certain emphasis on concrete historical realities. Thus Ignatius apparently finds it significant that Jesus suffered under Pontius Pilate (*Mag.* 11; *Tr.* 9.1; *Sm.* 1.2). He also correlates docetism with the avoidance of good deeds (*Sm.* 6.2–7.1) and connects the reality of Christ's passion with the meaningfulness of his own martyrdom (*Tr.* 10; *Sm.* 4.2). Similarly he sees things done by Christians "according to the flesh" as "spiritual" (*Eph.* 8.2). Yet Ignatius also takes it for granted that the spirit is of higher dignity than the flesh, and he goes beyond the NT in ascribing significance to things only insofar as they are subordinated to the revelation of Jesus Christ as God incarnate. Thus he radically dissociates "Judaism"

---

98 Cf. Corwin, *Ignatius*, 140–41.

99 Complications are possible in light of the antithesis of "Son of God" and "Son of Man" in *Eph.* 20.2 and the correlation of the "Father" and the "Son" in *Rom.* inscr.

100 For other christological images and titles in Ignatius see *Eph.* 3.2 ("intention"), *Eph.* 17.2 ("knowledge"), *Rom.* 8.2 ("mouth"), *Phd.* 9.1 ("door"). Note also *Sm.* 4.2 ("perfect human being").

101 There is as yet no critical reflection in Ignatius on how the divine and the human can be joined in Christ. The christological paradoxes of *Eph.* 7.2 and

Pol. 3.2 indicate that the bishop's concern was simply to affirm that such a union occurred. Indeed, so undifferentiated is his sense of the divinity of Christ that he can refer to the "blood of God" (*Eph.* 1.1) and the "suffering of my God" (*Rom.* 6.3). At the same time, Christ as "our God" (see on *Eph.* inscr) and the self-manifestation of God (cf. *Mag.* 8.2) is somehow God in a particular way. The Father is not the Son (see on *Sm.* 1.1). Ignatius hovers on the brink of an "economic" interpretation of the Godhead.

102 A concern for the problem of sin is almost totally absent from Ignatius (see on *Eph.* 14.2; *Sm.* 7.1).

from the OT and thoroughly Christianizes the prophets (see on *Mag.* 8–10). And having lost vital interest in eschatology except in individual terms he thinks almost exclusively of the destiny of an idealized church as he looks to the future. Ignatius' doctrine of the incarnation deepens the sense of God's involvement in the phenomenal world and the significance of what is done by human beings in the sphere of the flesh, but it also narrows the historical arena of divine activity and emphatically objectifies revelation.

5.3. Eucharist.

The eucharist is the center of worship for Ignatius (cf. *Eph.* 5.2; 13.1; *Phd.* 4; *Sm.* 7.1; 8.1) and serves as the focus for a sense of the presence of saving power in the Christian community (cf. *Eph.* 20.2).[103] There is really only one passage of which it can be said with any confidence that the very elements of the meal are associated with the flesh of Christ (*Sm.* 7.1). Yet that passage is sufficiently impressive as to suggest that sacramental realism is taken for granted (and even emphasized) by Ignatius.

At the same time, it is remarkable that this is made explicit so infrequently and that references to Christ's "flesh and blood" in a more or less symbolic sense are also to be found (see on *Tr.* 8.1; *Rom.* 7.3; *Phd.* 5.1; cf. *Sm.* 12.2).[104] This is not simply a matter of the spiritualization of cultic language however. Rather it reflects Ignatius' sense that an acknowledgment of the reality of the incarnation and passion (and thus also of the presence of Christ in the elements of the sacred meal) is correlated with a commitment to good deeds (see on *Sm.* 6.2–7.1). The sacred meal, to be sure, has another function: the bread that is broken is in some (probably not too literal) sense the "medicine of immortality" (*Eph.* 20.2), and there is a connection between participation in the meal and the believer's resurrection (*Sm.* 7.1). Nevertheless, references to Christ's flesh and blood evidently serve Ignatius primarily to mark the value of commitment to deeds of love and obedience.

It is this that explains the link regularly found in Ignatius between the eucharist and unity. The link is made all the clearer by the association of the sacred meal with the image of the altar which in Ignatius is not used to indicate the sacrificial character of the meal but to symbolize solidarity (see on *Eph.* 5.2; *Mag.* 7.2; *Tr.* 7.2; *Phd.* 4). In a sense it is this solidarity that is the fundamental reality for Ignatius (see on *Tr.* 2.3). And it is this solidarity that is signified by the presence of the Lord at or in the sacred meal.

The eucharist, then, has come to function in two ways in Ignatius—(a) as the bearer of a sacred power (however defined) that confers immortality and (b) as the sign of the inestimable importance of concrete acts of love and obedience in the church. This dual function (as we shall see) is not unrelated to other dualities in Ignatius' thought.

5.4. Unity.

The theme of unity may well represent the central concern of the letters of Ignatius. But in our view its significance has often been distorted. Thus it has been taken to include union with God, and a Gnostic background has been invoked to explain it. Gnostic or semi-Gnostic usage may be presupposed, yet in some passages Hellenistic or Hellenistic-Jewish parallels are clearly more relevant (see on *Eph.* 4.1–5.1; *Mag.* 7.1–2). In any event, it is significant that the term ἕνωσις ("union") as Ignatius uses it evidently refers primarily to the solidarity of the Christian community (see on *Mag.* 1.2) and that the same can be said with almost equal confidence of the term ἑνότης ("unity"; see on *Phd.* 5.2; 8.1). In particular, we argue that the expression "unity of God" means "unity from God" rather than "unity with God"[105] We also question an interpretation in mystical terms of statements that seem to identify God and unity (*Eph.* 14.1; *Tr.* 11.2). A sense of communion with God is not missing from Ignatius and is no doubt presupposed

---

103 But not (as we have seen) in the sense that the sacred meal represents a reenactment of the Lord's passion (see 4.1 above). Similarly, it is doubtful that Ignatius' application of eucharistic language to martyrdom amounts to a sacramentalization of the latter (see on *Rom.* 2.2; 4.1; 7.3).

104 Cf. S. M. Gibbard, "The Eucharist in the Ignatian Epistles," *Studia Patristica VIII* (TU 93; Berlin: Akademie-Verlag, 1966) 214–18.

105 Similarly, ὁμονοία θεοῦ ("concord of God") must mean "godly concord" (*Mag.* 6.1; 15; *Phd.* inscr).

whenever he speaks of union or unity. For the latter are conferred by God. But since Ignatius apparently avoids using the term union when he speaks of communion with God, we may assume that union has to do with the solidarity of the community in social and cultic terms and lacks deeper mystical significance.[106] The church, to be sure, is the body of Christ,[107] and Christ is God; but Christ as "*our* God" (see on *Eph.* inscr), God's self-manifestation (*Mag.* 8.2), presumably serves a function distinct from God simply as God. Ignatius does not dissolve everything into unity as indiscriminately as is sometimes thought.

These findings cohere with the role that unity plays in Ignatius' reflections on his relations with the churches. There (as we have seen) his call for union represents at the same time a call for support and recognition. Concrete social interaction is what is primarily involved.

5.5. Ministry.

Closely related to the theme of unity are Ignatius' reflections on the ministry. On the historical side, we conclude that the threefold ministry (bishop, elders, deacons) was surely in place in the communities known to Ignatius and that the authority of one bishop was recognized (see on *Tr.* 3.1).[108] But there are signs that the situation was still somewhat in flux (see on *Eph.* 2.1–2), and it seems likely that Ignatius gave greater weight

to episcopal authority than did most of those with whom he came in contact (see on *Mag.* 4). In any event, episcopacy does not yet seem to have been reinforced by the idea of succession (see on *Eph.* 3.2; *Tr.* inscr). And the ministry is still genuinely collegial. Thus a requirement to obey the elders along with the bishop is taken for granted.[109]

Of greater importance for our purposes is the question of Ignatius' understanding of the ministry. There has been a general tendency to find in the letters a view that all but divinizes the leaders of the church. At the heart of the discussion is Ignatius' treatment of the silence of the bishop (see on *Eph.* 6.1; *Phd.* 1.1), the analogies between the earthly hierarchy and the heavenly hierarchy (see on *Mag.* 6.1), the place of bishops in a line of authority proceeding from God and Christ (see on *Eph.* 3.2; cf. *Pol.* inscr), and the virtual interchangeability of God and the bishop as sources of authority (see on *Mag.* 3.1; cf. *Eph.* 5.3; 6.1; *Sm.* 9.1). We argue that in Ignatius the bishop does not occupy the place of God or Christ[110] and that we are still close to NT models. The authority of the ministry (the bishop in particular) is certainly strengthened,[111] but it is not legitimated in terms that are essentially new.

Ignatius' high view of the authority of the bishop is probably still the single most important reason for doubting the authenticity of the middle recension.[112]

106 The closely related theme of ὁμονοία ("concord"; *Eph.* 4.1, 2; 13.1; *Mag.* 6.1; 15; *Tr.* 12.2; *Phd.* inscr; 11.2) occurs most characteristically in cultic contexts. Even so, the emphasis is on the solidarity of the group, and it is likely that here (as still more clearly in *1 Clement*) a civic ideal has left its mark (see on *Eph.* 13.1; cf. *Eph.* 4.1–5.1). Note that in *Mag.* 1.2 Ignatius appears to model his activity on that of secular orators when he encourages unity in the churches.

107 In this regard it is doubtful that Ignatius goes beyond Paul (see on *Tr.* 11.2; cf. *Eph.* 4.2; *Sm.* 1.2).

108 No formal earthly authority (including that of the Roman church) was recognized beyond the local level (see on *Rom.* inscr).

109 Cf. Albano Vilela, "Le Presbytérium selon saint Ignace d'Antioche," *BLE* 74 (1973) 161–86.

110 Cf. Ekkart Sauser, "Tritt der Bischof an die Stelle Christi? Zur Frage nach der Stellung des Bischofs in der Theologie des hl. Ignatius von Antiocheia," in Victor Flieder, ed., *Festschrift Franz Loidl zum 65. Geburtstag* (2 vols.; Sammlung "Aus Christentum und

Kultur," Sonderband 1–2; Wien: Hollinek, 1970) 1. 325–39.

111 Note that prophetic gifts are also put directly in the service of episcopal authority (see on *Phd.* 7.1–2). Thus charisma is in process of routinization. Yet Ignatius' prophetic activity is not formally tied to his status as bishop, and he still conceives of the divine spirit as blowing where it wills.

112 See now Joly, *Ignace,* 75–85. Joly sometimes forces the argument. It is not true, for example, that Ignatius' use of the term πρεσβυτήριον ("presbytery") is totally isolated in the period (p. 83). For it is also used of a church council in 1 Tim 4:14.

But if our understanding of this matter is correct, it is not as advanced as is often thought. The situation in the Pastoral Epistles is not entirely clear, but it appears that the churches known to Ignatius have moved at most but a step beyond them.[113] And Ignatius' somewhat more emphatic personal view of the authority of the bishop seems comprehensible in light of his situation.

5.6. Flesh and Spirit.

It is characteristic of Ignatius to speak of unity in terms of polarities—some antithetical, others more or less complementary—that together serve to express totality.[114] It is frequently the case, then, that it is the polarity as such rather than the content of the polar terms that is significant (cf. *Mag.* 1.2; 13.1).[115] At the same time, the terms do have distinguishable content, and their separate meanings deserve attention.

One of the most important of these polarities is that of "flesh" and "spirit" or the corresponding adjectives (and adverbs) "fleshly" and "spiritual." Undoubtedly Ignatius' source here was the Christian tradition, although he hardly derived the theme directly from John or even Paul.[116] Ignatius treats flesh and spirit in the Pauline manner as two spheres within which human existence moves. At the same time, he goes beyond Paul in taking them more or less clearly as two metaphysically distinct substances. Quite unexpectedly (from either a Pauline or a Hellenistic point of view) he seeks to deny their incompatibility.[117] In one passage he reflects the older view in which flesh and spirit are opposed but goes on almost consciously to modify the tradition (*Eph.* 8.2).[118] Here the presupposition is that the flesh represents not the sphere of sin but the sphere of corruptibility. Thus Ignatius preaches a gospel of the spiritual transformation of all that is fleshly.[119]

An important application of the polarity by Ignatius is at the christological level. The two spheres are conjoined in the God-Man (*Eph.* 7.2; cf. *Sm.* 3.2–3).[120] It is more

---

113 The Pastorals may even presuppose the "monarchical episcopacy" (Hans von Campenhausen, *Ecclesiastical Authority and Spiritual Power* [Stanford, CA: Stanford University, 1969] 107–8). But there can be no certainty on the point.

114 The analogies used by Ignatius in his discussion of the ministry involve polar terms (and triadic patterns) that also express totality (cf. *Eph.* 3.2; 5.1; *Mag.* 6.1). The fact that the relation between the divine Father and Son is appealed to not only in his discussion of the ministry but also in the materials under discussion (cf. *Mag.* 1.2; 13.1) indicates the close relation between the two sets of data.

115 A similar function is served by the six terms in *Phd.* 11.2 that look like two triadic patterns conjoined.

116 Three reasons may be given for doubting direct Pauline inspiration of the polarity: (1) Ignatius seems to have known only 1 Corinthians at all well (as we will see), and that letter does not have the flesh/spirit polarity (moreover, the expression "according to the flesh" in 1 Cor 1:26 and 10:18 is relatively neutral). We do find a juxtaposition of the two corresponding adjectives in 1 Cor 3:1–3, but it is obscured by the complexity of the context (cf. Birger Albert Pearson, *The Pneumatikos-Psychikos Terminology in 1 Corinthians* [SBLDS 12; Missoula, MT: Society of Biblical Literature, 1973). (2) Ignatius' use of the polarity is at times stereotyped (e.g. *Tr.* inscr; 12.1; *Rom.* inscr; *Sm.* 1.1; *Pol.* 5.1). (3) Ignatius modifies the characteristic force of the polarity so fundamentally (see on *Eph.* 8.2) that it is hard to believe that he associated it with a revered apostle. At the same time, an antici-

pation of Ignatius' usage is to be found in a less characteristic Pauline expression like "both in the flesh and in the Lord" in Phlm 16.

117 Cf. Eduard Schweizer, "σάρξ, σαρκικός, σάρκινος," *TDNT* 7 (1971) 98–151.

118 Acting "according to the flesh" seems occasionally to be negatively evaluated by Ignatius. It happens, however, that here the contrast is between God (or Christ) and the flesh (*Mag.* 6.2; *Rom.* 8.3); and other such contrasts present the flesh in a more neutral light (*Eph.* 1.3; 16.2; *Mag.* 3.2; *Rom.* 9.3). Similarly neutral are expressions in which the human is contrasted with the spiritual (*Eph.* 5.1; cf. *Tr.* 2.1; *Rom.* 8.1). At a more elementary level, Ignatius refers to his own body as "my flesh" (*Rom.* 2.1) and to Christ's body as his flesh (*Sm.* 1.2; 3.1; *Pol.* 5.2). A special application of such usage is his discussion of the eucharistic flesh of Christ (*Sm.* 7.1; cf. *Tr.* 8.1; *Rom.* 7.3; *Phd.* 4; 5.1). Finally, his references to Christ's lineage "according to the flesh" are semi-credal in character (*Eph.* 20.2; *Rom.* 7.3; *Sm,* 1.1).

119 There is at least one polarity that resists such treatment—that of God and the world (*Mag.* 5.2; *Rom.* 2.2; 3.2, 3; 4.2; 6.1, 2; 7.1). Here the term "world" evidently refers to (a) a sphere opposed to God (cf. *Mag.* 5.2), (b) the world of people hostile to Christianity (cf. *Rom.* 3.3), (c) the realm of matter (cf. *Rom.* 6.2) insofar as Satan inflames an unhealthy affection for it (cf. *Rom.* 6.1; 7.1–2). The "world," then, is never simply the physical world.

120 As we have seen, it seems best to distinguish the spirit in the polarity flesh/spirit from the spirit (or holy

frequently applied at the anthropological level. In some passages Ignatius may be thinking of two components of human nature (cf. *Tr.* 12.1; *Pol.* 1.2; 5.1),[121] but it is difficult to distinguish these instances from the majority in which he has in mind the total commitment of Christ's people and (presumably) the interpenetration of the two spheres that attends being "in Jesus Christ" (*Eph.* 8.2).[122]

Finally, we note a distinctive application of the theme that correlates the flesh and the spirit with the visible and the invisible (the relatively superficial and the more profound). This is found most clearly perhaps in Ignatius' description of Polycarp as the ideal bishop who is both fleshly and spiritual (*Pol.* 2.2).[123] A similar point, however, lies behind the series of antitheses in *Rom.* 2–3, and these in turn hark back to the distinction between words and deeds in *Eph.* 14.2–15.2. Here again we find a fluctuation between anthropological and christological applications of the materials.

5.7. Flesh and Blood.

A correlation of some interest is that which connects flesh and blood with faith and love (*Tr.* 8.1; cf. *Rom.* 7.3; *Sm.* 12.2).[124] It is tolerably clear in the context of *Sm.* 12.2 that the mention of flesh and blood contributes first of all to an emphasis on total commitment to unity. At the same time, it also underscores the reality of the passion and resurrection as the ground for such unity.

Particular reference to the flesh and blood of Christ in the eucharist evidently hovers in the background (cf. *Phd.* 4; *Rom.* 7.3).[125] Yet the reference is not explicit either in *Sm.* 12.2 or (more importantly) in *Tr.* 8.1. Thus the mention of flesh and blood serves more generally to mark not only the reality of the passion and resurrection but also the seriousness of the commitment to faith and love that Ignatius associates with anti-docetic theology (see on *Tr.* 8.1; *Rom.* 7.3).

5.8. Faith and Love.[126]

(a) The most important polar terms in Ignatius are faith and love. Ignatius himself indicates that they are "everything" (*Sm.* 6.1). The noun "love" occurs sixty-four times, appearing sixteen times together with "faith" (and three more times with the corresponding adjective or verb)[127] and twenty-seven times alone (or in combination with words other than "faith"). It is significant that "faith" appears alone (or with words other than "love") only nine times. Ignatius probably did not derive the formula "faith and love" directly from Paul but from popular developments of Pauline themes.[128]

To some extent the formula "faith and love" appears in Ignatius as a stereotyped expression used along with other polarities simply to express the completeness and fullness of the happy state of affairs under discussion.[129] For the most part, however, it plays an independent role

---

spirit) conceived of as a divine force (cf. *Eph.* 18.2; *Phd.* inscr; 7.1–2; *Sm.* 13.1) and from the spirit mentioned in the trinitarian formulae (cf. *Eph.* 9.1; *Mag.* 13.2). A link between the spirit in the polarity and the spirit as a divine force is most nearly approached in *Phd.* 7.2.

121 In this connection it should be noted that Ignatius sometimes speaks of "my spirit" when he could just as well have said "I" (*Eph.* 18.1; *Tr.* 13.3; *Rom.* 9.3; *Sm.* 10.2) and talks of persons' interior disposition as their "spirits" (cf. *Mag.* 15; *Sm.* inscr; *Pol.* 1.3). There is also an echo of the anthropological triad "flesh, soul, spirit" (*Phd.* 11.2). None of this, however, lends much support to an interpretation of the flesh/spirit polarity in terms of the components of human nature.

122 Cf. *Eph.* 10.3; *Mag.* 1.2; 13.1, 2; *Tr.* inscr; *Rom.* inscr; *Sm.* 13.2.

123 Note the correspondence between "visible"/"unseen" and "with flesh"/"with God" in *Mag.* 3.2.

124 Note that *Sm.* 12.2 (a greeting) mentions "both his [Christ's] *flesh and blood*, both his suffering and resurrection, both *fleshly and spiritual*," and that *Sm.*

13.2 (also a greeting) speaks of "*faith and love*, both *fleshly and spiritual*."

125 References to (Christ's) flesh and blood are probably to be eliminated in two other passages on textual grounds (*Tr.* inscr; *Sm.* 3.2).

126 See especially Olavi Tarvainen, *Glaube und Liebe bei Ignatius von Antiochien* (Schriften der Luther-Agricola-Gesellschaft 14; Joensuu: Pohjois-Karjalan Kirjapaino Oy, 1967).

127 *Mag.* 5.2; 6.1; *Phd.* 9.2. "Faith" probably joins "love" by implication also in *Rom.* 7.3.

128 The formula is also presupposed in 1 John (3:23; 5:1–4) and elsewhere (cf. 1 Pet 1:8; 2 Pet 1:5–7; Jude 20—21; *Barn.* 11.8). But it is primarily in Pauline literature that faith and love are mentioned together (1 Thess 3:6; Gal 5:6; 1 Cor 16:13–14; Phlm 5; cf. Eph 3:17; 6:23; 1 Tim 1:4–5, 14; 2 Tim 1:13) or in combination with other terms (1 Cor 13:13; 1 Thess 1:3; 5:8; cf. Col 1:4; 1 Tim 4:12; 6:11; 2 Tim 2:22; 3:10; Tit 2:2). Yet Ignatius, who knew of Paul only 1 Corinthians at all well, fails ever to imitate the most striking combination of terms from that source—

comparable in importance to that of faith or faith and love in Paul. For faith and love in Ignatius are the primary expressions of the Christian life, reflecting an orientation deeper than the purely intellectual, ethical, or emotional elements involved. From them flows all that is good (*Eph.* 14.1). It is characteristic that faith and love (or love alone) are linked with the most desirable states of affairs. It is also characteristic that this link is established by words like "in accordance with"[130] or "in"[131] or by the use of the dative[132] or the genitive[133] (or by personifications of "love"[134] or other expressions that make of love a sphere within which Christ's people move[135]) so that there is a virtual equivalence between faith and love (or love alone) and Christian existence as such.[136] This close relation is further suggested by the identification of faith as the beginning of life and love as the end in *Eph.* 14.1 and by the connections made elsewhere between love and the realities associated with the sacrament (*Rom.* 7.3; *Sm.* 6.2–7.1; 8.2).

The state of affairs which faith and love (or love alone) express is primarily the unity and good order of the Christian community.[137] And one important manifestation of such loving unity is the recognition and support accorded Ignatius himself (especially in the sending of representatives to greet him).[138] This happy state of affairs is, of course, inconceivable apart from the presence of God or Christ in the churches.[139]

Occasionally faith and love appear to be thought of not as the happy state of affairs itself but as the way to it. One striking image compares faith to the guide and love to the road up to God (*Eph.* 9.1). Elsewhere the love of the Trallians for Ignatius is regarded as promoting his eternal felicity (*Tr.* 12.3). Associated with this turn to the other world is the sense that love itself is an otherworldly phenomenon that transcends the flesh (cf. *Eph.* 1.3) and is opposed to the corruptible things of this life (cf. *Rom.* 7.3). Thus Ignatius moves toward a more teleological mode of thought in which faith and love function as virtues that describe partly the desired end and partly the means to that end.

The diverse tendencies of Ignatius' ethical thought apparently coexist in his description of faith as the beginning of life and love the end (*Eph.* 14.1). These identifications, as we have seen, make of faith and love the all-embracing realities of the Christian community. This interpretation of the passage has been reinforced by an appeal to the possible mythological background of the polarity "beginning and end" (see on *Mag.* 6.1). But this may be going too far. For references to beginning and end are found in less dramatic contexts to express totality

---

faith, hope, and love (1 Cor 13:13). On the other hand, his linking of faith, love, and endurance (*Pol.* 6.2) echoes less immediately discernible combinations in the Pauline materials. Thus the three terms are brought together in Tit 2:2 (cf. 1 Tim 6:11; 2 Tim 3:10); and a connection between faith/hope/ love and faith/love/endurance is suggested already by 1 Thess 1:3 (work of *faith*/labor of *love*/endurance of *hope*); moreover, 1 Thess 5:8 links faith/hope/ love to parts of armor in the way that Ignatius links faith/love/endurance to parts of armor in *Pol.* 6.2. A similarly complex relation seems to obtain between *Eph.* 14.2 (faith as the beginning of life and love the end) and 1 Tim 1:4–5 (where the formulation is less complete). It seems likely, then, that Ignatius is dependent in such matters on tradition alive in circles affected by Pauline theology or a closely related stream of gentile-Christian thought.

129 *Mag.* 1.2; 13.1; cf. *Eph.* 20.1; *Rom.* inscr; *Phd.* 11.2; *Sm.* 1.1; 13.2.
130 *Eph.* 1.1; 2.1; *Rom.* inscr.
131 *Eph.* 1.3; 4.1; 20.1; *Mag.* 1.1; 5.2; 6.1; 7.1; *Tr.* 8.1;

12.3; *Rom.* 2.2; *Phd.* 1.1; 6.2; 9.2; *Sm.* inscr; 1.1; *Pol.* 1.2.
132 *Mag.* 13.1; *Phd.* 11.2; *Sm.* 13.2.
133 *Mag.* 1.1, 2.
134 *Eph.* 2.1; *Tr.* 6.1; 13.1; *Rom.* 9.1, 3; *Phd.* 11.2; *Sm.* 12.1.
135 *Eph.* 2.1; *Mag.* 14; *Tr.* 3.2; 12.3; *Rom.* 1.2; 7.3; *Pol.* 6.2.
136 Cf. Paulsen, *Studien*, 91–93.
137 Cf. *Eph.* 14.2; *Mag.* 1.1, 2; 5.2; 7.1; 13.1; 14; *Tr.* 6.1; 12.3; *Phd.* 1.1; 6.2; *Sm.* 6.1, 2; *Pol.* 1.2.
138 Cf. *Eph.* 1.1, 3; 2.1; *Mag.* 6.1; *Tr.* 3.2; *Rom.* 1.2; 2.2; *Pol.* 7.2. Love also forges bonds between the churches that support Ignatius and his cause (*Tr.* 13.1; *Rom.* 9.1, 3; *Phd.* 11.2; *Sm.* 12.1).
139 Cf. *Eph.* 4.1; 14.1; 20.1; *Mag.* 1.2; *Rom.* 2.2; *Phd.* 11.2.

(see on *Mag.* 13.1). Moreover, still other parallels suggest that their use in *Eph.* 14.1 may in fact echo ethical discussions in which the relation between various virtues is structured in terms of beginning and end. An interpretation of faith and love as virtues would place greater emphasis on the formation of character and would be more likely to move toward teleological conceptions. Such tendencies are not absent from Ignatius.

(b) Ignatius' use of the verb "to love" confirms the fact that for him love is associated primarily with the unity of the group. Most examples have to do with relations between Christians and their leaders (including also Ignatius),[140] Christians and other Christians,[141] or one Christian leader and another.[142] Thus it is basically a matter of loving unity (*Phd.* 7.2).[143]

There is little to go on in this connection when it comes to the relation between Christians and God. Ignatius twice speaks of a church beloved by God (*Tr.* inscr; *Rom.* inscr) and knows that the Lord loved the church (*Pol.* 5.1).[144] There are also three references to loving God or the Lord (*Eph.* 9.2; 15.3; *Pol.* 5.1) and one to loving his grace (*Eph.* 11.1). The context indicates, however, that in each instance the mention of such love serves to confirm the importance of good deeds and/or the maintenance of unity in the church.

(c) References to faith outside of the formula faith and love deserve attention. For the most part we find ourselves on familiar ground. Thus there is a connection between faith and concord (cf. *Eph.* 13.1; 20.2). Moreover, the realms of faith and unfaith constitute antithetical spheres comparable to the spheres of flesh and spirit (*Eph.* 8.2) and are thus oriented to the world and God respectively (*Mag.* 5.2).

Yet since faith is the beginning of life and love the end (*Eph.* 14.1; cf. *Phd.* 9.2), faith and love represent two distinct moments in the life of the Christian community. Objectively, faith refers to the body of Christian truth or (perhaps somewhat more accurately) the reality of the Christian revelation that determines the Christian way of life as a whole (*Eph.* 16.2; *Phd.* 8.2). Subjectively, faith has to do with firmness and endurance (*Eph.* 3.1; 14.2), sometimes with special reference to constancy on behalf of the truth in the face of error (*Eph.* 10.2). The term conviction may capture the blend of intellectual and moral elements involved. Such conviction presupposes a receptive attitude of the kind generally associated with faith in the Pauline sense (reliance on the promises of God). But in Ignatius the emphasis is on the settled state of mind to which such an attitude gives rise. Faith, in short, begins to take on more clearly the characteristics of a virtue.

The use of the verb points in the same direction.[145] The communal orientation that Ignatius brings to his reflections on faith and love is probably illustrated by two passages in which he speaks of believing in (divine) grace with a view to what others will be enabled to accomplish by way of unified action or support for Ignatius himself (*Phd.* 8.1; *Pol.* 7.3). One distinctive use of the verb seems related to the bishop's treatment of faith as an objective body of revealed truth. For he can speak of believing as a matter of following a Christian rather than a Jewish way of life (*Mag.* 9.1; 10.3). On the subjective side, believing has to do with reliance on Christ (cf. *Tr.* 9.2; *Phd.* 5.2). Even so, it is often more accurate to say that believing is a matter of having convictions concerning the reality of Christ's death and resurrection (*Sm.* 3.1, 2; 6.1). Thus when reliance on Christ's death is set in the context of anti-docetic polemic and closely allied with an emphasis on episcopal authority (*Tr.* 2.1), an acceptance of authoritative utterances is almost inevitably involved.

For Ignatius, as for Paul, faith is necessarily active in love (cf. *Phd.* 9.2). But whereas faith receives greater attention than love in Paul, the reverse is true of Ignatius. The fundamental reason for the difference is that Ignatius' thought revolves about the unity and concord of the church rather than the question as to the correctness of admitting non-observant Gentiles into the Christian community.

---

140 *Eph.* 1.3; *Mag.* 6.1; *Tr.* 3.3; *Phd.* 5.1; *Sm.* 9.2; *Pol.* 2.3.
141 *Mag.* 6.2; *Tr.* 13.2; *Sm.* 7.1; *Pol.* 5.1; cf. *Phd.* 5.2.
142 *Eph.* 21.1.
143 Ignatius' statement that he loves suffering (*Tr.* 4.2) represents an isolated use of the verb.
144 There is also an isolated reference to Jesus Christ as the "beloved" (*Sm.* inscr).
145 There are some eighteen uses of the verb in Ignatius.

Six of these have no theological significance (*Mag.* 6.1; *Tr.* 6.2; *Rom.* 8.2; 10.2; *Phd.* 9.1).

5.9. Hope.

Ignatius refers to hope eleven times (never in connection with faith and love). The word is most often used to designate Christ himself (*Eph.* 21.2; *Mag.* 11; *Tr.* inscr; 2.2; *Phd.* 11.2; *Sm.* 10.2) or the Christian reality as a whole (*Eph.* 1.2; *Mag.* 7.1; *Phd.* 5.2) as that on which Christians rely. In four of these instances hope is referred to as our "common" hope (*Eph.* 1.2; 21.2; *Phd.* 5.2; 11.2). Two other uses of the term are more general (*Eph.* 10.1; *Mag.* 9.1).

The significant point about the conception of hope in Ignatius is that it is no longer oriented primarily to the end of time. The development is in harmony with the treatment of other eschatological themes in the letters.[146] Thus Christ is the hope of Christians in the sense that they expect blessings to flow from him as ever-present Lord of the church. The designation of such hope as our "common" hope underscores the point (see on *Eph.* 1.2).

Ignatius, to be sure, links hope with the resurrection (cf. *Tr.* inscr). The impression left, however, is that the resurrection is itself something that takes place at death (*Eph.* 11.2; *Rom.* 4.3; cf. *Sm.* 5.3).[147] Ignatius evidently connects his thought about "resurrection"—ἀνάστασις "rising up"—with the fact that Christians are "carried up" (ἀναφερόμενοι) to the heights (*Eph.* 9.1) or that Ignatius himself hopes to "rise" (ἀνατείλω) to God at death (*Rom.* 2.2). The prophets are explicitly spoken of as already raised from the dead (*Mag.* 9.2). Yet Ignatius did not work with a spiritualized conception of the resurrection. For he connected the hope of resurrection with opposition to docetism (*Sm.* 7.1) and pictured a bodiless future state as undesirable (*Sm.* 2). Ignatius may well have resorted to a conception of the general resurrection to overcome the apparent inconsistency in his thought. It seems better, however, to allow for a certain vagueness on his part and to note the extent to which the shape of a doctrine is determined by the context in which it occurs. Thus Ignatius' emphasis on the physical reality of the resurrection represents an unusually precise statement of matters which he makes in the interest of upholding the value of suffering and the importance of concrete deeds of love (*Sm.* 3–7). But when he thinks of the individual's final destiny, his mind is dominated by imagery that is satisfied by nothing less than immediate access to God. These are very different concerns, and their religious and theological significance is lost when a premature synthesis is sought. Here is another piece of evidence that there are two foci in Ignatius' soteriology and that the desire to attain God does not deprive the earthly task of Christians of independent meaning.

5.10. Passion and Resurrection.

The terms passion and resurrection appear closely conjoined (with or without other terms) nine times in Ignatius (cross, death, and resurrection once in *Phd.* 8.2). In addition, the term passion is found six times alone;[148] the term resurrection two times alone.[149]

As is typical of Ignatius, passion and resurrection sometimes appear as one polarity among others to express totality and to emphasize the unity of the church (*Eph.* 20.1; *Sm.* 12.2; cf. *Tr.* inscr). Indeed, in one passage, concord, passion, and resurrection are explicitly named together (*Phd.* inscr).

Passion and resurrection also stand out, however, as the heart of the Christian gospel and the ground of faith (*Sm.* 7.2; *Phd.* 8.2). In this connection, Ignatius sometimes speaks of Christ's birth, death, and resurrection (*Mag.* 11; *Phd.* 9.2). The reality of all three are important to him, but it is the passion that receives the emphasis. For without the passion there can be no talk of resurrection (*Sm.* 5.3). And apart from the passion Christ's "life" is not "in us" (*Mag.* 5.2). Thus Christians are "from" the passion (*Sm.* 1.2) and are likened to branches of the cross (*Tr.* 11.2). It is "in" Christ's passion and resurrection in

---

146 See on *Eph.* 11.1 (cf. *Eph.* 15.3; 16.1–2; *Mag.* 5.1; 6.1; 9.2; *Tr.* 2.1; 9.2; *Phd.* 9.2; *Sm.*7.1; 9.1; *Pol.* 2.3; 3.2; 5.2; 6.2).

147 Cf. Ton H. C. van Eijk, *La résurrection des morts chez les pères apostoliques* (Théologie historique 25; Paris: Beauchesne, 1974) 99–126.

148 *Eph.* inscr; 18.2; *Mag.* 5.2; *Tr.* 11.2; *Rom.* 6.3; *Phd.* 3.3. The corresponding verb is used five times with reference to Christ's passion (*Tr.* 10; *Sm.* 2.1, three times; 7.1) and three times with reference to Ignatius' suffering (*Tr.* 4.2; *Rom.* 4.3; *Pol.* 7.1).

149 Cf. *Sm.* 3.1, 3 (perhaps also *Pol.* 7.1, where there is a textual problem). The corresponding verb (ἀνίστημι "raise") is used five times in Ignatius (*Eph.* 11.2; *Rom.* 4.3; 6.1; *Sm.* 2; 7.1), the verb ἐγείρω ("raise") four times (*Mag.* 9.2; *Tr.* 9.2, twice; *Sm.* 7.1).

some vague sense that Christians act and live.[150] Ignatius also thinks of the passion as having somehow cleansed the waters of baptism (*Eph.* 18.2). And the eucharist is identified with the flesh of Christ that suffered for our sins (*Sm.* 7.1). Thus the Christian finds himself "in agreement with" the passion (*Phd.* 3.3) in more than an intellectual sense. Similarly, in one striking statement Ignatius speaks of himself as being an "imitator of the passion of my God" and in the same context suggests that those who "have" Christ "in themselves" will "sympathize" with him (*Rom.* 6.3). Thus a present fellowship with Christ and participation in his passion is presupposed by Ignatius. Yet the complete destruction of death lies in the future (cf. *Eph.* 18.2)—a fact that evidently has special relevance to those who like Ignatius have reasons to doubt their worthiness. And although a present fellowship with Christ "apart from whom we do not have true life" is the presupposition of the future resurrection, reference to God and his power is still decisive; for the resurrection of Christ and the believer's resurrection are dealt with as comparable acts of God (*Tr.* 9.2). It is traditional material of this kind that limits any tendency in Ignatius to conform Christ's passion and resurrection to the model of a Hellenistic mystery religion.

5.11. Beginning and End.
The polarity of beginning and end is the most obvious expression of totality in Ignatius. He does not fall back on it often, however; and when he does, he makes rather diverse applications of it. In one passage it is the last in a list that includes three other polarities that have little in common in terms of content (*Mag.* 13.1). Elsewhere it is used most strikingly to describe the all-sufficiency of faith and love when they are united (*Eph.* 14.1). But it is evidently also involved in an expression of hope that Ignatius will remain firm "to the end" (*Rom.* 1.1; cf. *Eph.* 14.2) on the grounds that his "beginning" has been well ordered (*Rom.* 1.2). And it probably hovers behind the description of Christ as the one "who before the ages was

with the Father and appeared at the end" (*Mag.* 6.1).

It is clear that traditional eschatological and paraenetic themes are here woven into a broader pattern of thinking that resists sharp antitheses and dualities. At the same time, beginning and end express totality, not identity, just as flesh and spirit complement each other, yet remain metaphysically distinct spheres, or as faith and love belong together, yet represent distinct theological moments.

It is possible that Ignatius' treatment of beginning and end (and their union) has mythological prototypes.[151] But there are other (less "cosmic") models that seem at least as relevant (see on *Eph.* 14.1; *Mag.* 13.1). This may well explain the relative unimportance of the theme in the letters and the fact that it is used by Ignatius in relatively uninflated forms.

5.12. Attaining God.
Ignatius speaks three times of Christians (or prospective Christians) "attaining" (τυγχάνειν) God (*Eph.* 10.1; *Mag.* 1.2; *Sm.* 9.2; cf. *Pol.* 4.3), some fifteen times of himself "attaining" (ἐπιτυγχάνειν) God or Christ,[152] and once of Polycarp "attaining" (ἐπιτυγχάνειν) God (*Pol.* 2.3). He uses the strengthened form of the verb of himself and his colleague Polycarp.

"Attaining God" is a future possibility, and it is clear especially in the case of Ignatius himself that it refers to communion with God at death. This is less obvious (though by no means unlikely) as far as Christians in general are concerned (cf. *Mag.* 1.2; *Sm.* 9.2). In any event, Ignatius takes the realization of "attaining God" less for granted in his own case. A sharper difference is to be noted in his treatment of the theme of "being a disciple" which is connected with that of "attaining God" (cf. *Eph.* 1.2; 10.1). For it is apparently assumed that Christians (and their predecessors, the prophets) realize their discipleship here and now (*Mag.* 9.1, 2; 10.1; *Pol.* 2.1) whereas Ignatius' discipleship has only begun and depends on a successfully completed martyrdom for its

---

150 *Eph.* 20.1; *Mag.* 11; *Tr.* inscr; *Phd.* inscr; *Sm.* 12.2; cf. *Eph.* inscr; *Tr.* 11.2.

151 Paulsen, *Studien,* 93 n. 91; cf. Gerhard Kittel, "A–Ω," *TDNT* 1 (1964) 1–3.

152 *Eph.* 12.2; *Mag.* 14; *Tr.* 12.2; 13.3; *Rom.* 1.2; 2.1; 4.1; 5.3 (twice); 8.3; 9.2; *Phd.* 5.1; *Sm.* 11.1; *Pol.* 7.1. Ignatius also speaks of attaining his lot (*Tr.* 12.3) and of attaining grace (*Rom.* 1.2). The verb appears twice in an auxiliary capacity (*Eph.* 1.2; *Rom.* 1.1).

perfection (*Eph.* 1.2; 3.1; *Tr.* 5.2; *Rom.* 4.2; 5.1, 3; *Pol.* 7.1). This difference does not reflect a conception of the distinctive quality of martyrs in general but the self-doubt and self-effacement of Ignatius in particular (see 3.4 above).

It may be said that whereas resurrection is expected after death, attaining God is spoken of as realized in death—that is, in Ignatius' martyrdom and (presumably) in the death of any other whose discipleship has been proved. Attaining God, then, has to do more directly with the relation between God and the believer.

The nature of that relation is disputed. It appears that Ignatius is still alone in speaking of God himself as that which is to be attained. At the same time, Hellenistic sources (notably the Magical Papyri) occasionally speak of attaining things closely associated with God.[153] Moreover, a related expression in *Tr.* 5.2 ("that we may not lack God") suggests that for Ignatius "attaining God" in the future is comparable to "having God" here and now. The expression "to attain God," then, takes its place with others in the letters that describe the relation between God and human beings in terms of a deep communion verging on or passing over into mysticism (see 5.1 above). It may be significant that although Ignatius speaks of "attaining" God or Christ, he speaks only of "having" Christ ("my God"—that is, God in his self-revelation) here and now (*Rom.* 6.3; cf. *Mag.* 12). In any event, "attaining God" represents a future possibility and most characteristically a *post mortem* possibility. Thus an interpretation of the expression in mystical terms should not be pressed.

More important, however, is the place of "attaining God" in Ignatius' theology as a whole and its relation to his pastoral concern for peace and harmony in the churches. We have argued that his call to unity is at the same time a call for recognition and support (see 3.1–6 above). This indicates that Ignatius sees the achievement of unity in his own church and its realization in the churches of Asia as a certification of his ministry and a

sign that there is no further question about his worthiness to attain God and become a disciple.[154] Thus although a longing for immortality has an important place in his Christianity, pastoral activity and the activities of the Christian community are not given meaning solely in terms of otherworldly goals. For Ignatius' martyrdom is also understood as playing a role in the fulfillment of the requirements of his ministry. His understanding of these requirements and their fulfillment may strike some as odd or perverse, yet his view of the matter guarantees the mission of the church a significance independent of his personal destiny. Every Christian, to be sure, is thought to attain God as the reward for endurance (*Sm.* 9.2). But the language of reward does not subordinate an action to an end in such a way that the meaning of the action is derived solely from that end. Reward motivates action, it does not determine its value.[155] Thus faith and love and the life of concord and unity that flows from them are (as we have seen) characteristically dealt with by Ignatius as describing the quality of the Christian community as a whole and as requiring nothing to perfect them (see 5.8 above).

For the most part, then, the life of faith and love and the hoped-for ascent to God represent theologically distinct foci in Ignatius. This is evidently related to the duality noted above in his treatment of the resurrection (see 5.9) and the eucharist (see 5.3). In both cases, what Ignatius has to say on these matters differs depending on whether he has in view primarily the requirements of Christian living or the hopes for life after death.

5.13 Imitation.

The theme of imitating God (or Christ) is tied in with that of attaining God (or Christ) through *Rom.* 6.3 where Ignatius asks to be allowed "to be an imitator of my God" (that is, Christ) in martyrdom. The context displays a longing for death that seems to justify the attribution to Ignatius of a theology more or less exclusively focussed

---

153 Cf. Paulsen, *Studien*, 71; Hermann Hanse, '*Gott Haben' in der Antike und im frühen Christentum* (RVV 27; Berlin: Töpelmann, 1939) 14. Similarly *Mart. Pet.* 10 (ed. Lipsius, 1. 98): "you will attain those things (ἐκείνων τεύξεσθε) which he [Christ] says to you neither eye has seen nor ear heard. . . ." Especially relevant perhaps is a passage noted by Paulsen from *Corp. Herm.* exc. IIB. 5 (Walter Scott, ed., *Hermetica*

[4 vols.; Oxford: Clarendon, 1924–36] 1. 390–93): "It is the road our ancestors trod; and thereby they attained to the good" (ἔτυχον τοῦ ἀγαθοῦ).

154 Cf. Willard M. Swartley, "The Imitatio Christi in the Ignatian Letters," *VC* 27 (1973) 81–103.

155 Cf. David Little and Sumner B. Twiss, *Comparative Religious Ethics* (San Francisco: Harper & Row, 1978) 182.

on personal immortality. Nevertheless, the letter to the Romans is also shot through with themes that link Ignatius' plea for martyrdom with his quest for vindication as a Christian and as bishop of the church in Antioch. It is as true here as elsewhere, then, that Ignatius thinks of his martyrdom as fulfilling the requirements of his ministry and that he thus accords the mission of the church independent significance (see 5.12 above).

Considering the suggestiveness of *Rom.* 6.3, the imitation theme is surprisingly infrequent in Ignatius. And when it does occur elsewhere, it gives little support to the view that imitation is linked exclusively with the passion or a longing to leave the world. In every other instance it is Christians in general (not Ignatius in particular) who are referred to as "imitators" of God (or Christ). Moreover, such imitation is seen as issuing in the sending of representatives to greet Ignatius (*Eph.* 1.1; cf. *Tr.* 1.2), the willing endurance of wrongs at the hands of other people (*Eph.* 10.3), and the love of unity and avoidance of division (*Phd.* 7.2). The image of the suffering Christ hovers in the background in two of these passages, but there it is clear that the concern is not immortality but benevolence (*Eph.* 1.1) and patient endurance (*Eph.* 10.3). Similarly in the pastoral sphere, Polycarp is advised in words usually applied to Christ (*Pol.* 1.3) to put up with troublesome people in his care (*Pol.* 2.1). And it seems evident in this connection that Ignatius sees his own martyrdom in such terms (see on *Pol.* 2.3). The theme of imitation, then, is oriented primarily to the church and its needs, and its use in *Rom.* 6.3 is apparently no real exception.

A debate has arisen in Protestant circles, however, as to whether the theme of imitation in Ignatius is to be understood in NT terms as a matter of following after Christ (*Nachfolge*) or in non-biblical terms as a matter of replicating Christ-like qualities (*Nachahmung*).[156] The former is seen as a species of faith or obedience (conceived of as receptivity to divine grace and participation in the sufferings of Christ), the latter as an achievement of the saint. Clearly the discussion mirrors the problems of a later age. It is not therefore without value, but it must be approached somewhat differently. For some of the implications associated with the alternatives fall away once it is recognized that the ascent to God and the mission of the church represent distinct foci in Ignatius and that the imitation theme is not oriented exclusively to the passion or a longing to leave the world. The bishop may have his eyes turned upward as much as any religious thinker of his age, but he does not say with Philo (for example) that he was unhappily drawn away from the contemplation of things above and plunged "into a great sea of concerns" in this world (*Spec. leg.* 3.1–4). Ignatius does not regard the life of faith and love and the concord and unity that flow from them as requiring justification in higher terms. The question that remains is whether imitation in Ignatius has in view action directed by the grace of God or action springing from a godly character. It is unlikely, however, that these exclude each other. The problem is analogous to that of the interpretation of faith and love alternatively as spheres of grace or as virtues. In this connection, even Protestant ethicists have begun to recognize that the language of virtues does not necessarily do violence to NT Christianity.[157] If there is a difference between Ignatius and Paul on this score, it is a matter of emphasis, with Ignatius (apparently) taking the importance of fixity of purpose more for granted. Thus he evidently understands grace somewhat less paradoxically than Paul in terms of a cooperation between God and the human being (see on *Sm.* 6.2). But this shift of emphasis has more to do with his conception of the way in which people are empowered to live godly lives than with his view of the way in which godly living is related to the final destiny of the believer.

Finally, it should be noted that the comparisons drawn between the earthly and heavenly hierarchy by Ignatius are sometimes regarded as based on the idea of the

---

156 Cf. Hans von Campenhausen, *Die Idee des Martyriums in der alten Kirche* (2d ed.; Göttingen: Vandenhoeck & Ruprecht, 1964) 56–78.

157 Gene Outka, *Agape: An Ethical Analysis* (Yale Publications in Religion 17; New Haven and London: Yale University, 1972) 123–52; cf. Giuseppe Trentin, "Eros e Agape: A proposito di una interpretazione teologica delle lettere di Ignazio di Antiochia," *Studia Patavina, Rivista di scienze religiose* 19 (1972) 495–538.

imitation of God or Christ. And here the tendency has been to see the ministry as replicating divine qualities and thus as standing in the place of God or Christ. In our view, however, this is to misconstrue these comparisons (see on *Mag.* 6.1). It is interesting that the imitation idea is explicitly used in a comparison involving the people and Christ on the one hand and Christ and the Father on the other and that in this context imitation is apparently all but interchangeable with obedience (*Phd.* 7.2).

Ignatius

to the Ephesians

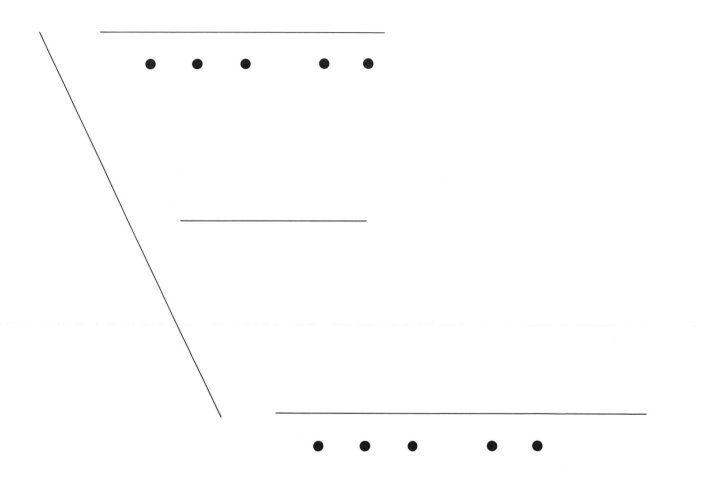

Salutation

Ignatius, also called Theophorus, to her who has been blessed with greatness by the fullness of God the Father, to her who has been foreordained before the ages, to be forever destined for enduring (and) unchanging glory, united and elect in (the) true suffering, by the will of the Father and Jesus Christ, our God, to the church most worthily blessed which is in Ephesus in Asia, abundant greeting in Jesus Christ and in blameless joy.

Ignatius' address to the Ephesians is an enrichment of the common Hellenistic form: so-and-so to so-and-so greeting. The use of the term "greeting" (χαίρειν) rather than "grace and peace" or any of the other Judaized and Christianized forms of greeting in the NT is but one of many indications that Ignatius is closer to pagan epistolary models and reworks them independently. The expression "abundant greeting" (πλεῖστα χαίρειν) is also common and occurs in the papyri as early as 22 B.C.E.[1]

Such opening formulae are sometimes expanded, but amplifications of the scope and type encountered in Ignatius are not characteristic either of the papyri or of the literary sources.[2] Paul seems to have set the style for Christian letters in this regard.[3] At the same time, apart from *Ephesians,* Ignatius does not reflect much of the actual content of the Pauline salutations. The amplifications in Ignatius often include (in a variety of sequences) the following elements attached to the mention of the addressees: (a) participles describing God's governance of the church addressed; (b) adjectives describing the spiritual greatness of the church addressed; (c) the location of the church. Numerous short phrases (and sometimes an ἀσπάζομαι formula) decorate the greeting proper.

Ignatius identifies himself in all his letters by two names (joined by ὁ καί). Such double names are widespread especially in inscriptions and papyri.[4] There is much debate about their purpose. In the papyri they regularly occur in business letters or official communications rather than in familiar letters.[5] Ignatius' usage is closest to that of rulers who added a laudatory appellative as a second name, as in "Cleopatra . . . also called Philometor [Mother-loving]."[6] For "Theophorus" is also a laudatory appellative used as a proper name.

The name Ignatius is a Greek form of the Latin Egnatius.[7] It is relatively rare yet frequent enough as a

1 Francis Xavier J. Exler, *The Form of the Ancient Greek Letter: A Study in Greek Epistolography* (Washington, D.C.: Catholic University of America, 1923) 63.

2 Cf. ibid., 24–60; Rudolph Hercher, *Epistolographi Graeci* (Paris: Didot, 1873).

3 Klaus Berger ("Apostelbrief und apostolische Rede: Zum Formular frühchristlicher Briefe," *ZNW* 65 [1974] 191–207) argues that Paul's opening formulae are based on Jewish models and attributes to them the character of words of blessing. Berger (199–200) finds echoes of the same tradition in features of Ignatius' letters such as the addresses to the churches as "blessed" (*Eph.* inscr; *Mag.* inscr), "elect" (*Eph.* inscr), "shown mercy" (*Phd.* inscr; *Sm.* inscr), and "at peace" (*Tr.* inscr) and the formulae "grace, mercy, peace" used near the end of *Smyrnaeans* (12.2). For a clearer example see below on the phrase "blessed is he" in *Eph.* 1.3. It is unlikely, however, that Hellenistic and personal elements are absent from Paul's salutations (Hans Dieter Betz, *Galatians* [Hermeneia; Philadelphia: Fortress, 1979] 37); and that is all the more true of Ignatius. In any event, it is probably from Paul that Ignatius derived the habit of elaborating his salutations so fully.

4 M. Lambertz, "Zur Ausbreitung des Supernomen oder Signum im römischen Reiche," *Glotta* 4 (1913) 78–143; 5 (1914) 99–170.

5 Cf. Exler, *Greek Epistolography,* 15–68.

6 Rita Calderini, "Ricerche sul doppio nome personale nell' Egitto greco-romano," *Aegyptus* 22 (1942) 9.

7 Thomas Münzer, "Ignatius," PW 9. 967; idem, "Egnatius," PW 5. 1993–2004 (usually a family name).

Greek name to occasion no surprise.[8] Some Syrian authors related the name Ignatius to the Latin word *ignis* (fire) and found in it a fitting description of the saint's temperament, but this is pure fancy.[9]

The meaning of the second name, Theophorus, has been much discussed. Rules of accentuation indicate that the adjective *theophóros* would mean "bearing God" whereas the adjective *theóphoros* would mean "borne by God."[10] In light of *Eph.* 9.2 (where the reading is clearly θεοφόροι) and the appearance of the metaphor of bearing God in the early period (Irenaeus *Adv. haer.* 3.16.3: βαστάζειν θεόν "to bear God"; Epictetus *Diss.* 2.8.12–13: θεὸν περιφέρεις "you bear God") the first meaning is to be accepted. Another consideration is the rule governing the accentuation of proper names formed from adjectives: generally, the accent changes (*chrēstós* becomes *Chrēstos*) with no change of meaning;[11] yet names formed from compounds ending in *phóros* regularly keep the accent on the penultimate and retain the active meaning.[12] The legend about Ignatius which builds on the passive meaning of the name (that Ignatius was the child carried by Christ in Mark 9:36) is attested first in the ninth century.[13] By that time the use of double names of the type found here was almost extinct (the second century C.E. was the high point). We may conclude that only after the ὁ καί formula was no longer current and Theophorus no longer taken as a proper name could the accent shift and a change of meaning occur.[14]

Theophorus could not have been given to Ignatius as a name at birth since it is not otherwise attested as a proper name. It may designate him as a martyr in the same way that later martyrs were said to be χριστοφόροι ("bearers of Christ"). This usage occurs for the first time in a letter of Phileus of Thmuis (in Eusebius *Hist. eccl.* 8.10.3); but already in 177 C.E. the "suffering Christ" is said to have accomplished great glories in the body of Sanctus the martyr.[15] Yet this interpretation gains little support from any other passage in Ignatius (including *Mag.* 1.2), and the image of bearing God in the parallels noted above has no special reference to martyrdom. It is more likely that Theophorus is a name adopted by Ignatius at his baptism despite the fact that the adoption of Christian names was not common until the middle of the third century.[16] Reasonable analogies are provided by Plutarch and Aelius Aristides, who associate the acquisition of a theologically significant name—Thespesius and Theodorus—with a religious crisis.[17]

The meaning of the name Theophorus is best elaborated in terms of other expressions in the letters: "to participate in God" (θεοῦ μετέχειν), *Eph.* 4.2; to be "entirely of God," *Eph.* 8.1; and "to be full of God" (θεοῦ γέμειν), *Mag.* 14. A parallel in Lucan (*Phars.* 9.564) joins the idea of being full of God and bearing him when it

---

8 W. Pape and Gustav Eduard Benseler, *Wörterbuch der griechischen Eigennamen* (3d ed.; Braunschweig: Vieweg, 1863) 533; Friedrich Preisigke, *Namenbuch* (Heidelberg: Selbstverlag des Herausgebers, 1922) 146; Daniele Foraboschi, *Onomasticon alterum papyrologicum* (Testi e documenti per lo studio dell' antichita 16; Serie papirologica 2: Milan: Istituto editoriale cisalpino, 1967) 143. To these may be added *P.Mich.* 12.639. In these instances "Ignatius" is usually part of a Roman name, but it also occurs independently as a Greek name (e.g., *SB* 5.7662; *P.Lond.* 4.1460; 5.1745). For the inscriptions see *CIG* 3.4129 (possibly a Jew); 4.6830; *SB* 5.7747; 8802b. See also the names Egnatius, Ignadius, and Ignatis in these sources.

9 Lightfoot, *Ignatius*, 1. 24

10 Raphael Kühner and Friedrich Blass, *Ausführliche Grammatik der griechischen Sprache*, 1. Teil: *Elementar- und Formenlehre* (3d ed.; 2 vols.; Hannover: Hahn, 1890–92) 1. 526.

11 John Pearson, *Vindiciae Epistolarum S. Ignatii* (2 vols.; Library of Anglo-Catholic Theology 69–70; Oxford:

Parker, 1852) 529–31.

12 See Pape/Benseler, *Eigennamen,* under the names Boulephórus, Daphnephórus, Doryphórus, Thesmophórus, Onesiphórus (also sometimes Onesíphorus however), Telesphórus, Phosphórus. Cf. Henry William Chandler, *A Practical Introduction to Greek Accentuation* (2d ed.; Oxford: Clarendon, 1881) 90.

13 Lightfoot, *Ignatius*, 1. 27.

14 The Syriac fragments (Lightfoot, *Ignatius*, 3. 93) and the Armenian version (Petermann, *Epistolae*, 3) take Theophorus to mean "wearing God"; but *Eph.* 9.2 fixes the meaning for Ignatius as "bearing God."

15 Eusebius *Hist. eccl.* 5.1.23; cf. Franz Joseph Dölger, *Antike und Christentum* (5 vols.; Münster: Aschendorff, 1929–36) 4. 73–80.

16 Adolf Harnack, *The Mission and Expansion of Christianity* (reprinted, New York: Harper, 1961) 422–30.

17 In Plutarch (*De ser. num. vind.* 24, 564c) Aridaeus dies and hears himself hailed by the soul of a kinsman as Thespesius ("Divine One"). When he objects that

describes stoical Cato (who refuses to inquire of the future from the God Ammon) as "full of God, whom he bore in the silence of his soul" (*ille deo plenus, tacita quem mente gerebat*). Thus Ignatius shares with a wide range of pagan, Jewish, Christian, and Gnostic writers a conception of God dwelling within human beings.[18] He goes beyond most of the NT writers (John is the major exception) in relating the Christian more or less mystically to God rather than Christ. Thus the "in God" of *Eph.* 1.1 has a parallel in 1 Thess 2:2 but is much more characteristic of Ignatius' theological outlook (see *Eph.* 6.2; *Mag.* 3.1; 14; *Tr.* 4.1; 8.2; *Pol.* 1.1; 6.1; 8.3). It is debatable whether such language is to be understood in Ignatius as a matter of personal fellowship or of transpersonal union (or whether these were felt as significant alternatives). A later discussion of "bearing God" (θεοφορία) by Iamblichus (*De myst.* 3.5) shows how indefinite the terminology could be (he distinguishes three levels of intimacy between God and human beings, moving from lowest to highest): "for either God has us, or we are entirely of God (ὅλοι θεοῦ γιγνόμεθα; cf. *Eph.* 8.2, ὅλοι ὄντες θεοῦ), or we exercise an activity in common with him; and sometimes we share (μετέχομεν) in the last power of God, sometimes in the middle power, sometimes in the first power; and sometimes there is a bare participation (μετουσία), sometimes also a communion (κοινωνία), and at other times even a union (ἕνωσις) with these inspirations; either the soul enjoys alone, or it participates also along with the body, or the very composite enjoys." Ignatius (as we shall see) reflects an outlook closer to the less highly developed possibilities indicated here (see Introduction, 5.4).

The address to the Ephesian church contains a series of themes reminiscent of the opening of Ephesians in the NT (1:3–23):

Ignatius	NT Ephesians
blessed, τῇ εὐλογημένῃ	1:3 ὁ εὐλόγησας ἡμᾶς
greatness, ἐν μεγέθει	1:19 τὸ ὑπερβάλλον μέγεθος
God the Father, θεοῦ πατρός	1:3 ὁ θεὸς καὶ πατήρ
fullness, πληρώματι	1:10, 23 τοῦ πληρώματος, τὸ πλήρωμα
foreordained, τῇ προωρισμένῃ	1:5 προόρισα.
before the ages, πρὸ αἰώνων	1:4 πρὸ καταβολῆς κόσμου
to be destined for glory, εἶναι . . . εἰς δόξαν	1:12 εἶναι . . . εἰς ἔπαινον δόξης
elect, ἐκλελεγμένην	1:4 ἐξελέξατο
suffering, ἐν πάθει	1:7 διὰ τοῦ αἵματος αὐτοῦ
by the will of the Father, ἐν θελήματι τοῦ πατρός	1:5 κατὰ τὴν εὐδοκίαν τοῦ θελήματος αὐτοῦ, and 1:11 κατὰ τὴν βουλὴν τοῦ θελήματος αὐτοῦ

The list may be deceptive: Some of these themes occur in other salutations (*Mag.*: "blessed"; *Rom.*: "by the will of him who wills all things"; *Tr.*: "elect"; "in the fullness"); not all the parallels are exact; and the ideas are connected in different ways by Pauline Ephesians and Ignatius. But Ignatius is generally very free in his use of Paul, and the cumulative effect of the parallels is impressive. It is tempting to think that (in spite of no references to Paul's Ephesians in *Eph.* 12.2, where it may have been expected) Ignatius felt it appropriate to address the Ephesians with language from an apostolic writing regarded as directed to them.

These additional points call for comment: (a) It would be possible to translate the first statement about the Ephesian church as "to her who has been blessed in the greatness of God the Father with (his) fullness" (τῇ εὐλογημένῃ ἐν μεγέθει θεοῦ πατρὸς πληρώματι).[19] This takes note of a common pattern in Ignatius ("in" + anarthrous noun + a reference to God or Christ in the

---

his name is Aridaeus, he is told, "Yes, previously; but from now on Thespesius." He then views the delights and sorrows of the souls beyond and finally returns to his own body. Similarly Aelius Aristides (*Or.* 50.53–54; ed. Keil) hears someone in a dream say, "Hail, Theodorus." He accepts the title "since everything of mine was a gift of the God." In another dream an old retainer appears to him and likewise refers to him as Theodorus. The story of these dreams is immediately preceded by this account of Asclepius' directions to Aristides: "He said that it was fitting that my mind be changed from its present condition, and having been

changed, associate with God (συγγένεσθαι θεῷ), and in association, be superior to man's estate . . ." (tr. C. A. Behr, *Aelius Aristides and the Sacred Tales* [Amsterdam: Hakert, 1968] 265).

18 Cf. Hermann Hanse, "ἔχω κτλ.," *TDNT* 2 (1964) 822–32; J. Haussleiter, "Deus internus," *RAC* 3. 794–842.

19 So the Armenian (Petermann, *Epistolae*, 3) and Coptic (L.-Th. Lefort, *Les pères apostoliques en Copte* [2 vols.; CSCO 135–36; Scriptores Coptici 17–18; Louvain: Durbecq, 1952] 1. 52). This rendering is made even easier if with L, g3, and S we insert an

genitive).[20] Especially important is *Rom.* inscr: "to her who has found mercy in the majesty of the most high Father" (τῇ ἠλεημένῃ ἐν μεγαλειότητι πατρὸς ὑψίστου). But μέγεθος is used elsewhere in Ignatius only of the church (*Rom.* 3.3; *Sm.* 11.2); consequently the expression is probably closer to the pattern of words in *Phd.* inscr: "whom . . . he established in strength by his Holy Spirit" (ἐν βεβαιωσύνῃ τῷ ἁγίῳ αὐτοῦ πνεύματι). If so, Ignatius' language here says more about the church than about God.

In any event, the "fullness" is the fullness of God. For background to *plērōma* as a term for the divine being see especially Col 1:19 and 2:9 (cf. John 1:16), and for its application to the church see Eph 1:23 and 3:19. It has been affirmed by some[21] and denied by others[22] that the Pauline use of the term derives from Hellenistic syncretism. It seems unlikely that it serves in Ignatius merely as a periphrasis to indicate the completeness and perfection of God's activity; rather it describes the very being of God as a unified sphere of divine life and power ("for the fullness of all things is one and in one" as *Corp. Herm.* 16.3 says of God).[23] We have moved beyond the biblical God from whom none can escape since he "fills heaven and earth" (Jer 23:24) to a God who no longer fills but *is* the fullness. Although there is no trace here of the Gnostic teaching about the *plērōma* as the harmonious totality of divine emanations (Irenaeus *Adv. haer.*

1.1.1–3; Hippolytus *Ref.* 6.32.1), a similar background is presupposed. Such a view of the divine deepens the sense of communion with God in Ephesians/Colossians and Ignatius without eliminating the personalism of biblical theism. (For a different use of the term *plērōma* in Ignatius see *Tr.* inscr.)

In Gnosticism, "greatness" (μέγεθος) also has connotations derived from its connection with the mysterious being of the unknown God (Irenaeus *Adv. haer.* 1.2.2; Epiphanius *Pan.* 31.5; *Treat. Seth* [NHC 7] 49,10; *Thom. Cont.* [NHC 2] 140,32). Ignatius' language may be similarly tinged especially if the variant translation noted above is followed.

(b) The foreordination of the church to glory may be illuminated both from Gnostic sources (Clement Alex. *Exc. ex Theod.* 41)[24] and sources with a more Jewish orientation (*Herm. Vis.* 2.4).[25] Again a common background may be presupposed. In any event, the Christian community at Ephesus is seen by Ignatius as a manifestation of the one transcendent church. A similar ambiguity affects the term "glory," which is used to describe the realm of the divine both in biblical and Gnostic sources.[26] Here in Ignatius the term is modified by adjectives[27] that take us into the realm of Hellenistic-Jewish theology (and Hellenistic syncretism) where divine permanence is conceived of in terms of changelessness.[28] It is also significant that Ignatius pairs the

"and" before πληρώματι. But the reading of S is probably a corruption (Petermann, *Epistolae*, 3), and the reading of L and g3 look like an effort to simplify the expression (though see *Pol.* 8.3 for just such a construction). Zahn translates: "blessed with the greatness of God richly" (*Ignatius*, 415).

20 *Eph.* inscr; 1.1, 3; 19.1; 20.1; *Mag.* inscr; 6.1; 15; *Rom.* inscr; 10.3; *Phd.* inscr; 1.1; 5.1, 2; 11.1; *Sm.* 12.2; 13.1, 2; *Pol.* 5.1, 2; 7.1; 8.3.

21 Cf. Martin Dibelius, *An die Kolosser, Epheser, An Philemon* (3d ed. Heinrich Greeven; HNT 12; Mohr [Siebeck], 1953) 18, 29–30.

22 Cf. Gerhard Delling, "πλήρης κτλ.," *TDNT* 6 (1968) 298–305.

23 For the Hermetic parallel see Eduard Lohse, *Colossians and Philemon* (Hermeneia; Philadelphia: Fortress, 1971) 57.

24 Cf. Schlier, *Untersuchungen* 84–85.

25 Cf. Daniélou, *Jewish Christianity*, 293–313.

26 Gerhard Kittel, "δόξα," *TDNT* 2 (1964) 252–53.

27 The sense requires that the two adjectives be taken with "glory." The sense also requires that the

following two participles, "united and elect," refer to the church as do the preceding participles ("blessed," "foreordained"). Grammatically they serve as predicates to the infinitive εἶναι (for εἶναι εἰς meaning "to be destined for" see Eph 1:12). There is a difficulty: "united and elect" are in the accusative case (and grammatically, therefore, could be taken with "glory") rather than the dative (as are "church" and the preceding participles); but such a shift of cases is grammatically defensible after εἶναι (Raphael Kühner and Bernhard Gerth, *Ausführliche Grammatik der griechischen Sprache*, 2. Teil: *Satzlehre* [3d ed.; 2 vols.; Hannover: Hahn, 1898–1904] 2. 25), and no emendation is required.

28 "Enduring" (παράμονον) is a rare word (cf. *Phd.* inscr) which was to have no significant theological future. "Unchanging" (ἄτρεπτον), on the other hand, became an important term in Christian theology (*LPGL s.v.* ἄτρεπτος II. A, p. 258). It is relatively insignificant in the Greek philosophical tradition but looms large in Philo's description of God and the God-intoxicated soul (e.g., *Leg. alleg.* 1.51; ´.32; 2.89; *Cherub.* 19),

election and unity of the church. Here again he is close to the world of Ephesians in the NT (1:3–14) and beyond that (perhaps) to the Gnostic conception of the *plērōma*.[29] But the theme is not pressed in Ignatius, and he generally emphasizes more concrete manifestations of unity (see Introduction, 5.4).

The church's unity and election are rooted in Christ's passion (see Introduction, 5.10). Ignatius proclaims a mystery of the cross (cf. *Eph.* 9.1), but already signals his unwillingness to have it evaporate into docetic symbolism in referring to it as "true" (cf. *Sm.* 1.1–2). The ultimate ground of the church's divine destiny is the will of the Father and Jesus Christ (see Introduction, 5.1). The two are so closely related that Jesus Christ is identified as "our God." It has sometimes been thought that since Ignatius regularly refers to Christ as "our" or "my" God (*Eph.* 15.3; 18.2; *Rom.* inscr; 3.3; 6.3; *Pol.* 8.3) or adds some qualifying phrase (*Eph.* 7.2; 19.3; *Sm.* 1.1), and since other more direct references to Christ as God are textually suspect (*Tr.* 7.1; *Sm.* 10.1), he did not view Christ as God in an absolute sense.[30] But such an interpretation seems forced, especially since Ignatius also speaks simply of "the blood of God" (*Eph.* 1.1) and "the passion of God" (*Rom.* 6.3).[31] "Our (my) God" may be compared with "our Lord," common especially in Paul's letters, as an expression of deep attachment to Christ; similarly, "my Lord and my God" (John 20:28; cf. 8:54); "our merciful God and Lord, Jesus Christ" (in a source quoted by Eusebius *Hist. eccl.* 5.28.11); "our God, Jesus Christ, higher and loftier than any epithet thought or spoken by us" (*Act. Ioann.* 107); and "my God, Jesus

Christ, who was unknown by the world but now revealed through us" (*Mart. Andr. pr.* 5; 12).

(c) The adjective applied to the church, "most worthily blessed" (ἀξιομακαρίστῳ), reveals a significant feature of Ignatius' style: his love of unusual words, especially compounds. Ἄξιος itself occurs seventeen times and there are eleven ἀξιο- compounds. "Eight of this group are found in no other Patristic writing, and four are hapax legomena of all extant Greek literature."[32] Richness of vocabulary is one characteristic of the Asianic style to which Ignatius seems to be indebted (see Introduction, 2.2). The "worthiness" terminology also reflects a preoccupation of Ignatius with the problem of his relation with the churches (see Introduction, 3.4).

(d) Asia need not have been mentioned with so famous a city as Ephesus. But Ignatius regularly (except in Romans) makes such specifications in his salutations (Irenaeus *Adv. haer.* 3.1.1 also refers to "Ephesus in Asia").

(e) The greeting reveals one other striking feature of Ignatius' thought and style: the pairing (or even identification) of Christ with things or states of being. Here Christ and "blameless joy" are conjoined (cf. *Mag.* 7.1, where "blameless joy" is more or less identified with Jesus Christ).[33] It seems likely that this compressed way of speaking serves to emphasize Christ as the source of that which is named together with him (see on *Eph.* 20.2).

---

where it is occasionally associated with the verb μένειν, "abide," "endure" (*Somn.* 2.221; *Mut. nom.* 24; 87). It is also used of God in *Corp. Herm.* 13.6 (and Exc. IIA, 9; 15) and of the "etherial and divine Element" in Ps-Aristotle *De mundo* 2.9 (392a 32). It becomes a name for the Valentinian first principle (Epiphanius *Pan.* 31.5). And Clement of Alexandria (*Strom.* 7.10, 57.5) uses it (in conjunction with φῶς ἑστὸς καὶ μένον ἀϊδίως "eternally stable and abiding light") to describe the state of individuals in the next world.

29   Schlier, *Untersuchungen*, 82–102.

30   Von der Goltz, *Ignatius*, 21–28.

31   Cf. Rackl, *Christologie*, 150–289.

32   Milton Perry Brown, *The Authentic Writings of Ignatius* (Durham, NC: Duke University, 1963) 15.

33   GL read "blameless grace" in *Ephesians*; but in light of the parallel (*Mag.* 7.1), the reading of SAg is to be preferred (χαραι "joy" was inadvertently replaced by χαρει "grace").

1

**Expression of Praise:
The Godly Affection of the Ephesians**

1   **Having received in God your much loved
name, which you possess by a just
nature according to faith and love in
Christ Jesus, our Savior—being imitators
of God, enkindled by the blood of God,
you accomplished perfectly the task
suited to you; 2/ for hearing that I was
put in bonds from Syria for the common
name and hope, hoping by your prayer to
attain to fighting with beasts in Rome,
that by attaining I may be able to be a
disciple, you hastened to see me. 3/ Now
since I received in God's name your
whole congregation in Onesimus, a man
indescribable in love, yet your bishop in
the flesh, whom I wish that you may love
according to Jesus Christ, and that all of
you may be like him; for blessed is he
who has granted you who are worthy to
have such a bishop.**

This section represents a form of the transitional device from salutation to body of letter which White refers to as "joy expressions."[1] This is often made up of a participial phrase (referring to what has been received or learned) followed by an expression of joy. The participle used by Ignatius (ἀποδεξάμενος) does not appear in White's examples but may be found elsewhere (Julian *Ep.* 30: "having received [δεξάμενος] your letter, I rejoiced . . .").[2] From *Tr.* 1.2 and *Pol.* 1.1 (cf. *Sm.* 1.1) we discover that Ignatius would normally have followed the participial phrase by saying "I gave praise" (which I take to be a Christianized expression of joy). Here (as in *Rom.* 1.1) we have instead an anakolouthon: Ignatius does not complete the thought but describes the behavior of the Ephesians that causes him to give praise. Only in 1.3 does he pick up the thread of his thought; but there again (as with the parallel passage in *Mag.* 2) he fails to complete the sentence. Consequently we must regard the concluding doxology in 1.3 ("blessed is he who . . .") as

replacing more conventional epistolary language just as such a "praise-giving" replaces the thanksgiving in a number of NT letters (2 Cor 1:3; Eph 1:3; 1 Pet 1:3). Schubert regards the substitution as "more liturgical, less personal" than the conventional formula.[3] The ultimate source of the expression "blessed is he who . . ." is Jewish prayers.[4] But it had also gained a place in Hellenistic-Jewish epistolography. The Jewish historian Eupolemus (ca. 150 B.C.E.) presents a letter of Suron (Hiram) to Solomon in which the blessing enriches a conventional Hellenistic expression of joy: "Blessed (εὐλογητός) is God, who created heaven and earth, who chose a good man born of a good man! When I read your letter, I greatly rejoiced and blessed God (σφόδρα ἐχάρην καὶ εὐλόγησα θεόν) on your succeeding to the kingdom" (in Eusebius *P.E.* 9.34.1).

■ **1.1** By the end of the passage, Ignatius' praise of the Ephesians comes to a focus in the bishop. But he begins in a more general way, saying that he has received (that

---

1   John Lee White, *The Form and Function of the Body of the Greek Letter: A Study of the Letter-Body in the Non-Literary Papyri and in Paul the Apostle* (SBLDS 2; Missoula, MT: Society of Biblical Literature, 1972) 39–40.

2   Other partial parallels include Julian *Ep.* 13 (δεξάμενος), *Ep.* 87 (ἐδεξάμην), and Libanius *Ep.* 1468 (ἐδεξάμεθα). Aeschines *Ep.* 7.1 (in Hercher, *Epistolographi Graeci*, 37) is close to Ignatius' practice (see especially *Tr.* 1.2 and *Pol.* 1.1) in speaking of having received not the letter itself but the good will of the addressees (καὶ τὴν μὲν ὑμετέραν ἀπεδεξάμην

φιλανθρωπίαν "and I received your good will").

3   Paul Schubert, *Form and Function of the Pauline Thanksgivings* (BZNW 20; Berlin: Töpelmann, 1939) 8, 50, 183.

4   Hermann W. Beyer, "εὐλογητός," *TDNT* 2 (1964) 764.

is, he has received a report—no doubt from the bishop—concerning) their "much loved name." The parallels in *Tr.* 1.2 and *Pol.* 1.1 show that this must have to do with the firmness and godly affection of the Ephesians.[5] Consequently it is hardly possible for the "name" to refer to their bishop. To be sure, Ignatius speaks more than once of a valued individual as a "name dear to me" (*Rom.* 10.1; *Sm.* 13.3; *Pol.* 8.3), but in these instances the expression is accompanied by the name of the person involved. Lightfoot builds on the same parallels but extends the meaning of the term "name" to include the "personality, character, worth" of the Ephesians themselves. That fits the general sense. But is there not a reference here to some definite name which belongs to the Ephesians? The medieval Latin scholiast (followed by Zahn and Bauer)[6] sees a hidden reference to the name Ephesus, and takes it to mean "desirable" (from ἔφεσις, ἐφίεσθαι). Perhaps Ignatius had in mind particularly the goodness of the Ephesians in "sending" their bishop to greet him (reflecting a derivation of Ephesus also from the active form of the verb: ἐφεῖναι). One of the suggestions of the *Etymologicon Magnum* will be that Ephesus is so named because Artemis "sent" (ἐφεῖναι) the Amazons salvation at Ephesus. An alternative is to find an oblique reference to the name of Christ or Christian by building on the absolute use of the term "name" in Ignatius (see on *Eph.* 1.2). The Ephesians may be regarded as having this name much as "Christianity" is elsewhere said to be the one indispensable "name" by which one should hope to be called (*Mag.* 10.1).[7] In any event, the context suggests that Ignatius sees the

Ephesians as having displayed their Christian character by having sent their bishop to greet him. The "name," in the last analysis, is the firmness and godly affection of the Ephesians, especially as shown on Ignatius' behalf.

Ignatius thinks of the Ephesians as a body (or as a body represented by their bishop, 1.3) since he speaks of "your" name ("your" in the singular). That is immediately followed by the plural, "which you [plural] possess." This is probably a form of enallage.[8] In any event, the godly ways of the Ephesians are accounted for by what can be expected of them simply as bearers of the name "Ephesians" or "Christians." They do what they do "by nature" (φύσει), and the task they perform is "congenital" or "suited to them" (συγγενικόν). But these Ephesians justly bear their name because its meaning has become a reality with them: their nature is "just according to faith and love in Christ Jesus, our Savior,"[9] they are "imitators of God" who have been "enkindled by the blood of God." As in the parallel provided by *Tr.* 1.1, a godly disposition has become second nature to them.

"Faith and love," as the primary expressions of the Christian life, represent a traditional theme of central importance in Ignatius (see Introduction, 5.8). Also traditional is the theme of the imitation of God (see Introduction, 5.13). The context suggests that here "God" refers to Christ. In any event, Ignatius thinks of the affection displayed by the Ephesians for him as an imitation of God's love for the world manifested in the incarnation (cf. Eph 5:1–2: "Become imitators of God as beloved children, and walk about in love just as Christ also loved us and gave himself for us . . .").[10]

---

5   As we have seen, the good qualities of the addressees can be said "to be received" (see n. 2). Moreover, the Ephesians are said to "possess" (κέκτησθε) this name; and the same verb is used elsewhere in connection with the possession of admirable dispositions (*Eph.* 14.2; 15.2; *Mag.* 15; *Pol.* 1.3; 8.1).

6   Zahn, *Epistulae*, 5; Walter Bauer, *Die Briefe des Ignatius von Antiochia und der Polykarpbrief*, in *Die Apostolischen Väter*, vol. 2 (HNTSup; Tübingen: Mohr [Siebeck], 1920) 196.

7   Paulsen, *Studien*, 93–98.

8   Cf. Sophocles, *Oed. Col.* 207: "O strangers [the chorus as a whole], do not ask thou [the leader in particular] me who I am." The reading of SAgl ("your [plural] name") represents a simplification.

9   Ignatius' reference to Christ as "Savior" here (and in *Mag.* inscr; *Phd.* 9.2; *Sm.* 7.1) is already formulaic

(Martin Dibelius and Hans Conzelmann, *The Pastoral Epistles* [Hermeneia; Philadelphia: Fortress, 1972] 100–3).

10   Ps-Ignatius recognized the relevance of Eph 5:1–2 for Ignatius here and added the final portion of it to *Eph.* 1.2. From there it was taken over also in G and involved the omission of "you hastened to see me." That has been restored by the editors from the versions (the Arabic also has "you were eager to see me").

What enflames the Ephesians is "the blood of God"—that is, the blood of Christ. The expression is found in important manuscripts (SB) of Acts 20:28. Tertullian also says that we are bought with a price—the "blood of God" (*sanguine dei; Ad uxor.* 2.3.1). That "God" suffered (see *Rom.* 6.3) was acceptable language before criticism required some refinement of the conviction that God (or God's Son) had become man and died on the cross.[11] Monophysites were later to appeal to precisely such unreflective remarks of Ignatius in defense of their christology.[12] By the term "blood" Ignatius has in mind the passion (*Phd.* inscr; *Sm.* 6.1) and/or the eucharist (*Phd.* 4). Such a reference is appropriate in this context since the eucharistic blood (*Tr.* 8.1; *Rom.* 7.3) and the blood of the passion (*Sm.* 1.1) are both closely linked with "love" by Ignatius (see Introduction, 5.7).

■ **1.2** The next sentence shows that the "task" suited to the nature of the Ephesians and "perfectly" accomplished by them had to do with visiting him. This is made all the more certain by the parallel construction of 1.1 and 1.2—lengthy participial phrases followed by somewhat abrupt conclusions ("you accomplished perfectly the task suited to you" and "you hastened to see me") which

themselves appear to be related (in spite of the distance between them) by homoeoteleuton (ἀπηρτίσατε, ἐσπουδάσατε). Note also the emphasis on "perfection" in *Sm.* 11.1–3 where the "perfect task" of the Smyrnaeans is to send an ambassador at Ignatius' request—a task not unlike that which he has in mind here.

Attention now shifts to Ignatius, the object of the Ephesians' affection. The hope that the prayers of other Christians will help the bishop realize his destiny worthily is often voiced by Ignatius and is an important part of his complex reflections on his role in the church (see Introduction, 3.4). Also frequent in the letters is Ignatius' description of his destiny as a martyr in terms of "attaining" (see Introduction, 5.12).[13] He usually speaks of attaining God or Christ. Here this destiny is spoken of as lying on the other side of "fighting with beasts" (θηριομαχῆσαι; cf. *Tr.* 10). This term has to do with the games in the arena (M. Aurelius 10.8; Vettius Valens 2.40, p. 129.33 Kroll) and is used of the punishment meted out to criminals who, insufficiently armed or bound to stakes, were exposed to animals (cf. Artemidorus 2.54; 5.49) for the delight of the public.[14] Among those treated in this way were Jewish revolutionaries

---

11 Cf. Adolf Harnack, *History of Dogma* (London: Constable, ca. 1900; reprinted New York: Dover, 1961) 1. 187 (n. 1); 2. 275–86.

12 Robert M. Grant, "The Use of the Early Fathers from Irenaeus to John of Damascus," in *After the New Testament* (Philadelphia: Fortress, 1967) 20–34; idem, "The Apostolic Fathers' First Thousand Years," *CH* 31 (1962) 421–29.

13 G reads ἐλπίζοντα τῇ προσευχῇ ὑμῶν ἐπιτυχεῖν ἐν Ῥώμῃ θηριομαχῆσαι ἵνα διὰ τοῦ μαρτυρίου ἐπιτυχεῖν δυνηθῶ μαθητὴς εἶναι, which is immediately followed by a line based on Eph 5:2, τοῦ ὑπὲρ ἡμῶν ἑαυτὸν ἀνενεγκόντος θεῷ προσφορὰν καὶ θυσίαν. The long recension merely substitutes πεποιθότα for ἐλπίζοντα and has all the rest except for the second ἐπιτυχεῖν. Lightfoot (*Ignatius*, 2. 30–31) is probably right in arguing that the interpolator substituted μαρτυρίου for the second ἐπιτυχεῖν to avoid the repetition of the verb and that the substitution came into G along with the line based on Eph 5:2 (which in turn caused the omission of the concluding words, "you hastened to see me"; see above n. 10). Ignatius uses the verb ἐπιτυχεῖν in one other passage (*Rom.* 1.1) to control an infinitive (corresponding to its first usage in *Eph.* 1.2) and in eighteen other passages with reference to his destiny as a martyr (corresponding to its second usage in *Eph.* 1.2). The sentence, then, is awkward

but not impossible. On the other hand, SA and the Arabic, which in all other respects have the original reading, apparently do not reflect the first ἐπιτυχεῖν. Consequently it may also have come into G from the long recension. In that event, the interpolator substituted μαρτυρίου for ἐπιτυχεῖν simply because of its apparent obscurity (for except in *Eph.* 1.2 and *Rom.* 8.3 the expression elsewhere occurs more clearly as "attain God" or the like; and note that the interpolator felt constrained to clarify the absolute use of the verb also in *Rom.* 8.3 by writing, "that I may attain my goal in the Holy Spirit"), and ἐπιτυχεῖν found its way into the earlier part of the sentence where it was put to new use. Joly (*Ignace*, 70–71) retains the reading of G: μαρτυρίου ἐπιτυχεῖν. He regards the absolute use of ἐπιτυχεῖν here as unintelligible, thinks that μαρτυρίου is required for the sense, and pronounces the appearance of the latter term as a sign of the lateness of Ignatius' letters. But he takes too lightly the other evidence of dislocation in the text and ignores the use of the absolute form of the verb in *Rom.* 8.3 (cf. *Phd.* 5.1).

14 See *Rom.* 5.1 for a metaphorical use of the verb. Probably also metaphorical is its use in 1 Cor 15:32 (see Abraham J. Malherbe, "The Beasts at Ephesus," *JBL* 87 [1968] 71–80; Malherbe also discusses the Stoic-Cynic background of the expression). In any

(Josephus *Bell.* 7.38; cf. 7.373) and Christian martyrs (*Mart. Pol.* 3). In Rome the Flavian amphitheater (Colosseum) was the popular place for such shows.[15]

Ignatius links martyrdom and "being a disciple." Although he calls all Christians "disciples" (*Eph.* 10.1; *Pol.* 2.1; cf. *Mag.* 9.2; 10.1), he characteristically thinks of himself as worthy of the title only after the successful completion of his martyrdom (*Eph.* 3.1; *Tr.* 5.2; *Rom.* 4.2; 5.1, 3). John also thinks of discipleship here and now as still incomplete (John 8:31; 15:8). But the link betwen discipleship and suffering is clearer in Luke 14:27 ("whoever does not bear his cross and follow me, cannot be my disciple"); and Ignatius' usage seems to represent an extension (probably by means of the idea of imitation; cf. *Rom.* 6.3) of the sentiment reflected there (cf. Acts 7:59–60 and Luke 23:46, 34). But in Ignatius the thought is related to his sense of inferiority to other Christians (see Introduction, 3.4) and has not yet hardened into hagiographical formulae.[16] Ignatius' orientation to Rome also represents a special feature of his self-understanding that transcends normal martyrological themes (see Introduction, 3.6).

Ignatius states the reason for his bonds in terms of loyalty to the "common name and hope." A reference simply to "the name"—meaning the name of Christ— may go back ultimately to Jewish-Christian theology;[17] but here, as elsewhere,[18] the absolute use of the term simply underscores the clear sense of identity enjoyed by Christians and suggests the depth of loyalty to Christ: one does extraordinary things "for the name" (cf. Acts 5:41; 3 John 7).[19] Ignatius also identifies Christ as "our

(common) hope" elsewhere (see Introduction, 5.9). In these passages the term "hope" has lost its earlier eschatological significance. It is worth noting that the expression "common hope" could be used by Libanius (*Or.* 59.30) to describe the expectations that the world had of Constantius and Constans (ἄξιοι δὲ τῆς κοινῆς ἐλπίδος "worthy of the common hope").

■ **1.3** The Ephesians, in the person of their bishop, Onesimus, "hastened to see" Ignatius (1.2). The idea is further explored in the next sentence (1.3) where the reception of the Ephesian bishop is seen as (in some sense) the reception of the Ephesian church itself. This vivid sense of the presence of the Ephesians in their representative probably builds on the thought in Hellenistic letters that the correspondents "see" one another in each other's words.[20] Ignatius elsewhere shows himself to be fully alert to this significance of the letter (*Eph.* 9.2; *Mag.* 15; *Rom.* 1.1; *Sm.* 9.2); and it may not be accidental that the verb ἀπολαμβάνω, used here of "receiving" Onesimus, is often used also of the reception of letters.[21] To judge from NT usage, a reception "in the name of God" would imply that Ignatius solemnly uttered the name of God when he welcomed his visitors from Ephesus.[22] Perhaps he would have used a variant of the common "peace" greeting (cf. Matt 10:13; 1 Pet 5:14; 3 John 15; Tertullian *Orat.* 26).[23]

The name Onesimus is a relatively common one,

---

event, it is likely that Ignatius is modelling his career on that of the apostle.

15 Ludwig Friedländer, *Darstellungen aus der Sittengeschichte Roms* (10th ed.; 4 vols.; Leipzig: Hirzel, 1921–23) 2. 89–91.

16 *Eph.* 3.1 shows that to Ignatius the figure of the disciple sometimes also suggests a comparison of the church to a school (cf. *Eph.* 6.2; 17.1; *Mag.* 6.2; *Rom.* 3.1; 8.2; *Phd.* 2.1; 8.2; *Pol.* 3.1). But the teacher and his disciples teach and learn in extraordinary ways (see on *Eph.* 15.1 and *Mag.* 9–10).

17 Daniélou, *Jewish Christianity*, 147–63.

18 Eph. 3.1; 7.1; *Phd.* 10.1; cf. *1 Clem.* 43.2; *2 Clem.* 13.1, 4; *Herm. Sim.* 8.10.3; 9.13.2; 9.28.3. The use of absolutes is a marked feature of Ignatius' style (Brown, *Authentic Writings*, 28–29).

19 Cf. Joseph Ponthot, "La signification religieuse du

'nom' chez Clément de Rome et dans la Didache," *EThL* 35 (1959) 339–61.

20 Heikki Koskenniemi, *Studien zur Idee und Phraseologie des griechischen Briefes bis 400 n. Chr.* (Annales Academia Scientiarium Fennica B, 102.2; Helsinki: Suomalainen Tiedeakatemia, 1956) 172–80.

21 Ibid., 187.

22 BAG *s.v.* ὄνομα I.4.c.γ, p. 576.

23 In 1 Pet 5:14 the pronouncement of peace follows a reference to greeting one another with a kiss. Note that the deacon who announces the kiss of peace in Cyril of Jerusalem (*Cat. myst.* 5.3) uses the same verb as does Ignatius here: "Receive (ἀπολάβετε) one another, let us greet one another." For a peace greeting that mentions God see the liturgical formula spoken by the bishop in *Const. Apost.* 8.13.1: "the peace of God be with you all."

especially (but not exclusively) for slaves.[24] There is little chance, however, that our Onesimus is (as John Knox argued) the Onesimus of Paul's letter to Philemon.[25] In any event, the bishop's person is described by means of an antithesis that unfortunately is not quite clear: he is "a man indescribable in love" (that is, he has qualities that all but exalt him above human nature?) yet functions at the mundane level as your bishop. The usual interpretation sees an implicit contrast between the bishop Onesimus and the divine bishop (cf. *Mag.* 3.1–2; *Rom.* 9.1; *Pol.* inscr). This depends on the translation "indescribable in love and (δέ) your bishop in the flesh." But the δέ is probably adversative ("yet") since "in love" and "in the flesh" seem to represent some kind of antithesis (see Introduction, 5.6).[26] It is likely that Ignatius wants to say that there is much more to the man than meets the eye. These words of praise for the Ephesian bishop prepare the way for requests that Ignatius is about to make.

---

24 Pape/Benseler, *Eigennamen*, 1062; Preisigke, *Namenbuch*, 241; Foraboschi, *Onomasticon*, 213. Onesimus means "useful" (cf. Phlm 11). Names that indicate such qualities were often given slaves. The papyri, however, know of many by the name of Onesimus who were farmers and merchants. And Livy (44.16) gives us a clear instance of a Macedonian noble by this name.

25 See Lohse, *Colossians and Philemon*, 186.

26 SAg and the Arabic simplify by omitting "in the flesh."

Unity with the Bishop [2.1–6.1]

2

Request for Assistance

1 **Now concerning my fellow slave Burrhus, your godly deacon blessed in all things: I pray that he stay here to the glory of you and your bishop. And Crocus too, worthy of God and you, whom I received as an exemplar of your love, refreshed me in every way; so may the Father of Jesus Christ refresh also him, along with Onesimus, Burrhus, Euplous, and Fronto, through whom I saw all of you in love. 2/ May I always have benefit from you if I am worthy. It is right, then, in every way to glorify Jesus Christ who glorified you, so that being joined in one obedience, subject to the bishop and the presbytery, you may be holy in every respect.**

■ **2.1–2** The formula "now concerning" ($\pi\epsilon\rho\grave{\iota}$ $\delta\grave{\epsilon}$) represents a transition in letters that often has to do with "a subject mentioned in previous communication."[1] Here it is a question of the deacon Burrhus and his continued attendance on Ignatius. Also note that the words "and Crocus too" employ two conjunctions ($\kappa\alpha\grave{\iota} \ldots \delta\grave{\epsilon}$) that together may be used to refer to additional items of importance in a series of requests.[2] The last sentence of section 2 begins with a phrase ($\pi\rho\acute{\epsilon}\pi o\nu$ $o\mathring{\upsilon}\nu$ $\acute{\epsilon}\sigma\tau\acute{\iota}\nu$ "it is right, then") that is used elsewhere in Ignatius to climax and summarize his appeal "with tact and courtesy."[3] This means that the request involving Burrhus (and Crocus) has something to do with praising Jesus Christ and submitting to the bishop and presbytery of Ephesus.

The connection is not made explicit. We learn from *Phd.* 11.2 and *Sm.* 12.1, however, that Burrhus went on with Ignatius at least as far as Troas and served as his scribe (or as carrier for his letters). We also learn that this luxury was supported by both the Ephesians and the Smyrnaeans. We may conjecture that expense was a problem and that the Ephesians who came to Smyrna were willing to agree to it only after their hosts cooperated by making a contribution. It seems likely that agreement had been reached concerning Crocus even earlier (perhaps when Ignatius' representatives first contacted the Ephesians). That would explain why without further discussion Crocus is here praised for his

attentions to Ignatius; why in *Sm.* 12.1 Ignatius uses the same language of Burrhus (now definitely at Ignatius' disposal) that he had already used of Crocus in *Eph.* 2.1 ("refreshed me," "exemplar"); and why (above all) Crocus alone is named in *Rom.* 10.1 when Ignatius says that he is writing to the Romans "through the Ephesians." Probably Crocus carried the letter to Rome. If that had been settled, it is not hard to see why there would be some discussion about further expenses involving Burrhus. Moreover, the threat to unity in Ephesus (of which we are soon informed) had to be taken into account in putting forward the new request. It appears that Onesimus (and his companions) were anxious to support Ignatius but felt that caution was necessary. Hence also Ignatius' caution. The words "may I have benefit from you" ($\dot{o}\nu\alpha\acute{\iota}\mu\eta\nu$ $\dot{\upsilon}\mu\hat{\omega}\nu$) in 2.2 represent a variant of a popular expression which reflects feelings ranging all the way from a conventional expression of good wishes ("bless me . . .") to vigorous protestation in situations of some uncertainty (Euripides *Helen* 645), delicacy (as in Phlm 20), or worse.[4] Ignatius' desire to see the Ephesians unified (that is, obedient to the ministry) is related to his request for support in his fateful journey to Rome. His doubt as to whether he is "worthy" of this support (the same language appears in *Mag.* 12.1) is part of the complex self-understanding of a man who is in some respects genuinely uncertain of himself, but whose self-

1   White, *Form and Function*, 31.
2   Ibid., 59.
3   Brown, *Authentic Writings*, 31; cf. *Mag.* 3.2; 4.1;
4   *Sm.* 7.2.
     Cf. LSJ (p. 1232) and BAG (p. 573) *s.v.* $\dot{o}\nu\acute{\iota}\nu\eta\mu\iota$. It is unlikely that $\dot{o}\nu\alpha\acute{\iota}\mu\eta\nu$ represents a play on the name

esteem also depends on gaining from others a positive response to his requests for support (see Introduction, 3.4). In particular, it is typical of Ignatius to affirm the worthiness of the Ephesians (1.3) while casting doubt on his own. To some extent this reflects epistolary convention. Thus the emperor Julian in writing to Priscus notes the latter's good will and adds, "of which may I be worthy (ἄξιος) that I might not dishonor your friendship" (*Ep.* 11). But Ignatius (as we shall see) has more at stake than the convention implies (see on *Eph.* 12).

The names of these Ephesian Christians are a mixed bag. Greek as well as Latin forms of the name Burrhus are found, but it is essentially a Latin name and in the existing examples seems never to be used of non-Romans.[5] Burrhus, then, may have been a Roman or the slave or freedman of a Roman. Or the name may have been in use by non-Romans in spite of the evidence. Crocus ("saffron"), a Greek name, is also rare; but we have enough examples to know that it was used by people of high and low social standing.[6] Euplous is a good Greek name.[7] Fronto, again, is a Latin name; but we also find it used occasionally of non-Romans.[8]

Ignatius' remark that he saw the Ephesian congregation in these visitors broadens the statement of 1.3 which speaks only of the bishop. Burrhus was a deacon, for Ignatius uses the term "fellow slave" (σύνδουλος) only of deacons (*Mag.* 2; *Phd.* 4; *Sm.* 12.2).[9] It is likely that

Crocus was also a deacon (see above). Euplous and Fronto were probably church officials too since Ignatius "sees" congregations in their leaders (cf. *Mag.* 2; 6.1; *Tr.* 1.1). There is an especially close bond between bishop and deacon in Ignatius. This may reflect an earlier stage in the development of the ministry when these two (Hellenistic-Christian?) offices had not yet merged with the (Jewish-Christian?) presbyterate.[10] But other factors probably suffice to explain the special attention given to deacons by Ignatius: their active role in practical matters; in particular, their service to Ignatius personally; and a special concern on Ignatius' part to support those whose position sometimes put them in difficult situations (see on *Tr.* 2.3). Whatever relation between bishop and deacon may have obtained, the presbyterate had won its place at or near the head of the Christian community.[11] Consequently, when Ignatius formally identifies the chief authority of the churches, he speaks either of all three orders or of the bishop and presbytery (as he does here in 2.2), not of the bishop and deacons. Of course he often also mentions the bishop alone, but there is a strong collegial element in Ignatius' view of the ministry, and the presbyterate is still very much alive (see Introduction, 5.5).

Some of the theological language in this section deserves comment: (a) "According to God" (κατὰ θεόν) is a common expression in Ignatius and (as in 2 Cor

---

Onesimus. Ignatius uses the expression elsewhere with reference to others (*Mag.* 2.1; 12.1; *Rom.* 5.2; *Pol.* 1.1; 6.2); and the suggestion gains little support from the parallel in Phlm 20 where there is also probably no play on words (Lohse, *Colossians and Philemon*, 205).

5   Pape/Benseler, *Eigennamen*, 225; Bauer, *Ignatius*, 199; it does not appear in Preisigke, *Namenbuch*, or Foraboschi, *Onomasticon*.

6   Pape/Benseler, *Eigennamen*, 722; Preisigke, *Namenbuch*, 187; Foraboschi, *Onomasticon*, 173.

7   Pape/Benseler, *Eigennamen*, 417; Preisigke, *Namenbuch*, 113; BAG *s.v.* Εὔπλους, p. 324.

8   Pape/Benseler, *Eigennamen*, 1649; Preisigke, *Namenbuch*, 468; Foraboschi, *Onomasticon*, 337.

9   It is most unlikely that Ignatius here identifies himself as a "deacon." In *Rom.* 2.2 he calls himself a "bishop," and there is no strong reason to separate the testimony of *Romans* from that of the other letters (see Introduction, 1.2, 4). Moreover, Ignatius no doubt reflects a usage familiar also from Col 1:7 (cf. 4:7) in which a subordinate—indeed, a "servant

(διάκονος) of Christ"—is called Paul's "fellow slave."

10 Cf. Hans Lietzmann, "Zur altchristlichen Verfassungsgeschichte," *ZWTh* 55 (1914) 97ff. (Reprinted in idem, *Kleine Schriften I* [TU 67; Berlin: Akademie-Verlag, 1958] 141–85); André Lemaire, "From Services to Ministries: 'Diakoniai' in the First Two Centuries," *Concilium* 80 (1972) 35–49.

11 We hear first of bishops and deacons (both in the plural) in one community (Phil 1:1). Probably such bodies of bishops later merged with bodies of elders (cf. Acts 20:17, 28) while deacons retained their subordinate position. Only when the monarchical bishop came to dominate these bodies of bishops/ elders would the active role of the deacons in practical affairs make a new relation likely between them and the bishop. Ignatius appears to be near the beginning of a development in this regard.

7:9–11) is used as a modifier with scarcely any stronger sense than "godly" (cf. *Mag.* 1.1; 13.1; *Tr.* 1.2; *Sm.* 11.3). (b) "According to love" is to be understood in light of the antithesis in 1.3 between "in love" and "in the flesh": he "saw" them in their representatives in a spiritual manner. (c) Finally, the mutual glorification of Christ and the community goes a step beyond the soteriological ideas of the NT.[12] But it is a short step in a tradition that not only speaks of glorifying God but also associates the being of God (and Christ) with glory and sees this glory as given to human beings (Rom 8:30; John 17:22).

---

12   Schlier, *Untersuchungen,* 65–67.

Unity with the Bishop [2.1–6.1]

3

Ignatius' Appeal and
the Authority of the Bishops

1   I do not command you as being someone;
for even though I have been bound in the
name, I have not yet been perfected in
Jesus Christ. Indeed, now I have but
begun to be a disciple, and I speak to you
as my fellow learners; for I must be
anointed by you with faith, admonition,
endurance, patience. 2/ But since love
does not permit me to be silent concerning you, I have accordingly taken it
upon myself to exhort you that you might
run together with God's purpose. Indeed
Jesus Christ, our inseparable life, is the
Father's purpose; as also the bishops,
appointed in every quarter, are in the
purpose of Jesus Christ.

■ **3.1** Having just made a strong recommendation, Ignatius feels compelled to say what gives him the right to do so. This is the first of several passages in which he self-consciously refuses to base his authority on his own importance.

Ignatius' diffidence in this regard (3.1) reflects in part conventional attitudes. Most examples in Greek literature of the expression "to be someone" (τις) or "something" (τι) have to do with people who are disapproved of for claiming an importance that they do not have, and Ignatius naturally seeks to avoid giving any such impression.[1] Ignatius' attitude may also be compared with that of other early Christian leaders who emphasize their insignificance or unworthiness and point to God's grace as the reason for their activity.[2] In particular, Ignatius has in mind (as the parallels in *Tr.* 3.3 and *Rom.* 4.3 show) his inability to give commands like the apostles who had by this time been invested with a special sanctity (cf. Eph 2:20) and who alone could be thought of as

exercising an authority that went beyond local congregations (cf. *Eph.* 11.2). This limited view of episcopal authority made it all the more natural for Ignatius to fall back on the diplomatic tone of requests for assistance in Hellenistic letters where exhortation but not commanding seemed appropriate.[3]

Yet Ignatius transforms these themes by linking them with his fate as a martyr.[4] His authority is limited because his discipleship is incomplete—that is, he has not yet been martyred (cf. *Eph.* 1.2). Elsewhere this attitude is further complicated by emphasis not only on his own possible unworthiness (even though "bound" for Christ) but also on the clear superiority of other Christians to himself (*Mag.* 12.1). In the passage before us Ignatius moves in the same direction, first self-consciously putting himself on the same level with the Ephesians as his fellow learners,[5] and then in some sense subordinating himself to them by comparing them to trainers who anoint the

1   *LSJ s.v.* τις II. 5, p. 1796; cf. Acts 5:36; Gal 6:3. According to Plutarch there was general agreement that it was odious for people to speak of themselves "as being something" (*De laude ipsius* 1, 539a; cf. Betz, *Plutarch's Ethical Writings,* 382).

2   Cf. 1 Cor 15:9; Eph 3:8; 1 Tim 1:15–16; Pol. *Phil.* 12.1; *Barn.* 1.8; 4.6, 9; Polycrates, in Eusebius *Hist. eccl.* 5.24.6.

3   As in Phlm 8—9; cf. Carl J. Bjerkelund, *Parakalô: Form, Funktion und Sinn der Parakalô-Sätze in den paulinischen Briefen* (Bibliotheca theologica Norvegica 1; Oslo: Universitetsforlaget, 1967) 188. See further

on *Tr.* 6.1.

4   It should be observed that from Plato's *Gorgias* (527b,d) to Plutarch's *De laude ipsius* (1, 539ab) the problem of what it means "to be something" is closely linked with the problem of merely seeming to be such and such as opposed to actually being so. As we shall see, variants of the latter theme also play an important role in Ignatius and are sometimes connected with reflections on his martyrdom (cf. *Eph.* 14–15; *Tr.* 10; *Rom.* 2–3).

5   Συνδιδασκαλίτης ("fellow learners") is a hapax legomenon in Greek literature (Brown, *Authentic*

athlete for the contest.[6] Schlier's view—that Ignatius models himself on the Gnostic redeemer who seeks release from the "bonds" of this world and feels inferior to the aeonic "church"[7]—falters here. The clause "even though I have been bound in the name" (cf. *Eph.* 1.2) presupposes that the bonds lend prestige (so also *Mag.* 12.1).[8] But Schlier was right in finding more than merely conventional self-effacement here (see Introduction, 3.4).

■ **3.2** What love (which transcends normal limitations) constrains Ignatius to say in spite of his unimportance or unworthiness is that the Ephesians should obey their bishop (and, we may assume, approve of Burrhus' staying with Ignatius). Ignatius explicitly mentions the Ephesian bishop only in 4.1. In the passage before us he sets the stage by referring to the purpose of God with which all the bishops in the world are in agreement. That the monarchical episcopate was universal in this period can hardly be so.[9] This is not a sign that our letters are forgeries but that Ignatius tends to shape the world about him in his own image (see Introduction, 3.3). All these bishops are thought of as deriving their authority from God independently of one another.[10] Ignatius takes

their agreement for granted since they all know the purpose of God (a conviction no doubt reinforced by the generally favorable reception which he received from the bishops of Asia Minor).

Knowledge of God's purpose, however, involves Christ as well as God, and the bishop is to be obeyed because he is to Christ as Christ is to the Father. In several other passages the relation between Christ and the Father is appealed to somewhat differently: the joint activity of Christ and the Father provides a model for the relation that should obtain between the people and the ministry (see *Mag.* 7.1; *Phd.* 7.2; *Sm.* 8.1; and for more complex instances, *Eph.* 5.1; *Mag.* 13.2). But *Phd.* 7.2 shows how much a comparison of two (or more) sets of paired terms can be linked together by Ignatius in such a way that a hierarchy emerges. For there the command to adhere to the bishop is based on the exhortation to imitate Christ as Christ imitated[11] the Father. The thought is that the people are to obey the bishop as Christ obeyed the Father. But the words set out a hierarchical pattern in which the people are related to Christ as Christ is to the Father. It is likely that we have some such pattern before us in *Eph.* 3.2, and this should warn us against pressing

---

Writings, 17). It was probably coined by Ignatius, who is fond of using σνν-compounds to stress the unity of the church (cf. *Pol.* 6.1).

6   "Anointing" is an athletic term often used metaphorically in the early church (BAG *s.v.* ἀλείφω, p. 34; *s.v.* ὑπαλείφω, p. 845; *LPGL s.v.* ἀλείφω B, p. 70; *s.v.* ὑπαλείφω, p. 1433). In particular, the spiritual preparation of the martyr could be regarded as a kind of anointing (Tertullian *Ad mart.* 3.4; cf. *Pass. Perp.* 10) since the martyr himself was often referred to as an "athlete" (*4 Macc.* 6.10; 17.15–16; *1 Clem.* 5.1; cf. Ign. *Pol.* 1.3). Here Ignatius, like Paul, works not from life but from literary culture (cf. Victor Pfitzner, *Paul and the Agon Motif* [NovTSup 16; Leiden: Brill, 1967]). The expression "run together with" in 3.2 is probably not, however, athletic imagery (see on *Pol.* 1.2; 6.1).

7   Schlier, *Untersuchungen*, 152–57.

8   Cf. Bartsch, *Gnostisches Gut*, 93.

9   Patrick Burke, "The Monarchical Episcopate at the End of the First Century," *JES* 7 (1970) 499–518.

10   A passing allusion to the idea of succession has been found in the expression "appointed in every quarter" (cf. *Eph.* 3.2; *Phd.* inscr) on the grounds that it applies to the present mission of the church language that had to do with the sending out of the apostles into all

the world (Peter Meinhold, "Die Anschauung des Ignatius von Antiochien von der Kirche," in Ernst Chr. Suttner and Coelestin Patock, eds., *Wegzeichen: Festgabe zum 60. Geburtstag von Prof. Hermenegild M. Biedermann* [Das östliche Christentum N.F. 25; Würzburg: Augustinus-Verlag, 1971] 8–10; Paulsen, *Studien*, 153–55). But when Ignatius mentions the apostles, it is to put distance between them and himself (cf. *Eph.* 12; *Tr.* 3.3; *Rom.* 4.3), to think of them as authorities from the past (*Eph.* 11.2; *Mag.* 7.1; 13.1, 2; *Phd.* 9.1; cf. *Tr.* 7.1; 12.2) or to work them into elaborate comparisons in which they correspond to the elders (see Introduction, 5.5). It is more likely, then, that he applies apostolic language to his own generation much as he thinks of his own career in terms that reflect Paul's ministry.

11   Here the term apparently covers both the notion of being like the Father and that of obeying him.

the theological significance of the passage too closely.[12] First, it is hardly correct to see evidence here of a subordinationist christology. The comparisons function within the sphere of exhortation and do not have in view the problem of the relation in the Godhead between the Father and the Son. It is the obedience of the historical Jesus that Ignatius has in mind (see especially *Mag.* 7.1). At most the designation of Christ as the "purpose" (γνώμη) of the Father, like the designation of him elsewhere as "word" (*Mag.* 8.2) and "mouth" (*Rom.* 8.2), is an image that expresses the revelatory function of Christ and that as such is linked with his historical appearance.[13] Second, we should be cautious about finding here any suggestion of a special presence of Christ in the bishop analogous to the presence of God in Christ. It is likely that (as we have seen) the hierarchical pattern conceals a simpler comparison and consequently that the bishop's knowledge of the mind of Christ has a significance comparable to the people's imitation of Christ in *Phd.* 7.2. Just as the people (in *Phd.* 7.2) are called on to look to Christ and mirror his obedience to the Father (in obeying their bishop), so the bishop (in *Eph.* 3.2) reflects the purpose of Christ and mirrors his likeness to the Father (in being worthy of the obedience of the people). A stricter emphasis on the symmetry of the hierarchical relations here has also this against it: that Christ is said to *be* the purpose of the Father, whereas the bishops are said to be *in* the purpose of Christ (although L may be right in dropping the preposition "in").[14] In any event, the term "purpose" (γνώμη) lends itself even less than the terms "word" or "mouth" to expressing the immanence of the divine in the bishop. As Brown notes, "purpose" (γνώμη) is frequently used by Ignatius in place of the more traditional "will" (θέλημα).[15] Ignatius uses the latter eight times (absolutely three times[16]), always of the divine will; he uses the former seven times of the divine will[17] and some nine times of human purpose, particularly that of the bishop.[18] But divine purpose and human purpose are closely related since the latter is regularly presented as purpose dominated by God and has to do with the achievement of unity. Most interesting is the fact that the command to do nothing "apart from the purpose" (or consent) of the bishop has secular analogies and echoes the requirement that people refrain from undertakings of consequence "apart from the purpose" of their superiors (see on *Pol.* 4.1). It is likely, then, that Ignatius often substitutes the term "purpose" for the term "will" not because it had an especially deep religious significance for him but because it reverberated with widely diffused notions of social and political discipline. The theological implications of Christ as the "purpose" of the Father are thus probably minimal.

At the same time, Christ not only gives life but *is* "our inseparable life" (3.2; cf. John 6:33; 10:28; 17:2); and such usage opens the way for more mystical conceptions of the relation between God and human beings. It may be noted, however, that the use of an attributive with an articular infinitive (τὸ ἀδιάκριτον ἡμῶν ζῆν; cf. *Eph.* 11.1; 17.1; *Mag.* 1.2; 5.2; *Tr.* 9.2; *Sm.* 4.1) is grammatically unusual[19] and may have more to do with adding weight to Ignatius' rhetoric than with furthering a particular spirituality.

---

12 Similar apparently innocent hierarchical patterns also occur in the NT (1 Cor 11:3, 7–9; John 15:9–10; 17:22).

13 Cf. Paulsen, *Studien,* 116–18.

14 Ibid., 75 n. 99.

15 Brown, *Authentic Writings,* 28. The parallel cited by Kathleen O'Brien Wicker (in Betz, *Plutarch's Theological Writings,* 145) from Plutarch *De def. orac.* 8, 413e, also refers anthropomorphically to the divine will: one explanation for the decline of oracles is that it comes about θεοῦ γνώμῃ "by the will of a god" (LCL 5. 371). More philosophically refined is another passage in Plutarch where the best things are said to take place θεοῦ γνώμῃ "by the will of God," since he is the soul of the universe (*Sept. sap. conv.* 21, 163e).

16 *Rom.* 1.1; *Sm.* 11.1; *Pol.* 8.1.

17 *Eph.* 3.2 (three times); *Rom.* 8.3 ; *Phd.* inscr; *Sm.* 6.2; 8.1. It is used once of Satan's purpose (*Phd.* 6.2).

18 Human purpose: *Eph.* 1.1; 2.2; *Rom.* 7.1 (of Ignatius); *Phd.* 3.3. The purpose (consent) of the bishop: *Eph.* 4.1; *Phd.* 1.2; *Pol.* 1.1; 4.1; 5.2.

19 BDF, §398.

Unity with the Bishop [2.1–6.1]

4

Harmony and Unity: Musical Metaphors

1 Consequently it is right for you to run together with the purpose of the bishop, which you indeed do; for your worthily reputed presbytery, worthy of God, is attuned to the bishop like strings to a cithara; therefore, in your concord and harmonious love, Jesus Christ is sung. 2/ And may each of you remain joined in chorus, that being harmonious in concord, receiving God's variation in unity, you may sing with one voice through Jesus Christ to the Father, that he may both hear you and recognize you through what you do well, as members of his Son. It is profitable, then, for you to be in blameless unity that you may always participate also in God.

■ **4.1** Ignatius is now in a position to replace the exhortation to "run together with the purpose of God" (3.2) with the recommendation to "run together with the purpose of the bishop." What this may mean is illustrated by Ignatius with the help of musical imagery (cf. *Rom.* 2.2; *Phd.* 1.2). The recommendation itself is softened by the remark that compliance is in fact the case (ὅπερ καὶ ποιεῖτε "which you indeed do"; cf. *Eph.* 8.1; *Tr.* 2.2; *Rom.* 2.1; *Sm.* 4.1; *Pol.* 1.2; 4.1). The same kind of remark occurs once in Paul (1 Thess 4:1), but Ignatius is unlikely to have picked it up there. It has a more general background in the diplomatic atmosphere of Hellenistic letters (both private and official) whose purpose is to make a firm but polite request (see on *Tr.* 6.1). A more or less precise parallel is found in *P.Freib.* 39: "So then I request you earnestly and exhort you to take good care of my horse, as indeed you always do (ὡς καὶ πάντοτε ποιεῖς), and I thank you profusely and will again thank you. . . ."[1]

In what follows Ignatius sees such compliance as a fact primarily in terms of the agreement between the bishop and the presbytery (4.1).[2] When he addresses the congregation directly (4.2),[3] he returns to the imperative mood. Evidently Ignatius had gained the confidence of the Ephesian clergy (see on *Eph.* 2) and now seeks to assure himself that the Ephesian church as a whole will continue to stand behind them (the imperative is present tense and so speaks of continuing a presumed state of affairs).

To illustrate his remarks Ignatius first compares the harmony between bishop and presbytery to a cithara and its strings. The latter was an elaborate form of the lyre. Both instruments figure in imagery that describes the harmony of the cosmos (cf. Philo *Cherub.* 110; Irenaeus *Adv. haer.* 2.25.2; Gregory Naz. *Or.* 14.23), of the human individual as microcosm (cf. Clement Alex. *Protr.* 1.5.1–6), or of relations between people (cf. Philostratus *Vit. Apoll.* 6.30). Appeal to the construction of the instru-

---

1 W. Aly, "Privatbrief aus der Freiburger Papyrussammlung, P. Freib. 39," *Aegyptus* 13 (1933) 487–92; cf. Bjerkelund, *Parakalô*, 128.

2 The term "presbytery" occurs some thirteen times in Ignatius. The only other contemporary example is found in 1 Tim 4:14. Such use of abstract for concrete expressions (that is, presbytery for presbyters or elders) fits the general development of the language of the period (G. J. M. Bartelink, *Lexicologisch-semantische studie over de taal van de Apostolische Vaders* [Utrecht: Beijers, 1952] 21–24.

3 "Each one of you" (οἱ κατ' ἄνδρα) is used in Ignatius

for the individual members of the congregation (cf. *Eph.* 20.2; *Sm.* 5.1); but in three passages the expression appears to have special reference to the laity as distinct from the ministry (*Tr.* 13.2; *Sm.* 12.2; *Pol.* 1.3).

ment is not usually as explicit as it is in Ignatius, but Heraclitus' familiar comparison of the universe with the bow and lyre (cf. Plato *Symp.* 187a) shows that this too was never far from people's minds. Ignatius may have emphasized the construction of the instrument because the number of strings (from three to twelve[4]) reminded him of the number of members of the presbytery.

In the last sentence of 4.1, however, Ignatius apparently also has the instrument's sound in mind and sees the congregation as singing harmoniously together to the cithara's music: "therefore, in your concord (ὁμονοίᾳ) and harmonious (συμφώνῳ) love, Jesus Christ is sung."[5] In 4.2 he repeats this language in connection with the image of the chorus (σύμφωνοι ὄντες ἐν ὁμονοίᾳ "being harmonious in concord") and speaks of the Ephesians as singing together "in unity" (ἐν ἑνότητι). The picture suggested in the last sentence of 4.1 is somewhat unusual. When harmony between rulers and citizens (or God and humankind) is compared to a chorus, the relation between the chorus and its leader is regularly invoked.[6] Instead, Ignatius appears to concentrate on the relation between the chorus and the accompanying instrument. If so, he cannot have the dramatic choruses in mind since there the flute was used almost exclusively.[7] Rather his imagery reflects the activity of choruses that sang and danced at public festivals in honor of the gods to the accompaniment of string music. It appears that the

instrumentalists often came to dominate in such settings.[8] And emphasis on the song (as opposed to the dance) also reflects late developments in choral practice.[9]

■ **4.2** When Ignatius turns directly to the congregation (note the transitional καὶ . . . δὲ as in 2.1), the imagery of the congregation as a chorus is made explicit. Probably the chorus is here said to "receive" God's "variation"[10] (from God? from the bishop?) since leaders were said to "give" (ἐνδίδωμι) the melody to the chorus—that is, to strike it up (Libanius *Or.* 59.172). Applications of the image of the chorus have an enormous range in classical and Hellenistic literature.[11] Close in spirit to Ignatius are the references in Gnosticism to the musical harmony (συμφωνία) of the aeons and their unity (ἑνότης).[12] Yet Ignatius' imagery is more specific and concrete and can be illustrated more adequately from the central cultural tradition of Hellenism.

Especially instructive is Theon of Smyrna who follows Pythagoras in describing music as "the union (ἕνωσις) of the many" and in stating its purpose as unification (ἑνοῦν) and harmonization. In the same passage God himself is said to be the harmonizer of diversities; music is linked with the "concord (ὁμονοία) of things"; and its benefits are thought to devolve on the cosmos, the city, and the home.[13] Similarly Plutarch (*De frat. amor.* 2, 479a) interprets the affection of brothers in terms of concord (ὁμονοία) and harmony (συμφωνία) and thinks of families

4   Curt Sachs, *The History of Musical Instruments* (New York: Norton, 1940) 129–35.

5   The expression "Jesus Christ is sung" may (especially in light of *Eph.* 5) not only function as part of the metaphor but may also reflect the actual practice of singing hymns to Christ (cf. Eph 5:9; Pliny *Ep.* 10.96.7). If so, hymns were also sung to the Father "through Jesus Christ" (4.2; cf. Eph 5:20). Similarly, the expression "what you do well" (4.2) probably refers not to good deeds in general but to worship "done" under the leadership of the bishop (cf. *Mag.* 7.1; *Tr.* 7.2; *Phd.* 4). Cf. Franz Joseph Dölger, *Sol Salutis: Gebet und Gesang im christlichen Altertum* (2d ed.; Liturgiegeschichtliche Forschungen 4/5; Münster: Aschendorff, 1925) 125.

6   Cf. Dio Chrysostom *Or.* 14.4; Themistius *Or.* 4, 53b; 16, 201a; Libanius *Or.* 59.172; Plotinus *Enn.* 6.9.8; Gregory Nyss. *In Psalmos* 6 (*PG* 44. 508b).

7   Reisch, "Chor," PW 3/2. 2400.

8   Ibid., 3/2. 2383. Cf. F. Castets and E. Pottier, "Cyclicus Chorus," *Dictionnaire des antiquités* (ed. Ch. Daremberg and Edm. Saglio; 5 vols.; Paris: Hachette,

1877–1919) 1/2. 1693.

9   Reisch, "Chor," PW 3/2. 2374, 2384.

10   The term χρῶμα ("color") is used in music of "a modification of the simplest music" (LSJ *s.v.* Χρῶμα IV. 3, p. 2012). It also has another highly technical meaning in ancient musical theory, but that is out of place here. Although cithara virtuosos were said to specialize in "variations" (Athenaeus *Deipn.* 14, 638a), Ignatius is probably no longer thinking of them here.

11   Lillian B. Lawler, "The Dance in Metaphor," *Classical Journal* 46 (1950/51) 383–91.

12   Hippolytus *Ref.* 8.9.2; cf. 6.32.1; Epiphanius *Pan.* 31.6.3–4; cf. Otto Betz, "συμφωνέω κτλ.," *TDNT* 9 (1974) 309.

13   Eduard Hiller, ed., *Theonis Smyrnaei Expositio Rerum Mathematicarum* (Leipzig: Teubner, 1878) 12. Cf. Plato *Symp.* 187c.

as flourishing together "as a harmonious chorus" (ὥσπερ ἐμμελὴς χόρος).[14] And in an idealized description of Hebrew society, Philo also brings together the themes of harmony, concord, and union and attributes such concord to "the creed concerning the one God" (*Virt.* 35; cf. *Mut. nom.* 200; *Migr. Abr.* 220; *Heres* 242; *Fuga* 112). It is significant that Ignatius shares so many of these themes. Note also that "concord" had a long independent history as a political term (as the orations especially of Dio Chrysostom and Aelius Aristides show) and that elsewhere Ignatius seems to echo this more purely political tradition (see on *Eph.* 13.1). A link is provided by the fact that this tradition also occasionally exploited musical imagery (cf. Dio Chrysostom *Or.* 39.4; Aelius Aristides *Or.* 24.55 [ed. Keil]).

It is likely that the reference in this context to the Ephesians as "members" (μέλη) of God's Son is to be explained as a play on words: they are also his "melodies" (μέλη).[15] Ignatius makes little use of the body imagery; and even though he may know a form of it that has moved in a Gnostic direction (see on *Tr.* 11.2; *Sm.* 1.2), the (apparent) play on words here suggests that it does not weigh heavily on him. It is possible that at least here Ignatius is closer to the body imagery that appears in Greek moral and political thought. Note that Plutarch (*De frat. amor.* 2, 478f) links the series of themes noted above with that of the body and (by implication) of the limbs. Chorus and limbs also appear together (clumsily conjoined) as images of the state in Hierocles.[16] And an analogy involving the "harmonious" relation of hands and feet to the soul is already used of the joint commitment to death of the Maccabean martyrs (*4 Macc.* 14.6).

The purpose of congregational unity is said by Ignatius to be that of continued participation also in God (ἵνα καὶ θεοῦ πάντοτε μετέχετε "that you may always participate also in God"). The possible mystical significance of the theme should not be exaggerated. It appears in pagan writers where it has in view primarily human kinship with the gods because of the possession of reason or more vaguely the participation of all things in God.[17] In Irenaeus the theme is further scaled down: being in God and participating in his brightness are compared to being in the light and participating in its brightness; and in this connection participation in God is defined as "knowing God and enjoying his goodness" (*Adv. haer.* 4.20.5). We have seen that even Iamblichus was prepared to think of participation in the divine as a relatively low level of intimacy between God and humanity (see on *Eph.* inscr). In favor of a minimalist interpretation of the theme in Ignatius is the fact that he addresses a group and correlates participation in God with the unity of the group. Such correlations must not be read too literally (see on *Eph.* 14.1).

---

14 Betz, *Plutarch's Ethical Writings*, 239.

15 Compare Plato's play on the word νόμος as both "law" and "melody" (*Leg.* 4, 722de).

16 Karl Praechter, *Hierokles der Stoiker* (Leipzig: Dieterich, 1901) 34–36.

17 Hermann Hanse, "μετέχω κτλ.," *TDNT* 2 (1964) 830–31.

Unity with the Bishop [2.1–6.1]

5

Unity in Worship Under the Bishop

1   For if I in a short time had such fellowship with your bishop, as was not human but spiritual, how much more do I count you blessed who are mingled together with him, as the church is with Jesus Christ and as Jesus Christ is with the Father, so that everything may be harmonious in unity! 2/ Let no one deceive himself: if anyone is not within the altar, he lacks the bread of God; for if the prayer of one or two has such power, how much more that of the bishop and the whole church! 3/ He, then, who does not come to the assembly, by that very fact displays arrogance and has judged himself. For it is written, "God resists the arrogant." Let us be eager, then, not to resist the bishop that we may be obedient to God.

6

1/ And the more anyone sees a bishop keep silence, the more he should fear him. For everyone whom the householder sends into his stewardship, him must we receive as the one who sent him. Clearly, then, one must regard the bishop as the Lord himself.

The theme of unity leads over to a more explicit affirmation of the need to be joined with the bishop and to worship together under him. The point is first made quietly with an *a minore* argument (5.1.)[1] Then with the words "let no one be deceived" (5.2) the mood grows more solemn. Such formulae occur elsewhere in Ignatius (*Eph.* 16.1; *Mag.* 8.1; *Phd.* 3.3; *Sm.* 6.1) as well as in the NT (1 Cor 6:9; 15:33; Gal 6:7; Jas 1:16). Ignatius is prompted to use it in part by Paul (in *Phd.* 3.3 it echoes 1 Cor 6:9–10), but it also has a wider background in the diatribe (Epictetus *Diss.* 2.20.7; 2.22.15; 4.6.23). There is no indication here that Ignatius has false teachers in mind. When he deals with them, his language is harsher.[2] Apparently there were Ephesians who simply exercised a measure of independent judgment (and

perhaps wondered about the wisdom of supporting Burrhus). Ignatius seems content to regard such behavior as merely conducive to false teaching (cf. 6.2). In 5.1 Ignatius hints that the Ephesians must learn to look beyond appearances. Such is the implication of the distinction between "human" and "spiritual" fellowship (cf. *Eph.* 1.3; and for the terminology, *Phd.* 7.2; 1 Cor 2:13). Apparently Ignatius here anticipates the problem of the bishop's silence (6.1). The independent ways of the Ephesians are construed by Ignatius as arrogance which he (like others in his day) meets with one of his rare[3] quotations from the OT (5.3).[4] The verse was probably drawn from an arsenal of passages used to bolster authority in the church.

■ **5.1** Ignatius continues to envelop his call for obedience

---

1   For the theological significance of the comparisons in 5.1 see on *Eph.* 3.2. The special characteristic of our passage is that not only does Ignatius compare sets of paired terms but he also organizes the second side of the comparison as a double set of hierarchically related pairs (the oneness of bishop and people is compared with that of the church and Jesus Christ and of Jesus Christ and the Father). Note that the comparison cuts across others in Ignatius in unpredictable ways. (For the conception of the relation between Christ and the universal church see on *Pol.* 5.1.)

2   Zahn, *Ignatius*, 344.

3   Ignatius introduces one other passage (also from Proverbs) by the formula "as it is written" (*Mag.* 12). For other quotations or allusions see *Eph.* 15.1; *Mag.* 13.1; *Tr.* 8.2; *Sm.* 1.2.

4   Prov 3:34. The passage is also quoted in 1 Pet 5:5; Jas 4:6; *1 Clem.* 30.2; Clement Alex. *Strom.* 3.6, 49.2; 4.17, 106.4. All these sources agree with Ignatius in reading "God" rather than (as does the LXX) "Lord" (the order of words in Ignatius is also found in Clement Alex. *Strom.* 3.6, 49.2).

in the language of musical metaphor: everything is to be "harmonious in unity." The term "mingled together" (ἐνκεκραμένους; cf. *Sm.* 3.2) probably reflects the same background: Plato (*Leg.* 8, 835b) speaks of harmony "mingled" with rhythms; Ps-Aristotle (*De mundo* 6, 399a17) likens the universe to a "chorus of men mingling (κεραννύντων) one melodious harmony"; and Athanasius (*Gent.* 38) refers metaphorically to God as putting the world together by "mingling" musical sound harmoniously (in a context that also refers to ὁμονοία and uses the images of the city, the "harmony of the limbs" of the body, and the lyre).[5] Perhaps Ignatius is suggesting that Christ's "melodies"—the Ephesian Christians (4.2)—are joined together with their bishop in one harmonious strain. There is also a possibility that the "altar" referred to in 5.2 has a connection with the musical imagery: the chorus that was apparently Ignatius' model in 4.1 sometimes sang to the accompaniment of a cithara around an altar of the gods (Callimachus *In Delum* 312; cf. Apollonius Rhod. *Argonaut.* 1.538). At the same time, it must be recognized that Ignatius uses the biblical rather than the pagan word for altar (θυσιαστήριον).[6]

■ **5.2** In any event, it is unlikely that Ignatius has a physical altar in mind (5.2). A few early Christian writers explicitly deny that there were such altars in the church (Minucius Felix *Oct.* 32.1; Origen *Cels.* 8.17); and the earliest term used in connection with the eucharist seems to have been τράπεζα "table."[7] Moreover, the Ephesians could scarcely be said to be "within" a physical altar in any intelligible sense; and the term is used symbolically by Polycarp (*Phil.* 4.3) and elsewhere in Ignatius (*Mag.* 7.2; *Tr.* 7.2; probably also *Phd.* 4).[8] From the latter passages it appears that the altar is the church, but it is also closely linked with Christ, the ministry, and unified worship. The appropriateness of the term was probably

suggested by the idea that prayer is true sacrifice.[9] The eucharist and the eucharistic prayer were naturally also linked with sacrifice in this way (cf. *Did.* 14.1), and Ignatius must reflect that connection here. It is likely, then, that the "bread of God"—a eucharistic expression from a Johannine milieu (cf. John 6:33)—is seen by Ignatius as the point of intersection between the prayers of the faithful and the presence of God or Christ. Against this background it is probable that here he is working primarily with the symbolic aspects of his eucharistic theology (see Introduction, 5.3). Note that the expression "bread of God" occurs once again in Ignatius (*Rom.* 7.3) and that there sacramental realism is scarcely in evidence.

In any event, the emphasis in *Eph.* 5.2 is on the power of corporate prayer. Such prayers are themselves expressions of unity in Christian communities (*Mag.* 7.1; *Tr.* 12.2; *Sm.* 7.1; cf. *Pol.* 1.3), but Ignatius sees them more often as serving a still larger purpose in assuring the success of his martyrdom and the peace of his church in Antioch (some thirteen passages),[10] the conversion of pagans (*Eph.* 10.1–2) or of false teachers (*Sm.* 4.1), and the writing of a theological tract (*Eph.* 20.1). A great cosmic conflict is presupposed in which Satan's powers are destroyed by the prayers of the worshippers (*Eph.* 13; cf. Origen, *Cels.* 8.73). Thus the theme of prayer in Ignatius again illustrates the high significance he attributes to his own martyrdom in bringing to expression the underlying unity of all the churches.

■ **5.3** Ignatius then appeals to a tradition (reflected in Matt 18:19–20) to underscore the power of corporate prayer.[11] Another *a minore* argument helps him bridge the gap between the tradition and his own more dramatic vision of the church's life of prayer. Although Ignatius must mean the local church of Ephesus when he

---

5   Consequently Schlier's (*Untersuchungen*, 100) Gnostic parallels to the theme of mingling (Clement Alex. *Exc. ex Theod.* 32.3; 36.2) need not be given the exclusive weight he gives them.

6   Bartelink, *Lexicologisch-semantische studie*, 14–16. Bartelink notes that Christian writers occasionally used the biblical term for pagan altars (e.g. Ps-Ignatius *Mar. ad Ign.* 4).

7   Cf. *LPGL s.v.* θυσιαστήριον, p. 660; *s.v.* τράπεζα A.4, p. 1399.

8   Cf. Heb 13:10.

9   Tertullian *Orat.* 28; cf. Johannes Behm, "θύω," *TDNT*

3 (1965) 189–90.

10   *Eph.* 1.2; 11.2; 21.2; *Mag.* 14; *Tr.* 12.3; 13.1; *Rom.* 9.1; *Phd.* 5.1; 8.2; 10.1; *Sm.* 11.1, 3; *Pol.* 7.1.

11   Matthew speaks of the power of the prayer of two who agree and of the presence of Christ among two or three who gather in his name. Ignatius mentions the power of the prayer of one or two. Similar themes are found in later Jewish and Christian sources. In this tradition the value of the piety of even one person is sometimes stressed. Thus 'Abot 3.7 teaches that the Shekinah is present when ten, five, three, two, or even one study Torah. And *Gos. Thom.*

speaks of the prayers of "the bishop and the whole church," the universal church provides the model for the local community and is not far from his mind (see 5.1). It seems evident that Ignatius' vision of the universal church is at least partly inspired by the role that he asks the local communities jointly to play in supporting him as he travels to Rome.

Ignatius concludes the section with a summary appeal to obey the bishop. It is cast in the form of a scriptural maxim (see n. 4 above) adorned by paronomasia (ἀντιτάσσεσθαι, ὑποτασσόμενοι), chiasmus (non-resistance to the bishop, to God obedience), and antithesis. The chain of reasoning in 5.3 is this: not coming together (under the bishop) is arrogance; God resists arrogance; therefore obey the bishop (come together) that we may be found obedient to God.[12] The call to obey the bishop is here another way of expressing the call to unity, and there is no real equation of God and the bishop (see on *Mag.* 3.1).

■ **6.1** To this is appended a statement about the bishop's silence that moves out of the sphere of the choral imagery[13] and perhaps also beyond the realm of worship. In any event, the bishop's silence was a matter of some embarrassment and seems to have represented a retiring nature (Lightfoot) or ineloquence (Bauer). Possibly he was not up to the demands of praying and preaching extemporaneously (cf. *Did.* 10.7; Justin *Apol.* 1.65.3; 1.67.4–5).[14] To judge from the parallels in *Eph.* 15 and *Phd.* 1, however, he seems to have lacked the ability in debate to turn back false teaching. Ignatius makes a virtue of this weakness. He fuses diverse elements from the tradition of Jesus' words[15] to show that silence (including, we may assume, the avoidance of dangerous debate with false teachers; cf. *Sm.* 7.2) is the mark of Christ's servant. Deeds, not words, are required of the bishop (see on *Eph.* 15; *Phd.* 1). And speech is not to be taken up lightly. It is apostles who give commands (cf. *Eph.* 3.1–2; *Tr.* 3.3; *Rom.* 4.3), and it is God who speaks loudly through the likes of Ignatius (*Phd.* 7.1). The unexpressed part of the argument is this: the bishop is to be respected all the more when he shows himself willing to remain silent and to point to the authority of the one who sent him.[16] We may conjecture that those who stayed away from worship found little in their inarticulate bishop to interest them.

The unexpressed part of the argument has been filled

---

30 says that Jesus is present where there are "two or one" (the Greek form of the saying in *P.Oxy.* 1. 1,5 mentions "one alone"). For further examples see Jacques-E. Menard, *L'évangile selon Thomas* (NHS 5; Leiden: Brill, 1975) 124–26. It is evident that the reference to "one or two" in Ignatius reflects a tradition independent of Matthew.

12 "Has judged himself" (ἑαυτὸν διέκρινεν) in 5.3 may mean "has separated himself." The latter reflects the more frequent sense of the verb, but it does not seem to advance the thought as required (he remains aloof, he brings on himself God's opposition, he has judged himself).

13 The hymn of Christ in the semi-Gnostic *Act. Ioann.* 96 calls for obedience to Christ's "dance" and silence concerning his mysteries. Very similar is the description in Athenaeus (*Deipn.* 1, 20d) of a certain Agrippa who is said to have been able to expound Pythagorean doctrine by dancing "in silence" and to do it more clearly than those using words. Here, then, choral imagery and silence are linked. But that is unlikely in Ignatius where the emphasis is on the song rather than the dance of the chorus.

14 Peter Meinhold, "Schweigende Bischöfe: Die Gegensätze in den kleinasiatischen Gemeinden nach den Ignatianen," in Erwin Iserloh and Peter Manns, eds., *Festgabe Joseph Lortz*, vol. 2: *Glaube und Geschichte*

(Baden-Baden: Grimm, 1958) 468–72; Christine Trevett, "Prophecy and Anti-Episcopal Activity: a Third Error Combatted by Ignatius?" *JEH* 34 (1983) 1–18.

15 There are two elements here: (a) the "householder" who sends his servants to his vineyard (Matt 21:33–41; cf. *Gos. Thom.* 65–66; *Herm. Sim.* 5.2); (b) "receiving" Christ's representative as Christ himself (cf. Matt 10:40; Gal 4:14) and accepting the one whom he "sends" (cf. John 13:20). Since the term "householder" (οἰκοδεσπότης) occurs only here in Ignatius and the term "stewardship" (οἰκονομία) only in a different sense elsewhere in the letters (*Eph.* 18.2; 20.1), it is likely that they come from his source; and since the term "stewardship" does not reflect the NT form of the parable, presumably Ignatius is drawing from independent tradition (cf. Koester, *Synoptische Überlieferung*, 39–42). The second element also probably goes back to an oral form of a saying subject to considerable variation in the tradition (see Kurt Aland, *Synopsis Quattuor Evangeliorum* [Stuttgart: Württembergische Bibelanstalt, 1964] 149, 433). It was the theme of "sending" that served to link the two elements in Ignatius' mind.

16 Luigi Franco Pizzolato, "Silenzio di vescovo e parola degli eretici in Ignazio d'Antiochia," *Aevum* 44

out in an entirely different way by others: God is silence (*Eph.* 19.1; *Mag.* 8.2); the bishop corresponds to God (*Eph.* 5.3; *Mag.* 6.1; *Tr.* 3.1; *Sm.* 8.1–2); therefore, the bishop's silence is a reflection of the divine silence—a silence for which Gnostic parallels may be found.[17] The correctness of this view depends on the exegesis of all the passages involved. It seems to us that *Eph.* 5.3–6.1 does not support it.

Ignatius' concluding remarks that the bishop is to be received as the one who sent him or looked upon as the Lord (probably Christ) should also not be read as supporting a view of authority more mystical in character. The words about receiving the one sent as the sender are traditional (see n. 15 above) and presumably reflect a traditional view of authority.[18] The *Didache* presents a sharpened form of the theme in urging Christians to honor or "receive" the travelling teacher or apostle "as the Lord" (*Did.* 4.1; 11.2, 4) but does not change its meaning. Ignatius applies all this to a stable figure who must constantly be "regarded" as the Lord, but the factor of stability alone does not necessarily imply a new form of legitimation (see on *Mag.* 3.1).

(1970) 205–18.

17 Henry Chadwick, "The Silence of the Bishops in Ignatius," *HTR* 43 (1950) 169–72.

18 Cf. Walter Grundmann, "δέχομαι," *TDNT* 2 (1964) 53–54.

The Ephesians and Outsiders [6.2–10.3]	**6**	Transition to the Problem of False Teachers

2   **Now indeed Onesimus himself praises highly your godly orderliness—that you all live according to the truth, and that no faction dwells among you; but you do not even listen to anyone except him who speaks truly concerning Jesus Christ.**

■ **6.2** The tandem particle μὲν οὖν ("now indeed"), followed in the next clause by δέ or ἀλλά ("but"), marks a passage that concludes one line of argument and goes on to set forth a contrasting point.[1] Such was Ignatius' intent here, but he was distracted from his purpose to some extent. He had apparently intended to say, "Now indeed there is no faction among you, but there are dangers (which increase when you do not listen to your bishop)." The explanation provided in 7.1 shows that he had in fact shifted attention to the problem of opponents who threaten the good order of the Ephesian church from without. But what he actually says is closer to this: "Now indeed there is no faction among you, but you do not even listen to anyone who speaks falsehood."[2] The intended contrast has become a clumsy reinforcement of the previous point. Ignatius seems anxious to avoid leaving the impression that the opposition has had any success at all. Evidently even to concede danger is dangerous. For Ignatius the basic danger is faction, but false teaching emerges here as a fundamental ingredient in faction.[3] (For the wider implications of this shift in emphasis see Introduction, 3.3.)

1   Kühner/Gerth, *Grammatik,* 2. 157–58; cf. Edwin Mayser, *Grammatik der griechischen Papyri aus der Ptolemäerzeit,* vol. 2: *Satzlehre* (3 vols.; Berlin and Leipzig: De Gruyter, 1926–34) 3. 152–53.

2   Our interpretation does not depend on the solution to the textual problem ("except him who speaks truly concerning Jesus Christ"). The reading of G, πλέον εἴπερ, is grammatically impossible. The Latin (*amplius quam,* πλέον ἤπερ, hence, "except Jesus Christ speaking in truth") makes tolerable sense but does not conform to language elsewhere in Ignatius where people are said to speak apart from or concerning Christ (*Tr.* 9.1; *Phd.* 6.1). Consequently we follow Lightfoot's emendation (πλέον ἢ περί): Ignatius is contrasting the false teachers with one who speaks about Jesus Christ. Support for the emendation comes from the Oriental versions: "and you do not listen to anyone *if he does not speak* truly with you *concerning* Jesus Christ" (A; cf. Petermann, *Epistolae,* 23); you do not accept anything "from anyone *except from him who teaches* you the teachings of our God Jesus Christ" (Arabic).

3   The word αἵρεσις points both back to the absence of strife ("faction") just discussed (cf. 4.1) and forward to the inability of false teaching ("heresy") to make inroads in Ephesus. Thus Ignatius' usage hovers on the borderline between that of Paul (1 Cor 11:19; Gal 5:20) and that of later writers (cf. 2 Pet 2:1). In *Tr.* 6.1 there is stronger emphasis on the false teaching that gives rise to "faction," and it seems fair to say that "from the time of Ignatius the sense of the term is defined and the first treatise on heresy will appear in the not too distant future"; see Marcel Simon, "From Greek Haeresis to Christian Heresy," in William R. Schoedel and Robert L. Wilken, eds., *Early Christian Literature and the Classical Intellectual Tradition* (Théologie historique 53; Paris: Beauchesne, 1979) 110; cf. Bartelink, *Lexicologisch-semantische studie,* 77–79; Adelbert Davids, "Irrtum und Häresie," *Kairos* 15 (1973) 175–76. For the view that Ignatius is still close to Paul in his use of the term see Martin Elze, "Häresie und Einheit der Kirche im 2. Jahrhundert," *ZThK* 71 (1974) 393–94.

The Ephesians and Outsiders [6.2–10.3]

7

The Infection of False Teaching and Its Cure

1   **For some are accustomed with evil deceit**
    to carry about the name, at the same
    time doing things unworthy of God,
    whom you must avoid as wild beasts; for
    they are rabid dogs, biting without
    warning, whom you must guard against
    since they are almost incurable.
      2/ There is one physician,
      both fleshly and spiritual
      begotten and unbegotten,
      come in flesh, God,
      in death, true life,
      both of Mary and of God,
      first passible and then impassible,
      Jesus Christ, our Lord.

■ **7.1** Ignatius issues a general warning about the false teachers in *Eph.* 7–8 before becoming more specific in *Eph.* 9. They are said to "carry about the name" (of Christ; cf. *Eph.* 1.2)—that is, they move from place to place looking for converts to their version of Christianity. The verb "carry about" is used elsewhere by Ignatius in connection with travel (cf. *Eph.* 11.2; *Mag.* 1.2; *Tr.* 12.2), and in *Eph.* 9.1 he explicitly refers to the journeys of these teachers. Polycarp speaks of those who carry about the name "in hypocrisy" (*Phil.* 6.3); and it is precisely hypocrisy that Ignatius has in mind when he refers to these teachers as dogs who "bite without warning" (λαθροδῆκται for the classical λαίθαργοι).[1] For "a dog biting without warning" was a widespread proverb that referred to a fawning behavior masking an intent to do harm.[2] The description suggests that they were reasonably attractive teachers. Their movement from place to place reminds us of the "apostles" and "prophets" of *Didache* 11–13, and it may be that they simply posed

problems for established local leaders. But doctrinal issues—specifically docetism—may also have been involved. For these same teachers seem to have come to Smyrna (see on *Eph.* 9.1), and Ignatius elsewhere warns the Smyrnaeans not to "receive" the "wild beasts" that teach docetism in that city (*Sm.* 4.1). Yet he makes surprisingly little of the doctrinal problem in the passage before us, and it may be that he is making connections without knowing certainly who or what was involved. In any event, Ignatius is at least as much concerned about the evil effects of their methods as about their "evil teaching" itself (*Eph.* 9.1; 16.1–2).

Ignatius reinforces the proverb by linking it with the metaphor of "rabid dogs" (cf. Josephus *Bell.* 6.196; *Odes Sol.* 28.13).[3] The false teachers are deeply infected, and little hope can be held out for them. Rabies was indeed hard to cure.[4]

In all likelihood the turn to medical imagery reflects a polemical stance traditional in Graeco-Roman society.

---

1   LSJ *s.v.* κύων, p. 1015. Ignatius also calls them "wild beasts" (cf. *Sm.* 4.1). This is a common metaphor (BAG *s.v.* θηρίον 2, p. 361) and is used of false teachers in Tit 1:12 (quoting Epimenides). Note also the reference to "wolves" in *Phd.* 2.2 (for false prophets as "wolves" see Matt 7:15). *Mart. Andr. pr.* 10 links both terms when it speaks of officials hostile to the Christians as "wild beasts and not men, like wolves." Gnostics were later to refer to the orthodox and their leaders as "dumb animals" and "wild beasts" (*Treat. Seth* 59,29; *Interp. Know.* 12,38; 13,33).

2   See Augustus Nauck, *Tragicorum Graecorum Frag-*

menta (Hildesheim: Olms, 1964) 318 (frg. 800 of Sophocles). The proverb is also listed by Zenobius (*Cent.* 4.90; *Paroem. Gr.* 1. 109).

3   The Syriac of the Ode (*klb' pqr'*) represents the exact equivalent of the Greek involved; cf. R. Payne Smith, *Thesaurus Syriacus* (2 vols.; Oxford: Clarendon, 1879–1901) 2. 3224.

4   Pliny *Nat. hist.* 25.6.17; 28.43.156; Galen *Sect.* 8 (Georg Helmreich, *Claudii Galeni Pergameni Scripta Minora*, vol. 3: ΠΕΡΙ ΑΙΡΕΣΕΩΝ ΤΟΙΣ ΕΙΣΑΓΟ-ΜΕΝΟΙΣ [Leipzig: Teubner, 1893] 18–22).

Conservative moralists represented themselves as the true healers of the soul in opposition to the flamboyance of wandering Cynic teachers. The latter were regarded as impudent, immoral, and greedy manipulators of people. Conservative churchmen (like the writer of the Pastoral Epistles) adopted the same attitude toward interlopers and enriched their polemics with similar imagery.[5] Ignatius' attack on the wandering teachers at Ephesus echoes the same tradition. Yet his discussion of them and his use of imagery seem original in many ways.

■ **7.2** First there is his appeal to Christ as the "physician." This is in the form of an acclamation ("there is one physician") modelled on a more familiar one, "there is one God" or "God is one" (cf. *Eph.* 15.1). The latter is not to be interpreted against the background of the late magical uses of it discussed by Peterson.[6] In the early period it overlaps with confession[7] and sometimes functions polemically as an antithesis to pagan acclamations (cf. 1 Cor 8:5–6).[8] Ott thought that here Ignatius was presenting Jesus in opposition to the pagan healing gods.[9] That may lie in the background. The immediate context, however, indicates that Ignatius opposes Christ's healing power to the efforts of the Ephesians to reply to the wandering teachers.[10] Or more precisely perhaps, he is showing again why Onesimus is correct in remaining silent before his opponents. There are some things too difficult and dangerous for human beings. Here Ignatius is elaborating an older theme. For Philo had already complained that people first try all the medical solutions before looking to God, "the only physician ($\tau \grave{o} \nu$ $\mu \acute{o} \nu o \nu$ $\grave{i} \alpha \tau \rho \acute{o} \nu$) of the soul's infirmities" (*Sacr.* 70).[11] Ignatius may

also have had a more specific model in mind. The physician Damocrates, in a poem setting forth a panacea for all kinds of bites (including those of animals "even though they may have given rabies"), hails it as the "one and only" ($\mu \acute{i} \alpha$ $\mu \acute{o} \nu \eta$ $\tau \epsilon$) salve that contains a particularly potent herb (Galen *Compos. medic.* 5.10).[12] Nicander (*Theriaca* 934) had also ended his famous poem on snake bites with a recipe for a panacea. An even more precise identification of the medicine involved may be possible (see on *Eph.* 20.2). Christ, then, is the panacea for the church's problems. But it is Christ as understood by Ignatius, and to question this understanding is (as Ignatius sees it) tantamount to calling into question Christ himself.

The first component of the striking list of antitheses that follows may ultimately be rooted in a semi-credal pattern that contrasted what Jesus was "according to the flesh" with what he became "according to the spirit" (Rom 1:3–4; cf. *Sm.* 1.1). In Ignatius, however, flesh and spirit represent two spheres or two dimensions that refer to human and divine reality respectively. We have here the kernel of the later two-nature christologies. To speak of this (with Loofs) as a "Geistchristologie" (Spirit christology) is to limit unduly Ignatius' use of the term "spiritual" and to misunderstand the function of the antithesis.[13] Thus if Ignatius reflects a semi-credal element here, he has completely transformed it in light of the familiar contrast between flesh and spirit known to us primarily from Paul (see on *Eph.* 8.2). The fifth antithesis about Christ's origin "both from Mary and from God" seems more clearly to reflect a semi-credal

5 Abraham J. Malherbe, "Medical Imagery in the Pastoral Epistles," in W. Eugene March, ed., *Texts and Testaments: Critical Essays on the Bible and Early Church Fathers* (San Antonio: Trinity, 1980) 19–35.

6 Erik Peterson, ΕΙΣ ΘΕΟΣ: *Epigraphische, formgeschichtliche und religionsgeschichtliche Untersuchungen* (FRLANT 24; Göttingen: Vandenhoeck & Ruprecht, 1926).

7 Reinhard Deichgräber, *Gotteshymnus und Christushymnus in der frühen Christenheit* (SUNT 5; Göttingen: Vandenhoeck & Ruprecht, 1967) 115–17.

8 Hans Lietzmann, "Symbolstudien," in idem, *Kleine Schriften III* (TU 74; Berlin: Akademie-Verlag, 1962) 235–37.

9 Jos. Ott, "Die Bezeichnung Christi als ἰατρός in der urchristlichen Literatur," *Der Katholik* 5 (1910) 454–58. For a fuller collection of references to Christ as

physician in the early church see Gervaise Dumeige, "Le Christ médecin dans la littérature chrétienne des premiers siècles," *Rivista di archeologia cristiana* 48 (1972) 115–41.

10 Zahn, *Ignatius*, 384.

11 In the same context (*Sacr.* 71) God is also referred to as "the only savior" ($\tau \grave{o} \nu$ $\mu \acute{o} \nu o \nu$ $\sigma \omega \tau \hat{\eta} \rho \alpha$). A contrast with pagan healing gods may be implied.

12 Kühn, *CGO* 13.821.

13 José Pablo Martin, "La pneumatologia en Ignacio de Antioquia," *Salesianum* 33 (1971) 379–454.

element (cf. *Eph.* 18.2; *Tr.* 9.1; *Sm.* 1.1), but it too is adapted to Ignatius' purpose. There is nothing else in the passage remotely credal in character.

It has been suggested that the passage is a hymn.[14] It has a rich poetic flavor. And similar strings of christological antitheses are found elsewhere.[15] There is also some formal and substantive similarity to the "hymnic" fragment in 1 Tim 3:16. But there is not enough in these parallels to suggest a coherent liturgical tradition.

It is Melito's *Paschal Homily* that gives us the clue to the form of our passage. For nothing is more characteristic of the homily than strings of parallel expressions heaped up for rhetorical effect. It has been shown that the homily reflects the same rhetorical impulses at work in Ignatius.[16] It seems more likely, then, that our passage is a rhetorical expansion of semi-credal paradoxes rather than a hymn.[17]

Concerning the second antithesis, "begotten and unbegotten" (γεννητὸς καὶ ἀγέννητος),[18] it should be noted that orthodox christology and theology later confined the adjective "begotten" to the Son and the adjective "unbegotten" to the Father. But there it is a question of the internal relations of the godhead. Ignatius thinks only of the incarnation and is restating the spirit/flesh antithesis in these terms.[19] Equally uncomplicated by later debates is the last antithesis, "passible and impassible." Similar language is found

elsewhere in the early fathers.[20] As to the third antithesis, the reading "come in flesh, God" (cf. John 1:14) is to be preferred to the reading from Patristic quotations "in man, God." The change can be ascribed to the desire of later theologians to avoid any suggestion of an Arian or Apollinarian christology which denied a human soul to Christ (hence "man" instead of merely "flesh" was required).[21]

Much of the terminology in this passage has a philosophical background. Thus ἀγέννητος "unbegotten" was regarded as an epithet peculiarly appropriate to God.[22] For background to other terms that appear here see on *Pol.* 3.2. These passages suggest that a deliberate emphasis on incarnation presupposes a theology that sets a gulf between God and humanity in terms drawn from the Graeco-Roman philosophical tradition.

The series of antitheses in *Eph.* 7.2 appears to move from the historical to the exalted Christ. This is emphasized in the last antithesis by the words "first" and "then." But the parallel series in *Pol.* 3.2 reverses the order, and it cannot be doubted that Ignatius is referring in both instances to the two-fold nature of "Jesus Christ our Lord." It is likely that he emphasized the historical side of Christ's being here in opposition to what he regarded as the heart of the false teaching of the opponents— namely, docetism. Note that the expression "from Mary" in Ignatius likewise emphasizes the true humanity of

---

14   Deichgräber, *Gotteshymnus*, 155–57; Gottfried Schille, *Frühchristliche Hymnen* (Berlin: Evangelische Verlagsanstalt, 1965) 39.

15   Melito frgs. 13 and 14; and especially Tertullian *Carn. Christ.* 5.7: *hinc natum, inde non natum; hinc carneum, inde spiritualem; hinc infirmum, inde praefortem; hinc morientem, inde viventem* ("in one respect born, in the other unborn; in one respect fleshly, in the other spiritual; in one respect weak, in the other powerful; in one respect dying, in the other living"). This may be an echo of Ignatius. But the similarity is probably explained by the fact that both writers were seeking to emphasize the true human reality of the divine Christ in opposition to docetism and both were familiar with the same rhetorical methods.

16   A. Wifstrand, "The Homily of Melito on the Passion," *VC* 2 (1948) 201–23; Othmar Perler, "Das vierte Makkabäerbuch," 47–72. The list of antitheses near the beginning of the *Paschal Homily* (2) describing the mystery of the passover—"new and old, eternal and recent, corruptible and incorrupt-

ible, mortal and immortal" —shows that the absence of the μέν-δέ construction in *Eph.* 7.2 is no indication of Semitic inspiration.

17   Cf. Hans von Campenhausen, "Das Bekenntnis im Urchristentum," *ZNW* 63 (1972) 248 n. 208.

18   This is the consistent witness of the manuscripts. For the confusion elsewhere between γενητός/γεννητός and ἀγένητος/ἀγέννητος see Lightfoot, *Ignatius,* 2. 90–94. Theodoret's variant, "begotten from the unbegotten," reflects post-Nicene perspectives.

19   For other uses of "unbegotten" of the Son in pre-Nicene sources see *LPGL, s.v.* ἀγέννητος C.3.a, p. 15. See now also *Teach. Silv.* 101,35–36 ("and even if [he is begotten], he is unbegotten").

20   Melito frg. 13; Irenaeus *Adv. haer.* 3.16.6; cf. *LPGL, s.v.* πάσχω A.3, p. 1049.

21   Othmar Perler, "Die Briefe des Ignatius von Antiochien," *Freiburger Zeitschrift für Philosophie und Theologie* 18 (1971) 381–96.

22   Plutarch *Sept. sap. conv.* 9, 153c; cf. David E. Aune, in Betz, *Plutarch's Ethical Writings,* 97.

Jesus and not the supernatural birth (cf. *Eph.* 18.2; 19.1).

Our passage also shows that Ignatius interprets redemption primarily in terms of victory over death. The emphasis is on the incarnation as the point at which divine power is brought to bear on human existence, and the passion is important largely because it is the necessary prelude to deathlessness. There is little about sin and forgiveness in Ignatius (cf. *Sm.* 7.1).

The Ephesians and Outsiders [6.1–10.3]

8

Remain What You Are

1   So let no one deceive you, as indeed you
are not deceived, being entirely of God;
for when no strife has become fixed
among you that can torment you, then
you live in a godly way. I am your lowly
offering and I dedicate myself to you,
church of the Ephesians, famous to the
ages. 2/ Fleshly people cannot do
spiritual things, nor yet spiritual people
fleshly things; just as faith cannot do the
things of faithlessness, nor yet faithlessness the things of faith. But what you
do even according to the flesh, that is
spiritual; for you do all things in Jesus
Christ.

Ignatius continues his exhortation to the Ephesians with a warning ("let no one deceive you") that echoes Pauline formulae (2 Thess 2:3; Eph 5:6) but that also has a wider background in the diatribe (see on *Eph.* 5.2). As so frequently, he immediately qualifies the imperative with an indicative: they are not in fact deceived (see on *Eph.* 4.1). This qualification dominates the whole section: they are "entirely of God,"[1] they live "in a godly way" (literally, "according to God"), and all that they do is spiritual.

■ **8.1** It is not immediately clear how the statement about Ignatius as περίψημα ὑμῶν "your lowly offering" functions in this context. It must somehow serve to affirm the established merits of a church "famous to the ages."[2] We may begin by observing that the statement belongs in

form and vocabulary together with several others in the letters: "I am your lowly offering (περίψημα ὑμῶν) and I dedicate myself to you (ἁγνίζομαι ὑμῶν)" *Eph.* 8.1;[3] "my spirit is a lowly offering (περίψημα) of the cross" *Eph.* 18.1; "I am your expiation (ἀντίψυχον ὑμῶν)" *Eph.* 21.1; "my spirit consecrates itself to you (ἁγνίζεται ὑμῶν)" *Tr.* 13.3; "my spirit and my bonds are your expiation" *Sm.* 10.2; "I and my bonds are your expiation" *Pol.* 2.3; "I am the expiation of those who . . ." *Pol.* 6.1. The word περίψημα occurs in three meanings: (a) "offscouring," (b) "scapegoat" (a Greek custom is attested of sacrificing a social outcast to purify the community), (c) "your humble servant" (a term of polite self-effacement).[4] The verb ἁγνίζω ("purify," "hallow") is a cultic term in biblical and pagan Greek.[5] Hesychius in his lexicon connects

---

1   "Being (entirely) of God" is one possible way of referring to the indwelling of God in human beings (see on *Eph.* inscr). But it is used here and elsewhere in Ignatius merely to express firm adherence and loyalty (cf. *Mag.* 10.1; *Rom.* 7.1; *Phd.* 3.2).

2   Schlier (*Untersuchungen*, 28) takes the term "ages" (αἰῶνες) here in the sense of (Gnostic) "aeons." Elsewhere, however, Ignatius uses the word in a temporal sense (*Mag.* 6.1) or spatially (perhaps) with reference to the world (*Eph.* inscr; *Sm.* 1.2). Only *Eph.* 19.2 offers a possible exception. Elze (*Untersuchungen*, 20) has made the interesting point that Ignatius would surely have used the term in *Tr.* 5 and *Sm.* 6.1 had he worked regularly with its mythological meaning. The singular of the noun is always used of "the present age" by Ignatius (*Eph.* 17.1; 19.1; *Mag.* 1.2; *Tr.* 4.2; *Rom.* 6.1; 7.1; *Phd.* 6.2).

3   Ἁγνίζομαι ὑμῶν ("I dedicate myself to you") is difficult to construe. Yet in view of *Tr.* 13.3, where the same expression occurs, no emendation should be made. Voss's (see Introduction, n. 17) suggestion (περίψημα ὑμῶν ἐγὼ καὶ ἅγνισμα ὑμῶν) involves too many changes. The rhetorical balance would be disturbed by Zahn's addition of ὑπὲρ after ἁγνίζομαι and in any event is unlikely to have been dropped both here and in *Tr.* 13.3. I follow Lightfoot in thinking that ἁγνίζομαι expresses Ignatius' (sacrificial) devotion or dedication to the church and thus functions as a verb of longing and desiring (which governs the genitive).

4   BAG *s.v.* περίψημα, p. 659; Gustav Stählin, "περίψημα," *TDNT* 6 (1968) 84–93. Purely conventional is the use of the term in *Barn.* 4.9; 6.5.

5   BAG and LSJ *s.v.* ἁγνίζω.

περίψημα with ἀντίψυχα and other sacrificial terms.[6] A possible background for the term ἀντίψυχον in Ignatius is *4 Maccabees* (6.29; 17.21) where it refers to the death of the Maccabean martyrs as vicarious expiation.[7] And Ignatius elsewhere uses sacrificial imagery of himself (*Rom.* 2.2; 4.2).

Sacrificial imagery is thus involved, but it is not clear that Ignatius thinks of his death as vicarious. It seems more accurate to say that he sacrifices himself "for God" to attain discipleship (cf. *Rom.* 2.2; 4.1–2). Particularly noteworthy is the formulaic character of these statements and the lack of any context to support a fuller sacrificial idea. Indeed, according to *Tr.* 13.3 his spirit "is consecrated" to his addressees not only now but also when he attains God, and that seems hardly appropriate if he is thinking in terms of vicarious sacrifice. Similarly he can hardly be a vicarious sacrifice of the cross (*Eph.* 18.1). It is more likely, then, that Ignatius' use of περίψημα and related terms expresses somewhat more conventional sentiments of devotion or dedication to Christ and the church. At the same time, however, the language does not reflect merely polite self-effacement.

What remains of sacrificial overtones is the presumption of the low and despised character of the victim.[8] Ignatius is building on what is surely one of the most obvious features of the use of περίψημα ("offscouring" or stronger) in Paul (1 Cor 4:13). In Ignatius the image thus becomes part of his whole concern about his worthiness. In some of the passages listed above he emphasizes the fact that he was not in fact despised by those to whom he is writing (see especially *Sm.* 10.2; *Pol.* 2.3) and once he emphasizes the extent to which he is dependent on their prayers (*Tr.* 13.3; cf. 12.3). It appears that Ignatius expects other Christians to look beyond appearances and to confirm the hidden value of his sacrifice. For what lay behind Ignatius' sense of possible unworthiness and his expressions of inferiority to the churches see Introduction, 3.4. In the passage before us he briefly recalls this line of thought to make the Ephesians conscious of their greatness (cf. *Eph.* 12) and to remind them of his dependence on their continued loyalty and unity (cf. *Eph.* 11.2). They are to remain what they are.

■ **8.2** Ignatius' strongest affirmation of the greatness of the Ephesians is his statement that what they do "even according to the flesh, that is spiritual." This is all the more striking in that he begins the passage by stating the contrast between "fleshly" and "spiritual" people in a Pauline manner (cf. Rom 8:5; 1 Cor 2:14–15; Gal 5:16–26) that he otherwise avoids (see Introduction, 5.6).[9] An almost conscious correction of the Pauline antithesis lies before us (cf. *Sm.* 3.2; *Pol.* 2.2). The contrast between faith and unfaith (cf. *Mag.* 5.2) seems to be rhetorically formulated by analogy to the previous antithesis, but the thought is also Pauline (Rom 14:27). This antithesis does not lend itself to the same resolution as the one before it, but Ignatius takes no notice of the problem.

The declaration of the coinherence of the spheres of flesh and spirit at the anthropological level mirrors their coinherence at the christological level (*Eph.* 7.2; cf. *Sm.* 3). Thus one pole of Ignatius' christology—the emphasis on the reality of the incarnation—sanctions the godly use of the things of this world. Everything is pure to the pure (cf. Tit 1:15). Another pole of Ignatius' christology—the emphasis on the reality of the passion—lends reality to Ignatius' own suffering (*Tr.* 10; *Sm.* 4.2) and provides a model for Christian forbearance in a hostile world (*Eph.* 10.3). Such world affirmation and world denial are not contradictory. Both are rooted in Ignatius' emphasis on the inescapable obligations that faith and love—and the incarnation—entail (see Introduction, 3.5).

---

6 BAG *s.v.* περίψημα, p. 659.

7 Perler, "Das vierte Makkabäerbuch," 51–52.

8 Note that even more normal sacrificial language could be used to denigrate. Aeschines (*Ctes.* 164) tells how Demosthenes derided him as a sacrifice made ready for political annihilation (χρυσόκερων ἀποκαλῶν καὶ κατεστέφθαι φάσκων "referring to me as having gilded horns and saying that I had been garlanded").

9 Schlier (*Untersuchungen*, 131–35) finds in this contrast a reference to the Gnostic doctrine of the two races of men. But there seems to be no compelling reason to look beyond Paul for Ignatius' source. Cf. Corwin, *Ignatius,* 161; Rathke, *Ignatius,* 55.

The Ephesians and Outsiders [6.2–10.3]

9

Itinerant Teachers and the Response of the Ephesians

1 I know that some have passed by on their way from there with evil teaching, whom you did not allow to sow among you, stopping your ears that you might not receive what was sown by them, since you are stones of the Father's temple, made ready for the building of God the Father, carried up to the heights by the crane of Jesus Christ (which is the cross), using the Holy Spirit as a rope; and your faith is your upward guide, and love the way which leads up to God. 2/ So you are all companions on the way, God-bearers and temple-bearers, Christ-bearers, bearers of holy things, in every way adorned with the commandments of Jesus Christ—you in whom I am very glad, that I was counted worthy through what I write to converse with you and rejoice together, that in your new way of life you love nothing except God alone.

■ **9.1** The verb ἔγνων ("I know that")[1] occurs elsewhere in Ignatius in transitional materials (*Mag.* 11.1; *Tr.* 1.1–2; 8.1; *Phd.* 1.1). In most of these passages it is best to treat the verb as an epistolary aorist. In the passage before us it marks what White has called a "disclosure formula."[2] Variants of the same formula appear in *Mag.* 11 and *Tr.* 8.1 (where the verb ἔγνων is also found). Although none of the examples given by White has exactly the same form as those in Ignatius, they are sufficiently close for comparison. An example of ἔγνων used much as it is in *Eph.* 9.1 occurs in an edict of T. Julius Alexander (68 C.E.) where the main issue of the communication is introduced by the expression "For I know (ἔγνων γὰρ) above all that your request is most reasonable . . ." (Dit., *Or.* 2. 669,10).

Also of interest from a formal point of view is Ignatius' statement in 9.2 of his purpose in writing—namely, "to converse with" (προσομιλῆσαι) his addressees. The terminology reflects one of three major characterizations of the essence of a letter that are to be found in the theory and practice of Greek letter writing of the period (cf. *Sm.* 9.2).[3]

What Ignatius wants to disclose to the Ephesians (9.1) is that the same travelling teachers who visited Ephesus have come to Smyrna "from there"—that is, from Ephesus.[4] But he refrains from saying anything more about them than necessary. For he immediately returns to the subject of the firmness of the Ephesians in the face of these very teachers. In language that reflects an early catholic view of authority, Ignatius praises them for not even having listened to their visitors (cf. *Sm.* 4.1; 7.2).[5]

Four images become involved in the description: (1) seed sown; (2) stones of a temple, an image elaborated

---

1 The verb is followed by accusative + participle to indicate the content of what is known (as in *Mag.* 3.1 and in the inscription referred to below). Ignatius is not claiming to have got to know them personally.

2 White, *Form and Function*, 11–15.

3 Koskenniemi, *Studien*, 42–47.

4 This interpretation of ἐκεῖθεν ("from there") has been challenged (Lightfoot). But ἐκεῖ means "where you

are" in a letter imbedded in Revelation (2:14), and ἐκεῖθεν means "from where you are" in a letter of Libanius (*Ep.* 400.1).

5 Cf. Irenaeus *Adv. haer.* 3.4.2: *statim concludentes aures longo longius fugient* "they immediately close their ears and run far away"(Zahn, *Epistolae*, 14).

along trinitarian lines[6] in terms of (a) a building,[7] (b) a crane, and (c) the crane's rope; (3) a road or way up; and (4) a religious procession.

(1) To speak metaphorically of planting and sowing teachings was as natural to the Greeks as to others.[8] The negative use of the metaphor here is reminiscent of the parable of the seeds sown secretly (Matt 13:24–30), but Plutarch also knows of "sowing words and reaping them immediately with strife" (*De Pyth. orac.* 1, 394e). It is possible that the close link between planting and building in the Bible (Jer. 1:10; 24:6) and between planting, sowing, and building in Philo (*Leg. alleg.* 1.48–49) reflects a tradition that made it easy for Ignatius to pass as quickly as he does from the image of sowing to that of being stones.

(2) Ignatius' use of the image of the temple—whether in reference to the individual (*Eph.* 15.3; *Phd.* 7.2) or the church (*Eph.* 9.1; *Mag.* 7.2)—is in harmony with that of Paul (1 Cor 3:16–17; 6:19; 2 Cor 6:16). This image along with the tradition about Christ as the keystone naturally led to the more elaborate picture of a "building" made up of Christians as "living stones" (1 Pet 2:4–6).[9] But more may be involved. Our passage has been connected with the image of the building in Eph 2:20–22 (4:12) which many regard as influenced by Gnostic ideas.[10] Or Ignatius may be read in light of the allegory of the stones and the tower in *Hermas* (*Vis.* 3; *Sim.* 9) which clearly owes much to the apocalyptic vision of the heavenly city (cf. Heb 11:10; 12:22; 13:14; Rev 21:10—22:5).

Schlier connects *Eph.* 9.1 with Gnosticism by linking the Ignatian image of the crane (μηχανή) with the cosmic wheel (also called a μηχανή) of the Manichees (*Act. Arch.* 7–9) and a (related) description of the heavenly building in Mandeanism. This in turn is felt to illuminate the description of the cross as a "crane of salvation" (μηχάνημα σωτηρίας) in the semi-Gnostic *Mart. Andr. pr.* 14.[11] Totally neglected, however, were other parallels which suggest that the Gnostic imagery was but one branch of a rich development of symbolism about the cross in the early church. Particularly important are the following: Hippolytus *Antichr.* 59, which speaks of the church as a ship whose "ladder, leading upwards to the sailyard, is an image of the sign of Christ's passion leading the faithful to climb up to heaven" and whose "ropes, joined at the yard on the masthead, are like the orders of the prophets, martyrs, and apostles at rest in Christ's kingdom"; and Methodius *Porph.* 1.7–10[12] where the cross is defined as "God's descent" and "the foundation of ascent to true day" and as "a crane (μηχανή) through which those who are suitable for the building of the church are drawn up from below like a square stone"; it is further compared with military standards, the mast of a ship, the shape of birds in flight, and a human being with outstretched arms;[13] and the whole thing concludes with a musical metaphor to underscore the harmony of the reality brought into being by the cross. These allegories presuppose mythic patterns of thought that are hardly exclusively Gnostic, and it seems reasonable to read *Eph.* 9.1 in light of them.[14] Even if Gnosticism was Ignatius' immediate source, his allegorization of the material robs it of its

---

6 The passage shows how firmly trinitarian language was rooted in the Christianity known to Ignatius (cf. *Mag.* 13.1–2). But it does not outweigh the many indications that the spirit as the third member of the trinity plays only a minor role in Ignatius. In this connection it seems evident that the characteristic antithesis between flesh and spirit does not intersect significantly with the spirit of the trinitarian formula, and that the same may be said of other uses of the term spirit as a divine force (Martin, "Pneumatologia," 446–54).

7 The awkwardness of mentioning the "building of God the Father" just after having introduced the "temple of the Father" is merely the result of Ignatius' attempt to break down the metaphor of the temple into three parts associated with the trinity (building, crane, rope). Thus a sharp distinction

between the Jewish-Christian background to the image of the temple and a Gnostic conception of the heavenly building (Schlier, *Untersuchungen*, 120) seems forced.

8 Ps-Plato *Amat.* 134e; Isocrates *Phil.* 104; *Corp. Herm.* 1.29.

9 For the image of "living stones" in the classical world see J. C. Plumpe, "Vivum saxum, vivi lapides," *Traditio* 1 (1943) 1–14. Building metaphors for social and political entities are also not unknown in the classical world (e.g., Plato *Leg.* 10, 902e; Xenophon *Cyrop.* 8.7.15; Diodorus Sic. 11.68.7; 15.1.3). But they are not developed.

10 Cf. Otto Michel, "οἰκοδομή," *TDNT* 5 (1967) 144–47.

11 Cf. Schlier, *Untersuchungen*, 110–24.

12 *PG* 18. 400c.

13 Justin (*Apol.* 1.55) already knows several of these

Gnostic overtones[15] or at least significantly mutes them.[16]

It may even be fair to say that we find ourselves near the beginning of a development in which the image of the temple was being elaborated with reference to the actual business of building. Corwin notes the feverish building activity in earthquake-prone Antioch.[17] The "crane" known to Ignatius would have had the same two basic elements reflected so clearly in his allegory: (a) a framework (two wood uprights apart at the base, together at the top, and held at a convenient angle by retaining ropes) and (b) a rope (with pulleys and wheels) for lifting stones.[18] It is likely that the wood of the crane was enough to associate it with the "wood" of the cross (cf. Gal 3:13). It is obvious why the mast of the ship became so much more common in later developments of this kind of imagery.[19]

(3) The language of ascent prompts another image—that of a guide[20] and a way or road leading up to God. A connection with the preceding image may have been traditional; note that Methodius also links metaphors of travel—κάθοδος and ἄνοδος ("way down" and "way up")—with the image of the crane. But the picture may change

in part simply to accommodate the theological formula of faith and love. In any event, language of ascent is not exclusively Gnostic.[21] It is well to recall that even the sober Roman Clement spoke of "the height to which love leads up" (τὸ ὕψος εἰς ὃ ἀνάγει ἡ ἀγάπη, 1 Clem. 49.4).

■ **9.2** (4) Apparently the image of travel further suggested that of the religious procession. Dölger in particular has shown that in 9.2 Ignatius refers to the small religious objects such as miniature temples that were carried in the parades in honor of the Ephesian Diana (cf. Acts 19:24).[22] Symbolic use of such language was also known to pagan writers (note the treatment of ἱεραφόροι "bearers of sacred things" in Plutarch De Isid. 3, 352b).[23] The list of epithets allows Ignatius to indulge in his love of -φορος compounds ("-bearers"),[24] including one that corresponds to his own second name, Theophorus, "God-bearer."[25] The democratization of the conception here indicates that it reflects a sense of the separation of the Christian community from the profane world at least as much as the indwelling of God in individual believers (see on Eph. inscr). The statement that the members of the procession are adorned with the "commandments" is reminiscent of Phd. 1.2, where the bishop is said to be

---

images (but not that of the crane).

14 Hugo Rahner, Greek Myths and Christian Mystery (New York and Evanston: Harper & Row, 1963) 46–68, 328–86; Jean Daniélou, Primitive Christian Symbols (Baltimore: Helicon, 1964) 58–70.

15 Bartsch, Gnostisches Gut, 30–34.

16 Philipp Vielhauer, Oikodome: Das Bild vom Bau in der christlichen Literatur vom Neuen Testament bis Clemens Alexandrinus (Diss. Heidelberg, 1939) 155–56.

17 Corwin, Ignatius, 37, 142.

18 O. Navarre, "Machina," Dictionnaire des antiquités, 3/2. 1462–66 (with illustrations).

19 The transition from the imagery of building to that of ships was hardly difficult. For "house" or "ship" as variant metaphors for the state see Demosthenes Olynth. 2.10.

20 Lightfoot found late examples for ἀναγωγεύς as a lifting device. In Ignatius, however, the word seems closer to usages in which it refers to the divine guide of souls (Proclus Hymni 1.34; cf. BAG s.v. ἀναγωγεύς, p. 53). Lightfoot's effort to see this sentence as a continuation of the mechanical metaphor also breaks down with the clear reference to love as a "way" (which can hardly be compared with the inclined plane used in building). Ignatius elsewhere joins only partially related images (cf. Tr. 6.1–2; 11.1–2).

21 Wilhelm Michaelis ("ὁδός," TDNT 5 [1967] 92)

rightly notes that the following metaphor of the procession weakens any possible Gnostic dimension in the imagery of the road upward. In any event, Philo already knows of a "way" that leads up to God (Post. Cain. 101; Deus immut. 142; Conf. 95). And the imagery is strikingly clear, e.g., also in Lucian (Hermot. 2–7). Ignatius and Gnosticism draw from a common stock of religious images.

22 Dölger, Antike und Christentum, 4. 67–80.

23 Bartelink (Lexicologisch-semantische studie, 73) presses his thesis too far when he sees Ignatius consciously opposing ἁγιοφόρος "bearer of holy things" to the pagan term ἱεροφόρος "bearer of sacred things." The whole passage unavoidably conjures up a picture of pagan religiosity.

24 Brown, Authentic Writings, 14–15.

25 Dölger (Antike und Christentum, 4. 72) notes an inscription from Frascati of a long list of religious functionaries of whom two are called θεοφόρος. See F. Messerschmidt, "Eine neue Bakcheninschrift," Gnomon 3 (1927) 250–51.

harmonized with the commandments "as the cithara is to the strings." Clearly Ignatius would think of the parallel musical imagery in *Eph.* 4.1 as in no way out of line with the metaphors of *Eph.* 9.[26] The context suggests that the "commandments" of Christ are conceived of not so much in terms of specific ethical injunctions as Christian revelation in general.[27] To be in harmony with this is to follow a "new way of life"[28] loving only God.

---

26 Similarly Methodius saw no incongruity between the analogies for the cross noted above and musical imagery. The passage (*Porph.* 1.10) includes reference to harmony, melody, strings, and the "mingling" of humanity with divinity (cf. *Eph.* 4.1–5.1). Note also that *Hermas* (*Vis.* 3.5.1–2) uses a musical term (συμφωνεῖν "to be in harmony") in connection with his building metaphors; that Irenaeus (*Adv. haer.* 1.10.2) likens the universal church to "one house" that hands its doctrine on harmoniously as though she possessed but "one mouth"; and that Ps-Hippolytus (*Pasch.* 6.5; *PG* 59. 745) connects the mystery of the cross with choral imagery.

27 Ignatius is like John in avoiding discussion of the content of the "commandments" (ἐντολαί) and in seeing obedience to them expressed in terms of the unity of the church under God. It is forced to see in *Eph.* 9.2 a view of Jesus as "legislator for Christians" (Gottlob Schrenk, "ἐντολή," *TDNT* 2 [1964] 556). What moralism there is in Ignatius expresses itself in other ways (see on *Sm.* 11.3).

28 I retain the difficult reading of G, κατ' ἄλλον βίον ("in your new way of life"; literally, "according to another way of life") and relate it to the proverb ἄλλος βίος, ἄλλη δίαιτα· ἐπὶ τῶν ἐπ' ἀμείνονα βίον μεταβαλόντων "another way of life, another life-style: said of those who change to a better way of life" (Zenobius *Cent.* 1. 22; *Paroem. Gr.* 1.7). The Arabic retains a clear reflection of the reading "(according to) another life."

10   Pray for Other People

1   But pray on behalf of other people unceasingly, for there is hope of repentance in them that they may attain God. Let them learn at least from your deeds to become disciples. 2/ Before their anger be gentle, before their boastfulness be humble, before their slanderings (offer) prayers, before their deceit be fixed in faith, before their fierceness be mild, not being eager to imitate them in return. 3/ Let us be found their brothers in gentleness; let us be eager to be imitators of the Lord—who was wronged more? who was defrauded more? who was rejected more?—so that no plant of the devil may be found among you, but that in all purity and sobriety you may abide in Jesus Christ, in flesh and in spirit.

■ **10.1** A distinct but related topic is again introduced by the tandem particle καὶ . . . δὲ (cf. *Eph.* 2.1; 4.2). Having warned against heresy (6.2–8.2) and commented directly on the itinerant teachers (9.1–2), Ignatius now speaks of all other people. The change in attitude is remarkable. False teachers are all but incurable (7.1), but there is still hope of repentance for pagans (10.1).[1] Ignatius' view is remarkably broad. Pagans are to be prayed for "without ceasing" (10.1)[2] and to be regarded (in a rare use of the term) as "brothers" of the Christians (10.3; cf. Justin *Dial.* 96.2; Clement Alex. *Strom.* 5.14, 98.1; 7.14, 86.1). The absence of an attitude of "gentleness"[3] toward them directly threatens the moral and spiritual health of the church (10.3).[4]

This attitude is sociologically significant in demonstrating the extent to which some Christians were prepared to go in coming to terms with the world (see Introduction, 3.5–6). An emphasis on prayer for pagans (and the authorities) emerges in the sub-apostolic period (1 Tim 2:1; *1 Clem.* 60.4–61.1) and is sometimes linked as it is in Ignatius with a willingness to suffer at the hands of persecutors (Pol. *Phil.* 12.3). The importance of influencing pagans by deeds (when words fail) is also stressed in 1 Peter (2:12; 3:1) in conjunction with a call to endure undeserved oppression (3:8–9; 3:16; cf. 1 Thess 5:15) and a reminder of the model provided by Christ's own unjust suffering (2:21–23).

■ **10.2** Ignatius delineates the Christian attitude of gentleness in a rhetorically constructed series of parallel clauses based on a free tradition of the words of Jesus (cf. Matt 5:39–42, 44; Luke 6:27–28).[5]

■ **10.3** The parenthetical trio of rhetorical questions has much in common with 1 Cor 6:7 ("why do you not rather suffer wrong? why do you not let yourselves be defrauded?") that in turn looks back to the same tradition (cf. 1 Thess 5:15; 1 Pet 3:9). Apparently we have a commonplace of early Christian preaching before us.

The image of the evil plant or weed opens up more

---

1   Elsewhere Ignatius is somewhat more hopeful of repentance for false teachers (*Sm.* 4.1; 5.3; *Phd.* 8.1).

2   Cf. *Pol.* 1.3. The theme of "unceasing" prayer is Pauline (1 Thess 5:17; cf. Rom 12:12; Col 4:2; Eph 6:18; see also Luke 18:1; Pol. *Phil.* 4.3; *Herm. Sim.* 9.11.7) and closely related to that of unceasing remembrance and thanksgiving (Rom 1:9; 1 Thess 1:2; 2:13). But Paul does not speak in this connection of praying for all people.

3   Cf. 2 Cor 10:1; Phil 4:5. Such "gentleness" was also widely commended in popular Greek ethics (Hans Dieter Betz and John M. Dillon, in Betz, *Plutarch's Ethical Writings*, 171).

4   The expression "purity and sobriety" (10.3) reflects central values of the early catholic church (*1 Clem.* 64; cf. 1 Tim 5:2; 2:9, 15). What is remarkable here is that their realization is felt to be contingent on loving pagans. Since purity and sobriety tend to refer to the sexual sphere (Jackson P. Hershbell, in Betz, *Plutarch's Ethical Writings*, 152–53), could Ignatius have been speaking primarily of the need to remain tolerant of pagan spouses throughout this section (cf. 1 Cor 7:12–16)?

5   Βλασφημίαι here means "slanderings" (cf. Rev 2:9). It

complex possibilities. Elsewhere it has to do with heresy (*Tr.* 6.1; *Phd.* 3.1), but in our passage the concern is more general (cf. Heb 12:15). In any event, we are reminded (as in *Eph.* 9.1) of the parable of the seeds sown secretly (Matt 13:24–30). But the word used for "plant" (βοτάνη) figures importantly only in *Hermas'* elaboration of the parable of the householder (*Sim.* 5.2; cf. Matt 21:33–41). The master's slave sees to it that no "weeds" spring up in the vineyard (*Sim.* 5.2.3–5). The same imagery joins that of the tower in another passage where it is connected with the question of the "hope of life"—that is, the hope of repentance (*Sim.* 9.26.4; for an exact parallel to the expression "hope of repentance" in *Eph.* 10.1 see *Sim.* 6.2.4; 8.7.2; 8.10.2).[6] In light of the apparent reference to the parable of the householder in *Eph.* 6.1, it is possible that the background here is a composite of parables of Jesus that arose in the tradition to illuminate the problem of fallen Christians.

Our passage is important for another reason:

"attaining God" (see Introduction, 5.12), "becoming disciples" (see on *Eph.* 1.2), and being "imitators" of the Lord (see Introduction, 5.13)—all themes connected especially with martyrdom in Ignatius—are used here of Christians (or potential Christians) in general. The context indicates that suffering is still closely associated with these themes. Yet becoming disciples and being imitators of the Lord are clearly thought of as attainable in this world and short of death. Presumably martyrdom represents a special focussing of the Christian stance in the world. It is to be noted that whereas Ignatius uses the simple verb τυγχάνειν when he speaks of Christians in general "attaining" God (cf. *Mag.* 1.2; *Sm.* 9.2), he uses the strengthened form ἐπιτυγχάνειν when speaking of himself and Polycarp. Yet Ignatius himself is merely beginning to be a disciple (*Eph.* 3.1). Thus he is both a special case and a problematic one (see Introduction, 3.4).

---

is best to take πλάνη as "deceit" (cf. 1 Thess 2:3) rather than "error" in this context; similarly, although "fixed (ἑδραῖοι) in the faith" (cf. *Sm.* 13.2) is reminiscent of Col 1:23, the meaning is best understood in light of Ign. *Pol.* 3.1 where Polycarp is urged to "stand fixed (ἑδραῖος) as an anvil struck"— that is, one is to endure quietly when pressure is applied.

6   Joly (*Ignace*, 56–57) suggests dependence of Ignatius on *Hermas* here. It is more likely that they have a common source.

**Eschatological Warnings
and Exhortations [11.1–19.3]**

11

Fear God's Patience

1   **These are the last times. Let us then
exercise restraint, let us fear God's
patience, that it may not turn to
condemnation for us. For either let us
fear the coming wrath, or let us love the
present grace—one or the other—only
that we be found in Christ Jesus to
possess the true life.**

■ **11.1** We may regard the whole of *Eph.* 11–19 as a loosely organized unit devoted to exhortation (11.1, 2; 13.1; 15.3; 16.1), frequently recalling last things and the defeat of Satan (11.1; 13.1–2; 14.2; 15.3; 16.2; 19.3), yet digressing often. Λοιπόν ("then"), the third word in the Greek sentence, seems to go not with the opening statement ("these are the last times") but with the following exhortation.[1] Even so it apparently functions like the initial λοιπόν in Paul (cf. 1 Thess 4:1; 2 Thess 3:1; Phil 3:1; 4:8; 2 Cor 13:11) and the papyri[2] as a transition to the final exhortations of the letter.

The appearance of the eschatological warning (cf. 1 John 2:18, 1 Cor 7:29; 1 Pet 4:7) is not as abrupt as it may seem, for the theme of repentance in 10.1 presupposes precisely such a background. Moreover, Ignatius presents traditional Christian eschatology in a much softened form. Note first of all that Plutarch also speaks about τὸν ἔσχατον . . . καιρόν "the last time" (*De ser. num. vind.* 10, 554e), meaning by that "the culminating moment in a process of progressive punishment,"[3] and in the same context comes close to Ignatius in denying the appropriateness of speaking of divine wrath and in tracing the delay of divine punishment to the exercise of

God's gentleness (*De ser. num. vind.* 5, 550f; see further on *Pol.* 6.2). Ignatius, to be sure, remains more biblical. If God's patience (in holding off judgment) is despised, the punishment will be all the greater (cf. Rom 2:3–4; 1 Pet 3:20; 2 Pet 3:9, 15; *Herm. Sim.* 8.11.1). Yet that sentiment is immediately softened by a standard linguistic device (though here less elegant than in classical usage) for presenting alternatives each of which can reasonably lay a claim on us.[4] The alternatives themselves—obeying God through fear of his wrath[5] or through love of his grace—reflect a problem that Hellenistic Jews[6] and Christians[7] faced in coming to terms with the Graeco-Roman devaluation of the passions and the rejection of fear as a worthy motive.[8] At the theological level, love and grace were somehow thought to escape anthropomorphism in a way that fear and wrath did not. Ignatius' concluding remark here shows that he too values the way of love more highly. Consequently the day of judgment is of secondary importance to him.

---

1   As in 1 Cor 7:29. For the same pattern see also Epictetus *Diss.* 1.24.1; 1.27.1–2.

2   Cf. *UPZ* 1. 78,43.

3   Hans Dieter Betz, Peter A. Dirkse, and Edgar W. Smith, in Betz, *Plutarch's Theological Writings*, 206.

4   Cf. Plato *Theaet.* 187c; *Gorg.* 475a: ἤ . . . ἤ . . . , δυοῖν θάτερον (Ignatius has ἓν τῶν δύο) "either . . . or . . . , one or the other."

5   For the expression "coming wrath" see Matt 3:7 (cf. 1 Thess 1:10).

6   Cf. Philo *Deus immut.* 69; *Migr. Abr.* 21; *Somn.* 1.163; *Spec. leg.* 1.300.

7   Cf. 1 John 4:18; Justin *Dial.* 67.9–10; Clement Alex. *Paed.* 1.7, 59.1–2; Origen *Hom. in Ies. Nave* 17.2.

8   Cf. Seneca *Ep.* 47.18; H. Schenkl, "Pythagoreersprüche in einer Wiener Handschrift," *Wiener Studien* 8 (1886) 264 (no. 8): "the gods mislead not because they have been angered, for wrath is foreign to the gods" (ὀργὴ γὰρ θεῶν ἀλλότριον).

Eschatological Warnings and Exhortations [11.1–19.3]	**11**	Do Nothing Without Christ (Ignatius and the Ephesians)

2 Let nothing have any attraction for you without him, in whom I carry about my bonds as spiritual pearls, in which may it be mine to rise by your prayer, of which may I always have a share, that I may be found a participant in the lot of the Ephesian Christians who always agreed with the very apostles in the power of Jesus Christ.

12 1/ I know who I am and to whom I write: I am condemned, you have been shown mercy; I am in danger, you have been strengthened. 2/ You are a passage for those slain for God; (you are) fellow initiates of Paul, (a man) sanctified, approved, worthy of blessing, in whose steps may it be mine to be found when I reach God, who in every letter remembers you in Christ Jesus.

■ **11.2** The second exhortation quickly becomes a digression on Ignatius' authority and his relation with the Ephesians. Here it is again clear (cf. *Eph.* 3.1) that his bonds as such are not the cause of any sense of unworthiness. They are in fact his "spiritual pearls"[1] in which he hopes to "rise."[2] Yet he regards himself as dependent on the Ephesians, whose prayer will prevent his martyrdom from failure and whose superiority consists in their full agreement with "the apostles." They still participate in the ideal of unity and order that their glorious past represents.

■ **12.1** These thoughts are elaborated (and complicated) in the next section (12.1–2), where it is not Ignatius' dependence on the Ephesians but his inferiority to them that is stressed. This is expressed by a set of antitheses. The parallel passages give us the following equivalences:

Eph. 12.1:	condemned	vs.	shown mercy
	in danger	vs.	strengthened
Tr. 3.3:	condemned	vs.	apostle
Rom. 4.3:	condemned	vs.	apostles
	slave	vs.	free

Consider also the link between the second antithesis noted above and *Tr.* 13.3: "my spirit is devoted to you

(cf. *Eph.* 8.1) . . . for I am still *in danger*" (followed by a reference to prayer on behalf of Ignatius). This parallel shows that our set of antitheses intersects with Ignatius' presentation of himself elsewhere as a "lowly offering" (see on *Eph.* 8.1). Thus we may say that Ignatius is "condemned" (κατάκριτος) just as the persons used as sacrifices for expiatory purposes were often drawn from the "condemned" (κατακριθέντων, Porphyry, in Eusebius *P. E.* 4.16.1). Consequently the same ambiguities are found here as in Ignatius' use of the sacrificial imagery. On the one hand, his bonds are his hidden glory which some learn not to despise (cf. *Sm.* 10.2; *Pol.* 2.3). On the other hand, his state as a condemned man also symbolizes his role as their "slave" (see on *Mag.* 12): he is not free, he does not speak with the authority of the apostles (with whom the Ephesians are in agreement), he lacks their strength,[3] and has not been "shown mercy" as they have (which, as in 1 Cor 7:25; 2 Cor 4:1; and Rom 11:30–31, seems to mean that they have been given special status). All of these statements must be treated as roughly equivalent. But more needs to be said: Ignatius is "in danger." Presumably this refers to the danger that his martyrdom may not succeed either because of

---

1 For other standard references to the bonds of martyrs as precious ornaments see Pol. *Phil.* 1.1; Eusebius *Hist. eccl.* 5.1.35; and Cyprian *Ep.* 76.2.

2 Especially in light of *Mag.* 9.2 and *Rom.* 2.2 (4.3) Ignatius probably thinks of resurrection as a state immediately after death. In any event, his talk of rising in his bonds is not intended to clarify the state of human beings in the other world but to express his

hope of seeing his martyrdom through. Hence also his reference to the prayer of the Ephesians on his behalf.

3 Both Schlier (*Untersuchungen*, 86–87) and Bartsch (*Gnostisches Gut*, 96, 105–7) read this verb (στηρίζειν) against a Gnostic (and sacramental) background. But the context does not call for this, and the only other use of the word in Ignatius (*Phd.* inscr) strongly

interference or because of loss of nerve (*Rom.* 6.2; 7.2). Consequently he needs the prayers of other Christians (cf. *Tr.* 13.3). But the intensity of the concern suggests that still more is involved.[4] We have argued that Ignatius feared that the value of his whole ministry had been called into question (see Introduction, 3.1; 3.4). He now looks to the united church of Ephesus (a church still in agreement[5] with the apostles) and the other churches to confirm the value of his mission by supporting him (materially and spiritually) in his last fight against the powers of darkness. The superiority of the Ephesians consists in their preservation of apostolic unity. The disunity that seems to have threatened Ignatius' own ministry (see on *Phd.* 10) is probably what brings him to view the Ephesians so favorably in this connection.

■ **12.2** Here Ignatius gives further reasons for the superiority of the Ephesians. They are a "passage" or "highway" ($\pi\acute{a}\rho o\delta os$) for martyrs[6] and are "fellow initiates" ($\sigma\nu\mu\mu\acute{\nu}\sigma\tau\alpha\iota$) of Paul. Paul's connection with the

Ephesians and the tradition that they formally "sent him off" conscious that they would never see him again (Acts 20:38) probably suffices to explain the reference to Ephesus as a highway for martyrs. For the whole passage is highly idealized and tends to make sweeping claims on the basis of few instances: thus the Ephesians are in agreement with "the apostles" (11.2; undoubtedly Ignatius means Paul and the twelve), and they are remembered in every epistle of Paul (12.2).[7] The second image ("fellow initiates") is drawn (ultimately) from the mysteries[8] and was to become fairly common in later Patristic Greek.[9] Paul had already used language from the same circle of ideas to describe his own spiritual readiness (Phil 4:12). The image of following in Paul's "steps" was a natural one,[10] and it occurs elsewhere in the early period in connection with suffering and martyrdom (1 Pet 2:21; *Mart. Pol.* 22.1). The expression "attain God" is employed here as it usually is of Ignatius' martyrdom.

---

4   An interesting parallel involving the attribution by a holy man of superiority to a group of city councillors is found in Apollonius *Ep.* 12. But Apollonius' remarks are merely polite and conventional by comparison.

5   The Arabic now supports the reading of gA and Zahn ($\sigma\nu\nu\hat{\eta}\sigma\alpha\nu$ "were together with") instead of $\sigma\nu\nu\acute{\eta}\nu\epsilon\sigma\alpha\nu$ "agreed together with." The meaning is not materially affected.

6   Schlier (*Untersuchungen*, 121) sees a reference here to the cosmic journey of the Gnostic. But he can do so only by translating the phrase "a passage for those taken up" ($\dot{\alpha}\nu\alpha\iota\rho o\nu\mu\acute{\epsilon}\nu\omega\nu$) to God. The verb $\dot{\alpha}\nu\alpha\iota\rho\acute{\epsilon}\omega$ occasionally has to do with picking something up, but more often with destroying it. Schlier extends its meaning to impossible lengths.

7   For similar hyperbole see 1 Thess 1:8; 1 Cor 1:2; Col 1:23; Pol. *Phil.* 11.3. Paul explicitly refers to the Ephesians only in 1 Cor 15:32 and 16:8 (as well as in 1 and 2 Tim). Our phrase ($\dot{\epsilon}\nu\ \pi\acute{a}\sigma\eta\ \dot{\epsilon}\pi\iota\sigma\tau o\lambda\hat{\eta}$) cannot mean "in a whole letter" (cf. LSJ *s.v.* $\pi\hat{a}s$, p. 1345)

and so refer to the NT letter to the Ephesians (even though Ignatius may have known that letter and connected it with Ephesus; see on *Eph.* inscr). Rathke (*Ignatius*, 13, 21–22) makes the ingenious suggestion that since Ignatius uses the verb $\mu\nu\eta\mu o\nu\epsilon\acute{\nu}\omega$ ("remember," "make mention of") elsewhere only in the formal epistolary sense (*Eph.* 21.1; *Mag.* 14; *Tr.* 13.1; *Rom.* 9.1; *Sm.* 5.3), he has in mind Paul's own use of the same verb and considers the Ephesians as included in every such apostolic reminiscence. For how else could it be said in Eph 1:16 that Paul never ceased remembering the Ephesians?

8   Franz Joseph Dölger, ΙΧΘΥΣ (5 vols.; Münster: Aschendorff, 1928–43) 2. 478–79. Philo had already used such language in a metaphorical sense (Bartelink, *Lexicologisch-semantische studie,* 152–53).

9   *LPGL s.v. $\sigma\nu\mu\mu\acute{\nu}\sigma\tau\eta s$*, p. 1284.

10   Cf. Lucretius *De rer. nat.* 3.1–8; Philo *Virt.* 64; Aelius Aristides *Or.* 35.39 (ed. Keil); Rom 4:12; 2 Cor 12:18.

Eschatological Warnings and Exhortations [11.1–19.3]	**13**	Meet Frequently for the Destruction of Satan

1 Be eager, then, to meet more often for thanksgiving and glory to God; for when you come together often, the powers of Satan are broken, and his destructiveness is shattered by the concord of your faith. 2/ Nothing is better than peace, by which all warfare of heavenly and earthly beings is destroyed.

■ **13.1–2** The previous exhortations receive their practical application in a call for frequent[1] meeting for worship. Elsewhere this call is closely associated with the arousal of a sense of personal or communal responsibility in light of the approaching end (Heb 10:24–25; *Did.* 16.1–2; *Barn.* 4.9–10; *2 Clem.* 17.3–7). Ignatius moves along similar lines, but he emphasizes the extent to which worship as such anticipates the eschatological drama by destroying the powers of darkness (cf. *Barn.* 4.10). A similar evaluation of worship is found in *Eph.* 5.2, and in both passages Ignatius alludes to the eucharist in particular. For "thanksgiving" (εὐχαριστίαν) here calls to mind the sacred meal (see also *Phd.* 4; *Sm.* 7.1; 8.1). But it is also to be observed that, as in other early sources, "thanksgiving" and "glory" are both still primarily terms for prayer to God that is employed at the celebration of the eucharist (Justin *Apol.* 1.65.3; cf. *Did.* 9.1).[2] The sacred meal for Ignatius is but one element in a whole pattern of worship and prayer.

Again the basic concern is unity, though here it is expressed in political metaphors: "concord" and "peace." The term ὁμονοία "concord" occurs eight times in Ignatius (*Eph.* 4.1, 2; 13.1; *Mag.* 6.1; 15; *Tr.* 12.2; *Phd.* inscr; 11.2). It is not, of course, an exclusively political term. But the following considerations point in that direction for Ignatius: the word does not appear in the NT; among the Apostolic Fathers only *1 Clement* makes significant use of it (otherwise it appears twice in *Hermas*), and it has been shown that a political model is involved there;[3] "concord" and (to a lesser extent) "peace" were central to the discussion of relations between citizens in the cities or between the cities themselves in Asia Minor at the time (see *Orations* 38–41 of Dio Chrysostom and *Orations* 23–24 [ed. Keil] of Aelius Aristides). This is not the only indication that Ignatius models the church to some extent on the Greek city (see Introduction, 3.5). Yet the political overtones of the theme are less vigorously exploited by Ignatius than in *1 Clement*. We have seen elsewhere how he encloses it in musical metaphors (*Eph.* 4.1–2). And in the passage before us it reaches out beyond mundane affairs. For such peace destroys "warfare," a term which, though it must allude to strife in the church (cf. *1 Clem.* 3.2; 46.5), also has to do with angelic hostility. Here (as in Phil 2:10) the expression "heavenly and earthly" does not distinguish sharply separated realms.[4] Ignatius anticipates the extraordinary description of the cosmic effects of the incarnation in *Eph.* 19.3. Unified activity in worship (with its corollaries of obedience to the bishop and support of Ignatius) carries forward the redemption set in motion by Christ.

---

1 For πυκνότερον in reference to "more frequent" meetings see *Pol.* 4.2 (cf. *Mag.* 4). The meaning "in larger numbers" would more naturally be represented by πυκνότεροι.

2 Cf. Bartelink, *Lexicologisch-semantische studie,* 113–14.

3 W. C. van Unnik, "Studies over de zogenaamde eerste brief van Clemens, I: Het litteraire genre," *Mededelingen der koninklijke Nederlandse akademie van wetenschappen, Afd. letterkunde,* 33/4 (1970) 149–204; idem, "'Tiefer Friede' (1. Klemens 2,2)," *VC* 24 (1970) 261–79; idem, "Noch einmal 'Tiefer Friede,'" *VC* 26 (1972) 24–28; cf. Paul Mikat, *Die Bedeutung*

der Begriffe Stasis und Aponoia für das Verständnis des 1. Clemensbriefes (Arbeitsgemeinschaft für Forschung des Landes Nordrhein-Westfalen 155; Köln and Opladen: Westdeutscher Verlag, 1969). For the view that these themes are filtered through an early Christian apologetic tradition rooted in Judaism see Karlmann Beyschlag, "Zur EIPHNH BAΘEIA (I Clem. 2,2)," *VC* 26 (1972) 18–23.

4 BAG *s.v.* ἐπίγειος, p. 290.

Eschatological Warnings
and Exhortations [11.1–19.3]

14

Faith and Love, Words and Deeds

1 None of these things escape you if you
have perfect faith and love in Jesus
Christ, which are the beginning and end
of life: the beginning is faith, the end is
love; these two, existing in unity, are
God; all other things leading to nobility
follow from them. 2/ No one professing
faith sins, nor possessing love hates. The
tree is known from its fruit; thus those
professing to be of Christ will be seen by
what they do. For the deed is not a
matter of what one now professes but of
being found in the power of faith to the
end.

15

1/ It is better to be silent and to be
than while speaking not to be. To teach is
good if the one who speaks acts. One,
then, is the teacher who "spoke and it
was so," and also what he has effected in
silence is worthy of the Father. 2/ He
who truly possesses the word of Jesus is
able also to hear his silence, that he may
be perfect, that he may act through what
he says, and may be known through that
in which he is silent. 3/ Nothing escapes
the Lord's notice, but even our secrets
are near him. Let us then do everything
knowing that he dwells in us, that we
may be his temples and he may be our
God within us—which indeed he is, and
he shall appear before our face because
we love him rightly.

Ignatius now turns to the spiritual and ethical presuppositions of the peace and concord that he has just
commended. The words faith and love link 14.1 with
14.2, and the concern for deeds links 14.2 with 15.1–3.
The imperative mood yields to the indicative here; but
there are clear indications that these statements also
serve as warnings, and the return to direct exhortation in
15.3 is not unexpected. The emphasis on deeds in this
passage has a particular aim within the context of the
letter as a whole: to encourage subordination to the
bishop (as the parallel in *Mag.* 4 also suggests). Eschato-

logical sanctions also continue to be invoked: one must
persist "to the end" (14.2);[1] the divine judge knows even
our secret thoughts (15.3). Again, however, this motivation for behavior is qualified by an emphasis on the
indwelling God whose temples we are (15.3).[2]

■ **14.1** Faith and love, as we have seen, are the primary
expressions of the Christian life (cf. *Eph.* 1.1). Here,
however, reflection on the pair is enriched by identifying

1   Cf. Matt 10:22; Mark 13:13 ; 1 Cor 1:8; Heb 3:14;
6:11; Rev 2:26. Note that the νῦν at the beginning of
the sentence and the εἰς τέλος at the end are
antithetical: it is not what we say "now" but how we
will be found "at the end" that is important. This
involves taking the adverb νῦν with the noun
ἐπαγγελίας ("profession"), which is unusual but by no
means impossible Greek (cf. Xenophon *Cyrop.* 4.25;

Hist. 6.2.39).
2   Ignatius' words bring more vividly to mind than do
the Pauline parallels (see on *Eph.* 9.1) the picture of
the temple with the god "dwelling" within it (cf. Acts
7:48; 17:24). This probably owes something to a
closer contact with the religious life of pagans (cf.
Eph. 9.3). The clumsiness of the expression, then, is
the result of the putting together of Ignatius' usual

faith as the beginning and love as the end of life.[3] The formula emphasizes the fact that faith and love belong together and represent the Christian way in its totality (see on *Mag.* 6.1; 13.1). Beyond that, however, it appears that here Ignatius also begins the long process of setting the theological and moral language of early Christianity within the framework of the Graeco-Roman virtues.[4] Thus Demosthenes (*Or.* 60.17) states that "the beginning of all virtue is wisdom, whereas the end is courage (ἔστιν γάρ, ἔστιν ἁπάσης ἀρετῆς ἀρχὴ μὲν σύνεσις, πέρας δ' ἀνδρεία); by the one what ought to be done is examined, by the other it is confirmed."[5] Also redolent of Greek ethics is Ignatius' identification of the consequence of faith and love as "nobility" (καλοκἀγαθία).[6]

At the same time, Ignatius connects faith and love directly with God; for "these two, existing in unity, are God." This peculiar statement has often been pressed to demonstrate the virtual identification by Ignatius of God and unity. But Ignatius is given to compressed forms of speech (see on *Eph.* 20.2) and is capable of expressing himself more normally elsewhere when he says that "where there is division and anger, God does not dwell" (*Phd.* 8.1). What Ignatius is saying, then, is that where

faith and love are joined (as beginning and end) in perfect unity, God is present. An instructive parallel to Ignatius' compressed form of speech is a maxim that appears in Pliny the Elder (*Nat. hist.* 2.18): *deus est mortali iuvare mortalem* (literally, "for a mortal to help a mortal is God").

■ **14.2** In the following sentences Ignatius goes on to emphasize deeds as the authentication of Christian lives. In terms reminiscent of 1 John he declares the incompatibility of faith and sin (3:4–10; 5:18) and of love and hate (4:20).[7] In a proverbial saying close to Matt 12:33 (Luke 6:44) he asserts that the tree is known from its fruit.[8] But behind all this (and behind 15.1 as well) hovers the Graeco-Roman commonplace that we are to be true to our profession not only in word but also (and especially) in deed[9]—a sentiment for which there are parallels also in Jewish[10] and early Christian sources.[11] The passage is immediately clarified when seen in these terms. In particular, Ignatius' definition of "the deed" here and in *Rom.* 3.3 (where it is all but identified with Christianity itself) may be taken as a conscious attempt to elaborate the significance of the word "deed" that figures in the commonplace. The expression "power (δύναμις) of

---

3   A verbal parallel to part of the statement is provided in 1 Tim 1:5, "the end of our instruction is love." A sense of progression from faith to love can also be found in other early texts (cf. 1 Cor 13:13; 2 Pet 1:5–7; *Herm. Vis.* 3.8.3–5; *Sim.* 9.15.2).

4   For a much more elaborate development along these same lines see Clement Alex. *Strom.* 7.10, 55.6.

5   A similar formula appears at almost the other end of the history of Greek literature in Hierocles *In aur. Pyth. carm. comm.* 7.9 (Fridericus Guilelmus Koehler, *Hieroclis in Aureum Pythagoreorum Carmen Commentarius* [Stuttgart: Teubner, 1974] 29): "for the end of the virtues is friendship, the beginning piety (πέρας μὲν γὰρ τῶν ἀρετῶν ἡ φιλία, ἀρχὴ δὲ ἡ εὐσεβεία); and the teaching of piety is the seed of all good things to us, the habit of friendship the most perfect fruit of the virtues." Ignatius' use of ἀρχή and τέλος instead of ἀρχή and πέρας represents a less elegant variant that reflects the linguistic horizons of the early Christians. Note that the prefatory poem (line 42) in the *Orphic Hymns* invokes (among others) the divinities 'Αρχήν τ' ἠδὲ Πέρας "Beginning and End" but that elsewhere the hymns speak of Heaven and Zeus as ἀρχὴ πάντων πάντων τε τελευτή "beginning of

all things and end of all things" (4.2; 15.7; cf. 34.15). The expression is often linked with the word "virtue" in Greek literature (LSJ *s.v.* καλοκἀγαθία, p. 869). It is frequent also in Philo where Hellenic connotations are to the fore (cf. Ioannes Leisegang, *Philonis Alexandrini Opera*, vol. 7: *Indices* [2 vols.; Berlin: De Gruyter, 1926–30] 2. 427–28) and in *4 Maccabees* (cf. Perler, "Das vierte Makkabäerbuch," 54).

6   identification of Christ as "our God" with the imagery of the god dwelling "within us" (his temples). No emendation is required.

7   Elsewhere Ignatius confronts the reality of shortcomings among Christians (cf. *Pol.* 2.1). In our passage he (like 1 John) may have in mind "the possibility of not sinning" that serves as a warning to Christians (Rudolf Bultmann, *The Johannine Epistles* [Hermeneia; Philadelphia: Fortress, 1973] on 1 John 3:9, pp. 52–53). In any event, a concern for "sin" is rare in Ignatius (only here and in *Sm.* 7.1) and it is likely that this piece of traditional teaching is used by him mainly to stress the inescapable requirement of deeds.

8   Koester (*Synoptische Überlieferung*, 42–43) draws attention to the proverbial character of the line and the appearance of something like it in *b. Ber.* 48a ("every pumpkin can be told from its stalk").

9   Usually λόγος or λόγοι are contrasted with ἔργον or ἔργα. Also common is a contrast between ὄνομα or ὀνόματα and πράξεις, τὰ πεπραγμένα, or πράγματα. See Demosthenes *Olynth.* 2.12; *Philip.* 3.15;

faith" is reminiscent of Paul's contrast between "word" and "power" in 1 Cor 4:20; but also note that in Dio Chrysostom (*Or.* 38.30) "names" and "the force of facts" (δύναμιν τὴν τῶν πραγμάτων) are contrasted.

■ **15.1–2** The same passage from Dio Chrysostom also illuminates the opening words of 15.1. Here the verb "to be" must mean "to be what one professes (a Christian)" just as in *Mag.* 4 we are urged not simply "to be called" (καλεῖσθαι) Christians but "to be" (εἶναι) Christians. Precisely the same contrast is presented by Dio Chrysostom (*Or.* 38.30) as he urges his audience not only "to be called" (καλεῖσθαι) leaders among the cities but also "to be" (εἶναι) leaders. Clearly Ignatius' rhetoric is shaped here as much by Graeco-Roman commonplaces as by early Christian tradition.

It is evident, then, that Ignatius has been circling back to the problem of the taciturn bishop of Ephesus (cf. *Eph.* 6.1). He is the one who is "silent" (σιωπᾶν) as Christ was "silent" (σιγῶν), he is the one who hears Christ's "silence" (ἡσυχίας). It is he who does not speak without backing up what he says with deeds. The clear implication is that precisely such empty talk characterizes the false teachers. And Ignatius sets up in opposition to them Christ the true teacher whose words are not mere words and whose silent deeds speak volumes. The perfect man (presumably Onesimus the bishop) is like Jesus in these respects. Such is the basic structure of Ignatius' argument, and it scarcely admits the profounder Gnostic themes that have been found here (see on *Eph.* 6.1).

As in *Eph.* 7.2 Ignatius sets Christ up in opposition to the false teachers by means of an acclamation: εἷς

διδάσκαλος, "there is one teacher."[12] Here again he is probably trying to defend the bishop's failure to confront the opposition effectively. He is suggesting that evil of such dimensions must be left to Christ and that the bishop's quiet demeanor is more in accord with the mind of Christ. It is wrong to think, however, that Ignatius sees silence alone as the true mark of Christ. For he says that teaching is good if deeds follow and that Christ is the one teacher whose words and deeds cohere perfectly (15.1). The success of the bishop in imitating the one teacher in this respect is explicitly set in terms of the complementarity of "possessing the word of Jesus" and "hearing his silence." Both elements are also given equal weight in the final clause "that he may act through what he says, and may be known through that in which he is silent" (15.2). The purpose of the oxymoron, "to hear his silence," is to underscore the fact that deeds too speak volumes.[13] To be sure, the passage as a whole gives special weight to the value of silence; the bishop's silence, after all, was the problem; but words are by no means completely devalued.

All this would be still clearer if we could tell exactly what Ignatius had in mind when he described Christ's speech and silence in 15.1. He "spoke and it was so" (εἶπεν καὶ ἐγένετο) is usually regarded as a reflection of Ps 32:9 (148:5). But the LXX here reads εἶπεν καὶ ἐγενή-θησαν. It is much more likely, then, that Ignatius reflects the basic elements repeated in the first chapter of Genesis where God "spoke" (εἶπεν) the various words of creation "and it was so" (καὶ ἐγένετο).[14] These verses were regarded as concealing the doctrine of the Logos

---

Aeschines *Ctes.* 152; Isocrates *Phil.* 120; 151; Thucydides 2.65.9; 8.78; 8.89; Plato *Lach.* 188d; Sophocles *Oed. tyr.* 517; *Oed. Col.* 782; 873; Euripides *Iph. Aul.* 128; Aelius Aristides *Or.* 24.6 (ed. Keil); Themistius *Or.* 2, 34bd; Livy 7.32.12; Cicero *Pro Cael.* 17.40. Note also the collection of materials in Stobaeus *Ecl.* 2.15. The theme is discussed by Felix Heinimann, *Nomos und Physis* (Schweizerische Beiträge zur Altertumswissenschaft 1; Basel: Reinhardt, 1945) 43–56. Similarly, popular wisdom proclaimed the superiority of silence to (idle) speech (cf. Sir 20:7; Apollonius *Ep.* 81; 82; Stobaeus *Ecl.* 3.33–34).

10   Cf. *m.* ʾAbot 1.17.

11   Cf. Matt 23:3; 1 Cor 4:20; Rom 15:18; *1 Clem.* 30.3; 38.2.

12   A similar statement appears in Matt 23:8 ("for one is

your teacher"), where it also follows closely on a discussion of the relation between words and deeds (Matt 23:3–7). Matthew and Ignatius are probably elaborating in their distinctive ways a traditional line of argument used by leaders in the early church to guard their followers from outside influences.

13   Even the high evaluation given to silence in the Pythagorean tradition (Philostratus *Vit. Apoll.* 1.14.16; 6.11.241) did not prevent the recognition "that silence is also speech" (ὅτι καὶ τὸ σιωπᾶν λόγος, *Vit. Apoll.* 1.1.2; cf. 6.11.245).

14   Cf. Joachim Jeremias, "Zum Logos-Problem," *ZNW* 59 (1968) 82.

(Irenaeus *Adv. haer.* 4.32.1; cf. John 1:1); and since Ignatius elsewhere refers to Christ as God's "mouth" (*Rom.* 8.2), it is understandable that Christ himself could be regarded as speaking the creative words. Thus it is easier to account for the change from God to Christ as the speaker in the case of Genesis 1 than in the case of Ps 32:9.

If this is correct, Ignatius views Christ as active in creation. The difficulty here is that elsewhere Ignatius associates the revelation of the Word with the incarnation (*Mag.* 8.2). But it is clear that the metaphorical dimensions of terms like "word" and "mouth" are particularly strong in Ignatius, and it does not seem impossible that he would have connected them freely with different events in the unfolding of divine purpose with no sense of contradiction.

The second part of the sentence ("and what he effected in silence is also worthy of the Father") represents the antithesis of the first: if Christ's creative word was effective, his silent deeds also proclaim his dignity. That his deeds are "worthy of the Father" reflects the Johannine theme that Christ pleased the one who sent him (cf. *Mag.* 8.2). This clearly has to do with the historical mission of Jesus, and the reference is probably to his silence before Pilate in particular. Even so, Ignatius would be characterizing Christ's mission in its totality just as he elsewhere universalizes the significance of a single event in Christ's ministry (see on *Eph.* 17.1). We are reminded of Melito's paradox (frg. 13) that "the Judge [Christ] is judged and is silent" (*iudex iudicatur et quietus est*). Possibly a still further extension of the theme is before us in Irenaeus' description of the incarnation as "the Word quiescing" (ἡσυχάζοντος τοῦ λόγου, *Adv. haer.* 3.19.3).

Our interpretation underscores the priority of speech in Ignatius' outlook. It is the transcendent Christ who speaks and it is done; it is the incarnate Christ whose silence speaks volumes. That Ignatius is thinking of two distinct stages in the unfolding of the divine purpose is suggested also by the fact that the two parts of the sentence are not simply antithetical but are also joined by the tandem particle καὶ . . . δέ which elsewhere marks the introduction of a separate but related point (see on *Eph.* 2.1).

For all these reasons we do not regard it as likely that Ignatius sees silence alone as the mark of Christ's person or that the Gnostic parallels which speak of the divine silence are relevant here.[15] Elsewhere, to be sure, Ignatius does speak of God's stillness (*Eph.* 19.1) and silence (*Mag.* 8.2). But as we shall see, this does not invalidate the interpretation of *Eph.* 6.1 and 15.1–2 developed here. The most that can be said is that the emphasis on the divine reserve in the theology of the period prompted Ignatius to spell out the meaning of the commonplace with which he was working in theological terms.

■ **15.3** It coheres with our view that Ignatius ends this section on no high mystical plane but with a warning (to those inclined to ignore the bishop?) that contains hints of future judgment and that invokes the theme of God's indwelling to reinforce the inescapability of his scrutiny of our deeds.[16] Characteristically, Ignatius immediately denies the need of such a reminder (see on *Eph.* 4.1) and states his conviction that the Lord (Christ) will "appear" (graciously) before us (in the judgment; cf. Matt 24:30) because of our love for him.

---

15 Bartsch, *Gnostisches Gut,* 54–61.
16 For God's knowledge of our secret deeds see Sus 42 (Theodotion) and Wis 17:3. But the best parallel to our passage is provided by *1 Clem.* 27.6, 3 ("nothing escapes the notice of his will," "all things are near him") in a context that has to do with resurrection and judgment. Apparently it was the previous mention of the (bishop's) silence that suggested to Ignatius the importance of also making reference to the silent thoughts of those inclined to resist the bishop. God knows the difference between these two forms of reticence.

Eschatological Warnings
and Exhortations [11.1–19.3]

16

Warning Against False Teachers

1   Be not deceived, my brothers: corrupters of
homes "will not inherit the Kingdom of
God"; 2/ if then they died who did these
things in the realm of the flesh, how
much more if someone by evil teaching
corrupts faith in God for which Jesus
Christ was crucified? Such a filthy being
will go into the unquenchable fire, likewise also the person who listens to him.

The final warning is now introduced (16.1–2). The vocative, as White has shown, often marks an important transition.[1] Ignatius turns again to the itinerant teachers previously discussed (*Eph.* 7–9). We may regard this section as an introduction to the three that follow (*Eph.* 17–19), and these in turn as answers to the views of the false teachers (as Ignatius understands them).

■ **16.1** The warning is based directly on the Pauline text that evil-doers (among whom adulterers figure prominently) "will not inherit the Kingdom of God" (1 Cor 6:9). The introductory formula, "be not deceived," echoes the same text but was no doubt also familiar to Ignatius from sources other than Paul (see on *Eph.* 5.2). In *Phd.* 3.3 the same elements of the Pauline passage are quoted and are applied to the person who encourages schism. Ignatius must have the same sort of person (or worse) in mind when he applied the passage to οἰκοφθόροι "corrupters of homes" in the present context. The following argument makes sense, however, only if the term refers in the first place to those who destroy households by committing adultery.[2] What we have, then, is an implied comparison between such adulterers and those who corrupt the church. But this comparison is

only indirectly worked out in 16.2 in the form of an *a minore* argument.

■ **16.2** The argument is that if such adulterers perished, how much more those who corrupt faith by their evil teaching. The corruption of homes is something that affects temporal well-being ("in the fleshly realm"; literally, "according to the flesh"); much more is at stake with "faith in God." The adulterers referred to by Ignatius are presumably the unchaste Israelites alluded to by Paul in 1 Cor 10:8 (cf. Num 25:1–9). The historical example is used by Ignatius to underscore the relative seriousness of the rule against adultery. The still greater importance of "faith in God" is brought out by a clause ("for which Jesus Christ was crucified") modelled on statements used in the early church to motivate brotherly love (cf. Rom 14:15; 1 Cor 8:11). The reapplication of the sentiment here serves to underscore the extent to which "faith" has become a matter of embattled beliefs. Ignatius may have chosen this language because it also pointed to the centrality of the crucifixion as an item of belief. Deny the crucifixion, he argues, and faith is denied. Faith, then, is the personified affirmation of the church "on behalf of which" Christ died.

---

1   White, *Form and Function*, 29–30.
2   Suidas (*s.v.* Ἱλάριος) uses the word in connection with an act of adultery that leads to the destruction of a household (cf. Plutarch *De educ. lib.* 16, 12b; *P.Grenf.* 1.53,19; Hesychius *s.v.* οἰκοφθόρος). Bauer (BAG *s.v.* οἰκοφθόρος, p. 564) argued that Ignatius means corrupters of "temples" when he says corrupters of "homes" (since the "home" of a God is his temple; cf. BAG *s.v.* οἶκος 1.a.β, p. 563) and has in mind the "temples" just mentioned in *Eph.* 15.3—that is, the Ephesians themselves (cf. 1 Cor 3:17; 6:19). This is ingenious and brings the passage more directly into

line with the parallel in *Phd.* 3.3. But it is difficult to read that much into the word, and it would be hard to construe the argument: what real difference would there be between corrupting (the faith of) the Ephesians and corrupting faith in God, and how could the former be regarded as something done merely in the sphere of the flesh?

The depth of Ignatius' feeling about those who destroy this faith may be gathered from the word "filthy" (ῥυπαρός) used to describe them. Here too occurs the bluntest language from the tradition about the judgment awaiting those who offend God (cf. Mark 9:43; Matt 3:12; Luke 3:17). Even more important, however, is the extension of the warning to include anyone who listens to such a teacher. Again Ignatius seeks to solve problems simply by cutting off contact between the Ephesians and the false teachers (see on *Eph.* 6.2).

Eschatological Warnings
and Exhortations [11.1–19.3]

17

The Aroma of Incorruptibiity

1   The Lord received ointment on his head for
this reason—that he might breathe
incorruptibility on the church. Do not be
anointed with the ill odor of the teaching
of the ruler of the age lest he lead you
captive from the life set before you. 2/
Why do we not all become wise, receiving the knowledge of God which is Jesus
Christ? Why do we foolishly perish, being
ignorant of the gift which the Lord has
truly sent?

■ **17.1** Ignatius opposes the aroma of incorruptibility (ἀφθαρσία) that Christ breathes (πνέη) on the church to the ill odor (δυσωδία) of the teaching of the evil one.[1] The language is interesting for two reasons: (a) the appeal to the sense of smell rather than that of sight or hearing lends a new subtlety to conceptions of revelation and redemption; and (b) the imagery seems somehow to move beyond metaphor to myth. Schlier sensed Gnostic affinities here, comparing particularly Irenaeus *Adv. haer.* 1.4.1 (Achamoth retains τινα ὀσμὴν ἀφθαρσίας "a certain aroma of incorruptibility") and 1.6.1 (the hylic element cannot receive the πνοὴν ἀφθαρσίας "breath of incor-ruptibility").[2] Fine parallels are also now available in the *Gospel of Truth* ([NHC1] 33,39–34,34) and the *Gospel of Philip* [NHC 2] 77,35–78,12). Both writings include references to the effect of the aroma on members of the community, and the latter also speaks of those who remain in their "ill odor" (stibōōn, i.e., δυσωδία).[3]

But it would be misleading to emphasize the Gnostic parallels too strongly. Paul already uses the image of the good aroma (2 Cor 2:14–16; cf. Eph 5:2);[4] and the (early?) parallel routinely cited from the *Odes of Solomon* (11.15: ηὐφράνθη ἡ ἀναπνόη ἐν εὐωδίᾳ χρηστότητος κυρίου "my breath rejoiced in the good aroma of the Lord's kindness")[5] is almost surely less heterodox than assumed by Schlier and others.[6] Moreover, Lohmeyer was able to trace the imagery of the good aroma as sign of the divine presence from early antiquity and found both Paul and Ignatius intelligible against that background.[7] The classical parallels adduced are often somewhat lifeless, but they demonstrate the wide appeal of such imagery. Not surprisingly it comes alive again not only in a Gnostically tinged writer like Clement of Alexandria (*Paed.* 2.8, 61.1, commenting on Luke 7:37, the same story reflected in Ignatius) but also in more sober thinkers like Irenaeus (*Adv. haer.* 3.11.8): The four Gospels are described as παντοχόθεν πνέοντας τὴν ἀφθαρσίαν "breathing immortality from every direction";

---

1   Ignatius often refers to the evil one in a traditional way as Satan (*Eph.* 13.1) or the devil (*Eph.* 10.3; *Tr.* 8.1; *Rom.* 5.3; *Sm.* 9.1). Here and in five other passages a somewhat more dualistic title appears: "ruler of this age" (*Eph.* 19.1; *Mag.* 1.2; *Tr.* 4.2; *Rom.* 7.1; *Phd.* 6.2). But this too has close analogies in both Paul (if 1 Cor 2:6–8 has to do with cosmic rulers; cf. Eph 2:2) and John (12:31; 14:30; 16:11). John's "ruler of this world" is practically equivalent to Ignatius' "ruler of this age" since the bishop treats "world" and "age" as interchangeable (*Rom.* 6.1). The exact terminology now appears in the Coptic *Gospel of the Egyptians* (59,22 in NHC 3; or 71,7 in NHC 4).

2   Schlier, *Untersuchungen*, 61–65, 82–84.

3   Cf. W. E. Crum, *A Coptic Dictionary* (Oxford: Clarendon, 1939) 363a.

4   The relation between Ignatius and 2 Cor 2:14–16 is particularly close (cf. Paulsen, *Studien*, 82–84).

5   Michel Testuz, *Papyrus Bodmer X–XII* (Cologne-Geneva: Bibliotheca Bodmeriana, 1959) 64.

6   Cf. James H. Charlesworth, "The Odes of Solomon —Not Gnostic," *CBQ* 31 (1969) 357–69; idem and R. A. Culpepper, "The Odes of Solomon and the Gospel of John," *CBQ* 35 (1973) 298–322; Henry Chadwick, "Some Reflections on the Character and Theology of the Odes of Solomon," in Patrick Granfield and Josef A. Jungmann, eds., *Kyriakon: Festschrift Johannes Quasten* (2 vols.; Münster: Aschendorff, 1970) 1. 266–70.

7   Ernst Lohmeyer, *Vom göttlichen Wohlgeruch* (Sitzungs-berichte der Heidelberger Akademie der Wissen-schaften, Philosophisch-historisch Klasse, 10/9; Heidelberg: Winter 1919) 32–37.

and Athanasius (*Contra Arian.* 1.8): the devil invents heresies διὰ τὴν ἰδίαν τῆς κακίας δυσωδίαν "through his own ill odor of evil."

In our passage the imagery is connected by Ignatius with the account of the woman who anointed Jesus with oil. He knew this story in a form close to that of Matthew (26:7; cf. Mark 14:3) where the oil is poured "on Jesus' head" and not (as in Luke 7:38 and John 12:3) on his feet. Apparent echoes in Ignatius of John's observation that "the house was filled with the aroma of the oil" (12:3) or that Jesus later "breathed" the spirit on his disciples (20:22) serve no more than to suggest the atmosphere in which the deeper meaning of such stories was being explored.[8] In any event, Ignatius goes beyond John in finding in this story resources for a characterization of the revelatory and soteriological significance of the ministry of Christ as a whole (see on *Eph.* 15.1).

There are a number of minute indications that Ignatius may also have been thinking of baptism: (a) He is about to make a striking reference to Jesus' baptism (18.2), and baptism was early associated with chrism (Tertullian *Bapt.* 7); (b) Ignatius may take up the unction first because of its unusual place before baptism in the Syrian liturgical tradition;[9] (c) the unusual reference to "Jesus the Christ" just below (in *Eph.* 18.2) may show that Ignatius is thinking of Jesus as "the anointed" and that this special interest is reflected also in 17.1 (note that Tertullian is fully alert to the meaning of Christ's name in connection with chrism); (d) the tradition connected both the baptism and the anointing of Jesus with his death (cf. Matt 26:12; and see on *Eph.* 18.2); Jesus' death

brings life in Ignatius (cf. *Mag.* 9.1); and life is what the anointing of Jesus confers in our passage.

In any event, the "incorruptibility" (ἀφθαρσία) that Christ breathes on the church is closely connected with sound teaching. That is suggested by the terminological links with *Eph.* 16 (the "corrupters of homes" in *Eph.* 16 "corrupt" faith by their evil teaching); by the antithesis which speaks of the ill odor of the "teaching" of the evil one; by the parallel in *Mag.* 6.2 (διδαχὴν ἀφθαρσίας "teaching of incorruptibility"); by the link in Paul between "knowledge" (γνῶσις) and the good aroma (2 Cor 2:14) and Ignatius' mention of "knowledge" that is "received" (17.2) just as Christ "receives" the ointment (17.1); and by the use of the unction of the gospel story as a symbol for teaching in later writers.[10] To the extent that Ignatius has sound teaching in mind here when he speaks of "incorruptibility," the metaphorical character of the language is maintained.[11] Of course Ignatius also has in mind the "incorruptibility" that such teaching and knowledge confers,[12] and he gives a more central role to "incorruptibility" than does the NT.[13] But he links "incorruptibility" elsewhere with the more traditional concepts of "resurrection" and "eternal life" (*Phd.* 9.2; *Pol.* 2.3), and it is likely that the link between teaching and incorruptibility is no more one of strict identification than that between knowledge and Jesus Christ in 17.2.

■ **17.2** Ignatius concludes the section with two rhetorical questions. In view of his general confidence about the theological integrity of the Ephesians (cf. *Eph.* 6.2), these questions are no doubt meant to be taken as warnings and not as indications that some of "us" have actually let

8   Antonio Orbe (*Estudios Valentinianos*, vol. 3: *La unción del Verbo* [Analecta Gregoriana 113: Rome; Università Gregoriana, 1961] 5–13) suggests that the enrichment of the gospel account in Ignatius may have come by way of Paul's view of Christ as the head of his body (the church) which in turn was connected with the anointing "upon the head" of Ps 132:2 (a connection made by Origen *Cels.* 6.79).

9   Richard Hugh Connolly, *Didascalia Apostolorum* (Oxford: Clarendon, 1929) xlviii–1, 146–47; cf. Robert M. Grant, *Ignatius*, 47.

10   Clement Alex. *Paed.* 2.8, 61.1; Theodore of Heracleia, in John Anthony Cramer, ed., *Catenae Graecorum Patrum in Novum Testamentum* (8 vols.; reprinted Hildesheim: Olms, 1967) 2. 323.

11   This is all the more likely since the following antithesis retains even more clearly its metaphorical

significance in carrying forward the image of being anointed and dropping that of breathing. Note also that the image of anointing in *Eph.* 3.1 and that of the ill odor of rotten food in *Mag.* 10.2 remain metaphorical.

12   Cf. Irenaeus *Adv. haer.* 4.36.7: "the knowledge of the Son of God, which is incorruptibility" (τὴν γνῶσιν τοῦ υἰοῦ τοῦ θεοῦ ἥτις ἐστιν ἀφθαρσία), i.e., the knowledge of the Son of God that effects incorruptibility.

13   Cf. Rom 2:7; 1 Cor 15:42, 50, 53, 54; Eph 6:2; 2 Tim 1:10.

curiosity lead to outright adherence to the false teachers. The content of the questions suggests the kind of false teaching that Ignatius has in mind: first he presents Jesus Christ as the ground of knowledge of God and emphasizes the fact by a blunt identification of the two (for this interpretation of such identifications in Ignatius see on *Eph.* 20.2);[14] he further defines his meaning when he says that the divine gift was "truly" (ἀληθῶς) sent, thus anticipating the emphasis in the next section on the reality of Christ's birth and passion (for the anti-docetic use of the adverb "truly" see *Tr.* 9.1–2 and *Sm.* 1.1–2.1). Although Ignatius' imagery may suggest a vague and otherworldly spirituality, he takes pains to tie it down to earth in the figure of Jesus Christ.

---

14 Since the identification is meant to emphasize the significance of Jesus Christ as the source of knowledge (compare the function of the identification in the passage from Irenaeus quoted above in n. 12), it is wrong to find here another quasi-hypostasized title—along with "word" (*Mag.* 8.2), "mouth" (*Rom.* 8.2), and "purpose" (*Eph.* 3.2)—for Christ. This is the only appearance of the term "knowledge" in Ignatius. The fact that it is linked with the image of the good aroma as in 2 Cor 2:14 suggests that Ignatius is in touch with traditional material at this point.

| Eschatological Warnings and Exhortations [11.1–19.3] | **18** | Defense of the Cross |

1 My spirit is a lowly offering of the cross, which is an affront to unbelievers, but to us salvation and eternal life. "Where is the wise man?" "Where the debater?" Where the boasting of those called intelligent? 2/ For our God, Jesus the Christ, was carried in the womb by Mary according to God's plan—of the seed of David and of the Holy Spirit—who was born and baptized that by his suffering he might purify the water.

■ **18.1** The allusions to Christ's passion in the preceding two sections are now filled out by a direct defense of its centrality and (implicitly) also its reality. The decisive elements in 18.1—the cross both as an "affront" (or "scandal") and as "salvation," the questions ("where is the wise man?" "where the debater?"), the challenge to the "intelligent"—are directly based on 1 Cor 1:19, 20, 23 (with an echo perhaps of Rom 3:27, "where is the boasting?").[1] Ignatius asserts his devotion to the cross with the help of the language of self-sacrifice (see on *Eph.* 8.1). In spite of this emphasis, he turns back to the incarnation in the following sections to develop his argument. For Christ's birth and passion (as we shall see) were closely related in his mind, and it is likely that the full reality of both of them was denied by the docetists of the day.

■ **18.2** It appears that Ignatius has recourse to quasi-credal material to defend his understanding of Christian teaching (cf. *Tr.* 9.1–2).[2] Clearly traditional is the description of Christ as being "of the seed of David and of the Holy Spirit." To be sure, in the formula preserved by Paul (Rom 1:3–4) Christ's dignity "according to the Spirit of holiness" is linked with the resurrection, whereas in Ignatius it is connected with Christ's birth. But this shift from eschatological to incarnational categories was no doubt effected before the time of Ignatius. The designation "Jesus *the* Christ" is also

extraordinary.[3] Ignatius generally prefers simply "Jesus Christ," which occurs about a hundred times and which apparently functions as a double name. The reverse order of the name, "Christ Jesus" (which is favored by Paul and which may make greater allowance for the original significance of "Christ" as a title), occurs only some thirteen times in Ignatius and probably functions as a double name for all practical purposes. The name "Jesus" rarely occurs by itself (*Eph.* 15.2; *Mag.* 1.2; *Phd.* 5.1), and the same is true of "Christ" (*Eph.* 14.2; *Sm.* 1.1; 6.1; 10.1) or "Christ" with the definite article (*Mag.* 13.2; *Rom.* 4.1, 2). "Jesus the Christ" (Ἰησοῦς ὁ Χριστός) appears only in our passage. It is very likely, then, that it derives from an older (perhaps adoptionist) tradition that still reflects a sensitivity to the name "Christ" as a title.

The clause "who was born and baptized" (ὃς ἐγεννήθη καὶ ἐβαπτίσθη) is marked as traditional by its first member and the characteristic use of the relative. Usually Jesus' baptism is not mentioned in credal material, but since Ignatius does not otherwise emphasize the importance of baptism (it does not figure as one of the mysteries in *Eph.* 19.1; and the emphatic ἀληθῶς "truly" is curiously missing from the reference to baptism in the list of quasi-credal items in *Sm.* 1.1), this too was probably traditional.[4] It is also likely that the clause "he was carried in the womb by Mary" was traditional since the verb (κυοφορεῖν) does not appear elsewhere

---

1 Rathke, *Ignatius*, 30–33; Paulsen, *Studien*, 33.
2 For a review of the scholarship and a careful treatment of the passage see Paulsen, *Studien*, 48–54.
3 For what follows see Ferdinand Kattenbusch, *Das Apostolische Symbol* (2 vols.; Leipzig: Hinrichs, 1894–1900) 2. 545 n. 113, 550–53, 555–56.

4 André Benoit, *Le baptême chrétien au second siècle, la théologie des pères* (Paris: Presses universitaires de France, 1953) 61.

in Ignatius.

On the other hand, the reference to Christ as "our God" seems distinctively Ignatian (see on *Eph.* inscr); and the expression "according to God's plan" (κατ' οἰκονομίαν θεοῦ) reflects a conception at home in Ignatius' theology just below (*Eph.* 20.1).[5] The term τῷ πάθει "by his suffering" also echoes Ignatius' special interests (see Introduction, 5.10), but the rest of the purpose clause ("that he might purify the water") may be traditional.[6]

Here baptism is subjected to a remarkable interpretation in the statement that Christ was baptized "that by his suffering he might purify the water." The view that τῷ πάθει means "by his experience (of baptism)" founders on the fact that πάθος always refers to the "passion" in Ignatius. Bartsch's emendation (τῷ πάτῳ "by the [Lord's] path" on the water)[7] seems awkward and unnecessary. It is generally recognized that the more or less magical idea that water was purified by Christ's baptism in the Jordan was known to both the orthodox[8] and the heterodox.[9] It is likely that the old Near Eastern mythology of the defeat of the dragon of the deep (alive in *Odes Sol.* 22.5; cf. 24.1–4) lies behind this theology. The idea is expressed in classical form by Cyril of Jerusalem who states that "to crush the heads of the dragon" (cf. Ps 73:13) Christ "descended into the waters and bound the strong one" so that we might receive the "power to tread upon serpents and scorpions" (*Catech.*

3.11).[10] The crushing of the "head of the dragon" of the deep still figured in the developed rites of the Syrian church for the blessing of the water or the benediction of the baptismal font. In the Byzantine rite the corresponding passage mentions "the opposing powers" (αἱ ἐναντίαι δυνάμεις). The exorcistic function of the rite is clear, and the link with Christ's baptism in the Jordan is explicit.[11] Ignatius' statement (and the material to which it is attached) may well reflect liturgical practice.

The connection between Christ's baptism and passion also seems to be traditional. It is apparently reflected in Luke 12:50 and Mark 10:38–39; and it may shine through small details in the Synoptic account of Christ's baptism.[12] Barnabas finds it relevant to inquire into the prophecies particularly "concerning the water and concerning the cross" (11.1). Justin has a collection of biblical testimonies in which the "wood" (the cross) and "water" (baptism) are connected in such a way that the former is thought of as energizing the latter (*Dial.* 86; cf. 138). In the *Sibylline Oracles* (8.244–47) the cross is said

---

5   Although οἰκονομία "plan" is not yet the synonym of "incarnation" in Ignatius, the two usages of it here frame the description of the soteriological events in *Eph.* 19 and so indicate that it already refers to the incarnation in particular as the "dispensation of divine purpose" (*LPGL s.v.* οἰκονομία C. 6, pp. 941–42).

6   Elze (*Untersuchungen*, 7) notes other uses of purpose clauses in formulaic materials (1 Pet 3:18; *Sm.* 1.1–2) and regards the clause here as belonging to the second of three stages of development. Bauer (*Ignatius*, 216) cites an interesting parallel from Clement Alex. *Eclog. proph.* 7.1: "and for this reason the savior was baptized . . . that he might purify all water for those being reborn" (καὶ διὰ τοῦτο ὁ σωτὴρ ἐβαπτίσατο . . . , ἵνα τοῖς ἀναγεννωμένοις τὸ πᾶν ὕδωρ ἁγιάσῃ). The clause may represent one more step in the history of tradition in which the reason for Jesus' baptism was being explored: he was baptized not to be purified but to purify (cf. *Sm.* 1.1).

7   Bartsch, *Gnostisches Gut*, 139.

8   Tertullian *Bapt.* 4.4; 9.2; *Adv. Jud.* 8.14; Clement

Alex. *Paed.* 1.6, 25.3; Methodius *Symp.* 9; Ps-Cyprian *Pasch. comput.* 22; Ephraem *Hymni de Epiphania* 10.2. Cf. Schlier, *Untersuchungen*, 44–48.

9   Clement Alex. *Exc. ex Theod.* 82.2; *Gos. Phil.* (NHC 2) 77,1–12. In *Paraph. Shem* (NHC 7) 32,5–18 whirlpools and flames rise up against the redeemer when he comes down to the water, but he emerges victorious (so it seems) and thus frees the Spirit imprisoned in creation "by the winds and the demons and the stars" and wipes out all "impurity" (ἀκαθαρσία). Later the treatise apparently criticizes ordinary baptism in water that is impure and filled with demons (37,14–25; 38,5–6; 45,20–23). In *Testim. Truth* (NHC 9) 30,20–28 Jesus alone sees the "power" (δύναμις) that comes down upon the Jordon river. Here, however, the Jordan is clearly symbolic of the body (30,30–32).

10 Cf. Daniélou, *Jewish Christianity*, 224–27. For still more parallels see *LPGL s.v.* δράκων 2.b, p. 386.

11 P. de Puniet, "Bénédictions de l'eau," *DACL* 2/1. 685–713 (for the text of the rite see pp. 697–98).

12 Oscar Cullmann, *Baptism in the New Testament* (SBT 1;

to "illuminate" the elect with water (cf. 8.310–17).[13] The connection could only have been strengthened by the mythology of the primeval dragon since conflict with the powers of darkness plays an especially important role with reference to the cross. Thus John Chrysostom (*Hom. in 1 Cor.* 24.4) will link Christ's resurrection with victory over the dragon of the deep. The connection between Christ's baptism and passion was also known in Gnostic circles. The *Gospel of Philip* ([NHC 2] 77,7–15) asserts not only that Jesus "made perfect the water of baptism" but also that he thereby "emptied death." It is, however, a matter of eliminating death, not of undergoing it.[14] Consequently the theme seems out of place, and Gaffron is surely right in suggesting that it is not "genuinely Gnostic" but stems from an older tradition.[15] The

underlying problem for a Gnostic is illuminated by Irenaeus' *(Adv. haer.* 1.21.2) observation on the Marcosians that they take Luke 12:50 and Mark 10:38 to refer not to the passion but to another baptism (the so-called redemption which has to do with "Christ" and "perfection") distinct from the first (which is connected with "the phenomenal Jesus" and "forgiveness of sins"). Ignatius has no such problem, and his overriding concern for the reality of the cross makes the link between the baptism and passion of Christ logical.

Naperville, IL: Allenson, 1958) 16–22.

13 Cf. Daniélou, *Jewish Christianity,* 277–78.

14 Jacques-É. Ménard, *L'évangile selon Philippe* (Paris: Letouzey & Ané, 1967) 226.

15 Hans-Georg Gaffron, *Studien zum koptischen Philippusevangelium unter besonderer Berücksichtigung der Sakramente* (Bonn: Rheinische Friedrich-Wilhelms-Universität, 1969) 120–23.

| Eschatological Warnings and Exhortations [11.1–19.3] | **19** | The Events of Salvation in Cosmic Perspective |

1 The virginity of Mary and her giving birth
eluded the ruler of this age, likewise also
the death of the Lord—three mysteries of
a cry which were done in the stillness of
God. 2/ How then was he revealed to the
aeons?
A star shone in heaven
brighter than all the stars,
and its light was ineffable,
and its novelty caused astonishment;
all the other stars
together with sun and moon
became a chorus for the star,
and it outshone them all with its light;
and there was perplexity (as to)
whence (came) this novelty (so)
unlike them.
3/ Thence was destroyed all magic,
and every bond vanished;
evil's ignorance was abolished,
the old kingdom perished,
God being revealed as human
to bring newness of eternal life,
and what had been prepared by God
had its beginning;
hence all things were disturbed
because the destruction of death was
being worked out.

■ **19** We must assume that the cosmic events described in this section were set forth by Ignatius to defend in greater detail the reality of their earthly components—the incarnation and passion. Ignatius attends primarily to the former here, but he was no doubt prepared to elaborate also on the latter.[1] For he indicates that he had more to say about such matters (*Eph.* 20.1). The themes discussed in this section are probably what Ignatius had in mind when he says elsewhere that he knew about angels and powers and that he thought such knowledge dangerous for the immature (*Tr.* 5). Consequently he and his opponents may well have stood on common ground when it came to such things. But since he also denies such knowledge the power to perfect (*Tr.* 5.2), he evaluated its importance differently; and we shall see that it was known to him in a form that is not yet markedly Gnostic.

A number of attempts have been made to read 19.2–3 ("a star shone . . .") as a hymn. Our translation follows the suggestion of Deichgräber that the passage breaks down into two sections of nine lines each.[2] Deichgräber also lists the following seventeen words as not otherwise

---

1   Ignatius knows that beings in heaven, on earth, and under the earth looked on as Christ was crucified (*Tr.* 9.1) and (so it seems) that he then descended into the underworld (*Mag.* 9.2). The former passage may contradict what is said in *Eph.* 19.1 about Christ's death. But it is more likely (as we shall see) that what eluded the evil one was not the crucifixion itself but an understanding of its implications.

2   Deichgräber, *Gotteshymnus*, 157–60. Deichgräber discusses other arrangements of the material by C. F. Burney, *The Aramaic Origin of the Fourth Gospel* (Oxford: Clarendon, 1922) 161–63; Ernst Loh-

meyer, *Kyrios Jesus: Eine Untersuchung zu Phil. 2,5–11* (Sitzungsberichte der Heidelberger Akademie der Wissenschaften, Philosophisch-historische Klasse 18/4; Heidelberg: Winter 1928) 64 (cf. R. P. Martin, *Carmen Christi* [Cambridge: University Press, 1967] 10–13); and Gottfried Schille, *Frühchristliche Hymnen* (Berlin: Evangelische Verlagsanstalt, 1965) 117–19.

found in Ignatius: star, shone, ineffable, novelty, sun, moon, outshone, perplexity, unlike, magic, vanish, evil, ignorance, eternal, disturbed, worked out, destruction. The variety of efforts (by Burney, Lohmeyer, Schille) to find a more precise versification suggests the difficulties involved, and Deichgräber is surely wise to settle for something less definite. On any division of lines, the first part (19.2) has rather uneven lengths[3] and often seems too awkward for a hymn. The second part (19.3) with its greater balance of lines at the beginning[4] and its figures of speech (chiasmus,[5] homoeoteleuton[6]) may seem more promising but may also reflect Ignatius' own rhetorical methods (see on *Eph.* 7.2). In any event, the last three lines of the section are again more shapeless. The list of peculiar words is impressive. But Brown has shown that the average rate of the appearance per line of peculiar words in Ignatius varies widely: .39 (*Eph.*); .34 (*Mag.*); .28 (*Tr.*); .46 (*Rom.*); .31 (*Phd.*); .25 (*Sm.*); .65 (*Pol.*).[7] It is evident that distinctive subject matter (especially in *Rom.* and *Pol.*) brings a dramatic change in vocabulary. Moreover, although the nine Greek lines (in the Funk/Bihlmeyer text) of the presumed hymn have seventeen words not otherwise used by Ignatius, the twelve Greek lines of *Rom.* 5 (clearly no hymn) contain twenty such words[8]—almost as high a proportion. It should also be noted that one important expression in *Eph.* 19.2 (χορὸς ἐγένετο "became a chorus") reflects Ignatius' own usage (*Eph.* 4.2; *Rom.* 2.2). It seems best, then, to regard *Eph.* 19.2–3 as a product of Ignatius' rhetorical methods and the distinctive subject matter.

The study of the substance of *Eph.* 19 has been dominated by the detailed analysis of Schlier, who emphasized the extent to which Ignatius reflects the Gnostic myth of redemption here.[9] Schlier found described in the passage (a) the hidden descent of the redeemer, his birth and death (19.1), (b) his glorious ascent as a star (19.2), and (c) the results of his epiphany on earth (19.3). Sources for parallels included especially the *Ascension of Isaiah*, the *Odes of Solomon*, the Mandaean scriptures, and a variety of Valentinian sources. Schlier recognized that the themes did not always combine in the literature precisely as expected, but he assumed that the anomalies were the result of dislocation of elements in the original pattern.

If we follow Schlier, we must read *Eph.* 19 as moving in simple linear fashion from the birth and death of Christ to his ascent. That is dubious as we shall see. We must also assume that when the theme of the star (or the disturbance of the powers) is connected with the redeemer's descent, this is the result of its migration from an earlier setting in which it was linked with his ascent. A number of treatises from Nag Hammadi now cast doubt on this solution. To be sure, the disturbance of the powers is described in the context of the ascension (*Ap. Jas.* [NHC 1] 15,9–20); but it also occurs in connection with the descent into the underworld (*Great Pow.* [NHC 6] 41,14–42,23); and more significantly for our purposes, it is sometimes part of the account of the coming of the redeemer even in documents that also teach his hidden descent (*Treat. Seth* [NHC 7] 51,24–31; 55,30–57,2; *Trim. Prot.* [NHC 13] 43,4–44,29; 49,9–20; cf. *Gos. Truth* [NHC 1] 26,4–23; Irenaeus *Adv. haer.* 1.30.11). The theme seems equally at home in all these contexts.

Schlier's perspective on his sources also calls for revision. He was right to emphasize the *Ascension of Isaiah* (9–11) as providing a significant early parallel to *Eph.* 19, but that writing should not be regarded as Gnostic in any full sense of the term.[10] A similar reevaluation of the Christianity of the *Odes of Solomon* has already been noted (see on *Eph.* 17.1). We are dealing, then, with develop-

---

3   The number of syllables per line in the division accepted by Deichgräber is as follows: 9, 8, 11, 13, 8, 9, 10, 16, 18.

4   Note the number of syllables (especially in the first six lines): 11, 9, 10, 12, 11, 11, 17, 10, 14.

5   "Loosed was all magic, and every bond vanished" (ἐλύετο πᾶσα μαγεία καὶ πᾶς δεσμὸς ἠφανίζετο).

6   Ἠφανίζετο, καθῃρεῖτο, διεφθείρετο (and later, συνεκινεῖτο). Length of lines and homoeoteleuton suggest that κακίας ("of evil") be taken with what follows rather than with what precedes.

7   Brown, *Authentic Writings*, 8. The statistics are based on the Funk/Bihlmeyer edition. They measure words "peculiar to Ignatius of all the Apostolic Fathers."

8   Sea, night, day, bound, ten, leopards, of soldiers, company, given gratuities, worse, mistreatment, devour, entice, force, indulge, be envious, wrenching, mangling, grinding, punishments.

9   Schlier, *Untersuchungen*, 5–81.

10   Daniélou, *Jewish Christianity*, 14. Naively docetic passages do occur (9.13; 11.7–9; 11.17).

ments in eschatological and cosmological speculation that lie at the base of many later theologies—orthodox and Gnostic alike.

A partial revision of Schlier's view was undertaken by Bartsch. It was the latter's concern to deemphasize the mythological elements in Ignatius and to locate the bishop's Gnosticism almost exclusively in his doctrine of God.[11] Thus Bartsch argued that in *Eph.* 19 there is no account of the redeemer's ascent (even though the description of the star was ultimately derived from ascent language) but only of a sign in heaven that marked the birth of Christ on earth. Bartsch perhaps limited too severely the mythological element here, but his view of the text is on the whole the more acceptable.

We may assume that fundamental to the theme of the hiddenness of the events of salvation (19.1) was a sense of awe at the noiseless entrance of divinity into the world (cf. Cyril Jer. *Catech.* 12.9) and a feeling of wonder that the pride of power unexpectedly met its match in apparent weakness and defeat. Ignatius' emphasis on the reality of Christ's suffering may be taken as an extension of that attitude. Complications arise when the role of the evil one in such transactions becomes a matter for speculation. A passage in Paul already seems to refer to demonic powers who unwittingly work their own defeat by crucifying the Lord of glory (1 Cor 2:6–8). They knew something but not enough. Why?

Two answers recommended themselves in the early period. (a) The evil one knew from OT prophecy that the Christ was coming but was uncertain whether Jesus was the one.[12] (b) The powers did not know with whom they were dealing when they persecuted Jesus since he eluded detection when he descended through the heavens.[13] Ignatius' language about the "economy" (*Eph.* 18.2; 20.1) and the "mysteries" (19.1) suggests a possible reference to the hidden purposes of God in the OT period.[14] But reminiscences of the language of hidden descent seem to be stronger. Thus Ignatius' reflections on the star (19.2–3) emphasize the cosmic dimensions of the event. And the treatment of the birth of Christ as miraculous and mysterious fits such a context. A noteworthy example is an interpolation[15] of the *Ascension of Isaiah* (11.2–22): we are told just after the description of Christ's painless (and almost non-physical) birth (11.2–15)[16] that "this was hidden from all the heavens and all the princes and every god of this world" (11.16).[17] Yet Ignatius does not actually describe the descent, and it is possible (c) that we are dealing with a more modest form of the theme in which the emphasis is on the events of salvation that take place here on earth and are hidden from the powers of darkness until the resurrection or ascension (cf. Justin *Dial.* 36.6). Apart from its present context the interpolation in the *Ascension of Isaiah* hardly says more. The text stresses the fact that Joseph continued as Mary's husband externally, telling no one of the virgin birth, and that the birth itself took place while he and Mary were alone. Similarly, in an interpretation of Ignatius' words, Origen (*Hom. in Luc.* 6) says that thanks to Joseph, Mary passed as a married woman and so escaped the notice of Satan. Jerome (*Comm. in Matt.* 1.18) repeats the point. Along the same lines, Hippolytus says that Jesus appeared in lowly human guise at his

11 Bartsch, *Gnostisches Gut,* 140–59.
12 Clement Alex. *Eclog. proph.* 53.2; cf. Justin *Apol.* 1.54–60; Irenaeus *Adv. haer.* 5.26.2; Hippolytus *Comm. in Dan.* 1.5. Clement adds that the demons once suspected Solomon of being the Lord (cf. Justin *Dial.* 36.5–6). *Treat. Seth* (NHC 7) 63,11–12 says that Solomon himself thought that he was the Christ. The role of Solomon as wise man and magician must lie behind this line of thought.
13 Cf. *Asc. Is.* 9.15; 10.7–31; 11.16; Irenaeus *Adv. haer.* 1.23.3; *Dem.* 84; Tertullian *Anim.* 24.4; *Epist. apost.* 13; Epiphanius *Pan.* 21.2.4; *Act. Thom.* 143; *Pistis Sophia* 7; *Treat. Seth* (NHC 7) 56,22–57,2; *Trim. Prot.* (NHC 13) 49,9–20. In the *Ascension of Isaiah* and related sources the seven heavens do not have planetary significance and are inhabited by more or less benevolent angels (Daniélou, *Jewish Christianity,*

174–79). Nevertheless, the descent is hidden from most of them—presumably because otherwise the secret could not be kept from the evil powers below in the firmament and air (cf. *Asc. Is.* 9.14–15; 10.9–11).
14 Cf. Rom 16:25; Col 1:26; Eph 3:9; Hippolytus *Comm. in Dan.* 1.5; Eusebius *Eccl. theolog.* 1.20.30; 2.18).
15 J. Flemming and H. Duensing, "The Ascension of Isaiah," in HSW, *NT Apocrypha* 2.643.
16 For early parallels see Daniélou, *Jewish Christianity,* 214–16.
17 The Flemming/Duensing translation (see n. 15) is used here and in what follows.

baptism ἵνα λάθῃ τοῦ δράκοντος τὸ πανούργημα "so that he might elude the wickedness of the dragon" (*Theoph.* 4). And in speaking of Jesus' trial, the *Sibylline Oracles* (8.292–93) predict that Jesus "will remain silent" (σιγήσει) to prevent any from knowing who he is so that he might speak to the dead.

The three mysteries—Mary's virginity and her child-bearing "likewise also" (ὁμοίως καί) the Lord's death—clearly break down into two groups and as such correspond to the birth and the baptism-as-death at the end of the previous section (18.2).[18] Thus there can be no emphasis on the number three. Elsewhere the expression ὁμοίως καί (*Eph.* 16.2; *Pol.* 5.1) emphatically affirms the relevance of what has just been said to another item. Thus Ignatius is not simply listing the events of Jesus' life in chronological order; and if it seems best, we are free to think that he goes on in 19.2–3 to comment on the birth of Christ in particular. Three things favor this solution: (a) According to *Eph.* 20.1 Ignatius regards himself as just "getting into" (ἠρξάμην) his exposition of the divine "plan"; and it is likely that he began at the beginning with the incarnation, especially since he links the birth of Christ and the divine "plan" so closely in *Eph.* 18.2. (b) The expression "God being revealed as human" in *Eph.* 19.3 may have in view the earthly epiphany of Christ as a whole, but surely refers to the incarnation in particular (cf. *Mag.* 8.2); in any event, the present tense of the participle indicates that Christ's manifestation in human form is thought of as contemporaneous with the shattering of the powers of evil; and such a statement seems out of place if Christ has just been described as having ascended and left this world behind.[19] (c) The tradition about the star is more securely tied (as we shall see) with the Christmas story. Yet the birth and the passion were clearly linked in Ignatius' mind, and here the older part of the *Ascension of Isaiah* may help us fill out the picture that Ignatius has left incomplete; for after the future descent of the Son is announced in heaven (9.12–13), the angel says, "and the god of that world will stretch forth his hand against the Son and they will lay hands on him and crucify him on a tree without knowing who he is; so his descent, as thou wilt see, is hidden from the heavens so that it remains unperceived who he is" (9.14–15).

Since such legends of Christ's birth are naively docetic and were soon appealed to by Gnostics (cf. Tertullian *Carn. Christ.* 23.2–3), it seems at first sight difficult to account for Ignatius' choice of themes in combatting the false teachers. But it must be remembered that *any* appeal to the birth of Jesus from Mary represents a threat to a theology that is consciously docetic. According to the apocryphal letter of the Corinthians to Paul, for example, the heretics deny "that the Lord came in the flesh" and "that he was born of Mary" (*Acta Pauli* 8.1.14); and Paul's rebuttal of these views is that "Christ Jesus was born from Mary of the seed of David, when the Holy Spirit was sent to her out of heaven from the Father" (*3 Cor.* 5).[20] Both Ignatius (*Eph.* 18.2) and the *Ascension of Isaiah* (11.2) agree with *3 Corinthians* that Mary was of the house of David. This (non-biblical) view, which was widely accepted by orthodox writers in the early period,[21] tied Jesus firmly to the Jewish people and no doubt effectively curbed overly docetic views of his being. That the virginity of Mary in itself did not necessarily serve as a strong weapon in the hands of Gnostics is shown by the Ophite discussion in Irenaeus (*Adv. haer.* 1.30.12). Here Mary's virginity is treated merely as giving assurance that the human Jesus was pure and capable of receiving the non-material Christ when it descended upon him. By insisting on the virgin birth to explain the being of Jesus as the Christ, Ignatius is making a vigorous anti-docetic statement. Against this background, the theme of Christ's hidden descent or hidden ministry may well have served a more obvious purpose in orthodox than in docetic circles. For incarnation puts the redeemer even more securely in Satan's realm and under his power; and thus it is all the more necessary to resort to the theme of Christ's hiddenness to

---

18 The twin theme of "birth and parturition" was suggested by Isa 7:14 ("a virgin shall conceive and bear a son"), as Tertullian (*Carn. Christ.* 23.1–2) indicates. The theme is also connected by Tertullian with a prophecy about the one "who bore yet did not bear" (23.6). This saying is much repeated in later sources, and the thought is reflected in *Asc. Is.* 11.13–14. Cf. Alfred Resch, *Agrapha* (TU 30; Leipzig: Hinrichs, 1906) 305–6.

19 Cf. Bartsch, *Gnostisches Gut*, 141, 150–51.

20 For this correspondence see Michel Testuz, *Papyrus Bodmer X–XII* (Cologne and Geneva: Bibliotheca Bodmeriana, 1959) 9–45.

21 Walter Bauer, *Das Leben Jesu im Zeitalter der neutestamentlichen Apokryphen* (Tübingen: Mohr [Siebeck], 1909) 13–15; cf. Grant, *Ignatius*, 48.

explain how his mission could have been accomplished.

Not unexpectedly the theme of Christ's hiddenness intersects that of the ἡσυχία "stillness" or "silence" of God (ἡσυχία "stillness" is synonymous with σιγή "silence," as *Eph.* 15.2 shows). This is usually taken either as a reference to the mysterious purposes of God brought to fulfillment in God's good time or as another indication of a growing emphasis on God's transcendence in Ignatius' theology. The latter in turn has been traced to the influence of Gnosticism.[22] Both solutions require us to take ἐπράχθη ("were done") as having to do with things effected within the purpose or sphere of the divine. But the use of the same verb in *Mag.* 11 (πραχθέντα) and *Sm.* 4.2 (ἐπράχθη) to refer to the same events under discussion here suggests that Ignatius is speaking of the birth and passion as historical events not openly commented on by God. "In the stillness (ἐν ἡσυχία) of God," then, means "while God remained silent" (just as a woman is counselled to learn ἐν ἡσυχία "while keeping silent" in 1 Tim 2:11).[23] Yet as in *Eph.* 15.2, these deeds without words speak volumes. With this in mind the paradoxical expression "three mysteries of a cry" and the antithesis between such revelations and the silence of God become intelligible. The unheralded events of salvation cry out their meaning to those who are able to grasp their significance. There is no need to try to locate cries of (say) Mary or Jesus uttered in connection with each of the three events.

■ **19.2** The question that follows apparently means, "If the events of salvation were hid from the evil one, how then did he and his hosts (the aeons)[24] come to level their animosity at Christ?" What arouses the envy of the powers in the interpolation of the *Ascension of Isaiah* 11.18–19 are the signs and wonders performed by Jesus. Ignatius finds a still earlier cause for their alarm in events at the time of the incarnation. The star indicated to the powers that something threatening was afoot, but they did not assess its significance accurately since they were unaware of the startling miracles that surrounded the birth of Christ. Had they known of them, presumably they would have tried more resolutely to cut Christ's mission short, and later they would not have been so foolish as to crucify him and so seal their own doom or let him enter the underworld and harrow hell. To be sure, Ignatius' question may be taken another way. Since he does not elsewhere use the term "aeons" to refer to evil powers (see on *Eph.* 8.1), the question may mean, "If the events of salvation were so completely hid, how then did the world (aeons)[25] learn that the time of salvation was at hand?" But such a question seems less natural in this context. For the description of the star concentrates on its effect in the heavens and the disturbance that it caused there. Moreover, the implied question of the stars—"Whence this novelty so unlike [us]"—is reminiscent of similar questions asked by the powers at Christ's ascent to the world above[26] or descent to the underworld[27] and presumably appropriate also at his descent into this world.[28] Ignatius, to be sure, does not explicitly present the star as marking Christ's downward path, but it can readily be seen that the parallel events—the hidden birth and the mysterious appearance of the star—either presuppose a unified descent theme or soon

---

22 Schlier, *Untersuchungen*, 27; cf. *Mag.* 8.2.

23 If any deeper background for the expression seems required, the relevant parallel is Wis 18:14–15 where we are told that all was in stillness as the divine word descended from heaven. Cf. Hans Lietzmann, *The Beginnings of the Christian Church* (New York: Scribner, 1937) 323–24; Allen Cabaniss, "Wisdom 18:14f.: An Early Christmas Text," *VC* 10 (1956) 97–102.

24 Although the word αἰῶνες elsewhere in Ignatius means "ages" (see on *Eph.* 8.1), it seems more likely to refer to supernatural beings here. This use of the term need not be Gnostic. "Lord of lords, God of gods, King of kings, and God of aeons" (τῶν αἰώνων) seems to be the original text of an old section of *1 Enoch* (9.4). See R. H. Charles, *The Book of Enoch or 1 Enoch* (Oxford: Clarendon, 1912) 20 (cf. BAG *s.v.*

αἰών 3, p. 27). The term later occurs predominantly in Gnostic sources, but not exclusively (cf. Ps-Ignatius *Tr.* 5; *Const. Apost.* 8.12.8). It is used of evil powers in particular in *Act. Phil.* 137.

25 For this use of the term see 1 Tim 1:17; *1 Clem.* 35.3; 55.6; 61.2 (Tob 13:7, 11). Cf. BAG *s.v.* αἰών 4, p. 27.

26 Justin *Dial.* 36.6; Irenaeus *Dem.* 84; *Asc. Is.* 11.24–29; *Pistis Sophia* 11.

27 *Gos. Nicod.* 17.3–11; *Great Pow.* (NHC 6) 41,14–42,15. Melito (frg. 13) says that at the crucifixion creation was troubled and cried out, "What is this new mystery?"

28 Cf. *Trim. Prot.* (NHC 13) 43,4–44,29. Here the powers say, "We are at a loss" (43,28).

lead over to it.

As we have indicated above, the theme of the disturbance of the powers stands side by side with that of Christ's hidden descent in other writings of the period. Schlier worked with too simple a scheme in associating such disturbance primarily with the ascent. It should also be noted that he offered no example in which a star marks the path of the ascending redeemer. The best parallels speak only of light and glory. The star of Matt 2:1–12, then, still presents the parallel most relevant to *Eph.* 19.2. But Ignatius reaches back to a more mythological version of the account. And the same tradition has apparently left its mark also on the frequently cited parallel from Clement Alex. *Exc. ex Theod.* 74, where the star is closely associated with the descending redeemer and referred to by language highly reminiscent of *Eph.* 19.2–3: it is "a strange and new star" (ξένος ἀστὴρ καὶ καινός); it destroys "the old astral order" (καταλύων τὴν πάλαιαν ἀστροθεσίαν); it "shines with a new light" (καινῷ φωτὶ . . . λαμπόμενος). It is arbitrary to think that this must originally have reflected the language of ascent. Daniélou has shown that these and other texts are held together by what looks like a very old exegetical tradition.[29] The vitality of the tradition of the star is also suggested by *Orac. Sib.* 12.30–33, which links the star (appearing in midday like the sun) with the hidden advent of the Word of the Highest. The brilliant light of the *Protevangelium of James* (19.2) which appears in the cave where Christ was born may likewise belong here.

What then is the relation between the star and the theme of the disturbance of the powers? Perhaps Ignatius has taken a fragment of a descent or ascent theme (the disturbance) and under the influence of the Epiphany star transformed it into a heavenly event parallel to the birth of Christ. But it seems at least as likely that the theme of the disturbance of the powers developed first in connection with the star and later came to be applied in other contexts.[30] The divine sign that marked the beginning of the hidden career of Christ came to be replaced by the hidden descent of Christ himself.

In any event, the emergence also of a chorus of lesser stars was natural enough. The wise men in the *Protevangelium of James* "saw a very great star shining among these stars and obscuring them from sight" (21.2)—though this passage is missing from the (earlier) form of the text represented by the Bodmer papyrus.[31] Early Christian art was also to supply the Epiphany star with a chorus of other stars.[32] It is tempting to try to account for the presence of sun and moon along with the stars as an interpretation of Joseph's dream (Gen 37:9) in Messianic terms. But the passage is hardly ever so employed.[33] Moreover, sun, moon, and stars often appear together as a collective designation for the heavenly bodies.[34] A frequently cited parallel from Origen that refers to their worship of God shows that they were conceived of as living beings (*Cels.* 8.67; cf. Philo *Opif. mund.* 73; *Plant.* 12) but hardly accounts for the more or less negative evaluation of them implicit in Ignatius' remarks about their surprise and disturbance. It may be easiest to regard the chorus of heavenly bodies as an elaboration intended to describe the role of the aeons more dramatically. There was good reason for making the connection. In *1 Enoch* (72.3; 75.1, 3; 82.10–20) the stars are thought of as having angels set over them; and in Clement Alex. (*Exc. ex Theod.* 70) they are said to express the influence of the "powers." In *1 Enoch* (18.12–19.3; 21.1–10) the stars and especially the planets (closely associated with fallen angels) have a place of torment prepared for them. In the Valentinian source the "powers," both good and evil, are said to strive together

29 Jean Daniélou, "The Star of Jacob," *Primitive Christian Symbols* (Baltimore: Helicon, 1964) 102–23.

30 It may be that the "disturbance" of Herod and "all Jerusalem with him" (Matt 2:1–12) represents an application on the historical plane of the disturbance of the stars. For, as the *First Apocalypse of James* will say, Jerusalem "is the dwelling place of many archons" ([NHC 5] 25,18–19). Herod's unsuccessful effort to slay Christ may also mirror the failure of the evil powers to have their way with the child.

31 Michel Testuz, *Papyrus Bodmer V* (Cologne and Geneva: Bibliotheca Bodmeriana, 1958) 112.

32 H. Leclercq, "Astres," *DACL* 1/2. 3016–18 (with figures 1047, 1050, and 1051 in particular).

33 Daniélou, *Jewish Christianity*, 220.

34 BAG *s.v.* ἀστήρ, p. 117. Cf. Plato *Leg.* 10, 898d; Dio Chrysostom *Or.* 30.28; Epictetus *Diss.* 2.16.32; 3.13.16.

and jointly to catch the world in the net of fate which the great star shatters (Clement Alex. *Exc. ex Theod.* 69–75). Somewhere in all this is the background to Ignatius' conception of the stars as more or less malevolent powers.

■ **19.3** What follows allows us to be somewhat more precise. We are told that with the appearance of the new star all magic, every bond, ignorance, and the old kingdom begin to break up. It is presumably the heavenly bodies that are here said to lose their grip on humankind. (a) Astrology and magic were closely associated in popular culture (cf. Apuleius *Golden Ass* 2.5, 11–12), and both contributed to the plain person's sense of being oppressed by occult powers. The Eastern magi in particular were conceived of as devoted to both,[35] and it is likely that Matthew represented a common view of Christians when he associated the tradition of the star with the subordination of the magi to the new faith. Thus Tertullian (*Idol.* 9) finds it significant that the magi first announced the birth of Christ and explains in this connection that the fallen angels (of Gen 6 and *1 Enoch* 6) discovered astrology and introduced magic. Similarly Origen (*Cels.* 1.60) traces the weakening of the demonic powers responsible for magic to the appearance of the Epiphany star. And Clement of Alexandria (*Eclog. proph.* 53) refers to the demons who are uncertain about Christ's identity as the fallen angels of *1 Enoch* who introduced astrology and other occult arts. The parallels again suggest the importance of the apocalyptic tradition for the development of the themes in *Eph.* 19. (b) The expression "every bond" (δεσμός) may refer in this context either to magical spells[36] or more generally to the constraints of evil powers[37] or of fate.[38] That ethical dimensions are not necessarily absent from the discussion is shown by *Phd.* 8.1, where "every bond" that is removed must refer to division and strife and where the malevolent influence of evil powers is no doubt presupposed (cf. *Eph.* 13.1).[39] It may be significant that the theme follows so soon on the semi-credal material of *Eph.* 18.2; for Justin (*Dial.* 85.2–3) associates such formulae with the name of the Son of God by which demons are to be exorcized, and he opposes this rite to the incense and "spells" (καταδέσμοι) of pagan and Jewish exorcists.[40] It seems fair to say that Ignatius reflects the theology that lay behind such practices and that here popular magic is being resisted in the name of a higher magic. (c) The term "ignorance" (ἄγνοια) is used with some frequency in early sources to describe the human state apart from God's grace.[41] And it appears with even more dualistic overtones in Gnostic or Gnosticizing contexts.[42] (d) The consciousness of standing at the end of the old era ruled by evil powers is deeply rooted in the tradition (cf. Matt 12:22–30; Luke 11:14–23)[43] and appears highly dramatized also in Gnostic contexts (cf. *Great Pow.* [NHC 6]

---

35 Joseph Bidez and Franz Cumont, *Les mages hellénisés* (2 vols.; Paris: Les belles lettres, 1938) 1. 131–50; 193–98; 2. 243.

36 Cf. Plato *Resp.* 2, 364c; *PGM* 4.296, 336; Plotinus *Enn.* 4.4.40; Iamblichus *De myst.* 3.27.

37 Cf. Luke 13:16; Hippolytus *Comm. in Dan.* 4.33; *Odes Sol.* 21.2; 25.1; 42.16; *Trim. Prot.* (NHC 13) 41,4–5; 44,14–17.

38 *Ap. John* 72,2–12 (Walter C. Till, *Die gnostischen Schriften des koptischen Papyrus Berolinensis 8502* [TU 60; Berlin: Akademie-Verlag, 1955] 184).

39 The verb λύω ("remove") used in *Phd.* 8.1 is regularly used in connection with the breaking of the bonds of evil powers (cf. Luke 13:16; Hippolytus *Comm. in Dan.* 4.33; Iamblichus *De myst.* 3.27). In *Eph.* 19.3 the verb is ἠφανίζετο ("vanished"), but it represents a stylistic variant of the preceding ἐλύετο ("destroyed"). The verb λύω is also found in *Eph.* 13.1, where it is a matter of destroying Satan's power through prayer.

40 In later Christian magic a star as well as the main events in the life of Christ figure on the amulets involved (cf. Peterson, ΕΙΣ ΘΣΟΣ, 93–94).

41 Cf. 1 Cor 15:34; Eph 4:18; Acts 17:30; 1 Pet 1:14; Justin *Apol.* 1.61.10; *Test. Levi* 18.9; *Test. Gad* 5.7; *Odes Sol.* 7.21; 18.11; 31.2.

42 Irenaeus *Adv. haer.* 1.15.2; *Corp. Herm.* 1.27; 7.1; 10.8; 13.7; *Mart. Andr. pr.* 16; *Act. Thom.* 97; *Act. Ioann.* 107; cf. Plutarch *De Isid.* 46, 369e. For the broad stream of late antique religiosity that lies behind this term see Paulsen, *Studien*, 179–80.

43 Ignatius' characterization of the "kingdom" of evil as "old" is not found elsewhere but represents a natural development in a tradition where the old and new are regularly contrasted (cf. Matt 9:16–17; Rom 7:6). Ignatius' reference here to "the *newness* of . . . life" may reflect Rom 6:4, which in turn is closely linked to a statement about "the *old* human being" (Rom 6:6).

42,13–15; *Trim. Prot.* [NHC 13] 43,4–44,29). For Ignatius the disturbance of the powers culminates in the victory over death (cf. 1 Cor 15:23–26).

The force of the passage as a whole is well illustrated by a frequently cited parallel from Irenaeus (*Adv. haer.* 2.20.3; cf. 1.15.2), who traces to the Lord's passion the destruction of death, error, corruption, and ignorance and the manifestation of life, truth, and incorruption. Ignatius focusses on the birth of Christ with its marvellous signs rather than the passion. But he clearly notes near the end of 19.3 that the star marked only the "beginning" of the fulfillment of God's purpose. All of the preceding verbs are imperfects and should be understood as inceptives—magic "began to be destroyed," every bond "began to vanish," and so forth.

Ignatius merely makes this more explicit with his remark that what God had prepared "had its beginning." He probably would have gone on to stress the passion as the culmination of God's plan (cf. *Sm.* 5.3), though he was also conscious of the fact that Satan's power had not even yet been completely destroyed (*Eph.* 13.1).

To conclude, *Eph.* 19.1–3 represents esoteric teaching based primarily on apocalyptic tradition enriched by legends about the birth of Christ. Something like it lay behind later developments in both orthodox and heterodox theology, but it is exploited by Ignatius with a view to undercutting docetic heresy. As an outgrowth of apocalyptic thinking the passage forms a fitting conclusion to the eschatological warnings that began in *Eph.* 11.1.

20   Closing and Farewell

1   **If Jesus Christ counts me worthy through your prayers, and it be the (divine) will, I will give you in the second document which I am going to write you further explanation of the (divine) plan which I was getting into regarding the new human being, Jesus Christ, having to do with faith in him and love of him, with his suffering and resurrection; 2/ particularly if the Lord reveals anything to me. All of you, severally and in common, continue to come together in grace, as individuals, in one faith and in Jesus Christ, who according to the flesh was of the family of David, the son of a human and son of God, that you may obey the bishop and the presbytery with undistracted mind, breaking one bread, which is the medicine of immortality, the antidote preventing death, but leading to life in Jesus Christ forever.**

21

1/ **I am your expiation and that of those whom you sent for God's honor to Smyrna from where I write to you, giving thanks to the Lord, loving Polycarp as I do also you. Remember me, as Jesus Christ remembers also you. 2/ Pray for the church in Syria from where I am being led off in bonds to Rome (being the least of the believers there) since I was thought worthy to serve God's honor. Farewell in God the Father and in Jesus Christ, our common hope.**

The letter ends with two conventional items: (a) a closing statement to the body of the letter (20.1–2) and (b) concluding formulae (21.1–2). The closing statement serves here, as it does in Hellenistic letters generally, "as a means of finalizing the principal motivation for writing" and "as a means of forming a bridge to further communication."[1] Ignatius avoids the most hackneyed formulae[2] but reflects the tendency to make "references to writing" at this point[3] (he says that he intends to write a second document to them)[4] and to employ conditional clauses (especially the future more vivid, as here) to remind recipients of an important responsibility previously touched on.[5] Another common feature of closing statements appears in 20.2. If we follow Zahn's reading

---

1   White, *Form and Function,* 42.

2   Cf. ibid., 45–51.

3   Ibid., 24–25.

4   The word βιβλίδιον "document" may describe any small writing of indefinite form (cf. Lucian *Alex.* 53; Plutarch *Cimon* 12.3; *Caes.* 65.1; Polybius 23.2.5; *Herm. Vis.* 2.1.3; 2.4.1). In the papyri it regularly refers to petitions in the form of letters to the authorities (James Hope Moulton and George Milligan, *The Vocabulary of the Greek Testament* [London and New York: Hodder and Stoughton, 1914–28] 110). It is the diminutive of βιβλίον which is also sometimes used of letters (1 Macc 1:44; Suidas *s.v.*).

5   White, *Form and Function,* 26–29. Ignatius reminds the Ephesians here of his need for their prayers (cf. *Eph.* 1.2; 5.2; 11.2) and no doubt also thereby indirectly reminds them of his request for assistance which in turn is connected in his mind with the question of his worthiness (cf. *Eph.* 2–3).

of the text,[6] we have an exhortation in which a major theme of the letter—the need to come together in unity (cf. *Eph.* 4–5; 13)—is recalled. There are often found in closing statements of Hellenistic letters set "expressions urging responsibility" which call for appropriate response to the message of the communication.[7] Although once again Ignatius avoids the conventional formulae, it seems likely that his exhortation represents a functional equivalent of them. In any event, we have examples in other letters of imperatives in comparable locations.[8]

■ **20.1** Ignatius hopes to use the second writing that he promises the Ephesians for the purpose of completing his discussion of the "economy"—the divine "plan"—manifested in Jesus Christ, "the new human being." It appears likely (as we have seen) that having discussed the incarnation (*Eph.* 19.1–3) he intended to go on to describe the significance of Christ's death and resurrection (which he in fact mentions here, though somewhat vaguely). It is also likely that he had in mind esoteric knowledge of the kind found in his discussion of the incarnation. If so, we understand why he hoped for further "revelation" on the subject (Zahn's reading seems appropriate also from this point of view). The expression "new human being" by which Ignatius summarizes his view of redemption also appears in Eph 2:15 and 4:24. It is evidently closely related to the expression "perfect human being" which

both writers also use (see *Sm.* 4.2 and Eph 4:13).[9] Such terminology evidently takes us a step beyond Paul's "last Adam" or "second human being" (1 Cor 15:45, 47) and, in presupposing an identification of the redeemer with the totality of the redeemed, represents a development that can be richly illustrated from Gnostic sources.[10] But views of Christ as representative humanity had a variety of possible roots (widely diffused notions about God as the Makroanthropos, speculation in many branches of Judaism on the figure of Adam, the interpretation of the image of God in Hellenistic Judaism), and it is not necessary to regard the Gnostic development of the theme as more than a special form of it.[11] In any event, Ignatius regards the divine plan as having to do (subjectively) with[12] faith and love[13] and (objectively) with Christ's passion and resurrection. These are standard anti-docetic themes in Ignatius.

■ **20.2** Although 20.2 (as we have seen) repeats the main point of the letter, comment is required on a number of points. (a) For the expression "as individuals" (ἐξ ὀνόματος) see *Pol.* 4.2 and 8.2 where it has to do with recognizing people individually "by name." Ignatius strongly emphasizes such recognition as an important element in the unity he seeks. (b) The formula describing Christ is again related to the tradition known to us from Rom 1:3. Ignatius alludes to this tradition frequently and in doing so alternates between a reference to David's

---

6 GL read ἀποκαλύψῃ ὅτι (if the Lord "reveals" to me "that" you come together). A and the Arabic reflect the same text but recognize its difficulty. Zahn (*Ignatius*, 568) emends this to ἀποκαλύψῃ τι (Theodoret reads εἴ τι "if indeed" and Gelasius treats συνέρχεσθε "come together" as an imperative) noting that the manuscript would have Ignatius base a revelation on what would surely be a human communication concerning the situation in Ephesus. It is also improbable that Ignatius would make the writing of a second letter contingent on hearing good news or that he would admit the situation in Ephesus to be as precarious as this formulation would suggest (cf. *Eph.* 6.2). And I would add that not only is the imperative ("come together") more in harmony with epistolary conventions (as we shall see) but also that similar exhortations occur in the closing of other letters of Ignatius (cf. *Mag.* 13; *Tr.* 12.2–3). (To take ὅτι as "because" yields improbable sense.)

7 White, *Form and Function*, 43–44, 46–48.

8 Cf. *P.Oxy.* 3.118; *P.Teb.* 1.58.

9 For the "new human being" and "perfect human being" in reference to the incarnate one see Hippolytus *Contra haer. Noet.* 17.

10 Schlier, *Untersuchungen*, 88 (n. 2).

11 See on *Sm.* 1.2. Cf. Joachim Jeremias, "Ἀδάμ," *TDNT* 1 (1964) 364–67; Carsten Colpe, "ὁ υἱὸς τοῦ ἀνθρώπου," *TDNT* 8 (1872) 400–77.

12 "Having to do with" translates Greek ἐν ("in"). I take the preposition to indicate vaguely the major themes associated with Christ and salvation in Ignatius' mind.

13 The Greek may mean, "having to do with his [Christ's] faith and his love." But elsewhere in Ignatius faith and love are always the religious affections of people.

"seed" (*Eph.* 18.2; *Rom.* 7.3) and his "race" (*Eph.* 20.2; *Tr.* 9.1; *Sm.* 1.1). Our present passage, including as it does the expression "according to the flesh," is closer than *Eph.* 18.2 to Paul; on the other hand, no mention is made of the spirit by way of antithesis. That lack is immediately made up, however, by Ignatius' juxtaposition of the titles "son of a human" and "son of God." These he apparently takes as pointing to Christ's human and divine origins respectively. Here is the first clear use of the title "son of a human" ("son of man") in this sense. No doubt the change of meaning is linked with the shift from eschatological to incarnational categories that we have met before in Ignatius (see on *Eph.* 18.2). Thus the expression "son of a human and son of God" represents an alternative formulation of the christological paradox (*Eph.* 7.2; cf. Tertullian *Adv. Prax.* 2.1). The fact that the title "son of God" is used in this context suggests that it refers to Christ before the incarnation and thus presupposes a correlative use of the terms Father and Son as designations of relations within the Godhead.[14] But in comparable contexts the title "Son" has no such significance (see on *Sm.* 1.1). It is the antithesis, then, not the possible implications of the terms of the antithesis, that is important to Ignatius here.

(c) Ignatius' description of the bread of the eucharist as the "medicine of immortality" is perhaps the best known passage from his letters. It is generally taken to support a very "realistic" (if not "magical") conception of the sacrament. The issue, however, is more complex than is generally realized. Schermann pointed out that not only are the words "medicine" and "antidote"

medical terms but that the word "immortality" itself is also the name of a drug.[15] Since Isis was said to have discovered the drug and to have used it to raise Horus from the dead (Diodorus Sic. 1.25.6), Schermann suggested that Ignatius was pitting the eucharist against the claims of a rival religion. But since that would seem to involve opposition also to the drug itself, Schermann probably overemphasized the importance of the parallel. *Athanasia* ("immortality") was a concoction very closely related to, if not identical with,[16] a famous medicine attributed to the Pontic king Mithridates VI. It served as a panacea against poisons, venomous bites, and problems of internal organs. Though it was technically an "antidote," it is also frequently called simply a "medicine" (φάρμακον).[17] Ignatius' emphasis here on the "*one* bread"[18] harks back to the "*one* physician" of *Eph.* 7.2 and suggests that there too the panacea dispensed by the one physician against the bite of mad dogs (false teachers) was being compared to the fabled drug (for a special connection between Mithridates' antidote and rabies see Pliny *Nat. hist.* 23.77.149). Two conclusions may be drawn: (a) The description of the eucharist here is to be taken no more literally than the medical language of *Eph.* 7 (or of *Tr.* 6.2). (b) The fame of the drug called *athanasia*[19] accounts for reference to it in a variety of non-medical contexts. Thus the story of Isis' invention of the medicine of immortality and (say) Clement of Alexandria's (*Protr.* 10.106.2) metaphorical use of the expression for the sound discipline of Christianity or Seneca's reference (*De prov.* 3.2) to the hemlock drunk by Socrates as the *medicamentum inmortalitatis*[20] can

---

14 The suggestion seems strengthened by another passage in which Ignatius speaks of the "Father" and "his only Son" (*Rom.* inscr). Yet as the Arian controversy later demonstrated, even the use of the term "only" does not prove that relations within the Godhead are necessarily under discussion (*LPGL s.v.* μόνος A, p. 883). The expression "only son" rarely occurs in the early period (Kattenbusch, *Das apostolische Symbol,* 2. 585).

15 Theodor Schermann, "Zur Erklärung der Stelle *epist. ad. Ephes.* 20,2 des Ignatius von Antiochien: φάρμακον ἀθανασίας κ.τ.λ.," *ThQ* 92 (1910) 6–19.

16 Cf. Galen *Antidot.* 2.8 (Kühn, *CGO* 14. 148).

17 The principal texts are these: Galen *Antidot.* 1.1; 2.1, 2, 8, 10 (Kühn, *CGO* 14. 1–3; 106–8; 115; 148; 154; 164–65); *Ad Pison.* 16 (Kühn, *CGO* 14. 283–84); *Composit. medic.* 8.7 (Kühn, *CGO* 13. 203). For other

references see Theodor Puschmann, *Alexander von Tralles* (2 vols.; Vienna: Braumüller, 1878–79) 2. 154–55.

18 Note also the "one faith" just above. Lightfoot (with Theodoret) also reads "in one Jesus Christ" (cf. *Mag.* 7.2) noting the ease with which ΕΝΕΝΙΙΗΣΟΥ could have become ΕΝΙΗΣΟΥ.

19 Galen regards Mithridates' antidote as displaced by the improved version (appropriately called *theriace*) put together by Nero's Greek physician. But the older drug was still important, and an Easterner like Ignatius may not have known the new product. In any event, the three drugs—Mithridates' antidote, *athanasia,* and *theriace*—were very closely related and often confounded.

20 Cf. Carl Weymann, "Zu lateinischen Schriftstellern," *Rheinisches Museum* 70 (1915) 152.

rightly be treated as independent appropriations of a widespread theme. Similar metaphors—"medicine of life" (Sir 6:16), "medicine of salvation" (Euripides *Phoen.* 893)[21]—had prepared the way. Later Christian liturgies also use such expressions for the eucharist: Serapion of Thmuis' (*Euch.* 13.15) "medicine of life" and the "medicine of immortality" from a papyrus quoted by Lietzmann.[22] And these may suggest the possibility of a liturgical source for our passage. But they may also represent independent appropriations of the theme or may themselves have been derived from Ignatius.[23] In any event, they can hardly determine the meaning of a passage so strongly marked by the author's own purpose. Thus although Ignatius elsewhere presents a realistic conception of the divine presence in the elements of the eucharist (see on *Sm.* 7.1), here the emphasis is on the unity under bishop and presbytery which provides the context within which the Ephesians "break bread" (cf. Acts 2:46; 20:7, 11; 1 Cor 10:16) together (cf. *Phd.* 4).

The two terms, "bread" and "medicine of immortality," are connected by ὅς ἐστιν ("which is"), that along with ἥτις ἐστίν and ὅ ἐστιν is a frequent stylistic feature of Ignatius' Greek. Here are their occurrences: (a) ὅς ἐστιν: *Eph.* 9.1; *17.2(L); 20.2; *Mag.* 7.1 (Lightfoot); **8.2; *10.2(L); *15; *Tr.* 8.1(G); *11.2(G). (b) ἥτις ἐστίν: **Eph.* 14.1; **Tr.* 6.1; *Phd.* inscr. (c) ὅ ἐστιν: *Eph.* 17.2(G); *18.1: *20.2(gL); *Mag.* 7.1(I.); 10.2(G); *Tr.* 8.1(LC); 11.2(L); *Rom.* 5.1; 7.3; *Sm.* 5.3. Passages marked with an asterisk (*) attract the gender of the relative to that of the following noun. The relative in passages marked with the double asterisk (**) joins two nouns of the same gender and naturally agrees with them. Attraction is common, then, in Ignatius. And in (a), since *Tr.* 8.1(G) is clearly impossible and must be rejected in favor of *Tr.* 8.1(LC), *Eph.* 20.2 alone does not follow the rule. It is likely, then, that (as many editors have seen) ὅ ἐστιν (the neuter) should be read. In (c) the neuter frequently joins nouns neither of which are neuter. There are textual problems in almost every case, as the list indicates. Yet in light of *Rom.* 7.3[24] and *Sm.* 5.3[25] (where there are no variants), it seems likely that all of the problematic passages (*Eph.* 17.2; *Mag.* 7.1; 10.2; *Tr.* 8.1; 11.2) should follow the neuter reading. This also suggests that *Eph.* 18.1 and 20.2 are not really cases of attraction and that a neuter noun is involved only accidentally. Yet as far as can be seen, there is no appreciable difference in Ignatius between this independent neuter and the masculines and feminines. All forms of the expression serve to connect two nouns, and there is no evidence that there is a difference in the character of the connection or that one rather than the other (usually this claim is made for the independent neuter) refers to the whole of the preceding expression rather than a single term. In other writers of the period the independent neuter occurs less frequently, and short clauses employing masculine, feminine, and (true) neuter relatives often function more like normal relative clauses. Otherwise, however, the function of these relatives is to connect two terms not so much for the purpose of equating them as of setting them in a striking or novel relation to each other.[26] This seems especially true of Ignatius. Here connections are drawn between abstract

---

21 Diogenes Oenoandensis frg. 2 (5, 14–6,2): τὰ τῆς σωτηρίας προθε[ῖναι φάρμα]κα "to set forth the medicines of salvation" (so Heberdey and Kalinka, William, Grilli [but not Usener]. This is part of an extended comparison between Epicurus' teaching and healing. For similar comparisons see Clement Alex. *Strom.* 7.11, 61.5; Athanasius *Virg.* 5. Irenaeus presents Christ himself as the *antidotum vitae* "antidote of life" (*Adv. haer.* 3.19.1).

22 Hans Lietzmann, *Messe und Herrenmahl* (Arbeiten zur Kirchengeschichte 8; Bonn: Marcus and Weber, 1926) 257 n. 2.

23 Cf. A. D. Nock, "Liturgical Notes," *JTS* 30 (1929) 392 n. 1.

24 Here the first of a pair of such expressions has the neuter relative joining a masculine and a feminine noun.

25 Here the first of the two nouns involved is neuter (this is also the situation in the second of the pair of expressions in *Rom.* 7.3). But since Ignatius regularly attracts the relative to the second noun (which is feminine here), this is probably a case of an independent neuter.

26 For examples of the use of the independent neuter see (most manuscripts of) Col 3:14; Eph 5:5; Hippolytus *Contra haer. Noet.* 15. For expressions employing masculine, feminine, or (true) neuter relatives see, e.g., Gal 3:16; 4:24, 26; 1 Cor 3:11, 17; 4:17; Col 1:7, 15, 18, 24, 27; 2:10, 17; 3:5; 4:9; Eph 1:22–23; 3:13; 4:15; 6:17; Pol. *Phil.* 3.3; *2 Clem.* 14.4; Philo *Heres* 78–79; Irenaeus *Adv. haer.* 4.36.7.

and concrete expressions (e.g., unity is God, knowledge is Christ, faith is flesh, and love is blood) and between images and their referents (e.g., the crane is the cross, the weed is heresy, the new leaven is Jesus Christ). Again, the two expressions joined may be mutually interdependent elements seen in a new light (e.g., the passion is the resurrection). And sometimes—as in other types of expression in Ignatius (cf. *Eph.* inscr; 14.1)—the bishop seems to be expressing in a compressed form a cause-and-effect relation (e.g., God is the ground of unity, Jesus Christ the source of joy). The order of words does not seem to make any difference (joy is Jesus Christ in *Mag.* 7.1, and the blood of Jesus Christ is joy in *Phd.* inscr). In *Eph.* 20.2 the formula does double duty: it connects an image to its referent, and it makes the bread the ground of immortality. Any further definition of the relation between the eucharist and eternal life, however, depends on the context and parallel passages. It is illegitimate to press the image itself too far. Thus our passage should not serve as the clearest expression of sacramental realism in Ignatius.

■ **21.1–2** In the final section of the letter a number of conventional elements are found. The most obvious is the "farewell" (ἔρρωσθε), which in pagan letters was often elaborated in comparable ways.[27] Its appearance here represents a notable instance in which Ignatius is closer to Hellenistic models than to Paul. The command to "remember me" echoes an expression commonly found in letters of friendship where it occasionally appears (as it does here) somewhere at the end.[28] The sentiment often takes on religious coloration[29] and may be connected with a request for prayer on behalf of the writer.[30] A request for such a prayer, independent of a call to be remembered, is found already in 1 Thess 5:25. Ignatius redirects the formula and asks for prayer on behalf of the church in Antioch. All of these elements are found at the end of most of Ignatius' letters but (as is true also of conventional items at the end of letters in the papyri) in many different positions.[31] The letter to the Ephesians

stands out as lacking the formal greetings which occur in all other letters of Ignatius. For the significance of that fact see on *Mag.* 15.

According to White, a sense of "the relationship between the two parties in the epistolary situation" often pervades the body closing.[32] Thus in *Eph.* 20.1 Ignatius' concern about his worthiness (cf. *Eph.* 2.2), his feeling of dependence on the prayers of the Ephesians (cf. *Eph.* 1.2; 11.2), and his submission to "the (divine) will" (θέλημα "will" used absolutely here as in *Rom.* 1.1; *Sm.* 11.1; *Pol.* 6.1) are all touched on. The farewell section goes further. In 21.1 the paradoxical union of Ignatius' self-depreciation and sense of authority is expressed in his reference to himself as their "expiation" (see on *Eph.* 8.1; 12.1). Such language, as we have seen, tends to the formulaic in Ignatius: he is presenting himself as their humble servant (a reference to vicarious sacrifice seems very unlikely here with the restricted application of the term to Ignatius' relations with the Ephesians and their representatives). But there are also deeper impulses at work, and they are hinted at here in Ignatius' request that prayer be made for the church in Antioch (rather than for himself as the convention would suggest), his reference to his bonds, and his identification of himself in Pauline terms (cf. 1 Cor 15:9; *Mag.* 14; *Tr.* 13.1; *Rom.* 9.2; *Sm.* 11.1) as "least" of the Antiochenes. The latter expression in particular is problematic. For though "least" of the Antiochenes, Ignatius immediately goes on to connect his confinement in bonds with the fact that he was found worthy of it (see Introduction, 3.4).

Ignatius refers simply to the church of "Syria" here and elsewhere (*Mag.* 14; *Tr.* 13.1; *Rom.* 10.2) but to the church in "Antioch in Syria" after he gets to Troas (*Phd.* 10.1; *Sm.* 11.1; *Pol.* 7.1). This must be connected with the fact that encouraging news about Antioch had reached him just before he wrote the letters from Troas

---

27 Exler, *Greek Epistolography*, 69–77.
28 *P.Ryl.* 235; Lucian *Dial. meretr.* 10.3; Chariton *Chaer. et Callirh.* 8.4.5–6; Col 4:18.
29 Cf. *SB* 5.8142.
30 Basil *Ep.* 259; cf. Koskenniemi, *Studien,* 145–48.
31 Gordon J. Bahr, "The Subscription in the Pauline Letters," *JBL* (1968) 39 n. 60.
32 White, *Form and Function,* 42 n. 37.

(*Phd.* 10.1). It seems likely that this news had to do with a victory for Ignatius' policies in his church and that only now can he bring himself to utter a name previously linked with such painful memories (see Introduction, 1.4).

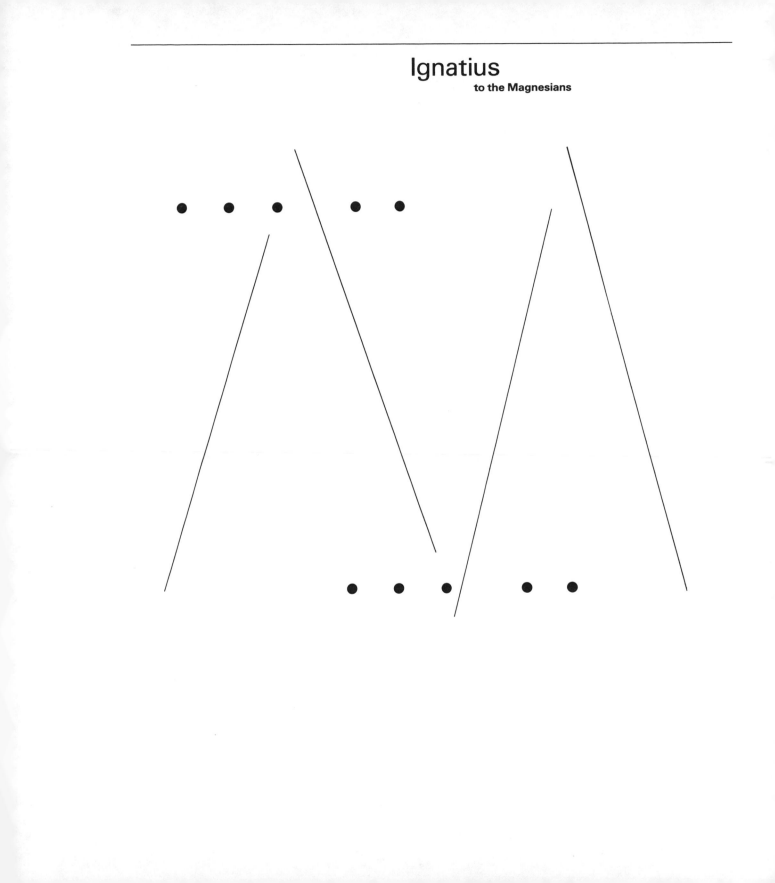

Ignatius
to the Magnesians

Salutation

Ignatius, also called Theophorus, to her who has been blessed in the grace of God the Father in Christ Jesus our savior, in whom I greet the church in Magnesia on the Maeander and wish her abundant greeting in God the Father and in Jesus Christ.

The address to the Magnesians (the shortest except for that to Polycarp) has two unusual features.[1] (a) The ἀσπάζομαι ("I greet") formula has an unusual location. In this period it had begun to appear not only at the end but also at the beginning of letters just after the salutation (in the first person, the form most suitable to establishing rapport with the addressee).[2] Here, however, it is incorporated in the salutation itself. (b) "I wish her greeting" (εὔχομαι ... χαίρειν), which is worked into the unusual construction occasioned by the ἀσπάζομαι formula (cf. *Tr.* inscr), must be modelled on the con-cluding expression, εὔχομαι ἐρρῶσθαι "I wish you fare-well," that begins to occur in place of the simple "fare-well" in the second century (cf. *Pol.* 8.3).[3]

Ignatius refers to Magnesia on the Maeander to distinguish it from other cities of the same name, especially its near neighbor "under (mount) Sipylus" (cf. Livy 37.44–45).[4]

---

1 For the theme of "blessing" see on *Eph.* 1.3, and for the term "savior" on *Eph.* 1.1.

2 Koskenniemi, *Studien*, 149.

3 Exler, *Greek Epistolography*, 70, 75–77.

4 Lightfoot, *Ignatius*, 106.

1
Expression of Joy and Reason for Writing

1 Having learned of the orderliness of your godly love, I gladly decided to address you in the faith of Jesus Christ. 2/ For having been deemed worthy of a most godly name, in the bonds which I bear I sing the churches, in which I pray for a union of flesh and spirit of Jesus Christ (our everlasting life) and of faith and love (than which nothing is preferable) and above all of Jesus and the Father, 3/ in whom, if we endure the whole abuse of the ruler of this age and escape, we shall attain God.

■ **1.1** The body of the letter opens with a formula more conventional than that met with in *Eph.* 1.1. Reception of information (indicated by a participle of the verb to know or learn) is followed by an expression of joy.[1] The formula is modified in such a way that it also serves a common purpose of opening statements in motivating the following communication ("having learned . . . I decided to address you").[2] In indicating that speaking to the Magnesians (προσλαλῆσαι "to address") is his reason for writing, Ignatius again reflects the Hellenistic view of the letter as a substitute for face-to-face relations (see on *Eph.* 9.2).

■ **1.2** What Ignatius had learned (no doubt from the representatives mentioned in the next section) had to do with the good order of the Magnesians—their unity and concord under their bishop. This information is the basis of his highly wrought expression of praise for "the churches" which follows. "I sing (ᾄδω)[3] the churches" has a poetic ring. When Ignatius uses the verb elsewhere, the image of choral singing is in the background (*Eph.* 4.1, 2; *Rom.* 2.2); and in one of these passages he leads over to the usage before us when he says that "Jesus Christ is sung" (*Eph.* 4.1). It is especially the extension of such praise to the churches that brings to mind the role of ancient poets in "singing" (the praises of) places, persons, and gods.[4] In Ignatius' day this task had been taken up also by rhetoricians like Aelius Aristides. Thus Aristides

says to the Romans, "all men sing and will continue to sing your city" (τὴν δὲ πόλιν ᾄδουσιν μὲν πάντες καὶ ᾄσονται, *Or.* 26.4). He opens his prose-hymn to Eleusis by declaring "O Eleusis, long since so sweet for me to sing" (ᾄδειν, *Or.* 22.1). And there are other such passages in his works.[5] The Christian bishop evidently went about his task of strengthening the churches (and focussing their attention on his martyrdom) by relying to a certain extent on models provided by contemporary rhetoricians. Thus his championing of unity and concord in this letter and elsewhere (see on *Eph.* 13) probably also builds on the widespread view that a major task of the orator was to stimulate people, as Demosthenes (*Coron.* 246) already declared, to "concord and friendship."

Ignatius says that he pursues this task because he was counted worthy of "a most godly name." Of the various suggestions concerning the name or designation which he had in mind—Christian, Theophorus, Damas,[6] bishop, martyr, and prisoner—the first two seem most likely. Elsewhere Ignatius uses the word "name" as follows: absolutely of the name of Christ or Christian (*Eph.* 1.1[?], 2; 3.1; 7.1; *Phd.* 10.1; cf. *Mag.* 10.1); of the name of God (*Tr.* 8.2; *Phd.* 10.2), including the expression "in the name of God" (*Eph.* 1.3); of Jesus Christ in the expression "in the name of Jesus Christ" (*Rom.* inscr; 9.3; *Sm.* 4.2; 12.2; *Pol.* 5.1); of the "names" of people who are not named (*Phd.* 6.1; *Sm.* 5.3); of the "dear"

---

1 White, *Form and Function*, 39–40.
2 Cf. *PSI* 4.299; Koskenniemi, *Studien*, 77–87.
3 Zahn (*Ignatius*, 569–70) emends to ἰδών, but his argument is complex and unconvincing.
4 Cf. LSJ *s.v.* ἀείδω II, p. 26.
5 Cf. *Or.* 25.60; 30.12; 40.1, 22; 42.6; 44.1 (ed. Keil).
6 Damas is the bishop of Magnesia mentioned in *Mag.* 2 as one through whom Ignatius "was thought

worthy" to see the Magnesians. Possibly relevant, then, is *Pol.* 1.1, where an expression similar to that used here—"having been counted worthy of your blameless face"—refers to having seen a bishop (Polycarp) face to face. If the "face" is Polycarp, the "name" may be Damas. But the solution does not fit the context very well.

name of an individual whom Ignatius names (*Rom.* 10.1; *Sm.* 13.2; *Pol.* 8.3; and perhaps somewhat similarly the "much loved" name of the Ephesians in *Eph.* 1.1 whose name, however, is not mentioned); of the name of individuals in the expression "by name" or "as individuals" (*Eph.* 20.2; *Pol.* 4.2; 8.2; *Sm.* 13.2). There is nothing in all this to justify thinking in terms of titles like martyr or prisoner. And the only analogy for finding a proper name referred to in *Mag.* 1.2 is the uncertain example of *Eph.* 1.1 which may allow for a reference to a name (like Theophorus) with a meaning (see on *Eph.* inscr). But there is very little to suggest this possibility here, and elsewhere in the letter Ignatius is preoccupied with the importance of living up to the name "Christian" or "Christianity" (*Mag.* 4; 10.1). The only difficulty is the lack of a definite article which otherwise marks the absolute use of the expression. But that is probably a subtle reflection of Ignatius' presentation of himself as unaccountably worthy of a name that other Christians have every right to bear (cf. *Eph.* 11.2). "The name," then, is also his name.

Ignatius' praise of the churches includes a prayer for the (continued) union (ἕνωσις) of their communities. The term does not figure in connection with the call for "concord" (cf. *Mag.* 6.1; 15.1) in the cities of Asia Minor by writers like Dio Chrysostom or Aelius Aristides. Aristotle probably still spoke for many when he criticized too organic a conception of political unity (*Pol.* 2.8, 1261b 10). A more Platonic regard for the ἑνότης "unity" of cities, however, can be found in Plutarch (*De ser. num. vind.* 15, 559a; cf. Plato *Resp.* 4, 423d),[7] and there is some evidence that Ignatius had contact with such conceptions of communal life (see on *Pol.* 1.2). Moreover, he also reflects metaphors and formulae of unity in Hellenism and Hellenistic Judaism that transcend purely political horizons (see on *Eph.* 4 and *Mag.* 7). Whatever the mixture of elements may be in Ignatius, such metaphors and formulae are focussed on the church under the influence of a transcendent conception of the

Christian community as the "body" of Christ (see on *Sm.* 1.2). Careful attention to Ignatius' usage shows, however, that he consistently refers to union within the individual communities and that he does not use the word to describe the communion between God and human beings (see *Mag.* 13.2; *Tr.* 11.2; *Phd.* 4; 7.2; 8.1; *Pol.* 1.2; 5.2). When Ignatius connects God with union, he speaks of him as the giver of it. The use of the verb ἑνόω "unite" (*Eph.* inscr; *Mag.* 6.2; 7.1; 14; *Rom.* inscr; *Sm.* 3.3) and the noun ἑνότης "unity" (*Eph.* 4.2; 5.1; 14.1; *Phd.* 2.2; 3.2; 5.2; 8.1; 9.1; *Sm.* 12.2; *Pol.* 8.3) is somewhat more complicated but basically reflects the same situation (see on *Phd.* 5.2).

Consequently we must assume that when Ignatius speaks here of a union "of flesh and spirit of Jesus Christ," he is referring to the Magnesians' flesh and spirit (cf. *Mag.* 13.2) and to a union of them given by or originating from Jesus Christ (a genitive of source; see *Phd.* 4 for a comparable problem). Here the pair of terms, flesh and spirit, and that which follows, faith and love,[8] serve to express the totality of the union in the Magnesian church (see Introduction, 5.6; 5.8). The same must be true of the reference to the union of "Jesus and the Father." This should not be taken as referring to union *with* Jesus and the Father. If the parallelism with the preceding pairs of terms seems awkward or inappropriate, we must remember that rhetorical balance sometimes came more easily to Ignatius than clarity of expression. Forced to explain himself, Ignatius would probably say what he does in *Mag.* 7.2 and 13.2—that the union of Father and Son is a model for the perfect concord of the Christian community. Consequently the mystical dimensions of the theme of unity in Ignatius should not be exaggerated.

■ **1.3** Much the same may also be said about the idea of "attaining God." For here such attaining is seen as the result of "enduring" and "escaping" the plots of "the ruler of this age" (cf. *Eph.* 17.1), and (as elsewhere) it describes the destiny of every Christian (see on *Eph.*

---

7   Cf. Hans Dieter Betz, Peter A. Dirkse, and Edgar W. Smith, in Betz, *Plutarch's Theological Writings*, 212–13.

8   Expressions like "than which nothing is preferable" are found elsewhere in Ignatius (*Mag.* 7.1; *Pol.* 1.2). Of the many short subordinate clauses that mark Ignatius' style, these are among the most empty in terms of content. But Ignatius was not alone in using

this method to underline important points. Thus Cicero (*De fin.* 5.13.38) says that the virtues of the soul are to be sought "because they spring from reason than which nothing in man is more divine" (*qua nihil est in homine divinius*).

10.1). To be sure, when Ignatius speaks of himself as "attaining" (some nineteen times) or of Polycarp as "attaining" (once), he uses the strengthened form of the verb.[9] Yet the trials of episcopacy, especially martyrdom, are apparently only heightened forms of those confronted by every Christian.

---

9   The ἐπί- of ἐπιτυγχάνειν "attain" is presumably used "to give force or intensity to the verb" (LSJ *s.v.* ἐπί G. III. 4, p. 623).

2

The Representatives from Magnesia

Since, then, I was thought worthy to see you in the person of Damas, your godworthy bishop, and the worthy presbyters Bassus and Apollonius, and my fellow slave the deacon Zotion, from whom may I benefit, because he is subject to the bishop as to the grace of God and to the presbytery as to the law of Jesus Christ—

This section consists of a sentence that is broken off at the end and resumed only in *Mag.* 6.1. The theme then continues on to the end of *Mag.* 7.2. Ignatius begins, as usual, by mentioning the representatives who have come to visit him from the church addressed (*Mag.* 2) and ends by urging continued attention to concord (6.1–2) and unity (7.1–2). Between are three digressions: (a) on the youth of the bishop (3.1–2); (b) on being Christian (4); (c) on the "two ways" (5.1–2).

■ **2** Ignatius had been visited by representatives of all three clerical orders at Magnesia. As Zahn, Lightfoot, and Bauer have shown in their commentaries, the names of these individuals are all common in Asia Minor, and the first three are known to us also from coins and inscriptions of Magnesia. The name Zotion is probably an orthographical variant for another reasonably familiar name, Sotion.

Ignatius' identification of himself as a "fellow slave" of the deacon Zotion is more striking here than the comparable identification in *Eph.* 2.1 since it is directly juxtaposed to the mention of the bishop and the presbyters (cf. *Phd.* 4; *Sm.* 12.2). To take this literally and to regard Ignatius as a deacon, however, involves denying the authenticity of *Romans,* which contains the one passage (*Rom.* 2.2) in which Ignatius calls himself bishop (see Introduction, 1.4b). It is more likely that Ignatius is taking cognizance of unusual difficulties and temptations affecting the office of deacon (see *Tr.* 2.3). His special praise for Zotion as obedient to bishop and presbytery probably reflects Ignatius' pleasure at finding unusually impressive evidence that the Magnesian deacon did not let his control of practical matters unduly swell his sense of importance. The expression "from whom may I benefit" may possibly indicate that (as in *Eph.* 2.2) Ignatius wanted the services of Zotion. Elsewhere,

however, the formula is used more loosely (*Mag.* 12.1; *Pol.* 1.1; 6.2; cf. *Rom.* 5.2); and in our passage the reasons attached to it presuppose that it is basically an expression of pleasure; consequently, it has its most conventional meaning ("bless me for him that he is subject to the bishop . . .").

The comparison of the bishop with the "grace" of God and of the presbyters with the "law" of Christ is atypical. More often Ignatius likens the bishop to God or Christ and the presbytery to the apostles (see on *Mag.* 6.1). An even greater range of variation is suggested, however, by passages in which it is not the presbyters but the bishop (*Tr.* 13.2; cf. *Phd.* 1.2) or the deacons (*Sm.* 8.1) who are compared to the "commandment" of God. This variety warns us not only against thinking that the details of the comparison may tell us something about the responsibilities of these offices but also against making too much of Ignatius' habit of comparing things human with things divine. For in *Mag.* 3.1 he will legitimate episcopal authority on grounds that are still recognizably biblical.

This is also the only passage in which "grace" and "law" appear as a pair.[1] Since bishop and presbyters together express a more or less unified authority (cf. *Eph.* 2.1), so grace and law are closely conjoined. Here they may be taken to refer to the totality of divine revelation—not, however, the two testaments (cf. John 1:17; Heb 10:28–29), but the new revelation as both gift and task.[2] Even this distinction has no finality, however, since grace and law are both presented here as realities to be obeyed. This overlap is in harmony with Ignatius' view of the grace of God elsewhere (see on *Sm.* 6.2).

---

1 The term "law" occurs only here and in two other passages where it refers to the law of Moses (*Mag.* 8.1; *Sm.* 5.1).

2 For Christ's "law" see also the expression χριστόνομος "under the law of Christ" in *Rom.* inscr (cf. 1 Cor 9:21; *Barn.* 2.6; *Herm. Sim.* 5.6.3).

Authority and Unity in Magnesia [2–7]

3

Digressions on the Theme
of Episcopal Authority

1 And you are not to take advantage of the youth of your bishop, but to show him all respect in accordance with the power of God the Father, just as I know that also your holy presbyters have not presumed on his apparent youthfulness but, as men wise in God, yield to him—not indeed to him but to the Father of Jesus Christ, the bishop of all. 2/ Thus to the honor of him who took pleasure in us it is right to obey without hypocrisy; for the point is not that a man deceives this bishop who is visible, but that he tries to cheat him who is unseen; in such a matter the reckoning is not with flesh but with God who knows our secrets.

4

1/ It is right, then, not only to be called Christians but also to be Christians; just as some certainly use the title "bishop" but do everything apart from him. Such people do not seem to me to act in good conscience because they do not meet validly in accordance with the commandment.

5

1/ Since, then, all things have an end, and two things are set before us together, death and life, and each person will go to his own place; 2/ for just as there are two coinages, the one of God, the other of the world, and each of them has its own imprint on it, the unbelievers that of this world, the believers the imprint of God the Father through Jesus Christ in love; through whom unless we freely choose to die unto his suffering, his life is not in us.

■ **3.1** (a) The first digression (set apart by the tandem particle καὶ ... δέ; see on *Eph.* 2.1) has to do with the youthfulness of the bishop of Magnesia. There is a tendency, apparently, to "take advantage" (συγχρᾶσθαι)[1] of him even though the elders did not "presume on" (προσειληφότας)[2] his "youthfulness" (νεωτερικὴν τάξιν).[3] Perhaps that is why Ignatius has just expressed special praise for the loyalty of the deacon Zotion (*Mag.* 2). The problem was evidently not isolated since it is also faced by the writer of the Pastoral Epistles (1 Tim 4:12). In calling the bishop's youthfulness "apparent" (φαινομένην), Ignatius either means that it is obvious or, more likely, that it is merely external. The contrast in 3.2 between the "visible" and the "unseen" bishop and between "flesh"

---

1   BAG *s.v.* συγχράομαι 1, p. 783.
2   BAG *s.v.* προσλαμβάνω 1.b, p. 724.
3   This expression has sometimes been taken to refer to the recent establishment of the episcopacy as an office in the church or (less remarkably) of the recent ordination of the bishop Damas. The context is against such interpretations, and they force the meaning of the words (Zahn, *Ignatius*, 302–6); and

now that parallels have been found for τάξις as "nature" or "appearance" (BAG *s.v.* τάξις 4, p. 811) there is no further reason to doubt that Ignatius is referring to Damas' youthfulness.

and the God who knows our "secrets" (cf. *Eph.* 1.3; 15.3) points toward the second solution (compare also the use of φαινόμενον "what appears" in *Rom.* 3.3).[4] Damas, we are being told, has the virtues usually associated with age.[5] The impression is left that youthful bishops were exceptional. The fact that they were to be found at all indicates that the episcopacy was beginning to be placed on a different footing from that of the presbyterate: the criterion of age had (at least in principle) lost its significance. The office is in an important state of transition.

Ignatius asks the Magnesians to respect their young bishop in light of God's power.[6] What that means is soon made clear: to yield to the bishop is not to yield simply to him but to God, "the bishop of all."[7]

■ **3.2** Unfeigning obedience in the church contributes to the honor "of him who took pleasure in us";[8] and deception of the bishop represents an effort to delude God. A similar point is made (though much more dramatically) in the story of Ananias and Sapphira where Peter says to Ananias, "you did not lie to men but to God" (Acts 5:4). In both instances the idea is that God concerns himself about the integrity of the relations between Christians and their leaders, not that the leaders stand in God's place. Similarly Josephus (*Bell.* 5.378) remarks to his countrymen that in refusing to yield to the Romans they "fight against not only the Romans but also God" (μὴ μόνον Ῥωμαίοις πολεμοῦντες ἀλλὰ καὶ τῷ θεῷ);

and he says (*C. Apion.* 2.193–94) concerning the high priest of the "one temple of the one God" (cf. *Mag.* 7.2) that "he who does not obey him will pay the penalty as one guilty of impiety toward God himself" (ὡς εἰς θεὸν αὐτὸν ἀσεβῶν).

■ **4** (b) Yet obedience to the bishop is of such decisive importance to Ignatius that he goes on virtually to define being Christian in terms of it. In this connection he appeals to the contrast between empty talk and actual deeds that he elaborates more fully in *Eph.* 14.2–15.2 (note especially the close parallel in *Eph.* 15.1). Some acknowledge[9] the bishop but "do" everything (probably in matters of worship; cf. *Mag.* 7.1; *Tr.* 7.2; *Phd.* 4) "without him." Here the contrast between words and deeds has been fused with another recurring theme in Ignatius: the call to do nothing without the bishop. In this connection Ignatius alternates between using ἄνευ "without" (*Mag.* 7.1; *Tr.* 2.2; *Pol.* 4.1) and χωρίς "without" (*Tr.* 7.2; *Phd.* 7.2; *Sm.* 8.2). Especially important is *Pol.* 4.1, where the expression "without (ἄνευ) your approval" (or "purpose") points to secular contexts in which authority (especially political and administrative) is asserted. For here one is frequently commanded to do nothing without (or without the permission of) those in charge.[10] The use of such language strengthens the impression left by Ignatius in our passage that he chose to define episcopal authority more strictly than others.

---

4 That God is ἀόρατος "unseen" (cf. *Pol.* 3.2) is a view unknown in the Hebrew Bible and rare in the NT (Col 1:15; 1 Tim 1:17; Heb 11:27; cf. Rom 1:20; John 1:18). It reflects a Hellenistic conception of divine transcendence; cf. Rudolf Bultmann, "Untersuchungen zum Johannesevangelium: B. Θεὸν οὐδεὶς ἑώρακεν πώποτε," *ZNW* 29 (1930) 169–92; reprinted in idem, *Exegetica* (Tübingen: Mohr [Siebeck], 1967) 174–97.

5 Deference to elders was not only a Jewish phenomenon. Special care had to be taken by a young man also in Hellenistic society if he expected to have his ideas respected (Plutarch *De defec. orac.* 47, 435e). Cf. Kathleen O'Brien Wicker, in Betz, *Plutarch's Theological Writings*, 176.

6 "In accordance with" (κατά) often marks the reason in light of which one acts (BAG *s.v.* κατά 5.a, p. 408).

7 For God as the universal "bishop" see *Rom.* 9.1; *Pol.* inscr; 8.3 (cf. 1 Pet 2:25).

8 The verb θέλειν ("to will") is used as the opposite of μισεῖν ("to hate") in *Rom.* 8.3 (cf. *Mag.* 8.1; *Rom.* inscr; 6.1). This is a development of the verb's meaning

("take pleasure in," "love") within biblical Greek (cf. Matt 27:43; Ps 21:9).

9 For καλεῖν "use the title" ("call") without the usual double accusative in ascribing names or titles see Matt 23:9 (cf. Heb 3:13). Possibly we should emend it (with Zahn) to λαλοῦσιν "use the term" (cf. *Mag.* 10.3; *Rom.* 7.1).

10 See on *Pol.* 4.1. Also note Dit., *Or.* 2.669,53–54: "I command also the generals to take nothing from the accountants without (χωρίς) the [license of the] prefect"; *P.Teb.* 1.20,6–7: " . . . in regard to the additions to the revenues letting him do nothing without you" (μηθὲν ἄνευ σοῦ ποιεῖν). For other examples of such uses of ἄνευ see Edwin Mayser, *Grammatik der griechischen Papyri aus der Ptolemäerzeit*, vol. 2: *Satzlehre* (3 vols.; Berlin and Leipzig: De Gruyter, 1926–34) 519–20.

At the same time, the appeal to secular models suggests that he did not (as Bauer thought) seek to reinforce discipline as the leader of a minority precipitating a split.[11] Groups within the churches known to Ignatius are just beginning to become conscious of distinct aims (and, in some instances, distinct theologies) which lead to separation (see on *Phd.* 7.2; 11.1; *Sm.* 5.2; 8.2). Ignatius does define situations more sharply in administrative and theological terms, but apparently the majority were prepared to follow (see Introduction, 3.3); and it is from the standpoint of the dominant group that the bishop speaks when he labels the separate meetings of others as "invalid" (cf. *Sm.* 8.2). When he also says that the separatists do not meet "in accordance with the commandment," it is unlikely that he is referring to any definite pronouncement (such as Matt 18:17). "Commandment" is as broad a term in Ignatius (cf. *Eph.* 9.2; *Tr.* 3.1 *v.l.*; 13.2; *Rom.* inscr; *Phd.* 1.2; *Sm.* 8.1) as it is in the Johannine writings (see 2 John 6 for the expression "according to his commandments"). What Ignatius probably has in mind is the principle of love and unity inherent in the very fabric of the life of the church as he has come to understand it (note Heb 10:25 which also criticizes the failure to meet together, "as the manner of some is," on general theological grounds). Thus Ignatius' definition of Christianity in terms of obedience to the bishop is not without its deeper ground.

■ **5.1–2** (c) The next section was apparently intended as a warning to those who might be tempted to act without the bishop. "Since the choice between death and life is before you," Ignatius is saying, "see that you choose life by adhering to the bishop." But he becomes so absorbed in sketching the alternatives that the exhortation itself is missing, and we are left with another incomplete sentence.

■ **5.1** The alternatives are first stated in a form reminiscent of the Christian and Jewish teaching about the "two ways" (cf. *Did.* 1–6; *Barn.* 18–20; 1QS 3.13–4.26). Ignatius, however, concentrates not on the ethical injunctions that constitute the two ways but on the goal of each (death or life). The language used of everyone going "to his own place" (heaven or hell) is traditional (Acts 1:25; cf. Pol. *Phil.* 9.2; *1 Clem.* 5.7). But when Ignatius speaks of the "end" which things have, he is referring not to judgment day but to the logical outcome of the activities associated with the two ways of life (cf. Rom 6:21–22).

■ **5.2** The second way of stating the alternatives—as a contrast between two coinages (νομίσματα)—is still less indebted to traditional eschatology. A good parallel is provided in Clement Alex. *Exc. ex Theod.* 86 (in an exegesis of Matt 22:20) which Schlier took as another indication of Gnostic influence on Ignatius.[12] But the passage may come from Clement himself rather than from his Gnostic source.[13] In any event, Clement (*Eclog. proph.* 24) works out the imagery of the two coinages independently, often basing it on the popular saying of Jesus, "be approved money-changers" (*Strom.* 1.28, 177.2; 2.4, 15.4; 7.15, 90.5). This saying was known also to many other writers in the early church, and it inspired interpretations reminiscent of Ignatius' use of the imagery of the two coinages.[14] But Ignatius may have been directly dependent on Hellenistic models. For Plutarch speaks of "testing these stories even as one tests foreign coins" (νομίσματα, *De defec. orac.* 21, 421a; cf. Aristotle *Hist. animal.* 1.6, 491a 21) and of distinguishing between false and true friends as one sorts out counterfeit and genuine coins (Plutarch *Quomodo adulator* 1, 49e). The dualities connected with this imagery in Ignatius are well within the range of Pauline and Johannine thought—God and the "world" (cf. 1 Cor 1:20–21; John 3:16), faith and unfaith (cf. 2 Cor 6:15; John 20:27). The acquisition of the imprint of God is described in Pauline terms (cf. Rom 6:5–11) as coming through participation in the death and resurrection of Christ. But Ignatius substitutes his own (less eschatologically oriented) terminology (suffering and life) and makes no allusion to baptism. Since participation in

11 Walter Bauer, *Orthodoxy and Heresy in Earliest Christianity* (tr. Robert A. Kraft and Gerhard Krodel; Philadelphia: Fortress, 1971) 61–70. Against Bauer see Bartsch, *Gnostisches Gut*, 11–17.

12 Schlier, *Untersuchungen*, 133.

13 Cf. F. Sagnard, *Clément d'Alexandrie: Extraits de Théodote* (SC 23; Paris: Cerf, 1948) 211.

14 Resch, *Agrapha*, 112–28.

Christ's death and resurrection is here only very loosely connected with worship (see *Mag.* 4), there is no reason to suspect a reference to the reenactment of these mysteries in eucharistic action (see Introduction, 4.1). It is more likely that the theme appears under the influence of Ignatius' view of the Christian community (and the Christian martyr) as following a way of life determined by the hostility of the "world" (cf. *Rom.* 3.3). Thus willingness to suffer as the Lord suffered (see *Eph.* 10.2–3)—and humble submission to the bishop is apparently regarded as a corollary—stamps the Christian.

Authority and Unity in Magnesia [2–7]

6

Concord

1   Since, then, in the persons already mentioned I have seen your whole community in faith and have loved it, I exhort you: be eager to do all things in godly concord, with the bishop set over you in the place of God, and the presbyters in the place of the council of the apostles, and the deacons, most sweet to me, entrusted with the service of Jesus Christ, who before the ages was with the Father and appeared at the end. 2/ All of you, then, keep a godly unity of spirit and respect each other, and let no one regard his neighbor in a fleshly way, but love each other in Jesus Christ forever; let there be nothing among you that will be able to divide you, but be united to the bishop and those set over you as an example and lesson of incorruptibility.

■ **6.1** The thought is at last picked up again from *Mag.* 2. Since Ignatius has seen their whole "community" (πλῆθος)[1] in their representatives (cf. *Eph.* 1.3; 2.1), he urges[2] them to "do" everything together (especially in worship, no doubt) in "godly[3] concord." Such concord (see on *Eph.* 4.1–2; 13.1) is maintained when the three orders of the ministry are seen (respectively) as (a) presiding "in the place" (εἰς τόπον)[4] of God and (b) "in the place" of the council (συνέδριον) of the apostles and (c) entrusted with the service of Jesus Christ.
    (a) The bishops are regularly compared with God or Christ by Ignatius (*Mag.* 13.2; *Tr.* 2.1; 3.1; *Sm.* 8.1).
    (b) The presbyters or elders are regularly compared with the apostles (*Tr.* 2.2 ; 3.1; *Phd.* 5.1; *Sm.* 8.1). This office almost certainly has roots in the administration of the Jewish synagogue. Yet here (and in *Tr.* 3.1; *Phd.* 5.1) it is probably modelled on the advisory "council of the elders" (συνέδριον τῶν πρεσβυτέρων) known in several communities of Asia Minor.[5] For a reference to the Judaean council (Sanhedrin) is very unlikely. It is not clear what lies behind the comparison between the elders and the apostles. In one passage the apostles appear as

---

1   The word is used in this sense also in *Tr.* 1.1; 8.2; *Sm.* 8.2 (cf. Acts 6:5; 15:12; *1 Clem.* 54.2).

2   The exhortation is introduced by the word παραινῶ ("I exhort"), which in Hellenistic epistolography may function as the equivalent of the more common παρακαλῶ (Bjerkelund, *Parakalô*, 84–85, 106). The first such exhortation in a letter usually contains the burden of the communication (see on *Tr.* 6.1).

3   Literally, "concord of God." But the reference to God is so conventional in such expressions (cf. *Mag.* 15; *Phd.* inscr) that the English adjective "godly" is more in place as a translation. The same is true of the expression ὁμοήθεια θεοῦ ("godly unity of spirit") in 6.2 (cf. *Pol.* 1.3). Unity and harmony with one another, not with God, is what Ignatius has in mind (see on *Mag.* 1.2).

4   The expression refers to the replacement of one authority by another, cf. Diodorus Sic. 38/39.2; Nicolaus of Damascus frg. 127.4 (ed. Felix Jacoby, *Die Fragmente der griechischen Historiker*, 2. Teil: *Zeitgeschichte*, A: *Universalgeschichte und Hellenika* [Berlin: Weidmann, 1926] 392). Its significance for

Ignatius may be partly illustrated by *Rom.* 9.1, where he says that the Syrian church has God as bishop "instead of " (ἀντί) himself. Another reading, "as an image of " or "like" (εἰς τύπον), is found in the Syriac (which uses a standard transliteration of the Greek word τύπος), the Arabic, and probably the Armenian. That gains support from *Tr.* 3.1 and *Const. Apost.* 2.26 (in a section that echoes many of Ignatius' views of the ministry). But this reading probably represents a simplification (occasioned by the expression εἰς τύπον καὶ διδαχὴν ἀφθαρσίας "as an example and lesson of immortality" in 6.2).

5   *CIG* 2.3417; cf. Carl Curtius, "Inschriften aus Ephesos," *Hermes* 4 (1870) 224; Albano Vilela, "Le Presbytérium selon saint Ignace d'Antioche," *BLE* 74 (1973) 174–75.

third in a list which includes the Father and Jesus Christ as its first two members (*Tr.* 12.2). This suggests that the apostles are conceived of as forming a heavenly council about God or Christ (like the elders of Rev 4:4) and that they represent the heavenly prototype of the elders just as God (or Christ) is the prototype of the bishop. But the text of this passage is uncertain and there is no other good evidence to support such an interpretation of the comparison. Indeed, in several passages, the apostles seem to be spoken of basically as figures from the past (*Eph.* 11.2; *Mag.* 7.1; *Tr.* 3.3; *Rom.* 4.3; *Phd.* 9.1). Consequently, there can hardly be any strict parallelism between the earthly and heavenly realms in Ignatius' treatment of the ministry. The apostles for him are venerable personages whose presence is still a reality among those who walk in the ways set down by them (cf. *Eph.* 11.2–12.2; *Phd.* 5.1). Thus the reference to "the precepts of the Lord and the apostles" in *Mag.* 13.1 suggests that when Ignatius links divine and apostolic authority, he has in view the historical events of the primitive period. He himself, we recall, cannot give commands as the apostles did (*Tr.* 3.3; *Rom.* 4.3; cf. *Eph.* 3.1), and presumably neither can the presbyters in spite of the comparison. It is primarily the universal and local, then, which is being compared by Ignatius rather than the heavenly and earthly. And the universal is rooted (at least in part) in an idealized past.

(c) As for the deacons, Ignatius' failure to carry through the comparison is in line with his treatment of them elsewhere. They are included in the comparisons only in three or four instances. Only in one of these are they compared with Jesus Christ (*Tr.* 3.1), and there the context is unusual. Otherwise vaguer expressions are the rule (*Mag.* 6.1; *Tr.* 2.3; *Sm.* 8.1). This is another indication that Ignatius stresses the bond between bishops and presbyters and sets the deacons apart from them (see on *Eph.* 2.1).

A more fundamental question is what kind of legitimation of the authority of the ministry Ignatius has in mind when he says that bishop and elders stand "in the place" of God and the apostles. Does this passage determine the meaning of the many parallels in which a comparison involving the particle ὡς "as" is made? Or is it just the reverse, that the expression before us is merely a more elaborate version of a simple comparison? A study of the relevant passages suggests the following classification:[6] (1) direct comparisons—for example, obey the bishop as Jesus Christ (such comparisons sometimes involve all three orders: *Tr.* 2.1–2; 3.1; *Sm.* 8.1; sometimes bishops and presbyters: *Mag.* 2; *Tr.* 13.2; cf. *Phd.* 5.1); (2) comparison of pairs (a) in which the pairs stand apart—for example, be united with your bishop as Jesus Christ is united with the Father (*Eph.* 5.1; *Mag.* 13.2; *Sm.* 8.1; *Pol.* 1.2; cf. *Mag.* 7.1); (b) in which the pairs are interconnected in step-wise progression—for example, Jesus Christ is the purpose of God as the bishops are in the purpose of Jesus Christ; or, you received them as the Lord received you (*Eph.* 3.2; *Phd.* 11.1; *Pol.* 1.2; cf. *Eph.* 2.1); (c) in which the pairs are interconnected in step-wise progression in such a way that they are virtually resolved into a direct comparison—receive the one sent as the one who sent him (*Eph.* 6.1). These types seem to be complexly interrelated. Especially interesting is *Sm.* 8.1, which begins with a comparison of type (2a)—follow the bishop as Jesus Christ followed the Father—but goes on with comparisons of type (1)—follow the presbytery as the apostles and respect the deacons as God's commandment. Evidently the two types of comparison are to be regarded as fundamentally the same.[7] Since type (2a) comparisons call for the imitation of exemplary relations

---

6 I include here all passages having to do with relations between people in the churches and based on comparisons of a similar form.

7 It may also be noted that *Eph.* 5.1 and *Mag.* 13.2 actually present a comparison of one set of relations with two others and that the latter interconnect in step-wise progression: you are intimately associated with your bishop as the church with Jesus Christ and as Jesus Christ with the Father; obey the bishop as Jesus Christ did the Father and the apostles did Christ. Evidently, then, statements of type (2a) and of type (2b) reflect the same habit of mind. Moreover,

there is a relation between type (1) comparisons and comparisons using step-wise progression occasioned by the fact that both compare one hierarchy with another. Basically, then, what is being compared is one cluster of harmonious relations with another, not one item in the cluster with another. That helps to account for the variety in the direct comparisons. And it helps to understand why the comparisons need not always be fully worked out in hierarchical terms.

in the sphere of the divine or of the idealized past (the Father and Christ, Christ and the church, Christ and the apostles), it seems unlikely that in type (1) comparisons Ignatius meant to present God, Christ, or the apostles as mystically present in the ministry itself. Or if we interpret type (2a) comparisons in light of type (1) comparisons in such a way that the relation between people and bishop is thought to embody the relation between the Father and Christ, then the divine must be thought of as present just as much in the community as in the bishop (see on *Mag.* 7.1). Some of the topics to which the comparisons are applied also suggest that Ignatius does not sharply distinguish the ministry from other Christians in terms of a special indwelling of the divine: thus the Magnesians are to obey the bishop *and one another* as Christ obeys the Father (*Mag.* 13.2); *husbands* are to love their *wives* as the Lord loves the church (*Pol.* 5.1); the *Philadelphians* received the *messengers* as the Lord received them (*Phd.* 11.1); *Polycarp* is to endure *all people* as the Lord endured him (*Pol.* 1.2). The last two examples (type 2b), in turn, seem to overlap with *Eph.* 6.1 (type 2c); and in the latter passage Ignatius not only states that we must receive the one sent as the one who sent him, but also goes on to draw the conclusion that we must view the bishop as the Lord himself. Here we apparently have an illustration of how a complex comparison is reduced to a direct one. The latter serves to dramatize the former, and such dramatization probably accounts for other direct comparisons in Ignatius' treatment of the ministry. It would be idle to deny that episcopal authority thereby receives sharper definition in Ignatius, but the comparisons apparently remain true comparisons in spite of the strong formulation of the idea in our passage.

A christological formula rounds out the comparisons. This formula is important in technical christological terms because it clearly states the pre-mundane (and separate) existence of Christ with the Father (cf. John 1:2; 17:5, 24). But Ignatius' concern lies elsewhere. For he couples Christ's preexistence with his manifestation at the end and underscores the polarity by the parallelism of lines. This polarity represented an early pattern for the bracketing of the world's history.[8] The idea that Christ had appeared in the last days long persisted,[9] and the terminology continued to be used in credal contexts (and elsewhere) still longer,[10] sometimes even where the same language was used of Christ's second coming.[11] Adjustments were required when another christological pattern (the Lord who comes from and returns to the Father) became more important and shifted attention to the center of history as the time of Christ's manifestation. We have such a pattern just below in *Mag.* 7.2, and there can be little doubt that it is the more important one in Ignatius. Yet both have similar symbolic value in projecting images of wholeness and completeness, and these are obviously appropriate in the context of *Mag.* 6–7.[12]

■ **6.2** The wholeness that Ignatius has in mind is one in which love of the "neighbor" is a key factor, and this is one important reason why his symbols do not lose themselves in an endlessly expanding world of myth. It is in people's relations with others that the transcendence of mere externals ("the flesh") is important, and it is by love that a fleshly outlook is overcome (cf. *Eph.* 1.3; *Mag.* 3.2). The result is "unity" and the lack of anything that will "divide" (μερίσαι) the Magnesians. This polarity, as Schlier notes, plays an important role in Gnostic speculation.[13] But Ignatius' thought lacks the mythological dimensions of the Gnostic sources, and more relevant parallels are to be found in Hellenistic and Hellenistic-Jewish discussions of cosmic and social unity (see on *Eph.* 4.2; *Mag.* 1.2; 7.1–2). The term that Ignatius uses for division, to be sure, does not regularly appear in these contexts. But it may not be as important to Ignatius as Schlier thought. The verb appears only here, and the uses of the corresponding noun are concentrated almost exclusively in *Philadelphians* (*Phd.* 2.1; 3.1; 7.2; 8.1; *Sm.* 7.2). In any event, Ignatius had

8   Cf. 1 Pet 1:20; *Herm. Sim.* 9.12.2–3; Irenaeus *Adv. haer.* 1.10.3.

9   Cf. 1 Cor 10:11; Heb 1:2; 9:26; *2 Clem.* 14.2; *Orac. Sib.* 8.456.

10   Cf. Athanasius *Synod.* 23; 24; 25; Socrates *Hist. eccl.* 2.10; Theodoret *Hist. eccl.* 1.4.54; Kattenbusch, *Das apostolische Symbol*, 2. 242.

11   Cf. *Const. Apost.* 7.41.

12   For reference to beginning and end to express totality and infinity see Gerhard Kittel, "ΑΩ," *TDNT* 1 (1964) 1–3; Gerhard Delling, "ἀρχή," *TDNT* 1 (1964) 479–84. Cf. Plutarch *De Isid.* 77, 382c; *De Pyth. orac.* 16, 402b; Plotinus *Enn.* 6.9.9.

13   Cf. Clement Alex. *Exc. ex Theod.* 36; *Treat. Seth* (NHC 7) 57,23–26; Schlier, *Untersuchungen*, 102.

surely read 1 Cor 1:13 where Paul asks, "Is Christ divided?" (μεμέρισται). And there are good examples in pagan sources of the use of the verb to designate the splitting up of people into factions.[14]

I understand the concluding statement about those set over you "as an example and lesson (τύπον καὶ διδαχήν) of incorruptibility" to be terminologically dependent on

Paul (Rom 6:17, "you obeyed . . . the standard of teaching" [τύπον διδαχῆς]), and to refer to the ministry as providing in their whole way of life a standard, pattern, or example of the teaching (a hendiadys) which leads to incorruptibility (including theological and moral purity as in *Eph.* 17.1).[15]

---

14   The following passages are noted in LSJ *s.v.* μερίζω III. 2, p. 1103: Polybius 8.21.9; Appian *Bell. civ.* 1.1; Herodian 3.10.4 (cf. Matt 12:25).

15   For the Christian leader as an "example" (τύπος) to his flock see Phil 3:17; 2 Thess 3:9; 1 Tim 4:12; Tit 2:7; 1 Pet 5:3. It seems much less likely that Ignatius takes the unity of the Magnesians with their leaders as the example. (For whom would they be the example?) Nor does it help much to translate τύπος as "image" or "copy." (Would not Ignatius have stated what their union copies?)

7   Unity

1   **As, then, the Lord did nothing without the Father—being united (with him)—neither by himself nor through the apostles, so you too do nothing without the bishop and presbyters, nor try to have anything appear right by yourselves; but (let there be) one prayer in common, one petition, one mind, one hope in love, in blameless joy, which is Jesus Christ, than whom nothing is better. 2/ All of you, hurry together as to one temple of God, as to one altar, to one Jesus Christ, who proceeded from the one Father and was with the one and returned (to him).**

The theme of unity is now more fully developed. In 7.1 this is done fundamentally in terms of a comparison between two sets of terms (the Lord and the Father, the Magnesians and their leaders). The appearance of such a comparison here just after the direct comparisons of *Mag.* 6.1 is further proof of the close relation between the two types. The Gospel of John provides good parallels to the theme of the Lord's oneness with the Father (John 10:30) and of his refusal to act alone (John 5:19, 30; 8:28). But the point is complicated here by the inclusion of the apostles in the scheme. The addition seems to be rhetorically motivated: the statement about the Lord doing nothing "without the Father" corresponds to the exhortation to do nothing "without the bishop and the presbyters"; but at the same time, the reference to bishop and presbyters as a pair corresponds rhetorically to the specification that the Lord acted alone "neither through himself nor through his apostles" (this is all the more evident when it is recalled that bishop and presbyters are compared elsewhere to the Lord and the apostles). It is evident that the details of the comparison cannot be pressed. If they are, the congregation is set in the place of the Lord and the bishop and presbyters correspond not only to this same Lord and the apostles (respectively) but also (collectively) to the Father. Ignatius, then, is basically interested in comparing clusters of harmonious relations, not in equating individual items in those clusters.

■ **7.1** The division that Ignatius fears is one that has to do with groups—not individuals—that go their own way. The expression ἰδίᾳ ("individually") when used with plurals (ὑμῖν "yourselves") refers to the private meeting of groups.[1] Opposed to such division is unity which in turn is closely linked with love and joy. Ignatius emphasizes the christological foundations of such joy with the help of two devices characteristic of his style—the linking phrase "which is" (see on *Eph.* 20.2) and the expression "than whom nothing is better" (cf. *Pol.* 1.2; see on *Mag.* 1.2).

The word "one" appears some nine times[2] in this section (7.1–2) and reflects the central concern of Ignatius' letters. We have seen that the bishop builds on ideas of concord and unity drawn from Greek political thought, but he orients them to a conception of the church as a transcendent reality (see on *Eph.* 4.1–2; 13.1–2). Our passage is another indication that Gnostic parallels are not the decisive ones for our understanding of the theme. Eph 4:5–6 with its repeated use of the word "one" provides the most obvious point of departure. But Dibelius[3] has shown that such formulae are ultimately rooted in Stoic language about the unity of the cosmos (cf. M. Aurelius 4.23; 4.40; 7.9). The link between Stoicism and the early church in this connection was Hellenistic Judaism: "one temple . . . and one altar

---

1   Cf. Matt 17:19; 24:3; Mark 4:34; Gal 2:2; Josephus *Bell.* 2.199.

2   Reading "one temple" (LA) instead of merely "temple" (G).

3   Martin Dibelius, "Die Christianisierung einer hellenistischen Formel," *Neue Jahrbücher für die klassische Altertumswissenschaft* 35/36 (1915) 224–36.

($\beta\omega\mu\acute{o}s$)" (Josephus *Ant.* 4.200); "one God and one Hebrew race" (ibid., 4.201); "one temple of the one God" (idem, *C. Apion.* 2.193); cf. Philo *Conf.* 170; *Opif. mund.* 171; *Spec. leg.* 1.67 (with a reference to $\acute{o}\mu o\nu o\acute{\iota}a$ "concord" in 1.70). Thus the history of the theme shows a progressive narrowing of its application from the cosmos to a holy people and from a holy people to a worshipping community. This background surely explains why both "altar" ($\theta\nu\sigma\iota a\sigma\tau\acute{\eta}\rho\iota o\nu$) and "temple" appear here as symbols of the new people of God (cf. *Eph.* 5.2).

■ **7.2** Ignatius develops such language in a christological direction. The threefold appearance here of the word "one" (*one* Jesus Christ, from the *one* Father, with the *One*, and returning to him) is clearly colored by the context. But the christological pattern itself is traditional and reflects in particular the atmosphere of the Gospel of John: Christ came from the Father (John 8:42; 13:3; 16:28; 17:8), is with him during his ministry (John 8:16; 8:29; 14:10),[4] and returns to him (John 13:3; 14:28; 16:10, 28). Unlike John, however, Ignatius uses the verb $\pi\rho o\epsilon\lambda\theta\epsilon\hat{\iota}\nu$ "proceeded" to describe Christ's coming from the Father (cf. *Mag.* 8.2). This verb is known primarily from Gnostic sources where it is used to describe

emanations from the godhead.[5] But it is unlikely that Gnostics alone found the term convenient. Its later use by Marcellus of Ancyra[6] suggests that it was appropriate wherever the relation between Father and Son was conceived of as especially intimate. In any event, Ignatius employs the term here of the incarnation (not of a precosmic generation), and in that sense it occurs elsewhere in early (non-Gnostic) texts (*Test. Jos.* 19.8; Justin *Dial.* 43.1; 64.7; Hippolytus *Contra haer. Noet.* 17), and at least once even in a strongly anti-Gnostic context where we would expect caution (*3 Cor.* 6: $\H{\iota}\nu a$ $\epsilon\H{\iota}s$ $\kappa\acute{o}\sigma\mu o\nu$ $\pi\rho o\acute{\epsilon}\lambda\theta\eta$[7] "that he might proceed into the world").[8] The emphasis on the unity of Christ with the Father and the theme of his derivation from and return to the Father are analogous to developments in Gnosticism, but Ignatius does not go beyond what had already become domesticated in Johannine circles.

---

4 For $\epsilon\H{\iota}s$ meaning "with," see John 1:18. The expression "being united (with him)" ($\H{\eta}\nu\omega\mu\acute{\epsilon}\nu os$ $\H{\omega}\nu$) in *Mag.* 7.1 (cf. *Sm.* 3.3) expresses the same idea.

5 Schlier, *Untersuchungen*, 35, cf. Clement Alex. *Exc. ex Theod.* 23.1; 35.2; 36.1 (where the angels assigned to the Gnostics are said to be "one, proceeding from the one"). For numerous other examples see the index in Alexander Böhlig and Frederik Wisse, *Nag Hammadi Codices III,2 and IV,2: The Gospel of the Egyptians* (NHS 4; Leiden: Brill, 1975) 228.

6 *LPGL s.v.* $\pi\rho o\acute{\epsilon}\rho\chi o\mu a\iota$ B.1, p. 1147.

7 EINA EIΣ KOΣMON ΠΡΟΕΛΘΗ (Michael Testuz, ed., *Papyrus Bodmer X–XII* (Cologne–Geneva: Bibliotheca Bodmeriana, 1959) 34.

8 Also non-Johannine is the verb $\chi\omega\rho\epsilon\hat{\iota}\nu$ ("go") used of Christ's "return" to the Father, but again it represents no more than a terminological variant. Ignatius uses it also when speaking of the place in the next world to which people will "go" (*Eph.* 16.2; *Mag.* 5.1). For Schlier's treatment of the word see on *Sm.* 6.1.

On Living Jewishly [8.1–10.3]

8

**The Divine Prophets
and the Word from Silence**

1   Be not deceived by erroneous opinions nor
by old fables, which are useless. For if we
continue to live until now according to
Judaism, we confess that we have not
received grace. 2/ For the most divine
prophets lived according to Jesus Christ.
For this reason they were also persecuted, inspired as they were by his grace
so that the disobedient might be persuaded that there is one God who
revealed himself through Jesus Christ his
Son, who is his Word which proceeded
from silence, who in every way pleased
him who sent him.

Ignatius now launches into a warning against living
Jewishly that forms the heart of the letter (*Mag.* 8–10).[1]
A similar issue is addressed in *Phd.* 5–9. These passages
have been taken by some (notably Lightfoot and Zahn) as
evidence that Ignatius confronted a movement in which
docetic ideas and Jewish practices were mixed (as in
Colossians and the Pastorals). Others have argued that
Ignatius was confronted by two different groups—Jewish
Christians (in Magnesia and Philadelphia) and proponents of docetism (especially in Tralles and Smyrna).[2]
The debate was turned in a new direction by Molland,
who tried to show that only one group was involved but
that it stood for an interpretation of Scripture which (in
the interests of a docetic christology) reflected the Jewish
view that the Messiah does not suffer (cf. Justin *Dial.*
90.1).[3] It is my view that in *Mag.* 8–10 Ignatius is
speaking about the observance of Jewish customs (based
on what he regards as a mistaken approach to Scripture);
that such Judaizing was not characterized by docetic
thinking; and that the link between Judaizing and
docetism was invented by Ignatius.

■ **8.1** The Magnesians are to avoid "erroneous opinions"
(cf. *Sm.* 6.2)—literally, "heterodoxies" ($\dot{\epsilon}\tau\epsilon\rho o\delta o\xi\acute{\iota}a\iota$). This
word and the verb $\dot{\epsilon}\tau\epsilon\rho o\delta\iota\delta a\sigma\kappa a\lambda\epsilon\tilde{\iota}\nu$ "to teach er7one-
ously" in *Pol.* 3.1 (cf. 1 Tim 1:3; 6:3) are evidently all but
technical terms for heresy.[4] Such false views are
characterized by Ignatius in language reminiscent of the
polemic of the Pastoral Epistles: they are "fables" that are
"useless" (cf. 1 Tim 1:4; 4:7; Tit 1:14).[5] But what mainly
concerns the bishop is the fact that some still ("until
now") wish to "live according to Judaism." The term
"Judaism" at this time stood for the whole system of
belief and practice of the Jews (cf. 2 Macc 2:21; 8:1;
14:38; *4 Macc.* 4.26); and "living Jewishly" in Christian
polemic meant insisting especially on the ritual requirements of that system (Gal 2:14; cf. 1:13). False views and
misguided practice are similarly linked in Tit 1:14 where
"Jewish fables" and "commandments of men" are

---

1   For the formula "be not deceived" see *Eph.* 5.2; 16.1.
2   For a review of the scholarship on the question see
C. K. Barrett, "Jews and Judaizers in the Epistles of
Ignatius," in R. Hamerton-Kelly and R. Scroggs,
eds., *Jews, Greeks and Christians: Essays in Honor of
William David Davies* (SJLA 21; Leiden: Brill, 1976)
220–44.
3   Einar Molland, "The Heretics Combatted by Ignatius
of Antioch," *JEH* (1954) 1–6.
4   The term "heterodoxy" seems to have philosophical
roots (cf. Plato *Theaet.* 193d). But it is in the early
church that it acquires "an unmistakably (indeed,
exclusively) pejorative sense" (Marcel Simon, "From
Greek Haeresis to Christian Heresy," in William R.
Schoedel and Robert L. Wilken, eds., *Early Christian
Literature and the Classical Intellectual Tradition*
[Théologie historique 53; Paris: Beauchesne, 1979]

111–12; cf. Bartelink, *Lexicologisch-semantische Studie,*
110–11).
5   The rejection of fables (myths) is part of a widespread pattern of polemics in Hellenism (cf. BAG *s.v.*
$\mu\tilde{\upsilon}\theta o\varsigma$, pp. 530–31). Especially interesting in this
regard is Plutarch's call for a correct interpretation
of the myth of Isis and Osiris (*De Isid.* 11, 355b) or
rejection of its more abhorrent features (20, 358e)
coupled with the demand "to have a true opinion
($\dot{a}\lambda\eta\theta\tilde{\eta}$ $\delta\acute{o}\xi a\nu$) about the gods" (11, 355d). Cf. Hans
Dieter Betz and Edgar W. Smith, in Betz, *Plutarch's
Theological Writings,* 51.

mentioned together.[6] But we cannot assume that the situation in the Pastorals and in Ignatius was the same simply because they share a common polemical vocabulary. Thus it may well be that the form of the polemic compelled Ignatius to look for a serious theological disagreement where none existed. In any event, the point on which Ignatius and the Pastorals seem agreed is that Judaism and the Scriptures have nothing to do with one another.

We may observe in this connection that Ignatius speaks of Judaism where Paul would more naturally have spoken of the law.[7] Thus Ignatius' contrast is between grace and Judaism and not, as in Paul, between grace and law (cf. Rom 6:14). For Ignatius the teachings and myths of Judaism are "old" (cf. *Mag.* 9.1; 10.2)—a term that he uses to describe what is opposed to God (cf. *Eph.* 19.3). "Judaism," then, is not granted even a historically limited role in the unfolding of God's plan. Consequently Ignatius radically Christianizes the "prophets" (as we shall see) and elsewhere also the "law" (*Sm.* 5.1). Thus the negative view of Judaism is more emphatic in Ignatius than in the Pastorals and approaches the extreme position of *Barnabas*.

■ **8.2** Ignatius calls the prophets "most divine"—an epithet borrowed from Hellenistic Judaism (cf. Josephus *Ant.* 10.35; *C. Apion.* 1.279; Philo *Mos.* 2.188). Clearly they are modelled to a certain extent on the "divine men" of Hellenistic piety and are thought of as transcending normal humanity (cf. Josephus *Ant.* 3.180; *C. Apion.* 1.279). Elsewhere, however, the prophets are called simply "holy" (*Phd.* 5.2)—an epithet shared by presbyters (*Mag.* 3.1) and indeed all Christians (*Sm.* 1.2). For Ignatius the main thing is that the prophets lived "according to Christ Jesus" and not (it may be inferred) "according to Judaism." Their way of life presupposes (as

we shall see) anticipation of the coming of Christ, but at this point the emphasis must be on their refusal to observe Jewish customs. In light of *Mag.* 9–10, Ignatius probably implies that the prophets did not even keep the Sabbath. For that he could have appealed to Isa 1:13 ("I cannot bear your new moons and sabbaths") which is quoted by *Barnabas* to make a similar point (*Barn.* 15.8; cf. 2.4–6; 9.4; 10.11–12). Presumably, divine men would know the true (spiritual) meaning of the seventh day (cf. John 5:17; Heb 4:4–11).

In any event, the proof of the prophets' Christianity is the fact that they were persecuted. Such persecution was often recalled by Christians in their quarrel with Judaism,[8] and the theme has special significance for Ignatius because of his emphasis on suffering as the mark of Christ and his disciples (cf. *Mag.* 9.1; *Eph.* 10.3). The reason for the persecution of the prophets is then further elaborated in a statement about their inspiration and the theological vision that determined their outlook. Here attention apparently shifts to their anticipation of the coming of Christ (cf. *Mag.* 9.2). As in other writers of the period such anticipation is traced to divine "inspiration"[9] (cf. 1 Pet 1:11; Justin *Apol.* 1.32–53; Irenaeus *Adv. haer.* 4.20.5) or to the influence of the "grace" of Christ (*Barn.* 5.6; cf. Irenaeus *Adv. haer.* 4.27.2). But apparently Ignatius also shared the widespread view that the prophets spoke primarily to persuade the "disobedient" (Jews?) of NT times. For the conviction said to be established by the prophets not only contains explicitly Christian components but also speaks of Christ's ministry as past ("revealed," "pleased"). This is not an anachronistic summary of the prophetic message to their contemporaries but a statement about the faith elicited by that message after the coming of Christ. The view is that for all except a few everything falls into place only after the

---

6 For the supposed connection between them see Dibelius/Conzelmann, *Pastoral Epistles*, 16–17.

7 The reading of G (preserved by Zahn), κατὰ νόμον Ἰουδαϊσμὸν ζῶμεν "we live Judaism according to the law," is unlikely Greek. The reading of gA, κατὰ νόμον Ἰουδαϊκόν "according to the Jewish law," represents an effort to correct G. The text of L (κατὰ Ἰουδαϊσμόν "according to Judaism") is to be accepted particularly in light of the κατὰ Χριστιανισμὸν ζῆν "to live according to Christianity" in *Mag.* 10.1. The word "law" probably crept in under the influence of the Pauline polemic.

8 Cf. Matt 5:12; 23:29–32; Luke 11:47–51; Acts 7:51–52; Irenaeus *Adv. haer.* 4.33.9; Cyprian *Ad Quirinum* 1.2.

9 The description of the prophets as "inspired" is another echo of Hellenistic conceptions (cf. BAG *s.v.* ἐμπνέω, p. 256). Similar notions are found in other statements about the Bible and the saints of old (cf. 2 Tim 3:16; 2 Pet 1:21; Theophilus *Ad Aut.* 2.9).

fulfillment of the prophecies (cf. Cyprian *Ad Quirinum* 1.4). Consequently, appeals to Scripture are indecisive apart from that fulfillment (cf. *Phd.* 8.2), and we see why the refusal to abandon Jewish ways "until now"—after the grace of Christ has become generally accessible—is what is so incomprehensible to Ignatius (8.1).

The conviction established by the prophets consists of the Jewish acclamation "God is one" and a three-line elaboration of it. Elaborations of the acclamation in Christian terms are particularly frequent in Syrian inscriptions from the days that the evidence becomes available,[10] and this may represent a well-entrenched tradition. However that may be, the elaboration in Ignatius presents many special problems.

In the first line of the elaboration a virtual identity of God and Christ is proclaimed. For God is said to have "revealed himself" ($\phi\alpha\nu\epsilon\rho\omega\sigma\alpha\varsigma$ $\dot{\epsilon}\alpha\nu\tau\dot{o}\nu$) through Jesus Christ. This is the presupposition also in *Eph.* 19.3 where Ignatius speaks of Christ as "God revealed as human being" ($\theta\epsilon o\hat{\upsilon}$ $\dot{\alpha}\nu\theta\rho\omega\pi\dot{\iota}\nu\omega\varsigma$ $\phi\alpha\nu\epsilon\rho o\upsilon\mu\dot{\epsilon}\nu o\upsilon$). The close relation between Christ and the Father is underscored by the fact that the separate existence of Christ as God's "Son" is associated here (as in *Sm.* 1.1) with the incarnation. From the perspective of later developments in christology, that is close to modalism. And the image of the "word which proceeded from silence" ($\lambda\dot{o}\gamma o\varsigma$ $\dot{\alpha}\pi\dot{o}$ $\sigma\iota\gamma\hat{\eta}\varsigma$ $\pi\rho o\epsilon\lambda\theta\dot{\omega}\nu$) in the next line reinforces the impression

that before Christ's coming the divine is conceived of as an undifferentiated unity.[11] Yet since Ignatius speaks in this very passage about the prophets being inspired by the grace of Christ (and just above in *Mag.* 6.1 about the preexistence of Christ—though not of the Son—with the Father), we must conclude that the modalism of the passage is not unmitigated.

The question that has preoccupied recent research is whether what obtains here is not so much modalism as a Gnostic conception of the relation between Christ and the Father. Here the second line of the elaboration is particularly important. The description of Christ as the "word [or speech] which proceeded ($\pi\rho o\epsilon\lambda\theta\dot{\omega}\nu$) from silence"[12] can be compared with *Mag.* 7.2 where Christ is said to be the one who "proceeded ($\pi\rho o\epsilon\lambda\theta\dot{o}\nu\tau\alpha$) from the one Father"; an identity of silence and the Father can be deduced; and a long list of Gnostic or Gnosticizing parallels to such a view of God can be found.[13] This explanation is reinforced by the fact that here the appearance of the divine Word or "speech" ($\lambda\dot{o}\gamma o\varsigma$) is associated not with creation or revelation in the OT period but with Christ's appearance.[14] It has reasonably been suggested that this represents an echo of the Gnostic view of Christ as the revealer of the unknown Father.

Yet it is doubtful that this interpretation is correct. (a) An identification of God and silence is not found

---

10 Peterson, ΕΙΣ ΘΕΟΣ, 1–46.

11 See the striking appropriation of precisely such language by the fourth-century modalist, Marcellus of Ancyra, who ascribed a certain "quiet" ($\dot{\eta}\sigma\upsilon\chi\dot{\iota}\alpha$) to God and said that "after the silence ($\sigma\iota\gamma\dot{\eta}$) and quiet ($\dot{\eta}\sigma\upsilon\chi\dot{\iota}\alpha$) the Word ($\lambda\dot{o}\gamma o\varsigma$) of God came forth ($\pi\rho o\epsilon\lambda\theta\epsilon\hat{\iota}\nu$) at the beginning of the making of the world" (Eusebius *Eccl. theolog.* 2.9).

12 GL read $\alpha\dot{\upsilon}\tau o\hat{\upsilon}$ $\lambda\dot{o}\gamma o\varsigma$ $\dot{\alpha}\dot{\iota}\delta\iota o\varsigma$ $o\dot{\upsilon}\kappa$ $\dot{\alpha}\pi\dot{o}$ $\sigma\iota\gamma\hat{\eta}\varsigma$ $\pi\rho o\epsilon\lambda\theta\dot{\omega}\nu$ "his eternal Word which did *not* proceed from silence." Recently this reading has again been defended and used to support the view that our letters were written against fully developed forms of Gnosticism (Joly, *Ignace*, 71–73). But Zahn and Lightfoot were surely right in seeing this reading as a correction introduced by later orthodox theologians perplexed by Ignatius' apparent acceptance of a Gnostic title for God. Zahn and Lightfoot have the support of Severus and of the Armenian and Arabic versions. And although it is correct that Ignatius nowhere else flatly identifies God and silence (if that is what he does here), the two are closely related in

Eph. 19.1.

13 See especially Irenaeus *Adv. haer.* 1.1.1; 2.12.2; Clement Alex. *Exc. ex Theod.* 29; *PGM* 4,559. Cf. L. W. Barnard, "The Background of St. Ignatius of Antioch," *VC* 17 (1963) 193–206; Schlier, *Untersuchungen*, 38; Bartsch, *Gnostisches Gut*, 57–61; Paulsen, *Studien*, 110–14. Numerous examples of the identification are also found in the Coptic *Gospel of the Egyptians* (NHC 3,2; 4,2). Especially interesting for our purposes are two passages: (a) Barbelo is said to have originated from herself, to have "proceeded" ($\pi\rho o\epsilon\lambda\theta\epsilon\hat{\iota}\nu$), and to have "agreed ($\epsilon\dot{\upsilon}\delta o\kappa\epsilon\hat{\iota}\nu$) with the Father [of the] silent [Silence]" (42,17–21 in NHC 3; 52,11–14 in NHC 4); (b) Doxomedon is regarded as the "word" who came forth from the silence ($\sigma\iota\gamma\dot{\eta}$) and still "rests in the silence" (43,21–24 in NHC 3; 53,20–26 in NHC 4). Other examples of a varied use of the theme from the Nag Hammadi materials include *Gos. Truth* (NHC 1) 37,10–12; *Disc. 8–9* (NHC 6) 58,20; 59,20–21; *Interp. Know.* (NHC 11) 7,3; *Trim. Prot.* (NHC 13) 42,4–5; 46,11–14.

14 Though *Eph.* 15.1 may presuppose a view of the

120

elsewhere in Ignatius. In *Eph.* 15.1–2 the reference is to the speech and silence of Christ. And although God is associated with quietness in *Eph.* 19.1, it is unlikely (as we have seen) that the passage reflects an identification of God and silence. (b) If Ignatius flatly equates God and silence in our passage, there is considerable tension between the image of speech proceeding from silence and the image in the following line of God sending the Son.[15] (c) If we look at the passage from the point of view of a tradition in which Christ had become known as the Word (cf. John 1:1), a desire to complete the image by referring to "silence" as well as to "speech" is comprehensible. That Ignatius is still very close to the purely metaphorical use of language is suggested by the way in which he plays with the relation between speech and silence in *Rom.* 2.1 and by his description of Christ as "the unlying mouth by which the Father spoke the truth" in *Rom.* 8.2. To be sure, even the latter image was probably not invented by Ignatius (cf. *Odes Sol.* 12.3; 12.11; *Gos. Truth* [NHC 1] 26,34–35). But he does not appear to exploit the possible mythological or metaphysical implications of his terminology. It should be noted that in our passage the connection between Christ and the word from silence is made by means of the expression ὅς ἐστιν ("who is") which elsewhere in Ignatius is used to set terms in a striking or novel relation to each other and thus sometimes also to link images and their referents (see on *Eph.* 20.2). The theme may have been prompted in part by Ignatius' reflections on the problem of the relation between words and deeds on which he builds elsewhere in his defense of the silence of the Ephesian bishop (see on *Eph.* 6.1; 14.2–15.2). There Christ's audible word is regarded as operative and his silent deed as speaking volumes, and it is this that puts Ignatius in a position to attribute profound religious significance to the silence of the bishop. Ignatius was not alone in deepening the meaning of an apparent commonplace in this way: Plutarch (*De garrul.* 4,504a) in a discussion of talkativeness calls its opposite, "silence" (σιγή), something "deep" and "mysterious."[16] What Plutarch had in mind was the silence required during initiation into the mysteries (cf. *De garrul.* 8, 505f), and a similar fascination with mystery and silence is known in various other strands of Hellenism as well (particularly Pythagoreanism).[17] The general respect for silence shared by Ignatius thus easily leads over to a theological application of the theme. Yet in Ignatius God's silence has value only in light of the revelation of the Word, and what he apparently had in mind (as in *Eph.* 19.1) was the fact that God did not comment openly on what he was about in the events of the incarnation.

For there are contexts in which (to speak more prosaically than Ignatius) the silence of God has to do with his hidden purposes in the unfolding of the divine plan. Thus Tertullian likens God's speech and reason to those of human beings, arguing that God contained his speech in his reason "as he silently (*tacite*) planned and arranged within himself what he was soon to utter through his speech" (*Adv. Prax.* 5.4; cf. 5.5, 7). The context is in favor of such an interpretation of the theme in Ignatius. For the bishop is claiming the prophets for Christ, the very prophets who await him yet whose message remains unclear to the majority until his coming. This obscurity is surely part of what is meant by God's silence. Thus Clement of Alexandria speaks of the "Word" as "unravelling the mystic silence (σιωπή) of the prophetic enigmas" (*Protr.* 1.10.1). In a more biblical vein, Paul or a later hand speaks in Rom 16:25–27 of the mystery "kept silent" (σεσιγημένον) for ages yet now

---

15 Cf. Elze, *Untersuchungen,* 56–59. Elze also notes the Jewish coloring of the language in the third line of the elaboration (Christ "pleased" the one who sent him as Enoch is said to have "pleased" God in Gen 5:24 LXX and Sir 44:16; the theme of God's sending in *Eph.* 6.1 is associated with the Jewish language of Matt 21:33–42) and concludes that Wis 18:14–15 (where God's word leaps down from heaven while all is pervaded by silence) still offers the best parallel to the second line of the elaboration.

Word as active already in creation.

16 Cf. William A. Beardslee, in Betz, *Plutarch's Ethical Writings,* 274.

17 Raoul Mortley, "The Theme of Silence in Clement of Alexandria," *JTS* N.S. 24 (1973) 197–202; cf. Odo Casel, *De philosophorum Graecorum silentio mystico* (RVV 16/2; Giessen: Töpelmann, 1919). Here the relation between speech and silence was also sometimes explored (cf. Philostratus *Vit. Apoll.* 1.1; 6.11).

"revealed" (cf. Col 1:26; Eph 3:9) and made known "through the prophetic writings."[18]

The theme of silence, then, should not be isolated from its context. For just as Ignatius' identification of Christ as the "unlying mouth" of God in *Rom.* 8.2 is brought to bear on the bishop's own desire to be believed, so in our passage the identification of Christ as the word from silence was chosen with an eye to the problem of the relation between the prophets and "Judaism." The silence of God is invoked to account for the supposed inability of the Jews and Judaizers to understand Scripture. And Christ is thought of as emerging from a sphere of silence only in the sense that his appearance brings the hidden purpose of God to light. It is possible, of course, that Ignatius is here revising a Gnostic theme. But we have also seen that there are alternatives to this. In any event, what Ignatius is announcing in our passage is the clarification with the coming of Christ of what was previously obscure.

---

18   Unless the reference to the prophets is a late addition intended to counteract Marcionite tendencies thought to be at work in the text, the writer must mean that the words of the prophets and the ministry of Christ support and illuminate one another and together set forth the mystery hid from the ages. That is precisely the view of Ignatius as I understand it. For the biblical background to this language of mystery and silence see L.-M Dewailly, "Mystère et silence dans Rom. xvi.25," *NTS* 14 (1967) 111–18.

On Living Jewishly [8.1–10.3]

9

The Abandonment of Judaism
by the Apostles

1   If, then, those who lived in old ways came
to newness of hope, no longer keeping
Sabbath, but living in accordance with
the Lord's day, on which also our life
arose through him and his death (which
some deny), through which mystery we
received faith, and therefore we endure
that we may be found disciples of Jesus
Christ, our only teacher; 2/ how shall we
be able to live without him of whom the
prophets also were disciples in the spirit,
him to whom they looked forward as
their teacher? And therefore he for whom
they rightly waited came and raised them
from the dead.

■ **9.1** Ignatius now turns to the early Christians who abandoned their allegiance to Judaism. The view that he still has the prophets in mind (Hilgenfeld, Molland[1]) must be rejected. It would be unnatural to attribute to the "most divine prophets" as described in *Mag.* 8.1–2 the need for conversion referred to here.[2] Ignatius is speaking of the early disciples who once lived as Jews (by observing the Sabbath) but came to live as Christians (by observing Sunday).[3] It seems only reasonable to suppose that the discussion was prompted by pressures exerted by some in favor of Sabbath observance. Yet that is not stated, and it may be that the question of the Sabbath was brought up or at least over-emphasized by Ignatius himself because it served as a convenient point of departure for illustrating the unacceptability of "Juda-

ism." The Judaizers of Magnesia (somewhat like the author of Hebrews or his audience) may have been more interested in the idea of Judaism than in the practice of it.[4] One possibility is that they seemed to Ignatius to devote too much attention to the problem of the meaning of biblical texts (about which Ignatius himself apparently knew little) and ran the risk from his point of view of forgetting the centrality of Christ and of falling back into Jewish practices (see on *Phd.* 5–9). This may account for the fact that the expressions "keeping Sabbath" and "living in accordance with the Lord's day" serve primarily to characterize two whole ways of life. The exact situation in regard to observance in Magnesia could thus be left conveniently up in the air.

In any event, Ignatius emphasizes the significance of

1   Adolf Hilgenfeld, *Ignatii Antiocheni et Polycarpi Smyrnaei epistulae et martyria* (Berlin: Schwetschke, 1902) 280; Einar Molland, "The Heretics Combatted by Ignatius of Antioch," *JEH* 5 (1954) 3.

2   And, as we have argued above, Ignatius is speaking of the contemporary relevance of the message of the prophets already in *Mag.* 8.2.

3   G reads κατὰ κυριακὴν ζωὴν ζῶντες "living according to the Lord's life." This is an awkward effort to improve on the more difficult expression κατὰ κυριακὴν (sc. ἡμέραν) ζῶντες "living according to the Lord's day," which is the reading of L. For other early references to some kind of observance on the first day of the week see 1 Cor 16:2; Acts 20:7; Rev 1:10 (?); *Did.* 14.1; *Barn.* 15.9. For the use of κυριακή alone to refer to "the Lord's day" see *Did.* 14.1 (?); *Gos. Pet.* 9.35; 12.50; Melito, in Eusebius *Hist. eccl.*

4.26.2 (cf. *LPGL s.v.* κυριακός 4.d, p. 786). Efforts to evade the reference to Sunday in the interest of Seventh-day Adventism are strained. Cf. Fritz Guy, "The Lord's Day in the Letter of Ignatius to the Magnesians," *AUSS* 2 (1964) 1–17; Richard B. Lewis, "Ignatius and the Lord's Day," *AUSS* 6 (1968) 46–59; Samuele Bacchiocchi, *From Sabbath to Sunday* (Pontificia Universitas Gregoriana; Rome: The Pontifical Gregorian University, 1977) 213–23.

4   Cf. Alexander C. Purdy, "The Epistle to the Hebrews," *The Interpreter's Bible* (12 vols.; New York and Nashville: Abingdon Press, 1952–57) 11. 591.

Sunday by connecting it with the Lord's resurrection. In saying that on that day "our life" (that is, Christ or the new being embodied in Christ) "arose" (ἀνέτειλεν), he uses a verb not usually associated with the resurrection but with the rising sun. Similar imagery (though not applied to Sunday) occurs also in *Rom.* 2.2. The meaning of Sunday was soon to be worked out more fully in such terms by Justin (*Apol.* 1.67.3, 7). The symbolism provided a significant point of contact with widely diffused patterns of thought in Hellenism.[5]

But Ignatius makes a characteristic move when he links the resurrection with the mystery of Christ's death and emphasizes the latter as that through which faith comes. For it is Christ's death that stands out as a "mystery" in Ignatius' mind (*Eph.* 19.1). One purpose of Ignatius here is to present the passion and resurrection (not Scripture as misinterpreted by the Jews and Judaizers) as that which determines the shape of Christian existence (and makes sense of Scripture). It is for this reason that Christ is called the "only teacher" whose "disciples" we must be (compare the use of the slogan "one teacher" in *Eph.* 15.1). Consequently, our "endurance" is a sign of our discipleship precisely because, for Ignatius, Christ's teaching consists of his enactment of his Father's will in being obedient to the point of death. This interpretation is strengthened by the reference in 9.2 to the prophets as also being "disciples" who awaited Christ "as teacher." For their discipleship was also evidenced by the fact that they were persecuted (*Mag.* 8.2); and no doubt Ignatius thought of the substance of their expectations as centered about the passion and resurrection (cf.

Sm. 5.1; 7.2). These expectations, now realized in Christ, preclude any Jewish interpretation of Scripture (or any observance of Jewish customs).

■ **9.2** The prophets are recalled for the purpose of putting the Judaizers to shame. The fact that the prophets were disciples "in the spirit" reminds us that they did not have the advantage of looking back to Christ's fleshly presence. Even so, unlike the Judaizers who had this advantage, they emphasized the centrality of Christ. And Christ confirmed their witness by raising them from the dead. In making this last point, Ignatius packs too much into one sentence: "for whom they rightly waited" refers to the activity of the prophets in this world (cf. *Phd.* 5.2), not in the underworld; "came," on the other hand, must refer to a descent of Christ into Hades;[6] and "raised them from the dead," unusual as it may sound in this context, reflects the language of some descriptions of Christ's victory in the underworld.[7]

The logic, then, of Ignatius' position in 9.1–2 is that Judaizing implies the denial of Christ's death and resurrection. This thought is explicitly formulated in 9.1 where Christ's death (or the fact that the resurrection life came "through his death") is said to be denied by some.[8] The pronoun "some" seems to have been chosen (as in *Sm.* 5.1) to serve as a warning to any who might be tempted to fall into this error. But the statement also suggests that Ignatius had in mind a denial of the passion more thoroughgoing than our argument has so far indicated. What "some deny" in *Sm.* 5.1 is the very reality of Christ's death. Ignatius' summary in *Mag.* 11 of the point of the letter suggests that it is precisely such docetic

---

5 Rahner, *Greek Myths*, 89–176.

6 Daniélou, *Jewish Christianity*, 233–48. Schlier's view (*Untersuchungen*, 72–76) that we have to do with an ascent to a supra-mundane sphere in which the prophets wait has no foundation in the text and is apparently determined by a desire to find additional support for his interpretation of *Eph.* 19.2 as the description of an ascent.

7 Tertullian *Anim.* 55.4 (*patriarchae et prophetae appendices dominicae resurrectionis ab inferis migraverint* "the patriarchs and prophets moved from the lower regions as appendages of the Lord's resurrection"); *Act. Thadd.* 3; Eusebius *Hist. eccl.* 1.13.20; Origen *Comm. in Rom.* 5.10 (*PG* 14. 1052A); *Gos. Nicod.* 19.12; 20.2; 21.2; cf. *Odes Sol.* 42.15–26. The resurrection of the saints in Matt 27:51–53 has sometimes been thought to presuppose the descent

theme. But that is uncertain; and in any event, Ignatius does not reflect the story as we have it in the Gospel of Matthew.

8 G reads οἵτινες ἀρνοῦνται. We may read either ὅ τινες with L or ὅν τινες with Lightfoot. In either case the reference will be to Christ's death or to the preceding remark as a whole (that life came through Christ's death). It is unlikely that the statement refers to the observance of Sunday (Bartsch, *Gnostisches Gut*, 38). Note that the parallel in *Sm.* 5.1 ("whom some deny") has in view Christ's passion.

theology that he is criticizing here (note especially the expression, "things truly and surely done"). Apparently the logic that enabled Ignatius to connect Judaizing with the denial of Christ's death is now stretched to the point that even allusions to docetic christology are deemed appropriate. Such allusions, then, cannot be taken too seriously. The expression "which some deny" (9.1) is purely parenthetical, and the summary in *Mag.* 11 is relatively anemic as an anti-docetic statement (contrast the emphasis gained by the repetition of the adverb ἀληθῶς "truly" in *Tr.* 9.1–2 and *Sm.* 1.1–2). We may conclude that Ignatius had been told about (relatively mild) Judaizing tendencies in Magnesia, that he construes them as a greater threat than they were, and that he seeks to deal with them by hinting at a link between them and the more dangerous threat of docetism.[9]

---

9 Some interpreters have tried to account for the view of the Judaizers in *Mag.* 9 by supposing that Ignatius is countering a Jewish-Christian denial of Christ's divinity. But the evidence for this is slight and is better accounted for by allowing for exaggeration on the part of Ignatius. For he goes so far as to find the Judaizers prepared to "live without (Christ)" (9.2). At the same time, when it comes to technical christological questions, the only danger that he seems to recognize here is docetism.

On Living Jewishly [8.1–10.3]

10   The Abandonment of Judaism Urged

1   **Let us not, then, be insensible to his goodness! For if he imitates us in our actions, we no longer exist! Therefore let us become his disciples and learn to live according to Christianity. For one who is called by any name other than this, is not of God. 2/ Set aside, then, the evil leaven, old and sour, and turn to the new leaven, which is Jesus Christ. Be salted with him to keep anyone among you from being spoiled, since you will be convicted by your odor. 3/ It is ridiculous to profess Jesus Christ and to Judaize; for Christianity did not believe in Judaism, but Judaism in Christianity, into which every tongue that has believed in God has been gathered together.**

■ **10.1** Finally, Ignatius turns directly to his own contemporaries and urges on them the rejection of Judaizing. The argument of the first two sentences apparently runs as follows: to Judaize is to ignore God's goodness (that is, to rely on something other than the death and resurrection of Christ); if God should imitate such neglect on our part, we are very badly off indeed. In short, Ignatius indirectly threatens divine punishment. To avert it, the Magnesians are to become "disciples" of Christ (see on *Mag.* 9.1) and to live "according to Christianity";[1] no other name (such as "Judaism") is to be adopted (cf. *Mag.* 8.1).

■ **10.2** Ignatius goes on to confirm the point with the help of images already traditional in the early church: the Magnesians are to eliminate the "old leaven" of Judaism and turn to the "new" leaven, Christ (cf. 1 Cor 5:7–8; Gal 5:9); they are to be "salted" with him (cf. Matt 5:13; Luke 14:34–35; Mark 9:49–50)[2] so that they will not rot (like unsalted meat) and give off a bad smell (see on *Eph.* 17.1).

■ **10.3** The final argument is a historical one: Judaism yielded to Christianity, not Christianity to Judaism. Here Ignatius comes closest to recognizing "Judaism" as a

legitimate stage in the unfolding of the divine plan. From this point of view it is possible that the opening argument in *Mag.* 8.1—that if we *still* live Jewishly, we have not received grace—implies that living Jewishly was once acceptable. But in light of everything else that is said, the most that can be meant is that living Jewishly once had some excuse (since the inspired prophets spoke a language that was intelligible only in light of later events). Christianity, for Ignatius, fulfills the prophets (Scripture) but negates "Judaism" (the misunderstanding of Scripture). Thus the curious remark that Judaism "believed in" Christianity makes sense only if Ignatius is recalling the first generation of Jewish Christians referred to in *Mag.* 9.1 who left their old (essentially godless) ways and turned to Christ. They are the ones who "believed in Christianity." Consequently this is not a comment on the preparatory role of the people of God in the OT period.

In his concluding remark, Ignatius touches on the universalism that was thought to set Christianity apart from Judaism. The expression "every tongue" is reminiscent of the end of the hymn to Christ in Phil 2:11 ("and every tongue confess that Jesus Christ is Lord") which in

---

1   This is the first appearance of the proper noun "Christianity" in Christian literature (cf. *Mag.* 10.3; *Rom.* 3.3; *Phd.* 6.1). Its appearance is not at all surprising (despite Joly, *Ignace,* 63). The proper noun "Christian" was already in use (cf. Acts 11:26; 26:28; 1 Pet 4:16), and the term "Judaism" (see on *Mag.* 8.1) provided a ready model for the creation of a noun to describe the distinctive identity of the Christian

movement (cf. *Mart. Pol.* 10.1).

2   For the literal and metaphorical value of salt in antiquity see Pliny *Nat. hist.* 31.41.87–89. The verb διαφθείρειν ("to corrupt") is a theological term in Ignatius (as in *Eph.* 17.1). But here it also refers to food that has "spoiled" (cf. LSJ *s.v.* διαφθείρω II, p. 418).

turn looks back to Isa 45:23 ("*every tongue* will confess"). The Isaianic passage is quoted in full elsewhere by Paul (Rom 14:11) and may have stood out for him and others because it occurs from an early period near the conclusion of the synagogue service in a prayer for a united humanity.[3] Even closer to Ignatius in some ways, however, is Isa 66:18 ("I am coming *to gather together all* nations and *tongues*"). This verse shares the theme of the Jewish prayer and the Christian hymn and evidently flowed together with Isa 45:23 in the mind of someone because of overlapping terminology ("every tongue"/"all . . . tongues"). What we have here, then, is an example of Ignatius' reading of the prophets—a reading probably mediated to him through a liturgical tradition and ultimately dependent on the very Judaism against which he spoke.

---

3   Joseph H. Hertz, *Daily Prayer Book* (New York: Bloch, 1961) 211; Tryggve Kronhelm, *Seder R. Amran Gaon,* Part 2: *The Order of Sabbath Prayer* (Lund: Gleerup, 1974) 70.

11 The Closing and Farewell [11–15]

11 (I write) these things, my beloved, not because I know that some of you are so disposed, but as one less than you I wish to forewarn you not to get caught on the hooks of vain opinion but to be convinced of the birth, and of the suffering, and of the resurrection which took place in the time of the rule of Pontius Pilate—things truly and surely done by Jesus Christ, our hope, from which may none of you be turned.

12 May I benefit from you in every way, if I be worthy; for even though I am in bonds, I am nothing in comparison with one of you who are free. I know that you are not conceited; for you have Jesus Christ in you. And further, when I praise you, I know that you blush—as it is written, "the just man is his own accuser."

13 Be eager, then, to be confirmed in the precepts of the Lord and the apostles that "in everything you do you may prosper," as to flesh and spirit, as to faith and love, in the Son and the Father [and in the Spirit], in the beginning and in the end, with your most right worthy bishop, and your worthily woven spiritual crown, the presbytery, and the godly deacons. 2/ Be subject to the bishop and to each other as Jesus Christ (was subject) to the Father [according to the flesh], and the apostles to Christ [and the Father and the Spirit], that there may be a union both fleshly and spiritual.

14 Knowing that you are full of God, I exhorted you briefly. Remember me in your prayers, that I may attain God, and (remember) the church in Syria, from which I am not worthy to be called; for I need your prayer and love united in God that the church in Syria may be judged worthy to be refreshed with dew from your church.

15 The Ephesians greet you from Smyrna—from which I also write you—being here for the glory of God—as you are too—who together with Polycarp, bishop of the Smyrnaeans, have refreshed me in every way. And the rest of the churches also greet you in honor of Jesus Christ. Farewell in godly concord, possessing an unwavering spirit, which is Jesus Christ.

The vocative ("my beloved") at the beginning of *Mag.* 11 marks a major transition,[1] and since a verb like ἔγραψα ("I write") must be understood here (as Zahn suggests; cf.

Rom. 8.3), we have before us an approximation of a "disclosure formula" (cf. *Eph.* 9.1).[2] It is closest to the type most frequently used for the closing section of the

---

1 White, *Form and Function*, 29–30.
2 Ibid., 11–15. The opening line of *Mag.* 11 reflects features of two of the standard types: ἔγραψα οὖν σοι

ἵνα εἰδῇς "*I write*, then, that you may know"; γινώσκειν σε θέλω ὅτι . . . "*I want* you to *know* that. . . ." (Ignatius uses no purpose clause to express his reason for

body of a letter[3] (which we have here in *Mag.* 11–13). The unusual length of the closing may be taken to reflect Ignatius' unwillingness to let slip the opportunity to make his meaning as clear as possible. An alternative would be to regard the first sentence of *Mag.* 14—which is also a type of "disclosure formula"[4]—as the body closing and *Mag.* 11–13 as an independent unit (cf. *Tr.* 8.1). But *Mag.* 11–13 more or less conforms to our expectations of a body closing and contains materials similar to those at the end of the other letters of Ignatius (see on *Eph.* 20–21). Consequently it seems better to regard the first line of *Mag.* 14 as a second formula of transition from the body to the conclusion of the letter.

■ **11** The reason for writing disclosed by Ignatius is not that he wanted to criticize the Magnesians for actually having fallen prey[5] to the erroneous opinions[6] discussed but that he desired to warn them against possible dangers. The same approach is taken elsewhere by Ignatius (*Tr.* 8.1; *Sm.* 4.1) and reflects the tendency in his letters to set forth recommendations as in principle already achieved (cf. *Eph.* 4.1) and to minimize the success of teachers not in harmony with the bishop (see on *Eph.* 6.2). But it may also be noted that in the same context in which Demosthenes defines the function of the orator as stimulating people to "concord and friendship" (see on *Mag.* 1.2; cf. *Mag.* 13.2; 15), we are also told that the orator is "to see things getting a foothold (ἀρχόμενα), to foresee (προαίσθεσθαι) what is coming, and to forewarn (προειπεῖν) others" (*Coron.* 246). Rhetoricians continued to play this role in Hellenistic cities, and it seems likely that Ignatius' self-understanding is partly shaped by such models.

The body closing fulfills its function of summarizing the point of the letter by urging adherence to the birth, death, and resurrection of Jesus Christ (the denial of which Ignatius sees as implied in Judaizing). The language here has contacts with the quasi-credal material of *Tr.* 9 and *Sm.* 1 particularly in the mention of the crucifixion under Pontius Pilate. Since this historical reference soon appears in widely scattered examples of the rule of faith,[7] it was evidently already traditional. Otherwise the passage appears to be freely formulated by Ignatius. The mention of Pilate was probably designed to underscore the reality of the passion in the face of docetic doctrine. A somewhat more definite expression of opposition to docetism is before us in the phrase "truly and surely done" (see on *Mag.* 9.2).

Ignatius' reference to himself as "one less (μικρότερος) than you" (cf. 1 Cor 15:9, ἐλάχιστος τῶν ἀποστόλων "least of the apostles") and the whole of the next paragraph (*Mag.* 12) reflect the function of body closings in bringing to expression the writer's conception of the relation between himself and his addressees.

■ **12** Ignatius begins with a statement consisting of a formula of polite request (presumably that his recommendations be not ignored) and an expression of his possible unworthiness (cf. *Eph.* 2.2). Ignatius elaborates on the latter in a paradoxical reflection on his bonds. On the one hand, "even though (εἰ καί) I am in bonds" (δέδεμαι) clearly presupposes that the bonds lend him prestige (cf. *Mag.* 1.2); on the other hand, they are also symbolic of his inferiority; for he is nothing in comparison with the Magnesians, "who are free" (λελυμένων). What follows shows that Ignatius has in mind first of all a tendency to pride that he elsewhere fears may destroy him (*Tr.* 4.1). Such pride has no hold on the Magnesians, whose lives are completely dominated by Christ.[8] This distinction between the "bound" Ignatius and the "free" Magnesians attributes to the latter an apostolic quality of life; for whereas Ignatius is a δοῦλος "slave," the apostles

---

writing, yet clearly presupposes the more conventional formulation.)

3   "I write that you may know" (cf. White, *Form and Function*, 45–46).

4   This type is characterized by the use of the verb "to know" in participial form (εἰδὼς ὅτι "knowing that"). It is not generally used in body closings, according to White (ibid., 45).

5   For the metaphorical use of the word "hooks" (fish-hooks) see Diogenes Laertius 4.47; Plutarch *De virt. moral.* 6, 446a; Aristaenetus *Ep.* 1.17; cf. Lucian *Pisc.* 47. From the same circle of metaphors comes the

word "lure" used in Jas 1:14 (cf. Plutarch *De ser. num. vind.* 10, 554f). For the full development of the imagery in connection with heresy see Theodoret *Hist. eccl.* 5.13.6.

6   Κενοδοξία has two meanings (conceit, vain opinion) of which the second is relevant here (compare the ἑτεροδοξία "false opinion" of *Mag.* 8.1). In *Phd.* 1.1, however, the first meaning obtains.

7   Cf. Justin *Apol.* 1.13.3; 1.61.13; *Dial.* 30.3; Irenaeus *Adv. haer.* 2.32.4; 3.4.2; Tertullian *Virg. veland.* 1.3.

8   For the theme of "having" God or Christ within (*Eph.* 15.3; *Rom.* 6.3; *Mag.* 12.1; cf. Gal 2:20; Rom 8:11)

are ἐλεύθεροι "free men" (*Rom.* 4.3). We have explored the connection between these sets of terms elsewhere (see on *Eph.* 12.1). Here it may be noted that the connection is supported by a similar use of images in Epictetus: "he who is free (λελυμένος) in body but bound (δεδεμένος) in soul is a slave (δοῦλος); he, however, who is bound (δεδεμένος) in body but free (λελυμένος) in soul is a free man (ἐλεύθερος)" (*Gnom.* 32). If we are right in thinking that the superiority of the Ephesians to Ignatius had to do with their possession of an apostolically inspired unity as opposed to the disunity of Ignatius' own Antiochene church (see on *Eph.* 11.2), then we also have the reason for the sequence of thoughts in *Mag.* 12: Ignatius is inferior to the Magnesians because they maintain an attitude of humility whereas he himself is conscious of impulses that push him in the opposite direction—impulses that may well have complicated his relations with his own church.

Ignatius' commendation of the Magnesians for blushing even when praised is illustrated by a quotation from Prov 18:17. The passage is not otherwise used in the early period.[9] But it is linked in a number of ways with the biblical passage quoted in *Eph.* 5.3: both quotations (and only these quotations in Ignatius) are introduced by the formula "as it is written"; both are from the Book of Proverbs; and both are on the theme of pride. And since the quotation in *Eph.* 5.3 appears in an unusual form in a number of different sources and consequently was probably known to Ignatius without direct recourse to the Bible, it is likely that the same is true also of the quotation before us.

■ **13.1** There follow in *Mag.* 13 exhortations that summarize the appeal of the letter as a whole (see on *Eph.* 20.2). The first of these begins with a call for obedience to the precepts of the Lord and the apostles.[10] The term δόγματα ("precepts") occurs only here in Ignatius but is found also elsewhere as an ethical term (precepts of the Lord are mentioned in *Barn.* 1.6 and precepts of the apostles in Acts 16:4). In Ignatius their content is as undefined as the "commandments" of Christ (*Eph.* 9.2), the "law" of Christ (*Mag.* 2), or the "commands" (διατάγματα) of the apostles (*Tr.* 7.1; cf. *Rom.* 4.3). For Ignatius thinks of the ordered life of the community as the manifestation of a unity rooted in the events of salvation. It is probably for this reason that there came to his mind at this point words from Ps 1:3 which in other early sources are connected with the cross through the preceding reference in the psalm to the "wood" (cross) planted by streams of water (*Barn.* 11.6, 8; cf. Justin *Dial.* 86.4). In any event, Ignatius goes on to list four sets of polarities that serve to express the totality of the "prosperity"—that is, unity (cf. 13.2)—of the Magnesians (see Introduction, 5.6, 8, 11). In *Mag.* 1.2 three of the same four sets occur in the same order and are there also connected with unity. The significance of the order is suggested more clearly in the passage before us: unity in the church (whose fullness is indicated by the polarities of flesh and spirit and of faith and love) is grounded "in" the divine unity (Son, Father, Spirit) and marked as total even more forcefully by the concluding reference to "beginning" and "end" (see on *Mag.* 6.1).[11]

The expression "in the Son and the Father and in the Spirit" calls for special attention. This is one of three trinitarian texts in Ignatius (cf. *Eph.* 9.1; *Mag.* 13.2). For rhetorical purposes the three resolve themselves into two (cf. *Eph.* 19.1): "*in* the Son and the Father and *in* the Spirit" is formally parallel to "*in* the beginning and *in* the end." Since the characteristic Ignatian teaching about spirit revolves about a polarity of flesh and spirit that has little to do with trinitarian thinking, our passage must

see on *Eph.* inscr; cf. Hermann Hanse, "ἔχω," *TDNT* 2 (1964) 822–24. Communal experience rather than mystical identification of human beings with God is at the root of the matter in Ignatius; cf. David E. Aune, "The Presence of God in the Community: The Eucharist in its Early Christian Cultic Context," *SJT* 2 (1976) 451–59.

9   It does not appear in the first two volumes of *Biblica Patristica*, ed. J. Allenbach and others (2 vols.; Paris: Éditions du Centre National de la Recherche Scientifique, 1975–77).

10   For the position of the apostles in such formulae see

11   on *Mag.* 6.1 and compare especially *Tr.* 12.2. "Beginning" (ἀρχή) and "end" (τέλος or occasionally πέρας) are also often conjoined in Philo to denote totality in connection with such diverse topics as the perfection of God and his activity (*Opif. mund.* 82; *Plant.* 77; 93; *Heres* 120–22), the full cycle of growth in nature and the life of the spirit (*Fuga* 171–72), the span of human existence (*Leg. alleg.* 3.253; *Spec. leg.* 1.266), and various interlocking cycles of development (*Migr. Abr.* 46; *Post. Cain.* 174).

reflect a traditional formula of secondary importance to him (for the order Jesus Christ, God, Spirit see 2 Cor 13:13).[12] But would he have set a formula consisting of three items among others consisting only of two? There is a good chance (in spite of the unanimity of the manuscripts)[13] that the text originally read "in the Son and in the Father" or even "in Jesus and in the Father." For as we shall see in a moment, the text of the very next line (13.2) seems to have been altered in the interest of trinitarianism; and the parallel in *Mag.* 1.2 mentions only "Jesus and the Father."[14]

■ **13.2** In exhorting the Magnesians to follow the Lord and the apostles, Ignatius naturally assumes that this will be done "with" the bishop, presbyters, and deacons.[15] An explicit exhortation to obey the bishop (and "one another" as in 1 Pet 5:5; cf. Eph 5:21) now follows. The significance of the comparisons which illustrate such obedience has been explored in our discussion of *Mag.* 6.1. But there are peculiarities of the text here that require comment. The phrase "according to the flesh" looks suspiciously like an addition made by an interpolator bent on eliminating any suggestion of subordinationism in the text. Such fears were groundless, as we have seen (see on *Eph.* 3.2), but in the age of trinitarian disputes there would have been great sensitivity on these points. The words are absent from the Armenian and Arabic versions. These versions also omit the reference to the Spirit in the following line, and this too looks like an addition made in the interest of trinitarianism. Moreover, the reference to the Father there (in spite of unanimous support for it from the manuscripts) may

represent an even earlier intrusion. For a text which read "as Jesus Christ [was subject] to the Father and the apostles to Christ" would conform to the comparisons discussed in our comments on *Mag.* 6.1. A theologically sensitive scribe may well have been disturbed by the implication that the relation between Christ and the Father was analogous to that between the apostles and Christ. The resulting doctrinal "correction" would be responsible for complicating the original structure of the comparison which seems still to be discernible here (two interlocking pairs arranged in step-wise progression).

■ **14** Following these exhortations come the concluding formulae (14–15). The first line of *Mag.* 14 represents a second "disclosure formula" (see on *Mag.* 11) and follows standard practice in attempting to put the communication as a whole in perspective (for the reference to brevity see on *Rom.* 8.2). What Ignatius claims to know, however, is somewhat unusual: "that you are full of God" (ὅτι θεοῦ γέμετε). Being full of the deity is attributed to a variety of individuals in the Hellenistic world: a person under the influence of Dionysus (Plutarch *Sept. sap. conv.* 4, 150b: θεοῦ μεστός "filled with God"); the giver of oracles (Pollux *Onom.* 1.15: πλήρης θεοῦ "full of God"); a self-reliant Stoic who refuses to consult an oracle (Lucan *Phars.* 9.564: *deo plenus* "full of God"); any whose rhetoric seems inspired (A. Seneca *Suas.* 3.5–7); the soul of the mystic (Plotinus *Enn.* 6.9.9: ψυχὴ πληρωθεῖσα θεοῦ "a soul filled with God"; cf. Iamblichus *De Myst.* 3.9).[16] But again Ignatius has in view the Magnesians' sense of solidarity (as he does in *Mag.* 12 where he says that they "have Jesus Christ in themselves"). Under the circum-

---

12 Also traditional are the references to the Spirit in Ignatius as a divine power that effects the incarnation (*Eph.* 18.2) or is at work in people (*Mag.* 8.2; *Phd.* inscr; 7.1–2). This usage is connected only very loosely, if at all, with trinitarian conceptions; and there is very little overlap (except perhaps in *Phd.* 7.1–2) of traditional usages of either kind with the flesh/spirit antithesis (cf. Martin, "Pneumatologia," 391, 400–1, 405–9, 447–49). The word "spirit" in Ignatius also sometimes refers to the self (*Eph.* 18.1; *Tr.* 13.3; *Rom.* 9.3; *Phd.* 11.3; *Sm.* 10.2) or to human dispositions (*Mag.* 15; *Sm.* inscr; *Pol.* 1.3; cf. Martin, "Pneumatologia," 396–99, 418–23).

13 Of the versions only the Arabic names but two members of the trinity ("in the Father and the Son"). This looks like the work of a translator who noted the difficulty of the text.

14 For Ignatius' "binitarianism" see *Eph.* 3.2; 5.1; 15.1; *Mag.* 7.1, 2; *Phd.* 7.2; 9.1; *Sm.* 3.3; 8.1.

15 The reference to the presbytery as the "crown" of the Magnesians echoes a popular metaphor for people who are the pride and joy of others (BAG *s.v.* στέφανος 2.b, p. 775; cf. Lycurgus *Leocrat.* 50; Plutarch *Apophth. Lac.* 28, 228e). It is later used of the "council and board" (συνέδριον καὶ βουλή) of presbyters in *Const. Apost.* 2.28 (cf. *Mag.* 6.1; *Tr.* 3.1; *Phd.* 8.1).

16 Cf. J. Haussleiter, "Deus Internus," *RAC* 3 (1957) 796, 798, 809, 822–23.

stances an exploitation of the mystical possibilities of the terminology is hardly possible. The thought serves primarily to motivate Ignatius' writing and to indicate why his exhortations are scarcely necessary (cf. *Mag.* 11).

There follows the familiar request to be remembered (see on *Eph.* 21). Ignatius, however, seeks prayers not only for himself but also for the church in Syria. The themes become curiously entwined. After having requested prayers for himself that he might "attain God," we expect Ignatius to go on to ask prayers for the church in Antioch that they might be "refreshed."[17] But he chooses to insert between the reference to the Antiochene church and the prayer on their behalf a statement about his own unworthiness to be named with them and a second more insistent request ("I need your united prayer and love"). These statements tie Ignatius' sense of need too closely in with the fate of the Antiochenes if what he had in mind were simply hopes for the success of his martyrdom and (say) an end to persecution in Antioch. It is more likely that the passage reflects tense relations between himself and his church (see Introduction, 3.1, 4).

■ 15 The letter ends with greetings and a farewell. Here (as in *Tr.* 13) greetings are passed on from the Ephesians and the Smyrnaeans (or the Smyrnaean bishop Polycarp). This must mean that the Ephesian representatives (or most of them) were still in Smyrna (their level of enthusiasm was higher than that of others, as their assistance to Ignatius shows). It will also be recalled that in the letter to the Ephesians there are no greetings from the Magnesians or Trallians to the Ephesians. Indeed there are no greetings at all. Since every other letter of Ignatius has greetings, this suggests that the Magnesians and the one Trallian representative had left for home with their letters before the letter to the Ephesians had been written. The modern order of Ignatius' letters is derived not from the manuscripts—which present a very confused picture on this score—but from Eusebius (*Hist. eccl.* 3.36), who must have worked out the order on

internal grounds. He saw that *Ephesians, Magnesians, Trallians,* and *Romans* were written from Smyrna, and *Philadelphians, Smyrnaeans,* and *Polycarp* from Troas. There are obvious enough reasons for putting *Romans* and *Philadelphians* where they are. But there are no comparable guides for the order of *Ephesians, Magnesians,* and *Trallians.* It is likely, then, that Eusebius (like those who first arranged the Pauline epistles) simply arranged them in the order of their length. The number of lines (following the Bihlmeyer text) for each is as follows: *Ephesians,* 186; *Magnesians,* 111; *Trallians,* 102. Eusebius' order, then, is artificial; and closer examination of the materials suggests that *Magnesians* and *Trallians* were written before *Ephesians.*

The Ephesians are said to "be here" as "you" (the Magnesians) are. Ignatius means, of course, the representatives of the Ephesians and the representatives of the Magnesians (who are waiting for their letter to be finished). Ignatius, as we recall, "sees" congregations in their representatives as a person sees a friend in the words of his letter (see on *Eph.* 1.3; *Mag.* 6.1). The term παρόντες "being here" reflects the same world of epistolary conventions. For "being here" and "being away," especially when paired (as in *Sm.* 9.2), emphasize the bond that exists between people whether present or absent.[18]

Greetings are also sent from "the rest of the churches." These presumably are others (such as the Trallians) who had also sent representatives to Smyrna. Ignatius may not have had a chance to write to all who visited him in Smyrna. He probably gave special attention to those whose representation seemed most to demand it.

The last sentence of the letter is a complexly worded farewell. The identification here of the "spirit" with "Jesus Christ" has sometimes been taken to show that Ignatius taught a " Spirit-christology" (cf. *2 Clem.* 14.4). This is not correct. As we have already seen, the Spirit of God and the Spirit of the trinitarian formula play roles independent of christology in Ignatius (see on *Mag.*

---

17 The imagery is biblical (Deut 32:2; Prov 19:12; cf. Philo *Migr. Abr.* 101) and is frequent elsewhere in early Christian literature (*Odes Sol.* 35.1; 36.7; *Mart. Lugd.,* in Eusebius *Hist. eccl.* 5.1.22; Clement Alex. *Quis div. salv.* 34; Origen *Exhort. mart.* 27; 33). In *Thom. Cont.* (NHC 2) 146,15–20 the "refreshing dew" is associated with "a sweet smell" (cf. *Eph.* 17.1). But Gnostic parallels have no special claims here.

(The substance of the request is arranged chiastically: εἰς τὸ ἀξιωθῆναι τὴν ἐν Συρίᾳ ἐκκλησίαν διὰ τῆς ἐκκλησίας ὑμῶν δροσισθῆναι "for to be judged worthy the church in Syria through your church to be refreshed").

18 Koskenniemi, *Studien,* 175–76.

13.1); and the spirit/flesh antithesis, though relevant to christology, has a different ambience (see on *Eph.* 7.2). In any event, here the "unwavering spirit" is almost certainly a human disposition since "possessing an unwavering spirit" further defines the attitude of those who are strong "in godly concord" (compare the "blameless and unwavering mind" of *Tr.* 1.1). Moreover, the "unwavering spirit" and "Jesus Christ" are connected by an expression, ὅς ἐστιν "who is," that in Ignatius does not flatly identify two terms but leaves open a whole range of possible relations between them (see on *Eph.* 20.2). It is used here to identify Christ as the source of the unwavering spirit of the Magnesians.

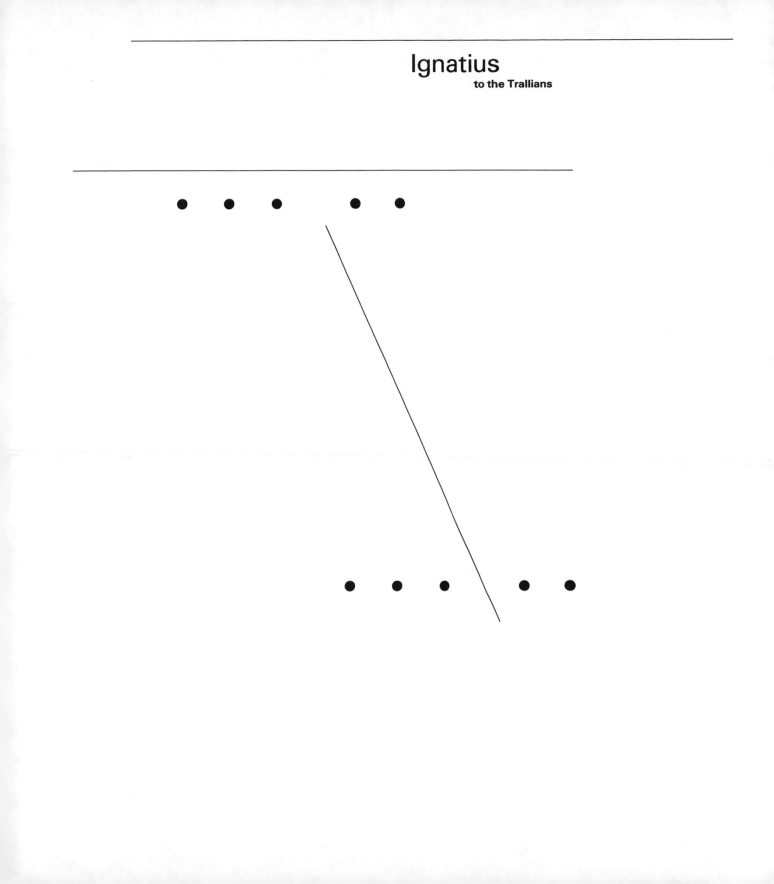

Ignatius

to the Trallians

Salutation

Ignatius, also called Theophorus, to her beloved by God, the Father of Jesus Christ, to the holy church which is at Tralles in Asia—elect and worthy of God, at peace in flesh and spirit by the suffering of Jesus Christ, our hope, through resurrection unto him—whom I also greet in the fullness, in apostolic manner, and wish abundant greeting.

The address to the church in Tralles shares with the address to the Magnesians the inclusion of the ἀσπάζομαι ("I greet") formula and the use of an expanded version of the standard greeting ("I wish abundant greeting"). Ignatius greets the Trallians "in the fullness"—he greets them as one who speaks from within the same sphere of divine grace and blessing in which they find themselves (see on *Eph.* inscr). He also greets them ἐν ἀποστολικῷ χαρακτῆρι "in apostolic manner"—he believes that his style of greeting echoes that of Paul. The expression does not mean "in my apostolic character." Rather it has literary significance (cf. Demetrius *De elocut.* 4.223; ὁ ἐπιστολικὸς χαρακτήρ "epistolary style"). Ignatius' disclaimer in *Tr.* 3.3 (that he does not command as an apostle) reinforces this point.[1]

According to the greeting, the Trallians are fully ("in flesh and spirit")[2] at peace. But special attention given to the passion and resurrection in this connection suggests that Ignatius already has in mind the theological problems discussed later in the letter (*Tr.* 9–10).[3]

---

1   Cf. Zahn, *Ignatius*, 415.
2   GLAC read "in flesh and blood" and the Arabic refers to "the blood of the body of Jesus the righteous." L adds "and" after "blood" to tie the expression to the following mention of Christ's "suffering" whereas AC and the Arabic drop the reference to the passion. The editors have rightly preferred the reading of g ("in flesh and spirit"). "Flesh" and "blood" occur together in Ignatius in reference to the eucharist (*Phd.* 4), in expressions echoing eucharistic language (*Tr.* 8.1; *Rom.* 7.3), and in reference to Christ's human reality (*Sm.* 12.2). In each instance they are modified by such expressions as "of the Lord," "of Jesus Christ," or "his." The same is true when the flesh and spirit of Christ are referred to (*Sm.* 3.2). But flesh and spirit as general anthropological terms require no such modification to be intelligible, and the absence of any modification here speaks in favor of the reading adopted. The formula expresses completeness or totality also in other passages (*Mag.* 1.2; *Rom.* inscr; *Sm.* 1.1).

3   Christ's suffering is presented as the basis of the church's peace. His resurrection is also alluded to in the expression "resurrection unto him." But the primary reference here is to the resurrection of the believers that brings them to Christ. The expression indicates in what way Christ is their "hope." There is as usual no emphasis on the last day as the context within which this hope is to be realized (cf. *Mag.* 9.2).

1   Expression of Praise

1   I know that you have a mind blameless and unwavering in endurance, not on loan but according to nature, as Polybius your bishop informed me, who was here in Smyrna by the will of God and Jesus Christ and so rejoiced with me, a prisoner in Christ Jesus, that I saw your whole congregation in him. 2/ Having received, then, your godly affection through him, I gave praise, since I found you, as I learned, to be imitators of God.

The transition to the body of the letter includes two closely related formulae: (a) a reference to the reception of information (1.1) in the manner of *Mag.* 1.1 (where another form of the verb γινώσκω "know" or "learn" is used) and (b) a second reference to the reception of information (ἀποδεξάμενος "having received") followed by an expression of praise (1.2) in the manner of *Eph.* 1.1–3 (but much less complex). The two formulae are tied together by the repetition of the verb ἔγνων "I know" (1.1) or "I learned" (1.2).

■ **1.1** What Ignatius learned came from the one Trallian representative—their bishop Polybius.[1] The latter presented a generally favorable picture of the spiritual health of the Trallians. Ignatius' enthusiastic response to the report is typical of him. But he has found an unusual phrase to convey his thought here: the Trallians are said to have their stability "not on loan (κατὰ χρῆσιν [literally, "according to use"]) but according to nature (κατὰ φύσιν)." An excellent Valentinian parallel is preserved by Irenaeus (*Adv. haer.* 1.6.2, 4) who reports that the Gnostics thought of ordinary Christians as having grace only ἐν χρῆσει "for use," while they considered themselves as having it as their own possession and (conse-

quently) as being spiritual φύσει "by nature." Ordinary Christians have been given grace to use and thus have it as a "loan."[2] Similar contrasting pairs of expressions are now found in the Nag Hammadi materials (*Exeg. Soul* [NHC 2] 134, 29–34; *Treat. Seth* [NHC 7] 62,23). Ignatius clearly wishes to attribute to the Trallians a spontaneous spirituality and to that extent approaches Gnosticism. But the contrast between natural endowments and acquired properties was an old one in Greek literature and lived on vigorously in our period.[3] Moreover it overlaps to some extent with the popular contrast between (hypocritical) words and (genuine) deeds that we have met elsewhere in Ignatius (see on *Eph.* 14.2).[4] It is surely not especially significant that the closest verbal parallel to our passage has been found in a Valentinian source. The Hellenistic preoccupation with the difference between natural endowments and acquired properties stands behind both. Especially instructive perhaps is a line from a letter of Apollonius of Tyana (*Ep.* 2) according to which "virtue comes by nature, possession, use" (φύσει, κτήσει, χρήσει), that is, by having it as one's own, by making it one's own, or by borrowing it.[5] Many writers recommended reliance on a

---

1   The name is not common in inscriptions and papyri. It is familiar enough in literary sources, however, and is used there of people of all classes (Pape/Benseler, *Eigennamen,* 1222–23). Polybius almost certainly carried the letter back to Tralles with him. If so, παρεγένετο ("was here") like ἔγνων ("I know") is an epistolary aorist, and we are being told that Polybius "*is* here."

2   For this meaning of the word see Aristotle *E.N.* 5.2, 1131a 4; Polybius 31.23.4; Ps-Phocylides 106 (cf. LSJ *s.v.* Χρῆσις, p. 2006).

3   Heinimann, *Nomos und Physis,* 99–106. In rhetoric

the relative values of φύσις "nature" and τέχνη "art" were much discussed. The contrast between φύσις ("nature") and θέσις ("arbitrary determination," "adoption") played an important role in the spheres of family relations, citizenship, and ethics. Note also that Philo (cf. *Migr. Abr.* 54) built up a theology of the three patriarchs on the basis of the relation between μάθησις "learning" (Abraham), ἄσκησις "practice" (Jacob), and φύσις "nature" (Isaac). The latter represents the highest form of life.

4   Heinimann, *Nomos und Physis,* 43–56.

5   Note that the familiar contrast between κτῆσις

blend of such elements, but the general tendency was to emphasize the importance especially of "nature." Ignatius (like the Valentinians) makes a choice of terms that stresses the opposition between the poles rather than their mediation. For here (as in *Eph.* 1.1) he seeks to present Christian existence as an extraordinary kind of second nature that manifests itself in a spontaneous overflow of obedience and love. But it is the solidarity of the Christian community (and not, as in Valentinianism, the special metaphysical endowments of the Gnostic) that determines Ignatius' use of the formula.

Also included in Ignatius' remarks on the stability of the Trallians is the familiar theme (prompted by the mention of Polybius) that Ignatius has seen the whole congregation in their representative (cf. *Eph.* 1.2–3).

■ **1.2** The expression of praise is Ignatius' substitute for the more usual expression of joy (see on *Eph.* 1.1). The phrase "imitators of God" recalls especially *Eph.* 1.1 and consequently probably has in view Christ as the model for the godly affection of the Christians for each other (cf. *Eph.* 10.3; *Phd.* 7.2).

"possession" and χρῆσις "use" (i.e., ownership vs. usufruct) occurs in the version of our passage given by g. It is easy to see how either φύσις ("nature") or κτῆσις ("possession") could be seen as the natural counterpart of χρῆσις ("use").

2   The Trallian Bishop

1 For when you are subject to the bishop as to Jesus Christ, it is clear to me that you are living not in human fashion but in the fashion of Jesus Christ who died for us, that by believing in his death you may escape dying. 2/ It is necessary then (as is your practice) to do nothing without the bishop; but be subject also to the presbytery as to the apostles of Jesus Christ, our hope, in whom we shall be found if we live in him; 3/ and it is also necessary for those who are deacons of the mysteries of Jesus Christ to please all people in every way; for they are not ministers of food and drink but servants of the church of God; thus they must be on their guard against complaints as against fire.

3 1/ Similarly let everyone respect the deacons as Jesus Christ, as also the bishop who is a type of the Father, and the presbyters as the council of God and as the band of the apostles. Nothing can be called a church without these, 2/ concerning which I am persuaded that you are so disposed. For I have received the exemplar of your love, and I have it with me in your bishop whose very demeanor is a great lesson, and his gentleness a (great) power, whom I think even the atheists respect.

■ **2.1** As in *Ephesians, Magnesians,* and *Philadelphians,* Ignatius first turns to the bishop and the other orders of the ministry as the focus of unity in the church. In 2.1–3 the comparisons which are used to dignify them conform to expectations (see on *Mag.* 6.1). Within the framework of Ignatius' theology the comparison between the bishop and Jesus Christ (2.1), though found only here, is scarcely more than a variant of the more usual comparison between the bishop and the Father. Obedience to the bishop indicates that a person has moved from the sphere of the merely human (κατὰ ἄνθρωπον "in human fashion"; cf. Rom 3:5; Gal 1:11; 3:15; 1 Cor 9:8; 15:32) to that of Jesus Christ.[1] Ignatius points especially to the death of Christ "for us" (cf. *Rom.* 6.1; *Sm.* 2; *Pol.* 3.2)—a death that paradoxically brings escape from death—as

the reality in which this new mode of existence is grounded. And he points to faith (i.e., a conviction conceived of both as assent to the reality of Christ's death and as reliance on its conquering power) as the presupposition of enjoying the benefits of that death.

It is not made clear, however, what makes the link between obedience to the bishop and the new mode of existence grounded in the passion so obvious to Ignatius. The clue is given in other passages in which he finds a connection between the denial of the reality of Christ's death and a neglect of communal responsibilities (see on *Sm.* 6.2) or in which he perceives his own martyrdom as having both anti-docetic and anti-separatist significance (see on *Tr.* 10). A community based on the passion is a community that stands united (with the bishop and with

---

1 Most translations soften the expression by rendering it, "you seem to me to be living. . . ." But that would require the infinitive rather than the participle with

the verb φαίνομαι "it is clear to me" (cf. LSJ *s.v.* φαίνω B.II.1, pp. 1912–13).

one another; cf. *Mag.* 13.2) in the face of a hostile world (see on *Eph.* 10.2–3).

■ **2.2** Consequently Ignatius goes on to give his familiar exhortation to do nothing (especially in worship) without the bishop (see on *Mag.* 4) and typically qualifies it with the remark that they already act accordingly (see on *Eph.* 4.1). Our passage is only unusual in presenting subordination to the bishop as all but identical with obedience to the presbytery. In any event, it is assumed that Jesus Christ presides over the relationship and that we shall be found in him—eternally, as the reference to Christ "our hope" indicates (cf. *Tr.* inscr)—if we live in him (taking ἐν ᾧ "in whom," both with ἄγοντες "if we live" and with εὑρηθησόμεθα "we shall be found").

The following discussion of the deacons—marked off by the tandem particle δὲ καί (see on *Eph.* 2.1)—is less typical of Ignatius. Here he uncharacteristically speaks of their duties rather than of the respect owed them. Polybius had evidently discussed special problems about the deacons of his own church. We may assume that their main task was to distribute "food and drink" to the poor of the congregation (cf. Acts 6:1–6), and it may be that (as in *Herm. Sim.* 9.26.2; cf. Pol. *Phil.* 5.2) they were using their office to their own advantage or were helping only some instead of "all." The word "fire" indicates how acutely aware Ignatius was of the destructive potential of any such self-serving or favoritism. He reminds the deacons that their work has other dimensions: they are deacons of the "mysteries" of Jesus Christ and servants of the church. There may be an echo here of 1 Cor 4:1 ("servants of Christ and stewards of God's mysteries"). If so, the term "mysteries" covers what in another reference to deacons Ignatius calls "the word of God" (*Phd.* 11.1; cf. *Sm.* 10.1; 1 Tim 3:9; Acts 6:8–10). But Ignatius may also have had the eucharist in mind since deacons are

soon found distributing the bread and wine (Justin *Apol.* 1.65.7; 1.67.5). Such a development was natural in a setting where a variety of links obtained between the eucharist, common meals, and charity.[2] In any event, the various channels of physical and spiritual nourishment are not sharply distinguished by Ignatius or by those to whom he writes. The solidarity of the community itself was experienced as the fundamental spiritual reality.

■ **3.1** Having exhorted the deacons to please everyone, Ignatius then goes on to state the corollary (such is the force of the word "similarly" here) in calling on everyone to respect the deacons. The remark is unusual in that it compares the deacons with Jesus Christ (see on *Mag.* 6.1). There is no compelling reason to reject the line on textual grounds,[3] and thus it properly serves to underscore the tentative character of all such comparisons in Ignatius (especially since it comes so soon after the comparison between the bishop and Christ in *Tr.* 2.1). The choice of language here was probably determined by the immediate context. Ignatius expresses himself more forcefully than usual to offset any possible negative impressions left by his preceding comments on the deacons of Tralles.

At this point Ignatius is driven to add to the remark about the deacons another about the bishop and elders. Having effected the addition by means of the conjunction ὡς ("as"),[4] that word is no longer available to him in making the comparison between the bishop and the Father. Instead, Ignatius resorts to speaking of the bishop as the τύπος ("type," "image," "copy") of the Father.[5] Since both *Barnabas* (19.7) and the *Didache* (4.11) speak of the master as "a type of God" to the slave, the meaning of the comparison does not go beyond what

---

2   Cf. Hans Achelis, *Das Christentum in den ersten drei Jahrhunderten* (2 vols.; Leipzig: Quelle und Meyer, 1912) 1. 189–98.

3   It is absent only in C, which also omits the (likewise unusual) comparison of the bishop with Jesus Christ in *Tr.* 2.1. The comparison in the Latin of *Tr.* 3.1 is between the deacons and "the commandment of Jesus Christ"; but this was probably derived from *Sm.* 8.1. Bartsch (*Gnostisches Gut,* 160 n. 1) would omit the comparison of the deacons with Jesus Christ in *Tr.* 3.1 as a dittography derived from the next line, i.e., from the next line as preserved in the Latin

version: *et episcopum ut Jesum Christum existentem filium patris* "also the bishop as Jesus Christ who is the Son of the Father." But it appears more likely that the Latin is simply trying to salvage a corrupt reading at this point (see below, n. 5).

4   This ὡς is missing in LSAC. But simplifying tendencies are at work in all of these texts.

5   G reads ὄντα υἱὸν τοῦ πατρός "who is Son of the Father," which is meaningless in reference to the bishop. This was apparently the reading known to the Latin translator (who attempts to salvage it as indicated in n. 3). But S (and the Arabic) and C read

we have set out above in our discussion of *Eph.* 6.1, *Mag.* 3.1 and 6.1. Authority is enhanced by such comparisons but not divinized.

The comparison involving the presbyters is more complex than usual. They are likened to the council of God and the band of apostles. Elsewhere the two expressions are collapsed into one—the council of the apostles (*Mag.* 6.1). The double formula makes more explicit the hierarchical relation involved. "God" in the expression "council of God" must correspond to the bishop (note that we hear of the "council" of the bishop in *Phd.* 8.1). Evidently Ignatius wants not only to compare the presbyters to the council of apostles but also to compare the relation between God and the apostles to that between the bishop and the presbyters. We have found other examples of such comparisons within comparisons (see on *Mag.* 6.1).

However subordinate to the bishop Ignatius makes the presbyters and deacons, here he is explicit in recognizing no church without the existence of all three. He must have found them in place wherever he went to make this statement in the matter-of-fact way that he does. It is only his exaltation of the role of the bishop that some-times strikes us as going beyond what was commonly accepted.

■ **3.2** Ignatius concludes this section with a standard theme: he is convinced that the Trallians are already "so disposed" (cf. *Mag.* 11), that is, that they recognize the need for submission to their leaders. He gives as his reason for this confidence the exemplar of their love that he has in their bishop. The word "exemplar" is a Latinism found in popular Greek.[6] In Latin sources *exemplar* is often used to refer to a person whose way of life is to be admired or abhorred (cf. Cicero *Resp.* 1.1; Horace *Ars poet.* 317; Pliny *Paneg.* 45.4; Tacitus *Ann.* 6.32). Polybius is said to be just such an exemplar whose humble demeanor and gentleness must surely awaken in the Trallians the appropriate attitude of submission. Even the "atheists"—pagans (as in Eph 2:12; *Mart. Pol.* 3.2; 9.2)[7] or, perhaps, the heterodox (as in *Tr.* 10)— must surely respect him.

τύπον "type" instead of υἱόν "son," and this fits the explanation of the passage developed above.

6   Cf. *P.Oxy.* 7.1066 where ἐξεμπλάριον refers to a pattern to be followed in making a tool.

7   Cf. *Tr.* 8.1–2 where gentleness is said to lead to approval from pagan society.

3   Ignatius' Authority and the Claims of Esoteric Knowledge

3 Because I love you I refrain, though I could write more sharply about this. <I was not empowered> for this that I, a condemned man, should give you orders as an apostle. **4** 1/ I have much knowledge in God, but I measure myself lest I perish through boasting. For now I must fear the more and not attend to those who puff me up; indeed, those who speak to me scourge me. 2/ Yes, I love the suffering, but I do not know if I am worthy; for the envy is not obvious to many, but it fights against me the more; therefore I need gentleness by which the ruler of this age is destroyed. **5** 1/ Surely I am not unable to write you of heavenly things? No, but I fear inflicting harm on you who are infants. Bear with me, then, lest you be choked by what you cannot take in. 2/ Even in my case, not because I am in bonds and am able to know heavenly things, both the angelic locations and the archontic formations, things both visible and invisible—not because of this am I already a disciple; for we need many things that we may not lack God.

In this section (3.3–5.2) Ignatius criticizes the Trallians and at the same time reflects on his right to do so. It appears that he is answering some who claim to have esoteric knowledge and that their activities have had considerable impact on the Trallians in spite of all that has been said about their stability (*Tr.* 1.1–3.2).

■ **3.3** Thus although the text is too corrupt to provide any certainty,[1] the transition seems abrupt—no doubt because the preceding high praise has made significant criticism awkward. In any event, Ignatius adopts the language of 2 Cor 12:6, where Paul also couples a statement about his restraint ("I refrain") with a claim to possess the secrets of the other world (cf. 1 Cor 2:6–7; 13:2). Ignatius, however, feels an even greater sense of

---

1   G reads ἀγαπῶντας ὡς οὐ φείδομαι ἑαυτὸν πότερον δυνάμενος γράφειν ὑπὲρ τούτου εἰς τοῦτο ᾠήθην ἵνα κτλ., which is unintelligible. The translation is based on the following reconstruction: ἀγαπῶν ὑμᾶς φείδομαι συντονώτερον δυνάμενος γράφειν ὑπὲρ τούτου· οὐκ εἰς τοῦτο ἱκανώθην ἵνα κτλ. The evidence for this is as follows: (a) gAC and the Arabic support ἀγαπῶν ὑμᾶς "because I love you" and (b) συντονώτερον "more sharply"; (c) AC do not reflect δυνάμενος "though I could," but this is probably because they felt uncomfortable with the isolated φείδομαι ("I refrain") and preferred to connect it directly with γράφειν (note, however, that φείδομαι is isolated also in 2 Cor 12:6); (d) AC and the Arabic omit ὑπὲρ τούτου ("about this" or perhaps "on his behalf"), but γράφειν ὑπὲρ τούτου is good Greek (cf. Polybius 1.1.4), and the ὑπὲρ τούτου may have been lost in translation only because of its vagueness; it is possible, however, that ὑπὲρ τούτου should be rejected as a gloss originally intended to make sense of εἰς τοῦτο (Zahn's γράφειν δυνάμενός περ οὐκ for δυνάμενος γράφειν ὑπὲρ τούτου introduces refinements unlikely in Ignatius); (e) οὐκ "not" finds support in AC and the Arabic and is required by the sense (it probably blended with the preceding ὑπὲρ τούτου); (f) since οὐκ εἰς τοῦτο ᾠήθην ἵνα κτλ. can hardly mean "I did not have this thought that . . . ," I suggest reading οὐκ εἰς τοῦτο ἱκανώθην ἵνα κτλ. "I was not empowered for this that . . . ," relying on a hint from A (Petermann, *Epistolae,* 100: *sed et non sum sufficiens* "but neither am I able") and the Arabic ("I have not been given the power"), the language of Paul (cf. 1 Cor 2:6–7; Col 1:12), and general usage (cf. *P.Teb.* 1.20,8: "you have full powers [ἱκανωθῆναι] until I arrive").

restraint since he, a condemned man, cannot command like an apostle (see on *Eph.* 12.1). He regards only apostles as having universal authority over the churches (cf. *Mag.* 6.1).

■ **4.1–2** Ignatius like Paul also follows Graeco-Roman models (familiar to us especially from Plutarch) in qualifying the "boasting" that seems imposed upon him by the situation.[2] He is sensitive to the dangers of self-praise and (as in *Mag.* 12) knows that it is right to feel embarrassed even when one is praised by others (cf. Plutarch *De laude ipsius* 1, 539d). He is aware that although he "has much knowledge" (for πολλὰ φρονῶ in this sense see Herodotus 9.16), he must "measure" (μετρῶ) himself—just as Paul will not let his boasting go εἰς τὰ ἄμετρα "beyond measure" (2 Cor 10:13) and as Plutarch admires Achilles because he ascribed glory to the deity καὶ μέτριος ἦν "and was moderate" (*De laude ipsius* 6, 541c; cf. 5, 541b; 12, 543a; 13, 543f; 18, 546b). And he yields to self-glorification only because it will benefit his addressees (cf. ibid., 22, 547f). For he knows that there are times when one ought not to "refrain" from speaking about one's achievements to effect a good purpose (cf. ibid., 2, 539ef; 6, 541de) and that boasting is sometimes required to deflate the headstrong (cf. ibid., 16, 544ef).[3]

But Ignatius' world is more intense than that of Plutarch. His concern "lest he perish" is specifically Pauline in thought (cf. 1 Cor 9:27) and language (cf. 1 Cor 1:18); and his own situation gives deeper significance to his use of the conventions. For he connects his concern about his possible unworthiness with temp-tations to self-assertion. Feelings of pride, we are told, are awakened by those who speak to him of his martyrdom.[4] The depth and complexity of these feelings is suggested by the words "they scourge me." But almost as startling are the words "I love the suffering" (cf. *Rom.* 7.2), which express what Ignatius regards as the healthy side of his spiritual state. What he goes on to suggest is that temptations to self-assertion call his commitment into question. And so subtle and powerful are these temptations that he attributes them (apparently) to the "envy" of supernatural forces invisibly urging on his well-wishers.[5] It seems likely that such evidence of unresolved anxiety is connected with the tense state of affairs that existed (as it seems) between Ignatius and his church in Antioch (see Introduction, 3.1; 3.4); and it is not improbable that an imperious temperament had something to do with his difficulties in that situation (see on *Mag.* 12). This would explain why Ignatius goes on to express his need for "gentleness" (cf. 1 Cor 4:21; 2 Cor 10:1; Plutarch *De laude ipsius* 5, 541c) in order to destroy "the ruler of this age" (cf. *Eph.* 7.1), that is, in order to destroy the source of his pride. (For a somewhat similar connection of themes see *Tr.* 8.1–2.)

■ **5.1** Here the bishop picks up the main theme again (cf. *Tr.* 3.3) and turns his attention more directly to the situation in Tralles. But now his attitude is more aggressive. For he says that he can write about heavenly things as well as anyone[6] and that his reason for refraining from doing so is merely the immaturity of the Trallians: he is afraid that they will choke on food too solid for them to swallow.[7]

---

2   Cf. Betz, *Plutarch's Ethical Writings*, 367–93.

3   Plutarch notes here (16, 545a) that according to Aristotle such boasting is permitted not only to military victors but also to "those who have true opinions about the gods."

4   The expression οἱ λέγοντές μοι ("those who speak to me") requires some such completion. But the text need not be corrected. As in Mark 7:36 the thought can be supplied from the context.

5   Here ζῆλος can hardly mean anything other than "zeal," "emulation," or "envy" (in spite of the subtler usages of the term that have attracted some commentators). Since zeal and emulation are qualities that Ignatius would not have rejected, we are left with "envy" as the likely meaning. Its significance is best illuminated by the parallel in *Rom.* 5.3 where Ignatius speaks of the envy of things seen and unseen which stands behind the misguided efforts of those who wish to save him from martyrdom. Similarly, in *Trallians* he must regard the words of his friends which instill pride in him as inspired by Satan. No doubt it is for this reason that he goes on to mention "the ruler of this age" and his defeat (cf. *Eph.* 13.1–2).—For Satan's envy of godly people see, e.g., Wis 2:24 and *Vita Adae et Evae* 12–17.

6   For μὴ οὐ δύναμαι ("surely I am not unable") see Xenophon *Mem.* 4.2.12. The translations usually weaken the expression unduly.

7   The imagery is Hellenistic: Persius *Sat.* 3.17–18; Cicero *De orat.* 2.39.162; Epictetus *Diss.* 2.16.39; 3.24.9; Philo *Agric.* 9; *Congr.* 19; *Sobr.* 8; *Somn.* 2.10. For NT parallels see 1 Pet 2:2; Heb 5:11–14; 1 Cor 3:1–2.

■ **5.2** We learn what esoteric knowledge Ignatius has in mind: "heavenly things" including both τὰς τοποθεσίας τὰς ἀγγελικάς "angelic locations" (τοποθεσία is an astrological term for the "location" of the stars)[8] and τὰς συστάσεις τὰς ἀρχοντικάς "the archontic formations" (συστάσεις is an astrological term for the patterns and conjunctions that emerge in the heavens),[9] that is, things both visible and invisible (cf. Col 1:16). The language suggests that Ignatius associates stars and planets with the angels or the "archontic" powers (as in Origen *Cels.* 6.27–33; cf. Justin *Dial.* 36.4–6). What we apparently have here is a mixture of astrological and apocalyptic ideas similar to that found in *Eph.* 19.1–3.[10]

But the point made by Ignatius is that neither his bonds nor his knowledge of heavenly things qualify him as a disciple (cf. *Eph.* 1.2; 3.1). "Not because of this"— the same expression as in *Rom.* 5.1 (based in turn on 1 Cor 4:4)—can any claims be made. An *a fortiori* argument lies just below the surface: If this is true (even) of me (καὶ γὰρ ἐγώ "yes, even I" or "even in my case"), how much more of those who disturb you with their claims of esoteric knowledge. In principle all are on the same footing. Both Ignatius and the Trallians fall far short of attaining God. This sentiment is somewhat obscured by an awkward play on words: "we lack (λείπει) many things that we may not lack (λειπώμεθα) God." Ignatius means that we still need many things before we can hope to gain God. "To lack God" is clearly the obverse of the more usual expression "to attain God" (as is confirmed by the previous reference to another martyrological theme— that of "being a disciple"). To "attain" God, then, must mean (in some metaphorical sense) to "acquire" him. Thus Augustine (*Sermo* 331.6.5) compares martyrs who "endured so much to acquire God" (*ut acquierent deum*) with lovers of gold who endure much to acquire riches. "Acquiring" God, then, is a future-oriented form of the theme of "having" God (cf. *Mag.* 12).

This section uncharacteristically emphasizes the incompleteness of the spiritual state of Ignatius' addressees. It was the special challenge to authority posed by the docetists of Tralles that forced such language from Ignatius and consequently contributed to the relegation of esoteric wisdom to the edges of Christian life and thought.

---

8   Seven uses of the word are listed in Wilhelm Kroll, *Vettii Valentis anthologiarum libri* (Berlin: Weidemann, 1908) 384 (cf. Epiphanius *Pan.* 24.7.3).

9   Ptolemy *Apotelesm.* 1.2.11; 2.10.3; 2.14.9, 10; cf. 4.7.6.

10 For another fragment from the same circle of ideas see *Sm.* 6.1.

6   Avoid False Teachers

1   I exhort you then—not I, but the love of Jesus Christ—make use only of Christian food; keep away from any strange plant —which is faction— 2/ who also mingle Jesus Christ with themselves, in a show of integrity, like people giving a deadly drug mixed with honeyed wine, which the unsuspecting gladly takes with evil pleasure, and therewith death.

7

1/ Be on your guard, then, against such people. So it will be for you if you are not puffed up and if you are inseparable from Jesus Christ, and from the bishop, and from the ordinances of the apostles. 2/ He who is within the altar is pure— that is, the person who does anything apart from bishop, presbytery and deacon, is not pure in conscience.

■ **6.1** A series of exhortations against false teachers follows. It is marked off by the word παρακαλῶ "I exhort" which functions similarly elsewhere in Ignatius (*Rom.* 4.1; 7.2; *Phd.* 8.2; *Pol.* 1.2; cf. *Mag.* 6.1). This epistolary παρακαλῶ appears in Paul (e.g., 1 Cor 1:10; 4:16; 16:15) but was no doubt also familiar to Ignatius from Hellenistic letters (whether personal or official) in which diplomatically worded requests were made. It was used where a course of action was being urged by one who felt that commands were not in place. Ignatius differs from Paul in not favoring a connection between the formula and a thanksgiving at the beginning of the letter or paraenetic material at the end.[1] But both writers seem to agree in taking the first appearance of the formula as an opportunity to drive home the burden of the communication.

Specifically Pauline is Ignatius' way of pointing beyond himself to Christ as the real reason for obedience—"not I, but the love of Jesus Christ" (cf. 1 Cor 7:10; 15:10).

The substance of his exhortation to the Trallians is that they use only Christian "food"—that they listen only to teaching approved by Ignatius and those who are in communion with him[2]—and avoid any "strange plant" (βοτάνη),[3] any weed. In *Eph.* 10.3 such weeds are regarded as planted by the devil (cf. Matt 13:24–30); and conversely in *Phd.* 3.1 they are said not to be the "planting of the Father" (cf. Matt 15:13). The image of the "planting of the Father" comes up again in *Tr.* 11.1, where it seems to acquire mythological or at least allegorical significance. But here, as Ignatius himself indicates, the "strange plant" (or weed) is a metaphor for αἵρεσις—"faction" or "heresy" (see on *Eph.* 6.2).

The metaphors that appear in 6.1 (food, weed) and 6.2 (drug) do not fit easily together.[4] The same is true of other series of metaphors in Ignatius (cf. *Eph.* 9.1–2; *Pol.* 2.1–3; 6.1–2). Nevertheless a link between weed (6.1) and drug (6.2) may be found if we recall that βοτάνη is also the term applied to plants used in drugs.[5] This link,

---

1   Bjerkelund, *Parakalô*, 104–6.

2   For "food" as a metaphor for teaching see Plutarch *De ser. num. vind.* 6, 551d; Philo *Fuga* 137; *Mut. nom.* 259; H. Schenkl, "Pythagoreersprüche in einer Wiener Handschrift," *Wiener Studien* 8 (1886) 277 (no. 99). See also on *Tr.* 5.1.

3   Plato regards badly trained people ὥσπερ ἐν κακῇ βοτάνῃ τρεφόμενοι "as though nurtured in an evil pasture" (*Resp.* 3, 401c). The imagery of weeds also hovers behind *Euthyphro* 3a where Socrates reports that the authorities regard him and his kind as choking out the young sprouts (cf. John Burnet,

Plato's Euthyphro, Apology of Socrates and Crito [Oxford: Clarendon, 1924] 13).

4   It is unlikely that the eucharist provides the link. "Food," as we have seen, is a common metaphor for teaching, and the possibility of eucharistic overtones seems limited in view of the parallel image of the "strange plant." To be sure, a connection between the "deadly drug" of 6.2 (and thus perhaps also the "strange plant" of 6.1 as the source of such a drug— see below) and the eucharistic bread (i.e., food) as the "drug of immortality" in *Eph.* 20.2 is evident. But that suggests the metaphorical character of the

as we shall see in a moment, strengthens the likelihood that the "Christian food" and the "strange plant" of 6.1 are images for true and false teaching respectively. But we should note first that in referring to the "strange plant" as "heresy" Ignatius is mainly concerned about the false teachers themselves rather than their teaching. For he moves forward without hesitation at the beginning of 6.2 with a plural relative. "Heresy," then, is still basically a matter of people who disrupt unity and create "faction."

■ **6.2** Ignatius' description of the methods of the false teachers depends heavily on medical imagery: (a) They "mingle" Jesus Christ with themselves[6] (παρεμπλέκω is used of mixing drugs).[7] (b) They administer a "deadly drug" (θανάσιμον φάρμακον)[8] and (c) disguise it "with honeyed wine" (μετὰ οἰνομέλιτος) to make it taste sweet (many drugs, including the drug athanasia presumably alluded to in *Eph.* 20.2, were administered μετ' οἰνομέλιτος "with honeyed wine";[9] and the same was true of

poisons).[10] Lacking serious instruction with pleasant topics or a pleasant style was often compared with getting children to drink bitter medicine by disguising it with sweet things like honey;[11] inevitably, evils dressed up to please were compared to poisons disguised by honeyed wine.[12] The gullible person happily swallows the mixture without recognizing that it represents death disguised as something pleasant (treating τὸ ἀποθανεῖν "and therewith death" as epexegetic of the relative pronoun ὅπερ "which").[13]

■ **7.1** The exhortation is renewed with a warning against such people. The advice to avoid being "puffed up" harks back to *Tr.* 4.1 and must refer to the danger of being impressed with esoteric theology. Such pride is characteristically coupled by Ignatius with separation from Jesus Christ[14] and the ministry (the bishop and

---

expression in *Eph.* 20.2 rather than the eucharistic character of the images in *Tr.* 6.1–2.

5   E.g., Galen *Sanit. tuend.* 3.6.7–8; 4.7.16; 5.5.22; 6.14.12 (ed. Konrad Koch, Georg Helmreich, Carl Kalbfleisch, and Otto Hartlich, *Galeni De sanitate tuenda* . . . [*CMG* V 4.2; Leipzig and Berlin: Teubner, 1923]); cf. Philo *Sacr.* 70.

6   Reading οἱ ἑαυτοῖς "who (mingle Jesus Christ) with themselves" (cf. SfA and the Arabic: "they mix themselves with Jesus Christ"; C is less clear). There is some connection between the meaningless οἱ καιροί of G and the reading reflected in L: *quae et inquinatis* = ἥ καὶ ῥυπαροῖς "which also (mingles Jesus Christ) with filthy things." Lightfoot may be right in seeing behind καιροί an earlier reading: οἱ καὶ ἰῷ "who also (mingle Jesus Christ) with poison" (compare g: καὶ τὸν ἰὸν προσπλέκοντες τῆς πλάνης τῇ γλυκείᾳ προσηγορίᾳ "and mingling the poison of error with sweet address"); and he is probably right in viewing ἥ καὶ ῥυπαροῖς as an effort to deal with the puzzling οἱ καιροί. Nevertheless, it is unlikely that Lightfoot's reading represents the earliest text. For the introduction of the word "poison" looks like an effort to tidy up the comparison, and it provides no convincing explanation for the reading of the Oriental versions. Ignatius elsewhere speaks of people being mingled with people (*Eph.* 5.1; *Sm.* 3.2).

7   Diphilus in Athenaeus *Deipn.* 2, 57c; Photius *Bibl.* 250.12 (cf. BAG *s.v.* παρεμπλέκω, p. 630). Παραπλέκω is also used in this sense (cf. Galen *Ad Glauc.* 2.3 [Kühn, *CGO* 11.88]).

8   For the expression see Plutarch *Quomodo adulator* 1, 49e; *Quaest. conviv.* 6.5, 691b; Philo *Plant.* 147 (cf. BAG *s.v.* θανάσιμος, p. 351).

9   Galen *Antidot.* 2.8 (Kühn, *CGO* 14. 148).

10   Diogenes Laertes 4.64; cf. Ps-Dioscurides *De venen.* proem (Carolus Gottlob Kühn, *Pedanii Discoridis Anazarbei tomus secundus: Libri spurii* [MGO 26.2]).

11   Lucretius *De rer. nat.* 1.936–50; Horace *Ars poet.* 343; Plutarch *De educ. lib.* 18, 13d; Maximus Tyr. *Or.* 4, 6d; Philo *Det. pot.* 117–18.

12   Diogenes Laertes 6.61; Irenaeus *Adv. haer.* 1.27.4; Theophilus *Ad Aut.* 2.12; Jerome *Ep.* 107.6. A connection here between Ignatius and *Odes Sol.* 38.8 ("all the drugs of error . . . which are considered to be the sweetness of death") is not likely. Ignatius' language is closer to the popular metaphor (even if the text of the *Ode Sol.* 38 is pressed to mean, "which they think to be honey-wine"; cf. Rendel Harris and Alphonse Mingana, *The Odes and Psalms of Solomon* [2 vols.; Manchester: University Press, 1916–20] 2. 40–42.

13   Cf. Kühner/Gerth, *Grammatik*, 2. 420 (section 556 n. 1).

14   GLC read θεοῦ Ἰησοῦ Χριστοῦ "from God Jesus Christ" (the translation "from the God of Jesus Christ" has the support of no parallel in Ignatius). We would expect "our God" or some other modification of the word "God" (cf. *Eph.* inscr.). Perhaps a comma should be placed after the word "God" to distinguish God from Christ. But for such purposes we would expect καί instead, and the parallels adduced for such

presbyters).[15]

■ **7.2** The warning concludes with a statement emphasizing unity in worship under the bishop.[16] Here Ignatius brings together two themes found elsewhere in the letters: being "within the altar" (see *Eph.* 5.2) and doing nothing apart from the ministry (see on *Mag.* 4). It is especially clear in this context that the word "altar" is used symbolically by Ignatius (cf. *Mag.* 7.2; *Phd.* 4). When the Christian is in harmony with his leaders, he is within the church. Also cultic is the theme of purity. It too is spiritualized by Ignatius, as the expression "pure in conscience" shows. Precisely such purity was later viewed as a requirement for participation in the eucharist,[17] and it is likely that this is what Ignatius had in view here. But for Ignatius the major test of purity of conscience is the very willingness to submit to the ministry (especially in acts of worship) and so to preserve unity. It should be noted that Ignatius' spiritualization of cultic terms is a spiritualization of notions associated with the sacrificial system of archaic religions and says nothing in itself about conceptions of the presence of Christ in the eucharist.

---

punctuation in Ignatius (*Tr.* 12.2; *Phd.* 9.2) are themselves textually or exegetically uncertain. In any event, the expression seems too doubtful to press in discussions of Ignatius' christology. The original text is probably that of A and the Arabic which omit the word "God" (cf. *Sm.* 10.1). Perhaps we have a contamination in GLC from g, which reads simply θεοῦ.

15 In this context, "ordinances of the apostles" looks like shorthand for presbyters, who stand in the place of the apostles (cf. *Mag.* 6.1). The term διατάγματα ("ordinances") is found only here in Ignatius; but the corresponding verb (διατάσσομαι) is twice connected with the apostles (*Tr.* 3.3; *Rom.* 4.3; cf. *Eph.* 3.1). Comparisons between the ministry and various legal entities occur elsewhere in Ignatius (*Mag.* 2; 13.1; *Tr.* 13.2; *Sm.* 8.1).

16 L reads: "he who is within the altar is pure, but he who is without the altar is not pure" (the second clause is represented as follows in gC: "but he who is without is he who acts without the bishop . . ."). The second clause is not found in GA and may have been dropped by homoeoteleuton. But it is more likely that it was added to facilitate the link between the statement of principle and Ignatius' comment upon it. As Resch (*Agrapha,* 268–69) notes, Ignatius' comment ("that is . . .") may take the form that it does because he is drawing out the negative implications of a traditional church rule.

17 Cf. *LPGL s.v.* συνείδησις G.2, p. 1316.

8   Reason for Writing

1   **Not because I know of any such thing among you, but I want to put you whom I love on your guard, foreseeing the snares of the devil. You, then, take up gentleness and renew yourselves in faith—which is the flesh of the Lord—and in love—which is the blood of Jesus Christ. 2/ Let none of you bear a grudge against his neighbor. Give no pretext to the gentiles so that because of a few fools God's congregation may not be slandered; for "woe to him through whom my name is slandered" among any through folly.**

■ **8.1** Something like "I have written these things" must be understood to complete the first sentence (cf. *Mag.* 11). Such an expression along with a form of the verb "to know" or "to learn" marks a disclosure formula and introduces a new section of the letter. What is disclosed here is Ignatius' reason for writing, namely, to forewarn (cf. *Eph.* 3.2; *Mag.* 11; *Sm.* 4.1). It is not clear whether or not the body closing should be thought of as beginning at this point (according to White the disclosure formula may serve as "a general transitional device" for any part of the letter).[1] It seems likely that Ignatius did intend to begin drawing to a close here but that he allowed himself to be carried away by fresh ideas in the following section, *Tr.* 9–11. Otherwise the kind of material that regularly precedes the ἀσπάζομαι ("I greet") formula (*Tr.* 12.1) in Ignatius' letters would be missing.

There is a remarkable similarity between the main theme of *Tr.* 8.1 and that of *Tr.* 4.2. In both instances the devil's activity is said to be overcome by "gentleness"[2] (for the devil's "snares" see also *Phd.* 6.2). In both instances that activity has something to do with engendering pride, the pride that Ignatius fears in himself and the pride that esoteric theology may arouse in the Trallians. But the lower level of intensity in the language used in *Tr.* 8.1 as compared with that of *Tr.* 4.2 indicates how much more uncertain Ignatius felt his own battle with Satan to be.

The ability of the Trallians to resist Satan is described in terms of a renewal of faith and love. These are the primary expressions of the Christian life for Ignatius, as we have seen (see on *Eph.* 1.1; 14.1). Here, however, we have an unusual feature: faith is connected with the flesh of the Lord, and love is connected with his blood. Our study of the formula (ὅ ἐστιν "which is")[3] by which the connection is made (see on *Eph.* 20.2) helps us gain some precision on the significance of the passage. First, it should be clear that flesh and blood are basically eucharistic terms (cf. *Phd.* 4). But more often than not they appear together in Ignatius in non-eucharistic contexts: they may be connected (as here) with theological terms from a different circle of ideas (*Rom.* 7.3; cf. *Phd.* 5.1); or they may be mentioned (without any obvious reference to the eucharist at all) to emphasize the reality of the incarnation or, more precisely, Christ's death (*Sm.* 12.2)—a purpose which is also served by the mention of Christ's "flesh" alone (*Eph.* 7.2; 20.2; *Sm.* 1.1, 2; 3.1), his "flesh and spirit" (*Sm.* 1.1; 3.2; cf. *Eph.* 7.2; *Sm.* 3.3; 12.2) or his "blood" alone (*Sm.* 1.1; 6.1; cf. *Eph.* 1.1; *Phd.* inscr). In one passage recognition of the eucharist as Christ's "flesh" is related to the theme of the reality of his death and resurrection (*Sm.* 7.1). What our study of the linking formula ("which is") has shown is that although Ignatius uses it to bring such elements of the tradition alive by juxtaposing them in striking ways, the formula does not determine the nature of the relation between

---

1   White, *Form and Function*, 11.
2   Πραότης (4.2) and πραυπάθεια (8.1) are synonyms for "gentleness" (BAG *s.vv.*, p. 705).

3   G reads ὅς ἐστιν in the first of the two expressions. But it joins two feminine nouns and must originally have been neuter (LC). See further on *Eph.* 20.2.

the items so joined. This must be supplied from context or parallel passages. We can say, then, that faith and love somehow express the meaning of Christ's flesh and blood,[4] but we cannot say (relying on the formula alone) that Ignatius here works with a spiritualized conception of the eucharist. What, then, do the parallels discussed above show? *Sm.* 7.1 indicates that a realistic conception of Christ's presence in the eucharist is probably presupposed by Ignatius throughout. But it is also noteworthy how frequently the bishop invokes Christ's flesh or blood (or both) to stress the reality of his death without any obvious reference to the eucharist or any special emphasis on the presence of Christ in the eucharist. The basic concern seems to be the affirmation of the reality of the flesh (and hence of the suffering) of the historical Jesus. And this, in turn, is linked by Ignatius with the maintenance of true obedience and love (*Sm.* 6.2; cf. *Tr.* 2.1). For in Ignatius' mind "faith and love" (cf. *Sm.* 6.1) can be maintained only when docetism is rejected. Thus he builds on realistic ideas of Christ's presence in the eucharist, and they serve him well; yet he directs his attention not so much to the meal itself as to the larger sacred unity of which it is a part. The various "means of grace" have not yet been clearly differentiated or set apart from the experience of the community as a whole.

■ **8.2** The corollary of the self-renewal of the Trallians against the snares of the devil (that is, against pride) is now stated: having nothing against one's neighbor. Apparently Ignatius had in mind animosity or criticism—"having something against someone" covers a wide range of attitudes (cf. Matt 5:23; Rev 2:4, 14)—emanating from those who are "puffed up" (7.1) against their fellow Christians. But he immediately goes on to reinforce the point by arguing that dissension in the

churches discredits Christianity in the pagan world and by quoting Isa 52:5 (or something like it) to drive home the lesson. A particularly important parallel is provided by *1 Clement* (47.7; cf. 1.1), where the argument is made more forcefully and where many of the same themes are found.[5] The concern for such social respectability is found already in Paul (1 Cor 10:32; 1 Thess 4:12) and became even more important in this period (e.g., 1 Tim 6:1; 1 Pet 2:15; cf. *Eph.* 10.1–3).

The concern often clustered (as in Ignatius) around allusions to Isa 52:5.[6] The text is used basically in two ways in this period: (a) against the Jews (Rom 2:24; Justin *Dial.* 17.2; Tertullian *Adv. Marc.* 3.23.3; 4.14.16; 5.13.7; cf. *Adv. Jud.* 13.26) and (b) as an exhortation not to cause offense to the heathen through dissension, immorality, or the failure to make deeds conform to words (Pol. *Phil.* 10.3; 2 Pet 2:2; *2 Clem.* 13.2–4). By Tertullian's day, secularized Christians were even using the passage to defend their participation in the Saturnalia and New Year's celebrations to avoid offending pagans (*Idol.* 14). It is likely that the passage first belonged to a collection of biblical testimonies against the Jews and was then adopted for paraenetic purposes. For there are two forms of the verse—one close to the biblical text and the other prefaced (as in *Tr.* 8.2) by a "woe" (Pol. *Phil.* 10.3; *2 Clem.* 13.2; *Const. Apost.* 1.10; 3.5); and it seems unlikely that all the passages which diverge from the Bible go back to Ignatius. Note in particular (a) that *2 Clement* provides both forms of the passage and treats them as distinct verses of the Bible (13.2–4) and (b) that in Justin the verse, though not itself in the woe-form, is followed by four "woes" from the Bible (*Dial.* 17.2). Thus it is likely that the woe-form of Isa 52:5 arose under the influence of other verses traditionally associated with it in a collection of texts.[7] Ignatius' use of Isa

---

4 Apart from the double formula here and in *Rom.* 7.3, Christ's blood is associated with love also in *Sm.* 1.1. But elsewhere it is associated with joy (*Phd.* inscr), and it would be artificial to think that Ignatius intends such correspondences to be pressed. It is the eucharist as a whole that is connected with faith and love (which in turn, as *Eph.* 14.1 shows, are also closely related).

5 Karlmann Beyschlag (*Clemens Romanus und der Frühkatholizismus* [Beiträge zur historischen Theologie 35; Tübingen: Mohr (Siebeck), 1966] 175) notes that Ignatius shares with *1 Clement* the following elements

(some of which are echoed also in other sources): the connection between the "foolishness" of a "few" and the "slander" of the gentiles; an application of the theme to the problem of disunity in the Christian community; language reminiscent of Isa 52:5.

6 The γάρ ("for") by which it is introduced probably indicates that Ignatius recognized it as Scripture (cf. Matt 24:7, 21; 1 Cor 2:16; 6:16; 10:26; 15:27; Rom 2:24; 11:34; 1 Pet 3:10).

7 For other parallels and a somewhat different evaluation of the evidence see W. C. van Unnik, "Die Rücksicht auf die Reaktion der Nicht-Christen als

52:5 illustrates the extent to which some Christians were willing to respect pagan opinion and at the same time how the possibility of pagan disapproval could be used to maintain the discipline of the churches.

Motiv in der altchristlichen Paränese," in Walther Eltester, ed., *Judentum, Urchristentum, Kirche: Festschrift für Joachim Jeremias* (BZNW 26; Berlin: Töpelmann, 1960) 221–34. Van Unnik attributes the woe-form of the verse to a lost prophetic-apocalyptic writing.

9   Against Docetism

1 Be deaf, then, when someone speaks to you apart from Jesus Christ, of the family of David, of Mary, who was truly born, both ate and drank, was truly persecuted under Pontius Pilate, was truly crucified and died, as heavenly, earthly, and sub-earthly things looked on, 2/ who was also truly raised from the dead, his Father having raised him, in whose likeness his Father will also so raise us up who believe in him through Jesus Christ, apart from whom we do not have true life.

10 1/ But if as some who are atheists—that is, unbelievers—say, that he suffered in appearance, whereas it is they who are (mere) appearance, why am I in bonds? why do I pray even to fight with beasts? I die, then, in vain! Then I lie about the Lord!

11 1/ Flee, then, the evil side-growths which bear death-dealing fruit, which if someone tastes, he immediately dies; for these are not the planting of the Father. 2/ For if they were, they would appear as branches of the cross, and their fruit would be incorruptible—(the cross) through which by his suffering he calls you who are his members. The head, then, cannot be born apart without the members since God offers union, which is himself.

A fresh set of exhortations follows that deals more directly with the views of the false teachers. Ignatius first tells the Trallians to close their ears to what the heretics say and identifies their denial of the reality of the incarnation and passion with speaking "apart from Jesus Christ" (9.1). We have noted the same refusal to debate and the same one-sided labelling of theological positions elsewhere (cf. *Eph.* 9.1; *Mag.* 8–10).

■ **9.1–2** The views of the false teachers can be gathered in part indirectly from the theology that Ignatius puts in their place. This theology is presented in quasi-credal form. According to Norden, such materials reflect fundamental features of an Oriental hymnic style—in particular, repeated relative clauses and participial expressions describing the divinity.[1] From this per-spective credal or quasi-credal materials may be said to represent a more prosaic adaptation of the hymnic style.[2] The appearance of repeated relative clauses in *Tr.* 9.1–2 (and to a lesser extent elsewhere) is particularly important in this connection and links Ignatius with earlier developments, even though comparable features in his letters apparently owe more to rhetoric than to hymnic style (see on *Eph.* 7.2). Yet there is an important difference between Ignatius and his Christian predecessors: The christological thought of the latter is dominated by the opposition between two periods—according to the flesh/according to the spirit (cf. Rom 1:3–4)—or two stages—humiliation/exaltation or death/resurrection (cf. 1 Cor 15:3–4; Phil 2:5–11; 1 Pet 3:18–22); whereas *Tr.* 9 (and similar material in Ignatius) presents us with a

---

1   Eduard Norden, *Agnostos Theos* (reprinted Stuttgart: Teubner, 1956) 166–76, 201–7, 263–76, 380–87.

2   Cf. Gottfried Schille, *Frühchristliche Hymnen* (Berlin: Evangelische Verlagsanstalt, 1965) 39.

list of moments in the ministry of Jesus that works to flatten out such opposition (and that puts relatively little emphasis on the exaltation of Christ). Ignatius' formulation is designed to answer docetism. No doubt the bishop uses traditional themes, but it is likely that he draws them from various sources and that he is at or near the beginning of a new way of putting them together.[3]

We meet elsewhere in comparable settings references by Ignatius to the family of David (*Eph.* 18.2; 20.2; *Sm.* 1.1; cf. Rom 1:3), Mary (*Eph.* 7.2; 18.2; 19.1), and Pontius Pilate (*Mag.* 11; *Sm.* 1.2). The statement that Christ "was born" ($\dot{\epsilon}\gamma\epsilon\nu\nu\dot{\eta}\theta\eta$) also occurs again (*Eph.* 18.2; cf. *Sm.* 1.1). That he was "persecuted" ($\dot{\epsilon}\delta\iota\dot{\omega}\chi\theta\eta$) by Pilate is an exceptional comment and seems to reflect Ignatius' interest in the theme of discipleship (cf. *Mag.* 8.2; 9.2). That Christ "was crucified and died" ($\dot{\epsilon}\sigma\tau\alpha\upsilon\rho\dot{\omega}\theta\eta\ \kappa\alpha\dot{\iota}\ \dot{\alpha}\pi\dot{\epsilon}\theta\alpha\nu\epsilon\nu$) is expressed in different words by Ignatius in comparable settings (cf. *Eph.* 18.2; *Sm.* 1.2; 2); and it is only in other contexts that we are told in so many words that Christ "was crucified" ($\dot{\epsilon}\sigma\tau\alpha\upsilon\rho\dot{\omega}\theta\eta$, *Eph.* 16.2; cf. *Rom.* 7.2) or that he was the one "dying" ($\dot{\alpha}\pi\theta\alpha\nu\dot{o}\nu\tau\alpha$) for us (*Tr.* 2.1; *Rom.* 6.1; cf. *Pol. Phil.* 9.2). That Christ "was raised from the dead" ($\dot{\eta}\gamma\dot{\epsilon}\rho\theta\eta\ \dot{\alpha}\pi\dot{o}\ \nu\epsilon\kappa\rho\dot{\omega}\nu$) is also expressed in different words by Ignatius elsewhere (see below) but echoes numerous NT passages.[4] Several of these themes are clearly traditional, and there is a good chance that taken together they constitute the core of such summaries in Ignatius. Yet they have no set wording, and the impression is left that traditional materials from a variety of sources come and go within the framework. Moreover the framework itself seems directly determined by the use to which Ignatius puts these themes. Such points become clearer when the elements in *Tr.* 9 so far not considered are also taken into account.

(a) First, the themes are chosen (as indicated above) with a view to their usefulness in the debate with docetism. The mention of the three proper names—David, Mary, Pontius Pilate—appears to reflect this purpose especially clearly (cf. *Eph.* 18.2; 19.1). It does not seem quite correct, then, to deal with the adverb "truly" ($\dot{\alpha}\lambda\eta\theta\dot{\omega}s$) as though it were fully detachable from its context as an addition made by Ignatius to earlier materials. It seems more likely that the desire of Ignatius (or the tradition in which he stood) to emphasize the reality of the historical Jesus led to a loose though also partly predictable selection of events from the story of the Lord's ministry. Later writers seem to be responding to the same impulse when they make use of the term "true" or "truly" in comparable contexts (cf. Tertullian *Carn. Christ.* 5.2; Origen *Cels.* 2.16; Augustine *Tract. in Ioann. evang.* 98.6; Agobard *Sermo de fid. verit.* 7).

(b) Second, it is largely our knowledge of the later standardized creeds that prevents us from recognizing that other elements in *Tr.* 9 are as primary as the ones discussed above. Certainly some themes are more likely than others to occur in such lists and some of these eventually establish themselves, but that does not deprive others of the weight that they obviously once had. An instructive illustration is provided by Ignatius' statement not only that was Christ "truly born" but also that "he both ate and drank." We usually meet this theme in connection with the story of the resurrection of Christ. It is reflected already in NT passages such as Luke 24:42–43 (eating), John 21:5, 10 (eating) and Acts 10:41 (eating and drinking). Justin (*Dial.* 51.2) also has Christ predict that he will "eat and drink" with his disciples after the resurrection (cf. *Const. Apost.* 6.30).[5] The theme could be important in the debate with docetism, as is evident from *Sm.* 3.3, where it is associated with quasi-credal materials (*Sm.* 1–2) and still more closely with a variant of the words of the risen Lord known to us from Luke 24:39 (*Sm.* 3.2). The form of Christ's words about the Son of Man in Justin—that he will "eat and drink again ($\pi\dot{\alpha}\lambda\iota\nu$) with his disciples" (*Dial.* 51.2)—illustrates how natural it would be to insist on the eating and drinking of Christ also before the resurrection (as in *Tr.* 9.1; cf. *Const. Apost.* 5.7), especially in the face of thoroughgoing docetism.[6]

---

3   For the general approach adopted here see Hans von Campenhausen, "Das Bekenntnis im Urchristentum," *ZNW* 63 (1972) 234–53.

4   E.g., Matt 14:2; 27:64; 28:7; John 2:22; Rom 6:4, 9; 7:4; 1 Cor 15:12, 20.

5   In Justin the notice is contained in a rephrasing of the passion prediction and thus has a stylized character. For the view that Justin is here dependent on "an extra-canonical source later than our synoptic gospels" and based on them, see A. J. Bellinzoni, *The Sayings of Jesus in the Writings of Justin Martyr* (NovTSup 17; Leiden: Brill, 1967) 30–32.

6   Matt 11:19 ("the Son of Man came eating and drinking") has a very different focus and is irrelevant here (Koester, *Synoptische Überlieferung*, 27–28).

The theme of eating and drinking may have been tied in with anti-docetism also in another way. In Tobit—a writing apparently known to Ignatius' fellow bishop Polycarp (Pol. *Phil.* 10.2)—the guardian angel reveals at the end of the adventure that he "did not eat or drink" with his charges while he was with them and that they saw only a "vision" (Tob 12:19 BA). Philo (*Migr. Abr.* 118) similarly regards it as marvellous that when the three strangers visited Abraham, though they did not eat or drink, they gave the appearance of doing so and, though "bodiless" (ἀσωμάτους), were transformed to look like men (cf. *Test. Abr.* 3). Note that the word ἀσώματος "bodiless" is one of the terms in *Sm.* 3.2 that distinguishes Ignatius' form of the Lord's saying from that of Luke. It does not seem impossible that for some Christians in Syria and Asia Minor angelology provided the clue to christology. And if we could overcome doubts about the link forged by Ignatius between Judaizing and docetism (see on *Mag.* 8–10), that would provide an attractive explanation for the appearance of docetism here. In any event, Ignatius and the docetists did not disagree about the essentially spiritual nature of Christ. They differed in their willingness to conceive of the spiritual as uniting with the physical.

Another traditional element in *Tr.* 9.1 is Ignatius' statement (a genitive absolute) that Christ was crucified "as heavenly, earthly, and subearthly things looked on."

This is reminiscent of the "things heavenly and earthly and under the earth" of the pre-Pauline Christ-hymn at Phil 2:10 (for another link with the same passage see on *Mag.* 10.3). And especially since a similar genitive absolute construction is used at 1 Pet 3:22 in quasi-credal material (Christ, we are told, went to heaven "as angels and authorities and powers became subject to him"), there seems no good reason to doubt that this element is as primitive as any in *Tr.* 9. Whatever its source, the line is not out of harmony with the cosmic conception of the events of salvation sketched by Ignatius in *Eph.* 19.[7]

Also traditional is Ignatius' attribution of Christ's resurrection to the Father in *Tr.* 9.2 (cf. *Sm.* 7.1).[8] This too is in the form of a genitive absolute ("his Father having raised him"). Although it spells out the meaning of the previous statement that Christ "was raised from the dead" (also traditional, as we have seen), it is unlikely that Ignatius is dealing with the latter as a fixed theme requiring elucidation. Rather he is providing an alternative formulation that eases the transition to the following point—a Pauline point by now traditional[9]—that the Father's raising of Christ is the presupposition of the resurrection of the believer who is "in Christ Jesus."[10] Here as elsewhere Ignatius seeks to strengthen the case against docetism by grounding the reliability of the believer's hopes on the reality of Christ's death and resurrection (cf. *Tr.* 10; *Sm.* 2). The fact that elsewhere

---

7 Elze (*Untersuchungen*, 11) thinks that there is a contradiction between the two passages since the events of salvation cannot both escape the notice of the demons (*Eph.* 19.1) and be seen by them (*Tr.* 9.1). But our comments on *Eph.* 19 show that that is too simple a conclusion to draw. Whether the reference to subearthly powers here presupposes the descent of Christ into Hades (cf. *Mag.* 9.2) is uncertain, especially since Ignatius is elsewhere satisfied with a division of the world into heavenly and earthly things (*Eph.* 13.2).

8 Gal 1:1 ("through Jesus Christ and God the Father who raised him from the dead"); cf. Acts 3:15; 4:10; 5:30; 10:40; 13:30, 37; Rom 4:24; 8:11; 10:9; 1 Cor 6:14; 15:15; 1 Pet 1:21; Heb 11:19. For God as the Father of Jesus Christ see Col 1:3 (cf. 2 Cor 1:3; Eph 1:3; 1 Pet 1:3).

9 Rom 8:11; 1 Cor 6:14; 15:12–22; 2 Cor 4:14; 1 Thess 4:14; cf. Pol *Phil.* 2.2.

10 The text of G (κατὰ τὸ ὁμοίωμα ὃς καί) is scarcely intelligible. The following are the major suggestions that have been made: (a) Several editors follow L: ὃς

καὶ κατὰ τὸ ὁμοίωμα "who [i.e., the Father of Christ] also in the same way" (will raise us). Note that the previous clause also begins with ὃς καί. But this reading requires us to deal with the second reference to "the Father" of Christ (which follows) as a clarification of the relative. That is very awkward. Elze (*Untersuchungen*, 11) thinks that the line was originally semi-credal material in which the relative referred to Christ and that it was Ignatius who then added the reference to the Father and changed the sense. Hence the awkwardness. But a link between Christ's resurrection and the believer's resurrection as comparable acts of God is more likely at any stage of the development (see the references in n. 9 above; cf. Paulsen, *Studien*, 65 n. 27). (b) The second reference to "his Father" should perhaps be dropped (Paulsen, *Studien*, 65 n. 28; cf. Petermann, *Epistolae*, 116). (c) Zahn reads: οὗ καὶ κατὰ τὸ ὁμοίωμα "in whose likeness" (Christ's Father will raise us). I suggest a slight improvement: οὗ κατὰ τὸ ὁμοίωμα καί. The οὗ may well have been absorbed by the preceding αὐτοῦ at which point someone added ὃς before καί by

this thought is linked with an emphasis on Christ's power to raise *himself* (*Sm.* 2; cf. John 2:19; 10:17–18) only underscores the extent to which anti-docetism controls Ignatius' selection and interpretation of traditional themes.

Finally, it is unlikely that the last clause ("apart from whom . . .") reflects traditional material, especially since the expression τὸ ἀληθινὸν ζῆν "true life" is typically Ignatian (*Eph.* 11.1; *Sm.* 4.1; cf. *Eph.* 3.2). Yet the line is the last of the series of relative clauses and illustrates the freedom with which the bishop worked in filling out the framework provided by the literary form that he had inherited.

■ **10** There now follows a direct statement about the teaching of the "atheists," that is, the false teachers (cf. *Tr.* 3.2). They say that Christ suffered only τὸ δοκεῖν "in appearance" (cf. *Sm.* 2; 4.2).[11] Although it is clear that denial of the true suffering of Christ was the heart of this teaching, it is also obvious that Ignatius took it as implying a denial of the reality of everything else said of the historical Jesus—from birth to resurrection (see *Tr.* 9; *Sm.* 1–3). Ignatius may not correctly represent his opponents on these points, but so emphatic are his words that evidently more than the logical extension of their thought is involved.[12] In particular, it is likely that they found in the vague atmosphere of the traditional accounts of the resurrected Christ models for their understanding of the rest of Christ's ministry (cf. *Sm.* 3). This flat denial of Christ's fleshliness is not common. Although Ignatius' polemic reminds us especially of 1 John 4:2–3 (cf. Pol. *Phil.* 7.1), it is not certain that 1 John

has in view the same absolute docetism.[13] In early Patristic discussions parallels can be found in the thought of Saturninus, Marcion, and (it seems) unnamed individuals attacked by Irenaeus (*Adv. haer.* 4.33.5; cf. 3.16.1; 3.18.6).[14] But there is nothing sufficiently precise in Ignatius' polemic to permit us to single out a particular sect of Gnostics as possibly known to the bishop. Indeed, it has become steadily clearer that docetism does not necessarily presuppose Gnosticism.[15] Perhaps no more was needed than an emphasis on divine transcendence, an identification especially with the resurrected Christ, and the group's sense of isolation from the world. In such a context traditional conceptions of angelic participation in the affairs of men (see on *Tr.* 9.1) could provide the categories for constructing an appropriate christology.

After setting out the position of the false teachers, Ignatius throws their teaching back at them by charging them with the same unreality they attribute to Christ. The same turn of thought is found in Irenaeus (*Adv. haer.* 4.33.5), from whom perhaps Tertullian (*Adv. Val.* 27.3) derived it.[16] Here, then, we have what looks like a traditional ploy.[17] The argument depends on the thought expressed more directly in *Sm.* 2 that an unworthy opinion about Christ becomes true of those who hold it. Thus Ignatius draws out negative implications from the teaching of his opponents that they would have rejected out of hand. It is likely that his argument relied for its cogency to some extent on the popular contrast between "appearance" (τὸ δοκεῖν) and "reality" (τὸ εἶναι). Originally it was a question of

---

analogy wih the preceding line to produce the reading of G.

11 The adverbial use of this expression (in the accusative) is also found in important manuscripts of Tertullian *Carn. Christ.* 1.4 (in a comparable context) and Philo *Leg. ad Gaium* 259 as well as in Josephus *Vita* 75; cf. *SB* 5.7696,55.

12 Cf. Zahn, *Ignatius*, 384–85.

13 Cf. ibid., 392; A. Grillmeier, "Doketismus," *LTK* 3 (1959) 470; Paulsen, *Studien*, 140 n. 42.

14 Zahn, *Ignatius*, 392–99. According to Irenaeus *Adv. haer.* 1.16.1: *alii vero putative eum passum, naturaliter impassibilem exsistentem* "others say that he only seemed to suffer, being naturally impassible" (these are contrasted with Gnostics who make distinctions between the historical Jesus and the heavenly Christ).

15 Cf. J. G. Davies, "The Origins of Docetism," *Studia*

Patristica VI (TU 81; Berlin: Akademie-Verlag, 1962) 13–35.

16 Lightfoot, *Ignatius*, 2. 175.

17 Note also that Philo (*Opif. mund.* 171) charges those who say that there are "infinite" worlds with being themselves "infinite and ignorant with regard to truth." The form of attack was evidently conventional, and it is likely that anti-Gnostic writers did not have to rely on one another in this regard.

155

"appearing to be just" as opposed to "actually being so."[18] The theme is treated by Heinimann in connection with other popular contrasts having to do with words and deeds, names and deeds, law and nature—all of which have left traces elsewhere in Ignatius (see on *Eph.* 14.2–15.2; *Mag.* 4; *Tr.* 1.1).[19] The verb εἶναι "to be" in the required sense does not appear in our passage, but it seems to be implied and is found in two other passages where it is correlated with deeds as opposed to (mere) words (*Eph.* 15.1; *Mag.* 4). It is also clear from Philo that the contrast between appearance and reality was alive in circles close to early Christianity. In Philo it serves to summarize a whole range of contrasts between the real and unreal (*Mut. nom.* 104), intersects the polarity of words and deeds (cf. *Migr. Abr.* 12; 40) and of law and nature (cf. *Ebriet.* 37; *Agric.* 43), and corresponds to ethical, epistemological, and metaphysical contrasts having to do with truth and hypocrisy (*Fuga* 156), opinion and truth (*Migr. Abr.* 86–88), shadow and reality, imitation and archetype (*Migr. Abr.* 12), and so forth. In one passage Philo tells us "that mortality is full of disbelief (τῆς ἀπιστίας) because it depends on appearance (τοῦ δοκεῖν) alone" (*Conf.* 57). Ignatius' reference to teachers of docetism here as "unbelievers" (ἄπιστοι; cf. *Sm.* 2; 5.3) may have this rather special significance. In any event, there is enough in all this to have given support to Ignatius' equating of docetism with devotion to unreality and his attribution of unreality to the faithless atheists themselves.

Ignatius' main argument against the docetic position is that it makes nonsense of his own bonds (cf. *Sm.* 4.2) and his desire to "fight with wild beasts" (cf. *Eph.* 1.2). This is yet another point at which Irenaeus' discussion of the unnamed docetists (*Adv. haer.* 3.18.6) echoes Ignatius. The argument is connected with the charge often

levelled at a later date that Gnostics denied the value of martyrdom.[20] But Gnostic theology and docetic christology were not always incompatible with a glorification of martyrdom, as the two Coptic *Apocalypses of James* (NHC 5) show. And since at least some of Ignatius' docetic opponents seem to have professed admiration for him (*Sm.* 5.2), he is evidently pressing conclusions on them which they did not necessarily share. Yet it also seems likely that the corollary of their theological sophistication (cf. *Tr.* 5) was an independence of mind that at least made credible the charge that they formed an exclusive society and neglected communal responsibilities (cf. *Sm.* 6–7). Ignatius' sharpening of the theological lines must represent in part a reaction to a growing threat to episcopal authority from that quarter. This meant claiming for the emerging orthodoxy the prestige of the martyr and associating an unquestioning willingness to die for the faith with the simplest and most direct requirements of Christian living. The insistence on the reality of the Lord's death, then, functions as a way of lending value and importance to obedience and to Ignatius' own (tortured) commitment to death. The underlying emotional currents come to the surface in the challenging tone of the concluding remarks that otherwise he dies in vain and his whole way of life is a lie which contradicts the truth about Christ (cf. 1 Cor 15:15).[21]

■ **11.1–2** Another exhortation to avoid the false teachers follows. It includes in a short space a rich variety of images involving (a) plant life, (b) the cross as a tree, (c) head and members. First, the false teachers are said to be extraneous "side-growths" (παραφυάδες) or "suckers"[22]— a term used in a variety of metaphorical senses elsewhere.[23] Here the image expresses Ignatius' view of the false teachers as illegitimate offshoots of the Christian community. Next, the fruit they produce is said to be

18 Aeschylus *Septem* 592; Plato *Resp.* 2, 361b; cf. Epictetus *Diss.* 4.6.24; 4.8.23; Arrian *Anab. Alex.* 4.11.5; *Sent. Sext.* 64.

19 Heinimann, *Nomos und Physis*, 57–58. Note that Stobaeus (*Ecl.* 2.15) also puts together materials that deal both with words and deeds and with seeming and being.

20 Irenaeus *Adv. haer.* 3.18.5; Clement Alex. *Strom.* 4.4, 16.3; 4.9, 73.1; Eusebius *Hist. eccl.* 4.7.7.

21 In the last clause read ἄρα οὖν "then" (with C) rather than the negative (which is absent also from g Severus A and the Arabic).

22 Cf. Ps-Aristotle *De Plantis* 1.4, 819a 24; Theophrastus *Hist. plant.* 2.2.4.

23 Aristotle, *E.N.* 1.6, 1096a 21; *4 Macc.* 1.28; Philo *Plant.* 4; *Herm. Sim.* 8.1.17–18; 8.2.1–2; 8.4.6; Eulogius, in Photius *Bibl.* 230.

"death-dealing" (θανατηφόρος). Since this term is used especially of poisonous plants (cf. Lucian *Hermot.* 62; Theophrastus *Hist. plant.* 9.15.2; 9.16.4), Ignatius must be harking back to the deadly drug (that is, false teaching) of *Tr.* 6.2. Yet since a connection between poisonous fruit and side-growths is not typical, here as in *Tr.* 6 Ignatius draws together only partially related images. Equally loose is the connection with the next image in which the bishop denies that the false teachers are a "planting of the Father." Schlier relates this to similar motifs in Gnostic and semi-Gnostic literature.[24] Yet again his perspective is one-sided. For not only is the image of the divine planter and his planting found in Matt 15:13 (cf. *Gos. Thom.* 40), but also it presupposes a wide range of biblical materials (see on *Eph.* 9.1), is impressively elaborated in the Dead Sea scrolls, and is long reflected in the main line of orthodox Christian theology.[25] Even if we regard the imagery of our passage as having acquired allegorical or mythological significance (see below), no less is true already of parallels from Qumran (1QH 6.15–17; 8.4–26). The image of the vine in John 15:1–8 (and its biblical background) may also be recalled.[26]

More clearly allegorical or mythological is the interpretation of the cross as a tree (or tree of life) of which true Christians are the branches. Although this too is found in Gnostic or semi-Gnostic sources (cf. *Gos. Truth* 18.24–27; *Mart. Andr. pr.* 14), it appears in non-Gnostic writers as well (Justin *Dial.* 86.1–8; *Barn.* 11.6–8; Irenaeus *Adv. haer.* 5.17.3)[27] and in early Christian art.[28] In any event, the bishop appeals to such imagery in opposition to docetism. To be a branch of the cross is to affirm the reality of the crucifixion and to enjoy the fruit of deathlessness which it alone guarantees.

The image of the branches (of the tree) flows together in Ignatius' mind with that of the members (of the body). Elsewhere Ignatius refers once to the church as Christ's body (*Sm.* 1.2) and once to the limbs (*Eph.* 4.2, unless he has in mind only "melodies" at this point). The paucity of references warns us against making too much of these notices in evaluating the bishop's view of the church. Nevertheless the striking form of the image here—suggesting as it does that Christ as head[29] and the people as his limbs are strictly interdependent—was taken by Schlier and Bartsch to go beyond Paul and even the deutero-Pauline literature in the direction of Gnosticism.[30] From this point of view Ignatius' understanding of the church is modelled on the Gnostic conception of the unity that obtains in the *pleroma*. And this was felt to be confirmed by the apparent identification of God and unity that follows. But we have already seen that the identification of God with unity elsewhere in Ignatius cannot be read too literally (see on *Eph.* 14.1), and our study of the linking formula used here ("which is") has shown that it is best understood as expressing a causal relation between God and unity (see on *Eph.* 20.2). The expression, then, serves simply to emphasize the fact that, as Ignatius has just said, God "offers" (literally, "promises") unity to the church. Moreover, the relation between head and members is hardly to be understood as involving strict interdependence. For it seems likely that Ignatius does no more than exploit the obvious physiological connection between head and members in order to stress the closeness of the bond between Christ and his people. As Ratramnus was to say centuries later, "because the people cannot exist without Christ, nor Christ without the people, so also can the head not exist without the body, nor the body without the head" (*De corp. et sang. dom.* 75). In neither instance need a consubstantiality between Christ and his people be presupposed. It is also just possible that the misleading impression left by the text owes something to a false reading and that we should substitute (as AC and the Arabic seem to suggest)

24 Schlier, *Untersuchungen*, 48–54.

25 Jean Daniélou, "The Vine and the Tree of Life," *Primitive Christian Symbols* (Baltimore: Helicon, 1964) 25–41.

26 Philo also refers to God as the divine planter in *Conf.* 61.

27 Cf. Rahner, *Greek Myths*, 61–68.

28 Ludwig von Sybel, "Ξύλον ζωῆς," *ZNW* 19 (1919/20) 85–91.

29 Cf. Col 1:18; 2:19; Eph 1:22–23; 4:15–16.

30 Schlier, *Untersuchungen*, 90; Bartsch, *Gnostisches Gut*, 27.

γενηθῆναι ("to exist") for γεννηθῆναι ("to be born"). Whatever the exact implications of the imagery may be, it is unlikely that the idea of a transcendent body of believers comes from Gnostic speculation in the first place.[31]

31 Cf. Karl Martin Fischer, *Tendenz und Absicht des Epheserbriefes* (FRLANT 111; Göttingen: Vandenhoeck & Ruprecht, 1973) 48–78. Fischer finds the source of the image in a widely diffused notion of the universal God as the "macroanthropos" (cf. Lohse, *Colossians and Philemon*, 52–55). In a writer like Ignatius the common metaphor of the body for human groups (cf. Plutarch *De defec. orac.* 29, 426a) may have blended with the cosmic symbol.

12 Closing Formulae and Farewell

1 I greet you from Smyrna along with the churches of God present with me, who in every way refreshed me both in flesh and spirit. **2/** My bonds exhort you, (bonds) which I carry about because of Jesus Christ with the prayer that I may attain God: persevere in your concord and in prayer with one another; for it is right for each one of you, but especially the presbyters, to refresh the bishop to the honor of the Father of Jesus Christ and of the apostles. **3/** I pray you to listen to me in love that I may not be a witness against you by having written. And pray also for me who need your love in the mercy of God, that I may be regarded as worthy of the lot which I am meant to attain, lest I be found a castaway.

13

1/ The love of the Smyrnaeans and Ephesians greets you. Remember the church in Syria in your prayers, from which I am not worthy to be named, being the least of them. **2/** Farewell in Jesus Christ, being subject to the bishop as to the commandment, likewise also to the presbytery. And love one another individually with undivided heart. **3/** My spirit is consecrated for you, not only now, but also when I attain God; for I am still in danger; but the Father is faithful in Jesus Christ to fulfill my entreaty and yours, in whom you may be found blameless.

It is possible, as we have seen, that Ignatius began to bring the letter to a close at *Tr.* 8.1, even though the exhortations in *Tr.* 9–11 prove to be unexpectedly complex for the purpose. If so, it is understandable that with the ἀσπάζομαι greeting in 12.1 ("I greet you") we are already into material associated with the closing formulae. A third-person form of the same greeting occurs in 13.1. Such an accumulation of greetings is not unusual in letters of the period[1] and occurs elsewhere in Ignatius (*Sm.* 12–13; *Pol.* 8). Other conventional items found here (see on *Eph.* 21) include: the request for prayer (12.3); the request to be remembered (13.1); the farewell (13.2). Expansions of the farewell are known in other letters of the period but are not as elaborate as they are here.[2]

Other elements here are less conventional but may also perform a recognizable epistolary function. (a) In 12.2 we have a fairly elaborate exhortation introduced by the curious expression "my bonds (δέσμα) exhort you." The personification intensifies what may be a Pauline model for the statement—"I exhort you . . . a prisoner (δέσμιος)" (Phlm 9–10; Eph 4:1)—by calling greater attention to Ignatius' situation. The content of the exhortation touches on major concerns of the letter—concord and corporate prayer (see on *Eph.* 13.1), both in turn regarded as dependent on obedience to the bishop.[3] (b) In 12.3 we find a brief request, buttressed by a mild threat, to listen to what Ignatius has said. The language associated with the threat ("so that I may not be a witness against you") elsewhere reflects a stance adopted by early

---

1   Exler, *Greek Epistolography,* 116.
2   Ibid., 74–77.
3   Bauer (*Orthodoxy and Heresy,* 68–69) took the special

reference to the presbyters and their responsibility in refreshing the bishop as an indication that even presbyters were involved in opposition to the bishop.

Christians in the face of an unreceptive world (cf. Matt 10:18; 24:14; Mark 6:11; Luke 21:13). Here it is applied to the relations between Ignatius and other Christians and betrays significant rifts within the church at Tralles. Similar tensions, though in a milder form, are reflected elsewhere in the letters (cf. *Phd.* 6.3).

Both of these elements—especially the second of them—recall "expressions urging responsibility" found in the body closings of Hellenistic letters (see on *Eph.* 20). For a threatening tone, as White has pointed out, sometimes characterizes such expressions.[4] To be sure, none of the conventional formulae appears in Ignatius at this point, but we may with some confidence regard his language as a substitution for them. If so, material associated with body closings and concluding formulae

interpenetrate each other in *Tr.* 12.

Intertwined with all this are expressions that illuminate the writer's conception of the relation between himself and his addressees. What we have along these lines in *Tr.* 12–13 is typical of Ignatius. There is the usual ambivalence (12.2–3): Ignatius' bonds give him an impressive authority and enable him to command unity; yet he requires the prayers and love of the Trallians to prove worthy of martyrdom[5] and not to become a castaway (cf. 1 Cor 9:27). There is the usual reference to the Antiochene Christians (*Tr.* 13.1): Ignatius requests prayers for them and states that he is the very least of them (cf. *Eph.* 21.2; *Rom.* 9.1–2; *Sm.* 11.1). Similarly self-depreciating is the recurring language about himself as a consecrated victim still in danger (see on *Eph.* 8.1; 12.1);

It is more likely that the remark is related to the fact that the bishop of Tralles came alone to meet Ignatius (*Tr.* 1.1). There is a difficulty with the text here. Support for the bishop according to GL redounds "to the honor of the Father of Jesus Christ and (to the honor of) the apostles." (For the title "Father of Jesus Christ" see *Eph.* 2.1; *Mag.* 3.1; *Tr.* inscr; and *Tr.* 9.2.) The translation "to the honor of the Father, of Jesus Christ, and of the apostles" neglects the tendency in Greek to set a καί between each member of such a series. To be sure, the required καί is reflected in AC and the Arabic (even more definite is g, which reads, "and to the honor of Jesus Christ"). But it probably represents an addition designed to simplify the relation between an awkward series of genitives. Moreover, Zahn (*Epistolae*, 53) was probably right in defending GL on the ground that the text was meant to recall the comparisons in Ignatius between God and bishop on the one hand and between apostles and presbyters on the other. (Note that the expression "to the honor of [God]" marks a comparison between God and bishop in *Mag.* 3.2.) To be sure, the allusion is easily missed, for since no presbyters had come with Polybius, they are included here not with the bishop as usual but with those who are exhorted to refresh the bishop. But in Ignatius' mind bishop and elders belong together (cf. 13.2), and it is not hard to imagine that habit immediately reasserts itself. There is little reason, then, to regard the reference to the apostles in 12.2 as going beyond Ignatius' usual treatment of them as venerable figures of the past who subordinated themselves to God or Christ as the elders subordinate themselves to the bishop (see on *Mag.* 6.1).

4 White, *Form and Function*, 46.

5 "To attain God" (12.2; cf. 13.3) and "to attain [one's lot]" (12.3; cf. *Rom.* 1.2; *Phd.* 5.1; *Eph.* 11.2) are evidently synonyms for martyrdom. It is significant that a word referring to one's lot or portion (here especially of martyrdom; cf. *Mart. Pol.* 6.2) as determined by God (cf. Acts 26:18; Col 1:12) can replace the name of God himself. Ignatius' talk about "attaining" is not without links to traditional biblical ways of structuring the relation between God and human beings. There is a textual problem here, but it does not seem to affect the general interpretation of the passage. G reads οὗ περίκειμαι ἐπιτυχεῖν, which (though repeated in g) hardly makes sense. Many suggestions involving compounds of other prepositions with κεῖμαι have been made, but none seems satisfactory. I suggest reading οὗπερ κεῖμαι ἐπιτυχεῖν. The relative with περ occurs some five other times in Ignatius. And κεῖμαι sometimes has to do with being appointed, set, or destined (BAG *s.v.* κεῖμαι 2.a, p. 428). Unfortunately the use of the verb with an infinitive is not easy to find (though note the impersonal construction in *P.Oxy.* 10.1297: ἅψαι αὐτὸν κεῖται "it is meant [for you] to burn it"). Of the versions, C ("clothed in," i.e., περίκειμαι), the Arabic ("stand," i.e., κεῖμαι "am set"?), and A ("called," i.e., κέκλημαι?) all omit ἐπιτυχεῖν "to attain" presumably because it cannot be construed with the controlling verb as the translators found it or understood it. The reading of L (*qua conor potiri* "which I am trying to attain") does not seem to shed much light on the problem.

160

and yet he is confident that "God is faithful" (cf. 1 Cor 1:9; 10:13) to fulfill the prayers of himself and the Trallians on his behalf (*Tr.* 13.3). Thus again Ignatius intimately links the preservation of concord in the churches with the possibility of the successful completion of his own martyrdom. And he shows himself a man used to achieving his aims by putting his destiny in the hands of others in such a way that they cannot refuse him the moral and physical support which he requests.

The churches who join in greeting the Trallians (12.1; 13.1) may include in addition to the Smyrnaeans and Ephesians (who are mentioned) also the Magnesians (for just as the Trallians are not mentioned in the letter to the Magnesians, so the Magnesians are not mentioned in the letter to the Trallians) and other unnamed parties also referred to in *Mag.* 15. It is clear that the most enthusiastic support of Ignatius came from the Ephesians and Smyrnaeans.

Ignatius
to the Romans

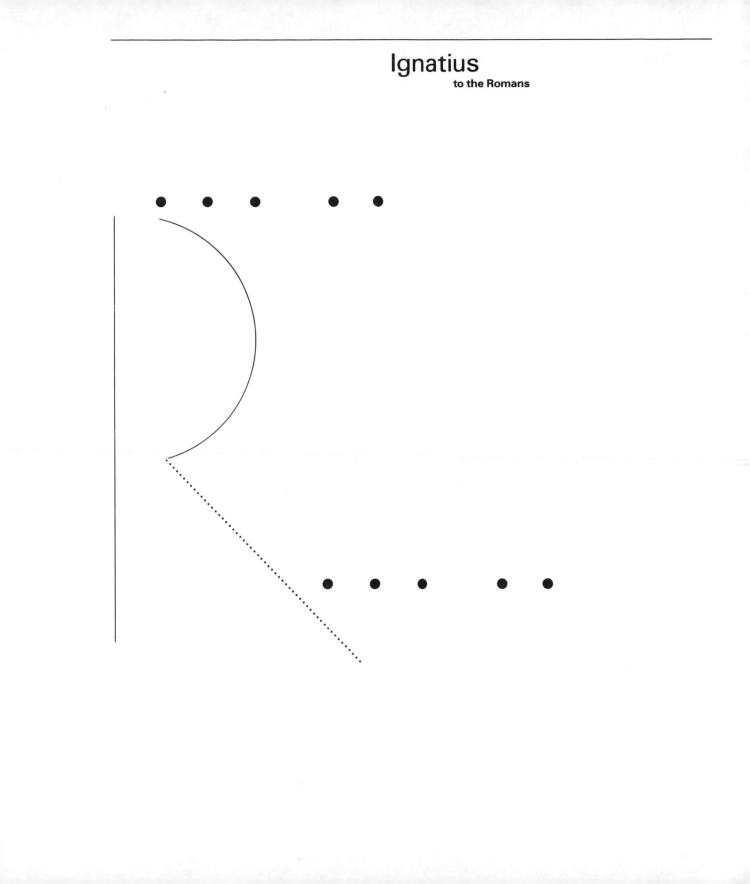

Salutation

Ignatius, also called Theophorus, to her who has found mercy in the majesty of the most high Father and his only Son Jesus Christ, to the church beloved and enlightened by the will of him who willed all things that are, in faith and love toward Jesus Christ our God, which presides in the place of the district of the Romans—worthy of God, worthy of honor, worthy of blessing, worthy of praise, worthy of success, worthy of sanctification, and presiding over love, under the law of Christ, bearing the Father's name—which I also greet in the name of Jesus Christ, son of the Father; to those united in flesh and spirit to every commandment of his, to those filled with the grace of God without wavering, and to those filtered clean from every alien color, abundant greetings blamelessly in Jesus Christ our God.

The salutation to the *Romans* is the most elaborate of all Ignatius' letters. Its basic formal elements are conventional, except that (as in *Magnesians, Trallians,* and *Philadelphians*) an ἀσπάζομαι greeting has been included ("which I also greet"). It is primarily the mention of the church of Rome that calls forth the astonishing flow of words, and the very length and complexity of the address (including the list of unusual adjectives compounded with ἀξιο-)[1] demonstrate the Syrian bishop's high regard for the Christian community of the capital. The exact nature of his attitude toward Rome, however, has been a matter of much dispute. But it appears that Protestant scholarship has been closer to the truth and that the best Roman Catholic commentators no longer read the text as teaching the primacy of the Roman church in a jurisdictional sense.[2]

The Roman church "presides in the place of the district of the Romans" (προκάθηται ἐν τόπῳ χωρίου ʽΡωμαίων). We may assume that, as in the other salutations, the geographical reference is simply to the place in which the church is located. The verb "presides," to be sure, normally takes a genitive of the place presided over; but to read the text as saying that the Roman church presides over "the district of the Romans" would require us to take ἐν τόπῳ (with Bunsen) in some adverbial sense or to alter it (with Zahn) to ἐν τύπῳ ("as an example"); and neither suggestion has much to recommend it. The phrase "place of the district of the Romans" is as pleonastic in Greek as in English. Yet although no exact parallel has been found, similar pleonasms occur: the word "place" is occasionally found together with the name of a province or city (Eusebius *Hist. eccl.* 1.13.6; Ps-Clem. *Hom.* 1.14); and the expression ὁ τόπος τῆς χώρας sometimes means simply "region" or "country" (Plato *Leg.* 4, 705c; cf. *Crit.* 114a). The word χωρίον used by Ignatius refers to any relatively small area such as a district, city, or town.[3] As expected, then, if Ignatius is speaking of the location of the church, he has Rome or

---

1   Two of these—ἀξιοεπίτευκτος "worthy of success" and ἀξιόαγνος "worthy of sanctification"—are hapaxlegomena for all of Greek literature (cf. Brown, *Authentic Writings,* 15).

2   Cf. Othmar Perler, "Ignatius und die Römische Christengemeinde," *Freiburger Zeitschrift für Philosophie und Theologie* 22 (1944) 413–51.

3   Cf. Thucydides 1.12, 13; 2.19, 47; Polyaenus 7.24; *CIG* 2.3137,94.

Rome and its immediate environs (not the Roman Empire) in mind.

It follows that the verb "preside" is used absolutely here as in *Mag.* 6.1–2 where it refers to those who exercise authority in the Christian community. Since the latter usage is evidently the primary one, its application to the church of Rome is already more or less metaphorical. The metaphor certainly leaves the impression that the preeminence of this church is one that it enjoys in the eyes of all Christians. But its scope is defined by Ignatius himself just below as a matter of "presiding over love" (προκαθημένη τῆς ἀγάπης). At one time Roman Catholic scholars (Nirschl, Funk) considered "love" to be a term for the (universal) church ("*Liebesbund*") and cited a number of parallels for the usage from Ignatius' letters (*Tr.* 13.1; *Rom.* 9.3; *Phd.* 11.2; *Sm.* 12.1). But when Ignatius says in these passages that the love of the churches or the brethren gives its greeting, his meaning is made clear by the genitives attached to the term. That is not the case in the passage before us. Rather the metaphor of presiding is extended here to include love as the territory, so to speak, over which the Roman church holds sway.[4] And the point has been appropriately illustrated from the letter to the Romans by Dionysius of Corinth (in Eusebius *Hist. eccl.* 4.23.10; cf. *1 Clem.* 55.2) which attributes to this church a long history of benefactions for the poor and those in mines. The primacy of the Roman church, then, is a spiritual one, and Ignatius singles out its love (for the outcast) precisely because a paradoxical "fear" of that very love dominates the request that follows (*Rom.* 1.2).[5] Thus Ignatius' words of praise—exaggerated as they may seem—are not to be understood apart from the circumstances in which he found himself and without taking into account the importance of the city as the place in which he was to attain God. The apostolic church of Rome, like the apostolic church of Ephesus, must play its role—a final and decisive one—in lending significance and meaning to the bishop's triumphant march to death (cf. *Eph.* 11.2–12.2). This attitude dominates Ignatius' other comments on the Roman church in what follows (see on *Rom.* 3.1; 4.3; 9.1).

Ignatius also praises the Roman church as totally ("in flesh and spirit") devoted to Christ's commandments (cf. *Eph.* 9.2), as in no way betraying the grace of God that has been given them (see on *Sm.* 6.2), and as "filtered clean from every alien color." The third statement requires special comment. The image of being filtered clean (cf. *Phd.* 3.1) occurs also in Valentinianism where it refers to the separating out of the spiritual "seeds" with Christ (Clement Alex. *Exc. ex Theod.* 41) or to the purification of the soul (Irenaeus *Adv. haer.* 1.14.8). Similarly, the "alien colors" referred to here by Ignatius have been compared with the good dyes used by God and with Christ's transformation of all dyes to white according to two different passages of the *Gospel of Philip* ([NHC 2] 61,12–20; 63,25–30).[6] Yet Ignatius' use of the image with its specification of what is being filtered out (namely, color) gives the impression of being derived directly from everyday life and probably should not be read exclusively in terms of the Gnostic parallels.[7] Presumably he has in mind the elimination of false

---

4 A weakness of Protestant interpretation of the passage (dominated by Harnack) has been the attempt to give a meaning other than "preside" to the verb (cf. John Chapman, "Saint Ignace d'Antioche et l'église Romaine," *Revue Bénédictine* 13 [1896] 385–400). The difficulty disappears when it is recognized that Ignatius is working metaphorically and the text is allowed to speak its high word of praise for the Roman Christians.

5 It seems much less likely that since Ignatius has a negative attitude toward the "love" of the Romans in the body of the letter, he must mean something very special by the "love" that he praises in the salutation. And it seems especially strained to read the latter as a martyrological term in light of the connections that can be drawn between love, the love feast, the eucharist, and martyrdom (cf. *Rom.* 4) in Ignatius

(Reinhard Staats, "Die martyrologische Begründung des Romprimats bei Ignatius von Antiochien," *ZThK* 73 [1976] 461–70).

6 Grant, *Ignatius*, 86.

7 Other metaphorical uses regularly noted are found in Archytas (in Stobaeus *Ecl.* 3.1.108: διυλισμέναν . . . ἀρετὰν ἀπὸ παντὸς τῶ θνατῶ πάθεος "virtue filtered clean of every mortal affection") and Clement of Alexandria (*Paed.* 1.6, 31.1; *Eclog. proph.* 7.3).

teachers from the Roman community (as in *Phd.* 3.1).[8] The verb used here, ἀποδινλίζειν "to filter," more often occurs in a simpler form (διυλίζειν or ὑλίζειν). It is applied to a number of processes such as the purification of drugs[9] or even of gold[10] but seems to play no role in connection with the preparation or use of dyes.[11] It most commonly has to do with wine.[12] And since almost all wine needed to be filtered,[13] it is likely that this use of filtering would have stood out in Ignatius' mind. To be sure, it seems hard to see what filtering out "colors" may mean, and it is no doubt this difficulty that has caused commentators to go so far afield.[14] Yet Plutarch's (*Quaest. conviv.* 6.7, 692b–693e) discussion of the straining or filtering of wine makes it clear that such filtering did cause the color to change, that the change could be a matter of lively discussion, and that those in favor of filtering wine saw it as eliminating not only the lees but dark and harmful elements as well.

The theological language in *Rom.* inscr also requires comment. The reference to the "greatness" or "majesty" (μεγαλειότης) of God, especially when linked with the description of the Father as the "most high," is reminiscent of *Eph.* inscr with its Gnosticizing talk of "greatness" (μέγεθος) and "fullness" (πλήρωμα).[15] Yet God's majesty and his exalted nature are common themes in Hellenistic Judaism[16] and the fact that they are brought together here is insufficient evidence that they have

taken on a Gnostic color. That they have a more biblical resonance is also suggested by their proximity to the expression "the will of him who willed all things that are." For it is difficult not to read this as a statement about God as Lord of heaven and earth: the verb θέλειν evidently has to do with willing things into being[17] (not with "taking pleasure in" as in *Mag.* 3.2; cf. *Rom.* 8.1), and "all things that are" sounds like a reference to the world and all that is in it (cf. Rom 4:17; 1 Cor 8:6; Eph 3:9; Heb 1:3; Rev 4:11; 5:13). The translation "by the will of him who willed all things that are according to the love of Jesus Christ" would presumably eliminate the reference to creation; but it seems unlikely that we should run the two parts of the sentence together in this way; and the possibility of doing so depends on a doubtful reading (GHKLSm) that omits the words πίστιν καί ("faith and"). Lightfoot's reading ("in faith and love toward Jesus Christ") is now even better attested (TAAmCg and the Arabic); it conforms to Ignatius' language elsewhere (cf. *Sm.* inscr; *Eph.* 14.1; 20.1); it may be taken easily enough as a prepositional phrase depending on the words "beloved and enlightened";[18] and it may well echo in reverse order those very words so that "faith" in Christ is the mark of one "enlightened" by God (cf. Justin *Apol.* 1.61.12; *Dial.* 122) and "love" for Christ the mark of one "beloved" by God. (For the imagery of light in Ignatius see on *Rom.* 6.2.)

---

8   For ἀλλότριος ("alien") as having to do with false teaching see *Tr.* 6.1 and *Phd.* 3.3.

9   E.g., Galen *Compos. medic.* 5.3 (Kühn, *CGO* 12. 836); Dioscorides *De mat. medic.* 3.7.3.

10   Clement Alex. *Strom.* 2.20, 116.2. But this seems very rare (cf. Hugo Blümner, *Technologie und Terminologie der Gewerbe und Künste bei Griechen und Römern* [4 vols.; Leipzig: Teubner, 1875–87] 4. 130–31).

11   Cf. ibid., 1. 215–53.

12   BAG *s.v.* διϋλίζω, p. 199.

13   Georges Curtel, *La vigne et le vin chez les Romains* (Paris: Naud, 1903) 156–57.

14   Notably Schlier (*Untersuchungen*, 86 n. 1). That "color" here refers to musical sound as in *Eph.* 4.2 (Bartsch, *Gnostiches Gut*, 107) seems incompatible with the verb.

15   Bartsch, *Gnostisches Gut*, 71–75.

16   BAG *s.v.* μεγαλειότης, p. 498; *s.v.* ὕψιστος, pp. 857–58.

17   *LPGL s.v.* θέλω B, p. 623.

18   It is likely that the reference to "faith" disappeared when the expression came to be taken with what immediately preceded. Talk of God willing all things according to the faith of Christ seemed incongruous.

1   Opening Statement of Request

1   Since by prayer to God I have attained my
    desire to see your God-pleasing faces, as
    I asked to receive still more; for as a
    prisoner in Christ Jesus I hope to greet
    you, if it be (God's) will for me to be
    judged worthy to reach the end; 2/ for
    the beginning has been well ordered, if I
    attain the grace to obtain my lot unim-
    peded; for I fear your love lest precisely it
    may do me wrong; for it is easy for you to
    do what you want; but it is hard for me to
    attain God if you do not spare me.

■ **1.1** The opening of the body of the letter is unusual for Ignatius, apparently because it serves to introduce a communication dominated by a request. Thus the opening ἐπεί ("since") clause may reflect widespread practice in the drawing up of petitions. Normally such a clause gives the reason for the petition and is followed by a verb of request, a vocative, and an expression indicating the content of the request.[1] But if in fact Ignatius had such a model in mind, his thoughts become so entangled in what he has to say about God's will and his own hopes that only a trace of the formula remains and the request itself appears in an obscure and indirect form. The awkwardness of the passage (with incomplete sentences as in *Eph.* 1.1–3; cf. *Mag.* 2) is one result, and the temptation to smooth out the text should be resisted.

The expression "as I asked to receive still more" is particularly difficult, but it probably represents what Ignatius dictated to his scribe. For it seems to conflate two thoughts that he was trying to express: (a) that he has gained his wish to see them (that is, he is on his way to Rome) as he had been asking; but (b) that in addition he had also been asking for "still more" (namely, to be regarded as worthy to the end). The beginning has been good (1.2), but he must now see things through. This sets the stage for turning from his past request (ὡς . . . ἠτούμην "as I asked") to his present request (not formally marked by an appropriate verb such as αἰτοῦμαι "I ask")

addressed to the Romans.

■ **1.2** The substance of the request to the Roman Christians is this: that they not seek to prevent Ignatius' martyrdom (for "lot" as a reference to martyrdom see *Tr.* 12.3; *Phd.* 5.1). This is expressed in paradoxical language (often misunderstood in the ancient versions): he "fears" their "love" (that is, their effort to get him released); such love may "harm" him (by preventing his martyrdom); they are to "spare" him (by not standing in the way of his death); it is "easy" for them to contemplate seeking his release (though no doubt Ignatius recognized the sacrifice that such an effort would represent) and "hard" for him to attain God if their efforts succeed (though again Ignatius must have recognized that such efforts sprang from godly motives).

There is evidence that in the early period Christians lavished attention on their coreligionists in prison, paid ransom for their brethren held captive by barbarians, attempted to obtain the release of fellow Christians also from Roman prisons, and apparently sometimes succeeded in doing so (once even from the mines)[2] through bribery or influence.[3] We are informed in *1 Clem.* 55.2 in an enigmatic passage that "many among us" (Roman Christians? Christians in general?) gave themselves into bondage to ransom others and sold themselves into slavery to feed others. Perhaps these were among the "easy" things that Ignatius had in mind. There is also

1   John L. White, "Introductory Formulae in the Body
    of the Pauline Letters," *JBL* 90 (1971) 93–94; cf.
    Terence Y. Mullins, "Formulas in New Testament
    Epistles," *JBL* 91 (1972) 380–81.

2   According to Hippolytus (*Ref.* 9.25.10–11), Marcia, a
    concubine of Commodus (emperor 180–92 C.E.),
    responded to a request of the bishop of Rome

(Victor) and obtained the release of Christians from
the mines in Sardinia.

3   Lucian *Peregr.* 12–13; Aristides *Apol.* 15.8 (Syriac);
    Cyprian *Ep.* 62.3–4; *Didascalia* 18; *Const. Apost.* 4.9;
    5.1. Cf. Adolf Harnack, *The Mission and Expansion of
    Christianity* (reprinted New York: Harper, 1961)
    162–65.

evidence—though most of it is vague or doubtful—of the existence of influential Christians in Rome in this period,[4] and they may have taken up the cause of imperiled brethren. But we do not have evidence of an instance in which a Christian condemned to the beasts was released, and the possibility seems remote.[5] It has been suggested that Ignatius may have thought otherwise because he had not actually been condemned but had only been sent to Rome with the recommendation that he be thrown to the beasts.[6] Although this is not impossible legally, it depends on a tenuous historical reconstruction of the situation; and it seems more likely that Ignatius instinctively exaggerates the possibility as he contemplates the enormity of the struggle that lies before him and the significance that it has for himself and (as he sees it) for the whole church (see Introduction, 3.4).

---

4   Adolf Harnack, *Mission und Ausbreitung des Christentums* (3d ed.; 2 vols.; Leipzig: Hinrichs, 1915) 2. 31–33, 41–42; Hans Achelis, *Das Christentum in den ersten drei Jahrhunderten* (2 vols.; Leipzig: Quelle & Meyer, 1912) 2. 366. The outstanding example was that of Titus Flavius Clemens and his wife Flavia Domitilla under Domitian. Yet it is not likely that they were Christians after all (cf. Paul Keresztes, "The Jews, the Christians, and Emperor Domitian," *VC* 27 [1973] 1–28).

5   Cf. Peter Garnsey, *Social Status and Legal Privilege in the Roman Empire* (Oxford: Clarendon, 1970) 67–85 (on the situation of provincials who brought their grievances before the emperor). The case of Ignatius would have been a desperate one since he had apparently already been condemned and belonged to the category of prisoner discussed in *Digest.* 48.19.31:

"The governor ought not, as a favor to the people, to release persons condemned to wild-beasts; but, if they are of such strength or skill that they would make a worthy spectacle for the Roman people, he ought to consult the emperor . . ." (for the translation and a discussion see Lightfoot, *Ignatius*, 1.342). There is earlier evidence that prisoners were sent to Rome by governors for the games (Cicero *In Pis.* 36.89; cf. *Ad fam.* 8.4.5).

6   Stevan L. Davies, "The Predicament of Ignatius of Antioch," *VC* 30 (1976) 175–80.

2

Word and Deed

1   For I do not want you to please people but to please God, as you do please him; for I shall never have such an opportunity to attain God, nor can you, if you remain silent, be credited with a better deed; for if you remain silent and let me be, I shall be a word of God, but if you love my flesh, I shall again be a (mere) voice. 2/ Grant me nothing more than to be poured out as a libation for God while an altar is still ready, that becoming a chorus in love you may sing to the Father in Jesus Christ because God judged the bishop of Syria worthy to be found at the (sun's) setting having sent him from the (sun's) rising. It is good to set from the world to God that I may rise to him.

3   1/ You never envied anyone; you taught others. I simply want that to stand fast which you command when you make disciples. 2/ Only ask power for me both within and without so that not only may I speak, but also will, that not only may I be called a Christian but also be found one; for if I am found one, I can also be called one and prove faithful then when I do not appear to the world. 3/ Nothing that appears is good; for our God Jesus Christ rather appears by being in the Father. The deed is not a matter of persuasive rhetoric, but Christianity is characterized by greatness when it is hated by the world.

Ignatius now elaborates his request to the Roman Christians that they not impede his martyrdom. He does so with the help of variations on the theme of word vs. deed and by the use of a number of remarkable images.
■ **2.1** Ignatius first urges the Roman Christians in Pauline terms to please not men but God (cf. 1 Thess 2:4; Gal 1:10) and characteristically adds that what he asks is already the case (see on *Eph.* 4.1). Since he is afraid that this golden opportunity may slip away, he expects the Romans to acquiesce and remain silent.[1] For if they do, it will not be possible for them to "be credited (ἐπιγρα-

φῆναι) with a better deed."[2] Here is another indication that for Ignatius silence (however singularly defined in this context) is a matter of letting deeds speak for themselves (see on *Eph.* 6.1; 15.1–2; 19.1). In our passage, however, the contrast between word and deed is replaced by a contrast between "voice" (φωνή) and "word" (λόγος).[3] The closest parallel is provided by the Gnostic Heracleon, who takes Johannine language as a point of departure in exalting Jesus as the "word" over John the Baptist as a mere "voice."[4] Behind this formulation, however, is an Aristotelian definition of "voice" as

---

1   The verb σιωπᾶν ("remain silent") is used twice in this passage. The second time it is followed by the preposition ἀπό ("remain silent and let be") and as such is found only in biblical Greek (Ps 27:1 LXX).

2   Bauer translates "be engaged in a better work" (BAG *s.v.* ἐπιγράφω, p. 291), appealing to Ps-Socrates *Ep.* 7.2: ἔργῳ ἐπιγραφείην ἀδίκῳ "subscribe to an evil deed" (Hercher, *Epistolographi Graeci*, 615). But in

our context it is likely that Ignatius relies on uses of ἐπιγραφῆναι that have to do with having one's name inscribed on something (originally on a piece of legislation) and so "claiming credit for" it (LSJ *s.v.* ἐπιγράφω II.1, p. 628).

3   The word "voice" is missing or corrupt in major witnesses to the text. We follow most recent editors in accepting the witness of LSSmC (and now

mere sound (including, for example, the utterances of animals) and "word" as sound that conveys meaning.[5] This definition lived on in popular discussions of language[6] and may well have been known to Ignatius. He was not, then, necessarily relying on Gnosticizing predecessors here, nor was he making a bold connection between himself as a word of God and Christ the Word. Rather he was contrasting an authentic and inauthentic witness to God. The silence of the Roman Christians will permit Ignatius to prove the profession of his faith by laying down his life. This (silent) deed will authenticate his claim to be a Christian and transform that claim from an empty sound to a meaningful word (see on *Eph.* 14.2–15.2).

■ **2.2** Before continuing with other such contrasts, however, Ignatius interprets for the Roman Christians the significance of his coming martyrdom with the help of a series of images that revolve about (pagan) sacrifice and the course of the sun through the sky. He may well have taken Paul as a point of departure in asking that they let him be poured out as a libation (Phil 2:17; cf. 2 Tim 4:6). But he adds to the picture a reference to the altar over which he is to be poured[7] (meaning the arena in which he is to give up his life); and he recalls the pagan practice of having a chorus (meaning the Roman Christians) sing about the altar (see on *Eph.* 5.2). Even the comparison between a libation and a religious devotee slain for his god is apparently not without parallel in paganism.[8]

Characteristically, this picture is quickly replaced by another. For the chorus of the Romans will sing because "the bishop of Syria"[9] has been judged worthy of coming from the east (where the sun rises) to the west (where the sun sets). And Ignatius goes on to liken his own person to the sun itself which in its daily journey across the sky sinks from the world only to rise again. We have already met a similar use of solar imagery in Ignatius' discussion of Sunday worship (*Mag.* 9.1). Dölger has discussed other examples from the church fathers in which the symbolic significance of the sun's journey under the earth is exploited.[10] One of the earliest is frg. 8b.2–4 of Melito where Christian baptism is discussed in terms of the sun being washed in the western ocean only to rise again in the east; and where Christ's baptism in the Jordan is then explained against the background of the same imagery and connected with the crucifixion through a comparison of the sun's passage under the earth with the descent into Hades.[11] Such a circle of ideas may explain why Ignatius can refer here to the martyr and in *Mag.* 9.1 to Christ as rising like the sun (and why in *Eph.* 18.2 we have a conception of the relation between Christ's baptism and passion not entirely unlike that of Melito). Yet it would be a mistake to rely too heavily on such a reconstruction. For the two appearances of solar symbolism in Ignatius give the impression of being separate and quite possibly unrelated applications of the same theme. Since in the passage before us the bishop mentions singing to the Father in Christ Jesus (as in *Eph.* 4.2), it may also be that he was inspired here at least partly by something like the primitive evening hymn in which Christ is hailed as the "gracious light" by those who "come to the setting of the sun."[12] In any event, a sense

4 also the Arabic).

4 Origen *Comm. in Joann.* 6.20.108–11; cf. 6.17.94–96. Less polarized are "word" and "voice" in *Trim. Prot.* (NHC 13) 37,5; 37,23–34; 40,8–9.

5 Aristotle *Interpr.* 4, 16b 26; cf. *Probl.* 11.55, 905a 20; *Gen. anim.* 5.7, 786b 20; *Polit.* 1.2, 1253a 10.

6 Cf. Plutarch *De anim. procr. in Tim.* 27, 1026a; Athanasius *Contra Arian.* 4.1.

7 Libations were sometimes poured over the burning flesh of sacrifices (cf. Homer *Il.* 1.462; 11.775; *Od.* 3.459; Aristophanes *Pax* 1102).

8 W. Schubart, "Aus einer Apollon-Aretalogie," *Hermes* 55 (1920) 190 (lines 25–28); cf. BAG *s.v.* σπένδω, p. 769. In spite of the parallels between our passage and *Eph.* 4.2–5.2 (which includes similar musical imagery and reference to an altar as well as mention of "the bread of God"), it is unlikely that Ignatius pictures

himself in *Rom.* 2.2 as a kind of eucharist (especially in light of the centrality of the image of libation). Rather we have two different applications of a similar range of cultic metaphors. (See further on *Rom.* 4.1.)

9 This is the only passage in which Ignatius refers to himself as a bishop (see Introduction, 1.4b).

10 Franz Joseph Dölger, *Sol Salutis: Gebet und Gesang im christlichen Altertum* (2d ed.; Liturgiegeschichtliche Forschungen 4/5; Münster: Aschendorff, 1925) 337–64. Compare already Philo *Heres* 263–66 where the setting and rising of the sun explain in symbolic form the mystical experience of Abraham in Gen 15:12. The setting of the human light is said to allow the rising of the divine light in the soul.

11 Othmar Perler, *Méliton de Sardes sur la Pâque et fragments* (SC 123; Paris: Cerf, 1966) 228–33.

12 Martin Joseph Routh, *Reliquiae sacrae* (2d ed.; 5 vols.;

of solidarity with Christ and his resurrection does not require cultic identification of the believer with his Lord (cf. *Tr.* 9.2).

A negative attitude toward pagan Rome may also be hinted at in the text. Although Rome is not mentioned here, the journey from east to west is seen by Ignatius as a journey from Syria to Rome (cf. *Eph.* 1.2; *Rom.* 5.1). There is a sense of movement here in the bishop's mental geography strikingly different from that of the defenders of Roman power who speak simply of Rome ruling from the rising to the setting sun.[13] Conceivably Ignatius shared the feeling of elements in Asian society that deliverance from Rome would come to them from the east where the sun arises.[14] In any event, it is significant that whereas elsewhere Ignatius is mildly disposed to pagan society despite its hostility (*Eph.* 10; cf. *Tr.* 8.2), in this letter he treats the importance of being hated by the world as the essence of Christianity (3.3; cf. John 7:7; 15:18–19; 17:14; 1 John 3:13). And whereas elsewhere he tells Christians that they are to prove "brothers" to the pagans with whom they have contact in their everyday life (*Eph.* 10.3), in this letter the representatives of Rome with whom the bishop deals are not seen by him as human at all (*Rom.* 5). We find corollaries of this bifurcation in Ignatius' view of the outside world elsewhere (see on *Pol.* 2). The situation is even more complex, however, since for Ignatius Rome is not only a place of inhumanity and death but also a goal that leads to God (*Rom.* 5.3). This very complexity indicates that Rome had come to play a crucial symbolic role in the mind of Christians like Ignatius and that it served as an important agent in shaping their identity and their understanding of the world about them (see Introduction, 3.6).

■ **3.1** Ignatius then reminds the Roman Christians of the fact that they taught others (to endure suffering and hardship, apparently), and he asks that they now do nothing to contradict their own teaching. There is probably a reference here to *1 Clement*, where (a) we hear much about "envy" (which in both sources is dealt with as inspired by Satan and is connected with martyrdom; *1 Clem.* 3.4; 5.2; cf. *Tr.* 4.2; *Rom.* 3.1; 5.3);[15] (b) there is a reference to Peter and Paul as martyrs (*1 Clem.* 5.3–5; cf. *Rom.* 4.3); (c) Paul's ministry in both the east and west and his glorious departure from the world after giving his witness in the west are mentioned (*1 Clem.* 5.6–7; cf. *Rom.* 2.2); and (d) instructions are given to imitate those who suffered and to endure all manner of hardship (*1 Clem.* 7.1; 46.1; 55.1). Yet as Beyschlag argues, Ignatius sometimes seems to reflect more clearly the original point of these themes and thus may be dependent on pre-Clementine tradition.[16] In any event, a Roman-Christian ideology has developed which Ignatius capitalizes on here. But it adds little to the picture of Roman preeminence which we gained from the salutation, par-

---

Oxford: E Typographeo Academico, 1846–48) 3. 515.

13   Wilhelm Gernentz, *Laudes Romae* (Rostock: Adler, 1918) 118–24.

14   Cf. Harald Fuchs, *Der geistige Widerstand gegen Rom in der antiken Welt* (Berlin: De Gruyter, 1938) 31–36. For some qualifications see John J. Collins, *The Sibylline Oracles of Egyptian Judaism* (SBLDS 13; Missoula, MT: Society of Biblical Literature, 1972) 38–44. The old anti-Roman oracles preserved by Phlegon (writing under Hadrian) deserve special mention. One of them predicts the day when ἥξει γὰρ στρατιὴ πολυφέρτερος ὀβριμόθυμος, τηλόθεν ἐξ Ἀσίης, ὅθεν ἡλίου ἀνατολαί εἰσιν "there will come [against Rome] a most brave and spirited host from Asia afar whence are the risings of the sun" (Phlegon *De mirab.* frg. 32, in Karl Müller, *Fragmenta Historicorum Graecorum* [5 vols.; Paris: Didot, 1841–70] 3. 616; cf. H. W. Parke, *A History of the Delphic Oracle* [Oxford: Blackwell, 1939] 281–82).

15   *1 Clem.* 3.4 describes envy (the same envy that caused the persecution mentioned in *1 Clem.* 5.2) as that "through which also death came into the world." There is an allusion here to Wis 2:24, from which we learn that "death came into the world by the envy of the devil." Similarly Ignatius' word ἐβασκάνατε "envied" in *Rom.* 3.1 still resonates with its original occult sense ("bewitch"). For as *Rom.* 5.3 shows, the "envy" that would impede Ignatius' martyrdom is attributed to supernatural powers. Ignatius and Clement both presuppose the thought that the devil inspires persecution, but Clement moralizes the theme and Ignatius chooses to stand it on end.

16   Beyschlag, *Clemens Romanus*, 299–306.

ticularly if there is no reference here to *1 Clement*. Certainly the verb ἐντέλλομαι ("command," "certify") does not imply formal authority (cf. *Rom.* 4.1; Pol. *Phil.* 13.2).

■ **3.2** In a sense Ignatius has just finished telling the Roman Christians to practice what they preach, and it is natural for him to apply the lesson again to his own case. And again a number of contrasts (set in the form of neat antitheses) are involved. The first is that between speaking and willing: λέγω ("I speak") vs. θέλω ("I will"). Here willing is the virtual equivalent of acting. This probably depends on the fact that the verb θέλω in Greek literature is sometimes used to refer to the "consent" given by the powerful as opposed to the mere "wish" of others (for which the verb βούλομαι is used).[17] The second contrast is that between being called and being found a Christian: λέγωμαι ("I may be called") vs. εὑρεθῶ ("I may be found"). Since "to be found" means as much as "to be" (cf. *Eph.* 14.2), the contrast is closely related to that between word and deed (*Eph.* 15.1; *Mag.* 4). If Ignatius is given the "power" (cf. *Eph.* 14.2), he will be able to live out his convictions and so also deserve the name Christian.

■ **3.2–3** To this Ignatius adds a complicated line of argument involving the word φαίνεσθαι "appear." The reality of his profession will be clear when he does not appear (that is, is not visible because he has died). He then states that nothing that appears is good and notes that Christ truly appears (that is, is seen for what he really is) when he has died and gone to the Father. It is no wonder that the text became altered by scribes who suspected Gnostic error. But that is to misunderstand Ignatius' peculiar way of expressing himself. First, he consciously reverses the meaning of the term: the negation of appearance in death makes true appearance possible. Second, the negation of appearance in this context must refer not only to the desirability of leaving the world behind but also to the negation of seeming to be what one is not. Ignatius will not only disappear

physically, but in seeing his martyrdom through to the end will also be free of any doubt as to whether he truly is what he now only appears to be (namely, a Christian). Only when the world no longer "sees" him will he be a disciple (*Rom.* 4.2; cf. John 14:19). It is surely this thought that leads him to say that "nothing that appears is good." The main point is that mere appearance is the Christian's worst enemy. Ignatius is not commenting on the nature of the physical world. Note that in Greek literature "appearing" (τὸ φαινόμενον) is frequently synonymous with "seeming" (τὸ δοκοῦν) to be something and opposed to actually being so.[18] We have seen Ignatius apply this same line of thought elsewhere in criticizing docetic christology and affirming the significance of his martyrdom (*Tr.* 10). In the passage before us he remains even more fully in the practical sphere. Thus also Origen says with reference to the hypocritical public praying criticized in Matt 6:5: οὐδὲν φαινόμενον καλόν ἐστι οἱονεὶ δοκήσει ὂν καὶ οὐκ ἀληθῶς "nothing that appears is good, only seeming to be and not truly existing" (*De orat.* 20). The parallel has often been noted. But it has not been observed that it has to do with the problem of the false profession of piety and that this too is Ignatius' concern. This is not a Gnostic theme.

Finally, then, Ignatius defines "the deed" (singling the term out as in *Eph.* 14.2) as a matter not of persuasion but of greatness. The word for "persuasion" (πεισμονή) is unusual, and it occurs for the first time in Greek literature in Gal 5:8, where it is set in opposition to truth. Similar themes occur in passages like Gal 1:10 and 1 Thess 2:4 (which are alluded to just above in *Rom.* 2.1) and in 1 Cor 2:4 where the "persuasive" (πειθοῖς) words of human wisdom are set in opposition to a display of spirit and power. There hovers in the background here the ancient quarrel between philosophy (the quest for truth and authentic living) and rhetoric (the art of persuasion).[19] And it is worth recalling that the first great anti-rhetorical treatise, Plato's *Gorgias*, ends with the contrast between seeming to be good and actually

---

17 Cf. Plato *Gorg.* 522e; *Alc.* 1, 135d; Demosthenes 2.20. Note that God's "willing" in *Rom.* inscr is also a form of action. Of the twenty-three uses of the verb θέλω in Ignatius, seventeen occur in *Romans* and eight of them in the first person singular. The passion with which Ignatius wills his own death in the letter no doubt has something to do with this.

18 Cf. Aristotle *E.N.* 3.4, 1113a 15–24; *Meteor.* 2.9,

370a 12; *Metaph.* 4.5, 1009a 8; Plato *Resp.* 10, 596e; Xenophon *Mem.* 1.7.3; Euripides frg. 698 Nauck.

19 Hans Dieter Betz (*Galatians* [Hermeneia; Philadelphia: Fortress, 1979] 54–55, 265) has shown that traditional philosophical criticism of rhetoric is reflected in Gal 1:10 and that the term "persuasion" in Gal 5:8 belongs to "Paul's anti-rhetorical arsenal."

being so (527b). Rhetoricians themselves, of course, soon made it a practice to claim to be speaking not mere words but the truth.[20] And it is likely that Ignatius was indebted primarily to rhetoric and Paul on this score. He gives a special turn to the theme by emphasizing the need to submit to death rather than yield to what is merely persuasive. But here too the example of Socrates would not have been far from peoples' minds, and pagans could not help admiring such fortitude in the Christians. At the same time, they sensed in Christian martyrdom a fanaticism that repelled them (cf. Epictetus *Diss.* 4.7.6; M. Aurelius 11.3.2). Various features of Christian teaching and the new social reality of the church made that reaction inevitable. But it should also be recognized that a writer like Ignatius instinctively turned to elements of popular Greek culture to spell out the significance of Christianity as a way of life.

---

20 Cf. Hecataeus, in Ps-Demetrius *De elocut.* 12; Papias, in Eusebius *Hist. eccl.* 3.39.3.

Ignatius' Voluntary Death [4.1–8.1]

4

Ignatius, the Wheat of God

1 I write to all the churches and certify to all that I die willingly for God provided you do not hinder me. I exhort you: do not become an inopportune kindness for me; let me be the food of wild beasts through whom it is possible to attain God; I am the wheat of God, and I am ground by the teeth of wild beasts that I may be found pure bread; 2/ instead, entice the wild beasts that they may become my tomb and leave behind no part of my body that when I fall asleep, I may burden no one. Then I shall truly be a disciple of Jesus Christ when the world will not even see my body. Pray Christ for me that by these means I may be found a sacrifice of God. 3/ I do not command you as Peter and Paul: they (were) apostles, I (am) a condemned man; they (were) free, I (am) still a slave; but if I suffer, I shall become a freedman of Jesus Christ, and I shall arise free in him; and now I am learning, as one bound, to desire nothing.

■ **4.1** The reference to "writing" represents a common non-formulaic transitional device in Greek letters.[1] What Ignatius seeks to emphasize here is the fact that he dies willingly. And he says that he writes this to "all" the churches. Presumably he has the Ephesians, Magnesians, and Trallians in mind. If so, he not only exaggerates in referring to "all" the churches (cf. *Eph.* 12.2), but also gives a one-sided impression of what he had written them. At the same time, there is a sense in which all that Ignatius says and does is oriented to the success of his martyrdom (see Introduction, 3.4). And Lucian (*Peregr.* 41) perhaps has Ignatius in mind when he reports that Peregrinus wrote "letters to all the famous cities" and takes that as one more indication of the Christian leader's quest for notoriety in pressing on to martyrdom (cf. Ign. *Pol.* 7.2). The attitude of people like Lucian soon gained tacit support in the Asian church itself where (as *Mart. Pol.* 4 shows) voluntary martyrdom came to be viewed as dangerous to the individual and the group. And the extreme character of Ignatius' protestations in what follows suggests why only a few could take such initiative without losing their bearings.

In repeating his request to the Romans to let him die, Ignatius resorts to an oxymoron derived from a proverb (εὔνοια ἄκαιρος "inopportune kindness")[2] in order to describe what gaining his release would represent. The intensity of his feelings is indicated by the language that follows. He wishes to become the food of wild beasts, and he likens himself (in a statement admiringly quoted already by Irenaeus *Adv. haer.* 5.28.4) to grain ground in a mill (the teeth of the wild beasts) and made into "pure bread."[3] The statement has often been regarded as

---

1 White, *Form and Function*, 24–25.
2 Zenobius *Cent.* 1.50 (*Paroem. Gr.* 1.20).
3 "Pure bread of Christ" is the reading of GHTLSmM; "pure bread of God" (cf. *Eph.* 5.2) of gSSfAAmC and the Arabic. For the text of Irenaeus *Adv. haer.* 5.28.4 see Adelin Rousseau, Louis Douteleau, and Charles Mercie, *Irenée de Lyon, Contre les hérésies, Livre V,* Tome 2: *Texte et traduction* (SC 153; Paris: Cerf, 1969) 362–63: the Latin version speaks of the "wheat of Christ" and the "bread of God"; a Greek fragment of the passage speaks of the "wheat of God" and the "bread of God." "Pure bread" without further qualification is read by Eusebius (*Hist. eccl.* 3.36.12) when he presents Irenaeus' quotation of our passage. And Lightfoot (*Ignatius,* 2. 208) is satisfied simply to read "pure bread." It seems probable that the scribes

inspired by eucharistic language (cf. *Eph.* 5.2) and thus as making of Ignatius' martyrdom a quasi-eucharistic event. It seems more likely that the image was selected from the realm of baking to express the transformation that Ignatius looked for as the result of his martyrdom.[4] It is true that "pure bread" was sometimes used in connection with sacrifices or religious meals.[5] But the word for "grinding" (ἀλήθομαι) was standard terminology in the baking business for milling grain,[6] and "pure bread" was the name of a high-quality product.[7] This, I suspect, is the relevant background to the passage before us.

■ **4.2** In what follows Ignatius apparently sees the complete disappearance of his body as desirable not only because he would no longer burden anyone (for this reapplication of a Pauline theme see on *Phd.* 6.3) but also because it would mark the completeness of his transformation and the attainment of true discipleship. Consequently, the Roman Christians should even "entice" the beasts. It seems that sometimes animals refused to approach a prisoner (see on *Rom.* 5.2) or left their victim half dead and "half eaten" (cf. Josephus *Bell.* 7.373–74). Ignatius sees the proper function of the Roman Christians as assisting him in overcoming such difficulties. For an animal to become a "tomb" for a human does not imply the disappearance of bones and all.[8] Ignatius is probably not that unrealistic about his martyrdom. Yet it is clear that to some extent he overdramatizes the event. At the very least, it is hard to see what he could have expected the Roman Christians to make of his request that they "entice" the beasts (cf. *Rom.* 5.2), that is, that they play the role of those who from the sidelines stirred reluctant animals to attack (cf. Eusebius *Hist. eccl.* 8.7.2).

■ **4.3** Finally, we may assume that Ignatius' interpretation of his death as "sacrifice" (4.2) is as metaphorical here as it is in *Rom.* 2.2 (cf. *Mart. Pol.* 14.1; Eusebius *Hist. eccl.* 5.1.51).[9] Indeed, it is probably the mention of sacrifice that leads over in the bishop's mind to reflection on his status as a condemned man (4.3). For both themes, as we have seen, express his sense of inferiority to the apostles and those in harmony with them (see on *Eph.* 8.1; 12.1). Some have sensed a somewhat different emphasis in this passage especially in Ignatius' use of the term "slave."[10] But our comments on *Mag.* 12 (and the comparison with Epictetus *Gnom.* 32 noted there) confirm the initial impression that "slave" is simply a variant for the terms "condemned" and "bound." It is also too literal a reading of our text, then, to conclude that it was martyrdom that made the apostles free. Martyrdom frees Ignatius because only so can he be a true disciple. But he evidently thinks of the apostles as having been on a different footing from the beginning (see on *Mag.* 6.1). They are not looked on as exercising authority from on high after their martyrdom but as having stamped their character on the churches in which they worked (cf. *Eph.* 11.2–12.2). Thus the selection here of Peter and Paul no doubt reflects Ignatius' awareness of a tradition about their joint presence and their martyrdom in Rome which significantly bolstered the prestige of that city's Christian community.[11] Surely Peter and Paul were thought of by Ignatius as "free" and capable of commanding obedience even apart from their martyrdom, and surely that is why

---

were puzzled by the boldness of the metaphor and that efforts to qualify the expression led to the variety noted above.

4   Note that Polycarp's fiery death is compared to the baking of bread or the refining of gold or silver (*Mart. Pol.* 15.2).

5   Cf. Herodotus 2.40; Hermeias, in Athenaeus *Deipn.* 4, 149e.

6   Hugo Blümner, *Technologie und Terminologie der Gewerbe und Künste bei Griechen und Römern* (4 vols.; Leipzig: Teubner, 1875–87) 1. 30 (n. 3).

7   Galen *Aliment. fac.* 1.2 (Kühn, *CGO* 6. 482); cf. M. Besnier, "Pistor," *Dictionnaire des Antiquités* 4. 497–98.

8   Gorgias, in Longinus 3.2; Aeschylus *Sept.* 1020–21; Lucretius *De rer. nat.* 5.993; Ovid *Heroid.* 10.123–24.

9   There is little support for the view that Ignatius saw

his death as an offering in the place of others (see on *Eph.* 8.1). Close to Ignatius in spirit are the words of Peter to his fellow Christians in a late martyrology: "If your love to me is true . . . , do not call me back as I go to the Lord, do not hinder me as I hasten to Christ. Stand then silent, rejoicing and glad, that I may offer my sacrifice to the Lord with joy" (*Mart. beat. Petr. apost. a Lino episc. consc.* 9).

10   Cf. Bartsch, *Gnostisches Gut*, 94–96.

11   Cf. *1 Clem.* 5.3–7; Dionysius, in Eusebius *Hist. eccl.* 2.25.8; Irenaeus *Adv. haer.* 3.1.1.

the bishop recognizes his inability to speak to the Romans with the same authority as they (cf. *Eph.* 3.1; *Tr.* 3.3). Ignatius differs from the apostles in that only through martyrdom can he become as they were. He is learning, then, to "desire nothing," that is, to give up his attachment to this world (cf. *Rom.* 7.1).

Ignatius' Voluntary Death [4.1–8.1]

5

The Victor

1   I am fighting wild beasts from Syria to Rome, through land and sea, by night and day, bound to ten leopards—which is a company of soldiers—who when well treated become worse. By their mistreatment I become more of a disciple, but "not for that reason am I justified." 2/ May I benefit from the wild beasts prepared for me, and I pray that they will be found prompt with me, whom I shall even entice to devour me promptly—not as with some whom they were too timid to touch; and should they not consent voluntarily, I shall force them. 3/ Indulge me; I know what is to my advantage; now I begin to be a disciple. May nothing of things visible and invisible envy me, that I may attain Jesus Christ. Fire and cross, and packs of wild beasts, the wrenching of bones, the mangling of limbs, the grinding of my whole body, evil punishments of the devil—let these come upon me, only that I may attain Jesus Christ.

■ **5.1** Ignatius' understanding of his martyrdom is now seen in a new light as he presents his journey to Rome in terms of the march of a military victor. Grant speaks of the bishop's use of the "regal-imperial style" here.[1] Something like it appears in Paul (2 Cor 11:23–27), but Paul and Ignatius both seem to draw on a form that (according to Fridrichsen) is found especially in inscriptions detailing the exploits and achievements of kings and generals (such as Augustus' *Monumentum Ancyranum*, the Silko inscription,[2] and the *Monumentum Adulitanum*[3]).[4] Thus Ignatius' opening words, "I am fighting wild beasts from Syria to Rome," though reflecting 1 Cor 15:32 ("I fought wild beasts") and oriented to his coming martyrdom (cf. *Eph.* 1.2; *Tr.* 10), are modelled on a line like "I fought from Whitetown to the land of the Sabaeans";[5] the expression "through land and sea" plays a natural role in the context of imperial claims to extraordinary achievements;[6] and the phrase "by night and day" is reminiscent of the theme of

sleepless toil which is found not only in Paul (cf. 2 Cor 11:27) but also (as Fridrichsen notes) in numerous descriptions given especially by Plutarch of the untiring activities of military leaders. Presumably the reference to the ten soldiers as leopards (like the expression "I am fighting wild beasts") blends the military metaphor and the anticipated struggle in the arena (where leopards were among the animals loosed on prisoners).[7] Ignatius' martyrdom will be but the last of a series of struggles in which he is already engaged.

The historical presuppositions of the passage require comment. (a) The troop guarding Ignatius represented perhaps a *contubernium* (later also called a *manipulus*), a division of the century which ideally consisted of ten soldiers.[8] The Greek word ($\tau\acute{\alpha}\gamma\mu\alpha$ "company") used here is apparently not technical, however, and had to do with military units of different sizes (in Polybius 6.24.5 of the maniple, but in the older sense of that term).[9] Ignatius would probably be attached to one of these soldiers by a

1   Grant, *Ignatius*, 90.
2   Dit., *Or.* 1.201.
3   Ibid., 1.199.
4   Anton Fridrichsen, "Zum Stil des paulinischen Peristasenkatalogs 2 Cor 11:23ff.," *Symbolae Osloenses* 7 (1928) 25–29; 8 (1929) 78–82.
5   Dit., *Or.* 1.199,29; cf. 201,16.
6   *Mon. Ancyr.* 3 (1,19–23); 4 (1,24–27); 13 (7,5–10).

7   Wild animals from Africa such as the panther or leopard "were the most commonly used of the non-European animals at *venationes,* in Rome and in the *municipia*" (Ludwig Friedländer, *Roman Life and Manners Under the Early Empire* [4 vols.; London: Routledge & Kegan Paul, 1907–13] 4. 182).
8   Vegetius *De re milit.* 2.13; Josephus *Bell.* 3.117; cf. Fiebiger, "Contubernium," PW 4/1. 1165. We have

chain.[10] (b) Ten soldiers are obviously too many for one man. But though Ignatius does not tell us, we may assume that there was more than one prisoner. At any rate, by the time Ignatius got to Philippi two other Christian martyrs were apparently part of the band (Pol. *Phil.* 9.1). Ignatius' sense of self-importance is such that we should not be surprised that he fails to comment on companions who may well have been morally indistinguishable in his eyes from his captors. (c) Ignatius could scarcely have been a Roman citizen if he had been condemned to be thrown to the beasts. Citizens were only exceptionally dealt with in that way, and there was a tendency even when dealing with Christians to distinguish citizens from aliens and to send only the latter to the beasts.[11] As has long been recognized, the reservation for spectacles in Rome of the best specimens among those condemned to this form of execution (*Digest.* 48.19.31) provides the natural background to the situation discernible in Ignatius' letters (see on *Rom.* 1.2). (d) It is not out of harmony with the supposed seriousness of his crime that Ignatius' coreligionists would have access to him and that (especially with the help of the bribes probably referred to in the remark that the soldiers were "well treated") they could assist in many ways[12] and make possible the writing of documents and letters.[13]

Although there is nothing, then, historically impossible about the situation, it is also clear that Ignatius had a highly personal interpretation of the events in which he was involved. For he turns his journey to the capital as a prisoner into a victorious campaign against opposing forces whose most immediate embodiment are the representatives of Rome—the ten leopards—who hold him bound. The Roman power is going down to defeat (see on *Rom.* 2.2), but in a paradoxical way. For Ignatius' victory will take the form of dying in the amphitheater and thus attaining God. Similarly the bishop's present sufferings are dealt with as teaching him to become a disciple (cf. *Rom.* 4.2) and readying him for his "justification." Ignatius speaks of his justification in terms that are directly dependent on 1 Cor 4:4 (echoed again in *Tr.* 5.2); but "justification" for Ignatius is apparently nothing other than becoming a disciple (cf. *Tr.* 5.2) and gaining perfection (cf. *Phd.* 8.2) through martyrdom;[14] Paul's words serve to emphasize the fact that Ignatius' justification is still future and thus to discourage the Roman Christians from interfering with his attaining it.

■ **5.2** Before working out in other ways the meaning of his journey to God, Ignatius pauses to express the hope that he may "benefit" from the beasts—using the very expression by which he also calls on people to aid and assist him (see on *Mag.* 12.1)—and that the beasts may be quick with him (5.2). Apparently the animals were themselves sometimes frightened (by the noise and excitement) and unwilling to touch their intended victims.[15] In such instances martyrs became famous for "forcing" these animals to attack.[16] It is debatable whether Ignatius here reflects simple human dread of a long-drawn-out affair or whether he betrays an unnatural bravado and a concern to enhance the significance of his death in the eyes of others.[17]

■ **5.3** In any event, there follows perhaps the most

---

evidence that legionary detachments quartered together in Rome were used for the transportation and guard of prisoners brought to the capital to be dealt with by the emperor (Theodor Mommsen, *Römisches Strafrecht* [Leipzig: Duncker & Humblot] 316). Ignatius may well have been included in a group of such prisoners.

9   "Which is a company of soldiers," though present in all the texts, may be a gloss. If so, it was a correct one, as the following words show. Laxness or ignorance of Greek on the part of the guard would have made it possible for Ignatius to dictate his harsh words about them.

10   Cf. Josephus *Ant.* 18.189, 196, 203 (though the situation here is somewhat different; cf. Hitzig, "Custodia," PW 4/2. 1898).

11   A. H. M. Jones, "I Appeal to Caesar," *Studies in*

Roman Government and Law (Oxford: Blackwell, 1960) 53–65; Peter Garnsey, *Social Status and Legal Privilege in the Roman Empire* (Oxford: Clarendon, 1970) 129–31.

12   Such at any rate was true of Christians in prison (cf. Lucian *Peregr.* 12; *Pass. Perp.* 3.7; *Didascalia* 19; *Const. Apost.* 5.1; *Act. Thom.* 151).

13   Cf. *Pass. Perp.* 2.3; 14; 16.1; Eusebius *Hist. eccl.* 5.3.4; 6.11.5; Lucian *Peregr.* 41.

14   This may represent a development of a strand of Paulinism in which justification had become more or less the equivalent of sanctification and redemption (cf. 1 Cor 1:30).

15   Cf. *Pass. Perp.* 19.6; *Act. Paul. et Thecl.* 32–35; Eusebius *Hist. eccl.* 5.1.42.

16   *Mart. Pol.* 3.1; Eusebius, *Hist. eccl.* 8.7.2.

17   In *Rom.* 4.2, Ignatius commands the Roman

extreme statement in the letter of Ignatius' eagerness to undergo any suffering to become a disciple and attain Jesus Christ. Tortures by fire and mutilation are found throughout the description of the Jewish martyrdoms in *4 Macc.* 4–18. Tortures and exposure to wild beasts[18] are mentioned together in *Mart. Pol.* 2 and in Irenaeus' description of the martyrs of Lyons (Eusebius *Hist. eccl.* 5.1). And Christians were hung on crosses in the reign of Nero (Tacitus *Ann.* 15.44). Thus Ignatius was not inventing these horrors. Yet he was extending the catalogue to its limits, and he seems to have left all

sobriety behind in the exultant tone of the passage.

The fact is that Ignatius had a greater fear than that of the wild beasts—namely, that the Roman Christians would be misled into seeking to prevent his martyrdom. Behind such an effort would stand the "envy" (ζηλῶσαι) of "things visible and invisible" (cf. *Tr.* 5.2; *Sm.* 6.1; Col 1:16)—the envy particularly of Satan, who would prevent Ignatius from attaining God (see on *Rom.* 3.1). That Ignatius has the devil in mind becomes still clearer in what follows (see on *Rom.* 6.1; 7.1–2).

Christians to "entice" the animals to devour him. In *Rom.* 5.2 it is Ignatius himself who will "entice" the beasts. The latter is perhaps more comprehensible, yet we are still presented with a figure who mentally enacts his last moments with an eye to their dramatic possibilities. (It seems best, though awkward, to take ἑκόντα "voluntarily"—assuming that that is the correct reading—as referring to the animals. The

sentiment grows in artificiality if it is taken to refer to Ignatius: κἂν αὐτὰ δὲ ἑκόντα μὴ θέλῃ "if they are unwilling [to attack me] who am willing.")

18 The words here may mean, "grapplings with wild beasts." But the use of the word συστάσεις in *Tr.* 5.2 makes the meaning "packs of wild beasts" somewhat more likely (BAG *s.v.* σύστασις, p. 802).

Ignatius' Voluntary Death [4.1–8.1]

6

Ignatius' Birth Pangs

1   Of no profit to me will be the ends of the world and the kingdoms of this age; it is "better for me to die" to Jesus Christ than to rule the ends of the earth. I seek him who died on our behalf; I want him who arose for our sake. The pains of birth are upon me. 2/ Indulge me, brothers: do not prevent me from living, do not want my death, do not give to the world one who wants to be God's, nor deceive him with matter; let me receive pure light— when I am there, I shall be a human being; 3/ allow me to be an imitator of the suffering of my God. If anyone has him within himself, let him understand what I want, and let him sympathize with me, knowing what constrains me.

7

1/ The ruler of this age wishes to carry me off and to corrupt my godly intent. So then let none of you present help him, rather take my side—that is, God's side. Do not profess Jesus Christ and desire the world. 2/ Let no envy dwell among you. Even if I should command you to when present, do not obey me; rather obey the things that I write to you. For I write to you (fully) alive, longing to die. My longing has been crucified, and there is no matter-loving fire in me. There is water living and speaking in me, saying from within me, "Come to the Father." 3/ I take no pleasure in the food of corruption nor yet in the pleasures of this life. I want the bread of God, which is the flesh of Jesus Christ, of the seed of David; and for drink I want his blood, which is incorruptible love.

8

1/ I no longer want to live in human fashion; and this will be so if you want it; want it, that you may also be wanted.

Ignatius continues to urge the Romans to let him die a martyr's death. But he now turns his attention more fully to the meaning of his journey to the Father and in so doing employs a wide range of otherworldly themes that sometimes strike a Gnostic note.

■ **6.1** Ignatius first denies the value to himself of the things of this world. In mentioning "the ends of the world" and "the kingdoms of this age" he may have in mind the grandiose claims of worldly princes which he parodies in drawing up his own short list of exploits in *Rom.* 5.1 (the reading "pleasures of this world" [GHTM, followed by

Zahn] instead of "ends of this world" [LSfSmAmg] probably represents an effort to ease the transition). In any event, faced with a choice like that presented to Jesus by Satan at his temptation (Matt 4:8), Ignatius too would reject the offer of universal rule;[1] for he knows that there is no "profit" in gaining the whole "world" (cf. Matt

---

1   Ignatius speaks of τὰ πέρατα τοῦ κόσμου ("the ends of the world") and αἱ βασιλεῖαι τοῦ αἰῶνος τούτου ("the kingdoms of this age"). Matthew speaks only of τὰς

βασιλείας τοῦ κόσμου ("the kingdoms of the world"). The variation suggests that Ignatius is not necessarily dependent on Matthew here (cf. J. Smit Sibinga,

16:26; Mark 8:36; Luke 9:25),[2] and with Paul he finds it better to die to Christ (1 Cor 9:15). In neatly balanced clauses marked by repetition of sound throughout, Ignatius proclaims his intention to seek Christ who died on our behalf and rose for our sake. The emphasis is on Christ as the one who died that death might be conquered (cf. *Tr.* 2.1) and who thereby opened up the path to God for believers.[3] What Ignatius hopes for is likened by him to the pangs of birth, apparently both because he will soon suffer like a woman in labor and because he will be born (that is, reborn) like a child. Other writers settled for the related but less complex metaphor of a birthday.[4]

■ **6.2** Death, then, is life and life is death, as the following paradoxes show (cf. Matt 10:39). But Ignatius goes on to describe the significance of those paradoxes in language that borders on Gnosticism. He does not want to be given back to the "world" or deceived[5] by "matter"; he wants to gain "pure light";[6] when he reaches it, he will be a "human being." (a) "Matter" (ὕλη) is frequent as a technical term in Gnosticism for substance that is hostile to God.[7] Yet God and matter are at times sharply opposed already by Philo,[8] and material things are closely associated by him with the passions.[9] Ignatius is also like Philo in that elsewhere the physical world is seen in a more positive light (cf. *Eph.* 8.2; *Pol.* 2.2). Moreover, the bishop's negative evaluation of the phenomenal world is connected just above with the thought that a person's deeds should match his words to the point of being ready to yield to martyrdom and to disappear from the "world" (see on *Rom.* 3.2–3). Thus also in *Rom.* 4.3 the rejection of the world's allure is linked by Ignatius rather to his resolve to die than to the nature of the world as such. The same seems to be true here. The material world is an inferior reality capable of being used by others to "deceive" the person who is reluctant to follow out his convictions, but it is not in and of itself hostile to God. (b) "Light" (φῶς) also is a favorite term in

---

"Ignatius and Matthew," *NovT* 8 [1966] 267–68). Yet neither is the terminology involved alien to him. For he mentions the ends of the earth elsewhere (*Eph.* 3.2); and his use of the Semitic expression "this age" may well have been derived from his view of the devil as the "ruler of this age" (*Eph.* 17.1; 19.1; *Mag.* 1.2; *Tr.* 4.2; *Rom.* 7.1; *Phd.* 6.2). For apart from this title Ignatius uses the expression only in our passage. This increases the likelihood that he has the temptation of Jesus in mind.

2 Ignatius is not necessarily dependent on the gospels for a sentiment so obviously traditional (Koester, *Synoptische Überlieferung*, 34).

3 The statement that Christ died ὑπὲρ ἡμῶν ("on our behalf ") is the oldest element of the formula (Rom 5:8; 14:15; 1 Cor 15:3; 2 Cor 5:14; *Tr.* 2.1; *Sm.* 1.2; cf. *Sm.* 7.1). The fuller form that we have here (that Christ died ὑπὲρ ἡμῶν "on our behalf " and rose διὰ ἡμᾶς "for our sake") apparently reflects later developments. But it is anticipated by Paul (cf. Rom 4:25) and is found in almost exactly the same words in Polycarp (*Phil.* 9.2). The ὑπὲρ ἡμῶν and διὰ ἡμᾶς of the fuller formula evidently function similarly and mark both the death and resurrection as gracious acts of God on our behalf. Thus the death of Christ is apparently deprived of meaning independent of the resurrection. In line with this is the fact that Ignatius does not dwell on the problem of sin (cf. *Eph.* 14.2; *Sm.* 7.1) but rather emphasizes the healing that Christ effects in the realm of the flesh and the spirit (cf. *Eph.* 7.2).

4 *Mart. Pol.* 18.3; *Con. Laod.* 51; cf. Seneca *Ep.* 102.26

("the day that you fear as the end is the birthday of your eternity").

5 The verb ἐξαπατήσητε ("deceive") is missing in the Greek texts. This seems to be the correct restoration, to judge from the Latin version of *Eph.* 8.1 where the same word as is used here (*seducare*) translates ἐξαπατάω ("deceive").

6 This supernal light is no doubt linked with the light that "enlightens" the church (*Rom.* inscr) and that characterizes the "children of light" (*Phd.* 2.1). It is typical of Ignatius that he ascribes to other Christians or the church what he himself still seeks (see Introduction, 3.4). The attainment of "pure light" lies before him as does his transformation into "pure bread" (*Rom.* 4.1). (For light that is half physical and half mythical see *Eph.* 19.2.)

7 Schlier, *Untersuchungen*, 148.

8 Cf. *Fuga* 198; *Spec. leg.* 1.329; 3.180; *Heres* 159–60; *Leg. alleg.* 1.88; 3.252.

9 Cf. *Post. Cain.* 114–19 (where Philo also notes that lovers of their bodies go on expeditions ἐπὶ τὰ πέρατα γῆς καὶ θαλάττης "to the ends of the earth and sea" to satisfy their desires; cf. Ign. *Rom.* 6.1); *Agric.* 22–25.

Gnosticism for the divine.[10] And it is undeniable that Ignatius (like the Gnostics) conceived of the divine light as a kind of substance or distinct sphere of reality. Yet the analogies to this conception in pre-Ignatian Jewish and Christian writings are so striking that it is one-sided to see Gnosticism as its only possible source.[11] Note that Plutarch (*Pericl.* 39.2) uses the phrase "purest light" (φῶς καθαρώτατον) to describe that by which the dwelling of the gods is illuminated. (c) "Human being" (ἄνθρωπος) as a term for the ideal "man" in whom individuals find their true being is important in Gnosticism.[12] At the same time, the idea of representative "man"—the "new man" or "perfect man"—has analogies also in non-Gnostic sources (see on *Eph.* 20.1; *Sm.* 4.2; cf. *Tr.* 11.2). All such parallels, however, may well be beside the point here. The expression ἄνθρωπος ἔσομαι ("I shall be a [true] human being") is reminiscent of another in *Rom.* 4.2: τότε ἔσομαι μαθητὴς ἀληθῶς ᾽Ιησοῦ Χριστοῦ "then I shall truly be a disciple of Jesus Christ." Just as discipleship in Ignatius' case presupposes his martyrdom, so also (it would seem) does his claim to being an authentic "human being." To be sure, it is the word ἀνήρ ("man") that is generally used in Greek literature to refer to one who is truly a man (see, for example, Herodotus 7.210: πολλοὶ μὲν ἄνθρωποι, ὀλίγοι δὲ ἄνδρες "many people, but few [real] men").[13] But there are also excellent examples of the word ἄνθρωπος being used in this sense: ἄνθρωπον ζητῶ "I am looking for a [true] human being" (Diogenes Laertius 6.41); πολὺς μὲν ὁ ὄχλος, ὀλίγοι δ' οἱ ἄνθρωποι "a large crowd, but few [real] human beings" (Diogenes Laertius 6.60).[14] In short, it is likely that what we have here once again is Ignatius' insistence that the authenticity of his Christianity depends on his readiness to act on his convictions. (d) The idea presupposed here of the ascent to the other world appears elsewhere in Ignatius and is comprehensible against a wider background than Gnosticism (see on *Eph.* 9.1).

The conclusion is that Ignatius and Gnosticism share a common set of otherworldly themes and symbols and are to some extent rooted in the same spiritual soil but that Ignatius' denial of the world does not yet amount to a Gnostic rejection of it.

■ **6.3** The implication of all this for Ignatius is that he should be allowed "to be an imitator of the suffering of my God." The line is a striking illustration of the extent to which the bishop regards Christian life in general and the life of the martyr in particular as dominated by the pattern of the crucified Lord. It is to be noted, however, that this is the only passage in which Ignatius connects the theme of imitation with his own suffering and death (cf. *Eph.* 1.1; 10.3; *Tr.* 1.2; *Phd.* 7.2; *Sm.* 12.1). That suggests how questionable it is to take the imitation theme in the letters as indicative of an unqualified preoccupation of the bishop with personal salvation. The one other passage in which it is joined with an emphasis on the suffering of God (expressed there in the reference to "the blood of God") has to do with the ethical consequences that flow from such imitation in the life of the Christian community (*Eph.* 1.1). The fact that the theme does not always have in view Christ's death or does so only to draw attention to the love of God or Christ's endurance also indicates how improbable it is to regard imitation in Ignatius as linked with the idea of cultic reenactment of the Lord's passion. And it is one-sided to find here decisive evidence that Ignatius had moved beyond the conception of following Christ in the NT and exalted the achievement of a special saintliness above the commitment to the Christian mission and its concern to illuminate the whole of human existence in light of the cross. Not only is it difficult to distinguish clearly between such alternatives in the early period, but also it is difficult to isolate our present passage from everything else in Ignatius that shows the sense of mission (in however strange a form) that dominates the activities of the bishop (see Introduction, 5.13). Finally, no sharp distinction is relevant here that opposes imitation as a human achievement to imitation as existence transformed by God or Christ. For presumably the imitation

---

10 Schlier, *Untersuchungen*, 172; cf. *Gos. Phil.* (NHC 2) 76,22–31 where such light is associated with the "perfect man" who cannot be seized or seen.

11 Cf. Hans Conzelmann, "φῶς," *TDNT* 9 (1974) 310–58.

12 Schlier, *Untersuchungen*, 172; cf. the "man of light" in *Gos. Thom.* 24 (NHC 2) 38,3–10 .

13 LSJ *s.v.* ἀνήρ IV, p. 138.

14 Cf. Clement Alex. *Strom.* 8.3, 5.3 (quoting Menander); M. Aurelius 10.15 (ἄνθρωπον ἀλήθινον "a true human being").

of Christ's passion in the case of Ignatius is dominated by the same sense of "having" God (Christ) within (cf. *Mag.* 12.1) that he here ascribes to the Roman Christians who (as he hopes) instinctively understand what constrains him to act as he does.

■ **7.1** Again, however, Ignatius thinks that there is a danger of being diverted from his goal. Here the role of "the ruler of this age" in any such eventuality is at last made plain. The devil seeks to change the martyr's mind, and the Roman Christians will be helping the evil one if they seek Ignatius' release and (as he adds in 7.2) yield to "envy." Although the word used for "envy" (βασκανία; cf. *Rom.* 3.1 for the corresponding verb) had long served as a moral term (and is thus synonymous with the word ζῆλος "envy" used in *Tr.* 4.2 and *Rom.* 5.3), it basically had to do with "bewitchment" by the evil eye; and in view of the reference to Satan it seems likely that the occult meaning of the term has not been entirely lost here (or in *Rom.* 3.1). Thus the possible "envy" of the Roman Christians (presumably based on their resentment of Ignatius and his glorious martyrdom in their own city) would arise from the enchantment of Satan, who had always envied the favor shown to human beings by God.[15] An early second-century mosaic from a villa near Antioch is mute witness to the fear of the "evil eye" in Ignatius' environment.[16] By turning the Roman Christians against Ignatius and effecting his release, Satan would demonstrate that their profession of Christianity was not genuine and that they still desired the world. They are expected to be free of such desire even though Ignatius thinks of himself as just now gaining a comparable freedom from earthly entanglements (cf. *Rom.* 4.3). Again it is the task of the apostolically inspired community to confirm the bishop in his appointed role. What Ignatius and the Roman Christians jointly "want"

(forms of the verb θέλειν, mostly in the first-person singular and second-person plural, appear some ten times in 6.1–8.3) is bound to prevail over the mere "wish" (βούλεται) of Satan (for this contrast see on *Rom.* 3.2).

■ **7.2** In light of this, Ignatius now sets out to guard against any eventuality: If he changes his mind at the end when he arrives, the Roman Christians are to ignore him and to remember what he is now writing while still "alive" or "living" (ζῶν). By "living" he must mean living in the fullest sense of the term and in full possession of his faculties—with his mind unclouded by the immediate threat of the arena and intent upon attaining God. The passage is important as an indication that a simple human fear of losing his nerve was a component in Ignatius' doubts about his worthiness (see Introduction, 3.4). This fear does not prevent him, however, from choosing his words carefully with an eye to their rhetorical effect. For his reference to writing while "living" is balanced by a reference to his "longing to die," and the parallelism is enhanced by rime at the beginning and end of the two clauses: ζῶν . . . ὑμῖν/ἐρῶν . . . ἀποθανεῖν.

Ignatius also goes on to play on the meaning of the word "longing": He "longs" or "loves" (ἐρῶν) to die,[17] but his "longing" or "love" (ἔρως) has been crucified. Origen initiated a long tradition of interpretation of the passage according to which Christ is spoken of as the soul's "longing" that was crucified.[18] But the use of the imagery of crucifixion in Gal 6:14 ("the world has been crucified to me and I to the world") and the parallel expression that follows in Ignatius—"matter-loving fire"—make it clear that he has in mind a "longing" for the things of the world.[19] This negative assessment of "love" (ἔρως) has been viewed as Gnostic,[20] but Philo in a number of instances deals with "love" and the longing for earthly things just as negatively (cf. *Leg. alleg.* 2.72; *Probus* 21;

---

15 Wis 2:24 (cf. Josephus *Ant.* 1.41); *2 Enoch* 31.3; *3 Baruch* 4.8.

16 Doro Levi, *Antioch Mosaic Pavements* (2 vols.; Princeton: Princeton University, 1947) 1. 33–34 (plate IVc in vol. 2).

17 The expression "longing to die" has good parallels in Greek literature and would not have seemed especially unusual (cf. Sophocles *Antig.* 220; Hippocrates *De arte* 7). In Ignatius' mind it must have had the same meaning as the parallel expression in *Tr.* 4.2: ἀγαπῶ . . . τὸ παθεῖν ("I love the suffering"). A positive evaluation of "longing" for the things of

God is frequent in Philo (cf. *Fuga* 58; *Somn.* 2.232; *Migr. Abr.* 170).

18 *Comm. in cant.*, prologus (ed. W. A. Baehrens, *Origenes Werke: Homilien zu Samuel I, Zum Hohelied und zu den Propheten, Kommentar zum Hohelied* [GCS 8; Leipzig: Hinrichs, 1925] 71).

19 The term "longing" in this sense evidently covers the same ground for Ignatius as the verb ἐπιθυμεῖν ("to desire").

20 Schlier, *Untersuchungen,* 152 (citing especially *Corp. Herm.* 1.18–19).

Spec. leg. 4.85; *Dec.* 151).

The background to other elements in this description of Ignatius' longing for the other world is no less difficult to identify. (a) Although intriguing parallels to the contrast between fire and water occur in Gnostic baptismal sects,[21] "fire" was a natural symbol for earthly passions,[22] and the imagery of "living water" was (as we shall see) also familiar; under the circumstances it is not hard to imagine that Ignatius with his fondness for striking metaphors would have seen the relevance of the traditional contrast between fire and water.[23] Note that the author of the description of the martyrs of Lyon makes a somewhat similar move when he opposes the Johannine "water of life" to the torturers' fire (Eusebius *Hist. eccl.* 5.1.22). (b) The adjective φιλόϋλον "matter-loving" (used of the fire) occurs elsewhere only in later patristic Greek.[24] Here again "matter" represents an inferior reality on which the fire of earthly desires feeds (cf. 6.2).[25] Similarly, Philo's Pharaoh, symbol of all the passions (*Somn.* 2.277–79), is called τῆς θηλείας ὕλης ἐραστής "a lover of matter, which is feminine" (*Leg. alleg.* 3.243). There is no reason to think that Ignatius goes beyond Hellenistic Judaism in this connection, especially since his resolve to leave the world is occasioned first and foremost by a call from God. (c) The "living and speaking water" (ὕδωρ ζῶν καὶ λαλοῦν) is reminiscent especially of the ὕδωρ ζῶν "living water" in John (4:10; 7:38)[26] and τὸ ὕδωρ τὸ λαλοῦν "the speaking water" of the *Odes of Solomon* (11.6) which "came near my lips from the spring of life of the Lord in his abundance." This water is apparently to be identified with the Spirit (cf. John 7:39)

which Ignatius experienced as extinguishing his love for the world by calling him from deep within: "Come to the Father." Thus the bishop is also a prophet who feels well up within him inspired utterances (cf. Rom 8:15) that have a direct bearing on what is to be done in a given situation (see on *Phd.* 7.1). This picture of prophetic activity may owe something to Hellenism, where the link between water and prophecy is traditional. Especially interesting is the reference in the *Anacreontea* (12.7) to some who are said to "drink the speaking water" (λάλον πιόντες ὕδωρ) of Apollo, the god of divination, and madly shout aloud.[27] Other references to "speaking water" in Hellenism are also found.[28] At the same time it must be recognized that if Ignatius borrowed the theme from Hellenism, he gave the prophetic waters a purely symbolic significance. For he could scarcely have been thinking of water that was actually drunk. Yet the thought of baptism may not have been totally absent from his mind, and even a connection with the "drink" of the eucharist (cf. 7.3) is not entirely impossible.

■ **7.3** The reference to water (with or without sacramental overtones) probably sufficed to bring food to mind and to prompt Ignatius' statement about his dissatisfaction with "the food of corruption." Although he may well have had real food in mind, the expression also stands for much more, as is indicated by the phrase with which it is coupled, "the pleasures of this life." Opposed to such food is the "bread of God" (cf. *Eph.* 5.2; *Rom.* 4.1) which is Christ's flesh and the drink, Christ's blood, which is "incorruptible love."[29] There is a curious lack of symmetry in the statement. We expect a comparison between

---

21 Schlier, *Untersuchungen*, 147; cf. *Thom. Cont.* (NHC 2) 141,20–30; 146,15–17.

22 Cf. 1 Cor 7:9; Philo *Heres* 64; *Leg. alleg.* 3.248–50; *Joseph.* 41; Justin *Dial.* 116.2.

23 Examples of the metaphorical use of the contrast include Sirach's observation that "water extinguishes flaming fire" as alms atone for sin (3:30), Cicero's (*Pro Roscio comoed.* 6.17) comparison of the power of an honorable life to stop slander with the power of water to extinguish fire, and especially the interesting juxtaposition in Philo (*Migr. Abr.* 99–101; cf. 210) of the "fire" of earthly passion with the "dew" and "rain" of God's blessing.

24 Cf. Bartelink, *Lexicologisch-semantische studie*, 55; *LPGL s.v.* φιλόϋλος, p. 1484.

25 Ignatius may have been playing on two meanings of the word ὕλη—"firewood" and "matter" (cf. Philo

Mos. 2.58).

26 Cf. Zech 14:8; Ezek 36:25; 1QS 4.21.

27 Carl Preisendanz, ed., *Carmina Anacreontea* (Leipzig: Teubner, 1912) 9; cf. Lightfoot, *Ignatius*, 2. 224.

28 Ps-Justin *Cohort.* 3 (Hercules is said to have sought ὕδωρ ἔναρθρον φωνὴν ἀποδιδόν "water producing an articulate sound"); Apuleius *Met.* 6.14 (*vocales acquae* "speaking waters"). Cf. Erwin Rohde, *Psyche* (2 vols.; 4th ed.; Tübingen: Mohr [Siebeck], 1907) 2. 390 (n. 1).

29 The link between the bread of God and Christ's flesh and between the drink and Christ's blood is reminiscent of John 6:26–59. But there is no clear evidence of literary dependence on John here or elsewhere (Paulsen, *Studien*, 36–37).

bread and flesh and between drink and blood (John 6:51, 55) *or* a comparison between flesh and faith and between blood and love (*Tr.* 8.1). Zahn thought the lack of symmetry significant and argued that the expression "which is incorruptible love" must refer to both the bread and drink and thus represent a reference to ἀγάπη as the "love-feast" (cf. *Sm.* 7.1; 8.2).[30] But Ignatius' use of the linking formula "which is" is against this solution (see on *Eph.* 20.2). It is more likely that the two sets of comparisons referred to above simply became conflated in the course of Ignatius' dictation of the passage. What Ignatius basically "wants," of course, is Jesus Christ who died and rose for us (cf. 6.1). The bread and drink (and all the rest) are simply specifications of that fundamental wish. The closest parallel here is *Tr.* 8.1, where the use of eucharistic language apparently echoes Ignatius' concern to emphasize the reality of Christ's death and thereby also the importance of the concrete requirements of faith and love. The reference in the passage before us to Christ being "of the seed of David" probably functions similarly to underscore the reality of the Lord's earthly ministry (cf. *Eph.* 18.2; 20.2; *Tr.* 9.1; *Sm.* 1.1). All of this is relevant to Ignatius himself who longs for death (7.2) and elsewhere makes the meaningfulness of his martyrdom dependent on the reality of Christ's passion (*Tr.* 10). It is likely, then, that the reference here to Christ's flesh and blood marks a reaffirmation of the bishop's desire to authenticate his Christianity in martyrdom.

■ **8.1** But Ignatius longs for death only because he also hopes for resurrection. The antithesis between "food of *corruption*" and "*incorruptible* love" dominates the passage. As Ignatius is about to say, he no longer "wants" to live at the merely human level. Thus the bread and cup that he "wants" (7.3) also have to do with the incorruption that he seeks. It is unlikely that Ignatius here expresses a longing to participate in the eucharist as one who had been deprived of it as a prisoner. For there was probably ample opportunity for Christians to eat with the bishop and to celebrate the sacred meal with him. He could speak to the Philadelphians of crying out while "among" them (*Phd.* 7.1); and Lucian (*Peregr.* 12) tells us that with the help of bribes (cf. *Rom.* 5.1) "variegated meals were brought in [by Christians to the martyr Peregrinus in

prison] and their sacred words were spoken." In any event, it is hard to prove that Ignatius attributes the exclusive preeminence to the eucharist that such an approach to the text assumes. It is likewise improbable that our passage presupposes a view of the eucharist as a reenactment of Christ's passion and thus a view of Ignatius' martyrdom as a quasi-eucharistic event by way of imitation (see on *Rom.* 2.2; 4.1).[31] As we have seen, eucharistic language of this kind serves to emphasize the reality of Christ's death and to link it with the need to practice love (7.3; cf. *Tr.* 8.1). And here his mention of (faith and) love indicates that his thoughts go beyond the meal itself. Indeed it is precisely love that is designated as "incorruptible." For it is love that causes one to transcend the limitations of this life (cf. *Eph.* 3.1) and that in its incorruptibility stands opposed to the "food of corruption" as well as to Satan's wish to "corrupt" the bishop's resolve (7.1). What we have here is a description, both in terms of Christ (his flesh and blood in the eucharist) and in terms of love, of what dominates Christian existence. A similar description is found in *Phd.* 8.2, where the mention of Christ's cross, death, and resurrection is followed by a reference to "faith through him." All of these are dealt with there as the realities in and through which Ignatius "wants" to bring his course to completion. We conclude, then, that Ignatius "wants" the eucharist, not in the sense that he does not have access to it, but in the sense that he prefers it to all other nourishment and seeks the special marks of being a Christian which are expressed in the sacred meal as well as in all the other words and actions of the Christian community.[32] Just as the "food of corruption" designates more than earthly food, so the "bread of God" and the sacred "drink" have to do with more than the elements of the Lord's supper. Essentially Ignatius "wants" Jesus Christ and all that flows from having him (including an authentic witness to him in death).

The section concludes with a summary statement of Ignatius' desire no longer to live κατὰ ἀνθρώπους "in human fashion."[33] He strives for rhetorical effect by placing forms of the verb ("want") at the beginning and end of each of the two units of thought and by playing with its meaning: He "wants" to live no longer at the

---

30 Zahn, *Ignatius,* 348–50, 405.
31 Bartsch, *Gnostisches Gut,* 84–85, 96–98.
32 Thus it seems unlikely that Ignatius is in some sense
33 It is characteristic of Ignatius that he can attribute

looking forward to the refreshment of the eucharist on the other side of the grave.

ordinary human level; that will be possible if the Romans "want" it—that is, "consent" to it (cf. *Rom.* 3.2); they should so consent that they themselves may be "wanted" —that is, "loved" (cf. *Mag.* 3.2; *Rom.* 8.3). The word-play cleverly catches up the delicate balance of factors that Ignatius thinks of as determining the relations between himself and the Christians of Rome.

---

the virtual attainment of such an existence to other Christians (*Tr.* 2.1) and find it lacking in himself (see Introduction, 3.4).

8	**The Closing and Concluding Formulae**
2	I make my petition to you in these few lines. Do believe me! Jesus Christ will make plain to you that I speak truly— (Jesus Christ) the unlying mouth by which the Father spoke truly. 3/ Make petitions on my behalf that I may attain. I am writing you not according to the flesh but according to the purpose of God. If I suffer, you wanted (it); if I am rejected, you hated (me).
9	Remember in your prayer the church in Syria which has God instead of me for its shepherd. Jesus Christ alone will oversee it—and so will your love. 2/ I am ashamed to be called one of them; for I am not worthy, since I am the last of them and a miscarriage; but I have been given the mercy to be someone if I attain God. 3/ My spirit greets you as does the love of the churches who received me in the name of Jesus Christ, not as a transient traveller; for even churches that do not lie on my way according to the flesh went before me city by city. 1/ I write you these things from Smyrna through the Ephesians, most worthy of blessing; and there is also with me, along with many others, Crocus, a name dear to me. 2/ Concerning those who preceded me from Syria to Rome to the glory of God, I believe you know. Do tell them that I am near. For they are all worthy of God and of you, whom it is right for you to refresh in every way. 3/ I am writing this to you on the ninth day before the calends of September [August 24]. Farewell to the end, in the endurance of Jesus Christ.
10	

■ **8.2** We may take the mention of the brevity of the communication as one form of the "reference to writing" that marks transitions at any point in the body of the Hellenistic letter including (as here) the body closing.[1] Brevity was one of the virtues of the ancient letter most admired,[2] and the end of the letter was the logical place to mention it or to apologize for unusual length.[3] Such a reference to brevity generally served as a vehicle to reaffirm bonds of friendship or to deal sensitively and diplomatically with the addressee.[4] And it was used (as here and in *Mag.* 14; *Pol.* 7.3) even when the letter was quite long.[5]

"Do believe me!" is an exhortation intended to recall the burden of the letter—that Ignatius dies voluntarily

---

1 White, *Form and Function*, 24–25.
2 Demetrius *De elocut.* 231; Isocrates *Ep.* 2.13; 3.1; Libanius *Ep.* 188; 342.
3 For the latter see Isocrates *Ep.* 4.13; 8.10.
4 Cf. Libanius *Ep.* 188.3; 112.8; 176.2; 194.3; 200.3; 1062.2; 1099.2.

5 Heb 13:22; 1 Pet 5:12; Ptolemaeus *Ad Flor.* 10 (Epiphanius *Pan.* 33.7.10); Libanius *Ep.* 390.1, 13; *P.Flor.* 3.296,56.

and that the Romans are to put no obstacle in his path. Ignatius expects that a little reflection will indicate (or, as he puts it, that Jesus Christ will reveal) that he speaks "truly" (ἀληθῶς). To confirm the point he names Christ (who shapes the thoughts of Ignatius as well as of the Romans) "the unlying mouth by which the Father spoke truly (ἀληθῶς)." The imagery of Christ as God's "mouth" occurs elsewhere in the early period, and (like the term "word") seems to have acquired mythological overtones (see on *Mag.* 8.2). But Ignatius has an eye particularly to its metaphorical qualities, as the comparison between his own truth-telling and God's veracity makes clear. Consequently it scarcely admits of Bartsch's interpretation according to which Christ in his role of "mouth" stands between the Father and the Word as a Gnostic emanation located within the divine Pleroma.[6] Rather, Ignatius likens Christ to the unlying mouth of God in much the same way that he likens himself to an authentic word of God in *Rom.* 2.1. Thus Ignatius speaks "truly" not only in the sense that he can be believed but also in the sense that his commitment to death confirms the authenticity of his Christianity and can be seen as logical and meaningful in light of God's own way of addressing the world in the crucifixion. The bishop's use of the term "truly" in anti-docetic settings is evidently relevant here (cf. *Tr.* 9–10).

■ **8.3** Consequently the Roman Christians, far from opposing Ignatius' will, are to petition God on his behalf that he "attain" (God), that is, that his martyrdom succeed. This request is not connected with the conventional request for "prayers" that we find elsewhere at the end of letters (for which Ignatius generally uses προσευχή and προσεύχομαι). Rather αἰτήσασθε ("make petitions") picks up the αἰτοῦμαι ("I make my petition") of 8.2 and thus emphasizes the responsibility of the Romans to encourage the bishop in his resolve. The following reference to the character of his writing—that he writes "according to the purpose of God" (cf. *Eph.* 3.2)—is another indication that we still have to do with the body

closing and its reaffirmation of the point of the letter. And Ignatius now summarizes that point in an antithesis set out in neatly balanced clauses (in which the opposition between θέλειν "to want" and μισεῖν "to hate" helps determine the unusual sense of θέλειν "to favor" or "to love" in *Mag.* 3.2 and *Rom.* 8.1): the Romans have shown their love if he suffers; they have shown their hatred if he is rejected (that is, if his martyrdom is stopped).

■ **9.1–3** A conclusion now follows that contains most of the items used elsewhere by Ignatius to close off his letters (see on *Eph.* 21; *Tr.* 12.1). Most conventional of these are the request that the church in Syria be remembered in their prayers (9.1), the ἀσπάζομαι ("I greet") formula (9.3), and the farewell (10.3). Beyond this the theme of Ignatius' unworthiness plays a particularly prominent role (9.2). Again it is clear that he cannot think of his own fate without reflecting on the situation of the church in Antioch. And again the ambivalence of his feelings comes to expression. On the one hand, the bishop's sense of importance is strikingly illustrated by the statements that in place of himself the Antiochenes now have God as their "shepherd" (cf. *Phd.* 2.1; Acts 20:28; 1 Pet 5:2) and that Christ and the love of the Roman church will "oversee" (ἐπισκοπήσει) them—serve as their "bishop" (9.1).[7] On the other hand, Ignatius uses the strongest language to stress his unworthiness over against these same Antiochenes (9.2): He has a sense of shame when he thinks of his relations with them. And in imitation of Paul (1 Cor 15:8–9) he calls himself the "last" of them (cf. *Eph.* 21.2; *Tr.* 13.1; *Sm.* 11.1) and a "miscarriage" (a term which he takes in a purely negative sense). Only through attaining God (his martyrdom) can the "mercy" shown him[8] lead to his actually being "someone" (see on *Eph.* 3.1). Particular attention has been given to the term "miscarriage" to determine more precisely Ignatius' self-conception as a martyr and his relations with the church in Antioch. There is scant reason for finding in it an echo of the special teaching of the Valentinians according to which the "miscarriage" of

---

6   Bartsch, *Gnostisches Gut*, 70–71.

7   Note that in 1 Pet 2:25 the terms "shepherd" and "bishop" (or "overseer") occur together. The idea that the bishop is replaced not only by Christ but also by the love of the Romans is another indication that Ignatius' comparisons between God (or Christ) and the bishop cannot be pressed (see on *Mag.* 6.1).

8   The language is that of 1 Cor 7:25 which Ignatius

applies to himself here and in *Phd.* 5.1 (even though in *Eph.* 12.1 he had set himself apart from those who had been "shown mercy").

Sophia is the spiritual seed that must find its way back to the Pleroma.[9] At the same time, the context is hardly in favor of reading the passage simply in light of Paul's situation and concluding that Ignatius denigrates himself because (like Paul) he once persecuted the church of God (cf. 1 Cor 15:8–9).[10] The image of "miscarriage" was capable of being used more broadly of moral and spiritual failings (cf. Philo *Leg. alleg.* 1.76), and it is likely that Ignatius would understand Paul's puzzling self-designation in light of his own experience.[11] It points to tension between Ignatius and the church of Antioch which he was seeking to resolve (see Introduction, 3.1). For the image is a strong one and can hardly be written off simply as a piece of polite self-effacement. It is true, of course, that by modelling himself on Paul in the first place Ignatius indicates the great importance that he attributes to his ministry; but it is an importance that has not yet been confirmed, and the bishop's concerns along these lines seem to transcend mere fear of losing his nerve at the end (see Introduction, 3.4).

The counterpart of Ignatius' unworthiness is the worthiness of the churches and the importance of their role in validating the significance of his ministry. That is shown in two ways here: (a) the "love" of the Romans is said to join Jesus Christ in overseeing the church left behind by Ignatius (9.1). Although the statement exalts the role of the Roman church, too much should not be made of this. For Ignatius elsewhere links Christ's guidance and the effective prayers of another church (*Eph.* 20.1), and he attributes to the "prayer and love" of still others comparable importance in providing refresh-ment to the Antiochenes (cf. *Mag.* 14). Rome's pre-rogatives, then, are simply the prerogatives of all the churches in a somewhat heightened form (see on *Rom.* inscr). Thus there is no hint that Ignatius is asking Rome to interfere in Antiochene affairs (*Phd.* 10 and *Sm.* 11 show what Ignatius had in mind along those lines).

(b) The activity of the Romans represents the last link in a chain of activity supporting Ignatius as he makes his way to martyrdom and to God. In their case it is appropriate that he say farewell εἰς τέλος "to the end," that is, with a completion and finality (cf. 1 Thess 2:16) that will seal their commitment to his martyrdom (10.3). Not only Ignatius' spirit (his own self)[12] but also the "love" of the various churches is said to greet them (9.3). Here the situation that the bishop sketches for the Romans is this: He has been "received" by the churches; they have treated him as more than a casual traveller; even those not on the road (Ephesus, Magnesia, Tralles) "went before" him—sent representatives on ahead (to Smyrna) to greet him. The atmosphere of a triumphal march permeates the text. Polycarp (*Phil.* 1.1) strikes a similar note when he speaks of Ignatius' hosts as having "received" (δεξαμένοις) and "sent on their way" or "escorted" (προπέμψασιν) the bishop and his companions. Note that the first of these terms occurs also in our passage. Talk of receiving and escorting visitors is naturally found in many settings,[13] but its use in con-nection with the reception accorded generals as they made their way from city to city on triumphal tours[14] may have special relevance here.[15] For Ignatius is also a kind of conquering hero (see on *Rom.* 5.1). Thus people

---

9   Schlier, *Untersuchungen*, 155–57.
10   Lightfoot, *Ignatius*, 2. 229–30.
11   For the obscurity of Paul's meaning see Johannes Schneider, "ἔκτρωμα," *TDNT* 2 (1964) 465–67.
12   Martin, "Pneumatologia," 398.
13   For "receiving" visitors see Matt 10:14; Luke 10:8; 2 Cor 7:15; Col 4:10. For "sending them on their way" see Acts 15:13; 20:38; 21:5; Rom 15:24; 1 Cor 16:6, 11; 2 Cor 1:16; Tit 3:13; 3 John 6. The special Christian conception that in "receiving" another one receives Christ himself (Matt 18:5; Mark 9:37; Luke 9:48) may hover behind the text. If so, Ignatius need not have been dependent on a written source for the thought (see on *Eph.* 6.1).
14   Cf. Plutarch *Pomp.* 13.4; 21.3; 43.3; 52.2; 57.1–2.
15   Although the verb προῆγον ("went before") has a wide and varied range of usages and cannot refer

here to an organized escort for Ignatius before he reached Smyrna (cf. Zahn, *Ignatius*, 254), it also evokes the picture of a procession. Thus Polycarp (in a figurative use of the verb) speaks of love going before faith with hope following after it (*Phil.* 3.3). And a reapplication of such imagery to geographical movement is found in the inscription of Abercius (line 12) where we learn that faith went before that intrepid traveller on his journeys to the great centers of Christianity. It may be worth noting that in two early papyri the verb is used of a statue of victory that leads a procession of other statues representing the imperial family (*P.Oxy.* 10.1265,10; 12.1449,2). What Ignatius has in mind is a procession that does not depend on mere physical proximity.

send representatives to see him even when they live off his "way." Here Ignatius hints at the deeper significance of his journey by speaking of his "way according to the flesh" (τῇ ὁδῷ τῇ κατὰ σάρκα) as opposed (presumably) to his way upward to God (cf. *Eph.* 9). His well-wishers have clearly become involved in both (cf. *Eph.* 11.2).

The ready support of the churches for Ignatius no doubt presupposes a recognition on their part that the martyr brought into focus their own deepest hopes and fears. At the same time, Ignatius and his friends evidently did not leave things entirely to chance. Messengers had gone on to Ephesus, Magnesia, and Tralles to rouse the Christians in those places to send representatives to Smyrna, and it now appears that messengers had been previously sent also to Rome to prepare for the bishop's arrival (10.2). Conceivably Ignatius was referring here to other martyrs. But messengers may be said to come and go "to the glory of God" (*Mag.* 15), and the expressions "worthy of God and you" and "refresh them" reflect what Ignatius says of others who travel on his behalf (*Eph.* 2.1; *Sm.* 10.1). Their task obviously was to make sure that the bishop's visit was known about. This and other evidence of the exchange of information through letters and couriers (see Introduction, 3.2) strongly suggest that more than a longing for martyrdom was involved in Ignatius' journey to Rome (see Introduction, 3.3–4).

■ **10.1–3** Other features of Ignatius' concluding remarks also indicate a special concern to alert the Romans to his coming. (a) The indication about the place of writing (10.1) and more especially the date of writing (10.3) are undoubtedly there to make it possible for people in Rome to calculate his time of arrival and to be ready for him. Ignatius does not otherwise indicate the date of his letters, and the omission of the year shows that the ordinary concerns in such dating are not apparent. Indeed the location and the form of the date are completely atypical of Hellenistic letters.[16] And although the Roman system followed in it was well known in the East,[17] it would have been especially helpful to a Roman audience in their calculations. By the time they received the letter it is likely that Ignatius would (as he says) be "near" (10.2). (b) The use of διά ("through") in the expression "through the Ephesians" (10.1) probably indicates that the Ephesian representatives carried the letter (cf. *Phd.* 11.2; *Sm.* 12.1; *Pol. Phil.* 14.1) rather than that they took part in drawing up the document (Eusebius *Hist. eccl.* 4.23.11; perhaps 1 Pet 5:12).[18] Presumably they carried the letter to Ephesus and sent it on from there.[19] The special mention of Crocus[20] makes sense if he was the one designated to carry it to Rome (by sea) and make sure that it got there before Ignatius did (see on *Eph.* 2.1; *Mag.* 15).[21]

---

16   Cf. Exler, *Greek Epistolography*, 78–100; Orsolina Montevecchi, *La papirologia* (Torino: Società Editrice Internazionale, 1973) 67–70.

17   Ludwig Hahn, *Rom und Romanismus im griechisch-römischen Osten* (Leipzig: Dieterich, 1906) 38, 85, 122, 124, 129, 229, 245.

18   Bauer (*Ignatius,* 254) observes that such a notice is missing in the letters to Ephesus, Magnesia, and Tralles but present in the letters to Rome, Philadelphia, and Smyrna. He argues that since Ignatius presumably used an amanuensis for all of them, his reference to people "through" whom he wrote would have to do with those who carried the letter. He suggests that the bearers of the letters to Ephesus, Magnesia, and Tralles would have been the very ones who had come to visit Ignatius and would not have needed to be mentioned, whereas the situation was different in the letters which contain the notice.

19   There were ships from Ephesus to the west (it was still sailing season), and it was generally faster to go by sea than by land (Lionel Casson, *Travel in the*

Ancient World [London: Allen & Unwin, 1974] 150–52, 176).

20   Ignatius identifies Crocus as τὸ ποθητόν μοι ὄνομα "a name dear to me" (cf. *Sm.* 13.2; *Pol.* 8.3). What appears to be a "complimentary epigram" of the late second century from a house in Ephesus suggests the everyday experience that gave meaning to the expression: "Hail, Eulalius, a noble name desirable to the gods (θεοῖς πεποθημένον οὔνομα σεμνόν)! May you ever live, and may your lifetime ever increase! For you offer friendship with good intentions to all and gifts of the divine good cheer which you have." I follow (with slight modifications) Miroslav Marcovich, "A New Graffito from Ephesus," *GRBS* 14 (1973) 61–63.

21   Without some such arrangement the letter would very probably have arrived late (cf. Casson, *Travel in the Ancient World*, 219–21).

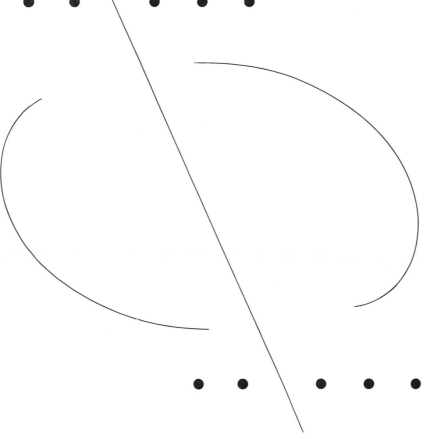

Salutation

Ignatius, also called Theophorus, to the church of God the Father and the Lord Jesus Christ which is in Philadelphia in Asia, shown mercy and established in godly concord, and rejoicing in the suffering of our Lord without wavering, and fully assured in his resurrection in all mercy—which (church) I greet in the blood of Jesus Christ, which is eternal and abiding joy, especially if they are at one with the bishop and with the presbyters and deacons with him, who have been appointed in the purpose of Jesus Christ, whom according to his own will he established in strength by his Holy Spirit.

The letter to the Philadelphians has a salutation second only to that of the letter to the Romans in length and complexity. The situation here (as we shall see) is also second only to that of *Romans* in delicacy, though for very different reasons.[1]

The salutation is surprising from a formal point of view not so much because it includes an ἀσπάζομαι ("I greet") formula (for that we have met also in the letters to Magnesia, Tralles, and Rome) but because it dispenses with the standard word of greeting. The omission is apparently not intentional: Ignatius mentions the bishop of Philadelphia, forgets that he has not finished the salutation, and plunges on into the body of the letter with a relative clause (1.1) that describes the sterling qualities of the Philadelphian leader.

Two themes dominate the salutation: (a) Christ's passion and resurrection and (b) unity with the ministry. The emphasis on Christ's passion and resurrection reflects Ignatius' fear that the centrality of these elements of the gospel is threatened by the views of some members of the Philadelphia church (cf. *Phd.* 8.2). The special mention of the "blood" of Christ[2] suggests that he again has in mind the dangers of docetism, and it may be

that (as in *Mag.* 9.1; 11) he sees a connection between the Judaizing tendencies of the Philadelphian community (*Phd.* 5–9) and the more disturbing christological error. The emphasis in the salutation on the importance of unity with the ministry is explained by what Ignatius regards as an unusual threat to authority in Philadelphia from dissident members of the community. The ministry is said to be appointed "in the purpose of Jesus Christ" (see on *Eph.* 3.2) and "established" (see on *Eph.* 12.1) by "the Holy Spirit." The latter is presumably conceived of not in distinctively trinitarian terms but in a more traditional way as a divine power closely connected with God or (as here) with Christ (cf. Rom 8:9–11; 2 Cor 3:17; Acts 16:6–7).[3] This divine power is operative in exceptional spheres—the incarnation (*Eph.* 18.2), the prophets (*Mag.* 8.2; 9.2), the charismatic bishop (*Phd.* 7.1–2; cf. *Rom.* 7.2), and (as here) the ministry (cf. Acts 20:28). Thus it is regularly connected with concrete manifestations of divine activity or with established authority.

---

1 The absence in the letter of any names of the members of the church in Philadelphia (Joly, *Ignace*, 50–51) probably owes something to the cooler relations that obtained between Ignatius and this community.

2 To judge from Ignatius' use of the linking formula "which is" (see on *Eph.* 20.2), it is the "blood of Jesus Christ" and not the church that Ignatius identifies

with "eternal and abiding joy" (cf. *Mag.* 7.1).

3 Martin, "Pneumatologia," 407–9.

1   Expressions of Blessing

1   **Of which bishop I know that he obtained a ministry for the community, not of himself, nor yet through any human beings, nor yet for vainglory, but in the love of God the Father and the Lord Jesus Christ, by whose gentleness I was struck, who though silent can effect more than they who talk vanity; 2/ for he is attuned to the commandments as a cithara to its strings. Therefore my soul blesses his godly mind, knowing that it is virtuous and perfect, (also) his freedom from disturbance and his freedom from wrath, as one living in all godly gentleness.**

In spite of the peculiar relation that obtains between the salutation and the opening of the letter, the first section (1.1–2) contains traces of the two essential elements of the transitional device most often used by Ignatius at this point: (a) a statement about information received or recalled (1.1) and (b) an expression which (like the blessing in *Eph.* 1.3 and the praise in *Tr.* 1.2 and *Pol.* 1.1) serves in place of the more conventional expression of joy (1.2). What Ignatius knows is that the bishop of Philadelphia has a divinely established authority and exercises his ministry in a most admirable way. And it is for this reason that his "soul" (a rare word in Ignatius and used only here of the self) "blesses" ($\mu\alpha\kappa\alpha\rho i\zeta\epsilon\iota$) the Philadelphian bishop's godly purpose (cf. *Eph.* 5.1).

■ **1.1** The authority of the (unnamed) bishop of Philadelphia is expressed in Pauline terms (cf. Gal 1:1) that emphasize his responsibility directly to God. Thus his authority is viewed as essentially charismatic. Yet the bishop of Philadelphia is not in full control of the situation (cf. *Phd.* 6–8) and apparently cannot deal to Ignatius' satisfaction with those who "talk vanity." Ignatius again seeks to make a virtue of necessity (as in *Eph.* 6.1; 15.2) by attributing more power to silence than

to words and by exalting the value of gentleness. It is probably also this that leads him to the unusual emphasis on "service" ($\delta\iota\alpha\kappa o\nu i\alpha$) as constitutive of the role of the bishop. For elsewhere it is only the deacons who are said to exercise "service" (*Mag.* 6.1; *Phd.* 10.2; *Sm.* 12.1).[1]

■ **1.2** The bishop's unconstrained submission to the "commandments" (see on *Mag.* 2) is explained with the help of a musical metaphor more fully elaborated elsewhere (see on *Eph.* 4.1). His freedom from "disturbance" (or "movement") and from "wrath" reflects the purpose of God himself (cf. *Eph.* 3.2), indeed the purpose of a somewhat Hellenized God devoid of passion (cf. *Eph.* 11.1).[2] The term "virtuous" ($\epsilon\nu\acute{a}\rho\epsilon\tau o\varsigma$) is equally Hellenic, for it was a "favorite word of the Stoics."[3] In such a context the expression $\epsilon\nu$ $\pi\acute{a}\sigma\eta$ $\epsilon\pi\iota\epsilon\iota\kappa\epsilon i\alpha$ $\theta\epsilon o\hat{v}$ $\zeta\hat{\omega}\nu\tau o\varsigma$ probably should not be taken to mean "in all gentleness of the living God." The biblical "living God" is mentioned nowhere else by Ignatius and seems out of place here. Thus the participle $\zeta\hat{\omega}\nu\tau o\varsigma$ ("as one living") may be taken with the preceding $\alpha\dot{v}\tau o\hat{v}$ ("his").

---

1   Note that it is service befitting $\tau\grave{o}$ $\kappa o\iota\nu\acute{o}\nu$ "the community"—a term that (like "council" in *Mag.* 6.1 and "ambassador" in *Phd.* 10.1) suggests the influence of Hellenic political and social models (cf. Herodotus 1.67; 5.109; Isocrates *Helen.* 36; *Plataic.* 21; Josephus *Vita* 65; *P.Oxy.* 1.53,2; 54,12; 84,3).

2   God's freedom from disturbance and wrath was taught by Hellenized Jews and by Christians other

than Ignatius (cf. Philo *Post. Cain.* 29; *1 Clem.* 19.3; *Diogn.* 8.8).

3   BAG *s.v.* $\epsilon\nu\acute{a}\rho\epsilon\tau o\varsigma$, p. 261.

2 Unity

1 Children of the light of truth, flee division and false teachings. Where the shepherd is, follow there as sheep. 2/ For many specious wolves take God's runners captive by evil pleasure, but they will have no place in your unity.

3

1/ Refrain from evil plants which Jesus Christ does not cultivate, because they are not a planting of the Father—not that I found division among you, but a filtering out. 2/ For all who are of God and Jesus Christ, these are with the bishop; and all who repent and come to the unity of the church, these too will be of God, that they may live according to Jesus Christ. 3/ Be not deceived, my brothers: if anyone follows a schismatic, he does not inherit the Kingdom of God; if anyone walks in an alien purpose, this person does not conform to the passion.

4

1/ Be eager, then, to celebrate one eucharist; for one is the flesh of our Lord Jesus Christ, and one the cup for union through his blood; one the altar, just as one the bishop along with the presbytery and deacons, my fellow slaves; that whatever you do, you may do it in a godly way.

■ **2.1** A vocative—"children of (the) light of truth"—marks the transition to the first main topic.[1] The expression looks like a combination of phrases like the Pauline "children of light" (Eph 5:8; cf. 1 Thess 5:5; Luke 16:8; John 12:36) and the Johannine "true light" (John 1:9; 1 John 2:8). The absence of the article in such a combination of words is no reason to question the text.[2]

The problem in Philadelphia had to do with "false teachings" (cf. *Eph.* 16.2) that divided the community (2.1). The term $\mu\epsilon\rho\iota\sigma\mu\acute{o}s$ ("division") occurs five times in our letter and only once elsewhere (*Sm.* 7.2). Though it was an appropriate word to designate social conflict (see the discussion of the corresponding verb in *Mag.* 6.2), it was not to have a future as technical language for schism

or heresy. The frequency of its use here reflects Ignatius' view of the seriousness of the situation in Philadelphia.

■ **2.2** The solution to the problem is given in terms of obedience to the bishop who fights such division as pastor or shepherd of his flock (cf. *Rom.* 9.1). For the shepherd protects the sheep from the wolves (2.1–2). The imagery is both biblical[3] and Hellenistic.[4] Ignatius probably knew it in a form closely related to Matt 7:15.[5] The athletic metaphor of "God's runners" ($\theta\epsilon o\delta\rho\acute{o}\mu ovs$), so oddly joined with that of the shepherd and his sheep,

---

1   White, *Form and Function*, 29–30.
2   Cf. Kühner/Gerth, *Grammatik*, 2/1. 608.
3   Matt 7:15; John 10:12; Acts 20:29.
4   Epictetus *Diss.* 3.22.35; Maximus *Or.* 6, 7d; Libanius *Ep.* 194.1.
5   In two sayings attributed to Jesus the imagery was used of the place of the Christian in a hostile world (Luke 10:3; *2 Clem.* 5.2–4). But it was the form of the

imagery in Matt 7:15 that was pressed into service against schism and heresy (cf. Justin *Dial.* 35.3). Indeed Matt 7:15 was to become an important text in orthodox polemics (G. Otranto, "Matteo 7,15–16a e gli $\psi\epsilon v\delta o\pi\rho o\phi\hat{\eta}\tau a\iota$ nell' esegesi patristica," *Vetera Christianorum* 6 [1969] 33–45; cf. Tertullian *Praescr.* 4.1–5). In all likelihood our passage provides evidence of the polemical use of the theme before its

may have been stimulated by Paul.[6] The same word occurs with a different application in *Pol.* 7.2 ("God's couriers").

■ **3.1–3** We have met elsewhere most of the themes and images used in the following section to underscore the sharp distinction between true and false Christians. (a) The false teachers are "evil plants" or "weeds" (cf. *Eph.* 10.3; *Tr.* 6.1) and the true Christians the "planting of the Father" (cf. *Tr.* 11.1). (b) There has been a "filtering out" of evil elements (cf. *Rom.* inscr). Note that Ignatius more or less corrects himself here: there was no real "division" in Philadelphia after all (cf. *Eph.* 6.2), rather only a "filtering out" of alien elements. As we shall see, it is unlikely that this had actually taken place or that the majority of the Philadelphians were as disturbed by the situation as was Ignatius (see on *Phd.* 11.1). Note also that the verb "I found" is the first definite indication that Ignatius had stopped in Philadelphia on his way to Smyrna. (c) Being of God and Jesus Christ means being with the bishop (see on *Mag.* 3.1). (d) Only false teachers who "repent" may return to the church (cf. *Eph.* 10.1; *Phd.* 8.1; *Sm.* 4.1; 5.3; 9.1). (e) The exhortation "be not deceived" is a warning against false teachers (cf. *Eph.* 5.2; 16.1). Its use was almost certainly stimulated directly by 1 Cor 6:9–10 since that passage is also echoed in what follows ("does not inherit the Kingdom of God").[7] Note that although the term "schismatic" (σχίζων) refers primarily to separatism, it also has in view false teaching (cf. 1 Cor 1:10; 11:18; 12:25). (f) Separatism is an indication that one does not agree with the passion, that is, disobedience and disunity have as a corollary the denial of the importance or reality of the passion (see on *Tr.* 2.1).

There is no real evidence in this mention of Christ's death and the subsequent discussion of the eucharist (*Phd.* 4) that Ignatius views separatism as a matter of having cut oneself off from the reenactment of the passion in the eucharist. Certainly worship and especially the eucharist are seen as the way in which unity is actualized (cf. *Eph.* 5.2; 13.1; *Sm.* 7.1; 8.1). And it is possible that there is a hint here of the need to discontinue separate celebrations of the sacrament (as in *Sm.* 7.1; 8.1) because of their potential for divisiveness. Yet the best commentary on the text is provided by the parallel in *Mag.* 7 where worship is the theme and where the repeated use of the word "one" also occurs. What is striking is that non-sacramental language sets the tone in *Mag.* 7 and that only the reference to the "one altar" is common to both passages. Thus Ignatius can speak of the unity actualized in worship with or without special reference to the eucharist. This would hardly be so if reenactment of the passion were the operative category in his view of worship. It is true, of course, that special attention was probably given to the eucharist in *Phd.* 4 because of the mention of the passion in *Phd.* 3.3. If this is so, it is not because the eucharist was seen as a reenactment of the passion but because Ignatius viewed Christ's presence in the sacred meal as one of the strongest confirmations of the reality of the passion and because he found a connection between this conviction and the desire to stand united, to follow the bishop, and to fulfill the requirements of love (see on *Tr.* 2.1; 8.1; *Sm.* 6.2–7.1). It is for this reason that in *Phd.* 4 he goes on to correlate the oneness of the flesh, cup, and altar with the oneness of the bishop and his colleagues. To conform to the passion is to submit to the bishop.

■ **4** Some problems of detail here may be examined in light of our general approach to the text. (a) Ignatius refers to the one "flesh" and the one "cup" of the eucharist. We expect him to speak of flesh and blood[8] or of bread and cup, but Ignatius does not value such consistency (cf. *Rom.* 7.3). The mention of the "cup" is reminiscent of the eucharistic traditions in the Synoptic Gospels and Paul.[9] But the reference to "flesh" (rather than "body") strikes a Johannine note (John 6:52–59), and it is the eucharistic terminology of this (interpolated?) passage in John that had evidently gained the upper hand in Ignatius' environment (see on *Rom.* 7.3).

---

incorporation into a written gospel (cf. Koester, *Synoptische Überlieferung*, 34).

6 Gal 5:7; 1 Cor 9:24–26; Phil 3:12–14; 2 Tim 4:7; cf. Heb 12:1–2.

7 Cf. Paulsen, *Studien*, 32–33.

8 Ignatius has flesh and blood in mind but refers to the latter only obliquely.

9 Matt 26:27; Mark 14:23; Luke 22:17; 1 Cor 10:16, 21; 11:25–28; cf. *Did.* 9.2.

This emphasis on Christ's "flesh" is probably linked in Ignatius' mind with the need to stress the historical reality of the incarnation and passion of the divine Lord. (b) In view of the fact that the repetition of the word "one" is designed to combat divisiveness, it is most likely that the term "union" refers (as usual) to the unity of the congregation. Thus the phrase εἰς ἕνωσιν τοῦ αἵματος αὐτοῦ does not mean "for union *with* his blood" but "for union *from* [or *through*] his blood." Similar uses of the genitive in such expressions are found elsewhere in the letters (see on *Mag.* 1.2; *Phd.* 5.2). Ignatius is saying that the reality of the passion is the ground of Christian unity. (c) The close connection between one flesh, one cup, and one altar has given rise to the view that here Ignatius surely had a physical altar in mind (and thus conceived of the eucharist in sacrificial terms). Yet this must remain doubtful in light of the symbolic use of the word "altar" elsewhere in the letters (*Mag.* 7.2; *Tr.* 7.2; *Rom.* 2.2). The only other passage in which there is a close connection between altar and eucharist is *Eph.* 5.2, where a symbolic sense of the term is also likely. The expression used there ("within the altar") is scarcely capable of being understood in terms of a physical altar, and we find it again in *Tr.* 7.2 in what is evidently a non-eucharistic setting. Thus Ignatius can mention altar and eucharist together without necessarily having in mind a cultic object. Moreover, the closest parallel to the language of *Phd.* 4 as a whole is provided by *Mag.* 7 with its comparable list of items prefaced by the word "one"; and there the expression "one altar" is clearly used in a symbolic sense of the oneness of the Christian community. It is likely, then, that the same is true of the passage before us.[10] It is probably significant that whereas the references to the flesh and cup are joined by the connective "and," the expression "one the altar" stands apart and is at least as closely linked with the words that follow ("just as one the bishop") as with those that precede.

---

10   For the altar as a symbol of Christ in later patristic writers see Dölger, *Antike und Christentum*, 2. 182–83.

The Judaizers in Philadelphia [5.1–9.2]

5   Ignatius' Authority and
His Theological Authorities

1   My brothers, I overflow in my love for you, and greatly rejoicing I watch out for your safety—not I, but Jesus Christ in whom, though I am bound, I fear all the more, since I am still imperfect; but your prayer will make me perfect unto God that I may attain the lot in which I was shown mercy, having fled to the gospel as to the flesh of Jesus and to the apostles as to the presbytery of the church. 2/ And we also love the prophets because they also made their proclamation with the gospel in view and set their hope on him and waited for him, in whom by believing they were also saved, being in the unity of Jesus Christ, saints worthy of love and worthy of admiration, attested by Jesus Christ and numbered together in the gospel of the common hope.

6   1/ But if anyone expounds Judaism to you, do not listen to him; for it is better to hear Christianity from a man who is circumcised than Judaism from a man uncircumcised; both of them, if they do not speak of Jesus Christ, are to me tombstones and graves of the dead on which nothing but the names of men is written. 2/ Flee, then, the evil arts and plots of the ruler of this age, lest, wearied by his scheming, you grow weak in love; but all of you, come together with undivided hearts.

Phd. 5–9 has many affinities with *Mag.* 8–10. Both passages are concerned with the problem of Judaizing Christians. In neither instance, however, does there seem to have been any debate over christology. Possible allusions to docetism in our letter (*Phd.* inscr; 3.3; 6.1; 8.2; 9.2) are even fainter than in *Magnesians* and even more likely to reflect Ignatius' own reading of the implications of the theology of his opponents.[1] It is equally difficult to find allusions to a "low" christology in either letter. Any emphasis in *Philadelphians* on the centrality of Jesus Christ (*Phd.* 8.2) or his high dignity

(*Phd.* 9.1–2) is more than matched in anti-docetic contexts (cf. *Sm.* 1.1–2) and therefore cannot serve as evidence that Ignatius was opposing Judaizers who held less exalted views of Jesus. On the other hand, neither is Christ presented in such a neutral fashion that Ignatius could be suspected of conceding anything to Jewish-Christian sensibilities.

It is more debatable whether the Judaizers of Philadelphia were interested in the observance of Jewish laws and customs. I shall suggest that it was the idea of Judaism rather than its practice that appealed to them

---

1   It is true that an attitude toward the prophets similar to that in the letter to the Philadelphians is found elsewhere in an anti-docetic setting (*Sm.* 5.1; 7.2). This could be taken as an indication that a similar polemic is concealed here and that the Judaizers had derived docetic christology from their interpretation of the OT (see on Christ's "eating and drinking" in *Tr.* 9.1). But it is more likely that Ignatius is adapting similar arguments to different situations. If he had been able to make a direct charge against the Judaizers of holding a docetic doctrine of Christ, he would surely have done so. (Cf. Bauer, *Orthodoxy and Heresy,* 88–89.)

and that this manifested itself principally in a display of exegetical expertise (see on *Phd.* 6.1; 8.2; 9.1). On this point the situation in Magnesia may have been different (see on *Mag.* 9.1).

■ **5.1** The vocative "my brothers" marks the transition to a new section of the letter.[2] Ignatius first emphasizes his love for the Philadelphians (cf. *Eph.* 3.2) and expresses his satisfaction in trying to safeguard them from harm (cf. *Mag.* 11.1; *Tr.* 8.1; *Sm.* 4.1). Here these themes are likely to have been put forward in self-defense since Ignatius was thought to have proceeded in a high-handed fashion in Philadelphia (cf. *Phd.* 6.3). Thus with a turn of phrase reminiscent of Paul (1 Cor 15:10; Gal 2:20) he traces his activities on their behalf not to self-will but to the presence of Jesus Christ within him (or, as in *Phd.* 7.1, to the Spirit). He immediately complicates this claim to authority, however, by recalling in compressed form a whole series of themes elsewhere associated with his paradoxical self-effacement: his bonds (see on *Eph.* 3.1; 11.2; *Mag.* 12.1), his fears of failure (*Tr.* 4.1), his imperfection (*Eph.* 3.1), his dependence on their prayers (*Eph.* 1.2; 11.2), his "lot" (*Tr.* 12.3; *Rom.* 1.2), the mercy shown him (*Eph.* 12.1; *Rom.* 9.2). But these points are passed over rapidly here, and Ignatius seems to be more confident than usual of the ultimate success of his mission—perhaps because things have gone his way in Antioch (see on *Phd.* 10.1). It is probably significant that, with but one exception (*Sm.* 11.1), all uses of the term ἄξιος ("worthy") to convey the bishop's concern about his possible unworthiness occur before his communication with the Philadelphians (cf. *Eph.* 2.2; *Mag.* 12.1; 14; *Tr.* 4.2; 13.1; *Rom.* 9.2). The same is true of other expressions of anxiety in the letters.[3]

Ignatius goes on to discuss the theological authorities in which he takes refuge (a discussion that is finally concluded only in *Phd.* 8.2). He first mentions the gospel and the apostles. From what follows, it is clear that this is tied in with the debate in Philadelphia that he is soon to describe (*Phd.* 8.2). He is already insisting on the precedence of the gospel and the apostles over the prophets (the OT). It is most unlikely that Ignatius has in mind written gospels and the letters of the apostles or is thinking of the gospel as put in the form of written

documents by the apostles. The term "gospel" in Ignatius seems regularly to refer to the good news about Jesus Christ (see on *Phd.* 8.2); when "apostles" are compared with presbyters (as they are here), they are dealt with as people rather than as scriptural authorities (see on *Mag.* 6.1); and the treatment of the "prophets" in 5.2—OT prophets (cf. *Phd.* 9.1–2)—shows that even when sacred books were known, Ignatius thinks of their authors primarily as people proclaiming a message. The linking of apostles and prophets, then, need not imply a comparison between classes of documents. Here (as in *Phd.* 8.2) Ignatius is setting the message about Jesus Christ—especially his death and resurrection (and indirectly Ignatius' own martyrdom)—above the words of the prophets (cf. *Sm.* 7.2).

Why, then, the peculiar comparison between the gospel and the flesh of Jesus and between the apostles and the presbytery? Just as Ignatius points to his (present) commitment to martyrdom as presupposing the (past) reality of the passion (see on *Tr.* 10), so he points to other contemporary elements of Christian life—the reality of Jesus' flesh (in the eucharist apparently) and the solidity of the presbytery—as presupposing the overwhelming significance of the gospel (the death and resurrection) as proclaimed by the apostles. The connection is not one established in terms of authoritative documents or an external historical continuity (there is no apostolic succession here or elsewhere in Ignatius) but in terms of a divine power which continually realizes itself in the institutions of the church. The church is based on the gospel, but the gospel is also confirmed by the church.

■ **5.2** Ignatius now turns to a discussion of the prophets and indicates by his use of the tandem particle καὶ . . . δέ that he is conscious of taking up a point requiring separate attention (see on *Eph.* 2.1). He echoes the traditional Christian view that the prophets awaited Christ; indeed he goes further and (as in *Mag.* 8.2; 9.2) virtually eliminates any distinction between the saints of the two testaments. Yet his main concern here is to suggest (however carefully) the incompleteness of the prophets. For fulfillment transcends anticipation and hope (cf. *Sm.* 7.2). Indeed Ignatius apparently sees the prophets as coming into their own only after the

---

2   White, *Form and Function*, 29.
3   Willard M. Swartley, "The Imitatio Christi in the Ignatian Letters," *VC* 27 (1973) 81–103.

appearance of Christ, who gave witness to them (cf. Matt 5:12) and so confirmed their participation in the gospel (see on *Mag.* 8.2). These cautious remarks are intended to take the edge off more radical statements about the OT made by Ignatius in Philadelphia (cf. *Phd.* 8.2).

Special comment is required on the meaning of the "unity of Jesus Christ" in which the prophets are said to be included (5.2). The term ἑνότης "unity" (like ἕνωσις "union") often clearly refers to unity within the church (*Eph.* 4.2; 5.1; *Phd.* 2.2; 3.2; see on *Mag.* 1.2). The reference of the term in other passages is less certain (*Eph.* 14.1; *Phd.* 5.2; 8.1; 9.1; *Sm.* 12.2; *Pol.* 8.3), and it has sometimes been taken to concern unity with God or Christ. But that is not where the emphasis lies. Thus in *Phd.* 8.1 the context shows that the "unity of God" has to do first and foremost with the social solidarity of the church ("if they turn in repentance to the unity of God and the council of the bishop"). Similarly in *Phd.* 5.2 and 9.1 the expression refers most naturally to the unity conferred on the church by God. Communion with God is presupposed, but the term "unity" is not used to cover that relationship or to suggest an interest in individual mystical experience. The prophets, we are being told, are united by God with all who adhere to "the gospel of the common hope." Consequently they are in harmony with the gospel and receive their significance from the events associated with Jesus Christ.

■ **6.1** Although the prophets are honored members of God's people, anyone who "expounds Judaism" is not. The term "Judaism" is apparently used by Ignatius to refer to an interest in Jewish observance (see on *Mag.* 8.1). The verb "expound" (ἑρμηνεύῃ), however, suggests that such "Judaism" is seen as the result of a misinterpretation of the prophets, that is, scripture (cf. *Phd.* 8.2; 9.1).[4] We may sketch Ignatius' train of thought in these three sentences as follows: (a) Anyone who expounds Judaism is not to be listened to. (b) For entanglement with Judaism negates Christianity. If entanglement seems inevitable, how much better to move (as did the earliest Jewish Christians) from Judaism (circumcision) to Christianity (cf. *Mag.* 9.1; 10.3) than from gentile Christianity (uncircumcision) to Judaism (thus the uncircumcised man who fosters Judaism is identical with the one who "expounds Judaism"). (c) Anyone—whether Jew or gentile—who does not speak of Christ (and in Ignatius' mind that is bound to be true of anyone devoted to "Judaism") is outside the church (cf. 1 Cor 7:19; Gal 5:6; 6:15).

It may be, however, that we should take Ignatius more literally and recognize that when he refers to "both of them" (ἀμφότεροι) in the third sentence, he has in mind the two groups precisely as they are mentioned in the second sentence.[5] In that event, he has in mind (a) a group of circumcised Jewish Christians and (b) a group of uncircumcised gentile Christians and regards the latter as followers of the former. We could assume that the gentile Christians would not have been circumcised because circumcision was not always required of proselytes.[6] Yet both groups would represent the same interests, and from Ignatius' point of view both would be guilty of not "speaking concerning Jesus Christ." The difficulty here is that Ignatius evidently thinks relatively highly of the circumcised person who proclaims Christianity. To be sure, the form of the statement about him ("it is better to hear Christianity from a man who is circumcised . . .") suggests that Ignatius senses some difficulty even here. But clearly such a person's witness to Christ is acceptable. What Ignatius is saying is this: Any entanglement with Judaism is unfortunate, but how much better to have moved—as especially the apostles

---

4   Ἑρμηνεύειν meaning "to expound" sometimes includes the idea of interpretation and sometimes does not (BAG *s.v.* ἑρμηνεύειν, p. 309). Philo uses it once (*Mut. nom.* 125) in clear reference to biblical exegesis (cf. Luke 24:27).

5   Zahn, *Ignatius,* 368–71; cf. C. K. Barrett, "Jews and Judaizers in the Epistles of Ignatius," in R. Hamerton-Kelly and R. Scroggs, eds., *Jews, Greeks, and Christians: Essays in Honor of W. D. Davies* (SJLA 22; Leiden: Brill, 1976) 220–44.

6   R. Joshua is said to have taught that circumcision was not necessary for the proselyte (*b. Yebam.* 46a). But it is not certain how accurate the report is or how much weight it carried (cf. Bernard J. Bamberger, *Proselytism in the Talmudic Period* [New York: Ktav, 1968] 42–43, 46).

202

did (cf. *Mag.* 9.1)[7]—from Judaism to Christianity than in the reverse direction. It is in this sense that Ignatius says in *Mag.* 10.3 that "Christianity did not believe in Judaism but Judaism in Christianity."

It seems better to assume, then, that in the third sentence Ignatius speaks more loosely of any—whether Jew or gentile—who do not put Christ first. This is probably Ignatius' adaptation of the Pauline statement that "neither circumcision counts for anything nor uncircumcision . . ." (1 Cor 7:19; Gal 5:6; 6:15). If our interpretation is correct, no one was actually recommending circumcision, and the issue had probably been injected into the debate by Ignatius under the influence of Pauline models. Ignatius' point is that the one expounding Judaism was himself uncircumcised, and the antithesis (in the second sentence) is intended to expose the absurdity of that fact. The suggestion has been made therefore that the Judaizers may have been interested in some other Jewish practice, for example, the observance of Sabbath as in *Mag.* 9.1 (as interpreted by most commentators).[8] But if so, it is strange indeed that Ignatius should have chosen to discuss circumcision. It is more likely, then, that he actually thought that the Judaizers of Philadelphia should logically have submitted to circumcision. And it is therefore also likely that he missed the point of their theology. But if neither Jewish practice nor christology was the issue, what was it? The following sections of the letter suggest that the Judaizers of Philadelphia may well have been more interested in the idea of Judaism than the practice of it (see on *Phd.* 8.2; 9.1). Thus perhaps it was the "expounding"

(exegetical expertise) that was the problem and not the "Judaism" (observance).

Ignatius' harsh words about the Judaizers as tombstones and graves (6.1) are reminiscent of the saying of Jesus in Matt 23:27 about the Pharisees as "whitewashed tombs." But, as the commentators note, there are better pagan parallels. Thus old age was said to render a man like a grave with nothing but a name left on it (Macrobius *Sat.* 2.7). Or a person ignored by others was compared to an old tombstone passed by and unread (Lucian *Tim.* 5). Also interesting are the references to the Pythagorean practice of building cenotaphs to those who abandoned the sect (Clement Alex. *Strom.* 5.9, 57.2–3; Origen *Cels.* 2.12; 3.51). For clearly Ignatius too has read the Judaizers out of the community. If he also intended to suggest that they were guilty of docetism since they were therefore mere names devoid of human reality (cf. *Tr.* 10), he did not dare to press the point.

■ **6.2** The section concludes with an exhortation to flee (cf. 1 Cor 6:18; 10:14) the devil's wiles. The main effect of the devil's activity is to negate "love." Common worship is the cure (cf. *Eph.* 13). Note that here disunity, not false teaching, is uppermost in Ignatius' mind (cf. *Phd.* 7).

---

7   The prophets as seen by Ignatius were never entangled in Judaism. The apostles, on the other hand, once were.

8   Bartsch, *Gnostisches Gut,* 39–42.

The Judaizers in Philadelphia [5.1–9.2]

6

Ignatius' Defense of His Behavior
in Philadelphia

3 I thank my God that I am clear in conscience as concerns you and that no one
can boast either in private or in public
that I burdened anyone in anything great
or small. And I pray for all among whom I
spoke that they may not have it as a
witness against them.

7

1/ For although some desired to deceive
me at the fleshly level, yet the Spirit,
which is from God, is not deceived; for it
knows whence it comes and whither it
goes, and it exposes hidden things. I
cried out while among you, I spoke with a
loud voice—the voice of God: "Attend to
the bishop and the presbytery and the
deacons." 2/ Those who suspected me of
saying this because I had advance information about the division of some—he is
my witness in whom I am bound that I
did not learn it from any human being. It
was the Spirit who made proclamation,
saying these words:
   "Do nothing without the bishop,
      keep your flesh as the temple of God.
   Love union,
      flee divisions.
   Be imitators of Jesus Christ,
      as he himself is of his Father."

8

1/ I, then, did my part as a man set on
union. Where there is division and anger,
God does not dwell. All, then, who repent
the Lord forgives, if they turn in repentance to the unity of God and the council
of the bishop. I believe the grace of Jesus
Christ who will remove every bond from
you.

■ **6.3** To put his argument in perspective, Ignatius recalls his stay in Philadelphia (where he was evidently given considerable freedom of movement by his captors). He begins with a word of thanks[1] that echoes Pauline passages in which the apostle expresses his satisfaction at not having depended on the resources of those addressed (1 Thess 2:7, 9; 2 Cor 11:9; 12:16; cf. *Rom.* 4.2). But that can hardly be the thought here (particularly in light of *Phd.* 7, which is presented as an explanation of 6.3), and it seems best to understand Ignatius as having put Pauline language to new use. The term "burden" (βάρος)

sometimes has to do with the weight of influence that a person has or claims (cf. 1 Thess 2:7),[2] and it is likely that Ignatius was regarded as having capitalized unfairly on his prestige as a martyr. His sensitivity on the point suggests that even his friends felt that he had gone too far. Note that although he regards his opponents as in principle excluded from the Philadelphian church (*Phd.* 3.1), they are apparently still part of the community (cf. *Phd.* 11.1).[3] In 7.2 Ignatius is on slippery enough ground that (again echoing words of Paul) he feels compelled to call on Christ as witness to the truth of his assertions.[4]

---

1   This is what Paul Schubert calls an expression of gratitude "on the colloquial, conversational level" (*Form and Function of the Pauline Thanksgiving* [BZNW 20; Berlin: Töpelmann, 1939] 83–84). Ignatius does not use the formal epistolary thanksgiving.

2   BAG *s.v.* βάρος 2, p. 133.

3   Cf. Bauer, *Orthodoxy and Heresy*, 86–88, 131–32.

4   Cf. Rom 1:9; Phil 1:8; 1 Thess 2:5; 2 Cor 1:23.

Similar appeals are found also in pagan sources: Polybius 11.6.4; Heliodorus *Aeth.* 1.25.1; Plutarch *Mul. virt.* 20, 258b; cf. Kathleen O'Brien Wicker, in Betz, *Plutarch's Ethical Writings*, 133.

The appearance of the tandem particle καὶ . . . δέ (see on *Eph.* 2.1) in the last sentence of 6.3 suggests that Ignatius turns his attention to "all" the members of a particular group with whom he had had an audience in Philadelphia. It was evidently not a pleasant interview (especially in retrospect) since he now issues a strong warning (of the type found in *Tr.* 12.3) to those with whom he had met.

■ **7.1–2** What follows reveals the source of the disagreement. As the discussion proceeded, Ignatius had become upset and had felt moved to cry out that the bishop must be obeyed. He was suspected of having been informed in advance of the situation and of having staged the response. The passage presupposes that Ignatius' opponents were part of the church and that they could not have been radically at odds with other members of the community since at first they made considerable headway with their visitor and (as he himself indicates) all but "deceived" him. Again it is hard to imagine that any serious theological disagreement—such as dispute over the person of Christ or over observance of the law— could have been involved. The words that Ignatius felt moved to utter contain no reference to such issues but only to matters of governance. Elsewhere, to be sure, the "division" (μερισμός) in the Philadelphian community is seen to involve "false teachings," but even there the main emphasis is on the problem of separatism (see on *Phd.*

2.1). If (as we shall argue) the opponents had become engrossed in problems of scriptural interpretation (see on *Phd.* 8.2; 9.1), their very expertise may have posed a threat to leaders who (like Ignatius himself) were neither skilled as exegetes nor particularly interested in the secrets of the Bible. That would explain why there was division in Philadelphia without any very obvious doctrinal dispute.

The likelihood is that Ignatius had not been informed of the situation in advance. The local bishop seems not to have been a person easily disturbed (cf. *Phd.* 1.2) and may well have seen his authority in less absolute terms than Ignatius thought appropriate. Even after the latter's visit the opposition appears to have been welcome in the Philadelphian church (cf. *Phd.* 11.1). Moreover, Ignatius' two prophetic utterances (7.1, 2) are so much part and parcel of what he always says about episcopal authority[5] that we can hardly doubt his sincerity.

Ignatius traces his outbursts to God's Spirit. He shared with many others in the Graeco-Roman world the belief that a sudden loud utterance marked the inrush of the divine.[6] The bishop clothes this perception in traditional Christian language when he denies that "human flesh" made the situation known to him (cf. Matt 16:17; Gal

---

5 Cf. *Pol.* 6.1; *Tr.* 7.2; *Sm.* 8.1, 2; *Eph.* 9.1; *Mag.* 7.2; 1.2; *Sm.* 7.2; *Eph.* 1.1; 10.3. The only unusual element is the exhortation, "keep your flesh as the temple of God" (7.2). But it is only unusual verbally. The line has a close parallel in *2 Clem.* 9.3 (cf. 8.4, 6) where it serves as a moral principle. But the same source also presents a complex (pre-Gnostic) development of the theme in which "keeping the flesh" acquires ecclesiological significance (*2 Clem.* 14.3–4; cf. Ton H. C. van Eijk, *La résurrection des morts chez les pères apostoliques* [Théologie historique 25; Paris: Beauchesne, 1974] 78–82). Thus the Christian's "flesh" is linked with the flesh of Christ which is the church. Similarly the temple is both the Christian's body (cf. 1 Cor 6:19) and the church (cf. 1 Cor 3:16–17; 2 Cor 6:16; Ign. *Eph.* 9.1; *Mag.* 7.2). (For the comparison between the believer and the hierarchy on the one hand and Christ and the Father on the other hand see on *Eph.* 3.2 and *Mag.* 6.1. For the theme of imitation see on *Rom.* 6.3.)

6 Dölger, *Antike und Christentum*, 5. 218–23; Peterson, ΕΙΣ ΘΕΟΣ, 191 (n. 3). Also note the remarkable

terminological similarities in Phlegon *De mirabilibus* 31: ἀνεκεκράγει μεγάλῃ τῇ φωνῇ λέγων τάδε "he cried out with a loud voice saying these words" (Carl Müller, *Fragmenta Historicorum Graecorum* [5 vols.; Paris: Didot, 1841–70] 3. 617); cf. Ign. *Phd.* 7.1, ἐκραύγασα . . . μεγάλῃ φωνῇ "I cried out . . . with a loud voice"; *Phd.* 7.2, λέγον τάδε "saying these words." As we have seen, other features of prophecy in Ignatius echo Hellenistic conceptions (see on *Rom.* 7.2). Note that the "spirit" also appears in descriptions of the activity of the Greek oracles (cf. Plutarch, *De defec. orac.* 40, 432de; Kathleen O'Brien Wicker, in Betz, *Plutarch's Theological Writings*, 171). Heinrich Weinel (*Die Wirkungen des Geistes und der Geister im nachapostolischen Zeitalter bis auf Irenaeus* [Freiburg: Mohr (Siebeck), 1899] 86–87) observes that the prophetic words of Ignatius in 7.2 fall into three groups of two lines of more or less equal length and that the last words of each group rime (ποιεῖτε/τηρεῖτε; ἀγαπᾶτε/φεύγετε; Χριστοῦ/αὐτοῦ). He attributes the poetic form to Ignatius' agitated state (cf. Phlegon *De mirabilibus* 31; Müller, *Fragmenta*

1:16; 1 Cor 2:13)[7] and in specifically Johannine terms when he describes the Spirit as knowing whence it comes and whither it goes (cf. John 3:8). Here we have the strongest possibility in Ignatius of a dependence directly on the Fourth Gospel. Yet in the absence of other positive evidence of such dependence the question must be left open.[8] Moreover, the Johannine writings speak of knowing the whence and whither of figures other than the Spirit,[9] and this suggests that we are dealing with a formula that could have been known to Ignatius apart from the gospel.[10] In any event, Ignatius appears before us here as one moved by the Spirit (cf. *Rom.* 7.2), yet as one who also takes it for granted that the Spirit speaks through and on behalf of established authority (cf. *Phd.* inscr).

■ **8.1** Ignatius concludes his self-defense with the remark that he did what he did because he was a man set on union. This (as we have seen) is a fair description of the bishop's dealings with everyone. But the fact that the statement is part of a self-defense is no doubt significant and reminds us that the emphasis on unity in Ignatius is intimately bound up with his desire to have the churches make a strong show of support for him and to have them close ranks behind him by eliminating dissident elements (see Introduction, 3.3). Some compromise, however, is noticeable here. For Ignatius is more ready than usual to grant the possibility of "repentance" to the errorists.[11] He is confident that Christ's "grace" (cf. *Phd.* 11.1) will release them from "every bond," that is, from the influence of Satan who prompts their separatism (cf. *Eph.* 13.1; 19.3). It is likely that his Philadelphian friends had convinced him (through the messengers mentioned in *Phd.* 11.1) to be somewhat more conciliatory.

It should be noted, in conclusion, that the "unity of God" to which Ignatius desires the schismatics "to turn in repentance" ($\mu\epsilon\tau\alpha\nu o\acute{\eta}\sigma\omega\sigma\iota\nu$) is not primarily unity with God but the unity of the church presided over by God (cf. *Phd.* 5.2). This is especially clear here since the "unity of God" and the "council of the bishop"—the circle of presbyters (cf. *Mag.* 6.1; *Tr.* 3.1)—evidently complement each other and refer to the solidarity of the community (under the ministry) of which Ignatius makes so much in this context (cf. *Phd.* 7).

Historicorum Graecorum, 3. 616).

7   For the bringing to light of "hidden things" see Rom 2:16; 1 Cor 4:5; 14:25. For the work of the Spirit in "exposing" evil see 1 Cor 14:24; John 16:8.

8   Cf. Paulsen, *Studien*, 36–37.

9   John 8:14; cf. John 7:27–28; 9:29; 12:35; 13:36; 14:5; 16:5; 1 John 2:11; Rev 7:13.

10   Gillis P:son Wetter, "Eine gnostische Formel im vierten Evangelium," *ZNW* 18 (1918) 49–63.

11   Cf. *Eph.* 10.1; *Sm.* 4.1; 5.3; 9.1.

The Judaizers in Philadelphia [5.1–9.2]

8

An Exhortation with Further Light on the Debate in Philadelphia

2   I exhort you to do nothing from partisanship but in accordance with Christ's teaching. For I heard some say, "If I do not find (it) in the archives, I do not believe (it to be) in the gospel." And when I said, "It is written," they answered me, "That is just the question." But for me the archives are Jesus Christ, the inviolable archives are his cross and death and his resurrection and faith through him—in which, through your prayers, I want to be justified.

9   **1/** The priests are also good; yet better the highpriest entrusted with the holy of holies, who alone is entrusted with the secrets of God, since he is the door of the Father through which enter Abraham and Isaac and Jacob and the prophets and the apostles and the church—all these—into the unity of God. **2/** Now the gospel has something distinctive: the coming of the Savior, our Lord Jesus Christ, his suffering and resurrection; for the beloved prophets made their proclamation with him in view; but the gospel is the completion of incorruptibility. All things together are good, if you believe with love.

■ **8.2** Ignatius now exhorts the Philadelphians—that is, his opponents among them—to abandon their contentiousness and to remember what it means to be Christian. His use of the expression παρακαλῶ ("I exhort") indicates that this is the main burden of the letter.[1]

But the need for the exhortation is immediately explained by a reference to a fragment of a debate in Philadelphia that had deeply disturbed Ignatius. What by now has become the standard interpretation of this much-disputed passage is the correct one.[2] (1) Ignatius had presented his view on some issue (we are not told

what it was). (2) His opponents say that if they do not find it in the OT, they do not "believe (it to be) in the gospel." (a) It is probably not correct on the slim authority of Mark 1:15 (πιστεύειν ἐν "believe in") to translate, "I do not believe in the gospel" (ἐν τῷ εὐαγγελίῳ οὐ πιστεύω). Ignatius could not have accomplished anything by twisting his opponents' words that badly (I take it for granted that they regarded themselves as believers in the gospel).[3] The object ("it") should be supplied in the second part of the sentence just as it is in the first. And something like the verb "to be" (or "to be found") can

---

1   Cf. Bjerkelund, *Parakalô*, 189.
2   For a review and bibliography concerning this question see William R. Schoedel, "Ignatius and the Archives," *HTR* 71 (1978) 97–106.
3   Conceivably a group of Christians could have declared rhetorically their unwillingness to believe the gospel unless it was backed up by Scripture simply to make clear the importance of Scripture to them. But then why would Ignatius have replied by saying, "It is written"? And why would they have challenged him on that as if to suggest that the truth of the gospel itself was in doubt? The answer may be

that the group was actually made up of Jews closely associated with Christianity but doubtful of its central tenets. But surely Ignatius has in mind Christians in danger of being attracted to Judaism (cf. *Phd.* 6.1)—people close enough to other members of the congregation that they almost "deceived" Ignatius (*Phd.* 7.1) and who still were (it seems) being given a hearing in Philadelphia (*Phd.* 11.1). When Ignatius indicates that "repentance" and a turning to the unity of the church is in order for this group (*Phd.* 8.1), it is likely that they were recognizably Christian.

also easily be supplied.[4] (b) The parallelism of the clauses would be needlessly destroyed by the translation "If I do not find it in the archives (that is, in the gospel), I do not believe."[5] Such a reference to a written gospel is unlikely in Ignatius.[6] (c) Any lingering doubt as to whether "archives"[7] can mean the Scriptures (OT)[8] is set aside by the curiously neglected parallel provided by Josephus.[9] In his *Contra Apionem* (1.29) the Jewish historian treats the Hebrew Scriptures (cf. 1.37–38) as literary phenomena parallel to the δημοσίαι ἀναγραφαί ("public records") of the Greeks (1.20–22) and of the societies of the Ancient Near East (1.28; cf. 1.9). Such public records, of course, are archives.[10] This is confirmed by the fact that elsewhere Josephus employs the term "archives" itself with particular reference to the Phoenician records (*C. Apion.* 1.143; cf. *Ant.* 8.144; 9.283, 287).[11] (In *C. Apion.* 1.31 and 1.35 the term "archives" is used to refer to the sources for priestly genealogies, but these play a subordinate role to the Scriptures as public records.) Note

that Philo also refers to the Scriptures as ἀναγραφαί ("records") or ἱεραὶ ἀναγραφαί ("sacred records").[12] (3) Ignatius replies that in fact, "It is written." This is the standard formula used to introduce quotations from Scripture. (a) Ignatius uses the expression only in reference to the OT (cf. *Eph.* 5.3; *Mag.* 12), and there is no convincing evidence that he puts any other source on the same level with it.[13] (b) The statement represents an effort by Ignatius to stake out his claim even on the territory claimed by his opponents. It is artificial to suppose that whereas *he* appealed to the OT, *they* appealed to (say) Jewish-Gnostic gospels ("archives").[14] The argument in *Phd.* 5.1–2 and 9.1 almost certainly presupposes that it is *they* who emphasized the importance of the OT. And it is the OT Scripture (as we have seen) that was called "archives" by Ignatius' Jewish contemporaries. (4) Ignatius' opponents retort: πρόκειται "it lies before us," that is, "that is just the question"[15] or (somewhat more mildly) "that deserves investigation."

---

4   For other examples of the omission of the verb "to be" after πιστεύω ("believe") see LSJ *s.v.* πιστεύω I.3, p. 1408.

5   The suggestion goes back especially to Zahn (*Ignatius*, 373–79).

6   A reference to a written gospel has been found in *Phd.* 8.2 without the help of Zahn's unusual punctuation of the passage. It has been argued that the opposition between (written) archives and the gospel presupposes that the gospel was also written (cf. Joly, *Ignace*, 66). But the uses of the term "gospel" elsewhere in our letter sound much more like references to a message than to a document (*Phd.* 5.1, 2; 9.2). And the remaining occurrences of the term in Ignatius by no means compel us to think that he was speaking of written sources (*Sm.* 5.1; 7.2). Ignatius' presentation of the alternative to the archives in terms of Christ's cross, death, resurrection, and (even more remarkably) faith through him (*Phd.* 8.2) surely indicates that he was not looking to anything written in this regard (cf. Paulsen, *Studien*, 43).

7   GL read ἀρχαίοις ("ancients") rather than ἀρχείοις ("archives") in the first of the three occurrences of the term. But we may assume that the same word was intended in all three places (for Ignatius to substitute "archives" for his opponents' reference to "ancients" would accomplish nothing). To reverse the procedure and read ἀρχαῖα ("ancient things") for ἀρχεῖα in the second and third places obscures rather than clarifies. The term ἀρχαῖα ("ancient things") for the OT is unparalleled and odd; and although the first

appearance of the term could be taken as a masculine (ἀρχαῖοις "ancients"), the second and especially the third (τὰ ἄθικτα ἀρχεῖα "the inviolable archives") are inescapably neuter. It should also be noted that the two terms were often confused by scribes. Thus ἀρχαῖα appears for ἀρχεῖα in Josephus *C. Apion.* 1.31 and 1.35 (but not in 1.143). Cf. Daniel Wyttenbach, *Animadversiones in Plutarchi opera moralia* (3 vols.; Leipzig: Kühn, 1820–34) 2. 422.

8   For misguided efforts to find here a reference to actual city archives, see Peterson, ΕΙΣ ΘΕΟΣ, 216–21; and Solomon Reinach, "Ignatius, Bishop of Antioch, and the ΑΡΧΕΙΑ," in W. H. Buckler and W. M. Calder, eds., *Anatolian Studies Presented to Sir William Mitchell Ramsay* (Manchester: University Press, 1923) 339–40.

9   See Schoedel, "Ignatius and the Archives," 99–101.

10   C. Dziatzko, "Archive," PW 2/1. 555.

11   He had included the Phoenicians along with the Egyptians and Babylonians in his earlier discussion of "public records" in the Ancient Near East (1.8–9).

12   *Congr.* 175; *Fuga* 132; *Somn.* 1.33, 48; 2.265, 301; *Praem.* 2.

13   Cf. Koester, *Synoptische Überlieferung*, 25.

14   Cf. Johannes Klevinghaus, *Die theologische Stellung der apostolischen Väter zur alttestamentlichen Offenbarung* (BFCTh 44/1; Gütersloh: Bertelsmann, 1948) 98–102.

15   BAG *s.v.* πρόκειμαι 2, p. 714; cf. LSJ *s.v.* πρόκειμαι I.3, p. 1485.

The verb has other meanings,[16] but none seems so appropriate as this. It is possible (in light of what follows) that Ignatius' opponents suggest engaging in exegesis: "[the archives] lie before us." But if so, it is still a challenge to the bishop's assertion that he can find what he wants in the OT. Evidently he was having difficulty in establishing his point from that quarter. (5) Consequently, Ignatius appeals to an even higher authority. For him the "archives" are Jesus Christ himself; or (as he rephrases it) the "inviolable archives"[17] are "his cross and death and his resurrection and faith through him." And Ignatius concludes by reminding his readers obliquely that the significance of his own martyrdom depends on the centrality of those same events.[18]

A similar link between Ignatius' martyrdom and Christ's passion serves elsewhere to turn back docetic error (cf. *Tr.* 10). But when Ignatius mentions the events of salvation in the passage before us, the all-important anti-docetic ἀληθῶς ("truly") is missing (cf. *Tr.* 9.1–2; *Sm.* 1.1–2.1; *Mag.* 11). It is likely, then, that the link between Christ's passion and Ignatius' martyrdom is one that he found possible to apply in more than one way. Thus the Judaizers were probably not docetists. But we have also found reason to doubt that they had a "low" christology. And we have argued that neither was the actual observance of circumcision (or the Sabbath) involved (see on *Phd.* 6.1). Perhaps, then, all that Ignatius means to say is that his opponents' preoccupation with Scripture prevented them from keeping Christ in the center of the theological stage to his satisfaction—or (to use his exaggerated words in *Phd.* 6.1) that "they do not speak concerning Jesus Christ."

The conclusion seems to be that Ignatius' opponents in Philadelphia were relatively harmless theologically. They probably represented a threat to the authorities simply because they surpassed them in exegetical expertise. The specific issue under debate may have come down to whether the Scriptures themselves anticipated a time when they would render themselves more or less obsolete and take second place to the gospel. If so, Ignatius was obviously much less skillful than writers like the authors of Hebrews or *Barnabas* in finding passages to support the thesis. The use of the term "archives" by Ignatius' opponents may give us a clue to the situation. Hellenistic Judaism's picture of the Jewish records as more ancient and impressive than Greek historical writings (Josephus *C. Apion.* 1.1–18) could have provided the spiritual anchor needed by Christians as well as by Jews. Such a Scripture would have proved attractive to gentiles for two main reasons: (a) as Josephus' discussion of the "constitution" of the Jews shows, a description of a way of life based on their archives could be remarkably free of reference to the observance of religious practices (*C. Apion.* 2.145–296); (b) as Philo's allegorization of the "sacred records" shows, Christians were left free to find Christian meaning in the Jewish texts and to lose themselves in endless theological speculation. It was the latter that evidently disturbed Ignatius.

■ **9.1** This interpretation is substantiated by what follows in *Phd.* 9.1–2. Here surely the priests of Israel are said to be good by way of concession: they are good, but the highpriest is better. Thus in Ignatius' view the excellence of the priests is of the same qualified kind as that of the prophets (*Phd.* 5.2; 9.2). The implication is that Ignatius' opponents more or less stopped at saying "the priests are good"—they found in the biblical priesthood an important subject of speculation in itself. Ignatius does not utterly refuse to become involved in such things. Thus he is close to Hebrews (9:1–12; cf. *1 Clem.* 61.3; 64.1; *Pol. Phil.* 12.2) in likening the highpriest to Christ to whom is entrusted the Holy of Holies. But his purpose in singling out the Holy of Holies is to suggest that only the highpriest should be concerned about certain "secrets of God." These "secrets" are probably exegetical secrets (as in *Barn.* 6.10) and may have had to do with details of the biblical sanctuary that even Hebrews does not attempt to elucidate. In any event, Ignatius subordinates such

---

16 See especially Lightfoot, *Ignatius*, 2. 272–73.

17 An expression most easily explained as a variant of Philo's "sacred records" (the OT Scriptures). For the close connection between what is "sacred" (ἱερός) and what is "inviolable" (ἄθικτος) see the metaphorical use of the two terms in Plutarch *Amat.* 16, 76a (Hubert Martin, in Betz, *Plutarch's Ethical Writings*, 500).

18 For the use of the term δικαιωθῆναι "to be justified"

virtually in the sense of "to attain God" see on *Rom.* 5.1.

secrets to Christ "alone" in much the same way that elsewhere he suggests leaving theological difficulties to the "one physician" (*Eph.* 7.2) or the "one teacher" (*Eph.* 15.1). Such things are not to be looked into too deeply. It is enough to recognize the sufficiency of Jesus Christ and to know that Scripture pointed forward to him.

Christ's sufficiency and his superiority over the priests is grounded in the view that he is the "door" of the Father. The closest parallel is John 10:7, 9; but the image is found in other early sources (*Herm. Sim.* 9.12–15; cf. *1 Clem.* 48.2–4) and may well have been prompted by Ps 117:20 LXX ("this is the gate of the Lord; the just will enter in it").[19] In any event, all God's people— patriarchs, prophets, apostles, the church—enter through the one door; through him "all these" (πάντα ταῦτα—all the items mentioned in the preceding list) enter "the unity of God"—are joined together as God's people in a unity that includes all generations of the faithful (cf. *Phd.* 5.2; 8.1). In all likelihood Ignatius is using themes spelled out more speculatively (though not necessarily in a Gnostic fashion) by others.[20]

The special attention to prophets and priests in this account may reflect the Hellenistic-Jewish views of Scripture already in evidence above. For prophets and priests play important and closely related roles in Josephus' account of the Jewish archives. The Jewish historian claims that only prophets (among whom is Moses; cf. Ign. *Sm.* 5.1) had the privilege of writing Scripture (*C. Apion.* 1.37, 41) but that the priests (whose pure genealogies recorded in public archives vouch for their reliability as spiritual guides) serve as the custodians

of the Bible (1.29–36). As a priest Josephus himself claims full familiarity with the sacred books and the ability to interpret them authentically (1.54). Thus when Ignatius speaks of "prophets" he also has in mind Scripture (OT) as a whole. And when he gives special attention to the priests, it is probably because others had thought of them as knowing "the secrets of God," that is, as those who were safeguarding and interpreting Scripture.

■ **9.2** Ignatius concludes the section with a summary statement of his view of the relation between the prophets (Scripture) and the gospel. The gospel goes beyond Scripture since it has something "distinctive," namely, Christ's "coming" (παρουσία is used here for the first time of the "first coming" of Christ and thus reflects the shift from eschatological to incarnational categories in Ignatius and elsewhere)[21] as well as his passion and resurrection. Yet at the same time the prophets anticipated Christ's coming. What makes the gospel distinctive is that it represents the "completion" of what the prophets could only foresee. What has been brought into being is "immortality" (cf. *Eph.* 17.1). Thus "everything" (πάντα)—Scripture and the gospel together (cf. 9.1)—is good if faith manifests itself in love (cf. Gal 5:6), that is, if it is seen that the fundamental points of Christian teaching are the burden of Scripture.

Again there is no suggestion in this summary that Ignatius has a christological heresy in view (cf. 8.2). The passage is not anti-docetic: the events of salvation are listed without elaboration, and the decisive ἀληθῶς ("truly") is missing. Nor is there any evidence that the

---

19 Bartsch, *Gnostisches Gut,* 48. Ps 117 (118) is quoted or alluded to some fifteen times in the NT (Nestle's enumeration). Verse 20 is cited for the first time in *1 Clem.* 48.2–3. The image of Christ as the door expresses the exclusive significance of the redeemer and the preeminence of spatial (rather than temporal) categories in the description of his saving work and thus lends itself to exploitation by Gnostics (Paulsen, *Studien,* 170–73).

20 Since the imagery of the "door" is probably related to that of the temple "curtain" in Hebrews (Heb 9:3; 10:20; cf. Paulsen, *Studien,* 172), this may be one of the items on which Ignatius' Philadelphian opponents were exercising their exegetical expertise.

21 Cf. Paulsen, *Studien,* 66–67. A fragment of the *Preaching of Peter* lists Christ's "coming" (παρουσία), "death," "cross," "resurrection," and "ascension"

(Clement Alex. *Strom.* 6.15, 128.1). The simpler three-member formulation of Ignatius (birth, passion, resurrection) is evidently but one among many possibilities (cf. *Mag.* 11). Ignatius is often satisfied to refer even more simply to Christ's passion and resurrection (*Eph.* 20.1; *Phd.* inscr; *Sm.* 2; 7.2; 12.2; cf. *Phd.* 8.2). It is in anti-docetic contexts that he sets out longer lists of the events of salvation (*Tr.* 9; *Sm.* 1; cf. *Eph.* 18.2).

passage is directed against a "low" christology. The title "savior," to be sure, is rare in Ignatius. But when it does occur, it does not stand opposed to any devaluation of Christ's high dignity (*Eph.* 1.1; *Mag.* inscr). On the contrary it once appears in an anti-docetic context (*Sm.* 7.1). More unusual is the term παρουσία ("coming"), which is otherwise absent from Ignatius and which is given a meaning atypical for the period. But its choice here was no doubt determined by the emphasis on Christ as the fulfillment of Scripture.[22] Ignatius is stressing the fact that for all practical purposes the christological

understanding of Scripture suffices. What the prophets announced has in fact appeared. The Christ has come. Preoccupation with Scripture from other points of view is irrelevant.

---

22 Compare the use of the term along with reference to the prophets in the *Preaching of Peter* (Clement Alex. *Strom.* 6.15, 128.1); Justin *Apol.* 1.52.3; *Dial.* 14.8; 40.4; 118.2; *Test. Levi* 8.15; *Test. Jud.* 22.2. Epiphanius cites the following logion of Jesus four times: ὁ λαλῶν ἐν τοῖς προφήταις, ἰδοὺ πάρειμι "he who speaks in the prophets—behold, I am here" (Resch, *Agrapha*, 207–8). The verb πάρειμι ("I am here") corresponds to the noun παρουσία ("coming").

10

The Closing and Farewell

1 Since it has been reported to me that in accordance with your prayer and the compassion which you have in Christ Jesus the church at Antioch in Syria is at peace, it is right for you as a church of God to appoint a deacon to undertake there an embassy of God to rejoice with them when they have assembled and to glorify the name. **2/** Blessed in Jesus Christ is he who will be counted worthy of such a service, and you too will be glorified. It is not impossible for you to do this for the name of God if you want to, just as the neighboring churches have sent bishops, and others presbyters and deacons.

11

1/ As to Philo the deacon from Cilicia, a man witnessed to, who is even now serving me in the word of God with Rheus Agathopous, an elect man, who has followed me from Syria having said farewell to life, both of whom also bear witness for you, I too thank God for you that you received them, as the Lord also receives you. But may those who dishonored them be redeemed by the grace of Jesus Christ.

2 The love of the brothers at Troas greets you whence I also write you through Burrhus who was sent with me by the Ephesians and Smyrnaeans as a token of honor. The Lord Jesus Christ will honor them, in whom they have hope in flesh, soul, spirit, faith, love, concord. Farewell in Jesus Christ, our common hope.

■ **10.1–2** The closing of the letter (10.1–11.1) is introduced by a "request formula" that includes background (marked by ἐπειδή "since") and the request proper (cf. *Pol.* 7.1). We have what appears to be an echo of the same formula in *Rom.* 1.1, where it functions more normally as a transition to the body of the letter.[1] In the passage before us the request serves to cement relations between the bishop and his addressees. Its effect is to broaden the usual purpose of the closing, however, by focussing attention on the church of Antioch.

At first sight the subject of the passage seems remote from the letter as a whole. Yet the last sentence of 11.1 almost certainly refers back to the Judaizers previously criticized by Ignatius, and his concern about the reception of the two messengers is not unrelated to his concern about his own reception among the Philadelphians. It is likely, then, that a major purpose of Ignatius' communication was not only to explain (or to defend) himself (cf. *Phd.* 6.3) but also in so doing to capitalize on what good will he had among the Philadelphians by convincing them to send a representative to his church in Antioch. The closing of the letter, then, has intimate (though not fully articulated) ties with the letter as a whole.[2]

The request for an ambassador is repeated in *Sm.* 11.2–3 and *Pol.* 7.2–3. We have assumed throughout this study that the purpose of the request was, in Harrison's words, "to confirm the Christians at Antioch in their present newly attained unity."[3] The traditional view has been that the purpose of the embassy was to

---

1 Cf. John L. White, "Introductory Formulae in the Body of the Pauline Letter," *JBL* 90 (1971) 93.
2 The situation is not unlike that in *P.Oxy.* 3.118 where a concluding exhortation picks up a special point not directly discussed in the letter but clearly related to it and obviously touched on in previous conversations.

congratulate the Antiochenes on the end of the persecution. The verb εἰρηνεύειν ("to be at peace") may be used in this way (cf. *4 Macc.* 18.4). But there are weighty objections to this interpretation: (a) "To be at peace" always refers to peace within the Christian community in the writings of the NT and the Apostolic Fathers.[4] "Peace" is also coupled with "concord" and "friendship" in the rhetorical tradition that apparently lies behind Ignatius' own preoccupation with "concord" (see on *Eph.* 13.1).[5] Moreover, the expression in 10.1, "when they have assembled" (ἐπὶ τὸ αὐτὸ γενομένοις), is always set in opposition to disunity elsewhere in Ignatius.[6] (b) Ignatius nowhere mentions a general persecution of Christians in Antioch (the arrest of one considered the leader of a disruptive group would probably have sufficed to maintain public order). (c) Ignatius' concern about unity in the church is intertwined (as we have seen) not with doubts about the endurance of the Antiochenes under persecution but with his own sense of unworthiness over against the churches—including especially the church in Antioch. Thus Ignatius now intimates (10.1) that his previous requests for prayers on behalf of the Antiochenes (*Eph.* 21.2; *Mag.* 14; *Tr.* 13.1; *Rom.* 9.1) have been answered; and such requests—requests that had been closely associated with the bishop's language of self-effacement—now cease.[7] (d) Consequently Ignatius' worry about his worthiness apparently also declines after he receives the good news from Antioch. That seems noticeable in *Phd.* 5.1 and is even more obvious here. (e) Ignatius' concern to have representatives sent to Antioch seems unusually strong if it is simply a matter of

congratulating the church after persecution. There is evidence of an elaborate plan, partly worked out in advance: nearby churches have already sent as weighty representatives as possible to Antioch (10.2);[8] from as far away as Philippi people respond to Ignatius' request to congratulate the church in Antioch (Pol. *Phil.* 13.1); the bishop makes his request even when there is some reluctance (as indicated in *Phd.* 10.2)[9] to accede to it (cf. *Sm.* 11.3; *Pol.* 7.2); and messengers have kept him informed about the situation in Antioch. All this makes sense if we recall how carefully planned Ignatius' whole journey appears to have been for calling out support from the churches on his route and how intimately such support figures in the bishop's reflections on the significance of his mission as a man set on unity (see Introduction, 3.2). It is only a short step in the argument to recognize that failure to unite the church in Antioch preyed on Ignatius' mind and that the good news had to do with the vindication of the role that he had played there. In that event, the failure of the bishop to specify more clearly the nature of the difficulty in Antioch is more understandable than his failure to mention a general persecution there.[10] The situation was delicate and required careful negotiations. It is probably not accidental that Ignatius uses the language of ancient intercivic diplomacy—χειροτονῆσαι ("appoint" or "elect"), πρεσβεῦσαι πρεσβείαν ("undertake an embassy")—to make his request.[11] The purpose of the embassies from the other churches was to make irrev-

---

3   Harrison, *Polycarp's Two Epistles*, 95.

4   Ibid., 84.

5   Dio Chrysostom *Or.* 39.2; Aelius Aristides *Or.* 27.40–46 (ed. Keil).

6   *Eph.* 13.1; *Mag.* 7.1; *Phd.* 6.2 (note that *Eph.* 13.1 is also linked with our passage by its mention of giving "glory" to God).

7   The Hebraism in 10.1—σπλάγχνα ("bowels") for "compassion"—was no doubt mediated to Ignatius through the early church (see especially Phil 1:8).

8   The argument is intended to convince the Philadelphians that Ignatius is not being unreasonable. Congregations nearer Antioch have sent bishops or at least presbyters and deacons. Ignatius is willing to settle for a deacon from Philadelphia. Even so he may have hoped for more. Note that Polycarp apparently got the impression that he himself was

being asked to represent Smyrna (Pol. *Phil.* 13.1) although Ignatius' letter to Polycarp only asks for "someone" to be sent (*Pol.* 7.2).

9   The expression "if you want to" (θέλουσιν δὲ ὑμῖν) recalls the use of the verb θέλω ("want") in *Romans*, where it is caught up in Ignatius' insistence on the importance of having deeds match words (*Rom.* 3.2; 6.1–3; 8.1).

10   Cf. Harrison, *Polycarp's Two Epistles*, 90–104.

11   R. Cagnat, "Legatio," *Dictionnaire des antiquités*, 3. 1025–27.

ocable the turn of events that vindicated Ignatius' leadership in Antioch.

■ **11.1** It remains to trace the movements of the messengers. The introductory formula περὶ δέ ("as to") forms a minor transition.[12] Having asked the Philadelphians to send a representative to Antioch, Ignatius now turns his attention to two men (Philo and Rheus Agathopous)[13] who presumably served as messengers in bringing the news of the peace in Antioch (cf. 10.1).[14] They too have had dealings with the Philadelphians. The formula περὶ δέ ("as to") implies that the role of the messengers has been a matter of some discussion. Presumably Ignatius is responding to hostile questions put to the messengers in Philadelphia and subsequently reported to Ignatius by the messengers themselves. There can be little doubt that it was their support of Ignatius (perhaps already coupled with a request to send a representative to Antioch) that caused the difficulty. The messengers were well enough received by the majority, but some "dishonored" them. Ignatius expresses the same hopes for these critics as he does for the Philadelphian Judaizers, namely, that by divine grace they may be freed from their delusion (cf. *Phd.* 8.1). No doubt we are dealing with the same group. This has always been recognized, but the corollary has not been emphasized: the Judaizers were still part of the Philadelphian congregation when Philo and Rheus Agathopous passed through. It was

Ignatius, then, and not the Philadelphians who regarded the Judaizers as excluded from the community (cf. *Phd.* 3.1–2). It is now easier to understand why the freshly confident Ignatius must proceed as cautiously as he does in this letter. People in Philadelphia were still on good terms with Judaizers and their disapproval of the messengers (and of Ignatius himself) required rebuttal.

We learn from *Sm.* 10.1 that Philo and Rheus Agathopous also passed through Smyrna. No doubt they thought that they might catch up with Ignatius there. But it was not until they reached Troas that they succeeded in doing so. And that, it seems, is why Ignatius heard there the good news that "peace" had been restored in Antioch.

■ **11.2** The concluding remarks of the letter are briefer than usual. There is a greeting of the type already met in *Tr.* 13.1 and *Mag.* 12.1 (where it is the "love" of the saints that gives the greeting). Burrhus is again mentioned, and it appears that the Smyrnaeans had joined with the Ephesians in making it financially possible for him to go on to Troas with the bishop.[15] He is said to serve either as Ignatius' scribe or (as seems more likely in light of *Rom.* 10.1) the bearer of this letter. If we were right in sensing some question about the expense involved (cf. *Eph.* 2.1), Troas would be a logical place for Burrhus to turn back (especially since Philo seems to have stayed on with the bishop from that point; cf. *Sm.*

---

12 White, *Form and Function*, 61.

13 (a) Philo was a common name (Pape/Benseler, *Eigennamen*, 1630–31; Preisigke, *Namenbuch*, 465; Foraboschi, *Onomasticon*, 332–33). (b) The name Rheus apparently does not occur elsewhere. The common Roman name Gaius is found instead in gC (and in the Berlin papyrus at *Sm.* 10.1). Lightfoot builds on this and plausibly suggests reading ῾Ραίῳ (appealing for support to the rare Latin name Raius). In any event, the Arabic (Rawus) supports the reading of a name beginning with R. (c) Agathopous ("well-footed") is not frequently encountered and serves most often as the name of slaves and freedmen or as a Roman cognomen (Pape/Benseler, *Eigennamen*, 6; Preisigke, *Namenbuch*, 5; Foraboschi, *Onomasticon*, 17).

14 (a) That Rheus Agathopous came "from Syria" probably means that he came from Ignatius' own church (cf. *Eph.* 21.2; *Mag.* 14.1; *Tr.* 13.1; *Rom.* 2.2; 5.1; 9.1; 10.2) and represented his side of the quarrel. That Philo was from Cilicia indicates that Ignatius had gained support in communities near

Antioch. (b) The statement that Philo serves Ignatius "in the word of God" does not appear to define the clerical function of the messenger but to describe his activity as dominated by the Christian message in an undifferentiated sense (cf. *Sm.* inscr: greetings are given "in a blameless spirit and the word of God"). (c) The expression used of Rheus Agathopous that he had "said farewell to life" denotes any serious commitment that counts the cost (cf. *2 Clem.* 6.5; Philo *Leg.* 325). That the messenger went on to martyrdom need not be implied.

15 (a) Ignatius' admiration for their generosity is expressed with the help of a kind of anastrophe (. . . εἰς λόγον τιμῆς· τιμήσει αὐτοὺς . . . " . . . as a token of *honor*; [the Lord] will *honor* them . . ."). (b) The list of terms used to describe the range of their hope in Christ looks like a conflation of several elements: a traditional cluster of anthropological terms—spirit, soul, body—that appears also in 1 Thess 5:23 (the Arabic supports the inclusion of the mention of the spirit in the list); faith and love (a common pair in Ignatius); and the term concord (also a favorite with

13.1) and to do one final favor by delivering the letter to the Philadelphians as well as that to the Smyrnaeans (cf. *Sm.* 12.1) as he returned.

Ignatius concludes with an only slightly adorned farewell (for the expression "our common hope" cf. *Eph.* 1.2; 21.2).

---

the bishop) added to balance the two parts of the list. In any event, the purpose of the list is to suggest the full scope of the Philadelphians' hope.

Ignatius

to the Smyrnaeans

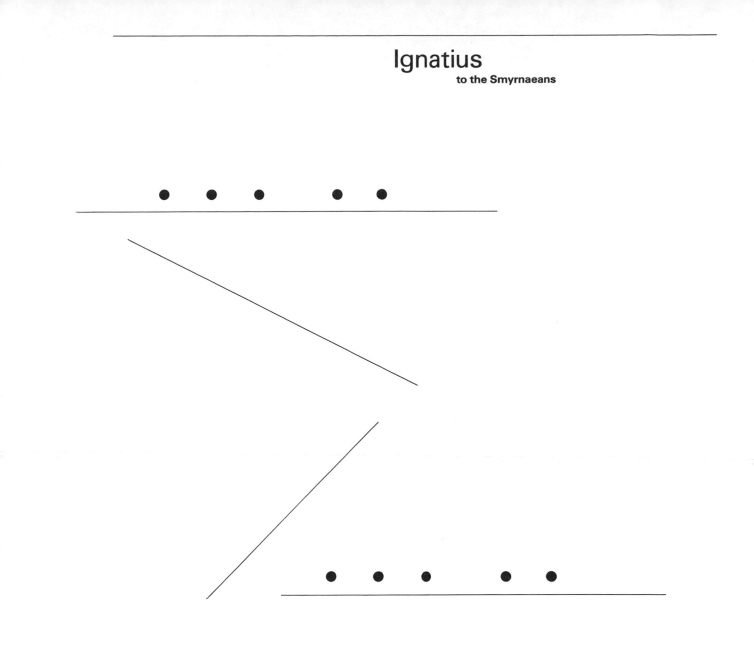

Salutation

Ignatius, also called Theophorus, to the church of God the Father and Jesus Christ the beloved—which has been shown mercy in every gift, which has been filled with faith and love, which is not lacking in any gift, most worthy of God and bearing holy things, which is in Smyrna in Asia—abundant greeting in a blameless spirit and the word of God.

The salutations in the letters to the Smyrnaeans and to Polycarp are among the shortest and simplest in the Ignatian letters, especially in comparison with those to the Ephesians, Romans, and Philadelphians. It appears that such simplicity is correlated with lack of complications in personal relations. The Smyrnaeans had provided a hospitable environment for the activity of Ignatius (*Eph.* 21.1; *Mag.* 15; *Tr.* 12.1; 13.1; *Phd.* 11.2); and their bishop, Polycarp, had made their visitor's cause his own (cf. Pol. *Phil.* 1.1; 9.1–2; 13.1–2). The Smyrnaean congregation was subject to what Ignatius regarded as disturbing external influences (*Eph.* 9.1), and the inroads of docetism were evidently significant (*Sm.* 4.1–9.2). Yet Ignatius appears more assured than usual that his audience will be responsive to him.

The theological language of the salutation has a few unusual features: (a) The identification of Jesus Christ as "the beloved" (ἠγαπημένου) is especially well illustrated from the *Ascension of Isaiah,* where it occurs frequently (3.17; 4.3; 8.18; 9.12).[1] But the many parallels from other early sources given by Lightfoot and Bauer show that the title is not necessarily associated with a particular theological tendency. (b) "Shown mercy in" means "by

God's mercy endowed with" (cf. *Eph.* 12.1; *Rom.* 9.2; *Phd.* 5.1). (c) The double appearance of the term χάρισμα ("gift" or "gift of grace"; cf. *Eph.* 17.2; *Pol.* 2.2) underscores the positive tone of the salutation. The expression "not lacking any gift" indicates that we are dealing with a reminiscence of 1 Cor 1:7. (d) "Bearing holy things" (ἁγιοφόρος) is a compound adjective of the type met with in *Eph.* 9.2. The parallel fixes the meaning as a cultic metaphor. The reference here is to the spiritual qualities that set the Smyrnaeans apart like participants in a sacred procession. (e) The use of the word "blameless" elsewhere in Ignatius (*Eph.* inscr; *Rom.* inscr; cf. *Mag.* 7.1) indicates that the expression "in a blameless spirit and the word of God" is to be taken with the final word of greeting. The phrase "blameless spirit," then, has to do with human innocence, and the expression "word of God" refers to the Christian message in the broadest sense (cf. *Phd.* 11.1) as that which shapes the believer's existence.

---

1   Cf. Daniélou, *Jewish Christianity,* 40.

1   Expression of Praise

1   I glorify Jesus Christ, the God who made
you so wise; for I perceived that you are
settled in immovable faith, having been
nailed, as it were, on the cross of the Lord
Jesus Christ both in flesh and spirit, and
established in love by the blood of Christ,
convinced as to our Lord (that he is)
    truly of the family of David according to
       the flesh,
    Son of God according to the will and
       power of God,
    truly born of a virgin,
    baptized by John
      that all righteousness might be
       fulfilled by him,

2   truly nailed for us in the flesh
    under Pontius Pilate and Herod the
       tetrarch—
       from the fruit of which are
        we,
       from his divinely blessed
        passion—
    that he might raise an ensign to the
      ages
    through his resurrection
    to his saints and believers
     whether among the Jews or
      among the Gentiles
     in the one body of his church.

■ **1.1** *Sm.* 1.1 begins with an expression of praise that serves as Ignatius' equivalent for the secular expression of joy.[1] The use of the finite verb ("for I perceived") instead of the participle to indicate the reason for rejoicing or praise is not without parallel in such formulae.[2] Here the reason for praise is based on Ignatius' memory of the Smyrnaeans from his visit with them. What he has in mind particularly is their firm opposition to docetism.

Such opposition is already hinted at in the reference to "Jesus Christ, the God who made you so wise." Like other references to Christ as teacher (*Eph.* 3.1; 15.1; *Mag.* 9.1–2), this one has in view his suffering and death which his followers learn to welcome. No doubt, as Bauer[3] notes, we have a reminiscence here of Paul's reflections on the wisdom of the cross (1 Cor 1:18–25). Ignatius goes beyond Paul in calling Christ "God." But he also adds to the title a qualifier ("who made you so wise") that has the effect of shifting attention to the estab-lishment of the bond between the Christians and their Lord (see the comments on the expression "our God" in *Eph.* inscr).

That Ignatius links Christian wisdom and the cross is made clear by the explanation that follows. For evidently the point is that the Smyrnaeans are committed to the reality of the passion. The thought is expressed with an odd play on words. The immovability of their orthodox faith is traced to the fact that they have been nailed (so to speak) to the cross. Their being nailed explains their "immovability," their being nailed to the cross indicates their acceptance of the passion. Underlying both levels of meaning is the Pauline theme of being crucified with Christ (Gal 2:19). Hints of the anti-docetic intention of the text occur in the expression "both in flesh and spirit"[4] and in the reference to the "blood" (see on *Tr.* 8.1).

■ **1.1–2.** These hints become explicit in the following collection of semi-credal statements about Christ dominated by the anti-docetic "truly." The best general

---

1   The closest parallels are provided by *Tr.* 1.1–2 and *Pol.* 1.1. But a similar pattern lies behind *Eph.* 1.1–3, *Mag.* 1.1, and *Phd.* 1.1.

2   Cf. Koskenniemi, *Studien*, 75–77.

3   *Ignatius*, 264.

4   Even though this passage (along with *Tr.* inscr; 12.1;

parallel is provided by *Tr.* 9.1–2 (and to a certain extent also *Eph.* 18.2). Many of the individual motifs, however, occur in a variety of contexts: "of the family of David" (*Eph.* 18.2; 20.2; *Tr.* 9.1; *Rom.* 7.3); "born[5] of a virgin" (*Eph.* 7.2; 18.2; 19.1; *Tr.* 9.1); "baptized" (*Eph.* 18.2);[6] crucified[7] "under Pontius Pilate" (*Mag.* 11; *Tr.* 9.1).

Other elements require more detailed attention: (a) The two lines, "of the family of David according to the flesh,[8] Son of God according to the will and power of God," apparently reflect the semi-credal tradition preserved in Rom 1:3–4 ("descended of the seed of

David according to the flesh, designated *son of God* in *power, according to* the spirit of holiness by his resurrection from the dead"). But the tradition has been significantly modified. Whereas Christ's designation as "Son of God" is connected in Paul with the resurrection, in Ignatius it is related to the Lord's birth (cf. *Eph.* 18.2).[9] Both sources agree in not associating the title "Son of God"

Rom. inscr; *Pol.* 5.1) represents one of the most perfunctory uses of the formula by Ignatius (Paulsen, *Studien*, 128 n. 31).

5   Zahn's (*Ignatius*, 467–76; *Epistolae*, 82) support of the reading of G (γεγενημένον "having come into being") and his punctuation ("truly having come into being as Son of God according to the will and power of God from the virgin") ignores the parallelism and presses unduly a correct observation about Ignatius' use of the title "Son of God."

6   The reference to Jesus as having been baptized "by John" is without parallel in such contexts but is probably traditional. For it is tied closely to the explanatory clause that follows which in turn reflects themes not typically Ignatian.

7   Ignatius speaks here of Christ being "nailed" for us in the flesh. Elze (*Untersuchungen*, 17) notes that the expression "nailed" is used in Ps 118:120 (LXX), a passage applied to the crucifixion by *Barnabas* (5.13) and Irenaeus (*Dem.* 79). Thus it is likely to be traditional. Elze also plausibly suggests that Ignatius' previous play on the word "nailed" in *Sm.* 1.1 was prompted by this tradition (just as the use of the words "bodiless" and "demonic" in *Sm.* 2 are thought to derive from the quotation in *Sm.* 3.2). The word is not used elsewhere by Ignatius. (For the formula "for us" see on *Rom.* 6.1.)

8   The expression "according to the flesh" does not occur in two parallel passages of semi-credal character in Ignatius (*Eph.* 18.2; *Tr.* 9.1; cf. *Rom.* 7.3). Elze (*Untersuchungen*, 13–15) takes this as one indication that it did not belong to the earliest form of the tradition reflected in *Sm.* 1.1. But it is hard to be very confident about that in light of the marked parallelism between our passage and Rom 1:3–4. Moreover, the appearance of the fuller formula also in *Eph.* 20.2 ("according to the flesh of the family of David") suggests that we are dealing with a traditional element that takes a variety of forms. It is true, however, that the antithesis of the Pauline formula becomes flattened out in *Sm.* 1.1 as it takes its place

in a list of events that serves to underscore the historical reality of the Lord's ministry. It is also true that this reorientation of the antithesis destroys the expected contrast between the two expressions introduced by the preposition κατά: thus "according to the flesh" now only faintly implies an opposition to what Christ is from another point of view and functions mainly to stress his humanity; and "according to the will and power of God" points to the plan that issued in the incarnation of God's Son and is thus virtually equivalent to the expression "according to God's plan" (κατ' οἰκονομίαν θεοῦ) in *Eph.* 18.2.

9   Elze argues that originally the first two lines (as he reconstructs them: "being of the family of David, Son of God according to the will and power of God") and the following two ("born of a virgin, baptized by John") refer respectively to the same two events and that consequently the designation of Christ as "Son of God" is to be associated with the baptism of Jesus (*Untersuchungen*, 14–15). This interpretation is tied in with his view that the christological tradition behind Ignatius was ultimately adoptionist (*Untersuchungen*, 23–26). Although Ignatius seems dependent on traditional material in our passage, it is possible that he drew from a variety of sources in constructing a list of the events of salvation for polemical purposes (see on *Tr.* 9) or that a predecessor had already worked along such lines. That would make the proposed distribution of lines unlikely. In any event, the situation is complicated here by the fact that when Christ's baptism is actually mentioned, it is given an explanation ("that all righteousness might be fulfilled by him") that does not reflect Ignatius' own theology and yet does not betray an adoptionistic view of the baptism. Moreover, as Elze recognizes, this explanation has a formal similarity with the purpose clause in 1.2 ("that he may raise an ensign . . .") that also looks traditional (*Untersuchungen*, 18). Thus it is not very obvious that Ignatius' source ever associated Christ's divine

with the preexistent Christ,[10] but in Ignatius the conferral of the title is pushed back in time. A corollary is that the category of incarnation emerges with greater definiteness in Ignatius. Yet his christology is not to be confused with the more highly developed specimens of a later period. Christ preexists as a distinct being (*Mag.* 6.1), but his preexistent state is not sharply defined (cf. *Mag.* 8.2). Thus the title "Son of God" no doubt expresses the fact that Christ has a divine origin (see on *Eph.* 20.2), but (at least in *Sm.* 1.1) it does not describe the relation between Father and Son in the godhead. To use the jargon of the historians of dogma, Ignatius tends to an "economic" interpretation of the godhead.

The expression "according to the will and power of God" looks like a terminological variant of the parallel in Rom 1:4 ("in power, according to the spirit of holiness"). It gathers up themes associated with Christ's birth in other sources such as John 1:13 ("will") and Luke 1:35 ("power") and later also in Justin (*Dial.* 128.4: δυνάμει καὶ βουλῇ αὐτοῦ "by his power and will"; cf. 61.1) and Tatian (*Ad Graec.* 5). Questions concerning God's power and will were to be taken up together as crucial criteria in the defense of Christine doctrine (cf. Athenagoras *De res.* 2.1–11.2). It is tempting to think that an apologetic aim accounts for their appearance as a pair already in Ignatius. If so, the phrase reflects an argument defending the incarnation on the grounds that it is consistent with God's purpose and within his power to effect.

(b) The reason given here for Christ's baptism—"that all righteousness might be fulfilled" (cf. Matt 3:15)—is different from the reason given in *Eph.* 18.2 (to purify the water).[11] The latter seems closer to Ignatius' own theological world. In any event, "righteousness" is not an Ignatian theme (cf. *Rom.* 5.1; *Phd.* 8.2). Indeed this is the one passage in which Matthew's own redaction of syn-

optic materials seems clearly evident in Ignatius.[12] Sibinga, to be sure, has denied this because of the similarity between our passage and the parallel from the *Ebionite Gospel* (Epiphanius *Pan.* 30.13.7–8: οὕτως ἐστὶ πρέπον πληρωθῆναι πάντα "thus it is right that all be fulfilled"): both use the passive form of the verb "fulfill."[13] But the word "righteousness" is missing from the Ebionite fragment. And the difference between Matthew's text, "to fulfill all righteousness" (πληρῶσαι πᾶσαν δικαιοσύνην), and that of Ignatius, "that all righteousness might be fulfilled by him" (ἵνα πληρωθῇ πᾶσα δικαιοσύνη ὑπ' αὐτοῦ), may reflect nothing more significant than the latter's desire to preserve a string of riming words at the end of the last four phrases of *Sm.* 1.1 (θεοῦ, παρθένου, Ἰωάννου, αὐτοῦ). Yet in view of the paucity of evidence elsewhere in Ignatius of reliance directly on Matthew, we must take Koester's[14] suggestion seriously that Matthew's language was mediated to Ignatius through a kerygmatic formula. Conceivably the materials on which the bishop relied were at some point used for apologetic purposes. For the reason given by Matthew for Christ's baptism aims to deflect possible misunderstanding, and other themes also possibly apologetic in character appear in *Sm.* 1–3.

■ **1.2** (c) Pontius Pilate and Herod the tetrarch are also mentioned together in connection with the crucifixion in Luke 23:6–12 (for Herod as "tetrarch" see Luke 3:1). Yet the gospel materials in Ignatius are not typically Lukan (see on *Sm.* 3.1–2), and it seems more likely that again we are in contact with a traditional theme. Koester notes that Pilate and Herod are brought together in Acts 4:25–28 where they are mentioned to prove that Ps 2 (with its reference to "kings" rising up against God's anointed) was fulfilled; and he observes that the same train of ideas in an independent form is still alive in

---

sonship with his baptism.

10 It is most improbable that Ignatius would have mentioned a pre-mundane generation of the Son from the Father between his references to Christ's lineage from David and his birth from the virgin.

11 *Gos. Phil.* (NHC 2) 72,30–73,1 brings together the baptism of Christ, purification, and the saying from Matt 3:15, giving the latter a mystical application. But although the text is broken, it seems unlikely that it spoke of the purification of the water. In any event, there is no sign of such a harmonization by Ignatius of the two explanations for Christ's baptism.

12 Koester, *Synoptische Überlieferung*, 57–59; Paulsen, *Studien*, 38–39.

13 J. Smit Sibinga, "Ignatius and Matthew," *NovT* 8 (1966) 275–77.

14 Koester, *Synoptische Überlieferung*, 57–59.

Justin (*Apol.* 1.40.5–18; cf. *Dial.* 103.4).[15] It is likely, then, that Luke 23:6–16 is an expansion of an older apologetic theme to which Ignatius is also indebted.

The phrase "from the fruit of which" probably means "from the fruit of the cross," which Ignatius has forgotten to mention but which is clearly implied.[16] If so, the fruit of the cross is the passion, as the parallel expression that follows indicates. The imagery is a variant of the picture of the cross as a tree elaborated in *Tr.* 11.2. The expression could mean "from the fruit of whom (Christ)" (Zahn) or "from which fruit (the passion)" (Lightfoot), but neither seems to yield as satisfactory a meaning. In any event, it is a parenthetical remark introduced by Ignatius to emphasize the importance of the passion.

(d) The purpose clause, "that he may raise an ensign to the ages . . . ,"[17] follows from the reference to the passion ("truly nailed"). The "ensign" ($\sigma\acute{u}\sigma\sigma\eta\mu o\nu$), then, is the cross; and as a military metaphor it anticipates the *labarum* of Constantine and the rich development of the theme in medieval piety.[18] The terminology itself ("raise an ensign"), however, is derived from Isaiah (5:26; 49:22; 62:10). An exegetical tradition probably hovers in the background. Thus the author of Ephesians offers a close parallel with his statement (Eph 2:16) that Jews and gentiles are brought together in "one body . . . through the cross" and with his allusion in the same context (Eph 2:17) to passages in Isaiah (an amalgam of Isa 52:7; 57:19).[19] Also relevant is Justin (*Dial.* 26.1–4), who quotes Isa 62:10—63:6 (and related material from the prophet) to show that the gentiles are the children of God along with the patriarchs, prophets, and the just ones born of Jacob.[20] It is perhaps from some such apologetic tradition that the reference to Jews and gentiles in Ignatius comes. In any event, the fact that this concern for the unity of the two societies in the church is not characteristic of Ignatius (cf. *Phd.* 6.1) and that the theme goes beyond his immediate purpose indicates that he is dependent on traditional materials here.

Also unusual for Ignatius is the reference to Christ's church as "one body" (cf. Eph 2:16). The image hovers in the background of two other passages (*Eph.* 4.2; *Tr.* 11.2), but only here does it come to clear expression. Although it no doubt echoes a mythological (though not necessarily Gnostic)[21] conception of the church, Ignatius (or his source) has in mind primarily the historical reality of the universal church that represents in its inclusion of

---

15 Ibid., 26–27.

16 Bauer, *Ignatius*, 265.

17 The expression "to the ages" ($\epsilon\grave{\iota}\varsigma$ $\tau o\grave{\upsilon}\varsigma$ $a\grave{\iota}\hat{\omega}\nu a\varsigma$) has primarily temporal significance ("forever") since the phrase "to ($\epsilon\grave{\iota}\varsigma$) his saints and believers" indicates the envisioned audience. In *Eph.* 8.1, on the other hand, the use of the dative in the expression "famous to the ages" ($\delta\iota a\beta o\acute{\eta}\tau o\upsilon$ $\tau o\hat{\iota}\varsigma$ $a\grave{\iota}\hat{\omega}\sigma\iota\nu$) suggests that "ages" has spatial significance and refers to the world. The difference may owe something to the influence of Ignatius' source in our passage. In any event, there can be no reference here to ages (or aeons) as heavenly powers (cf. *Eph.* 19.1). For a Gnosticized account of a "sign" that does appear to heavenly powers see *Great Pow.* (NHC 6) 41,14–42,23: at the success of the revealer's mission the archons rise up against him and bring him down into hell; they cannot master him and wonder about his identity; "they did not know that this is the sign ($\sigma\eta\mu\epsilon\hat{\iota}o\nu$) of their dissolution and the change of the aeon"; also mentioned is "the sign of the coming aeon" that will appear after he leaves hell.

18 Adolf Harnack, *Militia Christi* (Tübingen: Mohr [Siebeck], 1905) 20.

19 For the connection in early sources between the symbolism of the cross and the gathering together of the "two peoples" see Daniélou, *Jewish Christianity*, 279–80. It should be noted that whereas the Isaianic amalgam alluded to in Ephesians admits of application to both gentiles and Jews (those "far" and "near"), Isa 5:26 speaks only of the gentiles. But since the latter are referred to as those "far," it is likely that the passages were linked in the minds of the interpreter. In any event, the raising of the "ensign" to the gentiles in Isa 49:22 and 62:10 has in view the restoration of the people of Zion. And in Isa 11:12 the raising of a "sign" ($\sigma\eta\mu\epsilon\hat{\iota}o\nu$) has similar significance.

20 Note that in *Mag.* 10.3 the mission to the gentile world is also linked with the echo of an Isaianic passage.

21 For the view that the image of the body of Christ is rooted in a widely diffused conception of God as the "Makroanthropos" see Karl Martin Fischer, *Tendenz und Absicht des Epheserbriefes* (FRLANT 111; Göttingen: Vandenhoeck & Ruprecht, 1973) 48–78.

Jews and gentiles the fulfillment of Isaiah's prophecies. There is some justification, then, for comparing the bishop's reference to the church as "one body" with the more mundane use of the expression in Graeco-Roman political and social thought.[22]

It is possible, as Elze[23] has argued, that the reference to the resurrection in this context has been awkwardly interpolated into the source by Ignatius. Ignatius would not have been alone, however, in seeing the power of the cross (as a symbol) confirmed by the resurrection.[24] In any event, the mention of the resurrection here has the effect of making a separation between *Sm.* 1 and the closely related materials in *Sm.* 2–3.

In its present form *Sm* 1.1–2 has a clear anti-docetic purpose. Yet the explanation of the character of some of the events of salvation (such as the birth and baptism) and the defense of the reliability of the reports about others (particularly the resurrection; see on *Sm.* 3.2) seem to echo arguments more broadly conceived. Thus the anti-docetic thrust of the passage may represent a development of apologetic concerns.[25] In any event, the structure of the traditional themes involved became significantly modified as they were adapted to new purposes. In particular, the antithesis between the earthly and exalted Christ has all but disappeared so that even the resurrection serves primarily to account for the significance of the "ensign" (the cross) as the center of the church's mission in unifying people. Apologetic concerns and fear of docetism, then, helped shift attention from exaltation to incarnation and from eschatology to ecclesiology.

---

22 See Kathleen O'Brien Wicker (in Betz, *Plutarch's Theological Writings,* 167) commenting on Plutarch *De defec. orac.* 29, 426a.

23 *Untersuchungen,* 19. He follows the commentators in noting that the "ensign" of Isa 5:26 was associated exclusively with the cross by Jerome (who was probably dependent on Origen here) in his commentary on the passage (*In Isaiam* 2).

24 Cf. Daniélou, *Jewish Christianity,* 266–70. Note especially *Gos. Pet.* 10.39–42 where we are told that the cross followed Christ from the tomb (cf. *Barn.* 12.1).

25 The list of the events of salvation in the *Preaching of Peter* (Clement Alex. *Strom.* 6.15, 128.1) where they are associated with proof from prophecy, indicates that the practice of cataloguing the major incidents of the Lord's ministry could also serve an apologetic purpose: Christ's coming, death, cross, punishments, resurrection, and ascension are mentioned. Note that the list of events here in Ignatius also reflects an interest in the fulfillment of prophecy (*Sm.* 1.2).

2   **The Reality of Christ's Passion and Resurrection**

For he suffered all this for us that we might be saved; and he truly suffered just as he also truly raised himself, not as some unbelievers say that he suffered in appearance, whereas it is they who are (mere) appearance; and just as they think, so it will happen to them, being bodiless and demonic.

3   1/ For I know and believe that he was in the flesh even after the resurrection. 2/ And when he came to those about Peter, he said to them: "Take, handle me, and see that I am not a bodiless demon." And immediately they touched him and believed, being intermingled with his flesh and spirit. Therefore they despised even death and were found to be above death. 3/ And after the resurrection he ate and drank with them as a being of flesh, although spiritually united with the Father.

The next two sections (2.1–3.3) are more openly argumentative than the preceding one and may be regarded as reflecting more directly Ignatius' own views. Yet the subject matter (though narrowed to the passion and resurrection) is the same, and the special material on the resurrection in 3.2–3 may well have had a connection with the semi-credal material in 1.1–2.

■ **2** At the heart of Ignatius' discussion of the reality of Christ's passion and resurrection[1] is his reflection on the term "appearance." This reflection has its closest parallel in *Tr.* 10, where docetism is also said to tell us more about the unreality of its proponents than about the nature of Christ.[2] Here, however, the argument is more fully elaborated. For Ignatius goes on to deny his docetic opponents any share in salvation by arguing that the beliefs of those who deny the reality of the passion will turn against them: they will have no share in the resurrection. For resurrection implies the reality of Christ's passion, and a denial of the latter eliminates the hope of

the former. That the docetists deprive themselves of resurrection by their beliefs is the argument again in *Sm.* 7.1 (cf. 5.3). In the present passage, however, Ignatius refers to this loss in terms of their being—and so also becoming—"bodiless" ($\dot{\alpha}\sigma\dot{\omega}\mu\alpha\tau\omega$) and "demonic" ($\delta\alpha\mu\nu\nu\iota\kappa\omega$). This surprising variation—all the more surprising because Ignatius draws a conclusion about the resurrection of the docetists from what they think about the passion without mentioning his reading of their view of Christ's resurrection which (as we shall see) he actually has in mind—is more likely to have been prompted by the expression "bodiless demon" in the tradition presently cited (3.2) rather than to have been created by Ignatius for this context.[3] At the same time, however, the docetists apparently spoke of the resurrection positively and probably taught a spiritualized version of it;[4] and thus Ignatius' reference to their becoming bodiless and demonic must also have functioned to make

---

1   Only here does Ignatius speak of Christ raising himself. For this there are Johannine parallels (John 2:19; 10:18). Elsewhere Ignatius reflects the more common view of the NT that God raised Jesus from the dead. Since the latter formulation appears not only in an anti-docetic context that relies on semi-credal material but also in one that does not (*Tr.* 9.2; *Sm.* 7.1), it is unlikely that a reference to Christ's self-

resuscitation had special anti-docetic significance for Ignatius and that he necessarily used it here to replace the more conventional formulation.

2   The other point made in *Tr.* 10, that docetism makes nonsense of Ignatius' martyrdom, is taken up again in *Sm.* 4.2.

3   See nn. 5–7 below.

4   Ignatius' statement that he believes Christ to be in

225

the point not only that they would lack bodily substance (which would not have concerned them) but also that what they thought of as a rarefied spiritual state would in fact be "demonic" in character.[5]

■ **3.1** Ignatius emphasizes the reality of the passion by declaring his certainty that Christ was in the flesh even after the resurrection (this subordination of arguments about the resurrection to those about the passion explains why in section 2 above Ignatius derives a cheerless view of the future of the docetists directly from their denial of the passion without explicitly mentioning his reading of their view of Christ's resurrection that he has in mind).

■ **3.2** The proof of this assertion follows in 3.2 where a tradition about the resurrection is quoted.[6] This tra-

dition is closely related to Luke 24:39 ("see my hands and my feet that it is I; handle me and see that a spirit does not have flesh and bones as you see me have"). Yet Ignatius is probably not simply presenting a loose version of the Lukan text since further evidence for dependence on Luke is virtually absent in Ignatius (see on *Sm.* 1.2; *Pol.* 2.1) and because the terms "bodiless and demonic" in *Sm.* 2, otherwise foreign to his vocabulary, were presumably prompted by the exact wording of the tradition under discussion.[7] Jerome claims to have found the source of this tradition in the *Gospel according to the Hebrews* (*De vir. ill.* 16; *In Isaiam* 18. prol.). But especially since Eusebius (who had studied the gospel) had previously failed in an effort to locate the source of Ignatius' quotation (*Hist. eccl.* 3.36.11), either Jerome

---

the flesh "even" (καί) after the resurrection (3.1) suggests that his opponents could have found support for their docetism especially in the mysterious coming and going of the resurrected Christ.

5 The positive assessment of all that is bodiless in Hermetic and Gnostic texts (cf. Paulsen, *Studien*, 142 nn. 50–51) is perhaps the strongest reason for believing that Ignatius picked up language used by his opponents and turned it against them both here and in his version of the saying of Jesus in 3.2. If they said, "In the resurrection Christ was bodiless and spiritual" (or, to take a clue from Luke 24:39, "spirit without flesh and bones"), it would make sense for Ignatius to reply, "Thus you too are (and will be) bodiless—and demonic!" But would he have gone on to change the saying of Jesus in 3.2 (assuming that he knew it in a form closer to Luke 24:39) to reflect the polemical distortion of the language that we have here? Would he not have accomplished more by letting the traditional form of the saying known to him ("a spirit does not have flesh and bones . . .") stand in 3.2 so that the point of his choice of words in 2 (the reference to what is "demonic" in place of that which is "spirit") would be more marked and he could gain the advantage of quoting the saying in a familiar form? Is it not more likely, then, that he derived his language from the saying of Jesus as reported in 3.2 and that he found it a convenient vehicle for bringing into focus what he took to be the implications of docetic theology? Thus it would be from the saying that he derived his view that his opponents spoke of the resurrected Christ as bodiless and demonic and on that basis took the opportunity to assess their own prospect as one of being bodiless and demonic. A play on the word "spiritual," then, would be secondary. For it is not hard to imagine

that Ignatius would have recognized the opportunity presented to him by the saying of Jesus to throw his opponents' enthusiasm for all that is spiritual back at them. Or more simply, the wordplay did not involve the term "spiritual" but had to do with the use of the term "demonic" (phantom-like) in the saying of Jesus, taken more or less accurately as the key to docetic theology by Ignatius, and his use of the same term in a different sense (anti-divine) to express disapproval. (See also n. 7.)

6 Zahn (*Epistolae*, 85–87) suggested that instead of καί ὅτε ("and when") we expect ὅτε γάρ ("for when") in the introduction to the saying and that the abrupt transition betrays Ignatius' reliance on an apocryphal tradition. At the same time, it must be noted that the comment that follows the saying flows from it without a break even though it apparently reflects the language of Ignatius himself. But Ignatius' contribution to the line may well be confined (as we shall see) to the expression "being intermingled with his flesh and spirit."

7 P. Vielhauer ("Jewish-Christian Gospels," HSW, *NT Apocrypha*, 1.129–30) views our passage as dependent on Luke 24:36–43. His argument depends on seeing Ignatius' use of the words "bodiless and demonic" (in *Sm.* 2) as his own—the first an echo of the Gnostic understanding of redemption as liberation from the body, the second a polemical distortion of the term "pneumatic" applied by the Gnostics to themselves. But it is quite unsure that Ignatius' docetic opponents had Gnostic views as highly developed as such a polemical distortion would presuppose. We have dealt with what may be regarded as a refined form of the same argument above (see above n. 5) and have concluded that although a wordplay is involved, it apparently does not depend on having Ignatius

was confused,[8] or found no more than a partial parallel in this gospel,[9] or had a copy of it to which the saying had been added later (Lightfoot). Origen knows a saying from the *Teaching of Peter* (in this instance probably the *Preaching of Peter*)[10] in which Jesus says, "I am not a bodiless demon" (*De princ.* praef. 8). But direct literary dependence by Ignatius on this document is hardly the only possibility, and "the attribution of the sentence to this Kerygma or to a lost Teaching of Peter remains an assumption."[11] Thus it is perhaps most likely that Luke and Ignatius rely on common tradition.[12]

The tradition was admirably suited to Ignatius' antidocetic purpose, especially since he or his source makes it explicit that the disciples actually touched Jesus.[13] The point appended to this (that they were "intermingled with his flesh and spirit") reflects Ignatius' own vocabulary: "flesh and spirit" is an expression of which he is fond (see Introduction, 5.6), and *Eph.* 5.1 offers the best commentary on the meaning of the term "intermingled."

■ **3.2-3** After a puzzling line about the apostles and their attitude toward death (to which we shall return in a moment) traditional material is again clearly in evidence (3.3). Here Ignatius joins Luke in pointing out that Jesus proved the reality of his resurrection by eating (Luke 24:41-43; cf. John 21:5, 13), although as in *Tr.* 9.1 Ignatius refers to both eating and drinking (cf. Acts 10:41). Once again, however, the point appended to this (that Christ was all the time "spiritually united with the Father") echoes Ignatius' own theology (cf. *Mag.* 7.1).

The puzzling remark that the apostles "despised even death . . ." (3.2) may be said to anticipate the discussion of Christian martyrdom in *Sm.* 4.2; but it does so in terms not characteristic of Ignatius and leaves the impression of being at least partly unassimilated. "Despising death" was

---

change the wording of the saying of Jesus. It remains significant, then, that this terminology appears only in close proximity to the saying in 3.2 and not elsewhere (including *Tr.* 10, which presents the same kind of argument). Another background for it is perhaps suggested by Theophilus of Antioch (*Ad Aut.* 1.10) who after referring to the pagan gods as mere "idols" (εἴδωλα), "works of men's hands," and "impure demons" (δαιμόνια ἀκάθαρτα) adds a wish reminiscent of Ignatius' argument here: "May those who make them and hope on them become such as they" (cf. Zahn, *Epistolae*, 85). There is the possibility (as we shall see) that Ignatius' source originally insisted on the reality of the resurrection against pagan criticism and thus reflects language associated with debates about the reality of gods and divine men (see n. 21).

8 Cf. Koester, *Synoptische Überlieferung*, 45–56.

9 Resch, *Agrapha*, 246–47.

10 Cf. Ernst von Dobschütz, *Das Kerygma Petri* (TU 11/1; Leipzig: Hinrichs, 1893) 82–84, 134.

11 Vielhauer, "Jewish-Christian Gospels," 1.129. He suggests that the saying may have passed from Ignatius to the *Teaching of Peter* (ibid., 130). The opposite view is defended by Joly (*Ignace*, 53–54), who believes that *Sm.* 3.2 betrays its relatively late date by its dependence directly on the *Teaching of Peter*. He points to the identity of the saying in the two sources and the fact that in Ignatius it is precisely to the circle of Peter that it is spoken. Although this ignores too easily other possibilities, it may be significant (as we shall see) that the account figured in an apologetic context.

12 Paulsen (*Studien*, 39–41, 141–42) also favors this conclusion in spite of his judgment that direct dependence on Luke cannot be ruled out. It is not possible, however, to confirm this view (as was once done) by treating the Lukan and Ignatian passages as variant translations of a Semitic original (cf. Resch, *Agrapha*, 96–98; Dobschütz, *Das Kerygma Petri*. Since Luke has "the Eleven" and those with them affirm that Christ first appeared to Peter (Luke 24:34; cf. 1 Cor 15:5) and then goes on to say (in introducing the exchange about the reality of the resurrected Christ) that Christ also appeared to the whole group of disciples (with no special mention of Peter), we may have evidence that the third evangelist has reduced Peter's role and that *Sm.* 3.2 preserves an original feature in this respect. But it seems equally possible that in some circles the theme of Peter's leadership would have intruded itself into contexts from which it had originally been absent.

13 The clarification could well have been part of the tradition. Cf. John 20:24–29 (Thomas is invited to put his finger on the marks of Jesus' wounds); *Epist. apost.* 11–12 (Christ denies being a ghost or demon; Peter is the first to be invited to put his finger on the nail-prints; Christ is described as having arisen "truly in the flesh"; and the apostles are said actually to have felt him). Cf. Carl Schmidt, *Gespräche Jesus mit seinen Jüngern nach der Auferstehung* (TU 43; Leipzig: Hinrichs, 1919) 298–300.

widely admired especially as a military virtue in Hellenism.[14] And in Josephus such behavior is often attributed to the heroes of the Jewish War.[15] At the same time, the theme becomes an important one in Josephus' defense of the Jewish way of life.[16] And it plays a similar role also in early Christian apologetics.[17] It seems likely, then, that we are dealing with an apologetic theme which Ignatius found associated with the resurrection tradition under discussion.

The question arises whether this resurrection tradition was itself originally apologetic in character. Skepticism about the resurrection was no doubt expressed at an early point by Jews and pagans. And an insistence on the bodily nature of the resurrected Christ could be expected to counter suggestions that the disciples had been deceived by hallucinations. If Luke's version of the tradition under discussion is not clearly anti-docetic, that may be because it reflects a broader purpose.[18] The following observations support the view that an earlier function of the tradition was apologetic: (a) The reference to the eating and drinking of the disciples with Christ after the resurrection in Acts 10:41 is in a speech that Peter makes at the conversion of Cornelius (Acts 10:34–43). The theme is associated with an emphasis on the reliability of the disciples as witnesses. Note that there is possible contact between *Sm.* 1–3 and Peter's speech in Acts 10 also in the emphasis on the openness of

Christianity to gentiles in light of prophecy (cf. *Sm.* 1.2) and in the listing of events from the ministry of Christ. (b) The same resurrection tradition or something like it was apparently taken up into the *Preaching of Peter,* an early document more or less apologetic in character.[19] (c) Also more or less apologetic in character are the Christian elements in the *Sybilline Oracles* (8.318–19) which emphasize the fact that the resurrected Christ will have the same flesh as he had before. (d) Justin (*Dial.* 51.2) mentions Christ's eating and drinking with his disciples in his version of the passion predictions. This is presented as proving that, however ambiguous the words of OT prophecy may seem, the predictions of Christ himself were clearly fulfilled. Again the apologetic function of the theme is obvious. (e) A fascinating parallel is found in Philostratus' *Life of Apollonius* (8.12) where we learn that near the end of his life Apollonius mysteriously disappeared from the court room in which he was being tried before the emperor Domitian (cf. 8.5; 8.8) and afterward reappeared to two disciples, one of whom asks whether the sage is alive or dead. Then "Apollonius stretched out his hand and said, 'Take me (λαβοῦ μου);[20] if I slip from your grasp, I am a phantom (εἴδωλον)[21] come to you from Persephone . . . ; if I remain firm under your touch (ἀπτόμενον),[22] persuade also Damis that I am alive and that I have not thrown off my body (καὶ μὴ ἀποβεβληκέναι τὸ σῶμα).' They were no

---

14 E.g., Dio Cassius *Hist. Rom.* 46.26.2; 46.28.4; 62.25.1.

15 *Bell.* 2.60, 377; 3.356, 475; 5.458; 6.33, 42; 7.406.

16 *C. Apion.* 2.146, 232–35, 294; cf. *4 Macc.* 7.16; 13.1.

17 Justin *Apol.* 1.25.1; 2.10.8; 2.11.8; Tatian *Ad Graec.* 11.1; 19.1; cf. Lucian *Peregr.* 13. Also note the grudging recognition by Epictetus (*Diss.* 4.7.2) and Marcus Aurelius (11.3.2) of Christian fortitude in the face of death and other misfortunes.

18 The "original purpose" of Luke 24:36–43 "may have been polemical—to allay any suspicion that the disciples had been victims of an apparition or hallucination in their resurrection faith" (S. MacLean Gilmour, "The Gospel According to Luke," *The Interpreters' Bible* [12 vols.; New York and Nashville: Abingdon-Cokesbury, 1952–57] 8. 430). The passage may be anti-Gnostic (Charles H. Talbert, *Luke and the Gnostics* [New York and Nashville: Abingdon, 1966] 30–31), but this is by no means certainly so (cf. Richard J. Dillon, *From Eye-Witness to Ministers of the Word: Tradition and Composition in Luke 24* [AnBib 82; Rome: Biblical Institute, 1978]

184–203). The issue is complicated by the problem of the relation between Luke 24:36–43 and (another possibly anti-Gnostic passage) John 20:19–29 (cf. Jean-Marie Guillaume, *Luc interprète des anciennes traditions sur la résurrection de Jésus* [EtBib; Paris: Lecoffre, 1979] 163–201).

19 Cf. Edgar Hennecke, *Neutestamentliche Apokryphen* (2d ed.; Tübingen: Mohr [Siebeck], 1924) 143–46.

20 In *Sm.* 3.2 Jesus says λάβετε ("take"). This word is not found in Luke 24:39 ("see my hands and my feet . . . ; handle me and see . . .").

21 See n. 7 for a passage from Theophilus in which the word εἴδωλον (in a different sense, yet one that emphasizes the unreality of the "idol") is closely related to the word "demon." Whatever may be thought of these linguistic links, Philostratus' "phantom come to you from Persephone" and Ignatius' "bodiless demon" both refer to spiritual beings that lack corporeal substance.

22 In *Sm.* 3.2 Jesus says ψηλαφήσετέ με ("handle me"), which is exactly parallel to Luke 24:39. Ignatius goes

longer able to disbelieve (ἀπιστεῖν). . . ."[23] This shows either how pagans regularly defended the credentials of a holy man like Apollonius or (as seems more likely) how certain pagan opponents of Christianity went about providing an alternative to the story of Christ. In any event, the theme has no connection with docetism or anti-docetism but shows how accounts of bodily reap-pearance were taken to confirm the authenticity of the divine man and his message. There is a good possibility, then, that the tradition preserved by Ignatius was an apologetic one refashioned by the bishop for anti-docetic purposes.

---

right on to say, however, that "they touched him" (αὐτοῦ ἥψαντο).

23 Ignatius says that the apostles "touched him and believed (ἐπίστευσαν)."

4   Warning Against Docetic Doctrine

1   Now I urge these things on you, beloved, knowing that you are of the same mind; but I am guarding you in advance from beasts in human form, whom not only ought you not receive, but if possible not even meet; rather only pray for them if somehow they may repent, which is difficult. That is in the power of Jesus Christ, our true life. 2/ For if those things were done by our Lord (only) in appearance, I too am in bonds (only) in appearance. And why indeed have I given myself up to death, to fire, to sword, to wild beasts? But near the sword, near God; with the beasts, with God; only in the name of Jesus Christ to suffer with him! I endure all things since he, the perfect human being, empowers me.

5   1/ Whom some in their ignorance deny, or rather have been denied by him, being advocates of death rather than of the truth; whom the prophecies did not persuade nor the law of Moses, nor indeed until now the gospel nor our own individual sufferings. 2/ Indeed they have the same opinion about us. For what benefit will anyone do me, praising me but blaspheming my Lord by not confessing that he is the bearer of flesh? Anyone who does not say this denies him completely and is the bearer of a corpse. 3/ Their names, which are faithless, it did not seem right to me to record; indeed, I would rather not even remember them until they repent in regard to the passion, which is our resurrection.

6   1/ Let no one be deceived: even heavenly powers and the glory of angels and the rulers, both visible and invisible, if they do not believe in the blood of Christ, are also subject to judgment. He who can receive this, let him receive it. Let (high) position inflate no one; for faith and love are everything, to which nothing is preferable.

Warning (mixed with argument) against docetic doctrine is the substance of *Sm.* 4.1–6.1.

■ **4.1** The opening exhortation is marked by the use of the verb παραινῶ ("I urge"), which serves (both here and in *Mag.* 6.1) as a variant of the more usual παρακαλῶ ("I exhort"). It draws attention—as the first appearance of the formula in a letter regularly does—to the burden of the communication: avoid docetic teaching. The use of the vocative ("beloved") is a frequent feature of exhortations of this kind.[1] The impression of polite interchange between equals—an impression that such formulae seek to convey even when a ruler and cities under his authority deal with one another[2]—is underscored by the fact that Ignatius makes his exhortation

---

1   Bjerkelund, *Parakalô,* 17.
2   Ibid., 59–74.

"knowing" (εἰδώς) that his addressees agree with him. For such phraseology one may compare *P.Oslo.* 3.148: "although knowing (εἰδώς) that you need no exhortation because you have a different [that is, the correct] view and good sense (and I should not think it fit to explain more fully to one who can exhort others), I adjure you. . . ."[3] There are other expressions in Ignatius that have the same epistolary function (see on *Eph.* 4.1).

As in *Mag.* 11 and *Tr.* 8.1, Ignatius claims merely to be guarding his addressees from trouble in advance. We have seen that this kind of statement cannot be taken too literally in those letters. Yet the language still suggests a reasonable sense of security. Ignatius himself is apparently reminded of the situation in Ephesus: the false teachers are "beasts" (as in *Eph.* 7.1);[4] they are not to be "received" (παραδέχεσθαι as in *Eph.* 9.1, although there Ignatius speaks of not receiving their teaching);[5] their repentance is difficult (cf. *Eph.* 7.1; 10.1); and that is to be left in the hands of Jesus Christ (as in *Eph.* 7.1–2). The Smyrnaeans, to be sure, are to pray for the false teachers, whereas the Ephesians are only asked to pray for their pagan persecutors of whose repentance Ignatius is more hopeful (*Eph.* 10.1). But the difference seems inconsequential.

Thus the false teachers of *Sm.* 4.1 may have a connection with the troublesome persons mentioned in *Eph.* 9.1 (cf. 7.1) who had travelled from Ephesus to Smyrna. Moreover, *Phd.* 11.1 shows that Ignatius elsewhere has travellers in mind when he talks about "receiving" people. Yet we have also seen how uncertain it is that the unwelcome visitors mentioned in *Eph.* 9.1 were teachers of docetism, and the notices about the false teachers in Smyrna seem to indicate that they were local people (cf. *Sm.* 5.3; 6.1; 7.1; 8.1). It may only be, then, that Ignatius would like to have thought that the docetists were the dupes of outside agitators.

■ **4.2** The argument against docetism—that it makes nonsense of Ignatius' martyrdom—has been met before (*Tr.* 10). The bishop reinforces the point with a dramatic rhetorical question in which he envisions his death in terms of fire, sword, and wild beasts. Elsewhere he clearly expects to die by being thrown to the beasts (*Eph.* 1.2; *Tr.* 10; *Rom.* 4.1). Yet there is nothing problematic here. For the words "fire, sword, wild beasts" function rhetorically to underscore Ignatius' commitment to martyrdom;[6] and they may well move to a climax, as the expressions that follow almost certainly do: "near (ἐγγύς) the sword . . . , with (μεταξύ) the beasts. . . ." Apparently Ignatius is referring to three possible ways in which criminals and other undesirables were done away with in the arena. An instance of men thrown to beasts and a writer of farces burned in the middle of the amphitheater under Caligula is mentioned by Suetonius (*Calig.* 27.4). By "sword" Ignatius may refer to the *coup de grâce* administered to victims of other forms of execution (cf. *Mart. Polyc.* 16.1), but it is more likely that he had in mind another possibility known to us particularly from Seneca (*Ep.* 7.3–5), who speaks of men thrown to wild beasts in the morning and of criminals executed at midday by having them slay one another with a single sword passed along in succession.[7]

Ignatius responds to his own question by saying in effect that death will bring him to God. "Near the sword, near God" has clear affinities with a saying of Jesus reported in *Gos. Thom.* 82; Origen (*Hom. in Jer.* 20.3); and Didymus (*In Psalm.* 88.8: ὁ ἐγγύς μου ἐγγὺς τοῦ πυρός, ὁ δὲ μακρὰν ἀπ᾽ ἐμοῦ μακρὰν ἀπὸ τῆς βασιλείας "he who is near me is near the fire; he who is far from me is far from the kingdom"). Also involved in the discussion, however, is a pagan proverb noted by Bauer[8] from a late

3 Ibid., 41–42.

4 The expression "beasts in human form" has, as Lightfoot notes, good parallels in Philo (*Migr. Abr.* 33; cf. *Mos.* 1.43; *Dec.* 80).

5 For a demand to avoid contact with false teachers as stringent as *Sm.* 4.1 see 2 John 10–11 (cf. Titus 3:10; *Did.* 11.1–2; *Sm.* 7.2).

6 Similarly Cyprian (*De habit. virg.* 6) throws out what is probably a traditional list of horrors when he speaks of the fate awaiting martyrs as *ignes aut cruces aut ferrum aut bestias* "fire or cross or sword or wild beasts."

7 Cf. George Lafaye, "Gladiator," *Dictionnaire des antiquités*, 2. 1573. Seneca's mention of "fire and sword" in this connection is not directly relevant since it has to do with the oath in which the gladiator swears to fight to the death (Giuseppe Scarpat, *Lettere a Lucilio libro primo epp. I–XII* [Brescia: Paideia, 1975] 144). Ignatius could not have been referring to beheading by the sword since that was reserved for people of standing (see on *Rom.* 5).

8 BAG s.v. ἐγγύς 3, p. 213; cf. *Paroem. Gr.* 2.228.

collection attributed to Aesop: ὁ ἐγγὺς Διός, ἐγγὺς κεραυνοῦ "he who is near Zeus is near the lightning" (*Aesop. prov.* 7). (a) If Ignatius was dependent on the saying of Jesus, he was interested only in the first part of it and reversed its meaning. The substitution of sword for fire was natural enough if the words "fire, sword, beasts" move to a climax and if Ignatius felt constrained to limit the following elaboration to two of the three items. But the change in meaning is still significant. (i) If the word "fire" in the saying refers to a time of trouble,[9] the first part of the saying has to do with counting the cost of discipleship. Ignatius, on the other hand, speaks of the glorious outcome of enduring suffering. (That may be an implication of the saying of Jesus taken as a whole; but the condensation and reorientation of the thought as we have it here changes its whole character.) (ii) If the word "fire" refers (or was taken to refer) to a divine power,[10] Ignatius presents an entirely new application of it (by taking the word more literally and substituting something more or less equivalent to it). In any event, the reversal of the order in Ignatius' form of the saying (sword/God *vs.* Christ/fire) represents more than a superficial variation. (b) If Ignatius was dependent on the proverb, he reversed not only the order of its parts but also its meaning. For the proverb is best explained in light of another that is taken as a recommendation to avoid tyrants: "far from Zeus and the lightning" (Diogenianus *Cent.* 7.77b; Apostolius *Cent.* 14.65).[11] We would be on firmer ground if the relation between the saying of Jesus and the pagan proverb(s) could be made out. It seems *a priori* more likely that the saying was based on the proverb(s).[12] The lateness of the collection containing *Aesop. prov.* 7 need not indicate a late date for the proverb itself. Certainly it seems bold to claim (as does Jeremias)[13] that a saying so thoroughly pagan owed its form to its Christian parallel. Thus, even if the saying of Jesus was in existence by the time of Ignatius (or, for all that we know, went back to Jesus himself), Ignatius was not necessarily dependent on it

here. Since the shift of meaning involved in deriving his sentence from the proverb is not much greater than in deriving it from the saying, and since his sentence shows no trace of the antithesis (near/far) found in the saying, it seems likely that the sentence and the saying represent independent applications of the same pagan proverb.

The next line, "only in the name of Jesus Christ," means "whatever the form of death, may it be in the name of Jesus Christ," as is shown by the parallel in *Eph.* 11.1: we are to fear God's wrath or love his grace, μόνον ἐν Χριστῷ Ἰησοῦ εὑρεθῆναι εἰς τὸ ἀληθινὸν ζῆν ("only that we be found in Christ Jesus to possess true life"). The same parallel suggests that the expression εἰς τὸ συμπαθεῖν αὐτῷ ("to suffer with him")[14] in the passage before us is to be taken with "only in the name of Jesus Christ" (so Lightfoot) rather than with what follows.

The paragraph concludes with the affirmation that Ignatius endures everything (cf. 2 Tim 2:10) because Christ empowers him (cf. Phil 4:13). Instead of mentioning Christ directly, however, he speaks of him as "the perfect human being" (τοῦ τελείου ἀνθρώπου). This is the reading of PC and the Arabic. Thus Lightfoot was probably correct in regarding the more widely attested text—"the one who became perfect human being" (τοῦ τελείου ἀνθρώπου γενομένου)—as a modification prompted by more mature christological doctrine. It seems likely that the expression "perfect human being" has a close connection with the expression "new human being" in *Eph.* 20.1 (and perhaps the term "human being" in *Rom.* 6.2). Both titles already occur in the NT—"perfect human being" (ἀνὴρ τέλειος) in Eph 4:13 and "new human being" (καινὸς ἄνθρωπος) in Eph 2:15 and 4:24 (cf. Col 3:10, νέος ἄνθρωπος "new human being")—where they are associated especially with the theme of unity in the body of Christ.[15] Thus it is probable that both titles have as their background a conception of Christ as Representative Human Being.[16] Yet in the passage before us the reference to Christ as "the perfect human being" is preceded by an emphasis on

---

9   Joachim Jeremias, *Unknown Sayings of Jesus* (2d ed.; London: S.P.C.K., 1964) 66–73.

10   Cf. Jacques-E. Ménard, *L'évangile selon Thomas* (NHS 5; Leiden: Brill, 1975) 182–84.

11   *Paroem. Gr.* 1.300; cf. 2.620.

12   Cf. Johannes B. Bauer, "Echte Jesusworte?" in W. C. van Unnik, *Evangelien aus dem Nilsand* (Frankfurt: Scheffler, 1960) 123–24.

13   See above n. 9.

14   Cf. Pol. *Phil.* 9.2: ᾧ καὶ συνέπαθον "with whom [i.e., the Lord] they [i.e., Ignatius and the martyrs with him] suffered." The thought represents one aspect of the theme of the imitation of Christ (cf. *Rom.* 6.3).

15   Cf. Schlier, *Untersuchungen*, 88 n. 2. For the title "perfect human being" in Gnosticism see *Gos. Phil.* (NHC 2) 55,12; 75,19; 76,23; *Hyp. Arch.* (NHC 2)

the importance of suffering with him (4.2) and followed by the statement that he is denied by the docetists (5.1). There must be some truth, then, in the connection drawn by the older commentators between our passage and frg. 6 of Melito (against Marcion) where Christ is spoken of as "both God and perfect human being" (ἄνθρωπος τέλειος).[17] Perhaps the best way to account for the evidence is to compare the treatment of the title "Son of God" in *Sm.* 1.1: though it indicates Christ's divine origin (cf. *Eph.* 20.2), it is applied to him only at the incarnation. Similarly, we may say that the title "perfect human being" marks the transcendent nature of the Representative Human Being, yet finds its actualization only in Christ as a historical figure—perhaps especially in Christ as the crucified one (note that the "perfect athlete" of *Pol.* 1.3 is one who, like Christ, "bears the illnesses of all").[18] Such a treatment of the title is consistent with the fact that the expression "perfect man" (ἀνὴρ τέλειος) in Eph 4:13 builds on the metaphor of the life-cycle, that is, the contrast between one who is "mature" (τέλειος) and one who is a "child" (νήπιος).[19] There we who are children are said to attain the perfect (or mature) human being by being incorporated into the body of Christ (Eph

4:11–16). In Ignatius, however, it is the perfect human being himself who brings human nature to mature expression in his incarnation, death, and resurrection. Thus the perfect human being, like the perfect athlete of *Pol.* 1.3, embodies the highest form of the type. If this is correct, the expression "perfect human being" here anticipates later usage where it designates the complete humanity of the God-Human.

■ **5.1** In the next paragraph, the argument against docetism based on Ignatius' own martyrdom is taken up again and broadened. Ignatius begins by asserting that those who deny the perfect human being have in turn been denied by him (5.1)[20]—they are denied eternal life.[21] They are said to argue for death (cf. *Sm.* 3.2) and not truth. "Truth," in light of expressions like "Jesus Christ our true life" (4.1), must refer to the truth that brings life—a truth that depends on Christ's being "truly" human. And thus "truth" serves as a natural antithesis to "death." Those who reject such truth are said not to have been swayed by the most powerful witnesses. They have not been convinced by prophecies

---

91,1–2; *Ap. John* (NHC 3) 22,8–9; 35,4–5.

16 Cf. Joachim Jeremias, "ἄνθρωπος," *TDNT* 1 (1964) 366. Yet parallels for the concept of the "new human being" in non-Christian sources have not been found (cf. Lohse, *Colossians and Philemon*, 142 n. 60). In particular, the logic of Gnostic anthropology calls for the identification of the inner self with *original* humanity itself, not with the "*new* human being."

17 Cf. Hippolytus *Contra haer. Noet.* 17, where Christ is seen as καινὸς ἄνθρωπος γενόμενος ("having become new human being") and as ἄνθρωπος τέλειος προελθών ("having come forth as perfect human being") since his humanity was "not a matter of illusion or of conversion [of divinity into flesh], but he was truly a human being (ἀληθῶς γενόμενος ἄνθρωπος)."

18 The connection beween the "new human being" and the "economy" in *Eph.* 20.1 may well point in the same direction. For there the plan regarding the new human being is said to have to do not only with faith and love for Christ but also with his suffering and death.

19 Cf. Gerhard Delling, "τέλειος," *TDNT* 8 (1972) 75–77; idem, "πλήρωμα," *TDNT* 6 (1968) 302. Note that the expression ἄνθρωπος τέλειος ("perfect human being," "mature human being") in *P. Hamb.* 1.88,7–8 is a legal term for one no longer a minor (cf. Paul M.

Meyer, *Juristische Papyri* [Berlin: Weidmann, 1920] 31).

20 The pattern of the expression "whom some . . . deny, or rather have been denied" has parallels elsewhere in Ignatius (*Tr.* 5.2; *Rom.* 8.1; *Sm.* 9.1; *Pol.* inscr) and Paul (1 Cor 13:12; Gal 4:9). Such manipulations of the active and passive were never given a name by the ancients, though they probably deserved one (cf. Richard Volkmann, *Die Rhetorik der Griechen und Römer* [Leipzig: Teubner, 1885] 481). In any event, it is primarily a rhetorical and not a theological phenomenon. We may regard ἠρνήθησαν as a "perfective aorist" (meaning "have been denied," not "were denied"). Since in Koine Greek not only the perfect passive of this verb but also the aorist middle were regularly used with an active meaning, the aorist passive came to be employed to express all aspects of passive meaning with reference to the past (cf. Basil G. Mandilaras, *The Verb in the Greek Non-Literary Papyri* [Athens: Hellenic Ministry of Culture and Science, 1973] 147, 162).

21 As the parallels (cf. Matt 10:33; 2 Tim 2:12) and the present context (see on *Sm.* 2) suggest.

and the law of Moses. They have not even been convinced "until now" (that is, not even after Christ's coming; cf. *Mag.* 8.1) by the gospel and the sufferings of individual martyrs. Elsewhere Ignatius treats the gospel as the Christian message (*Phd.* 5.1, 2) and provides no real evidence that he thought of it as a written document (see on *Phd.* 8.2; 9.2). The fact that here he links the gospel and the sufferings of Christians so closely also suggests that nothing written is involved.[22] In any event, what all these witnesses—written and unwritten—have in common is that they confirm the reality of Christ's humanity. As we have seen, Ignatius thinks of the appeal to the Scriptures as making sense only if it is recognized that they point forward to Christ and find their fulfillment there. The prophets and Moses gain their significance from the events of the Lord's ministry (cf. *Phd.* 5.2; 8.2; 9.2) and the commitment of the martyr (cf. *Phd.* 5.1; 8.2). Thus, arguments that Ignatius had used against Judaizers to subordinate the Scriptures to Christ are used here (in a modified form) against docetists to confirm the reality of the humanity of Christ. Consequently, here too the gospel and the sufferings of Christians are given greater importance than the Scriptures. And thus the "gospel" for Ignatius is likely to have been a collection of traditions about Christ such as we have in *Sm.* 1.1–2 and 3.2–3 that not only represent the fulfillment of prophecy but also confirm the reality of Christ's birth, death, and resurrection. Additional confirmation of Christ's true humanity is provided by the sufferings of Christians themselves. The fact that Ignatius refers not only to his own martyrdom in this connection but also to the sufferings of others suggests that he is reexpressing in his own theological idiom the apologetic theme of *Sm.* 3.2 about the disciples' contempt for death.

But why does Ignatius appeal to the Scriptures at all in dealing with this issue? Zahn was convinced that only people brought up in Judaism could have been expected to respond to this appeal.[23] Corwin, on the other hand, read the passage as indicating a contempt for Jewish

writings on the part of Gnosticizing elements in Smyrna.[24] But the passage has a neutral tone (see also on *Sm.* 7.2). Ignatius is neither offering a defense of the Scriptures nor speaking by way of concession (as in *Phd.* 5.2; 9.1) to people overly enthusiastic about them. Their authority is simply taken for granted in the Christian community. There are, to be sure, similarities between the line of argument here and in *Philadelphians* (as we have seen), but it has been turned to a different purpose. In particular, the theme of the superiority of the gospel is expressed in *Sm.* 5.1 with none of the polemical spirit of *Phd.* 8.2. Thus the passage cannot be taken to prove that the Judaizers and the docetists represented one and the same group. It is still possible, however, that the docetists derived their christology in part from a Hellenistic-Jewish interpretation of Scripture (see on the expression "ate and drank" in *Tr.* 9.1). That may be the reason why Ignatius speaks of the Scripture as not "convincing" them: they accepted its authority but interpreted it differently.

■ **5.2** Ignatius now goes on to discuss more fully his argument against docetism based on the suffering of martyrs. "They (the docetists) have the same opinion about us," must mean, "they deny the reality and significance of our sufferings if they deny the reality of Christ's sufferings." Apparently the logic of that escaped the docetists since (as we are explicitly informed) they actually "praised" Ignatius. This remarkable statement indicates that their theology ran along different lines and that it was Ignatius and not they who polarized the situation.[25] Docetism, then, did not necessarily imply a lack of respect for martyrs and martyrdom (see on *Tr.* 10). Why did Ignatius think that it did? The answer is likely to lie in the bishop's call to the churches for unquestioning obedience to their leaders and for unqualified support of his own ministry (see on *Phd.* 8.1). It is quite possible that in fact docetism presupposed greater sensitivity than usual to theological difficulties and greater independence of judgment, and that this

---

22 The most that can be said is that Ignatius' emphasis on Christ's birth, death, and resurrection as the content of the "gospel" (cf. *Phd.* 8.2; 9.2) anticipates the view that the written accounts of Christ's ministry represent the gospel in the truest sense of the term (Paulsen, *Studien*, 43; cf. Adolf Harnack, *The Constitution and Law of the Church in the First Two Centuries* [London: Williams & Norgate; New York:

Putnam, 1910] 315–20).
23 Zahn, *Ignatius*, 370 (in support of his thesis that the docetists and the Judaizers were one and the same).
24 Corwin, *Ignatius*, 56.
25 Ignatius' reaction to them is all the more remarkable since he evidently knew the rules concerning self-praise laid down by Hellenistic moralists and would have realized that although a decent person feels

suggested to Ignatius a link beween docetism, lack of love, disrespect for bishops, and failure to appreciate martyrdom (cf. *Sm.* 6.2–8.2).

The anti-docetic polemic here is furthered by two wordplays: (a) The one who denies that Christ is σαρκο-φόρος ("the bearer of flesh")[26] is himself νεκροφόρος ("the bearer of a corpse"). Lightfoot notes that the latter term normally refers to "a bearer in a funeral" (Polybius 35.6.2; Appian *Bell. civ.* 4.27). Thus the docetist presides over his own loss of eternal life: such a person will not rise from the dead (see on *Sm.* 2). The language is reminiscent of *Phd.* 6.1 (where Ignatius' opponents are called "graves" and "tombs"), but there it apparently has no anti-docetic thrust. (b) The statement that the docetists "have denied" Christ "completely" (τελείως "perfectly") plays on the previous reference to Christ as the "perfect human being" (4.2) whom they "deny" (5.1). The reference reinforces the point that Ignatius used the title "perfect human being" especially with a view to affirming Christ's true humanity.

■ **5.3** The next words are the first reasonably clear indication that Ignatius is reacting to individuals known to the Smyrnaeans. He says that he will not record their names and will even try to blot them out of his memory until they regain their senses and recognize the reality of the passion which alone can assure our resurrection.[27] Such words make no sense unless the Smyrnaeans knew well enough of whom he spoke.[28] He certainly cannot be referring to old enemies in Antioch, and it seems unlikely that he has the travellers from Ephesus in mind (see on *Sm.* 4.1).

■ **6.1** The local origin of the opponents becomes clearer in the concluding lines of the section. This is introduced by a solemn warning (derived from Paul or the diatribe): "let no one be deceived" (see on *Eph.* 5.2). Ignatius traces the difficulty to someone who has τόπος. Evidently the term has come to refer to a "position" of leadership. It has no such meaning in normal Greek and begins to acquire technical significance along these lines only in the Christian literature of the period (cf. *Pol.* 1.2; *Pol. Phil.* 11.1; Acts 1:25).[29] Ignatius cannot be thinking,

26 For a christologically significant use of the term σαρκοφόρος see Clement Alex. *Strom.* 5.6, 34.1; Origen *Cels.* 7.13; cf. Bartelink, *Lexicologisch-semantische studie,* 26. With Ignatius it is more likely to be enthusiasm for compound words rather than dependence on technical vocabulary that accounts for its appearance (cf. Brown, *Authentic Writings,* 14–17).

27 For the way in which the formula ὅ ἐστι ("which is") links the "passion" with the "resurrection" see on *Eph.* 20.2.

28 I can see little force in Joly's (*Ignace,* 50) objection that if our letters were authentic, Ignatius would not have refrained from naming his opponents. It is likely that here again the bishop reflects an aspect of ancient political life. Thus the Roman concern to expunge the name and memory of traitors was not without its antecedents in the Mediterranean world (cf. Friedrich Vittinghoff, *Der Staatsfeind in der römischen Kaiserzeit* [Neue Deutsche Forschungen, Abteilung Alte Geschichte 2; Berlin: Junker und Dünnhaupt, 1936] 18–43). Also note that Xenophon (*Hist. Graec.* 2.3.1) mentions a past official "whom the Athenians do not name (οὐκ ὀνομάζουσιν)" to show their disapproval of his politics. It is not only here that Ignatius regards those who oppose him as dead to the Christian community (cf. *Phd.* 6.1). embarrassed even when praised by others (see on *Mag.* 12), it was precisely the witness to our good deeds by others that was acceptable (cf. *1 Clem.* 30.7; 38.2; Betz, *Plutarch's Ethical Writings,* 384).

29 Cf. Helmut Koester, "τόπος," *TDNT* 8 (1972) 207–8. Schlier's interpretation of the passage is extraordinary (*Untersuchungen,* 126–28). Τόπος, he thought, must refer to the "place" reached by a Gnostic who had ascended (spiritually) to a high level in the heavenly realms. It is unlikely, however, that Ignatius could have spoken of τόπος in this sense as "inflating" a person. In any event, Schlier's effort to show that the term has local significance involves a strained exegesis of the preceding words, ὁ χωρῶν χωρείτω ("he who can receive this, let him receive it"). We are asked to believe that to Gnostics the line had come to mean, "he who goes (to the heavenly realms), let him go" (for χωρεῖν in this sense see Irenaeus *Adv. haer.* 1.6.4; 1.13.3); and that Ignatius (playing on yet another meaning of the verb) throws the saying back at them, "he who goes (to the heavenly realms), let him understand (that the Gnostic ascent gives no advantage)."

then, of social prominence in general[30] but of ecclesiastical prestige in particular. Apparently the individual involved used his position to further docetism and to strike out on his own organizationally. Ignatius seeks to undercut his authority by saying that even the heavenly powers will be judged if they do not believe in the "blood" of Christ (that is, the reality of his passion).[31] Not office but faith and love (which inevitably involve submission to the bishop for Ignatius) are the indispensable elements in Christianity.

The solemnity of the warning is underscored by the choice of theological themes. They are intended to expose the theological immaturity of the opposition. Thus Ignatius' reference to "heavenly powers," "angels" in their glory, and rulers "both visible and invisible" echoes the triple division of heavenly things discussed in *Tr.* 5.2;[32] and his suggestion that the Smyrnaeans may be unable to "receive" (χωρείτω) such mysteries reflects his doubts about the ability of the Trallians to "receive" (χωρῆσαι) them (*Tr.* 5.1). The expression "he who can receive this, let him receive it" (ὁ χωρῶν χωρείτω) is close to Matt 19:12 (ὁ δυνάμενος χωρεῖν χωρείτω "he who is able to receive this, let him receive it"). It is evidently a homiletical formula used to commend hard sayings. For in Matthew it has to do with the difficult text about becoming eunuchs for the sake of the kingdom; and it has the same form as the expression that occurs in Mark 4:9 and elsewhere to mark theological challenges: "he who has ears to hear, let him hear."[33] Thus the formula is appropriate here both in light of the esoteric quality of the theology and the use to which it is put.

It is unlikely that the unnamed opponent was (as Bauer thought) an anti-bishop in Smyrna.[34] Ignatius apparently assumes that there was only one who claimed the office of bishop in Smyrna (cf. *Sm.* 8). Otherwise he would surely have counterattacked more vigorously than he does here and would probably have made use of his impressive formula about the importance of recognizing ". . . one altar, one bishop . . ." (cf. *Phd.* 4). The unnamed opponent, then, is more likely to have been an elder.[35] The discussion apparently assumes that he was a member of the church in Smyrna. And it seems very likely that he was behind the separate meetings presently mentioned (*Sm.* 7.1). If so, the command in *Sm.* 8.1 to celebrate a eucharist only under the guidance of the bishop himself or his representative was necessary precisely because of

---

30   Though Pseudo-Ignatius couples τόπος with "rank and wealth" in his paraphrase of the passage.

31   Lightfoot (building on hints from two Syriac witnesses) thought that the text may originally have read τὸ αἷμα Χριστοῦ τοῦ θεοῦ "the blood of the God Christ" (cf. *Eph.* inscr). The Arabic now joins all the important witnesses against the reference to Christ as God in this passage.

32   The reference to the heavenly powers as possible believers or unbelievers in the passion is partly *ad hoc*. But it also indicates that Ignatius conceives of the heavens in apocalyptic fashion as occupied by angels who have fallen as well as by those who have not. In particular, he may have in mind the powers mentioned in *Eph.* 19.2–3 as thrown into confusion by the star and destroyed by the incarnation. For the "judgment" reserved for fallen angels see especially Jude 6, which in turn harks back to the apocalyptic tradition (cf. *1 Enoch* 10.4–16).

33   Koester, *Synoptische Überlieferung*, 35; cf. Josef Blinzler, "Justins Apol I,15,4 und Matthäus 19,11–12," in A. Descamps and André de Halleux, eds., *Mélanges Bibliques en hommage au R. P. Béda Rigaux* (Gembloux: Duculot, 1970) 45–55. These connections are not arbitrary. Resch (*Agrapha*, 208–9) cites Ps-Ignatius' version of our passage, ὁ χωρῶν χωρείτω, ὁ ἀκούων ἀκουέτω ("he who can receive this,

let him receive it; he who can hear, let him hear") and a saying quoted by Epiphanius (*Pan.* 78.24), ὁ ἀκούων ἀκουέτω, καὶ ὁ ἀπειθῶν ἀπειθείτω ("he who can hear, let him hear; and he who disobeys, let him disobey"; cf. Rev 22:11).

34   Bauer, *Orthodoxy and Heresy*, 32.

35   Cf. *Asc. Is.* 3.23–24: "And in those days there will be many who will love *office* though they are devoid of wisdom, and many *elders* will be lawless and violent shepherds to their sheep . . ." (J. Flemming and H. Duensing, "The Ascension of Isaiah," HSW, *NT Apocrypha*, 2.648).

this individual's high position in the church. It was apparently an unusual situation since no such direction is given elsewhere in Ignatius' letters. And it indicates that Polycarp was not in complete control of the situation. That may have been because the office of bishop did not mean as much in Smyrna as Ignatius would like to have thought. In his letter to the Philippians, Polycarp makes nothing of the office either in reference to himself or in his discussion of problems in Philippi. That seems significant even though it must be admitted that Polycarp's reticence about his position is hardly greater than that of Ignatius (see on *Rom.* 2.2) and that there may not yet have been a monepiscopate in Philippi (cf. Phil 1:1). In any event, the situation in Smyrna suggests that the presbyters retained a greater measure of independence there than Ignatius thought suitable.

6   **Warning Against Docetic Practice**

2   Now observe those who hold erroneous opinions about the grace of Jesus Christ which came to us, how they are opposed to God's purpose: for love they have no concern, none for the widow, none for the orphan, none for one distressed, none for one imprisoned or released, none for one hungry or thirsty;

7   1/ they remain aloof from eucharist and prayers because they do not confess that the eucharist is the flesh of our savior Jesus Christ which suffered for our sins, which the Father raised by his goodness. They, then, who speak against the gift of God die in their disputing; it would profit them to love that they may also rise. 2/ It is right, then, to avoid such people and to speak about them neither privately nor publicly, but to pay attention to the prophets and in particular the gospel, in which the passion is shown us and the resurrection accomplished. Flee divisions as the beginning of evils.

8   1/ You must all follow the bishop as Jesus Christ (followed) the Father, and (follow) the presbytery as the apostles; respect the deacons as the commandment of God. Let no one do anything apart from the bishop that has to do with the church. Let that be regarded as a valid eucharist which is held under the bishop or to whomever he entrusts it. 2/ Wherever the bishop appears, there let the congregation be; just as wherever Jesus Christ is, there is the whole church. It is not permissible apart from the bishop either to baptize or to celebrate the love-feast; but whatever he approves is also pleasing to God, that everything you do may be sure and valid.

Ignatius turns to the practical consequences of docetic doctrine. First he exhorts the Smyrnaeans to "observe" (καταμάθετε) the behavior of the false teachers (6.2). The implication (explicitly stated in 7.2) is that they are to "avoid" (ἀπέχεσθαι) them. The dual theme—"observe and avoid"—is expressed in somewhat different language by Paul in Rom 16:17: "I exhort you, brothers, to note (σκοπεῖν) those causing divisions . . . and shun them (ἐκκλίνετε ἀπ' αὐτῶν)." This is evidently a traditional polemical theme.

■ **6.2** The false teachers are said to hold "erroneous opinons" (ἑτεροδοξοῦντας)[1] about the "grace" of Jesus Christ. A similar opposition between "erroneous opinions" (ἑτεροδοξίαι) and grace occurs also in *Mag.* 8.1.

---

1   Bartelink (*Lexicologisch-semantische studie*, 110–11) notes the anticipation of this pejorative use of the term in Plato (*Theaet.* 190e; cf. 193d), but suggests that it was familiar to Christian writers from less remote sources. Thus in Philo the word ἑτερόδοξος is applied to those whose lives reflect distorted beliefs and values (*Sobr.* 68; *Migr. Abr.* 175; *Spec. leg.* 2.193; cf. Josephus *Bell.* 2.129). Ignatius' usage moves toward a still narrower conception of "heterodoxy" as doctrinal error (see on *Mag.* 8.1).

In both passages "grace" refers to a whole pattern of life and thought bestowed on the church by God or Christ. Elsewhere it refers more particularly to God's favor freely bestowed (*Rom.* 1.2; *Sm.* 11.1) or is set in opposition (but by no means radical opposition) to his wrath (*Eph.* 11.1); or it designates a sphere of divine favor within which Christian life as a whole moves (*Eph.* 20.2; *Mag.* inscr; *Rom.* inscr; *Sm.* 9.2; 12.2; *Pol.* 1.2; 8.2) so that the prophets may also be said to be inspired by it (*Mag.* 8.2) and the redemption of errorists said to flow from it (*Phd.* 8.1; 11.1). Consequently the relation between grace and action is complex. On the one hand, the doing of good is said to flow from grace (*Pol.* 7.3). On the other hand, Ignatius uses "grace" and "law" as parallel expressions and compares submission to grace with submission to the bishop (*Mag.* 2). Ignatius appears to connect grace as divine favor with the realm of religious and ethical obligations in three ways: (a) grace clarifies obligations since it is connected with a distinctive way of life (as in *Mag.* 8.1, where grace stands opposed to Jewish practices, or as in *Sm.* 6.2–8.2 where the ethical implications of grace are explored); (b) grace provides assistance in both knowing and fulfilling one's obligations (*Mag.* 14, "knowing that you are full of God I exhort you briefly," may be taken as a model);[2] (c) grace is that which makes sense of moral effort (thus "grace" is said to reward kindness in *Sm.* 12.1), and its benefits are in turn made secure by acts of love (see on *Sm.* 7.1; and note that in *Rom.* inscr "grace" is something that is to be maintained "without wavering"). When Ignatius says that the docetists have mistaken opinions about grace, he is not saying that they held views on the subject which would have directly challenged any of these assumptions. Rather, it is his way of indicating what he takes to be the implications of their position, much as elsewhere he charges Judaizers with having rejected grace (*Mag.* 8.1) or docetists with having denied Christ (*Sm.* 5.1).

Ignatius sets out two ways in which the docetists oppose God's γνώμη or "purpose" (for the term see on *Eph.* 3.2). The first is given in 6.2, the second in 7.1. In 6.2 Ignatius claims that they have no concern for love, that is, no concern for the needy. In this connection he provides a list of unfortunates for which Lightfoot, Zahn, and Bauer have collected many parallels from early Christian literature (note especially *Barn.* 20.2, which mentions the widow, the orphan, and others in distress; Pol. *Phil.* 6.1, which mentions the widow, the orphan, and the poor man; and Matt 25:31–46, which mentions the hungry, the thirsty, the stranger, the naked, the sick, and the prisoner). The reference not only to one "imprisoned" but also to one "released" has raised the question as to whether Ignatius (or perhaps a scribe) added an irrelevant item for the sake of rhetorical balance. AC mention only one "imprisoned," but all the other witnesses to the text (including the Arabic) have both terms. The difficulty has been exaggerated. Rehabilitation could not have been without its problems.[3]

Such works of love made the Christian church stand out as a social phenomenon in the Graeco-Roman world.

---

2 There are other passages in which Ignatius bases an imperative on an indicative; and some of these—notably *Sm.* 11.3 ("you who are perfect, be intent also on perfect things")—are paradoxically formulated. Rudolf Bultmann found here "an existentiell attitude" rooted in the Pauline paradox of the "already" and the "not yet" ("Ignatius and Paul," in Schubert M. Ogden, ed., *Existence and Faith* [New York: Meridian, 1960] 267–77). But Ignatius (if not Paul) thinks more conventionally, as the examination of *Sm.* 11.3 will show. Such passages are readily intelligible against the background of the bishop's insistence that Christians should live up to their profession (see on *Eph.* 14.2). Even when Ignatius calls for radical obedience ("a Christian has no power over himself but devotes himself to God"), he naturally assumes that "this is God's work *and yours*"

(*Pol.* 7.3). A cooperative effort between God and the Christian is the logical model when "grace" is conceived of as a gift that is preserved by holy living.

3 Ignatius may have been thinking of Christian "confessors" who on being released from prison continued to be supported by the church until they had established themselves again (Paulsen, *Studien,* 79).

In this respect it was the inheritor of values developed especially in Judaism. Humanitarian impulses were not absent from Hellenic society, but they were not always directed at those most in need. In particular it is noteworthy how small a part the concern for widows and orphans played.[4] The church, then, found itself able to fill a social vacuum with its small close-knit units. And Dodds is surely right in seeing such solidarity as a major reason for the success of Christianity.[5] Ignatius is no doubt sensitive to all this as he charges the docetists with neglecting the works of love. It would be naive, however, to think that the bishop was describing the behavior of his opponents accurately. What is true, perhaps, is that they valued their theology highly enough to be unwilling to sacrifice it simply to avoid the threat of disruption to the community (cf. 7.1). Even at that, they need not have felt that they were the ones responsible for precipitating the split. For apparently they had gone out of their way to be friendly to their visitor (*Sm.* 5.2). Thus it is evidently Ignatius who polarizes the situation by insisting that the theology of the docetists logically leads to the destruction of what he can take for granted as the aim of all (because it corresponds to the deepest social needs of the early Christians): unity and love.

■ **7.1** Ignatius presents the deeper reason for the presumed neglect of deeds of love by pointing to a second way in which the docetists oppose God's purpose: they stay away from the eucharist and prayer. There is considerable evidence that in the early period there was a morning service of prayer and an evening meal or eucharist.[6] But the eucharist was also closely associated with prayer (cf. Justin *Apol.* 1.65–67); and since that connection seems to be reflected in *Eph.* 5.2, our passage probably refers to but one service. In any event, Ignatius puts all the emphasis on the eucharist.[7] Here again his charge is exaggerated. For it is clear enough from *Sm.* 8 that the docetists celebrated their own eucharists or love-feasts. It is not even fair to say that that in itself necessarily represented a divisive act. For the group seems to have been led by an elder (see on *Sm.* 6.1), and there can be little doubt that separate meetings in different houses were usual in the early period. At the same time, it would be hard to deny that this particular group had gained a distinct identity and avoided eucharists in other settings because of the eucharistic theology involved. It seems only logical that they would not be willing to identify the eucharist as the flesh of Christ any more than they were willing to accept Christ's death and resurrection as physical realities. For once this does not seem to be a logic imposed by Ignatius on his opponents. The argument presupposes that he could count on wide agreement in Smyrna with a realistic doctrine of the presence of Christ in the elements of the eucharist.[8] And from that he works back to the reality of the passion and the resurrection. In the process it is likely that he goes beyond usual expectations. For when he identifies the eucharist with the flesh that suffered and was raised, he harks back to his longer discussion of *Sm.* 2–3 and in so doing draws what even many of his friends may have regarded as an overly direct line between the presence of Christ in the bread (and wine)[9] of the eucharist and the resurrected body of Christ.[10] (Note the considerably

---

4 Hendrik Bolkenstein, *Wohltätigkeit und Armenpflege im vorchristlichen Altertum* (Utrecht: Oosthoek, 1939) 275.

5 E. R. Dodds, *Pagan and Christian in an Age of Anxiety* (Cambridge: Cambridge University, 1965) 136–38.

6 Hans Achelis, *Die Canones Hippolyti* (TU 6/4; Leipzig: Hinrichs, 1891) 194–97.

7 The term "eucharist" in Ignatius has a flexible range of interrelated meanings: in *Eph.* 13.1 it apparently refers both to the offering up of "thanksgiving" and to the celebration of the sacred meal; in *Phd.* 4 the cultic sense dominates; in *Sm.* 7.1 there seems to be special reference to the elements of the meal; and in *Sm.* 8.1 the term serves as a general designation for the whole complex of liturgical acts and prayers that constitute the celebration of the sacred meal (Bartelink, *Lexicologisch-semantische studie*, 113–14).

8 Although the verb ὁμολογεῖν ("confess") means little more than "admit" in *Mag.* 8.1, it seems to have a more technical significance in our passage (and in *Sm.* 5.2) and to refer to the affirmation of true doctrine. Thus it may mark the following clause ("that the eucharist is the flesh of our savior Jesus Christ") as an extension of traditional anti-docetic material (cf. 1 John 4:2–3: "every spirit which confesses that Jesus Christ came in the flesh is from God"; Pol *Phil.* 7.1: "for everyone who does not confess that Jesus Christ came in the flesh is antichrist"). If so, this material seems to have been combined with still more primitive traditions (see n. 10 below).

9 Evidently the "flesh" stands for the eucharist as a whole just as the "breaking of bread" (recalled by Ignatius in *Eph.* 20.2) includes the whole meal (cf. *Eph.* 5.2).

more subtle connection drawn by Tertullian in *Adv. Marc.* 4.40.3 and even by Irenaeus in *Adv. haer.* 5.2.2–3.)

It is also important to recognize, however, that this realistic doctrine of the eucharist plays a limited role in Ignatius. First, he appeals to it openly and clearly only here where it owes its importance to the use made of it to oppose docetism. Second, even in this passage the connection between the believer's resurrection and participation in the eucharist is balanced by an emphasis on the role of love in assuring salvation. For "it would profit them to love (ἀγαπᾶν) that they may also rise." To be sure, the line has been taken to refer primarily to the sacred meal. For since Ignatius mentions celebrating the "love-feast" (ἀγάπη) in 8.2, it has been conjectured (by Zahn and many others) that the verb ἀγαπᾶν means "to hold a love-feast" (which would include the eucharist). It has also been suggested that just as the word "rise" is set in opposition to the word "die," so the verb ἀγαπᾶν is set in opposition to the expression "to speak against the gift of God," and that this in turn can be taken as a direct reference to opposition to the eucharist. If this interpretation is followed, then the presence of Christ in the eucharist affects the resurrection, and the sacred bread truly functions as a "medicine of immortality" (*Eph.* 20.2). Yet, as universally admitted, the verb ἀγαπᾶν does not mean "to hold a love-feast" elsewhere, and such a development of its meaning is not very likely. At most the verb may be taken (and, I think, *should* be taken) to *allude* to the love-feast (and eucharist). But its primary reference must be to the works of love that figure so importantly in 6.2. It is these, then, that are said to affect

resurrection. Moreover, it also seems likely that the expression "gift of God" refers only indirectly to the eucharist. It occurs in John 4:10, where it is possibly connected with eucharistic imagery but clearly has a much broader range of connotations.[11] The use of the phrase by Irenaeus (*Adv. haer.* 5.2.2–3) in an important passage is also worth noting since it is part of an argument that bases the possibility of the (general) resurrection on the reality of Christ's presence in the eucharist. Even here, however, the "gift of God" is not the eucharist itself but "eternal life" bestowed on the Christian's flesh especially in the eucharist. If this is the reference in Ignatius, his thought has moved beyond preoccupation with the eucharist itself to its benefits. It is probably significant, then, that he makes so much of the danger of "disputing" and "speaking against" God's gift. For thus attention is focussed on those who deprive themselves of eternal life by introducing division in the church. If that is where the emphasis lies, the natural antidote to such strife is the call to love (and only secondarily to celebrate the eucharist). It is important, then, to ask how Ignatius related doing the works of love to acknowledging the reality of Christ's presence in the eucharist.

A possible key to this problem is the fact that the ancient love-feast (which must often have included the eucharist)[12] served as an important agency for taking care of the needs of the poor including especially widows and orphans.[13] In a very obvious way, then, to avoid the

---

10 Ignatius says that Christ's flesh suffered ὑπὲρ τῶν ἁμαρτιῶν ἡμῶν ("for our sins"). Sin is referred to only one other time by Ignatius, and that too in a passage where he is dependent on special materials (*Eph.* 14.2). "For our sins," then, is doubtless a traditional formula (cf. 1 Cor 15:3, Χριστὸς ἀπέθανεν ὑπὲρ τῶν ἁμαρτιῶν ἡμῶν "Christ died for our sins"; see also on the expression τὸν ὑπὲρ ἡμῶν ἀποθανόντα "who died for us" in *Rom.* 6.1). The remark that "the Father raised" Christ's flesh also reflects an old theme (see on *Tr.* 9.2). But as Elze (*Untersuchungen*, 35–38) suggests, the form of the expression σάρκα . . . τὴν . . . παθοῦσαν ("the flesh which suffered") evidently goes back to Ignatius himself (cf. τὴν χάριν . . . τὴν . . . ἐλθοῦσαν "the grace which came" in 6.2). Less probable is Elze's view that the original form of the material ran as follows: Ἰησοῦς Χριστὸς . . . ὃς ἔπαθεν

ὑπὲρ τῶν ἁμαρτιῶν ἡμῶν, ὃν τῇ χρηστότητι ὁ πατὴρ ἤγειρεν "Jesus Christ . . . who suffered for our sins, whom the Father raised by his goodness." For it seems at least as likely that it was Ignatius who brought the two older motifs together here and adapted them to his purpose (see on *Tr.* 9). In any event, it is evidently Ignatius himself who made this direct connection between the flesh of Christ in the eucharist and the crucified and resurrected body of the Lord.

11 Cf. Rudolf Bultmann, *The Gospel of John: A Commentary* (Oxford: Blackwell, 1971) 180 n. 4.

12 Felix L. Cirlot, *The Early Eucharist* (London: S.P.C.K., 1939) 17–49.

13 Tertullian *Apol.* 39.16–19; Hippolytus *Trad. apost.* 26; *Can. Hipp.* 32.164–65.185; Justin *Apol.* 1.67.6; cf. Hans Achelis, *Die Canones Hippolyti* (TU 6/4;

common meal was to avoid doing the works of love. It is this threat to the community that controls the argument, as 6.2 shows.[14] To some extent Ignatius is playing on words: to deny the reality of Christ's presence in the eucharist leads to separation from the ἀγάπη (the love-feast); to stay away from the ἀγάπη is to refrain from doing the works of ἀγάπη (love). At a deeper level, however, the bishop apparently sensed a connection between the concreteness of revelation in the incarnation and the concreteness of the obligations that love imposes (cf. *Tr.* 8.1; *Rom.* 7.3). Sociologically, the presence of Christ in the elements lends special weight to the common meal as it functions to sanctify the pattern of authority in the community and to confirm the value of love (cooperation and the suppression of dissent). Theologically, the presupposition is evidently this: works of love that maintain the bond of unity preserve the gifts of grace that are conferred on the community through the historical flesh of Christ and its extension in the sacred meal.

No doubt Ignatius' opponents would have rejected his analysis and would have had little difficulty showing the compatibility of docetism and love (8.2 indicates that they also celebrated the love-feast). Yet it is likely that the bishop had an advantage in the dispute. For part of even the most elementary docetism is an emphasis on spirit that brings readier dissatisfaction with the "cruder" elements of the religious tradition. The history of Gnosticism where docetism and elitism went hand in hand provides relevant commentary on this point. By the same token, Ignatius was probably more closely attuned to the religious impulses of a majority who opted for a "cruder" conception of the eucharist, a greater insistence on the importance of unity and mutual assistance, and a more authoritarian government of the community.

■ **7.2** Having analyzed the behavior of the docetists, Ignatius now makes his recommendations to the Smyrnaeans. The first is that they are to avoid such people. The language is even more severe than in *Sm.* 4:

these people and their views are not to be discussed either privately or publicly. Instead, the Smyrnaeans are to pay attention to the prophets and especially the gospel. As in *Sm.* 5.1, the thought is close to *Phd.* 5.2 and especially *Phd.* 9.2.[15] Again there is no reason to think that Ignatius is speaking of a written gospel (see on *Phd.* 8.2; *Sm.* 5.1). Nor is there any evidence either that the docetists overemphasized the prophets (in spite of the parallels with the letter to the Philadelphians) or that they despised them. (a) On the one hand, although it is likely that the docetists saw nothing in the scriptures that contradicted their theology, Ignatius' remarks here are too neutral to suppose that they put special emphasis on the prophets to support their views (*Sm.* 2–3 suggests that they worked primarily with resurrection traditions). (b) On the other hand, Ignatius seems to be working from a traditional view of the relation between the Scriptures and Christianity (the theme of prophecy and fulfillment) rather than arguing for the acceptability of the OT as such. What he does is to sharpen the traditional view (for he emphasizes fulfillment in terms of the passion and resurrection) as a weapon against docetism. His opponents may not have known much about the Scriptures, but that does not mean that they would have rejected them. As we have seen, Ignatius' own knowledge of the OT is not profound. In any event, his arguments rely most heavily (ἐξαιρέτως "in particular") on the nature of the gospel, and he finds it possible to adapt his views on the subject either to those who over-emphasize the Scriptures (as in Philadelphia) or to those who teach docetism (as in Smyrna).

It is probably significant that the bishop ends the paragraph with an exhortation to flee "divisions" (cf. *Phd.* 2.1) as the "beginning of evils."[16] Unity is still the dominant concern.

■ **8.1** The second recommendation to the Smyrnaeans is that they follow the bishop, presbyters, and deacons. Here and in what follows occur some of the most striking of Ignatius' comparisons beween local and universal

---

Leipzig: Hinrichs, 1891) 198–205.

14 Note that *Sm.* 6.2 is itself but an extension of the concluding words of *Sm.* 6.1 which identify faith and love as "everything." Clearly Ignatius is trying to establish lack of love as the key to the behavior and beliefs of the docetists.

15 Compare "and in particular (ἐξαιρέτως) the gospel" (*Sm.* 7.2) with "the gospel has something distinctive

(ἐξαίρετον)" (*Phd.* 9.2).

16 The expression "beginning of evils" has a quasi-proverbial ring. The closest parallels are provided by 1 Tim 6:10 ("love of money is the root of all *evils*") and Pol. *Phil.* 4.1 ("love of money is the *beginning* of all difficulties"). Bauer (BAG *s.v.* ῥίζα 1.b, p. 743) cites Greek parallels that mention the "root of evils" or the "root of goods." The interchangeability of

authority in the church. Yet they remain true comparisons and do not indicate that the local leaders are conceived of as representatives of their heavenly counterparts or are in any way divinized. Indeed, the peculiarly mixed form of the comparison in *Sm.* 8.1 plays an important role in establishing that conclusion (see on *Mag.* 6.1). Also familiar to us from a number of other passages is the command to do nothing relevant to the life of the church without the bishop (see on *Mag.* 4). From the same circle of ideas is the insistence that only a eucharist held under the bishop is "valid" (βέβαιον, cf. *Mag.* 4: βεβαίως "validly"). But here there is a new element: Ignatius speaks of a eucharist under the bishop "or him to whom he has entrusted it." The addition makes most sense if it is seen as called forth by the appearance of rival eucharists held by the docetists under the leadership of the officer mentioned in *Sm.* 6.1. Ignatius wishes to make it doubly clear that only the bishop can give approval to such meals. Confusion on the point would have been easy since a person of high position (perhaps a presbyter) was involved, and it was probably not unusual for such persons to preside over church events held in one or another of the houses in which Christians met.

■ **8.2** A second comparison follows.[17] The bishop is to the local congregation as Christ is to "the whole church" (or "the catholic church"). Although the thought is formulated in an unusual way, it does not go beyond what is said of the status of the bishop in other such comparisons (see on *Eph.* 5.1). The perplexing problem is the meaning of the term καθολική ("whole," "catholic") which

is applied for the first time to the church in this passage. The literature is dominated by the view of Lightfoot that here καθολική means "universal" (with reference to geographical extension) rather than "catholic" (with reference especially to the church's orthodoxy). Zahn's solution was similar except that he did not think that the universality of the church was conceived of by Ignatius in geographical terms.[18] In any event, both scholars were concerned to deny to Ignatius a use of the term considered impossible early in the second century. We may regard it as generally agreed that the word καθολικός does mean "universal" in a wide variety of senses in the Greek of the period and that in Ignatius some kind of reference to universality is demanded by the comparison between the catholic church and the local congregation. Yet the study by Garciadego, however unsatisfactory in some ways, has made revision of Lightfoot's view necessary.[19] Three points deserve special attention: (a) Despite the wide variety of uses of the word "catholic" in the Greek of the period, it rarely (if ever) refers to geographical extension. (b) It sometimes carries with it an idea of organic unity or completeness.[20] (c) Opposition to division plays some role in Ignatius' reference to the catholic church, for the sentence is immediately preceded and immediately followed by statements attacking the problem of unauthorized assemblies.[21] The evidence can be accounted for if we build on the recognition that in *Sm.* 8.2 the local congregation and the catholic church are presented not only as in some ways unlike one another (local *vs.* universal) but also as in some

---

"beginning" and "root" in such expressions is shown by a statement of Epicurus which refers to pleasure as the ἀρχὴ καὶ ῥίζα παντὸς ἀγαθοῦ "beginning and root of every good" (Athenaeus *Deipn.* 12, 546f). The reference both to the "root of wisdom" and to the "beginning of wisdom" in Jewish wisdom literature may also be recalled (Sir 1:6, 20; Ps 110:10 LXX; cf. Sir 10:13). Note that schoolchildren learned to write Greek by using as models such maxims as the following: ἀρχὴ μεγίστη τοῦ φρονεῖν τὰ γράμματα "letters are the true beginning of knowledge" (H. I. Marrou, *A History of Education in Antiquity* [New York: Sheed and Ward, 1956] 138, 218).

17   *Sm.* 8.1 and 8.2 take up the same three themes with variations: (a) comparison between local and universal authority; (b) exhortation to do nothing

without the bishop; and (c) discussion of the "validity" of liturgical acts.

18   Zahn, *Ignatius*, 428–29.

19   Alejandro Garciadego, *Katholiké Ekklesia: El significado de epíteto "Catholica" aplicado a "Iglesia" desde san Ignacio de Antioquía hasta Orígenes* (Mexico City: Editorial Jus., 1953).

20   Here Garciadego builds on the suggestions of Kattenbusch (*Das apostolische Symbol*, 2. 920–27). Note that the adjective καθολικόν describes what is undivided and permanent in *Treat. Seth* (NHC 7) 57,26 as opposed to what is μερικός "fragmentary" (57,23).

21   This is also rightly emphasized by Joly (*Ignace*, 63–64). But opposition to division is not yet opposition to heresy in the narrow sense of the term.

ways like one another: the local congregation (πλῆθος)[22] for Ignatius is an organic unity under its bishop just as the universal church is an organic unity under Christ. Thus we may say that the "catholic" church here is not the universal church opposed to heresy, but the whole church resistant by its very nature to division. All other references to the universal church in Ignatius are compatible with such a definition (*Eph.* 5.1; 17.1; *Phd.* 5.1; 9.1; *Sm.* 1.2). From this undifferentiated conception there later emerged specialized applications of the term "catholic" to the church as orthodox or to the church in its geographical extension.

The second comparison is followed by a second exhortation to do nothing without the bishop. Here again, however, the statement is interestingly varied. It is not permitted to baptize or "to celebrate the love-feast" (ἀγάπην ποιεῖν) apart from the bishop.[23] There can be little doubt that there is in fact a reference here to the love-feast since the expression ἀγάπην ποιεῖν is used elsewhere of the celebration of the meal (*Con. Gangr.* can. 11; *Con. Laod.* can. 28). Nor can there be much doubt that the love-feast was thought of as including the eucharist since baptism and love-feast are juxtaposed as the two cardinal liturgical acts of the church. Ignatius probably chose to speak of the love-feast rather than the eucharist (as he regularly does; cf. *Eph.* 13.1; *Phd.* 4; *Sm.* 7.1) because he wanted his regulation to cover events

that he himself could not regard as true eucharists (as defined in 7.1) and that others may have been tempted to regard as harmless communal meals.

A final variation in 8.2 of the themes found in 8.1 occurs in Ignatius' comment on what constitutes "valid" activity in the church ("all that you do" must refer to liturgical activity in particular). His point is that whatever the bishop approves is pleasing to God. Note that just as a previous line ("*wherever* Jesus Christ is, *there* is the whole church") recalls Matt 18:20 ("*where* two or three are gathered in my name, *there* I am in their midst"; cf. *Eph.* 5.2), so the statement about God's satisfaction with what the bishop approves recalls Matt 18:18 (whatever the apostles bind on earth will be bound in heaven). The differences between Ignatius and Matthew suggest that the two writers are drawing on a common body of developing church regulations. But the parallel also shows that Ignatius' high claims for the authority of the bishop are embedded in ideas still very close to the NT (see on *Mag.* 3.2).

---

22 The term is used of the local church elsewhere in Ignatius (*Mag.* 6.1; *Tr.* 1.1; 8.2; cf. *Eph.* 1.3) and in other writings of the period (BAG *s.v.* πλῆθος 2.b.δ, p. 674). Since Ignatius can speak of seeing a whole "congregation" in their bishop (*Mag.* 6.1; *Tr.* 1.1; cf. *Eph.* 2.1), it is likely that for him the term refers not only to the full number of members but also to their organic unity.

23 Elze (*Untersuchungen*, 66–67) plausibly suggests that here Ignatius is applying a recognized rule about baptism to the love-feast since it is apparently taken for granted in the case of baptism.

9 Final Exhortation

1 Finally, it is sensible for us to regain sobriety while we still have time to repent unto God. It is good to acknowledge God and the bishop: he who honors the bishop is honored by God; he who does anything without the bishop's knowledge serves the devil. 2/ May all things abound for you in grace, for you are worthy. You refreshed me in every way, and Jesus Christ (will refresh) you. You loved me when I was absent and present. God is your reward, whom you will attain if you endure everything for him.

The adverb λοιπόν ("finally") marks a transition (see on *Eph.* 11.1). What follows is a final exhortation to obey the bishop (9.1) joined with a word of encouragement for the Smyrnaeans (9.2).

■ **9.1** The exhortation begins with a call to regain sobriety. The image was common in the early church (cf. 1 Thess 5:6, 8; 2 Tim 4:5; 1 Pet 1:13; 4:8; 5:8). In 2 Tim 2:25–26 it is associated (as here) with the theme of repentance which in Ignatius refers (as usual) to the return of the separatists (cf. *Phd.* 3.2; 8.1; *Sm.* 4.1; 5.3). The theme of repentance is in turn associated with a reference to the shortness of the time before the end (cf. *2 Clem.* 8.2: "let us repent . . . while we have time for repentance"; Gal 6:10 provides only a verbal parallel). A similar association of ideas occurs elsewhere in Ignatius (see on *Eph.* 10.1–11.1; cf. 2 Pet 3:9); yet the eschatological language is again quickly left behind, and it is evident that Ignatius is not preoccupied with thoughts about the end of the world.[1] His real concern is that men should acknowledge God and the bishop—an abbreviated formula for more complex thoughts on the matter that come to partial expression in the following antithesis. There, in spite of the strong sanction given to episcopal authority, the underlying argument is not without biblical precedent (see on *Mag.* 3.1–2). Disobedience to the bishop is in the last analysis disobedience to God—and service to the devil (cf. Acts 5:3–4)!

The antithesis is made more telling by figures of speech: note especially the repetition of sounds at the beginning and end of each part of the statement: ὁ τιμῶν . . . τετίμηται "he who honors . . . has been honored" (for the interchange of active and passive voices see on *Sm.* 5.1); ὁ λάθρα . . . λατρεύει (this cannot be imitated in the translation).[2]

■ **9.2** The following word of encouragement to the Smyrnaeans reflects Ignatius' satisfaction with the majority of his addressees. In particular, he recalls their enthusiastic support of him, both materially and spiritually, as he journeys to Rome (cf. *Sm.* inscr). His statement that they loved him ἀπόντα καὶ παρόντα ("when absent and present") may reflect Pauline language (1 Cor 5:3; 2 Cor 10:1–2, 11; 13:2, 10; Phil 2:12); but the terminology played an important role in Hellenistic epistolography as a whole in reinforcing good relations and in lending a sense of personal presence to the communication.[3]

Ignatius' statement "God is your reward" (ἀμοιβὴ ὑμῖν ὁ θεός) is formulated in less striking terms by a number of our witnesses to the text (who were probably trying to deal with the meaningless αμοιβει of G): "may God reward you" (L); "God will reward you" (g, Arabic). Many editors (Jacobson, Zahn, Lightfoot, Funk, Hilgenfeld) have followed the lead of L and printed ἀμείβοι. But this reading ignores the fact that the verb is

---

1 This may be because the theme was understood partly against the background of Graeco-Roman rather than biblical views of the relation between sin and its recompense. Thus Plutarch speaks of providing opportunity for μετάνοια ("repentance") as the purpose for the delay of divine punishment (*De ser. num. vind.* 6, 551d–551e; Betz, *Plutarch's Theological Writings*, 200).

2 Cf. Perler, "Das vierte Makkabäerbuch," 58–60.

3 Koskenniemi, *Studien*, 169–80 (see also on *Eph.* 1.3). Ps-Demetrius regards the formula as especially characteristic of the letter of friendship, though in the same context he notes that letters in such a style were often sent by superiors to inferiors (Hercher, *Epistolographi Graeci*, 1).

used in the middle when it means "reward" and regularly takes the accusative (rarely the dative) of the person rewarded[4] (which is precisely how it is used in *Sm.* 12.1). The correct reading—ἀμοιβή (so also Bauer)[5]—is given by P and is strongly suggested by the reading of G. It fits with what follows since, as we have seen, "attaining God" in Ignatius has to do with "acquiring" God in some metaphorical sense (see on *Tr.* 5.2). Here (as elsewhere) Ignatius speaks of Christians in general (not only the martyr) as "attaining God," and draws a close connection between "enduring" and "attaining" (see on *Eph.* 10.1;

Mag. 1.2). The language of exchange should not be understood too crudely in a writer who emphasizes the divine indwelling (*Eph.* 15.3) and the grace of God (*Sm.* 6.2); yet it is also a warning against a one-sided interpretation of the letters in mystical terms.

---

4   LSJ *s.v.* ἀμείβω B.I.3, p. 80; BAG *s.v.* ἀμείβομαι, p. 44.
5   *Ignatius,* 271.

10

Closing and Farewell

1 Philo and Rheus Agathopous, who followed me for the sake of God, you did well to receive as deacons of God, who also give thanks to the Lord for you that you refreshed them in every way. Nothing (of this) will perish for you! 2/ My spirit and my bonds are your expiation, which you did not despise or feel ashamed of. Neither will the perfect hope, Jesus Christ, be ashamed of you.

11

1/ Your prayer went out to the church in Antioch in Syria; whence having come bound in the most God-pleasing bonds, I greet everyone—not being worthy to be from there, being the least of them; but by the (divine) will I was counted worthy, not because of the witness of my own conscience, but because of the grace of God, which I pray may be given to me perfect that by your prayer I may attain God. 2/ So, then, that your work may be perfect both on earth and in heaven, it is right for God's honor that your church appoint a godly ambassador to visit Syria and rejoice with them because they are at peace and have regained their own greatness and have had restored to them their own corporate body. 3/ It appeared to me, then, a deed worthy of God for you to send one of your people with a letter that he might join in giving praise for the godly tranquility granted them and because they have now reached a harbor by your prayer. You who are perfect be intent also on perfect things; for if you want to do well, God is ready to grant it.

12

1/ The love of the brothers in Troas greets you, whence I am also writing you through Burrhus whom you along with your brothers, the Ephesians, have sent with me, who refreshed me in every way. Would that all imitated him, since he is an exemplar of service to God. Grace will reward him in every way. 2/ I greet your God-worthy bishop, and godly presbytery, and my fellow servants, the deacons, and all of you, individually and corporately, in the name of Jesus Christ, and (in) his flesh and blood, (in) both his passion and resurrection, both fleshly and spiritual, in unity of God and of you. Grace to you, mercy, peace, endurance forever.

13

1/ I greet the households of my brothers with their wives and children, and the virgins called widows. Farewell, I say, in the power of the Father. Philo, who is with me, greets you. I greet the house of Tavia, whom I boast is established in faith and love both fleshly and spiritual. I greet Alce, a name dear to me, and the

■ **10.1** "You did well" (καλῶς ἐποιήσατε) reflects a common formula in Hellenistic letters. It most often appears in the future at the beginning or end of a letter to emphasize a request.[1] White provides examples of such a use of the expression in connection with the transitional device that he names a "responsibility statement."[2] In the aorist the formula evidently serves a somewhat different purpose (to express thanks), but it no less clearly marks the transition to the closing of the body of the letter.

As in *Phd.* 11.1, the reception accorded the two deacons (Philo and Rheus Agathopous) figures importantly in the closing section of the letter. And once again Ignatius' remarks on the subject are not unrelated to what precedes it. For the bishop has not only expressed satisfaction with the Smyrnaeans in a general way but has also brought the previous discussion to a conclusion (in *Sm.* 9.2) with high praise particularly for their attention to his cause. The two deacons (as *Phd.* 11.1 shows even more clearly) are regarded by Ignatius as important allies in this same cause. They are said to have followed him "for the sake of God" (εἰς λόγον θεοῦ)[3] and to have been received as "deacons (διακόνους)[4] of God."[5] Apparently they had learned from the Philadelphians of Ignatius' transit to Smyrna and had followed him there only to find that he had already gone on to Troas. Their reception in Smyrna had been unmarred by any of the resistance met with in Philadelphia; and it is linked by Ignatius with his own by his use of almost exactly the same words to describe it: "you refreshed them (me) in every way" (*Sm.* 9.2; 10.1). Moreover, the assurance that the Smyrnaeans will be rewarded eternally for their treatment of the two deacons ("nothing [of this] will perish for you") echoes the sentiment expressed at the end of *Sm.* 9.2 concerning their treatment of Ignatius himself ("God is your reward").

■ **10.2** What follows underscores Ignatius' appreciation of the Smyrnaeans and their support with the help of a compendium of unusual expressions that he applies to himself elsewhere: I am your ἀντίψυχον "expiation" (cf. *Eph.* 21.1; *Pol.* 2.3; 6.1); or more precisely, "my spirit . . . is your expiation" (cf. *Eph.* 18.1: "my spirit is a lowly offering"; cf. *Tr.* 13.3: "my spirit is consecrated for you"); "and my bonds" (cf. *Tr.* 12.2: "my bonds exhort you"). Such language, as we have seen, evidently does not designate Ignatius as a vicarious sacrifice for the churches (see on *Eph.* 8.1; 18.1). Rather it points to an ambivalence in Ignatius' self-understanding: he has reason to question his own worthiness and anticipates having his bonds misunderstood as symbols of his spiritual inferiority; at the same time, he expects that the value of his ministry will be confirmed and is confident that his bonds lend him a special authority (see Introduction, 3.4). Thus here he explicitly notes that the Smyrnaeans looked beyond appearances and did not despise, or feel ashamed of, his bonds. To this he immediately adds the corollary: neither will Christ ("the perfect hope")[6] be ashamed of them. It is clear, then, that the offering of thanks and the assurance of reward dominate 10.2 no less certainly than 10.1. Thus the positive side of Ignatius' self-understanding is to the fore.

■ **11.1** Equally positive (it appears) is the treatment in 11.1 of standard closing themes. As in *Phd.* 10.1, the request

---

1 Friedrich Preisigke, *Wörterbuch der griechischen Papyrusurkunden* (3 vols.; Berlin: Selbstverlag der Erben, 1925–31) 1. 731–32.

2 White, *Form and Function,* 18–20, 46–48.

3 Cf. *Phd.* 11.2: εἰς λόγον τιμῆς "as a token of honor."

4 Or "servants" of God. But in every other instance διάκονος is used in a technical sense in Ignatius.

5 GL read διακόνους Χριστοῦ θεοῦ "deacons of the God Christ." But with one doubtful exception (*Tr.* 7.1; cf. *Sm.* 6.1) this way of speaking of Christ is not characteristic of Ignatius (see on *Eph.* inscr). I follow PAC (now supported also by the Arabic) in omitting "Christ."

6 GL read "the perfect faith"; PAg and the Arabic, "the perfect hope." Either change is textually explicable: (a) ΤΕΛΕΙΟΣΠΙΣΤΙΣ became ΤΕΛΕΙΟΣΠΙΣ (by homoeoteleuton) and was corrected to ΤΕΛΕΙΟΣΕΛΠΙΣ (the scribe assumed that the two appearances of ΕΛ had confused his predecessor); (b) ΤΕΛΕΙΟΣΕΛΠΙΣ became ΤΕΛΕΙΟΣΠΙΣ (since the two appearances of ΕΛ and the repetition of other letters had in fact caused confusion) and was corrected to ΤΕΛΕΙΟΣΠΙΣΤΙΣ (the first and most obvious word that would come to

for prayer on behalf of the church in Antioch has become a statement that the bishop's prayer has been answered. There are added here, however, motifs elsewhere associated with Ignatius' sense of inferiority to the Antiochenes: he is "not worthy to be from there, being last of them." Moreover this sense of inferiority seems to cast its shadow over Ignatius' view of his martyrdom: unworthy as he is to be from Antioch, he consoles himself with the thought that although he did not deserve being selected for martyrdom, he was chosen by God's grace;[7] and he expresses the hope that such grace to him may be perfect. But if (as we have argued) the bishop's self-doubts were connected with a feeling of having failed in Antioch, and if now the situation there had changed in his favor (see on *Phd.* 10.1), we may expect this positive development to be reflected here. Three things suggest that in fact it is: (a) The more evident signs of anxiety found in the parallel passages are missing: the urgency of the request in *Mag.* 14 to pray for the Antiochene church; the indication in *Tr.* 13.3 (cf. 13.1) that Ignatius is still "in danger"; the reference to himself in *Rom.* 9.2 as a "miscarriage." *Sm.* 11.1 is closer to *Eph.* 21.2 in that it balances a statement of Ignatius' unworthiness with one of his worthiness.[8] This is probably one reflection of the fact that he had his most active supporters in the Ephesians and Smyrnaeans. In any event, he now has even better reason to view the matter of his worthiness in a more favorable light. (b) The whole last section of Ignatius' letter is dominated by the ἀσπάζομαι ("I greet") formula. It occurs in the first person here (11.1), in the third person in 12.1 and in

13.1, and three more times in the first person in 12.2–13.2. Similarly in *Pol.* 8.2 it occurs four times. No doubt the abundant use of the formula in these letters reflects Ignatius' familiarity with and positive feelings about the Smyrnaeans. But more is involved. If we compare *Sm.* 11.1 ("Antioch in Syria whence having come as a prisoner in the most God-pleasing bonds I greet [ἀσπάζομαι] everyone") with *Eph.* 21.2 ("the church in Syria whence having come as a prisoner I am being led off [ἀπάγομαι] to Rome"), the contrast seems obvious. In *Sm.* 11.1 the church in Antioch becomes for the first time involved in a greeting, Ignatius' bonds become distinguished as "most God-pleasing," and he greets "everyone" (cf. 13.2). In *Eph.* 21.2 he regards it as an honor to be led away a prisoner from Antioch, but there is no temptation to include a happy greeting in the remark. (c) Even more important is the role of the term τέλειος ("perfect") in 10.2–11.3. Of the ten uses of the word in Ignatius, six occur in the letter to the Smyrnaeans and five in this context. These five are obviously interrelated. First, Christ is our "perfect hope" (10.2; cf. 4.2), and Ignatius' confidence in Christ must color all the following uses of the term "perfect." Second, Ignatius prays that the grace which will enable him to face martyrdom may be "perfect" (11.1). He has still not attained God, but gone is his anxious way of talking

---

mind). Perhaps (b) is somewhat more likely; in any event, Christ is regularly identified as our "hope" or our "perfect hope" by Ignatius (*Eph.* 1.2; 21.2; *Mag.* 11; *Tr.* inscr; 2.2; *Phd.* 5.2; 11.2), and it seems gratuitous to accept the more unusual reading here. Schlier (*Untersuchungen*, 77) reads "faith" and regards it as modelled on a pagan deity (cf. Richard Reitzenstein, *Hellenistic Mystery-Religions* [Pittsburgh: Theological Monograph Series 15; Pittsburgh: Pickwick, 1978] 293–96). But Franz Joseph Dölger (ΙΧΘΥΣ [5 vols.; Münster: Aschendorff, 1922–43] 2. 481–86) has collected numerous references to personifications of faith in early Christian sources that are not mythological.

7   Two unusual expressions are involved in Ignatius' attribution to God of his good fortune in being selected for martyrdom: (a) "By the (divine) will." For

this absolute use of θέλημα ("will") see *Eph.* 20.1; *Rom.* 1.1; *Pol.* 6.1. (b) "Not because of the witness of my conscience (οὐκ ἐκ συνειδότος), but because of the grace of God." This seems to be based on 1 Cor 4:4: "for I am conscious of nothing against me (οὐδὲν . . . σύνοιδα), but not because of this am I justified." The same passage is also reflected in *Rom.* 5.1, and it is apparently given a specifically Ignatian turn in *Tr.* 5.2 (also note the use of the verb δικαιωθῆναι "to be justified" in *Phd.* 8.2).

8   And even though Ignatius attributes his selection as a martyr solely to the grace of God in *Sm.* 11.1, the use of the verb καταξιόω ("count worthy") in this connection reflects the positive side of the bishop's self-understanding (*Mag.* 1.2; *Tr.* 12.3; *Rom.* 2.2; cf. *Phd.* 10.2; *Pol.* 1.1; 7.2; 8.2).

about being "still in danger" (*Eph.* 12.1; *Tr.* 13.3). Third, such perfect grace immediately reminds him of what will make the work of the Smyrnaeans "perfect" (11.2).[9] Now that their prayer has helped restore the congregation in Antioch, they should send an ambassador to confirm what has been accomplished. Clearly the success of Ignatius' own martyrdom (that is, the result of perfect grace) can be more easily anticipated since the cooperation of churches like Smyrna to confirm the peace in Antioch (that is, to achieve their perfect work) can be confidently envisioned. Finally, Ignatius' last exhortation to the Smyrnaeans that they send a messenger to Antioch is reinforced by the following line: "you who are perfect, be intent also on perfect things" (11.3). Ignatius is speaking of people who had supported him strongly and are now being asked to make a final sacrifice on his behalf by sending a messenger to Antioch. The line is intended to emphasize the importance of this activity and to suggest the relative ease with which it can be carried out (see on *Sm.* 6.2). Thus it is immediately explained by a statement to the effect that God is prepared to assist them if they are willing. It should also be noted that the expression θέλουσι ὑμῖν ("if you want") connects this statement with *Phd.* 10.2 ("if you want [to send a messenger], it is not impossible for you"). Human effort and divine help are both involved. The main point, however, is that the use of the word "perfect" ties together the fate of Ignatius and the situation in Antioch and suggests that both were coming to a happy conclusion. Ignatius' journey to the west was about to be answered by a journey of messengers to the east, and the

prospect of success for the latter[10] could be expected to relieve his mind about the prospect of success for the former. This connection of ideas makes most sense if Ignatius saw his ministry vindicated by the turn of events in Antioch.

■ **11.2** Ignatius' description of the messenger's task in 11.2 is obscure particularly in one respect. The messenger is to join with the Antiochenes in rejoicing over their good fortune. But what is the "greatness" (μέγεθος) which they have regained and the "corporate body" (σωματεῖον) which has been restored? The word μέγεθος can refer to physical "size," but that is inappropriate here especially in light of the uses of the word elsewhere in Ignatius (*Eph.* inscr; *Rom.* 3.3). A reference to the restoration of the "greatness" of a church (cf. *Rom.* 3.3) makes most sense if it has to do with the recovery of unity in the congregation at Antioch.[11] The word σωματεῖον (GP), unfortunately, also occurs as σωμάτιον (g)—a confusion met with elsewhere in ancient manuscripts.[12] The former was a legal term meaning "corporate body";[13] the latter occurs in a number of senses, the most relevant of which is "small," "poor," or "sick body."[14] The word σωμάτιον, then, could serve as an image of the persecuted church (in *Mart. Pol.* 17.1 it refers to the martyr's tortured body). And it may be significant that the verb ἀπεκατεστάθη ("restored") is sometimes used of healing.[15] But the adjective ἴδιον ("their own") is used with both nouns and presumably in both instances has to do with some desirable state that the Antiochenes once had and have now regained. What could it mean that they had had their small, poor, sick

---

9   The expression "on earth and in heaven" may reflect the language of Matthew about how what is decided on earth by Christ's followers is ratified in heaven (Matt 16:19; 18:19). If so, it is one more indication that the problems in Antioch had to do with authority rather than with persecution.

10   Ignatius evidently had strong assurances in this connection, for we know that his requests were taken very seriously (cf. Pol. *Phil.* 13.1).

11   It is improbable that Ignatius would regard relief from persecution as a mark of restored "greatness." On the contrary, Christianity is a matter of "greatness" when it is hated by the world (*Rom.* 3.3). Thus it is far more likely that Ignatius saw "greatness" restored to the Antiochenes when they set aside merely being called Christians and actually behaved as such (cf. *Rom.* 3.2)—meaning (in this instance) that

they demonstrated the reality of their Christianity by submitting to their bishop and making peace with one another (cf. *Mag.* 4; *Eph.* 13–16). Thus the bishop's insistence that deeds match words probably lurks in the background, and his application of that theme to church governance seems the relevant one in this context.

12   LSJ *s.v.* σωμάτιον, p. 1749. Henricus Stephanus, *Thesaurus Graecae linguae* (8 vols.; Paris: Didot, 1831–65) 7. 1713–14.

13   LSJ *s.v.* σωματεῖον, p. 1749.

14   BAG *s.v.* σωμάτιον, p. 807.

15   BAG *s.v.* ἀποκαθίστημι 1, p. 91.

body (their condition as a persecuted community) given back to them? Since the verb ἀπεκατεστάθη ("restored") also refers frequently to the restoration of a polity,[16] it seems probable that Ignatius is speaking of the restoration of their "corporate body"[17]—the recovery of peace and unity in Antioch.

■ **11.3** In the next section Ignatius first repeats in different words what he has said in 11.1: send a messenger to rejoice with the church in Antioch. One more point about the ambassador's role is added that may reflect standard diplomatic practices of the day: he is to carry a letter.[18] We learn later that the Smyrnaean messenger to Antioch actually took letters from more than one community with him (Pol. Phil. 13.1). Another distinctive feature of our passage is the image of fair weather and the harbor used in the description of the good fortune of the Antiochenes (cf. Pol. 2.3). The image occurs frequently in Hellenistic literature and designates all manner of good fortune.[19] Its use is fully compatible with our view that Ignatius had in mind the peace of the church.[20]

■ **12.1** The ἀσπάζομαι ("I greet") formula is taken up again (from 11.1) and is repeated five more times before the end. For the greeting given by the "love" of the brethren see on Tr. 13.1. For Burrhus' role in carrying the letter and for the joint support of his mission see on Phd. 11.2. The wish that "all" would have found in Burrhus an "exemplar"[21] no doubt reflects Ignatius' dissatisfaction with some in Smyrna and may represent a final allusion to the docetists (like the final allusion in Phd. 11.1 to the Philadelphian dissidents). But the context—along with

the fact that the docetists of Smyrna seem to have been friendly with Ignatius (Sm. 5.2)—makes it more likely that the bishop has in mind some difficulty over the expenses involved in catering to his requests for attendants (see on Eph. 2.1). In any event, Ignatius again emphasizes the reward for such devotion to his cause: "grace," he says, will repay Burrhus in every way (cf. 9.2; 10.1; 10.2). Grace, then, is thought of here as divine favor providing assurance that kindness (especially in such a cause) meets with God's approval and reward.

■ **12.2** The second greeting refers to all the Smyrnaeans, beginning with their bishop. The list is designed to emphasize their common purpose as Christians. Similarly, the function of the set of antitheses that follows is to suggest the completeness of the unity that prevails in Smyrna. At the same time, they also hint at the anti-docetic presuppositions of such unity. Thus the expression "flesh and blood" probably alludes to the eucharist (cf. Tr. 8.1; Rom. 7.3) and recalls the anti-docetic eucharistic doctrine of Sm. 7.1. Similarly, the reference to the "passion and resurrection," especially when linked with the insistence on the reality of the resurrection in both the realm of the flesh and that of the spirit, recalls a major preoccupation of the letter (cf. Sm. 1–3). Yet the main point is still the "unity of God and of you." What

16 BAG, ibid.; LSJ s.v. ἀποκαθίστημι 1, p. 200.

17 Paulsen adopts a similar view of the term (Studien, 147–50). But he goes on to draw theological conclusions: in Ignatius the local "corporate body" is the "ecclesiological concretion" of the universal "body" of Christ (cf. Sm. 1.2). But if our interpretation of the passage is correct (see especially n. 11 above), Ignatius has less abstract matters in mind. It is doubtful that he saw the link between σῶμα (i.e., of Christ) and σωματεῖον that we are inclined to find.

18 R. Cagnat, "Legatio," Dictionnaire des antiquités, 3. 1027 (see further on Phd. 10.1). At the same time, the practice of sending letters with messengers for diplomatic reasons was known in the church before the days of Ignatius (cf. 1 Cor 16:3).

19 For a partial collection of materials see Campbell Bonner, "Desired Haven," HTR 34 (1941) 49–67.

Note particularly Philo Fuga 50; Somn. 2.225; Lucian Pisc. 29; Plutarch Consol. ad uxor. 6, 610b; De tranq. anim. 19, 477a.

20 Note that even in 4 Macc. it designates not peace after the persecution but victory over the fear of death (7.3; 13.7).

21 For this Latinism see Eph. 2.1 and Tr. 3.2. In Eph. 2.1 it is used of Burrhus' fellow deacon, Crocus.

precisely does this peculiar phrase mean? It may be that Ignatius finally speaks clearly about union with God as well as with one another ("unity *with* God and *among* you"). But since the two genitives need not have the same force, it seems better to conform to Ignatius' usage elsewhere (cf. *Phd.* 8.1; 9.1; *Pol.* 8.3) and to take the expression to mean "unity *from* God and *among* you." Thus Ignatius has in mind the unity of the congregation from two somewhat different points of view (source and scope).[22]

The section concludes with a benediction that begins with the mention of "grace" as do the benedictions at the end of Paul's letters. But the other words used here by Ignatius reflect language found in the salutations of early Christian letters (such as "grace, mercy, peace" in 1 Tim 1:2; 2 Tim 1:2; 2 John 3).[23]

■ **13.1** In his next greeting Ignatius turns to the two main social groups that constituted the community: (a) house-holders with wives and children; (b) "virgins called widows" (τὰς παρθένους τὰς λεγομένας χήρας). The latter expression has elicited a flood of comment. The solution once advanced by many (including Lightfoot) that Ignatius means widows who may be regarded as virgins fails because of the order in which the terms occur and because the expression τὰς λεγομένας ("called") indicates that the term widow is used of the virgins in an unusual or improper sense.[24] The correct solution is probably that argued most forcefully by Zahn: the order of "widows" (cf. 1 Tim 5:3–16)[25] was opened up also to virgins (especially older women) who had no other means of support.[26] The crucial parallel is provided by Tertul-

lian (*Virg. vel.* 9), who expresses disapproval of the fact that a virgin no more than twenty years old was assisted by being enrolled among the widows. It may be objected that Tertullian would not have been so critical if the custom had had precedents. Tertullian, however, had an independent mind. Another objection to the proposed solution has been that it unnaturally supposes that Ignatius chose to address only the virgins from among the widows (or that all the widows happened to be virgins). It is likely, however, that the virgins associated with widows were still regarded as distinct in important respects (Tertullian's complaint that the twenty-year-old virgin continued to leave her head unveiled is perhaps one indication of this); and we know that there was special enthusiasm in Smyrna for virginity (*Pol.* 5.2). Thus it is not impossible that virgins formed a distinct (and relatively large) subgroup in Smyrna and that they had been given special responsibilities in connection with their visitor.

There follows the first statement of farewell—this one "in the power of the Father."[27] To this is appended a greeting from the deacon Philo. The fact that only Philo is mentioned may indicate that he alone stayed on with Ignatius in Burrhus' place (cf. *Phd.* 11.1–2). Philo's companion, Rheus Agathopous, was more closely associated with Antioch and may well have turned back to bring news about Ignatius to his congregation and to make sure that affairs continued to develop favorably there.

■ **13.2** At this point it apparently occurs to Ignatius to greet various individuals in Smyrna.[28] All the names

---

22 Analogous are expressions like "worthy of God and of you" (*Eph.* 2.1; cf. *Rom.* 10.2) or "to the honor of you and the bishop" (*Eph.* 2.1).

23 The background to these terms is Semitic (cf. Klaus Berger, "Apostelbrief und apostolische Rede: Zum Formular frühchristlicher Briefe," *ZNW* 65 [1974] 199 n. 35).

24 BAG *s.v.* λέγω II.3, p. 471 (a more neutral use of the expression is out of the question here).

25 Ignatius expresses concern for such "widows" in *Pol.* 4.1. The term "widows" in *Sm.* 6.2 is used in a less technical sense. But since the order of widows was "in no sense an active order" in the first two centuries (J. G. Davies, "Deacons, Deaconesses and the Minor Orders in the Patristic Period," *JEH* 14 [1963] 5), the distinction is not significant.

26 Zahn, *Ignatius*, 334–38. From this point of view, the

arrangement in Smyrna marks an early stage of a development (complete in *Const. Apost.* 2.26.3, 8; 2.57.12; 3.6.4; 3.15.5) which saw the interpene-tration of the order of widows and the ideal of virginity (A. Kalsbach, "Diakonisse," *RAC* 3. 919).

27 "Father" (LlA) rather than "Spirit" (Gg) also appears in the Arabic (cf. *Mag.* 3.1: "the power of God the Father").

28 Joly (*Ignace*, 48–49) makes much of the fact that although Polycarp, bishop of Smyrna, is mentioned in letters to others (*Eph.* 21.1; *Mag.* 15), he is not named here or elsewhere in the letter to the Smyrnaeans. Joly attributes this to the temporary lapse of a forger. But it is at least as likely that Ignatius regarded his allusion to Polycarp in 12.2 as sufficient. These names, in any event, are something of an afterthought.

involved are somewhat unusual. Tavia[29] is not otherwise found. But there are names very much like it,[30] and it may be a feminine form (as Bauer suggests) of the Latin name Tavius.[31] Alce is a rare name.[32] This woman is referred to again by Ignatius (*Pol.* 8.3), and she is probably the same person mentioned in *Mart. Pol.* 17.2: "Nicetes the father of Herod [the police official responsible for the arrest of the aged Polycarp], brother of Alce." If the parallel can be trusted, Alce evidently belonged to a family of some standing since Herod was an *eirenarch* (an office that in this period was filled by members of the superior classes).[33] Daphnus[34] is a somewhat more common name.[35] Eutecnus (Εὔτεκνος), on the other hand, does not occur elsewhere as a proper name.[36] Some analogy is provided, however, by the name Εὐτέκνιος (attested once);[37] or it may be that the Smyrnaean's name was actually Εὔτεχνος (attested once).[38] The last reference to "everyone individually" (πάντας κατ᾽ ὄνομα) has numerous parallels in the greetings of ancient letters.[39]

The second and final statement of farewell—this one "in the grace of God"—concludes the letter.

---

29 Read by GL. The Arabic (Natawiya) also seems to be working with this name. The remark associated with the name here may be translated, "of whom I pray (εὔχομαι) that she is established." But it seems more likely that Ignatius mentions those whom he fondly remembers as firm in the faith. It is better, then, to take εὔχομαι to mean, "I boast" (cf. LSJ *s.v.* εὔχομαι III, p. 739).

30 Cf. Preisigke, *Namenbuch*, 413; Foraboschi, *Onomasticon*, 308.

31 BAG *s.v.* Ταουΐα, p. 811.

32 Pape/Benseler, *Eigennamen*, 61; cf. BAG *s.v.* Ἄλκη, p. 37.

33 Theodor Mommsen, *Römisches Strafrecht* (Leipzig: Duncker & Humblot, 1899) 308 n. 2.

34 To take the epithet associated with Daphnus—τὸν ἀσύγκριτον "the incomparable"—as another name (Asynkritos as in Rom 16:14) would require the elimination of the article that precedes it.

35 Pape/Benseler, *Eigennamen*, 277; Preisigke, *Namenbuch*, 84; *Supplementum epigraphicum Graecum* (Leiden: Sijthoff, 1923ff.) 12.115,41; 22.167,4; 23.112,20; 23.602,1.

36 As an adjective it means "blessed with children," and may represent a second epithet associated with the name of Daphnus (BAG *s.v.* εὔτεκνος, p. 327). But the adjective seems out of place in this context (and to give spiritual significance to it appears forced).

37 Pape/Benseler, *Eigennamen*, 427.

38 Foraboschi, *Onomasticon*, 116.

39 Cf. Koskenniemi, *Studien*, 150.

Ignatius

to Polycarp

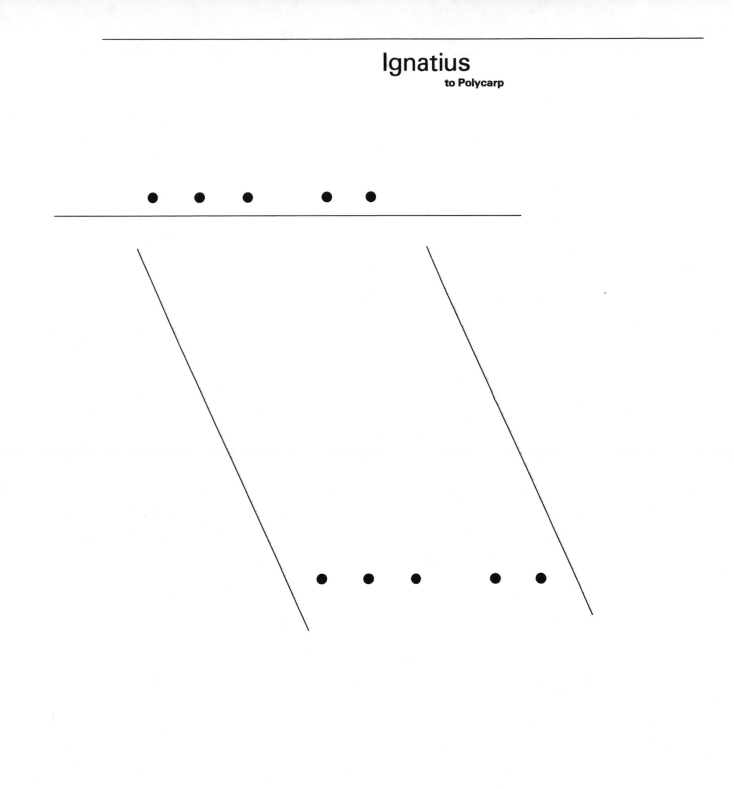

Salutation

Ignatius, also called Theophorus, to Polycarp, bishop of the church of the Smyrnaeans, or rather, one who has God the Father and the Lord Jesus Christ as bishop, abundant greetings.

This is the shortest salutation in the letters of Ignatius. The less problematic the situation, the briefer the salutation tends to be (the exception is the salutation to the Magnesians). In this instance Ignatius also seems to have been pressed for time (see on *Pol.* 8.1). Thus the whole letter is shorter and the style more abrupt than usual. (For Ignatius' reason in addressing a second communication to the church in Smyrna, i.e., in the form of a letter to its bishop, see on *Pol.* 6.1.)

The only unusual feature of the salutation is the reference to Polycarp as "bishop" (ἐπισκόπῳ) of Smyrna followed by the correction that it is rather he who "has (God and Christ) as bishop" (ἐπισκοπημένῳ). It is a play on words approaching the use of active and passive forms of the verb in *Sm.* 5.1 ("whom some deny, or rather have been denied by him"). The closest parallel in thought is *Mag.* 3.1 where obedience to the bishop is recommended as due "not indeed to him, but to the Father of Jesus Christ, the bishop of all (τῷ πάντων ἐπισκόπῳ)" (cf. *Rom.* 9.1: "Jesus Christ alone will oversee [ἐπισκοπήσει] the church in Antioch"). In our passage, the studied correction is apparently intended to suggest to the Smyrnaeans that Polycarp's authority to guide the life of their community (and to champion the cause of Ignatius) rests on the special guidance of their bishop by God.

1   Expression of Praise

Receiving your godly purpose, established as on an immovable rock, I glory exceedingly, having been counted worthy of your blameless face, from which may I benefit in God.

■ **1.1** The body of the letter opens with a transitional device previously encountered: the participle, "receiving" (ἀποδεχόμενος), points particularly to *Eph.* 1.1 and *Tr.* 1.2; the latter passage and *Pol.* 1.1 also agree in completing the thought with an expression of praise. What is regularly "received" is news communicated through letters or messengers. Yet Ignatius uses the formula here to speak of information which he himself had gathered from the personal encounter to which he immediately alludes: "having been counted worthy of your blameless face" (i.e., having visited Polycarp in Smyrna). The passage illustrates the force of epistolary conventions for our author.

Also a matter of polite convention is Ignatius' wish that he may "benefit" from Polycarp. The expression, as we have seen, often means little more than "bless me for you" and expresses strong admiration (see on *Eph.* 2.2; *Mag.* 2; 12). Under such circumstances what is hoped for is assumed to be forthcoming. For Ignatius knows Polycarp's "godly purpose"—Polycarp's firm guidance of the church in Smyrna and his support of Ignatius in this connection (cf. *Pol.* 1.2–5.2).

The use of the image of a "rock" to suggest such firmness and reliability is natural enough (cf. Homer *Od.* 17.463, where Odysseus is said to have "stood like a rock"). But here the situation is more complex: Polycarp's purpose is said to be "established (ἡδρασμένη) as on an immovable rock." The obvious parallel is Matt 7:24–26 where one who does Jesus' words is likened to a man whose house stands because he built it on rock. The language has a close rabbinic parallel and seems to reflect building practices in Palestine.[1] Digging down to rock for the foundation apparently struck Luke (6:48) as more plausible (cf. Vitruvius *De arch.* 1.5.1; 3.4.1; 6.8.1); but he probably misunderstood the saying. Thus Ignatius knew Matthew or the tradition behind Matthew. Since another application of the theme seems to be found in Sirach and is in one respect closer to Ignatius than to Matthew ("a heart established [ἡδρασμένη] upon a mind of understanding"), we may be justified in preferring the second alternative (Sir 22:17).[2] In any event, there is no reason to import into the passage a reference to Christ as the "rock" (cf. *Herm. Sim.* 9.2.1; Justin *Dial.* 113.6).

---

1   Gerald G. Friedlander, *The Jewish Sources of the Sermon on the Mount* (New York: Ktav, 1969) 259–61; cf. *'Abot R. Nat.* 24.

2   Cf. Koester, *Synoptische Überlieferung*, 33.

Exhortations to Polycarp [1.2–5.2]

1

The Role of the Bishop

2   I exhort you by the grace in which you are clothed to continue on in your course and to exhort all people so that they may be saved. Justify your office with all diligence, both fleshly and spiritual; be concerned about union, than which nothing is better. Bear with all people, as the Lord also bears with you; put up with all people in love, as you in fact do. 3/ Take time for constant prayer. Ask for greater understanding than you have. Be watchful with a sleepless spirit. Speak to people individually in a godly unity of spirit. Bear the illnesses of all as a perfect athlete. Where there is greater labor, great is the gain.

The first five sections of the letter are addressed to Polycarp. Here the duties of the bishop are sketched by Ignatius. The topics addressed include (a) general comments on the bishop's role (1.2–3), (b) his treatment of less cooperative members of his congregation (2.1–3), (c) his resistance to false teachers (3.1–2), (d) his care for widows and slaves (4.1–5.1a), and (e) his advice to the married (5.1b–2). All these matters are taken up with a view to the importance of unity in the church, and these sections show once again that Ignatius conceives of unity in terms of the complete subordination of individual interests to the group and the suppression or elimination of dissent. It follows that the bishop is conceived of as embodying the community and taking upon himself all its ills. For where concord means the absence of conflict, underlying tensions must be resolved in the person of the one who guarantees symbolically and organizationally the coherence of the group. The relevance of all this for Ignatius' own self-understanding should not be neglected. For his language of self-effacement (see on *Eph.* 8.1; 12.1) represents only a slightly more extreme statement of the conception of the bishop's role as sketched here.

■ **1.2** Ignatius begins his advice to Polycarp with the παρακαλῶ ("I exhort") formula (see on *Tr.* 6.1). Its unusual prominence here reflects the fact that this letter, beyond any of the others, is a matter of exhortation from beginning to end. The basic content of the exhortation is that Polycarp, relying on the "grace" (see on *Sm.* 6.2) with which he is "clothed" (cf. 1 Cor 15:53–54; Gal 3:27; Rom 13:14; Col 3:12; Eph 4:24; 6:11, 14), should prosecute his ministry vigorously and exhort all people. The exact meaning of these lines is not clear, however. (a) The verb προσθεῖναι with the dative ("continue on in") literally means "to add to." What is added is usually clear from the context. Thus "to add to sins" (*Herm. Vis.* 5.7) means to add more sins to those already committed. But what does it mean to add to one's course? "Course" (δρόμος) may refer to the track or the race run on the track.[1] Although Ignatius must be thinking of the progress that Polycarp is making on the track of life, it is unlikely that he is calling for an increase in speed. For in his athletic imagery Ignatius concentrates not on the race (as does Paul) but on more brutal sports (cf. *Pol.* 1.3; 2.3; 3.1) in which endurance, not speed, is the basic requirement.[2] Since the immediate context also emphasizes the

---

1   Cf. BAG *s.v.* δρόμος 1, p. 206.
2   The verb συντρέχειν (used in *Eph.* 3.2; 4.1; *Mag.* 7.2; *Pol.* 6.1) literally means "to run together." It may allude to the world of sports in *Pol.* 6.1 (cf. *Eph.* 3.2), but that is not likely. The word scarcely means more than "to agree" in Ignatius. Moreover, this metaphorical meaning seems originally to have derived

from the activity of people in running together to meet or assemble (cf. LSJ *s.v.* συντρέχω 2, p. 1728).

need for endurance, Ignatius is probably thinking of a person adding distance to his course rather than speed to his running.[3] (b) The basic content of Ignatius' exhortation is that Polycarp himself should exhort others. But it is not clear whether Polycarp is instructed to exhort people "to be saved" (the ἵνα clause indicating the content of the appeal) or whether he is to direct their lives by exhortation "so that they may be saved."[4] The latter is more in harmony with Ignatius' view of the ministry and the Christian community. Salvation presupposes obedience to the bishop and unity in the church. Exhortation is one very natural focus of pastoral activity under these circumstances.

A bishop can expect, however, that such exhortation will not go unquestioned: he must "justify" (ἐκδικεῖν) his "office" (τόπος). We have found τόπος in the sense of "office" before (Sm. 6.1). The verb ἐκδικεῖν basically means to "avenge" a crime or to "vindicate" a person.[5] Commentators generally regard Ignatius' usage here as an extension of the usual meaning and render it "to do justice to." Support for this is found in Origen (Comm. in Matt. 12.14) and Eusebius (Hist. eccl. 6.43.9). But in Eusebius the reference is to someone who deceitfully "claims" the episcopacy (a secondary meaning of the verb recognized by the lexicographers). And Origen seems to be speaking of "those who defend the office of bishop" (οἱ τὸν τόπον τῆς ἐπισκοπῆς ἐκδικοῦντες) by appealing to the Bible. Relevant parallels occur in the papyri where the verb comes to mean (among other things) "to defend" someone or "to plead for" something.[6] We may regard the usage in Origen and Ignatius as a legal metaphor having to do with the advocacy of the cause of episcopal authority. In Polycarp's case the defense of his office is to be effected by a "diligence" that will touch on the total life of the community in both its "fleshly" and "spiritual"

aspects (see on Eph. 8.2).

The bishop is not only to defend his office but also to "be concerned about union." The juxtaposition of the two commands indicates that the furtherance of episcopal authority is closely linked with concern for the unity of the church. The importance of unity is marked by the formula "than which nothing is better" (cf. Mag. 7.1, where it refers to Christ). No doubt the assumption is that episcopal authority and the coherence of the group are mutually interdependent. But it is also immediately made clear that such interdependence rests on the willingness of the bishop to "bear with all people" (cf. "bear the illnesses of all" in 1.3) "as the Lord also bears with you" (for the significance of the comparison see on Mag. 6.1); or to "put up with all people in love" (cf. Eph. 4.2) "as you in fact do" (for the use of this formula to soften commands see on Eph. 4.1).

■ **1.3** There follows a list of exhortations that shows in greater detail how the bishop is to carry out his task. The first three focus on the bishop's personal piety but at the same time have in view his readiness for assuming the burden of pastoral work. Traditional paraenetic material lies behind these commands. The bishop is to "take time" (σχολάζειν, cf. 1 Cor 7:5) for "constant" prayer (cf. 1 Thess 5:17).[7] He is to ask especially for more "understanding" (σύνεσιν) than he has in order to deal with the problems of the church.[8] And he is to maintain this prayerful attitude by "being watchful" (γρηγορεῖν) and keeping a "sleepless" (ἀκοίμητον) spirit.[9]

Ignatius then turns to the bishop's dealings with the community. He is to speak to people "individually" (for the importance of such personal contact see on Pol. 4.2) but with a view to their integration in the community.[10] The climax of the passage is reached with the command "to bear the illnesses of all as a perfect athlete." The

3   Otto Bauernfeind, "τρέχω," TDNT 8 (1972) 234: "Polycarp still has some distance to go."

4   Cf. BAG s.v. παρακαλέω 2, p. 622.

5   LSJ s.v. ἐκδικέω, p. 504.

6   Friedrich Preisigke, Wörterbuch der griechischen Papyrusurkunden (3 vols.; Berlin: Selbstverlag der Erben, 1925–31) 1. 442.

7   For other parallels see on Eph. 10.1.

8   Cf. 2 Tim 2:7, where the author draws special attention to the fact that "the Lord will give understanding (σύνεσιν) in everything" to Timothy. It is interesting to note (in light of Ignatius' use of

athletic imagery here) that the preceding verses call upon Timothy to suffer and labor on behalf of the community like a soldier, athlete, or farmer. Perhaps the request for understanding originally drew on 1 Kgs 3:5–14 where Solomon asks the Lord to give him σύνεσις to make sound judgments for the people.

9   Prayer and wakefulness are mentioned together in Col 4:2 (γρηγορεῖν "be watchful") and Eph 6:18 (ἀγρυπνεῖν "be sleepless"); cf. Matt 26:41; Luke 21:36.

10   The phrase κατ᾽ ἄνδρα ("individually") is linked elsewhere with expressions that emphasize the importance of the individual as a member of the

sentence contains two parts whose connection is perhaps not immediately obvious. (a) "Bear the illnesses (τὰς νόσους βάσταζε) of all" reflects a form of Isa 53:4 found in Matt 8:17. It has been suggested that Ignatius derived the verse from some other Greek version of the Bible (Aquila and Symmachus say of the servant of the Lord τὰς νόσους ἡμῶν ἀνέλαβεν "took up our illnesses"; and in Aquila the verb βαστάζειν "to bear" appears in Isa 53:11). But the similarity between Matthew and Aquila (or Symmachus)—the reference to τὰς νόσους "(our) illnesses"—depends on the fact that both are closer to the Hebrew than the Septuagint; consequently the disagreement between Ignatius and Aquila (or Symmachus) on the verb is significant; and it seems improbable that Ignatius and Matthew would independently have taken the verb βαστάζειν ("to bear") from Isa 53:11 (Aquila) and combined it with Isa 53:4 (or that there was some other version which had such a reading).[11] Thus Ignatius is likely to reflect Matthew here, a tradition dependent on Matthew, or a source used by Matthew. Neither of the last two possibilities should be discounted. For Irenaeus (*Adv. haer.* 4.33.11–12) at the end of a dossier of texts from Isaiah quotes the Matthaean form of Isa 53:4 to refer to Jesus as healer (as does Matthew) and follows it immediately by an allusion to the Septuagint form of Isa 53:3 which (along with other material) he takes to refer to the events of Christ's passion; and in his popular exposition of Christian teaching (*Dem.* 67–68) he provides the same double treatment of the text again (the Matthaean form of Isa 53:4 followed this time by a full quotation of the Septuagint form of Isa 52:13—53:5). This suggests the existence of a list of biblical prophecies that made use of two forms of Isa 53:4. The form reflected by Ignatius may have come into the tradition from Matthew himself or from the school out of which the evangelist apparently worked. And Ignatius' teaching about the imitation of Christ (*Rom.* 6.3) would make the application of the text to episcopal activity appropriate.[12] (b) In any event, Polycarp is to endure as "a perfect athlete." The author of the Pastoral Epistles also associates this image with the gift of pastoral understanding (2 Tim 2:5, 7). Thus the preceding exhortations are all to be seen as addressed to the spiritual guide who must sustain hard blows. The image of the athlete is used widely in Hellenistic literature of the man who strives for virtue,[13] and in Judaism and Christianity with particular reference to the martyr (*4 Macc.* 6.10; 17.15–16; *1 Clem.* 5.1–2). Philo has the expression "perfect athlete" (ἀθλητὴς τέλειος) which he uses of Abraham's spiritual victory in journeying from Haran to Palestine (*Migr. Abr.* 27). Epictetus' call (in *Diss.* 3.15.11; cf. 1.7.30) to the philosophic athlete (cf. *Diss.* 3.10.7–8) to "be awake" (ἀγρυπνῆσαι), "to labor" (πονῆσαι), and "to conquer" (νικῆσαι) provides an additional link between Ignatius' use of the image of the athlete and the preceding exhortations to Polycarp.

The concluding aphorism in 1.3 seems to have been coined by Ignatius, although a remark of Tertullian's about athletes in his reflections on martyrdom is comparable: "the more they labor in exercise, the more they hope of victory" (*Ad. mart.* 3). The thought is made all the more striking in Ignatius by the neat parallelism and the alliteration: ὅπου πλείων κόπος, πολὺ κέρδος ("where there is greater labor, great is the gain").[14] It is worth noting that πόνος rather than κόπος is the word used for athletic effort ("labor") in Hellenistic sources, and that it was apparently Paul (Gal 6:17) who first spoke of κόπος in this connection.[15] The use of the Pauline term underscores the pastoral significance that the imagery has for Ignatius.

---

group (*Eph.* 4.2; 20.2; *Tr.* 13.2; *Sm.* 5.1; 12.2). (For ὁμοήθεια θεοῦ as "godly unity of spirit" see on *Mag.* 6.1.)

11 Krister Stendahl, *The School of St. Matthew* (Philadelphia: Fortress, 1968) 106–7.

12 For precedents to such an application of the text see Joachim Jeremias, "παῖς θεοῦ," *TDNT* 5 (1967) 712. In this connection it seems evident that Ignatius is thinking primarily of Christ's suffering rather than his healing activity. For the verse is applied to Polycarp as the "perfect athlete" (see on the "perfect human being" in *Sm.* 4.2) whose "labor" brings reward. And the verb βαστάζειν ("to bear") suggests the need to endure (cf. Rom 15:1; Gal 6:2). Yet the word "illnesses" cannot be slighted, especially since Ignatius immediately goes on to address Polycarp also as a spiritual physician (*Pol.* 2.1). Apparently there was a confluence of the two images in his mind (see on *Pol.* 2.3).

13 Cf. Plutarch *De ser. num. vind.* 18, 561a; Epictetus *Diss.* 1.24.1–2; 3.10.7–8.

14 Cf. Perler, "Das vierte Makkabäerbuch," 58–60.

15 Victor C. Pfitzner, *Paul and the Agon Motif* (NovTSup 16; Leiden: Brill, 1967) 102–3.

Exhortations to Polycarp [1.2–5.2]

2

**Dealing with
the More Troublesome**

1   If you love good disciples, you have no credit; rather, bring the more troublesome into subjection by gentleness. "Not every wound is healed by the same salve." "Stop attacks by embrocations." 2/ Be prudent as a serpent in everything and always pure as the dove. You are both fleshly and spiritual that you may humor things visible to your eyes; ask that things unseen be revealed, so that you may lack nothing and abound in every gift. 3/ The occasion requires you, as pilots (require) winds, and as a storm-tossed sailor a port, to attain God. Be sober, as God's athlete; the prize is incorruptibility and eternal life, concerning which you too are persuaded. In every way I am your expiation, as are my bonds which you loved.

The reason for the emphasis on endurance becomes clear in *Pol.* 2.1–3 where the bishop is instructed as to how he is to deal with the more troublesome. Presumably Ignatius has in mind ordinary troublemakers as opposed to false teachers. For the latter (it seems) are dealt with later (*Pol.* 3.1). Although the treatment of the troublemakers is less severe than that of the false teachers, the medical imagery indicates that even here the aim of the Smyrnaean bishop is to be the total eradication of opposition.

■ **2.1** The paragraph begins with the admonition to pay attention not only to "good disciples" but also to the "more troublesome." The similarity of the first part of the admonition to Luke 6:32 ("if you love those who love you, what credit have you?") suggests an indebtedness to common tradition (presumably reflected also in 1 Pet 2: 18–19; cf. *Did.* 1.3; *2 Clem.* 13.4). The metaphorical significance of the expression τοὺς λοιμοτέρους ("the more troublesome")—literally, "the pestilential"—was often scarcely felt[1] but is probably more alive here than usual. For Ignatius has just spoken of bearing the "illnesses" (νόσους) of all,[2] and he is about to launch into more medical language. In any event, the expression is a

strong one, and it may be that Ignatius himself felt affronted by the more troublesome in Smyrna. For in *Sm.* 12.1 he complains that not all (presumably in Smyrna) were as solicitous for his needs as Burrhus, who had been sent along at the expense of the Ephesians and Smyrnaeans. Here, too, then, there may have been some feeling that Ignatius' expectations were too high (see on *Eph.* 2.1). In any event, the troublemakers are to be brought into line. The control over the community is to be total.

At the same time, the troublemakers are to be handled "with gentleness."[3] The two medical maxims make that point. (a) That the physician should vary treatment depending on the person or the problem was a strong emphasis in medical sources. Thus Galen notes that "as has often been said, one drug cannot suit all bodies";[4] and later in the same context he uses the same terminology as Ignatius in speaking of "salves" (ἔμπλαστροι) and the attempt "to heal wounds" (τραύματα θεραπεύειν).[5] A metaphorical use of the rule was common in advising philosophers, lawyers, and rulers to adopt remedies fit for the occasion.[6] (b) The emphasis on gentleness is even clearer in the command to stop "attacks" (paroxysms) by

---

1   Cf. BAG *s.v.* λοιμός, p. 480.

2   Note that λοιμός ("plague") and νόσος ("illness") occur together in Aelian *Var. hist.* 14.11 as metaphors for an overbearing person.

3   Ignatius' use of medical language is like that of the Pastorals in stressing the need for mild treatment. Traditional philosophers made a similar use of the imagery in opposition to the radical methods of the

Cynic teachers (Abraham J. Malherbe, "Medical Imagery in the Pastoral Epistles," in W. Eugene March, ed., *Texts and Testaments: Critical Essays on the Bible and Early Church Fathers* [San Antonio: Trinity University, 1980] 19–35). This is another indication of the appreciation of conservative aspects of Greek culture by Ignatius.

4   *Compos. medic.* 2.1 (Kühn, *CGO* 13. 468).

"embrocations." In ancient medicine the term "paroxysm" referred to the events leading up to a crisis and was contrasted with the "quieting" that follows it (Hippocrates *Aph.* 1.12). An embrocation or fomentation was a liquid (such as oil and water) used for (among other things) the soothing of paroxysms (cf. Celsus *De medic.* 3.7.2 where embrocation is recommended for fevers *in ipsis accessionibus,* i.e., when the paroxysms strike). Numerous passages show that the advice to use embrocations was associated with efforts to soothe and to avoid anything harsh.[7] Nor was Ignatius alone in applying such advice to interpersonal relations or spiritual matters.[8]

■ **2.2** The same combination of fixity of purpose and gentleness (verging on craft) is expressed in the proverbial wisdom that follows here. The maxim puts into the singular what is given in the plural in Matt 10:16. But the sentiment was also more widely spread. According to the Midrash on the Song of Songs, "R. Judah said in the name of R. Simon: God spoke concerning the Israelites: to me be simple as the doves, but to the peoples of the world sly as the serpents" (2.14).[9] Another application of the theme is apparently made in Rom 16:19 ("I want you to be wise as to good, and pure as to evil"). Thus Ignatius is probably in touch with a traditional saying.

Ignatius immediately translates these thoughts into his own theological idiom. Since Polycarp is both "fleshly and spiritual" (cf. *Eph.* 8.2), not only can he come to terms with what is visible to his eyes (πρόσωπον "face"), but he is also in a position to ask for insight into deeper matters. In this connection, the term ἀόρατα ("things unseen") evidently refers to theological mysteries (cf. *Mag.* 3.2; *Tr.* 5.2; *Rom.* 5.3; *Sm.* 6.1; *Pol.* 3.2); the verb φανερόω ("reveal") has to do with God's activity in revealing them (cf. *Rom.* 8.2); and the "gift" (χάρισμα)

that Polycarp is to receive designates the spiritual endowment that follows (cf. *Eph.* 17.2; *Sm.* inscr). But since the purpose of this endowment is to enable Polycarp to deal with the spiritual diseases of his congregation, it seems likely that the contrast between "things visible" (τὰ φαινόμενα) and "things unseen" (τὰ ἀόρατα) owes something to the medical contrast between open symptoms and underlying causes of illnesses. It may not be accidental that Ignatius also refers to Christ, "the one physician," as "both fleshly and spiritual" (*Eph.* 7.2). As Galen indicates, the traditional dogmatic or rationalist school of medicine used "the method of inference from the visible to the invisible" (*On Medical Experience* 10.1; cf. 10.6; 11.1, 2).[10] In this connection the Greek sources oppose τὰ φαινόμενα ("things visible") to τὰ ἄδηλα ("things unclear").[11] Our suggestion is that Ignatius gives a theological turn to the contrast by substituting "things unseen" (τὰ ἀόρατα) for "things unclear" (τὰ ἄδηλα). The substitution was an easy one. For as Hippocrates (*De art.* 11) notes, one who sees with the eyes alone cannot be a good doctor since most diseases are "unclear" (ἄδηλα) and "not easily seen" (οὐκ ἐν εὐόπτῳ). And Galen later opposes the methodist school of physicians with the words: "And how do you see (βλέπεις) the strength [of the patient]? For surely it is not visible (μὴ γὰρ φαίνεται)."[12] The peculiar notion of "humoring" (κολακεύειν) the things that are visible probably also reflects medical language. One source (admittedly a late one) uses the verb in describing the need to "soften" or "make mild" the "substance" (ὕλην) of an illness by

---

5   Ibid. (Kühn, *CGO* 13. 469).

6   Chalcidius *In Plat. Tim. comm.* 1 (ed. Wrobel, p. 70); Quintilian *Inst.* 4.2.84; Plutarch *Adulat.* 36, 74d; Philo *Joseph.* 33; Libanius *Or.* 59.150.

7   Cf. Galen *Vict. rat.* 4 (Kühn, *CGO* 19. 193; *CMG* V,9/1. 375); 8 (Kühn, *CGO* 19. 210; *CMG* V,9/1. 385); Oribasius *Coll. med.* 89.7 (*CMG* VI,2/2. 268).

8   Plutarch *Adulat.* 37, 74d; Dio Chrysostom *Or.* 17.6.

9   Wilhelm Bacher, *Die Agada der Palästinensischen Amoräer* (3 vols.; Strassburg: Trübner, 1892–99) 3. 197 n. 3.

10   Translated from the Arabic by Richard Walzer,

Galen on Medical Experience (London: Oxford, 1944) 100.

11   Cf. Galen *Sect.* 5–6 (Kühn, *CGO* 1. 78–82); *Method. med.* 2.5 (Kühn, *CGO* 10. 104).

12   *Vict. rat.* 4.7 (Kühn, *CGO* 19. 206; *CMG* V,9/1. 379).

suitable ointments and baths.[13] Polycarp, then, will be able both to treat the symptoms and to explore the underlying causes.[14] Note that this interpretation of the text coheres with Ignatius' use of the verb φαίνεσθαι ("to appear") in *Rom.* 3.2–3 to point up the contrast between words and deeds, that is, between what appears on the surface and what is actually the case.[15]

■ **2.3** At this point Ignatius shifts from medical to nautical imagery. The bishop is compared to the pilot of a ship. The image of the ship of state is old and widespread in Hellenism.[16] Particularly relevant, however, is a passage in Plutarch (*Praec. gerend. reipubl.* 19, 815b; 815d) where the Greek statesman is referred to both as a physician who heals the "diseases" (νοσήματα) of the people (cf. *Pol.* 1.3; 2.2) and as one who guides the city when storms strike. The parallel has more than literary significance.[17] Plutarch is describing the risks faced by the Greek statesman in trying to direct the affairs of Greek cities subject to the Romans. On the one hand, the statesman must deprive the Romans of excuses for intervention by healing the citizens of reckless behavior and disunity. On the other hand, he must pilot them through troubles when they come. Much is made by Plutarch (*Praec. gerend. reipubl.* 32, 823f–825a) of the value of ὁμόνοια or "concord"—the same term that figures so importantly in Ignatius (see on *Eph.* 4.1–2; 13.1). The church, then, is in some respects like the Greek city (see Introduction, 3.5).[18] Both regard themselves as threatened from without. That in turn may explain Ignatius' relatively hopeful view of pagans in the immediate environment of the churches (see on *Eph.* 10) and the fact that the

"world" looms larger as a hostile power when he thinks of Rome (see on *Rom.* 2.2; 3.3; 5.1).

But the situation is still more complex. For whereas Ignatius' emphasis on the reality of the incarnation is linked with his relatively positive attitude toward the things of this world (see on *Eph.* 8.2), his emphasis on the reality of Christ's passion is connected with his awareness of the marginal position of Christianity in society as a whole (see on *Eph.* 10). Ignatius as martyr embodies this marginality in a particularly striking form; yet it has significance for him primarily as he seeks to define his ambivalent relation to the churches—including the church in Antioch (see especially on *Eph.* 8.1; 12.1). Since every bishop is in principle similarly situated, Polycarp too must be prepared to be misunderstood and to bear up under attack. He must be prepared to think of himself as something of a martyr in his own congregation.

Several elements in the passage underscore this point: (a) The situation is one that puts Polycarp under great pressure. He must face dreadful calms and dangerous storms. In this connection the expression ὁ καιρός ("the occasion") is not eschatological (as, for example, in Mark 13:33) but reflects common Greek usage for the "need of the moment" (Sophocles *Philoct.* 466; cf. Lucian *Nav.* 17; *Jupp. Trag.* 15). (b) The result of Polycarp's endurance in responding to the occasion is described in martyrological terms as "attaining God" (see on *Eph.* 1.2). This is the only passage in which Ignatius uses the strengthened form of the verb (ἐπιτυγχάνω "attain") of anyone other than himself (see on *Eph.* 10.1). The path to salvation for

---

13 Alexander of Tralles 1.11 (Theodor Puschmann, *Alexander von Tralles* [2 vols.; Vienna: Braumüller, 1878–79] 1. 493).

14 Another intriguing possibility is that Ignatius' devotion to ἕνωσις "union" (cf. *Pol.* 1.2) also had medical overtones. For Galen treats disease as the dissolution of the "union" (ἕνωσις) of the body (*Method. med.* 6.1; Kühn, *CGO* 10. 384–85).

15 Galen also quite naturally knows the traditional contrasts between "being" and "appearing," "truth" and "seeming" (*Method. med.* 2.5 [Kühn, *CGO* 10. 114]), and "name" and "deed" (*Method. med.* 3.7 [Kühn, *CGO* 10. 204]) or "word" and "deed" (*Vict. rat.* 4.6 [Kühn, *CGO* 19. 197; *CMG* V,9/1. 197]).

16 Aeschylus *Sept.* 1–3; Plato *Resp.* 6, 488a–e; Polybius 6.44.3–7; Demetrius *De elocut.* 78; and the scholiast on Aristophanes *Vesp.* 29 (also see on *Sm.* 11.3 the

discussion of the term "harbor").

17 Philo (*Joseph.* 33) also links the images of pilot and physician in a discussion of political activity. Ignatius was evidently building on a commonplace.

18 More purely literary and homiletical is the later use of the figure of the pilot in the church where it is regularly applied to God and where bishops are often seen as subordinate officers on the ship (Campbell Bonner, "Desired Haven," *HTR* 34 [1941] 63).

Polycarp, as for Ignatius, lies through suffering (a suffering occasioned in both instances by the effort to maintain unity in the church). (c) Ignatius underscores this thought by returning to the image of the athlete (cf. *Pol.* 1.3). If Polycarp is "sober" like an athlete in training (cf. Epictetus *Diss.* 3.15.2–3; *Ench.* 29.2; Plutarch *Adulat.* 17, 59f), there lies before him a "prize" in the same way that a prize lies before the athlete.[19] Just how hard the trials of the athlete are will become apparent in a moment (in *Pol.* 3.1). (d) The expression "you too" (καὶ σύ) in the clause "concerning which you too are persuaded" (namely the prize of incorruptibility and eternal life) seems to mean "you as well as I" and suggests that Ignatius' own sufferings are not indeed far from his thoughts as he portrays the role of the bishop of Smyrna. This, then, prepares the way for the reference to Ignatius and his "bonds" as "your (sing.) expiation" (σου ἀντίψυχον) and the grateful reminder of the fact that Polycarp "loved" his visitor's bonds. The line expresses respect for Polycarp, partly because Ignatius must relate to him in the ambivalent role of an "expiation" (the expression draws attention to his humble and degraded condition and his sense of inferiority to the churches; see on *Eph.* 8.1), partly because Polycarp (who must also learn to endure much) saw beyond appearances and recognized the true significance of Ignatius' bonds (see on *Sm.* 10.2). The appearance of this complex compliment at this point links the fate of the two bishops and may have in view especially Polycarp's willingness to endure troubles for the sake of unifying the Christians in Smyrna and gaining their support for Ignatius' cause.

---

19 For θέμα as the athlete's "prize" see Karl F. W. Dittenberger, *Sylloge Inscriptionum Graecarum* (3d ed.; 4 vols.; Leipzig: Hirzel, 1915–24) 2.867,67; 3.1063,21 (see n. 4).

Exhortations to Polycarp [1.2–5.2]

3

Dealing with False Teachers

1 Let those seemingly worthy of confidence, yet holding erroneous teachings, not strike fear in you. Stand firm as an anvil when struck. It is the mark of a great athlete to be battered and yet be victorious. Especially for God's sake we must put up with everything, that he may also put up with us. 2/ Become more diligent than you are. Observe the times. Look for him who is above time—
   non-temporal,
   invisible,
      for our sakes visible,
   intangible,
   impassible,
      for our sakes passible,
one who endured in every way for our sakes.

■ **3.1** The bishop is to respond with even greater firmness to false teachers. The latter give the impression of being worthy of trust (in *Tr.* 6.2 they are said to disguise their views) yet must be recognized as "holding erroneous teachings" (ἑτεροδιδασκαλοῦντες; cf. *Mag.* 8.1: ἑτεροδοξίαι "erroneous opinions"; *Sm.* 6.2: ἑτεροδοξοῦντες "holding erroneous opinions"). Ignatius is referring to the docetists of *Sm.* 4–8. Here healing is beside the point (see on *Sm.* 4.1; 7.2). The bishop can only endure. The image of the anvil is used elsewhere in Greek literature of people who bear up under blows in battle or fighting (Aeschylus *Pers.* 51; Aristophon, in Athenaeus *Deipn.* 6, 238b); and the scholiast who comments on Callimachus' description of Heracles as the "Tirynthian anvil" (*Hymn.* 3.146) offers this explanation: "one who does not grow weary in contests" (ὁ μὴ καμὼν ἐπὶ τοῖς ἄθλοις). The participle τυπτόμενος ("when struck") is used in *4 Macc.* 6.10 of the "noble athlete" who endures out of loyalty to God's law. And the most important terms in what follows appear elsewhere as agonistic metaphors for personal endurance: "to be battered" (δέρεσθαι; cf. Epictetus *Diss.* 3.10.7); "be victorious" (νικᾶν; cf. Epictetus *Diss.* 3.15.11; *4 Macc.* 17.11, 15); "put up with" or "endure" (ὑπομένειν; cf. Aristotle *E.N.* 3.12, 1117a 29–b 22; *4 Macc.* 6.9; 17.12; ὑπομένειν πληγάς "endure blows" occurs in the passage from Aristophon referred to above). Ignatius plays on the meaning of the last term (ὑπομένειν "put up

with") by taking it to refer both to our "endurance" and to God's "toleration" for us.

■ **3.2** The call to "be more diligent" that opens the next section apparently has to do with Polycarp's handling of the docetists. For we have seen that the theological lines in Smyrna were not as strictly drawn as Ignatius would have liked (see on *Sm.* 4.1; 5.2, 3; 6.1; 7.1; 8.2); and the appearance in our passage of an impressive list of essentially anti-docetic christological antitheses indicates what concerns him here. The second exhortation ("observe the times") points in the same direction. For although the line has eschatological overtones (cf. the "last times" of *Eph.* 11.1), the focus of attention is elsewhere. In ordinary Greek the expression οἱ καιροί ("the times") refers to critical or difficult times,[1] and the singular of the word has just been used in *Pol.* 2.3 of the situation brought about by troublemakers in Smyrna. Note that in *Sm.* 6.2 the Christians are told to "observe" (καταμάθετε) those who cause divisions in Smyrna (the verb occurs only in these two passages in Ignatius).

The command to "observe the times (τοὺς καιρούς)" is linked with the following christological attributes through the exhortation to "look for him who is beyond time (τὸν ὑπὲρ καιρόν)"—to wait on Christ for release from troubles. Under the circumstances the phrase ὑπὲρ καιρόν ("beyond time") must mean something like "beyond every vicissitude." At the same time, the phrase

---

1   LSJ *s.v.* καιρός III. 4, p. 860.

was also selected to lead over (by a play on the word) to the theologically more precise attribute "non-temporal" (ἄχρονον). The imperative, "look for" (προσδόκα), suggests that the help of the Timeless One is expected in eschatological terms (somewhat similarly, προσδοκᾶν in *Mag.* 9.2 is used in connection with a discussion of the prophets' expectations of the coming of Christ; cf. Matt 11:3; 24:50; 2 Pet 3:12–14). Note that the exhortation to mark and avoid false teachers in Rom 16:17–19 is likewise followed by encouragement in an eschatological form (Rom 16:20, "the God of peace will soon crush Satan under your feet"). At the same time, the christological attributes in Ignatius are evidently designed to encourage Polycarp to "endure" or "put up with" everything (3.1) by reminding him of Christ "who in every way endured (ὑπομείναντα) for our sakes." And since this expression stands apart at the end of the list, it presumably reveals Ignatius' overriding concern. Once again eschatological language is made to serve a new function (see on *Eph.* 11.1). "Look for," then, virtually means to "endure as you wait for." Thus the christological attributes are meant not only to underscore the reality of the incarnation and the passion (in opposition to docetism) but also to motivate the suffering of the bishop. We have seen that the union of the two themes is of fundamental importance to Ignatius (see on *Tr.* 10; *Sm.* 4.2).

The christological attributes of *Pol.* 3.2 find their closest parallel in *Eph.* 7.2, but there are also important differences between the two texts. First, we have seen that the last element in our passage ("one who endured . . .") stands apart and determines the purpose of the passage as a whole. Second, *Pol.* 3.2 is dominated to a greater extent by negative attributes of God (or Christ) and is thus closer to its philosophical sources. This probably explains the fact that whereas in *Eph.* 7.2 mention of Christ's earthly condition precedes that of his heavenly status, the reverse is true in *Pol.* 3.2: the preponderance of negative attributes is correlated with the fact that Ignatius here chose to speak first of Christ's place in the sphere of the divine. The second and fourth of these attributes ("invisible" and "impassible") are followed by antitheses ("visible for our sakes" and "passible for our sakes") appropriate in an anti-docetic context ("passible"/"impassible" occurs in *Eph.* 7.2). The first and third attributes ("non-temporal" and "intangible") lack antitheses only because they are linguistically impossible ("temporable") or theologically odd ("tangible"). Christological antitheses of some kind represent an old element in the tradition. But they have undergone important revision in Ignatius. As we have seen, he (or his source) adapts the two-stage christological thinking of Rom 1:3–4 to a more sharply articulated incarnational theology (see on *Eph.* 18.2; *Sm.* 1.1); and he leaves behind the earlier more or less poetic descriptions of the entrance of Christ into the world (Phil 2:6–11; cf. 2 Cor 8:9) for language that is more precise metaphysically. These revisions are bound up with dependence on Hellenic views of the divine and the use of negative (anti-anthropomorphic) attributes for God. In their new context such attributes require paradoxically worded antitheses in order to bridge the widening metaphysical gulf between God and the world. Thus the early apologetic *Preaching of Peter* says that "God is one who made the beginning of all things and has power over the end; and he is the unseen (ἀόρατος) who sees all, the uncontained who contains all, the one beyond need whom all things need . . ." (Clement Alex. *Strom.* 6.4, 39.1–2). Such language, as van Unnik suggests, probably arose in circles of educated Christians.[2] And it is surely in such circles that the possibility of applying the same approach to christology was appreciated.[3] In any event, the new theology proved relevant in the encounter with docetism, and its usefulness was evident to churchmen like Ignatius. It was not long before others were also saying that in Christ the invisible became visible, the incomprehensible comprehensible, and the impassible passible (Irenaeus *Adv. haer.* 3.16.6; cf. Melito frg. 13).

---

2   W. C. van Unnik, "Die Gotteslehre bei Aristides und in gnostischen Schriften," *Theologische Zeitschrift* 17 (1961) 166–74. For further discussion of the philosophical background see Paulsen, *Studien*, 118–21. Hellenistic Judaism probably played the decisive role in mediating these themes to Christians (cf. William R. Schoedel, "'Topological' Theology and Some Monistic Tendencies in Gnosticism," in Martin Krause, ed., *Essays on the Nag Hammadi Texts in Honour of Alexander Böhlig* [NHS 3; Leiden: Brill, 1972] 88–108). For other possible contacts with the *Preaching of Peter* in Ignatius see on *Sm.* 3.2.

3   Cf. Paulsen, *Studien*, 121–22.

For God as "non-temporal" (ἄχρονος) compare Plutarch *De E* 20, 393a (God "exists according to no time but according to an immovable and *non-temporal* eternity"); Philo *Sacr.* 76 ("God's swift and *non-temporal* power"). For God as "invisible" (ἀόρατος) see especially Maximus of Tyre *Or.* 2, 10a (God is "greater than time and the passage of time" and "*invisible* to the eyes"); Diodorus Siculus 2.21.7; Philo *Opif. mund.* 69; *Conf.* 138; *Leg.* 318; cf. John 1:18; Rom 1:20; Col 1:15 ("the image of the *invisible* God"); 1 Tim 1:17 ("the incorruptible, *invisible,* only God"); Heb 11:27. That God is "intangible" (ἀψηλάφητον) apparently cannot be directly illustrated from ancient sources; but the equivalent is found: Maximus of Tyre *Or.* 11, 9d ("the divine is invisible to the eyes" and "impalpable to flesh" [ἀναφὲς σαρκί]; and

note that Hesychius defines ἀναφής as ἄψαυστος, ὁ μὴ ψηλαφώμενος "untouched, not tangible");[4] Philo *Leg.* 6 (τὸν ἄψαυστον καὶ ἀναφῆ πάντῃ θεόν "the wholly untouchable and impalpable God"; and note that Hesychius defines ἄψαυστον "untouchable" as ἀψηλάφητον "intangible"). As for God's impassibility, Sextus Empiricus (*Pyrr. hypot.* 1.162; cf. 1.225) rightly regards it as a "dogma of the philosophers" that ἀπαθές ἐστι τὸ θεῖον "the divine is impassible."

---

4 Ignatius' use of the term ἀψηλάφητον in particular may have been determined by the tradition in which the resurrected Jesus says, "handle me (ψηλαφήσατέ με) and see . . ." (*Sm.* 3.2).

4

The Social Order of the Church

1   Let the widows not be neglected; after the Lord, you be their guardian. Let nothing take place without your approval; nor do you do anything without God, which indeed you do not; stand firm. 2/ Let meetings be held more often; seek out all individually; 3/ do not despise slaves, male or female, but neither let them be puffed up; rather let them serve all the more to the glory of God, that they may attain a greater freedom from God; let them not desire to be set free out of the common fund, that they may not be found slaves of lust.

5

1/ Avoid evil arts; better yet, preach sermons about them.

■ **4.1** Ignatius now turns to somewhat less problematic areas of church life. First of all, the widows are to be cared for (cf. *Sm.* 6.2; 13.1). The centrality of the concern was no doubt one of the things that made membership in Christian communities attractive. By the same token, control of the funds involved was obviously important (as may be seen from the struggle over such control at Carthage in the days of Cyprian and Novatus).[1] That may be one reason for Ignatius' instruction to Polycarp in this context to "let nothing take place without your approval." The issue is important: the bishop must "stand firm" ($\epsilon \dot{v} \sigma \tau \acute{a} \theta \epsilon \iota$).[2] The expression "without your approval" ($\ddot{a} \nu \epsilon v$ $\gamma \nu \acute{\omega} \mu \eta s$ $\sigma o v$) finds a good parallel already in Isocrates' advice to the prince Nicocles (54). The latter is provided a model speech to the people that contains the following command: "do not create private clubs or societies without my approval" ($\ddot{a} \nu \epsilon v$ $\tau \hat{\eta} s$ $\dot{\epsilon} \mu \hat{\eta} s$ $\gamma \nu \acute{\omega} \mu \eta s$). In the papyri $\ddot{a} \nu \epsilon v$ $\tau \hat{\eta} s$ $\gamma \nu \acute{\omega} \mu \eta s$ (and its opposite, $\mu \epsilon \tau \grave{a}$ $\tau \hat{\eta} s$ $\gamma \nu \acute{\omega} \mu \eta s$) is regularly used to indicate failure (or success) in getting permission of appropriate authorities or interested parties.[3] Again Ignatius apparently looks to the sphere of political and legal activity for models (see on *Mag.* 4).[4] At the same time he grounds episcopal authority theologically: there is a chain of command from God through the bishop to the people (see on *Pol.* inscr). The call not to neglect that responsibility is softened (as so often) by the formula "which indeed you do not" (see on *Eph.* 4.1).

■ **4.2** Again the cure for any difficulties is given in terms of

---

1   Hans Lietzmann, *The Founding of the Church Universal* (Beginnings of the Christian Church 2; New York: Scribner, 1938) 303.

2   A popular ethical term (M. Aurelius 5.18; 6.10; Epictetus *Diss.* 3.9.17; cf. Edward J. O'Neil, in Betz, *Plutarch's Ethical Writings,* 310).

3   Edwin Mayser, *Grammatik der griechischen Papyri aus der Ptolemäerzeit,* vol. 2: *Satzlehre* (3 vols.; Berlin and Leipzig: De Gruyter, 1926–34) 2. 519. Compare also the edict in Dit., *Or.* 2.669,53–54: there is to be no transfer of title "without the permission of the prefect" ($\chi \omega \rho \grave{\iota} s$ $\tau \hat{\eta} [s$ $\dot{a} \delta \epsilon \acute{\iota} a s$ $\tau o \hat{v}]$ $\dot{\epsilon} \pi \acute{a} \rho \chi o v$). Note that Ignatius uses $\chi \omega \rho \grave{\iota} s$ and $\ddot{a} \nu \epsilon v$ interchangeably in such expressions (see on *Mag.* 4).

4   Paul reflects the same background when he speaks to Philemon of wanting "to do nothing without your approval" ($\chi \omega \rho \grave{\iota} s$ $\tau \hat{\eta} s$ $\sigma \hat{\eta} s$ $\gamma \nu \acute{\omega} \mu \eta s$ $o \dot{v} \delta \grave{\epsilon} v$ . . . $\pi o \iota \hat{\eta} \sigma a \iota$, Phlm 14). That a less formal use of such language was possible is shown by Plutarch, who speaks of his wife as possibly awaiting his approval (*Consol. ad uxor.* 1, 608b: $\epsilon \dot{\iota}$ $\delta \acute{\epsilon}$ $\tau \iota$ $\beta o v \lambda o \mu \acute{\epsilon} \nu \eta$ $\mu \grave{\eta}$ $\pi \epsilon \pi o \acute{\iota} \eta \kappa a s$ $\dot{a} \lambda \lambda \grave{a}$ $\mu \acute{\epsilon} \nu \epsilon \iota s$ $\tau \grave{\eta} \nu$ $\dot{\epsilon} \mu \grave{\eta} \nu$ $\gamma \nu \acute{\omega} \mu \eta \nu$ "if you want to do something that you have left undone while you await my approval"; cf. Hubert Martin and Jane E. Phillips, in Betz, *Plutarch's Ethical Writings,* 416).

meeting more frequently (see on *Eph.* 13.1). The word συναγωγαί ("meetings") was not peculiar to the Jewish synagogue. Other groups, including the Hellenistic clubs, also used it.[5] At such meetings the bishop is to deal with people as individuals. The expression ἐξ ὀνόματος is used elsewhere in Ignatius to mean "individually";[6] but in our passage (and in *Pol.* 8.2) the more natural meaning—"by name"—is equally likely and is in any event implied. Being able to call people by name was admired as much in antiquity as it is today (Thucydides 7.69.2; Petronius *Satyr.* 44). The effort was no doubt intended to reinforce the solidarity of the Christian community.

■ **4.3–5.1** Ignatius then turns to a special problem raised by the presence of slaves in the church. That the bishop (and through him the congregation) is instructed not to despise them is one indication that slaves did not dominate the churches known to Ignatius.[7] At the same time, slaves had found a natural home in Christian circles. For the church, like many of the Hellenistic clubs[8] and the private religious associations,[9] was open to all classes—perhaps even more consistently so.[10] The situation was not entirely without its difficulties. Some slaves apparently came to expect help from the common fund in gaining manumission. Such help is known to have been forthcoming elsewhere as part of the church's efforts to aid its members materially.[11] And some Hellenistic clubs (perhaps largely servile in makeup) are known to have lent money from the common fund to members seeking manumission.[12] Since there are certain similarities in the organization of the club and the

church,[13] the expectations of the slaves in Smyrna were perhaps quite natural.

But Ignatius prefers to see them remain slaves. His attitude is paternalistic: one is not to despise slaves, but neither are slaves to forget their place. For their comfort he provides justification for this view in religious terms: slaves gain greater freedom before God the more faithfully they serve their masters. The paradox has some of the flavor of 1 Cor 7:21–22 where Paul also is usually understood to encourage slaves to remain as they are.[14] One reason for such advice is that it was hard to believe that even Christian slaves could be answerable for themselves. Thus a later writer speaks as follows about the slave who desires baptism: "and if he is the slave of one of the faithful, let his master be asked [for a character reference]. . . . But if he is a slave of a Gentile, let him learn to please his master 'so that' the Word 'be not blasphemed'" (*Const. Apost.* 8.32; cf. Isa 52:5). The author of the Pastoral Epistles already evinces the same attitude when he advises slaves to honor their (pagan) masters so that "the name of God . . . be not blasphemed" (Isa 52:5; cf. *Tr.* 8.2) and not to "despise" their Christian masters by taking advantage of the fact that they share the same faith (1 Tim 6:1–2). It is some such doubt about slaves that Ignatius reflects when he speaks of the danger of their being "puffed up." He evidently values the stability that masters provided in the lives of those who as a class had no very good reputation.

That evaluation of slaves is more directly suggested in what follows. To desire freedom at communal expense is to run the risk of becoming a slave of "lust." It seems

5   BAG *s.v.* συναγωγή, p. 790; Franz Poland, *Geschichte des griechischen Vereinswesens* (Leipzig: Teubner, 1909) 155–56.

6   In *Eph.* 20.2 it reinforces the expression κατ᾽ ἄνδρα ("severally") as the context suggests ("all individually come together").

7   Cf. Hennecke Gülzow, *Christentum und Sklaverei in den ersten drei Jahrhunderten* (Bonn: Habelt, 1969) 26–28, 93–100.

8   Reginald Haynes Barrow, *Slavery in the Roman Empire* (New York: Barnes and Noble, 1928) 165: many clubs drew membership from only one class, "but it is possible to find all classes blended together." Cf. S. Scott Bartchy, *First-Century Slavery and 1 Corinthians 7:21* (SBLDS 11; Missoula, MT: Society of Biblical Literature, 1973) 76–77.

9   Karl F. W. Dittenberger, *Sylloge Inscriptionum*

Graecarum (3d ed.; 4 vols.; Leipzig: Hirzel, 1915–24) 3.985,14–16 (from Philadelphia, first century B.C.E.): πορευόμενοι εἰς τὸν οἶκον τοῦτον ἄνδρε[ς καὶ γυναῖκες] ἐλεύθεροι καὶ οἰκέται "those entering this house, men [and women], bond and free."

10 As Gülzow argues (see n. 7 above).

11 *1 Clem.* 55.2; *Herm. Man.* 8.10; *Sim.* 1.8; *Const. Apost.* 4.9.2; cf. Gülzow, *Christentum und Sklaverei*, 91 n. 4.

12 Herbert Rädle, "Selbsthilfeorganisationen der Sklaven und Freigelassenen in Delphi," *Gymnasium* 77 (1970) 1–5.

13 Erich Ziebarth, *Das griechische Vereinswesen* (Leipzig: Hirzel, 1896) 130–32; Poland, *Geschichte des griechischen Vereinswesens*, 534.

14 For another view of the text see now Bartchy, *First-Century Slavery*, 127–83.

unlikely that dependence on the common fund would in itself have been regarded as leading to the general moral breakdown of the slave. It is more likely that Ignatius fears the effects of the removal of restraints. In fact, freedmen frequently had little choice but to take up low trades and often came to be associated with prostitution in particular.[15] This may be the ἐπιθυμία ("lust") to which Ignatius refers (the word has clear sexual significance in *Pol.* 5.2). If this is correct, we should follow Zahn and include the first line of *Pol.* 5.1 in this section and see in τὰς κακοτεχνίας ("evil arts") a reference to the low trades that minister to pleasure (note that Cicero *De off.* 1.42.150 regards the trades "that minister to pleasure" as especially reprehensible; cf. Dio Chrysostom *Or.* 7.117–18).[16] Lexicographical support for this is found in Strabo (7.3.7: "luxury and pleasures and evil arts [κακοτεχνίας] that lead to innumerable acts of greed") and Plutarch (*Apophth. Lac.* 19, 228b: Lycurgus "made Sparta off limits to all those artisans who concerned themselves with beautifying the body on the grounds that they damaged the arts by evil art [διὰ τῆς κακοτεχνίας]").[17] Polycarp and through him the Christians in Smyrna are instructed to avoid all such low trades. Indeed Polycarp is to give the

topic special attention in his sermons (for ὁμιλίαν ποιεῖν "to preach sermons" as a fixed reference to the presentation of a discourse intended to instruct or persuade see already Justin *Dial.* 28.2; 85.5).[18] There were, then, a sufficient number of people of low social standing in the community to make such sermons relevant. Clearly, pressure was to be brought to bear on them not to step beyond the bounds of respectability—not to allow the name of God to be blasphemed among the heathen (cf. *Tr.* 8.2). Slaves in particular were not to push for manumission for fear that they would find themselves in morally questionable situations.

The expression "out of the common fund" (ἀπὸ τοῦ κοινοῦ) appears in ordinary Greek to designate state expenditures[19] or the disbursements of Hellenistic clubs.[20] Neither model can be excluded here. City, club, and church all shared the emphasis on the commonality (see on *Phd.* 1.1) just as "concord" (ὁμονοία) was also highly valued by each.[21] At the same time, the church found its relation to the world as distinctly more problematic (cf. *Eph.* 10; *Rom.* 3.3).

---

15 Isaeus *De Philoctem. hered.* 19–20; Ps-Demosthenes *In Neaeram* 18; Epictetus *Diss.* 4.1.35–40; cf. Aristide Calderini, *La manomissione e la condizione dei liberti in Grecia* (Milan: Hoepli, 1908) 350–71; Arnold M. Duff, *Freedmen in the Early Roman Empire* (Oxford: Clarendon, 1928) 103–15.

16 Zahn, *Ignatius,* 321.

17 See also *LPGL s.v.* κακοτεχνία, p. 696. In *Phd.* 6.2 Ignatius refers to the "evil arts [τὰς κακοτεχνίας] and deceits" of Satan. That opens up a very wide range of possibilities for the meaning of our term. Yet a reference to "magical arts" (cf. Cyril of Jerusalem *Cat.* 19.8) seems out of place in *Pol.* 5.1. And talk of "malice" or "slander" (cf. Lucian *Alex.* 4; *Calumn.* 12), "deception" or "fraud" (*P.Teb.* 2.393,22; Dit., *Or.* 2.669,55), seems almost equally remote from the context.

18 Bartelink (*Lexicologisch-semantische studie,* 136–37) regards this meaning of the term ὁμιλία ("sermon") as derived from its use in reference to philosophical lectures.

19 BAG *s.v.* κοινός 1.b, p. 439.

20 Poland, *Geschichte des griechischen Vereinswesens,* 488–89.

21 See on *Eph.* 4.1; 13.1; and for the clubs Franz Poland, *Geschichte des griechishen Vereinswesens,* 501.

5

Marriage

1 Tell my sisters to love the Lord and to be satisfied with their mates in flesh and spirit. Likewise command also my brothers in the name of Jesus Christ to love their mates as the Lord loves the church. 2/ If anyone is able to remain continent to the honor of the Lord's flesh, let him remain (so) without boasting; if he boasts, he is lost; and if it is known beyond the bishop, he is destroyed. It is right for men and women who marry to establish their union with the approval of the bishop that the marriage may be according to the Lord and not according to lust. Let everything be done to the honor of God.

■ **5.1** The presumed reference to the immorality of slaves may have prompted this special section on marriage in general. The requirements are high. Wives are to be "satisfied" (ἀρκεῖσθαι; cf. Josephus *Bell.* 2.116; *Const. Apost.* 8.32) with their husbands. Husbands are to be equally self-controlled. The rules of the private religious association in Philadelphia (see on *Pol.* 4.3) are also strict in such matters: "A man [is not to take] another woman in addition to his own wife. . . . Woman and man [alike], whoever does any of the things above written, let them not enter this house. . . ."[1] The appearance of a strict sexual ethic in such groups is probably best explained as a corollary to marginal status in society. The group requires coherence to survive, and control of sexuality is a vital factor in maintaining such coherence (see further on 5.2). Thus (in Ignatius) marriage, a matter of the "flesh," receives a religious interpretation and becomes also a matter of the "spirit." Satisfaction with one's mate is directly linked with "loving the Lord"; and a man is instructed to love his wife "as the Lord loves the church" (a traditional theme shared by Ignatius especially with Eph 5:25, 29).[2]

■ **5.2** The tendency for Ignatius to see the union of flesh and spirit as the special mark of life in the church (see on *Eph.* 8.2) provides one reason for his cautious attitude in this section toward celibacy. A closely related concern is the potential challenge that it poses to episcopal authority (evidently most church leaders in this period were married; cf. Pol. *Phil.* 11). A symptom of Ignatius' general attitude in this regard is the fact that he can use the same word here of marriage (i.e., ἕνωσις "union") that he elsewhere uses of the solidarity of the church (for the comparison see on *Mag.* 6.1); and it is to be noted that the same drawing together of opposites—namely, flesh and spirit—is involved in the bishop's thinking about both. The emergence of a polarized ascetic elite poses a challenge to such a conception of the Christian community.

---

1 Frederick C. Grant, *Hellenistic Religions* (New York: Liberal Arts, 1953) 29. (For the Greek text see n. 9 of the preceding section.)

2 The imagery presupposes a sense of the abiding presence of Christ in the church and may depend on the speculative idea of a preexistent syzygy (Christ/ Church) in the style of Christian Gnosticism or of *2 Clement* (Paulsen, *Studien*, 146–47). We have found a similar background to the exhortation "keep your flesh as the temple of God" in *Phd.* 7.2. That passage indicates how freely Ignatius (or his source) moved from concern for the purity of the flesh to reflection on the integrity of Christ's "flesh," namely, the church (cf. *2 Clem.* 8.4–6; 14.3). Ignatius works with some such moralized version of the thought here. This background points to some of the deeper factors involved in the link between control of sexual mores and social control in general (cf. Samuel Laeuchli, *Power and Sexuality* [Philadelphia: Temple, 1972]).

The theological reason for celibacy[3] in Smyrna was given in terms of showing honor to "the flesh of the Lord." The expression may refer to the imitation of the Lord's own celibacy (Tertullian *Monog.* 5.6: "But giving the example of his own flesh to your weakness, the more perfect Adam—that is, Christ [who was unmarried]— came in the flesh"; 11.7: pagans converted in Paul's time wondered whether they could still enjoy their marriages "because they had believed in the holy flesh of Christ"; cf. Cyprian *De habit. virg.* 3). Psychologically more complex factors—including the idea that physical union adulterates the purity of the relation with Christ (cf. 1 Cor 6:12–20) or that the virgin is wedded to Christ (cf. Tertullian *Virg. vel.* 16.4)—also seem to be involved.[4]

Ignatius does not reject the ascetic way of life[5] but adds considerations that qualify its value. The first consideration is given in the form of a parallelism that shows how closely related the religious and social aspects of the situation are: if the ascetic boasts, he is lost; if his celibacy is known "beyond [πλέον, GL] the bishop,"[6] he is ruined (cf. *1 Clem.* 38.2).[7] Episcopal authority is also the main issue in the words about marriage that follow. Marriages are to take place "with the approval of the bishop." It is impossible to tell how deeply the bishop was involved. It is in Tertullian for the first time that we find reference to something like a marriage ceremony (*Ad uxor.* 2.8.6; *Pud.* 4.4; *Monog.* 11.1–2). Yet the bishop's interest was hardly superficial. "With the approval (μετὰ γνώμης) of the bishop" recalls "nothing without your approval" in *Pol.* 4.1 as well as all the other passages that make the health of the church's life depend on the presence of the bishop (see on *Mag.* 4). Marriage, then, an essentially secular event in the Graeco-Roman world, gains clear religious significance.[8] Paul had stipulated that Christians should marry "in the Lord," that is, marry other Christians (1 Cor 7:39). Ignatius takes the matter a step further by requiring Christian couples to seek the blessing of the bishop. It is only then that marriages are regarded as pleasing to God and not prompted by lust. This development put into the hands of the bishop a potent instrument of social control—"group endogamy"[9] —and no doubt contributed significantly to the tightly knit texture of the Christian community.

3 For ἐν ἁγνείᾳ μένειν ("to remain continent," "to remain in purity") of celibacy see *Act. Phil.* 119 (cf. BAG *s.v.* ἁγνεία, p. 10).

4 The background to Ignatius' argument discussed in n. 2 above (see on *Phd.* 7.2) may have been involved also in the growth of the ideal of celibacy. For purity of the flesh in this more extreme form could also be seen as a presupposition for participation in the Spirit and (hence) for union between Christ and the church symbolized in Gen 1:27 by the terms "male and female" (cf. *2 Clem.* 14.2, 4). It is significant that Ignatius does not exploit this possibility but chooses to emphasize the direct analogy between the love of a husband for his wife and the love of Christ for the church.

5 There is no indication that it was practiced by the docetists in particular. Ignatius would probably have rejected it outright if that had been so.

6 For πλέον in the sense of "beyond" see *Mag.* 10.1: "whoever is called by another name beyond this one (πλέον τούτου)." Cf. A. d'Alès, ΕΑΝ ΓΝΩΣΘΗΙ ΠΛΕΟΝ ΤΟΥ ΕΠΙΣΚΟΠΟΥ, ΕΦΘΑΡΤΑΙ, *Recherches de science religieuse* 25 (1935) 489–92.

7 Paulsen (*Studien*, 66 n. 34) suggests that these lines reflect the structure of NT "sentences of sacred law" and like them are eschatologically colored. Again, however, the eschatology presupposed has primarily individual rather than cosmic significance for Ignatius.

8 Cf. Alfred Niebergall, "Zur Entstehungsgeschichte der christlichen Eheschliessung, Bemerkungen zu Ignatius und Polykarp 5,2," in G. Müller and W. Zeller, eds., *Glaube, Geist, Geschichte, Festschrift für Ernst Benz* (Leiden: Brill, 1967) 107–24.

9 Bryan R. Wilson, *Patterns of Sectarianism* (London: Heinemann, 1967) 37.

6   Exhortations to the Smyrnaeans

1   Heed the bishop, that God may also heed you. I am an expiation of those subject to the bishop, presbyters, and deacons; and may I obtain my lot with them in God. Labor together with one another. Contend together. Run together. Suffer together. Sleep together. Rise together as God's stewards, assistants, and servants. 2/ Be pleasing to him whose soldiers you are, from whom you also receive your wages; let none of you be found a deserter. Let your baptism serve as (your) arms; your faith as (your) helmet; your love as (your) spear; your endurance as (your) panoply; your works are your deposits that you may have the savings you deserve. Be patient, then, with one another in gentleness, as God is with you. May I always benefit from you.

This section (6.1–2) is not addressed to Polycarp but to the congregation in Smyrna as a whole.[1] Thus the second-person plural obtains throughout. There seems to be no parallel in ancient letters for such a shift from singular to plural. Evidently Ignatius wished to communicate with the Christians in Smyrna a second time after the lapse of only a very short time and found it advisable to address them through their bishop. He expected that the letter would be read to the group and now drops the mask. The reason for the second letter was probably to guard against any slackening of support for the request that Ignatius had previously made of the Smyrnaeans (*Sm.* 11; repeated in *Pol.* 7) and to generate enthusiasm for the additional burden that he is about to lay on them (*Pol.* 8.1). Their bishop, Polycarp, was especially important in seeing to it that Ignatius' journey was properly announced and escorted (see on *Eph.* 2; *Rom.* 10; *Phd.* 11; *Sm.* 12.1) and (in particular) properly appreciated in Antioch (*Phd.* 10; *Sm.* 11; *Pol.* 7; 8.1). Thus the martyr's advice to Polycarp—and through Polycarp to the church in Smyrna—was intended to discourage any disobedience to Polycarp and thereby also to ensure the fulfillment of Ignatius' requests. The return to the second

person singular in *Pol.* 7.2 (and the surprising alternation between singular and plural from there to the end) shows just how impossible it was for Ignatius to think of the Christians in Smyrna without thinking first of their bishop and the latter's activity on behalf of his colleague from Antioch.

■ **6.1** This reconstruction of the situation explains the whole tenor of the passage. It begins with a command to heed the bishop[2] and presents such obedience as the ground of God's care for his addressees. There follows Ignatius' identification of himself as their "expiation"—a theme that (as we have seen) expresses admiration for those whom Ignatius chooses to regard as spiritually superior to himself and who at the same time are viewed as grasping the true significance of his bonds and lending him their support (see on *Pol.* 2.3); here their presumed superiority is emphasized by the wish that Ignatius may have a share with them in the life to come (see on *Eph.* 11.2). As the following imperatives indicate, this compliment is intended to reinforce the solidarity and resolve of the Smyrnaeans.

The first command—"labor together" ($\sigma\upsilon\gamma\kappa\omega\pi\iota\hat{\alpha}\tau\epsilon$)—conceivably involves an athletic metaphor (see on $\kappa\acute{o}\pi\sigma\varsigma$

---

1   This section cannot be regarded as directed to presbyters and deacons. The sentence "I am an expiation of those subject to the bishop, presbyters, and deacons" is a compliment that names in the genitive ($\tau\hat{\omega}\nu$ $\dot{\upsilon}\pi\sigma\tau\alpha\sigma\sigma\sigma\mu\acute{e}\nu\omega\nu$ "those subject") the ones addressed (as in the last sentence of *Pol.* 2.3).

2   Alternatively (as he says in the next sentence), the bishop, presbyters, and deacons. Ignatius emphasizes

the solidarity of the clerical orders by this substitution. But the bishop is clearly first and foremost.

"labor" in *Pol.* 1.3). Greater certainty on this score may seem to be possible in the case of the second and third commands—"contend together" (συναθλεῖτε), "run together" (συντρέχετε). Nevertheless, the verb ἀθλεῖν ("to contend") covers a wide range of physical exertions (including fighting in battle) and in metaphorical usage is often very neutral (cf. Phil 1:27; 4:3). Similarly, the verb συντρέχειν ("to run together") scarcely means more than "to agree" elsewhere in Ignatius and depends on the picture of people running together to an assembly (see on *Pol.* 1.2). Nor do suffering, sleeping, and rising together suggest any readily identifiable circle of images. To be sure, these verbs have been taken to refer to suffering, dying,[3] and rising together with Christ,[4] or the last two of them to services of worship in the evening and morning.[5] But it is hard to believe that two or three of the items in the list should be set apart from the others in this way and given such special significance. It seems evident that the σύν ("together") associated with each verb is more important than the verbs themselves. If we begin with the fact that only the concluding comparison of the Smyrnaeans with servants is clear, two solutions seem possible: (a) all the verbs describe the common labor and mutual efforts of servants (including their retiring and rising together);[6] or (b) all the verbs (including the last two) refer to the alertness required of servants. Note that "to rise" may mean to leave indolence

or carelessness behind (Rom 13:11; Epictetus *Diss.* 2.20.15);[7] that κοιμᾶσθαι ("to sleep") occasionally means "to keep watch at night";[8] and that the two verbs could be taken together to refer to alertness by night and day.

The three words used here for servants do not seem to be otherwise found together. The first two ("stewards," "assistants") are especially likely to be used for subordinates with high responsibilities.[9] "Stewards" and "servants" are mentioned together in 1 Cor 4:1 and have rich associations as applied to believers.[10] Two things speak against finding in the three terms a reference to the three orders of the ministry: the passage appears to be addressed to all the Christians in Smyrna; and it would be odd for Ignatius to refer to the one bishop by a plural term.

■ **6.2** The imagery shifts in the next section from the household to the army. But just as those who obey the bishop are regarded as servants of God, so the Christian soldiers are called on to please God ("him whose soldiers you are"). The writer of 2 Tim 2:4 also speaks of "pleasing" the one who enlists the Christian soldier. Military metaphors are found across a wide range of religious and philosophical (especially Stoic) literature of the period and were familiar to Jews as well as pagans.[11] Ignatius' method of comparing parts of the armor with aspects of the Christian faith is reminiscent particularly of Eph 6:11–17 (cf. 1 Thess 5:8); but he introduces a

---

3   "To sleep" means "to die" in *Rom.* 4.2 and frequently in the NT (cf. BAG *s.v.* κοιμάω 2, p. 438); but it is not the verb used in expressions that have to do with dying and rising "with Christ" (Rom 6:2–11; Col 2:12, 20; cf. *Mag.* 5.2; *Tr.* 9.2; *Sm.* 4.2); it is used, rather, of the state of affairs after bodily death when, at most, one can be said to sleep "in Christ" (1 Cor 15:18; cf. *Herm. Sim.* 9.16.5). Thus the suggestion is most unlikely.

4   BAG *s.v.* συγκοιμάομαι, p. 781; Bartsch, *Gnostisches Gut*, 123–24.

5   Zahn, *Ignatius*, 353.

6   The most serious difficulty here is the use of the verb συμπάσχειν ("suffer together"). For πάσχειν and συμπάσχειν always refer to Christ's passion elsewhere in Ignatius (for the latter see *Sm.* 4.2). Nevertheless, the full expression in our passage is, "suffer (together) . . . with one another" (ἀλλήλοις . . . συμπάσχετε); and it finds a nearer parallel in *2 Clem.* 4.3: "and we ought to sympathize with one another" (συμπάσχειν ἀλλήλοις); moreover, Ignatius uses the closely related verb συμπαθέω ("sympathize with") of

human relations in *Rom.* 6.3. Thus there is no real difficulty here for our proposed interpretation.

7   Cf. BAG *s.v.* ἐγείρω 2.a, p. 214.

8   Aeschylus *Agam.* 2; Xenophon *Cyrop.* 1.2.4, 9; *P.Oxy.* 6.933,25. Cf. Eduard Fraenkel, *Aeschylus, Agamemnon* (3 vols.; Oxford: Clarendon, 1950) 2. 3.

9   LSJ *s.vv.* οἰκονόμος (p. 1204), πάρεδρος (p. 1332), ὑπερέτης (p. 1872).

10   BAG *s.vv.* οἰκονόμος (p. 562), ὑπερέτης (p. 850).

11   Dibelius, *An die Kolosser, Epheser*, 96–97; Victor C. Pfitzner, *Paul and the Agon Motif* (NovTSup 16; Leiden: Brill, 1967) 42–43, 157–64; cf. Philostratus *Vit. Apoll.* 6.16, 36.

different range of vocabulary and handles the comparisons so didactically that there is less reason here than in the parallel to suspect the influence of Gnostic conceptions of a cosmic conflict between the forces of light and darkness. Three Latinisms occur in the passage: "deserter" (*desertor*), "deposits" (*deposita*), and "savings" (*accepta*). "When gifts of money were given the army on special occasions, the individual soldier received only half of what was due him; the rest was deposited to his credit in the regimental treasury, and he received it (as ἄκκεπτα) if and when he was honorably discharged."[12] Hahn could find no other instance of these Latinisms in Greek sources.[13] But Preisigke gives an example of δησέρτωρ ("deserter"),[14] and Kiessling several examples of δηπόσιτον or δηπόσειτον ("deposit") from the papyri.[15] The Latinisms may be as concentrated as they are here because of the conversation of the bishop's Roman guard. As for his references to the parts of armor, there seems to be some impreciseness: "weapons" (any defensive or offensive weapon is covered by the term), "helmet," and "spear" are clear enough; but "panoply" generally included at least shield, sword, lance, and helmet[16] and seems unnaturally narrowed here. It may be that the passage moves to a climax. In that event, the theological entities may follow some more or less logical order: baptism[17] provides the basic protection and corresponds to the "arms" (ὅπλα) by which the soldier is protected; faith and love represent the fundamental Christian virtues (see on *Eph.* 1.1; 14.1) and correspond more particularly to the two important weapons named;[18] finally, endurance corresponds to the whole armor

(πανοπλία "panoply") because it must characterize the exercise of all the previously mentioned arms if they are not to fail. Endurance is probably treated as the climax here because Ignatius seeks to confirm the Smyrnaeans in their unity and their support for his cause (see on *Pol.* 6.1). These are the "deeds" (ἔργα) put on deposit for the Smyrnaeans that will have their reward. Note that support of Ignatius' plans is shortly to be identified as a "deed" (ἔργον) in which God and the Smyrnaeans cooperate (*Pol.* 7.3). In our passage the emphasis is on the deeds that make the deed on Ignatius' behalf possible, namely, those acts in which the Smyrnaeans demonstrate their willingness to bear with one another (in imitation of God's gracious dealings with them). In any event, Ignatius assumes compliance with his recommendations. For the concluding wish is a formula that he uses to express satisfaction with what he can expect of his addressees (see on *Pol.* 1.1).

Ignatius' remark about the "gentleness" (πραότης) of God that the Smyrnaeans are to imitate bears a trace of the theory alluded to elsewhere that divine punishment is delayed because of God's goodness (see on *Eph.* 11.1; *Sm.* 9.1). The thought, as we have seen, has a Hellenic coloring; and it is worth noting that Plutarch (*De ser. num. vind.* 5, 550f) speaks specifically of God's πραότης ("gentleness") in discussing reasons for the delay of the punishment of evil-doers.[19]

---

12 BAG *s.v.* δεπόσιτα, p. 174; *s.v.* ἄκκεπτα, p. 30 (cf. Suetonius *Domit.* 7; Vegetius *De re milit.* 2.20).

13 Ludwig Hahn, *Rom und Romanismus im griechisch-römischen Osten* (Leipzig: Dieterich, 1906) 168.

14 Friedrich Preisigke, *Wörterbuch der griechischen Papyrusurkunden,* 1. 341.

15 Ibid., ed. Emil Kiessling (Berlin: Selbstverlag des Verfassers, 1944ff.) 4. 506; Emil Kiessling, *Wörterbuch der griechischen Papyrusurkunden* (Supplement 1; Amsterdam: Hakkert, 1971) 69.

16 Cf. LSJ *s.v.* πανοπλία, p. 1298; Albrecht Oepke, "ὅπλον," *TDNT* 5 (1967) 296.

17 Baptism is dealt with elsewhere by Ignatius in contexts that reflect traditional material (see on *Eph.* 18.2; *Sm.* 1.1; 8.2). Here, then, we may have themes that echo post-baptismal instruction (cf. Paulsen, *Studien,* 80). At the same time, the material seems to be thoroughly at home in this context and reflects Ignatius' own concerns. That is suggested especially by the mention of faith and love (see Introduction, 5.8). Also note that the quality of "endurance" (ὑπομονή) is elsewhere important to Ignatius (*Eph.* 3.1; *Tr.* 1.1; *Rom.* 10.3; *Sm.* 12.2; and note that the corresponding verb occurs several times: *Mag.* 1.2; 9.1; *Sm.* 4.2; 9.2; *Pol.* 3.1, 2). For the possibility that what we have here is a popular development of Pauline themes see Introduction, 5.8 n. 128.

18 Conceivably faith and love are compared to helmet and spear respectively because faith is, so to speak, defensive (a matter of basic orientation) and love offensive (the active expression of faith in deeds).

19 Hans Dieter Betz, Peter A. Dirkse, and Edgar W. Smith, in Betz, *Plutarch's Theological Writings,* 197.

7 Conclusion and Farewell

1 Since the church at Antioch in Syria is at peace (as I have been informed) thanks to your [plural] prayer, I too have become more content in a godly freedom from care, if through suffering I may attain God that I may be found a disciple by your entreaty. 2/ It is right, Polycarp most blessed of God, to convene a most God-pleasing council and to appoint someone whom you [plural] consider very dear and resolute, who can be called God's courier; to consider him worthy of going to Syria and glorifying your [plural] resolute love to the glory of God. 3/ A Christian is not his own master, but devotes himself to God. This is God's deed and yours [plural] when you [plural] accomplish it; for I rely on grace that you [plural] are ready for a good work of a God-pleasing kind.

8 Knowing the fervor of your [plural] fidelity, I exhorted you [plural] with these few lines. 1/ Thus since I was unable to write to all the churches because I am sailing any moment from Troas to Neapolis, as the (divine) will requires, you [singular] will write to the churches on this side as one who has the purpose of God, that they may also do the same thing, those who can by sending messengers, others (by sending) letters through those whom you [singular] send, that you [plural] may be glorified by an eternal deed, since you [singular] are worthy.

2/ I greet all individually, including the wife of Epitropus with the whole household of her and her children. I greet my beloved Attalus. I greet the one soon to be considered worthy of going to Syria. Grace will be with him always and with Polycarp who sends him. 3/ I wish that you [plural] may always fare well in our God Jesus Christ, in whom may you [plural] remain in the unity and care of God. I greet Alce, a name dear to me. Farewell [plural] in the Lord.

It would appear that the concluding section opens with a "request formula" of the type found in *Phd.* 10.1. In both passages the background for the request is given in an ἐπειδή ("since") clause; and the request is marked in both instances by the expression "it is right" (πρέπει in *Pol.* 7.2; πρέπον ἐστίν in *Phd.* 10.1). In the passage before us the "since" clause (7.1) is completed by a statement other than the request, and the latter delayed until 7.2. But this probably represents no more than the kind of variation that we have come to expect from Ignatius in the use of epistolary formulae (see especially on *Eph.* 1.1; *Rom.* 1.1).

■ **7.1** The "since" clause repeats the information previously given to the Smyrnaeans that the church in Antioch "is at peace" (cf. *Sm.* 11.2). The request to send someone to Antioch (7.2) had also been communicated previously to the Smyrnaeans (cf. *Sm.* 11.3). These repetitions are not surprising. Ignatius, as we have seen, had much at stake in this connection; and he is taking what seems to him to be a final opportunity (cf. 8.1) to confirm his supporters. Moreover, he remains sensitive to the dynamics of the situation. For although he still has in view the whole community in 7.1 ("your prayer" and "your entreaty" are both plural) and the request itself in 7.2 touches all of them ("you consider" and "your resolute love" are both plural), the latter is actually addressed directly to Polycarp (see on *Pol.* 6.1). This permits Ignatius to repeat himself somewhat less awkwardly. In any event, the "since" clause (7.1) breathes the confident mood of a person who (as we have argued) saw affairs settled in Antioch to his satisfaction (see on *Phd.* 10; *Sm.* 11). For that reason he is now more content and apparently easier in his mind[1] that he will see his martyrdom[2] through to a successful conclusion. For since the church in Antioch is now at peace through the "prayer" of the Smyrnaeans, he "too" has become more confident "if"—that is, "in the hope that" ($\dot{\epsilon}\dot{\alpha}\nu\pi\epsilon\rho$)[3]—he will attain God and be found a disciple by their "entreaty."[4] Thus both projects are made to depend on the intercession of the churches. And the end of troubles in Antioch is evidently taken to indicate that Ignatius may expect his own troubles to be over; or more precisely, vindication of Ignatius in Antioch is taken to mean that the bishop may now have higher hopes of God's final approval.

■ **7.2** Among the arguments in favor of finding an allusion here to the vindication of Ignatius in his own church is the insistent request in the next sentence that a representative be sent to congratulate the Christians in Antioch. Ignatius again uses terminology redolent of diplomacy. Polycarp is to call a "council" ($\sigma\nu\mu\beta\omicron\acute{\nu}\lambda\iota\omicron\nu$)[5] and "appoint" ($\chi\epsilon\iota\rho\omicron\tau\omicron\nu\hat{\eta}\sigma\alpha\iota$) someone (see on *Phd.* 10.1; *Sm.* 11.2). The name invented by Ignatius for this person—"God's courier" ($\theta\epsilon\omicron\delta\rho\acute{o}\mu\omicron\varsigma$)—may, as Zahn suggests,[6] be modelled on the term $\dot{\eta}\mu\epsilon\rho\omicron\delta\rho\acute{o}\mu\omicron\varsigma$ or "courier" (although the force of the parallel is weakened by the fact that Ignatius also refers to Christians in general as "God's couriers" in *Phd.* 2.2). In any event,

---

1   "I too have become more content in a godly freedom from care" ($\kappa\dot{\alpha}\gamma\grave{\omega}\ \epsilon\dot{\upsilon}\theta\nu\mu\acute{o}\tau\epsilon\rho\omicron\varsigma\ \dot{\epsilon}\gamma\epsilon\nu\acute{o}\mu\eta\nu\ \dot{\epsilon}\nu\ \dot{\alpha}\mu\epsilon\rho\iota\mu\nu\acute{\iota}\alpha\ \theta\epsilon\omicron\hat{\upsilon}$). The term $\epsilon\dot{\upsilon}\theta\nu\mu\acute{\iota}\alpha$ or "contentment" is the center of Plutarch's discussion of tranquility of mind (Betz, *Plutarch's Ethical Writings*, 202–8); and such contentment is naturally associated with $\dot{\alpha}\mu\epsilon\rho\iota\mu\nu\acute{\iota}\alpha$ or "freedom from care" (Hesychius gives the latter as a synonym for $\epsilon\dot{\upsilon}\theta\nu\mu\acute{\iota}\alpha$). Since neither of the two words is found elsewhere in Ignatius, they underscore the relative serenity of the bishop at this point and his growing confidence that his martyrdom will prove a glorious one. Another word used here from the same linguistic circle—$\dot{\alpha}\nu\alpha\pi\alpha\acute{\upsilon}\omega$ "refresh"—has less special significance and is spread out more evenly in Ignatius (*Eph.* 2.1; *Mag.* 15; *Tr.* 12.1; *Rom.* 10.2; *Sm.* 9.2; 10.1; 12.1).

2   Both "attaining God" and becoming a "disciple" refer to martyrdom in Ignatius (cf. *Eph.* 1.2; *Tr.* 5.2; *Rom.* 4.2; 5.3). Lightfoot suspects that a proverb accounts for the link between "suffering" ($\pi\alpha\theta\epsilon\hat{\iota}\nu$) and being found a "disciple" ($\mu\alpha\theta\eta\tau\acute{\eta}\varsigma$). Cf. Aeschylus *Agam.* 177 ($\pi\acute{\alpha}\theta\epsilon\iota\ \mu\acute{\alpha}\theta\omicron\varsigma$ "learning comes by suffering"); Herodotus 1.207; Plato *Symp.* 222b; Diogenianus *Cent.* 2.31; Philo *Heres* 73; *Somn.* 2.107; *Spec. Leg.* 4.29 ($\dot{\iota}\nu$' $\dot{\epsilon}\kappa\ \tauο\hat{\upsilon}\ \pi\alpha\theta\epsilon\hat{\iota}\nu\ \mu\acute{\alpha}\theta\eta$ "that you may learn from suffering").

3   For $\dot{\epsilon}\acute{\alpha}\nu$ meaning "in the hope that" see Herbert W.

4   Smyth, *A Greek Grammar* (Cambridge, MA: Harvard University, 1956) 533 (section 2354).

4   $A\grave{\iota}\tau\acute{\eta}\sigma\epsilon\iota$ ("entreaty") is read by g (and the plural of the same word by A and the Arabic). GL have $\dot{\alpha}\nu\alpha\sigma\tau\acute{\alpha}\sigma\epsilon\iota$ ("resurrection"). That Ignatius should hope to be ranked with the Smyrnaeans "in the resurrection" is a possible thought for him (see on *Eph.* 11.2; *Pol.* 6.1). Yet it is unlikely that he would speak specifically of being "your disciple"—the disciple of the Smyrnaeans—in the resurrection. For elsewhere the term "disciple" refers to a disciple or disciples of Jesus Christ or is used without specification in the same sense (cf. *Eph.* 1.2; 3.1; 10.1; *Mag.* 9.1, 2; 10.1; *Tr.* 5.2; *Rom.* 4.2; 5.1, 3; and presumably also *Rom.* 3.1 and *Pol.* 2.1). Moreover, as Bauer notes, Ignatius elsewhere speaks of the fulfillment of the "entreaty" ($\alpha\dot{\iota}\tau\eta\sigma\iota\nu$) of both himself and his addressees when he thinks of his end (*Tr.* 13.3; cf. *Eph.* 20.1; *Phd.* 5.1; 8.2; *Sm.* 11.1).

5   The term is especially frequent of councils called by officials (cf. LSJ *s.v.* $\sigma\nu\mu\beta\omicron\acute{\nu}\lambda\iota\omicron\nu$, p. 1677).

6   Zahn, *Ignatius*, 286 n. 3.

this is clearly the "godly ambassador" (θεοπρεσβευτής) of *Sm.* 11.2. Lucian (as Lightfoot and others have suggested) probably had Ignatius in mind when he wrote the following concerning Peregrinus: "they say that he sent letters to almost all the famous cities more or less as testaments, counsels, and laws; and he appointed (ἐχειροτόνησε) certain of his companions as ambassadors (πρεσβευτάς) for the purpose, calling them messengers of the dead and couriers of the shades (νεκραγγέλους καὶ νερτεροδρόμους)" (*Peregr.* 41). "Couriers of the shades" in Lucian looks very much like a parody of "God's couriers" in Ignatius. If this is so, it is all the more likely that Ignatius' language reflects more or less directly the language of inter-city diplomacy. In any event, the double appearance of the word "resolute" or "unhesitating" (ἄοκνος) in this section underscores the urgency of Ignatius' appeal. Such urgency seems relevant particularly if the concern was the defense of Ignatius' policies in Antioch. The cessation of persecution would hardly have called for requests of such intensity.

■ **7.3** Similarly suggestive are the following remarks about the devotion of the Christian to God. For these lines were apparently intended to confirm the Smyrnaeans in their willingness to support Ignatius by sending the messenger to Antioch (the second-person plural is found throughout). This is the "deed" in which God and they will cooperate (cf. 8.1). (For the conception of the relation between God's grace and human achievement here see on *Sm.* 6.2.)

The concluding statement of 7.3 represents a "disclosure formula" of the type already found in *Mag.* 14.1.

It is marked by the participle εἰδώς ("knowing") and serves to call attention to a point already made[7]—here, that the "fidelity"[8] of the Smyrnaeans may be assumed (cf. *Pol.* 6.1). Other agreements between *Mag.* 14.1 and our passage include the reference to the brevity of the letter (which also introduces the conclusion in *Rom.* 8.2) and the identification of the content of the letter as "exhortation." In both instances the disclosure formula also represents a second transition to concluding material (for the first see *Mag.* 11; *Pol.* 7.1). Here it prepares the way for a new request.

■ **8.1** This request (marked like the first one in 7.1 by ἐπεί "since") is addressed directly to Polycarp. Ignatius had planned to write to "all the churches" to ask them to send representatives to Syria. Suddenly he was to be moved from Troas to Neapolis,[9] and he requests Polycarp[10] to finish the task of writing for him. Polycarp is to ask "the churches on this side" to send people to Antioch if possible and failing that to write letters that will be carried by those[11] dispatched by Polycarp. Presumably "all the churches" means the churches of Asia Minor previously contacted by Ignatius—Smyrna, Philadelphia, Ephesus, Magnesia, and Tralles. Note that "all the churches" in *Rom.* 4.1 also seems to include the churches of Asia Minor contacted up to that point. Who, then, are "the churches on this side (ἔμπροσθεν)" to whom Polycarp is to write? The spatial meaning of the adverb ἔμπροσθεν ("before" or "in front") may be clarified as follows: let A and B represent two geographical points; in moving (mentally) from A to B, the adverb is used attributively (as in Ignatius) of territory between A and B—that is,

---

7   Cf. White, *Form and Function*, 11, 45.

8   For ἀλήθεια ("truth") in this sense see BAG *s.v.* ἀλήθεια 1, p. 35.

9   He ascribes the move to "the will"—God's will (cf. *Eph.* 20.1; *Rom.* 1.1; *Sm.* 11.1). Neapolis was the harbor of Philippi in Macedonia (cf. BAG *s.v.* νέος 3, p. 538).

10   Whom he regards as having "the purpose (γνώμη) of God" (see on *Eph.* 3.2) and as being "worthy" (the expression, though far separated from the subject, clearly refers to him since it is in the singular). Polycarp's unquestioned worthiness in this connection may be taken as a reflection of the superiority that Ignatius attributes to the churches who support him (see on *Eph.* 11.2–12.1).

11   Previously Ignatius talked of selecting "someone" to be sent to Antioch (*Pol.* 7.2; cf. 8.2). And Polycarp

(*Phil.* 13.1) himself speaks of the messenger to Antioch in the singular. Lightfoot is probably right in thinking that Ignatius is referring here to the numerous messengers required to get in touch with the various churches. Such messengers would bring the letters back to Smyrna, and one "courier of God" (*Pol.* 7.2) would carry them on to Antioch. This in turn presupposes that Ignatius is thinking of localities relatively near Smyrna and relatively far from Antioch.

territory *on this side of* B rather than beyond it.[12] Presumably Ignatius has in mind the churches that lay between Polycarp (that is, Smyrna) and Antioch (the glance westward from Troas to Neapolis seems to presuppose a more fundamental orientation to the east). In other words he has in mind Ephesus, Magnesia, and Tralles. From this point of view, Philadelphia should also be regarded as among "the churches on this side," but Polycarp would know that the request had already been made of them by Ignatius (more precise information was often carried by the messenger). Ignatius himself, as we learn from Polycarp's own letter, extended his campaign into Europe and convinced the Philippians to send a letter of congratulations as far as Smyrna that it might be carried on from there to Antioch (*Phil.* 13.1).[13] Polycarp indicates that he was thinking seriously of making the trip himself. All of this adds up to an impressive amount of activity, and it makes most sense if we see it as Ignatius' attempt to confirm decisions made in Antioch that vindicated his ministry. Certainly the expression "eternal deed" (cf. 7.3) to describe the sending of messages and letters by the churches attests to the high importance that Ignatius ascribes to these activities.

■ **8.2** The letter then draws to a close. First come the greetings. There are three in all (with a fourth appended to the farewell in 8.3)—less than in *Smyrnaeans* but more than in any other letter. Ignatius' familiarity with the

church in Smyrna partly explains the phenomenon. Yet only the last two of the seven greetings in *Smyrnaeans* actually mention people by name—first the household of Tavia and then Alce with Daphnus and Eutecnus. And of these Alce is mentioned again (and similarly described) in the greeting appended in *Pol.* 8.3. The names mentioned in the first two greetings of *Pol.* 8.2—"the wife of Epitropus"[14] and Attalus[15]—are new (unless Tavia is meant by the first). The third greeting has to do with the as yet unknown messenger to Antioch. Thus Ignatius seizes the opportunity again to remind the Smyrnaeans of what he wants of them and to underscore its importance by a special word of blessing for the messenger and for Polycarp who is mainly responsible for having him sent.

■ **8.3** The letter concludes with two standard expressions of farewell—both in the plural. The first is the more complex: ἐρρῶσθαι ὑμᾶς . . . εὔχομαι ("I wish that you may fare well"). This variant is well known from the papyri,[16] and it influenced the form also of other parts of Ignatius' letters (see *Mag.* inscr; *Tr.* inscr). The simpler "farewell" (ἔρρωσθε) occurs at the very end after the special greeting to Alce. The elaboration of the first farewell mentions Jesus Christ as "our God" (see on *Eph.* inscr) and speaks of abiding in him "in the unity and care of God." It appears that just as the care of God is care exercised by God, so the unity of God is unity given by God. For

---

12   Thus Herodotus (4.24–25) speaks of "the peoples on this side" (τῶν ἔμπροσθεν ἐθνέων) of the distant land of bald men (the usage in 7.126 is less clear). I can find no basis for James A. Kleist's statement that "the adverb, when not further qualified, is used in the sense of 'preferred'; hence, 'principal, chief '" (*The Epistles of St. Clement of Rome and St. Ignatius of Antioch* [ACW 1; Westminster: Newman, 1946] 146). We do have the prepositional expression ἔμπροσθεν δικαίου "preferred before justice" (Demosthenes *Or.* 56.50; cf. LSJ *s.v.* ἔμπροσθεν, p. 548); but I have found no example in which some such meaning is extended to the attributive use of the word. For numerous examples of the attributive use in a temporal sense see Edwin Mayser, *Grammatik der griechischen Papyri aus der Ptolemäerzeit*, vol. 2: *Satzlehre* (3 vols.; Berlin and Leipzig: De Gruyter, 1926–34) 2. 170.

13   Polycarp says that the Philippians and Ignatius wrote to ask him to have the letter of the Philippians forwarded. But this does not mean that Ignatius wrote another letter to Polycarp (since the views of the former were no doubt reflected in the letter of

the Philippians) or that Polycarp understood "the churches on this side" to include Philippi (and other points west). In responding to the request from Philippi, Polycarp was adjusting to changed circumstances.

14   The name Epitropus is most unusual, though it does occur (Karl F. W. Dittenberger, *Sylloge inscriptionum Graecarum* [4 vols.; Leipzig: Hirzel, 1915–24] 3.957,34). An alternative translation—"wife of the procurator"—may be preferred. The term ἐπίτροπος ("steward," "procurator") covered a wide range of administrators (cf. LSJ *s.v.* ἐπίτροπος, p. 669), and Lightfoot notes a number of inscriptions from Smyrna that mention such an officer. That the woman was a widow is suggested by the fact that she is pictured as in charge of "the whole household." This, then, may be the "household of Tavia" greeted in *Sm.* 13.2.

15   A common name (Preisigke, *Namenbuch*, 65).

16   Exler, *Greek Epistolography*, 70, 75–77.

God's "care" (ἐπισκοπή) see on *Pol.* inscr where Polycarp
the "bishop" (ἐπίσκοπος) is said to "have (God and Christ)
as bishop" (ἐπισκοπήμενος)—that is, to be cared for by
God and Christ. For "unity" as God's gift to the church
see on *Mag.* 1.2 (cf. *Phd.* 8.1; 9.1).

**Bibliography
Indices**

Bibliography

1. Commentaries (listed in order of their publication)

Zahn, Theodor
Ignatii et Polycarpi Epistolae Martyria Fragmenta (Patrum Apostolicorum Opera, ed. Oscar de Gebhardt, Adolph Harnack, and Theodor Zahn, 2; Leipzig: Hinrichs, 1876).

Lightfoot, J. B.
The Apostolic Fathers, Part 2: S. Ignatius, S. Polycarp (3 vols.; London: Macmillan, 1885, 2d ed. 1889).

Bauer, Walter
Die Briefe des Ignatius von Antiochia und der Polykarpbrief, in *Die Apostolischen Väter,* vol. 2 (HNTSup; Tübingen: Mohr [Siebeck], 1920).

Grant, Robert M.
Ignatius of Antioch (The Apostolic Fathers 4; Camden, N.J.: Nelson, 1966).

2. Studies (alphabetically)

Bammel, C. P. Hammond
"Ignatian Problems," *JTS* N.S. 33 (1982) 62–97.

Barnard, L. W.
"The Background of St. Ignatius of Antioch," *VC* 17 (1963) 193–206.

Barrett, C. K.
"Jews and Judaizers in the Epistles of Ignatius," in *Jews, Greeks and Christians, Essays in Honor of W. D. Davies,* ed. R. Hammerton-Kelly and R. Scroggs (SJLA 21; Leiden: Brill, 1976).

Bartelink, G. J. M.
Lexicologisch-semantische studie over de taal van de Apostolische Vaders (Utrecht: Beijers, 1952).

Bartsch, Hans-Werner
Gnostisches Gut und Gemeindetradition bei Ignatius von Antiochien (Gütersloh: Bertelsmann, 1940); review by Ernst Käsemann, in *Verkündigung und Forschung, Theologischer Jahresbericht 1942–46* (München: Kaiser, 1946) 131–36.

Bauer, Walter
Orthodoxy and Heresy in Earliest Christianity (ed. Robert A. Kraft and Gerhard Krodel; Philadelphia: Fortress, 1971).

Berthouoz, Roger
"Le père, le fils et le saint-esprit d'après les lettres d'Ignace d'Antioch," *Freiburger Zeitschrift für Philosophie und Theologie* 18 (1971) 397–418.

Bieder, Werner
"Das Abendmahl im christlichen Lebenszusammenhang bei Ignatius von Antiochia," *Evangelische Theologie* 16 (1956) 75–97.

Idem
"Zur Deutung des kirchlichen Schweigens bei Ignatius von Antiochia," *Theologische Zeitschrift* 12 (1956) 28–43.

Bommes, Karin
Weizen Gottes, Untersuchungen zur Theologie des Martyriums bei Ignatius von Antiochien (Theophaneia 27; Köln and Bonn: Hanstein, 1976).

Bosio, C.
"La dottrina spirituale di Sant' Ignazio d'Antiochia," *Salesianum* 28 (1966) 519–51.

Bower, Richard A.
"The Meaning of ΕΠΙΤΥΓΧΑΝΩ in the Epistles of St. Ignatius of Antioch," *VC* 28 (1974) 1–14.

Brown, Milton Perry
The Authentic Writings of Ignatius (Durham, NC: Duke University, 1963).

Bultmann, Rudolf
"Ignatius und Paulus," in *Studia Paulina, in honorem Johannes de Zwaan septuagenerii* (Haarlem: Bohn, 1953) 37–51; English trans.: "Ignatius and Paul," in *Existence and Faith,* ed. Schubert M. Ogden (Cleveland and New York: World, 1960) 267–77.

Burke, Patrick
"The Monarchical Episcopate at the End of the First Century," *JES* 7 (1970) 499–518.

Cabaniss, Alan
"Wisdom 18:14f.: An Early Christmas Text," *VC* 10 (1956) 97–102.

Camelot, Pierre-Thomas
"Ignace d'Antioche," in *Dictionnaire de spiritualité* 7 (Paris: Beauchesne, 1971) 1250–66.

Campenhausen, Hans Freiherr von
Die Idee des Martyriums in der alte Kirche (2d ed.; Göttingen: Vandenhoeck & Ruprecht, 1964).

Idem
Ecclesiastical Authority and Spiritual Power in the Church of the First Three Centuries (tr. J. A. Baker; Stanford, CA: Stanford University, 1969).

Idem
"Das Bekenntnis im Urchristentum," *ZNW* 63 (1972) 210–53.

Carlozzo, G.
"L'ellissi in Ignazio di Antiochia e la questione dell' autenticità della recensione lunga," *Vetera Christianorum* 19 (1982) 239–56.

Chadwick, Henry
"The Silence of Bishops in Ignatius," *HTR* 43 (1950) 169–72.

Corwin, Virginia
St. Ignatius and Christianity in Antioch (Yale Publications in Religion 1; New Haven: Yale University, 1960).

Daniélou, Jean
Primitive Christian Symbols (Baltimore: Helicon, 1963).

Idem
The Theology of Jewish Christianity: A History of Early Christian Doctrine before the Council of Nicaea, vol. 1 (London: Darton, Longman and Todd; Chicago:

Regnery, 1964).

Dassmann, Ernst
"Zur Entstehung des Monepiskopats," *Jahrbuch für Antike und Christentum* 17 (1974) 74–90.

Daube, David
"Τρία μυστήρια κραυγῆς: Ignatius, Ephesians, XIX,1" *JTS* N.S. 16 (1965) 128–29.

Davids, Adelbert
"Irrtum und Häresie: 1 Clem.—Ignatius von Antiochien—Justinus," *Kairos* 15 (1973) 165–87.

Davies, Stevan L.
"The Predicament of Ignatius of Antioch," *VC* 30 (1976) 175–80.

Deichgräber, Reinhard
Gotteshymnus und Christushymnus in der frühen Christenheit (SUNT 5; Göttingen: Vandenhoeck & Ruprecht, 1967).

Donahue, P. J.
"Jewish Christianity in the Letters of Ignatius of Antioch," *VC* 32 (1978) 81–93.

Eijk, Ton H. C. van
La résurrection des morts chez les pères apostoliques (Théologie historique 25; Paris: Beauchesne, 1974).

Elze, Martin
Überlieferungsgeschichtliche Untersuchungen zur Christologie der Ignatiusbriefe (Tübingen: Univ. Bibl., 1963).

Goltz, Eduard Freiherr von der
Ignatius von Antiochien als Christ und Theologe: Eine dogmengeschichtliche Untersuchung (TU 12,3; Leipzig: Hinrichs, 1894).

Grant, Robert M.
"The Appeal to the Early Fathers," *JTS* N.S. 11 (1960) 13–24.

Idem
"The Apostolic Fathers' First Thousand Years," *CH* 31 (1962) 421–29.

Idem
"The Odes of Solomon and the Church of Antioch," *JBL* 63 (1944) 363–77.

Idem
"Scripture and Tradition in Ignatius of Antioch," in *After the New Testament* (Philadelphia: Fortress, 1967) 37–54.

Idem
"The Study of the Early Fathers in Modern Times," in *After the New Testament* (Philadelphia: Fortress, 1967) 3–19.

Idem
"The Use of the Early Fathers, From Irenaeus to John of Damascus," in *After the New Testament* (Philadelphia: Fortress, 1967) 20–34.

Gribbard, S. M.
"The Eucharist in the Ignatian Epistles," in *Studia Patristica VIII* (TU 93; Berlin: Akademie-Verlag, 1966) 214–18.

Halleux, A. de
"'L'église catholique' dans la lettre Ignacienne aux Smyrniotes," *EThL* 58 (1982) 5–24.

Harnack, Adolf
"Bishop Lightfoot's 'Ignatius and Polycarp'," *The Expositor*, 3d Series, 2 (1885) 401–14.

Idem
"Lightfoot on the Ignatian Epistles," *The Expositor*, 3d Series, 3 (1886) 9–22.

Harrison, Percy Neale
Polycarp's Two Epistles to the Philippians (Cambridge: Cambridge University, 1936).

Hörmann, Karl
"Das Geistreden des heiligen Ignatius von Antiochia," *Jahrbuch für Mystische Theologie* 2 (1956) 39–53.

Joly, Robert
Le dossier d'Ignace d'Antioche (Université libre de Bruxelles, Faculté de Philosophie et Lettres 69; Brussels: Éditions de l'Université de Bruxelles, 1979).

Jouassard, G.
"Les épîtres expediées de Troas par saint Ignace d'Antioche ont-elles été dictées le même jour en une série continue?" in *Memorial J. Chaîne* (Bibliothèque de la Faculté Catholique de Théologie de Lyon 5; Lyon: Facultés catholiques, 1950) 213–21.

Kannengiesser, Charles
"Bulletin de théologie patristique," *Recherches de science religieuse* 67 (1979) 599–623; 69 (1981) 443–79.

Klevinghaus, Johannes
Die theologische Stellung der apostolischen Väter zur alttestamentlichen Offenbarung (BFCTh 44,1; Gütersloh: Bertelsmann, 1948).

Koester, Helmut
"Geschichte und Kultus im Johannesevangelium und bei Ignatius," *ZThK* 54 (1957) 56–69; English trans.: "History and Cult in the Gospel of John and in Ignatius of Antioch," *Journel of Theology and the Church* 1 (1965) 111–23.

Idem
Synoptische Überlieferung bei den Apostolischen Vätern (TU 65; Berlin: Akademie-Verlag, 1957).

Kraft, Heinrich
Clavis Patrum Apostolicorum (München: Kösel, 1963).

Laeuchli, Samuel
"The Drama of Replay," in *Searching in the Syntax of Things*, essays by Maurice Friedman, T. Patrick Burke, and Samuel Laeuchli (Philadelphia: Fortress, 1972).

Lemaire, André
Les ministères aux origines de l'église, Naissance de la triple hiérarchie: évêques, presbytres, diacres (Lectio divina 68; Paris: Éditions du Cerf, 1971).

Liébaert, J.
Les enseignements moraux des Pères Apostoliques (Recherches et synthèses, section de morale 4; Gembloux: Duculot, 1970).

Lusk, D. C.
"What is the Historic Episcopate?" *SJT* 3 (1950) 255–77.

McCue, James F.
"Bishops, Presbyters and Priests in Ignatius of Antioch," *TS* 28 (1967) 828–34.

Idem
"The Roman Primacy in the Second Century and the Problem of the Development of Dogma," *TS* 25 (1964) 161–96.

Malina, Bruce J.
"The Social World Implied in the Letters of the Christian Bishop-Martyr Named Ignatius of Antioch," in *Society of Biblical Literature 1978 Seminar Papers,* ed. Paul J. Achtemeier (Missoula, MT: Scholars Press, 1978) 2.71–119.

Martin, José Pablo
"La pneumatologia en Ignacio de Antioquia," *Salesianum* 33 (1971) 379–454.

Maurer, Christian
Ignatius von Antiochien und das Johannesevangelium (AThANT 18; Zürich: Zwingli, 1949).

Meinhold, Peter
Studien zu Ignatius von Antiochien (Veröffentlichungen des Instituts fur Europäische Geschichte Mainz 97; Wiesbaden: Steiner, 1979). A collection of papers that includes all the articles by Meinhold referred to in this commentary.

Molland, Einar
"The Heretics Combatted by Ignatius of Antioch," *JEH* 5 (1954) 1–6.

Munier, Charles
"À propos d'Ignace d'Antioche," *RevScRel* 54 (1980) 55–73.

Idem
"À propos d'Ignace d'Antioche: Observations sur la liste épiscopale d'Antioche," *RevScRel* 55 (1981) 126–31.

Niebergall, Alfred
"Zur Entstehungsgeschichte der christlichen Eheschliessung, Bemerkungen zu Ignatius an Polykarp," in *Glaube, Geist, Geschichte, Festschrift Ernst Benz,* ed. G. Muller and W. Zeller (Leiden: Brill, 1967) 107–24.

Norris, Frederick W.
"Ignatius, Polycarp, and I Clement: Walter Bauer Reconsidered," *VC* 30 (1976) 23–44.

Padberg, Rudolf
"Das Amtsverständnis der Ignatiusbriefe," *Theologie und Glaube* 62 (1972) 47–54.

Idem
"Geordnete Liebe: Amt, Pneuma und kirchliche Einheit bei Ignatius von Antiochien," in *Unio Christianorum, Festschrift für Erzbischof Dr. Lorenz Jaeger* (Paderborn: Bonifacius, 1962) 201–17.

Idem
"Vom gottesdienstlichen Leben in den Briefen des Ignatius von Antiochien," *Theologie und Glaube* 53 (1963) 337–47.

Paulsen, Henning
Studien zur Theologie des Ignatius von Antiochien (Forschungen zur Kirchen- und Dogmengeschichte 29; Göttingen: Vandenhoeck & Ruprecht, 1978).

Perler, Othmar
"Das vierte Makkabäerbuch, Ignatius von Antiochien und die ältesten Märtyrerberichte," *Rivista di archeologia cristiana* 25 (1949) 47–72.

Idem
"Die Brief des Ignatius von Antiochien: Frage der Echtheit—Neue Arabische Übersetzung," *Freiburger Zeitschrift für Philosophie und Theologie* 18 (1971) 381–96.

Idem
"Ignatius von Antiochien und die römische Christengemeinde," *Freiburger Zeitschrift für Philosophie und Theologie* 22 (1944) 413–51.

Pizzolato, Luigi Franco
"Silenzio del vescovo e parola degli eretici in Ignazio d'Antiochia," *Aevum* 44 (1970) 205–19.

Preiss, Th.
"La mystique de l'imitation du Christ et de l'unité chez Ignace d'Antioche," *RHPhR* 18 (1938) 197–241.

Prigent, Pierre
"L'hérésie Asiate et l'église confessante, de l'Apocalypse à Ignace," *VC* 31 (1977) 1–22.

Rackl, Michael
Die Christologie des heiligen Ignatius von Antiochien (Freiburger Theologische Studien 14; Freiburg: Herder, 1914).

Rathke, Heinrich
Ignatius von Antiochien und die Paulusbriefe (TU 99; Berlin: Akademie-Verlag, 1967).

Richardson, Cyril Charles
The Christianity of Ignatius of Antioch (New York: Columbia University, 1935).

Riesenfeld, Harald
"Reflections on the Style and the Theology of St. Ignatius of Antioch," in *Studia Patristica* IV (TU 79; Berlin: Akademie-Verlag, 1961) 312–22.

Rius-Camps, J.
The Four Authentic Letters of Ignatius, the Martyr (Christianismos 2; Rome: Pontificium Institutum Orientalium Studiorum, 1979).

Rogge, Joachim
"Ἕνωσις und verwandte Begriffe in den Ignatiusbriefen," *. . . und fragten nach Jesus, Beiträge aus Theologie, Kirche und Geschichte, Festschrift Ernst Barnikol* (Berlin: Evangelische Verlagsanstalt, 1964) 45–51.

Rohde, Joachim
"Häresie und Schisma im ersten Clemensbrief und in den Ignatius-Briefen," *NovT* 10 (1968) 217–33.

Rüsch, Theodor
Die Entstehung der Lehre vom Heiligen Geist bei Ignatius von Antiochien, Theophilus von Antiocheia und Irenäus von Lyon (Studien zur Dogmengeschichte

und systematischen Theologie 2; Zürich: Zwingli, 1952).

Sauser, Ekkart
"Tritt der Bischof an die Stelle Christi? Zur Frage nach der Stellung des Bischofs in der Theologie des hl. Ignatius von Antiocheia," in *Festschrift Franz Loidl*, ed. Victor Flieder (Vienna: Hollinek, 1970) 1.325–39.

Schermann, Theodor
"Zur Erklärung der Stelle epist. ad Ephes. 20,2 des Ignatius von Antiocheia: φάρμακον ἀθανασίας κ.τ.λ.," *Theologische Quartalschrift* 92 (1910) 6–19.

Schilling, Frederick Augustus
The Mysticism of Ignatius of Antioch (Philadelphia: University of Pennsylvania, 1932).

Schlier, Heinrich
Religionsgeschichtliche Untersuchungen zu den Ignatiusbriefen (BZNW 8; Giessen: Töpelmann, 1929).

Schoedel, William R.
"Ignatius and the Archives," *HTR* 71 (1978) 97–106.

Idem
"Theological Norms and Social Perspectives in Ignatius of Antioch," in *Jewish and Christian Self-Definition: The Shaping of Christianity in the Second and Third Centuries*, ed. E. P. Sanders (Philadelphia: Fortress; and London: SCM, 1980) 30–56.

Shepherd, Massey H.
"Smyrna in the Ignatian Letters, A Study in Church Order," *Journal of Religion* 20 (1940) 141–59.

Sibinga, J. Smit
"Ignatius and Matthew," *NovT* 8 (1966) 262–83.

Sieben, Hermann Josef
"Die Ignatianen als Briefe: Einige Formkritische Bemerkungen," *VC* 32 (1978) 1–18.

Snyder, Grayden R.
"The Historical Jesus in the Letters of Ignatius of Antioch," *Biblical Research* 8 (1963) 3–12.

Idem
"The Text and Syntax of Ignatius πρὸς Ἐφεσίους 20:2c," *VC* 22 (1968) 8–13.

Staats, Reinhart
"Die martyrologische Begründung des Romprimats bei Ignatius von Antiochien," *ZThK* 73 (1976) 461–70.

Story, Cullen I. K.
"The Text of Ignatius' Letter to the Trallians 12:3," *VC* 33 (1979) 319–23.

Swartley, Willard M.
"The Imitatio Christi in the Ignatian Letters," *VC* 27 (1973) 81–103.

Tarvainen, Olavi
Glaube und Liebe bei Ignatius von Antiochien (Schriften der Luther-Agricola-Gesellschaft 14; Joensuu: Pohjois-Karjalan Kirjapaino Oy, 1967).

Torrance, Thomas F.
The Doctrine of Grace in the Apostolic Fathers (Edinburgh and London: Oliver and Boyd, 1948).

Trentin, Giuseppe
"Eros e Agape, A proposito di una interpretazione teologica delle lettere di Ignazio di Antiochia," *Studia Patavina, Rivista di Scienze Religiose* 19 (1972) 495–538.

Idem
"Rassegna di studi su Ignazio di Antiochia," *Studia Patavina, Rivista di Scienze Religiose* 19 (1972) 75–87.

Trevett, Christine
"Prophecy and Anti-Episcopal Activity: A Third Error Combatted by Ignatius?" *JEH* 34 (1983) 1–18.

Vilela, Albano
"Le Presbytérium selon saint Ignace d'Antioche," *BLE* 74 (1973) 161–86.

Vogt, Hermann J.
"Ignatius von Antiochien über den Bischof und seine Gemeinde," *ThQ* 158 (1978) 15–27.

Walter, Johannes Wilhelm von
"Ignatius von Antiochien und die Entstehung des Frühkatholizismus," in *Reinhold-Seeberg-Festschrift*, vol. 2: *Zur Praxis des Christentums*, ed. Wilhelm Koepp (Leipzig: Deichert, 1929) 105–18.

Weijenborg, Reinoud
Les lettres d'Ignace d'Antioche (Leiden: Brill, 1969).

Winling, R.
"À propos de la datation des Lettres d'Ignace d'Antioche: notes de lecture à l'occasion d'une recherche thématique," *RevScRel* 54 (1980) 259–65.

Winslow, Donald F.
"The Idea of Redemption in the Epistles of St. Ignatius of Antioch," *Greek Orthodox Theological Review* 11 (1965) 119–31.

Zahn, Theodor
Ignatius von Antiochien (Gotha: Perthes, 1873).

Zañartu, Sergio
El concepto de ΖΩΗ en Ignacio de Antioquia (Publicaciones de la Universidad Pontificia Comillas 1,7; Teologia 1,4; Madrid: Eapsa, 1977).

Idem
"Les concepts de vie et de mort chez Ignace d'Antioche," *VC* 33 (1979) 324–41.

Zanetti, Paolo Serra
"Bibliografia eucaristica Ignaziana recente," in *Miscellanea liturgica in onore di sua eminenze il cardinale Giacomo Lercaro* (Rome: Desclée, 1966) 1.341–89.

Idem
"Una nota Ignaziana: ΑΝΤΙΨΥΧΟΝ," in *Forma futuri, Studi in onore del cardinale Michele Pellegrino* (Torino: Bottega d'Erasmo, 1975) 963–79.

1. Passages[2]

a / Old Testament and Apocrypha

Gen

1	77
1:27	273(4)

1 Kgs

3:5–14	260(8)

Ps (LXX)

1:3	130
32:9	77
110:10	243(16)
117:20	210
118:120	221(7)

Prov

3:34	54(4)
18:17	130

Isa

1:13	119
5:26	223, 223(19), 224(23)
11:12	223(19)
45:23	127
49:22	223, 223(19)
52:5	150–51, 270
52:7	223
52:13—53:5	261
53:4	261
53:11	261
57:19	223
62:10	223, 223(19)
62:10—63:6	223
66:18	127

Jer

23:24	38

Tob

12:19	154

Wis

2:24	172(15)
18:14–15	91(23), 121(15)

Sir

1:6, 20	243(16)
3:30	185(23)
10:13	243(16)
22:17	258

4 Macc

6:9	266
6:10	261, 266
6:29	64
7:3	251(20)
13:7	251(20)
14:6	53
17:11, 15	266
17:15–16	261
17:21	64
18:4	213

b / Old Testament Pseudepigrapha and Other Jewish Literature

'Aboth

3.7	55(11)

Asc. Is.

3.23–24	236(35)
9.12–13	90
9.14–15	90
11.2	90
11.2–22	89
11.13–14	90
11.18–19	91

b. Yebam.

46a	202(6)

1 Enoch

18.12–19.3; 21.1–10	92
72.3; 75.1, 3; 82.10–20	92

Josephus

Ant.

4.200	117
4.201	117

Bell.

5.378	109
7.373–74	176

C. Apion.

1.1–18	209
1.20–22	208
1.28	208
1.29	208
1.29–36	210
1.37, 41	210
1.54	210
2.145–296	209
2.193	117
2.193–94	109

Philo

Abr.

33	231(4)
54	138(3)
118	154

Conf.

57	156
61	157(26)

Congr.

175	208(12)

Dec.

151	185

Fuga

132	208(12)

Heres

263–66	171(10)

Jos.

33	264(17)

Leg. alleg.

1.48–49	66
1.76	190
2.72	185
3.243	185

Legat.

6	268

Migr. Abr.

27	261
99–101	185(23)

Mut. nom.

24	39(28)
87	39(28)

Opif. mund.

171	155(17)

Post. Cain.

29	196(2)
114–19	182(9)

Praem.

2	208(12)

Probus

21	185

---

1 Numbers in parentheses following page citations for this volume refer to footnotes.

2 The following lists contain a selection of the references made to primary sources in this volume.

2:20	201, 220
4:14	56(15)
5:6	203, 210
5:8	173
6:10	245
6:14	184
6:15	203
Eph	
1:3–14	39
1:3–23	37
1:16	73(7)
1:23	38
2:15	96, 232
2:16	223
2:17	223
2:20–22	66
3:19	38
4:1	159
4:5–6	116
4:13	96, 232, 233
4:24	96, 232
5:1–2	41
5:2	42(13)
5:8	197
5:25, 29	272
6:11–17	275
6:18	260(9)
Phil	
1:1	46(11), 237
2:6–11	267
2:10	154
2:11	126
2:17	171
4:12	73
4:13	232
Col	
1:7	46(9)
1:15	268
1:19	38
2:9	38
3:10	232
4:2	260(9)
1 Thess	
1:3	25(128)
2:2	37
2:4	170, 173
2:7, 9	204
4:1	51
5:17	260
5:23	214(15b)
5:25	99
1 Tim	
1:2	252
1:4–5	25(128)
1:5	76(3)
1:17	268
4:12	108
4:14	51(2)
5:3–16	252
6:1–2	270
6:10	242(16)
2 Tim	
1:2	252
2:4	275
2:5, 7	261
2:7	260(8)
2:10	232
2:26	245
Tit	
1:12	59(1)
1:14	118
2:2	25(128)
Phlm	
9–10	159
14	269(4)
16	23(116)
Heb	
9:1–12	209
9:3	210(20)
10:20	210(20)
10:25	110
1 Pet	
2:18–19	262
2:25	189
3:22	154
5:14	43(23)
1 John	
2:8	197
3:4–10	76
4:2–3	155, 240(8)
4:20	76
5:18	76
2 John	
3	252
6	110
10–11	231(5)
Jude	
6	236(32)

d / Early Christian Literature and the Ancient Church

Abercius Inscription	
12	190(15)
Acta Archelai	
7–9	66
Acta Ioannis	
96	56(13)
107	39
Acta Pauli	
8.1.14	90
Acta Philippi	
119	273(3)
Apocalypse of James (First)	
25,18–19	92(30)
Apocryphon of James	
15,9–20	88
Apocryphon of John	
22,8–9; 35,4–5	233(15)
Athanasius	
Contra Arian.	
1.8	82
4.1	171(6)
Gent.	
38	55
Athenagoras	
De res.	
2.1–11.2	222
Augustine	
Sermo	
331.6.5	145
Barnabas	
1.6	130
4.9	63(4)
5.13	221(7)
6.5	63(4)
6.7	15(76)
6.10	209
11.1	85
11.6, 8	130
15.8	119
18–20	110
19.7	141
20.2	239
1 Clement	
3.4	172
5.1–2	261
5.2, 3–5, 6–7	172
7.1	172
19.3	196(2)
27.3, 6	78(16)
46.1	172
47.7	150
48.2–4	210
49.4	67
55.1	172
55.2	168
2 Clement	
4.3	275(6)
8.2	245
8.4–6	272(2)
9.3	205(5)
13.2–4	150
14.2, 4	273(4)
14.3	272(2)
14.3–4	205(5)

---

3   This list includes references to passages in Ignatius discussed outside the normal sequence of the commentary.

e / Greek and Latin Authors

2. Greek Words

ἀγαπᾶν 241
ἀγάπη 186, 241–42
ἀγαπην ποιεῖν 244
ἁγνεία 273(3)
ἁγνίζομαι ὑμῶν 63(3)
ᾄδω 104
ἀθανασία 97
ἄθικτος 209(17)
αἵρεσις 58(3), 146–47
αἰών, αἰῶνες 63(2), 91,
    181(1),
    223(17)
ἀλήθομαι 176
ἀληθῶς 125, 153, 189,
    221
ἀμεριμνία 278(1)
ἀμοιβή 245–46
ἀναγραφαί 208
ἀναπαύω 278(1)
ἀνάστασις 27
ἀνατέλλω 27, 124
ἀναφερόμενοι 27
ἄνευ 109, 269(3)
ἄνευ γνώμης σου 269
ἀνήρ 183
ἀνὴρ τέλειος 232
ἄνθρωπος 183
ἄνθρωπος τέλειος 232–33,
    233(17, 19)
ἀνίστημι 27(149)
ἀντίψυχον 13, 63–64,
    248, 265
ἄξιος 39, 46, 201
τὰ ἀόρατα 263
ἀόρατος 109(4), 268
ἀπαθές 268
ἀπέχεσθαι 238
ἀποδεξάμενος, ἀπεδεξάμην 40, 138
ἀποδεχόμενος 258
ἀποδιυλίζω 167
ἀπολαμβάνω 43
ἀπόντα καὶ παρόντα 245
ἀπὸ τοῦ κοινοῦ 271
ἀρχεῖα 208(7)
ἀσπάζομαι 35, 103
ἀσώματος 154, 225–27
ἄτρεπτος 38(28)
ἀφθαρσία 81, 82
ἄχρονος 267, 268
ἀψηλάφητος 268

βάρος 204
βασκανία 184
βαστάζειν θεόν 36
βαστάζω 261
βιβλίδιον 95(4)
βοτάνη 70, 146–47
βούλομαι 173, 184

γεννητὸς καὶ ἀγέννητος 61
γνώμη 50, 269

δαιμονικός 225–27
δεδεμένος 129–30
δεξάμενος, ἐδεξάμην 40, 190
δεσμός 93
διακονία 196
διατάγματα 148(15)
δικαιωθῆναι 209(18),
    249(7b)
δόγματα 130
τὸ δοκεῖν 155
δοκεῖν vs. εἶναι 156
τὸ δοκοῦν 173
δοῦλος 129–30
δρόμος 259
δύναμις 76–77, 173
δυσωδία 81

ἐγείρω 27(149)
ἔγνων 65, 138
εἰδώς 279
εἶναι vs. καλεῖσθαι 77
εἰρηνεύω 213
εἷς διδάσκαλος 77
εἰς τόπον 112
ἐκδικέω 260
ἐκεῖθεν 65(4)
ἐλεύθερος 130
ἔλπις 248(6)
ἔμπροσθεν 279, 280(12)
ἐνάρετος 196
ἐν θεῷ 19
ἑνότης 21, 52, 105,
    202
ἑνόω 52, 105
ἕνωσις 21, 37, 52,
    105, 199,
    264(14), 272
ἐξ ὀνόματος 96, 270
ἐπεί, ἐπειδή 168, 212, 277,
    279
ἐπιγραφῆναι 170
ἐπιθυμία 271
ἐπιτυγχάνω 28, 42(13), 70,
    106(9), 264
ἔργον 76(9)
ἑρμηνεύω 202, 202(4)

ἔρρωσθε 99, 280
ἐρῶν 184
ἔρως 184
ἑτεροδιδασκαλέω 118, 266
ἑτεροδοξία, ἑτεροδοξέω 118, 238,
    238(1)
εὐθυμία 278(1)

ζῆλος 144(5), 184

ἠγαπημένος 219
ἡσυχία 77, 91,
    120(11)

θανατηφόρος 157
θέλημα 50, 99,
    249(7a), 279(9)
θέλω 109(8), 167,
    173, 173(17),
    184, 189,
    213(9), 250
θέμα 265(19)
θεοδρόμος 197, 278
θεοπρεσβευτής 279
θεοφορία 37
θηριομαχῆσαι 42, 178
θυσιαστήριον 55, 117

ἱερός 209(17)

καθολική 243
καινὸς ἄνθρωπος 232, 233(17)
καιρός 264, 266
κακοτεχνία 271, 271(17)
καλοκἀγαθία 76
καλῶς ἐποιήσατε 248
κατὰ ἄνθρωπον 140
κατὰ ἀνθρώπους 186
κατάδεσμος 93
κατὰ θεόν 19, 46
καταμάθετε 238, 266
κατ᾽ ἄνδρα 260(10),
    270(6)
κατὰ φύσιν 138
κατὰ χρῆσιν 138
τὸ κοινόν 196(1), 271
κοινωνία 37
κολακεύω 263
κόπος 274
κυριακή 123(3)

λαθροδῆκται 59
λελυμένος 129–30
λόγος 120, 120(12)
λόγος vs. ἔργον 76(9)

4. Modern Authors[4]

Achelis, H.
240(6)
Alès, A. d'
273(6)

Bamberger, B. J.
202(6)
Barnett, A. E.
9–10
Barrow, R. H.
270(8)
Bartchy, S. S.
270(8,14)
Bartelink, G. J. M.
55(6), 67(23), 238(1),
240(7), 271(18)
Bartsch, H.-W.
2, 15, 16, 72(3), 89,
141(3), 157, 167(14,15),
189, 203(8), 210(19)
Bauer, W.
56, 85(6), 110, 159(3),
191(18), 220, 223(16),
231–32, 236, 253, 278(4)
Bellinzoni, A. J.
153(5)
Berger, K.
35(3)
Betz, H. D.
17, 35(3), 71(3), 173(19),
278(1)
Beyschlag, K.
150(5), 172
Bjerkelund, C. J.
146(1), 230(1,2), 231(3)
Bolkenstein, H.
240(4)
Brown, M. P.
39(32), 45(3), 50, 88
Bultmann, R.
3(14), 76(7), 239(2)

Calderini, R.
35(6)
Campenhausen, H. F. von
9(50), 23(113), 30(156),
153(3)
Casson, L.
191(19,21)

Corwin, V.
3(14), 5(31), 16, 67, 234

Daniélou, J.
16, 92
Davies, J. G.
252(25)
Davies, S. L.
169(6)
Deichgräber, R.
87
Dibelius, M.
116
Dillon, R. J.
228(18)
Dodds, E. R.
240
Dölger, F. J.
67, 67(25), 171, 249(6)

Eijk, T. H. C. van
15(74), 27(147)
Elze, M.
9(49), 15(76), 63(2), 85(6),
121(15), 154(7,10),
221(7,8,9), 224, 241(10),
244(23)
Exler, F. X. J.
35(1,2,5)

Fischer, K. M.
158(31), 223(21)
Fridrichsen, A.
178
Friedländer, L.
178(7)

Garciadego, A.
243
Garnsey, P.
169(5), 179(11)
Gilmour, S. MacL.
228(18)
Goltz, E. von der
2
Grant, F. C.
272(1)
Grant, R. M.
1(4), 178
Gülzow, H.
270(7,10,11)

Harnack, A.
1(3), 5(30)
Harrison, P. N.
10, 212–13
Heinimann, F.
156
Hilgenfeld, A.
123

Jeremias, J.
232
Joly, R.
1(2), 6–7, 22(112), 42(13),
120(12), 195(1), 208(6),
227(11), 235(28), 243(21),
251(28)
Jones, A. H. M.
179(11)

Kalsbach, A.
252(26)
Kattenbusch, F.
243(20)
Kleist, J. A.
280(12)
Knox, J.
44
Koester, H.
9, 9(51), 56(15), 76(8),
198(5), 222
Koskenniemi, H.
65(3), 220(2), 245(3)
Kroll, J.
8(48)

Laeuchli, S.
272(2)
Lambertz, M.
35(4)
Lietzmann, H.
98
Lightfoot, J. B.
1(3), 2, 4–5, 5(30),
11(63,64), 42(13), 56,
58(2), 61(18), 63(3),
67(20), 97(18), 118,
120(12), 147(6), 167,
169(5), 175(3), 190(2),
214(13), 223, 227, 231(4),
232, 235, 236(31), 243,

252, 278(2), 279, 279(11),
280(14)
Lohmeyer, E.
81
Lohse, E.
233(16)
Loofs, F.
1(2)

Malherbe, A. J.
42(14), 60(5), 262(3)
Massaux, E.
9(51)
Meinhold, P.
49(10), 56(14)
Molland, E.
118, 123
Mommsen, T.
179(8)
Marcovich, M.
191(20)
Marrou, H. I.
243(16)

Niebergall, A.
273(8)
Norden, E.
7, 152

Orbe, A.
82(8)
Ott, J.
60
Outka, G.
30(157)

Pannenberg, W.
3(14)
Paulsen, H.
3(14), 16(81), 28(151),
29(153), 154(10), 226(5),
227(12), 239(3), 251(17),
272(2), 273(7), 276(17)
Pearson, J.
2
Perler, O.
7–8, 61(21), 165(2)
Peterson, E.
60
Pizzolato, L. F.
56(16)

---

4   The following list contains a selection of the
references made to modern studies in this volume.

In the design of the visual aspects of *Hermeneia*, consideration has been given to relating the form to the content by symbolic means.

The letters of the logotype *Hermeneia* are a fusion of forms alluding simultaneously to Hebrew (dotted vowel markings) and Greek (geometric round shapes) letter forms. In their modern treatment they remind us of the electronic age as well, the vantage point from which this investigation of the past begins.

The Lion of Judah used as visual identification for the series is based on the Seal of Shema. The version for *Hermeneia* is again a fusion of Hebrew calligraphic forms, especially the legs of the lion, and Greek elements characterized by the geometric. In the sequence of arcs, which can be understood as scroll-like images, the first is the lion's mouth. It is reasserted and accelerated in the whorl and returns in the aggressively arched tail: tradition is passed from one age to the next, rediscovered and re-formed.

"Who is worthy to open the scroll and break its seals . . ."
Then one of the elders said to me
"weep not; lo, the Lion of the tribe of David,
the Root of David, has conquered,
so that he can open the scroll and
its seven seals."
Rev. 5:2, 5

To celebrate the signal achievement in biblical scholarship which *Hermeneia* represents, the entire series will by its color constitute a signal on the theologian's bookshelf: the Old Testament will be bound in yellow and the New Testament in red, traceable to a commonly used color coding for synagogue and church in medieval painting; in pure color terms, varying degrees of intensity of the warm segment of the color spectrum. The colors interpenetrate when the binding color for the Old Testament is used to imprint volumes from the New and vice versa.

Wherever possible, a photograph of the oldest extant manuscript, or a historically significant document pertaining to the biblical sources, will be displayed on the end papers of each volume to give a feel for the tangible reality and beauty of the source material.

The title-page motifs are expressive derivations from the *Hermeneia* logotype, repeated seven times to form a matrix and debossed on the cover of each volume. These sifted-out elements will be seen to be in their exact positions within the parent matrix. These motifs and their expressional character are noted on the following page.

Horizontal markings at gradated levels on the spine will assist in grouping the volumes according to these conventional categories.

The type has been set with unjustified right margins so as to preserve the internal consistency of word spacing. This is a major factor in both legibility and aesthetic quality; the resultant uneven line endings are only slight impairments to legibility by comparison. In this respect the type resembles the handwritten manuscripts where the quality of the calligraphic writing is dependent on establishing and holding to integral spacing patterns.

All of the type faces in common use today have been designed between 1500 A.D. and the present. For the biblical text a face was chosen which does not arbitrarily date the text, but rather one which is uncompromisingly modern and unembellished so that its feel is of the universal. The type style is Univers 65 by Adrian Frutiger.

The expository texts and footnotes are set in Baskerville, chosen for its compatibility with the many brief Greek and Hebrew insertions. The double-column format and the shorter line length facilitate speed reading and the wide margins to the left of footnotes provide for the scholar's own notations.

Kenneth Hiebert

304

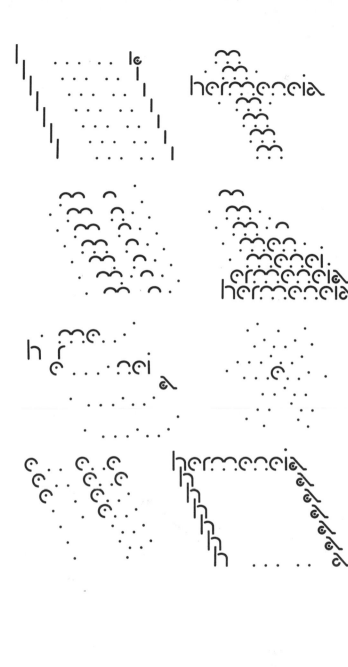

Category of biblical writing,
key symbolic characteristic,
and volumes so identified.

1
Law
(boundaries described)
  Genesis
  Exodus
  Leviticus
  Numbers
  Deuteronomy

2
History
(trek through time and space)
  Joshua
  Judges
  Ruth
  1 Samuel
  2 Samuel
  1 Kings
  2 Kings
  1 Chronicles
  2 Chronicles
  Ezra
  Nehemiah
  Esther

3
Poetry
(lyric emotional expression)
  Job
  Psalms
  Proverbs
  Ecclesiastes
  Song of Songs

4
Prophets
(inspired seers)
  Isaiah
  Jeremiah
  Lamentations
  Ezekiel
  Daniel
  Hosea
  Joel
  Amos
  Obadiah
  Jonah
  Micah
  Nahum
  Habakkuk
  Zephaniah
  Haggai
  Zechariah
  Malachi

5
New Testament Narrative
(focus on One)
  Matthew
  Mark
  Luke
  John
  Acts

6
Epistles
(directed instruction)
  Romans
  1 Corinthians
  2 Corinthians
  Galatians
  Ephesians
  Philippians
  Colossians
  1 Thessalonians
  2 Thessalonians
  1 Timothy
  2 Timothy
  Titus
  Philemon
  Hebrews
  James
  1 Peter
  2 Peter
  1 John
  2 John
  3 John
  Jude

7
Apocalypse
(vision of the future)
  Revelation

8
Extracanonical Writings
(peripheral records)